MW01623158

Snap Judgments

Snap Judgments

New Positions in Contemporary African Photography

Okwui Enwezor

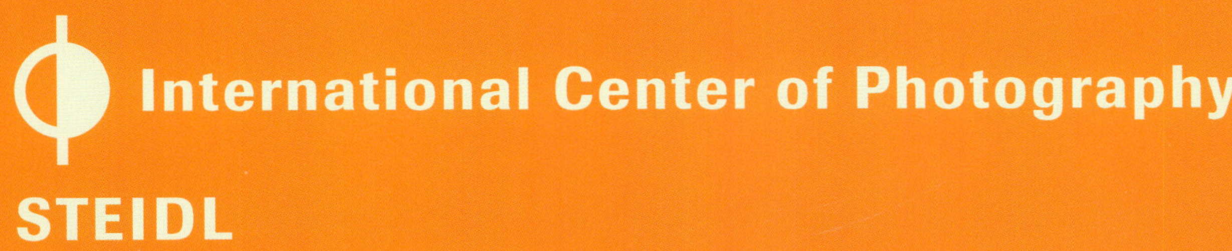

International Center of Photography

STEIDL

Published in conjunction with the exhibition *Snap Judgments: New Positions in Contemporary African Photography* organized by the International Center of Photography, New York.

Exhibition Dates: March 10 through May 28, 2006

This exhibition was organized by the International Center of Photography with lead support from Altria Group Inc., and the ICP Exhibitions Committee. Additional funding was generously provided by The Andy Warhol Foundation for the Visual Arts, Christian K. Keesee, Roberta and Steven Denning, Eni S.p.A., Marjorie G. and Jeffrey A. Rosen, Artur Walther, Association Française d'Action Artistique, Robert Scully and Nancy Peretsman, Meryl and Robert Meltzer, Andrew and Marina Lewin, Jane K. Lombard, Prince Claus Fund, Mondriaan Foundation, Pamela and Arthur Sanders, and the British Council. Support for the exhibition catalogue has been provided by the Elizabeth Firestone Graham Foundation.

First edition 2006

Copublished by the International Center of Photography, New York, and Steidl Publishers, Göttingen, Germany

Director of Publications: Karen Hansgen / Copyeditor: Philomena Mariani / Research: Bassem Barzani, Koyo Kouoh, Mona Marzouk, Allison Moore, Kevin Mulhearn / Design: Claas Möller, Steidl Design
Separations: Steidl's digital darkroom / Production: Steidl, Göttingen

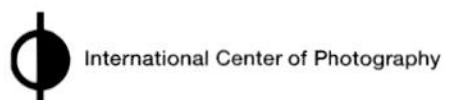

1114 Avenue of the Americas / New York, NY 10036 / www.icp.org

STEIDL

Düstere Str. 4 / D-37073 Göttingen / Phone +49 551-49 60 60 / Fax +49 551-49 60 649 / E-mail: mail@steidl.de

ISBN 3-86521-224-7 / ISBN 13: 978-3-86521-224-5
Printed in Germany

Front cover: Zwelehtu Mthethwa, Untitled (detail), 2003. Courtesy the artist and Jack Shainman Gallery, New York
Frontispiece: Yto Barrada, *Belvédère 2—Tangier 2003*, from the series "A Life Full of Holes: The Strait Project" (detail), 1998–2004. Courtesy the artist and Galerie Polaris, Paris
Back cover: Moshekwa Langa, *Untitled XVI* (detail), 2005. Courtesy the artist and Goodman Gallery, Johannesburg

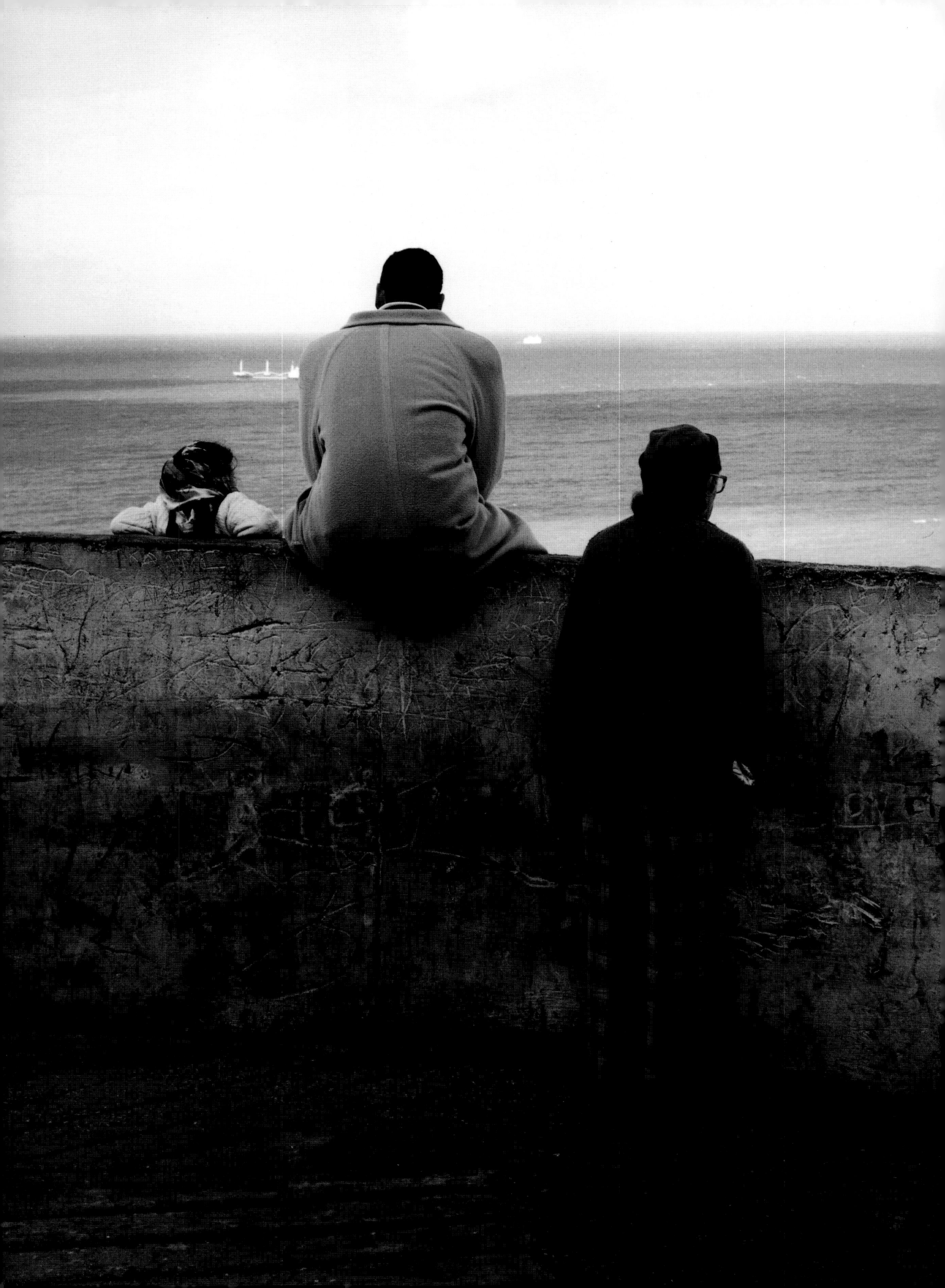

Director's Foreword

The world is changing swiftly in the early twenty-first century, sometimes at a pace too rapid to comprehend. The International Center of Photography has sought to give early recognition to those photographic artists who help us to understand the social, political, and economic transformations that are reshaping the globe. In 2003, with *Strangers*, our first Triennial exhibition of contemporary photography and video, ICP's curators made a special effort to seek out compelling new works not only from North America and Europe but also from around the planet. In 2004, the extraordinary emergence of China on the world stage was vividly conveyed by the works in *Between Past and Future: New Photography and Video from China*. The current exhibition, *Snap Judgments: New Positions in Contemporary African Photography*, aims at an equally ambitious goal: to illuminate the enormous social and cultural shifts now taking place across the African continent.

Snap Judgments has been organized by Okwui Enwezor, whom I am delighted to welcome to ICP as an adjunct curator. One of the world's most highly regarded curators of contemporary art, Mr. Enwezor will help to bring a continuing global scope to ICP'S exhibition program in the coming years. In 1996, Mr. Enwezor's exhibition *In/Sight: African Photographers, 1940 to the Present* at the Solomon R. Guggenheim Museum, highlighted a group of remarkable African portrait photographers, including such figures as Seydou Keïta and Malick Sidibé, whose work has since gained international acclaim. During the past decade, photography has won a place as a major medium within the expanding field of African contemporary art. As *Snap Judgments* reveals, photography now serves as a vehicle for considering the fate of the African landscape, exploring the dynamics of urban culture, and recording fascinating experiments in self-portraiture and performance.

As Mr. Enwezor points out in his catalogue essay, one of the exhibition's underlying purposes is to provide an alternative to the current of "Afro-pessimism" that runs through much of the global media reporting about the continent. Instead of reducing Africa to a set of images of famine, disease, and warfare, the artists in *Snap Judgments* set out to examine the drama of contemporary life in Africa in all of its richness and complexity, without resorting to sensationalism or romanticization. Seen in this light, *Snap Judgments* is a significant as well as a historic accomplishment, and all of us at ICP are proud to have played a role in its realization.

An exhibition as ambitious as *Snap Judgments* could not take place without the commitment of many organizations and individuals. For their generous lead support, I wish to express my deepest appreciation to the Altria Group Inc. and to the ICP Exhibitions Committee, chaired by Artur Walther and Meryl Meltzer. Additional funding was contributed by The Andy Warhol Foundation for the Visual Arts, Christian K. Keesee, Roberta and Steven Denning, Eni S.p.A., Marjorie G. and Jeffrey A. Rosen, Artur Walther, the Association Française d'Action Artistique, Robert Scully and Nancy Peretsman, Meryl and Robert Meltzer, Andrew and Marina Lewin, and Jane K. Lombard, among others. The Elizabeth Firestone Graham Foundation was instrumental in furnishing support for the exhibition catalogue.

I would also like to acknowledge the contributions of the many dedicated individuals who brought this complex project to completion. They include Brian Wallis, ICP Director of Exhibitions and Chief Curator; Assistant Curator Vanessa Rocco, who played an important role in coordinating the exhibition; Assistant Curator Kristen Lubben, who guided the exhibition through its final phases of preparation; and interns Allison Moore and Kevin Mulhearn, who provided invaluable assistance with myriad details of the exhibition and publication. I wish to express my gratitude to Karen Hansgen, Director of Publications, who supervised the preparation of the catalogue; Gerhard Steidl, our publications partner, designer Claas Möller, and the entire staff at Steidl Publishing; and Philomena Mariani for her superb editing. I also wish to thank Registrar Barbara Woytowicz, and Preparator Karlos Carcamo for their work on the exhibition, as well as Alicia Cheng and her colleagues at mgmt., who expertly designed the exhibition and its accompanying graphics.

Finally, I wish to extend my deepest thanks to the artists participating in the exhibition. Their works open up a host of new and surprising perspectives on the changes that are sweeping the African continent.

Willis E. Hartshorn

Ehrenkranz Director

Curator's Acknowledgments

When the luminous, incomparable photographs of Seydou Keïta came to the attention of a wide discerning public in the early 1990s, his nearly forgotten work, shut away for almost half a century, called for a reassessment of the history of photography. Keïta's take on the art of portraiture did more than merely register the richness of the lives of ordinary people and the not-so-ordinary alike—most of whom he photographed as if they were nobility in a distinctive style all his own—in mid-twentieth-century Bamako. The large body of work Keïta left behind not only generated excitement, it offered a considerable challenge to historians of African art, and to wit photography. Though *Snap Judgments* does not present the work of Seydou Keïta, its basic premise begins with the deeply moving stories he captured in thousands of portraits. This book and exhibition are dedicated to him not only for his example but also for his photographic aesthetic and ethic.

The opportunity to curate this exhibition at ICP began with the generous invitation of Brian Wallis, Director of Exhibitions and Chief Curator, whose support and enthusiasm for the work undertaken here cannot be properly reciprocated by these few lines of thanks. I am grateful to Brian for the initial invitation and for helping me see the project through to a successful conclusion. As the scope of the exhibition grew, he knew exactly on whom to call for support, and none supported our work more committedly than Artur Walther. During the course of the project, Artur was more than a supporter, he was also a co-traveler, advocate, and friend. The Exhibition Committee deserves as much credit for their support as well.

Special thanks go to Vanessa Rocco, without whom the formidable challenge of coordinating the project on three continents would have been impossible. Vanessa has been an expert guide, project leader, and curatorial partner whose insight, advice, judgment, patience, and brio made the course of the exhibition a smooth one. I am especially privileged to work with Vanessa and thank her also for her astute and engaging essay. Christopher Phillips was always an invisible force behind the scene. His wise counsel made a key difference in delicate matters of protocol and scholarship.

Many more people have contributed to this project; though I cannot thank them all, a few stand out in matters of professionalism. For her editorial stewardship of the catalogue, I have boundless respect for Karen Hansgen, ICP's Director of Publications. It has been a delight to work with Kristen Lubben, who stepped in at a late stage to oversee the final aspects of the exhibition and handled every detail with precision. I was fortunate to be the beneficiary of the expertise, dedication, and stamina of two outstanding curatorial assistants and researchers: Allison Moore and Kevin Mulhearn. Their scholarly interest in African photography resulted in written contributions and an extensive bibliography which further elucidate the work of artists in the exhibition. Few editors have the ability to retain the writer's voice and make him look and read better on the page than Philomena Mariani, whose scrupulous editorial skills were diligently applied to all the texts in this book. Project interns Alexandre Therwath, Kirsten C. Springer-Delgado, and Scott Campbell have capably supported the exhibition. I wish to thank Alicia Cheng of mgmt. design for her elegant graphic interpretation of the spirit of the exhibition. The team of ICP preparators and handlers contributed enormously in the invisible but necessary elements that make an exhibition look beautiful.

Beyond ICP there are many others whose efforts and generosity have been essential. Mona Marzouk and Bassam Barzini assisted the research coordination in Alexandria and Cairo and introduced me to artists during my visit to Egypt. William Wells and Osama Dawod of Townhouse Gallery, Cairo, served as hosts and made the gallery's lovely library the site of my work there. Ramez Elias provided contacts and advice. Research in Algeria was aided by the kindness and generosity of Stefan Roessll at the French Embassy; Volker Redder, Goethe-Institut, Algiers; Andreas Rost, Pat Binder, and Gerhard Haupt; Galerie Kamel Mennour, Paris; and Michket Krifa, who offered superb contacts and advice. In Ethiopia, we were the beneficiaries of the hospitality and expertise of Elizabeth Giorgis, Director, Institute of Ethiopian Studies, Addis Ababa; Meskerem Assegued, Curator, Zoma Contemporary Art Center, Addis Ababa; Heran Sereke-Brhan, University of Addis Ababa; and Konjit Seyoum-Pankhurst, Asni Gallery, Addis Ababa. In Mali, we were assisted by Moussa Konaté, Director, Bamako Biennial of Photography; Amadou Sow, Moussa Konaté, and Alioune Bâ, President, Association Seydou Keïta, Bamako; Malick Sidibé; and Chab Touré, Galerie Chab. We were enormously helped in Morocco by Abdellah Karroum of Appartement 22, Rabat; Claire Lamotte, Institut Français, Rabat; Yto Barrada, Tangier; Sakina Gharib, Marrakech; Hassan Darsi and Zhor Rehill, Casablanca. In Nairobi, Carol Kaminju and Antony Kaminju introduced us to many photographers and artists. Joy Mboya, Director, Godown Centre; Patricia Kyungu of Kuona Trust; Barbara Meyer-Marroth, Director, and Barbara Reich, Programme Coordinator, Goethe-Institut, Nairobi; and James Muriuki provided invaluable support. In Dakar, I wish to thank the artists of Villages des Arts for their hospitality; and Joëlle le Bussy Fal, Director, Arte Gallery, Dakar. Koyo Kouoh opened doors and smoothed paths in Dakar; her knowledge and expertise are immeasurable. In Johannesburg and Cape Town, I want to thank Makgati Molebatsi; Clive Kellner, Director, and Khwezi Gule, Curator of Contemporary Collections, Johannesburg Art Gallery; John Fleetwood, Director, Market Photo Workshop; Colin Richards, University of the Witwatersrand; Emma Bedford, Chief Curator, South African National Gallery, Cape Town; Geoffrey Grundlingh, University of Cape Town and Cape Town Month of Photography; David Brazier, Zimbabwean Association of Photographers; João Ferreira, João Ferreira Gallery; Linda Givon, David Brodie, Neil Dunda and Melissa Goba, Goodman Gallery, Johannesburg; Michael Stevenson and Kathy Grundlingh, Michael Stevenson Contemporary, Cape Town; Warren Siebrits and Lunetta Bartz, Warren Siebrits Modern and Contemporary Art, Johannesburg; Monna Mokoena, Gallery Momo, Johannesburg; Sue Williamson, Artthrob, Cape Town; and Rory Bester.

Thanks to Dagmar Wittek, Van Laere Contemporary Art, Antwerp, Belgium; Galerie Gabriele Rivet, Cologne; Jack Shainman, Claude Simard, Zuleika Milan, and Judy Sagal, Jack Shainman Gallery, New York; Factum Arte, Madrid; Bernard Utudjian, Galerie Polaris, Paris; Dominique Boutin, Maxppp (Agence France Presse); Pierre Brullé, Galerie Pierre Brullé, Paris; Deepak Talwar, Talwar Gallery, New York; Galeria Rafael Pérez Hernando, Madrid; Nuria Enguita Mayo, Fundació Antoni Tàpies, Barcelona; Catherine David, Humboldt-Universität, Berlin; Serge Aboukrat, Galerie Serge Aboukrat Éditions, Paris; Jeffrey Uslip, Projectile Gallery, New York; Pernilla Holmes, Haunch of Venison Gallery, London; Thomas Erben, Thomas Erben Gallery, New York; Els Vanderplas, Prince Claus Fund for Culture and Development, The Hague. I would like to thank Barbara Vanderlinden for her support.

If I neglected to acknowledge anyone who provided support for this project, I sincerely apologize for the oversight and proffer my thanks. Rest assured, though, that this exhibition is testament to your assistance. However, in concluding I want to mention a number of people who have been exceptionally important in seeing me through the full realization of the project. My boundless gratitude goes to Willis E. Hartshorn, Director of ICP, without whose early support and encouragement there would have been no exhibition. Lea Green was more than an able translator during difficult discussions with artists in Morocco and a reassuring presence as the exhibition took shape. Isabella Brancollini deserves special recognition and thanks for her delicacy and energy. Chika Okeke-Agulu and Marcia Kure were, as usual, both friends and family, and Arinzechukwu made his parents' environment all the more congenial for the nights of endless discussion with his dad. Chika, I owe you, as always. I thank Chris Bratton for his support. None of the work that went into this book and exhibition would have come to much without the special discernment and patience of two beautiful girls: Nora Sophia Chin, who surprised and delighted her parents midway through preparation of the show; and my beloved, beautiful daughter Uchenna Soraya, who has served as my able unpaid assistant and endured my long absences. As you will all see, Uchenna's incandescence has touched every stage of this project. Finally, I want to extend my gratitude to all the artists in the exhibition for their generosity.

Okwui Enwezor
Adjunct Curator

Snap Judgments

New Positions in Contemporary African Photography

Part One

The Uses of Afro-Pessimism

Part One

The Uses of Afro-Pessimism

To begin, it is necessary that the reader confront the "idea" of Africa as a substance. But to do so requires us to struggle with a central paradox of this substance, by virtue of the fact that Africa is always perched on a precipice, on the threshold between something and nothingness, between survival and the negativity of life cycles. At the core of our consideration is the unrelentingly grim view of the world Africans occupy. This is the terrain of Afro-pessimism, that impossibility of fathoming another kind of understanding of what Africa stands for in the larger imagination. It could be said without exaggeration that Afro-pessimism is as old as the invention of Africa as the darkest of all places in human history. Afro-pessimism proceeds by first invalidating the historical usefulness of African experience. This is often based on the belief that "nothing good ever happens in Africa"; that her peoples possess nothing of value for the advancement of humanity. The media is filled with this pernicious objectification. Accompanying this notion are those others that seek to explain Africa's inadequacy. Here, emphasis is placed on the point that the more contact one has with Africa, the better the understanding of the deficiency of its human development index. And therefore the more obvious the backwardness that plagues the continent and her peoples.[1]

It is always tempting to begin discussions of Africa against this familiar backdrop. Depending on the critic's intellectual disposition, he or she may defend or contest the sins and scandals committed and waged against the continent. As entrenched as Afro-pessimism has been as the dominant way to describe Africa, it has not escaped the careful rebuttal of African intellectuals and artists (following this lead, photography has emerged as fertile ground for this dispute).[2] Some African thinkers take a nuanced and ambivalent position toward the subject, striking a balance between stressing nonessentialism and a critique of problems in African governance.[3] But others may take the tack, like earlier apologists of violence against colonized societies, of justifying the state of things in Africa by completely excoriating her in the harshest, most pitiless terms, as the German philosopher Hegel, writing in *Reason in History*, famously did at the beginning of the nineteenth century. We all know the caricature and set-up: the despotic, corrupt "African Big Man" rules a Potemkin state (a banana republic of some sort), the kind novelist V. S. Naipaul gave us in noxious writings like "The Crocodiles of Yamoussoukro." The British press has recently regaled its readers with the cruel stories of Zimbabwean misanthrope Robert Mugabe, and, with no sense of irony, even brought Ian Smith, former racist leader of the now expired Southern Rhodesia, as expert witness against him.

It is in the nature of the struggle to understand what Africa is and her place among other cultural spaces in history that it excites a lot of passion and sometimes regret. We choose which Africa suits our intentions, or, as it were, inventions.[4] Each of these choices surely will correspond to a "correct" representation. In this way, Africa ceases to exist as a concrete reality. Instead, it becomes phosphorescent like the proverbial will-o'-the-wisp, a dazzling dark ember in the figment of our imaginations.

In thinking about Afro-pessimism and the opaque glass it places on our vision of Africa, we are here primarily concerned with the photographic attributes of its manufacture. Specifically, we are interested in exploring photography's specular and blasphemous enterprise and the visual narratives that drive it, particularly if we are to interrogate the way it shapes images of Africa and uses them to telegraph reports which the global public absorbs as the events of life "over there." Careful consideration of photography's wild hallucinations about "phantom Africa"[5] is not simply about its dimension but also the depth of photographic uses of Afro-pessimism to perpetuate a uniform, fixed, and singular approach to the study of Africa. This approach, given many of its assumptions, tends to offer sweeping impressions whereby spatial and cultural distinctiveness and diversity become one blurry, indistinguishable thing.

Can the photographic event of Afro-pessimism be overcome? And if so, how? To do so, we must look at one major impediment. Most reasonable observers would agree that Africa fares poorly in the lens of the global media industry and the twenty-four-hour news cycle that drives it today. Though the global media is by no means the only agent of this sordid affair, it is infinitely the most saturating. To live in the West is to be intimately acquainted and ruthlessly confronted with the evil eye the media casts on Africa. Africans are turned into specters haunting the photographic imaginary and Western conscience. Entire industries that are dependent on this haunted scene have been sustained by a fiction that has been almost impossible to eradicate. For decades now, the photographic imaginary of Africa has circled the same paradoxical field of representation: either showing us the precarious conditions of life and existence, in which case the African subject always appears at risk, on the margins of life itself, at that intersection where one is forced to negotiate the relationship between man and animal. Or we are confronted with the heartbreaking beauty of its natural world, where man is virtually absent except on the occasion when the landscape is left to the whims of tourists and researchers with dollars and fat grants.

Both Africanists and African scholars have condemned the execrable representations which the media deploy to reduce a landmass ten times the size of Europe into a veritable unknowable. If I, like many others, have become inured to such impressions, it has little to do with wanting to inoculate my sensibility against the depredations that constantly leap at us whenever Africa is, as it were, in the picture. Neither is it apathy toward the African condition, nor the visceral need to shut my cognitive and mental vision against stories of debilitation that accompany much of the reporting. My single and sole reason, after decades of absorbing no other kind of information about the continent, is that these stories are no longer plausible. The disaster mongering of the media and its concentration on those scenarios (many abstracted from larger and more complex pictures) that make Africa seem less than a nurturing place for any imaginative and fulfilling life stretch credulity. This calls for a kind of counter-reporting, one driven by an informed, balanced approach to writing or picturing Africa, which is what the group of artists and photographers in this project are carefully sketching. The works they present do not offer palatable impressions and accounts of Africa; rather, what is important is that they bring to bear on the subject in question a different set of lenses guided by a scrupulous attention to images that form their photographic investigations.

To avoid undue sentimentality, it is important to state that there are reasons for reexamining representations of Africa other than the wish to construct "positive" views and stories. The development of such stories will in itself be a good thing. But that will be the job of an advertising and marketing campaign.[6] The role of intellectuals and artists is another matter. It is their task to provide a different environment for reasonable discourse on Africa and, through such discourse, call into question the prejudicial misrepresentations that characterize the work of thinkers and writers like Hegel, Naipaul, Joseph Conrad, Ryder Haggard, and many others. The reasons are both ethical and epistemological. To transform the epistemology of Afro-pessimism is to dismantle an entire intellectual edifice and with it a seemingly incorrigible world view. Ethically, placing the quest for truth above newsworthiness is essential. An ethical commitment to Africa requires the recognition of the complexity of each situation, seeing and writing about what is at hand in any given context as part of a larger world and not merely as a series of disjointed, fragmentary narratives.

An Atlas of Disorder

For more than 150 years, photography has been an intractable ogre in the visual life-world of modernity. Photography either sees through the caked-layer of life and reality, or it obfuscates them in a relentless production of sentimentality, spectacle, and fragmented rumors of existence. For Roland Barthes, photography's final scenes—often wrought as textures of life and experience—are neither necessarily true nor real, but instead encode a visuality of mythmaking that is today collectivized in the daily consumption of mass media images.[7] In contrast to the first, in which a laborious, studied affect of quasi-scientific observation is applied, the frenzy of mass media photography speaks less to the specificity of the photographic image as a carrier of meaning native to a singular subject, but to a whole eschatology of the industry, what Walter Benjamin called an image world.[8] The photographic meaning of Africa is buffeted—perhaps we should say sandwiched—between these two points of view. In Africa, photography has carried the fragmented rumors of existence and mythmaking to another level. In particular, a type of photographic practice has repeatedly staged a veritable phantasmagoria. The manner in which photography frames the African body makes the body appear peculiarly defamiliarized, if not altogether monstrous. To survey these photographic images—in newspapers, on television, in film documentaries and magazines—is to encounter an atlas of disorder. One is immediately struck by the uniformity of the pictorial focus, namely, a resolute commitment to images of entropy. Though such a focus may not perturb most observers of the global photographic industry, the images are clearly at odds with those being made by a large number of

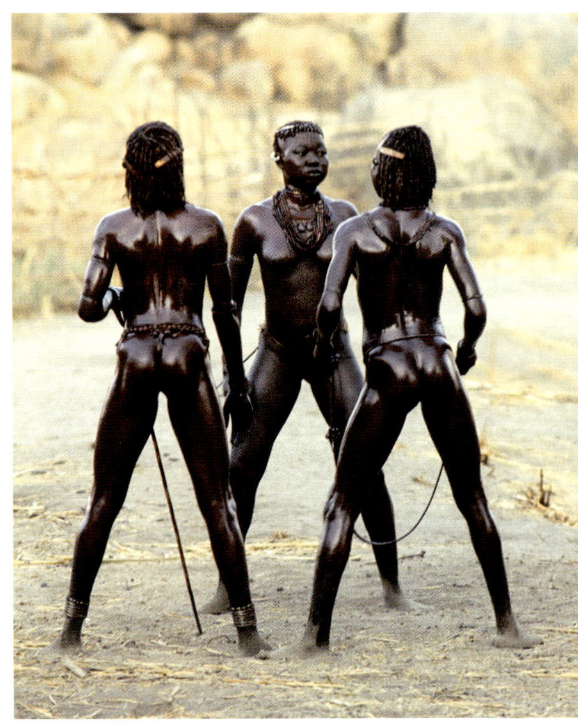

Leni Riefenstahl, *Liebestanz* (Dance of Love, Three Women), 1975–76. Estate of Leni Riefenstahl

African practitioners.[9] Not discounting the censor's black marker, take any number of images published in an African newspaper or magazine and compare them to those that appear in Europe and the U.S. The dissonance is striking.

The gap between these two photographic discourses points us to a historical disjunction in the relationship between photography and Africa.[10] This relationship is both rich and troubling. From the earliest recorded history of the photographic encounter, Africa has made for a fascinating and elusive subject, at once strange, intoxicating, carnal, primitive, wild, luminous.[11] At first the desire to record the exotic, mysterious beauty of the *black* continent may have provided the incentive to invent a kind of sport in which a hunterlike figure wielding congeries of instruments stalks a gamelike subject—suspended between an abyss of indeterminacy and plenitude—waiting to be literally captured. This early phase of the photographic sport (dominated by ethnographers, prospectors, speculators, prosecutors of the colonial enterprise) yielded a huge archive of visual tropes about Africa that have persisted in the popular imagination. Today, hunter and game remain more or less the same, except that the result has become not only outlandish but also has acquired a quality of myth impossible to dislodge from the real. In this latter phase, Africa has been transformed into a wasteland of the bizarre and outrageous.

No other cultural landscape has had a more problematic association with the photographic medium: its apparatus, various industries, orders of knowledge, and hierarchies of power. As already mentioned, the act of photographing Africa has often been bound up with a certain conflict of vision: between how Africans see their world and how others see that world. In a way, this is a clash of lenses, a struggle to locate and represent Africa by two committed but disparate sensibilities—one intensely absorbed in its social and cultural world, the other passing through it, fleetingly, on one assignment or another. The latter sensibility has come to represent specters that haunt Africa. It is constituted around an accumulation of myths. This photographic sensibility works on assumptions based not so much on what it sees but on a preordained, fragmented, and internalized view of the world Africans seem to occupy. This view feeds a phantom essence and releases it as a readymade canon of fascination and repulsion. The image of Africa that I am describing, and which has overwhelmed every other pictorial value, has been produced as much from processes of estrangement as from positions of engagement.

A Vampiric Machine

Consider for example the work of Peter Beard, the socialite and expatriate American photographer who has spent more than forty years living and photographing in Kenya. What is immediately evident in Beard's work is its utter ambivalence toward Kenyans. His photographic pastiches of wild, edenic Africa and the cultivated languor of settler lifestyle, published in American fashion magazines and glossy coffee table books, give us a glimpse into a troubled image machine. Beard's photographs, in which graceful and unpredictable animals and Africans are commingled in a disjointed colonial fantasy, perfectly express the ethos of the vampiric ma-

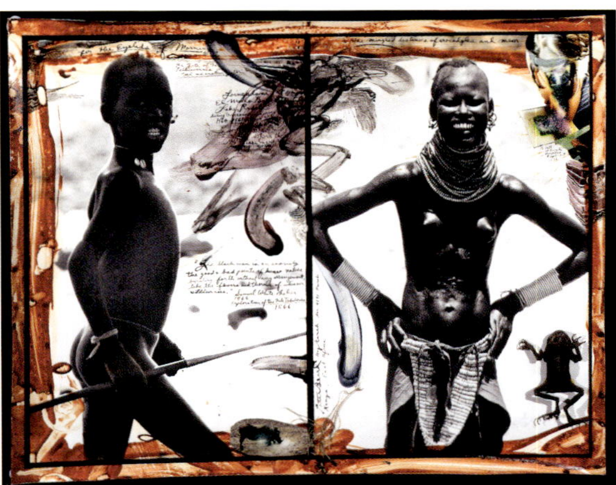

Peter Beard, *Lake Rudolf, Ferguson's Gulf Turkana Bibi*, 1968. Peter Beard / Art + Commerce

chine and its primitivizing capacities. Beard appears simultaneously close to and distant from his subjects; the sleight of hand that permits this form of visualization is the simple trick of the telescopic lens, a tool of surveillance that enables the photographer to feign a kind of intimacy, even if the real intent is to remain untouched by that artificial proximity. The telescopic lens allows the photographic hunter to act as both ethnographer and surveyor, the more to underscore the cultural distinctions between himself and his subject. This distance is placed at the liminal point of the dichotomy of spatial and temporal relations. It exposes a civilizational gap, and at the same time eschews any kind of empathy in social relations. What I am describing here ought to be familiar to us, since it is not at all different from the ideology that supports the geopolitics of North and South relations.

To make sense of the spatial formatting (distance and closeness) and temporal remoteness at the core of Beard's photographic values, one may turn to the rich research that has been initiated in anthropology. In his remarkable book *Time and the Other: How Anthropology Makes Its Object*, Johannes Fabian explains this phenomenological separation: "When modern anthropology began to *construct* [my italics] its other in terms of topoi implying distance, difference, and opposition, its intent was above all, but at least also to construct ordered Space and Time—a cosmos—for Western society to inhabit rather than 'understanding other cultures …'"[12] According to Fabian, at the root of the separation of Self and Other is the severance of temporal connection, to circumvent and deny coevalness.[13] The denial of coevalness is usually based on the principle that even if the Self and Other share space, they may not share the same time; in other words, there is no intersubjective link between them. This lack offers one explanation for the dichotomy that has been a principal problem in modernity between the idea of the modern and primitive, civilized and savage, developed and underdeveloped, and ultimately Self and Other.

Photography reflexively encodes these orders of civility and lack of civility in its approaches to the Other. Photography, which is an art about time, inverts the structure of time in order to create an unnatural temporality that it does not wish to share or coexist in with the Other. However, Fabian observes, "To recognize *Intersubjective Time* would seem to preclude any sort of distancing almost by definition. After all, phenomenologists tried to demonstrate with their analyses that social interaction presupposes intersubjectivity, which in turn is inconceivable without assuming that the participants involved are coeval, i.e. share the same time."[14] In Beard's photographs, human qualities of the subjects are placed at the zero-degree of recognition, the more to focus on the exotic potentials of both man and animal. What we experience—looking at the pictures—is an anthropological machine[15] at work, in which the qualities of man (the African) are always embedded in the environment of the animal. Beard's photographs thus exemplify the problems of coevalness in the documentation of life and people in Africa by Western photographers. The collages that constitute his primary technique of display play off the contrast between man and animal. The images are usually torn, painted, colored, and pieced together pell-mell to create a dizzying agglomeration of bodies, objects, landscapes, and animals. Consequently, there is never a settled point at which Africa is not photographically coextensive with the carefully organized jumble of images, much like the chaos one is subtly meant to perceive in its social reality. This is the sphere of photographic meaning that must be engaged and cleared away in any project concerned with photography and Africa.

If it has been impossible to write about photography and Africa without drawing attention to the vampiric machine—which has been mostly a history of the Western photographic relationship to Africa—it is partially because this photographic archive[16] and its apparatus have remained largely intact and their capacity for mischief undiminished. The reason is simple: Western photographers have the broadest access to distribution systems and reach far more of the global public because of the Western control of global media and institutions of visual and archival modernity. Consequently, photographic depictions of Africa in the global media are shaped primarily by the subjectivity of Western photographers, many of whom wield a controlling influence over visual meaning.[17] But beyond professionals, what of the amateur photographer on a backpacking trip through Africa? Consider another example: a European tourist comes upon a group of women sitting in their stalls in a West African market (say Mali or Senegal) and, seeing them in their resplendent attire, has an overwhelming desire to photograph them. He politely asks their permission, the women good-naturedly decline, but he persists. The question is, why would anyone want to photograph people with whom there is mutual estrangement? What would be the nature and final outcome of this transaction? The photographic sport between hunter and game often assumes the features of a low-intensity courtship, blurring the boundary between assent and violation, license and exploitation.

A good part of the research for this project was spent observing such encounters and pondering the meaning of the photographic sport. As the research progressed, a clear fact emerged—the touristic eye has entered a new era of conflict with Africans who no longer enjoy the unsolicited attention of the lens. We can see in this conflict the emergence of new measures toward the eradication of the touristic eye. Yet, at the same time, the invasive aspect of photography needs to be balanced by the common fact of praxis (artistic or otherwise) within which photography is continuously staged in Africa. To get to this story, which is the result of my research, we would still need to account for the mass media industry and the pixilated remainders that make up its photographic archive.

Suffocation of Images

It is a shocking photograph. The tremor it set off on the first viewing remains palpable, a blunt-edged blow to conscience and the humanitarian conceit.[18] Kevin Carter's photograph of an emaciated, exhausted, naked child crouched on the ground—his/her head bowed down like a supplicant—in the dusty, rutted landscape of Sudan is as iconic as it is disturbing. The child is surrounded by an eerie silence, the outlines of a straw bivouac barely visible in the background. The nakedness of the solitary figure is rendered all the more stark by two ornaments attached to his/her body: a heavy white bead necklace that weighs down the fragile neck and a white hospital tag—as if marked like a statistic—still intact around the skeletal right wrist. Published on the front page of the *New York Times* on March 26, 1993, this picture accompanied a story of the mass exodus of families driven from their homes by famine and a stubborn drought that engulfed and laid waste to formerly productive farmlands. Carter's photograph is distressing not only because of the suffering it records, but also because it is an image with little meaning.[19]

The photograph is also an emblem, registering how the world links Africa to the precariousness of life: hunger, disease, civil strife, genocidal madness, debt, anomie. It encapsulates and seems to feed an intractable addiction—the fascination with Africa's ostensibly futile struggle to slip the clutches of a perpetual nightmare. The photograph therefore serves the function of a double image: it depicts, on the one hand, the actuality of the child's predicament, his/her utter helplessness and inability to reach the feeding center, and, on the other, the persistent image of Africa as "the land of motionless substance and of the blinding ... and tragic disorder of creation."[20] This disorder is often organized into a visual spectrum from where the image begins its journey into inscription. One tragic event, such as a famine, is illuminated, and from this a deductive perspective is drawn, a specificity accrues into a generality. An image repertoire is developed. Every photograph of Africa created in this mode repeats the same appropriation of singular scenes as stand-ins for a larger collective scene, turning the practice of photography into a mythology factory. Every image exists under the aegis of a particular typology: there is the grotesque, the despot; the fetid shantytown that is the very picture of disorganized geometry; the dank, frightful hospital scene crowded with patients dying from diseases not yet known to science; the wild, undisturbed beauty of primeval forests full of animals. All of which signify and represent one and the same thing: Africa. A condemnation to be born stoically until the next Live Aid or Live 8, or whatever indignity Bob Geldof and his fellow miracle workers can muster to rattle the tin can of mercy for an unfortunate people and place.

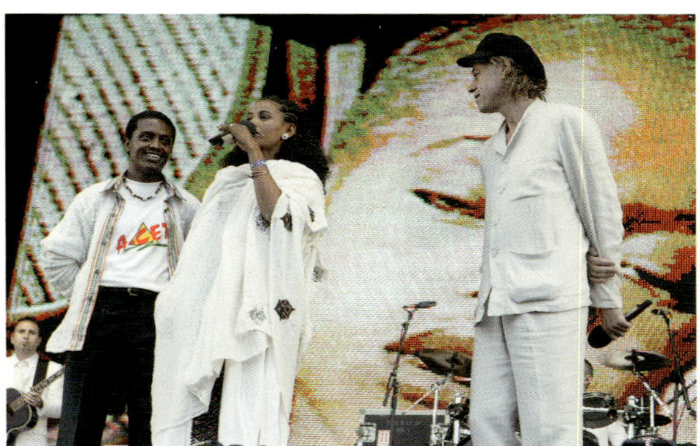

Jo Hale, 24-year-old student Birhan Woldu, former Ethiopian famine victim and the inspiration for Live Aid 1985, speaks on stage as Sir Bob Geldof looks on during *Live 8 London* in Hyde Park on July 2, 2005 in London, England. Twenty years ago, Woldu's face was featured in a video at Live Aid as a dying child with only 10 minutes to live before she was saved by aid workers, 2005. Getty Images

"In a framework in which every word [or image] spoken is spoken in a context of urgency—the urgency of ignorance—it is only possible to take the path from sense to reason in the opposite direction by saturating the words, resorting to an excess ... provoking a suffocation of images."[21] On the day that Live 8, the follow-up to Live Aid from twenty years earlier, opened in London's Hyde Park, Geldof reenacted that scene of excess via a slide presentation of the 1984 Ethiopian famine. Projected in slow-motion across several gigantic screens in the capacious park were photographic images of an emaciated child collapsed like a sack of shredded cloth in the arms of a delirious looking mother while a dense nest of flies played havoc on the child's

Sudan Is Described as Trying to Placate the West

By DONATELLA LORCH
Special to The New York Times

JUBA, the Sudan — The Sudanese Government has made a series of gestures that are meant to placate the West but are also emblematic of the country's need to become more flexible and pragmatic, relief officials say.

The moves come as the United States threatens to add the Sudan to the list of countries that sponsor terrorism and considers creating safety zones for refugees in the south, which is devastated by war and famine.

More than a million people are at risk of starvation in the swampy southern Sudan, the relief workers say. The people of the south, mostly Christians and animists, have been forced from their homes both by famine and by the Islamic fundamentalist Government's offensives in 10 years of fighting.

The plight of the south's people is aggravated by their isolation. More than half the year, rains make the area inaccessible, and in recent years the Government has kept visitors out and offered only limited entry to relief agencies.

Food Is Provided

This year, the Government has donated enough food to provide for all the grain needs for the hundreds of thousands of displaced people in the south.

The Government and rebel factions are allowing the United Nations greater access to devastated and contested areas. Government-controlled areas in the south, previously closed, are granting visas to Western journalists, but they are not permitted to travel freely, but rather to spend the allotted 24 hours under Government supervision.

And one of the biggest concessions has been the permission to allow food delivery by barge in the south to areas cut off in the wet season.

In the southern military outpost of Juba on the banks of the White Nile where more than 230,000 people displaced by fighting and famine rely on airlifted rations, food arrived by barge recently for the first time since the civil war began a decade ago.

"I think the Government has realized that relief needs to be addressed, and we have never gotten so much cooperation," said Manuel Da Silva, director of operations for the World Food Program in Khartoum. "If we are stopped from reaching the people, then the situation will deteriorate."

Empty of Vitality

Dreary, dusty and empty of vitality, Juba is bounded by roads that are mined. Neighboring areas are controlled by rebels. Shops are barricaded shut, but a few foods, like onions and garlic, are laid out on dirty burlap bags on the streets. There is electricity every other day for a few hours.

But Juba is better off than most other towns, largely because it is the most important Government stronghold in the south. There are no starving people here, and officials say some of the displaced are filtering back to their villages. For the first time since 1989, the food rations have reached the recommended level of 400 grams a person.

But Juba is also the most notorious town, a symbol of the vicious Government crackdown. Last fall, when the rebels almost gained control in heavy fighting, the Government retaliated with torture and execution. Priests and Westerners who fled the onslaught said that more than 300 people were accused of being collaborators and were brutally punished by the Government.

Denial by Government

The Government response is denial, as it has been throughout the Government of Gen. Omar Hassan al-Bashir.

In an office empty of books and even visible paperwork, but equipped with a baby blue telephone, Gasim Barnaba Kisanga, the Minister of Political Affairs, insisted that those killed were caught in Government-rebel crossfire.

In an interview videotaped by an aide, he preferred to speak of newfound freedoms in the Sudan.

"People are leading a normal life," Mr. Kisanga said. "We can all move around freely. Everything should be settled for lasting peace."

But the Sudan has lately been considered the breeding ground for some of the most zealous Islamic fundamentalists operating in the world today. Hassan al-Turabi, widely believed to be the real power behind the Bashir Government, has worked with Iran to build training camps in both countries for hundreds of militant Muslim recruits.

It is unclear whether the Sudan's conciliatory gestures are merely reactions from a Government concerned with the threat of intervention or whether they reflect a schism between the relative pragmatists in the Government and the Islamic fundamentalists who favor a theocratic government.

Whatever the motivation, the blanket of silence that has cloaked one of the world's most repressive governments, where hundreds of thousands of people have died in the last several years in a policy that officials have called "ethnic cleansing," appears to be lifting ever so slightly.

The United Nations Human Rights Commission recently accused the Sudan of widespread executions, torture, detention and expulsions and voted to appoint a special investigator. The United States accused Khartoum of having close ties to Iran and Libya and harboring known terrorist groups, including the Palestinian group Hamas, Islamic Holy War and the Party of God. The American list of countries accused of sponsoring state terrorism, which is expected to be reissued in April, now consists of Libya, Iran, Syria, North Korea, Iraq and Cuba.

Rebels Strong in Countryside

Although the military balance favors the Government, which last year won back 14 towns and villages, Khartoum still does not control the countryside. Last year, the Sudanese People's Liberation Front splintered, and the factions fight with one another.

There have been isolated Government bombings this year but no official offensive in the dry season.

Last year the Government executed a Sudanese employee of the United States Agency for International Development, and two agency workers are still missing. The Government has promised to investigate. And relief agencies are concerned that the Government, while talking peace, intends to seal the borders to the south to prevent weapons from reaching rebels.

"The Government has systematically raped the country," said a relief official who spoke on condition of anonymity. "This is definitely a change in tactics. I'd call it a charm offensive. They just deny. We mustn't forget that the Government is superior at delay tactics. It's amazing how you can lose six or eight months before a promise comes through."

Many Displaced and Hungry

Forced to leave their lands and with their cattle herds virtually decimated, hundreds of thousands of mostly nomadic southern Sudanese are either on the brink of starvation or face severe malnutrition, relief officials say. In the area around the town of Kongor, 625 miles south of Khartoum, 145,000 displaced people face starvation, and more than 15 are dying each day. About 100,000 more, mostly from the cattle-herding Dinka, have been pushed to camps along the Kenyan border.

In some areas there are no children under 5 years of age. In Bahr el Ghazal Province, 530 miles southwest of Khartoum, more than 200,000 people are surviving by gathering wild food, relief officials say. In the same region, United Nations officials estimate that since 1989, a wasting disease carried by a sand fly has killed more than 60,000 people hemmed in by fighting. The disease, Kala-Azar or visceral leishmaniasis, can be cured in 30 days with proper medical attention.

United Nations workers and relief agencies, whose money as well as access is restricted, say keeping the people alive requires regular but not necessarily costly intervention. While airlifts cost about $2 million per planeload, barge shipments, which are much larger, cost only about $200,000 a ton.

The arrival of the barge in Juba with wheat, lentils and vegetable oil was more of a symbolic delivery meant to spread hope to the 200,000 Sudanese living along that stretch of the White Nile who have not yet been reached.

2-Day Trip Takes 59 Days

And it was far from easy. A trip scheduled to last two weeks took 59 days, delayed by negotiations and eight hijackings. The World Food Program crew was shot at and in one instance lost 1,300 tons of food to looters. But all 2,400 tons went out to the Sudanese, said Russell L. Ulrey, the barge coordinator. Another barge convoy is scheduled to begin as soon as possible.

The assessment teams, riding into the countryside on motorcycles, found hardly any cattle, the main stock animal. In most villages, there was no corn or wheat in the houses, and people were surviving on water lilies and papyrus roots. There were no seeds, and most everyone appeared to have some visible form of skin disease or illness.

Even the hijackings appeared to have been acts of desperation by groups who thought they were being bypassed. After the rebel looting, the crew expected the crowds on the banks to disappear into the swamps.

"We raised our hands, and then they raised theirs," said David Steele, one of the crew. "Then they began singing. It was beautiful. We went from frustration and anger to the most moving moment of the trip."

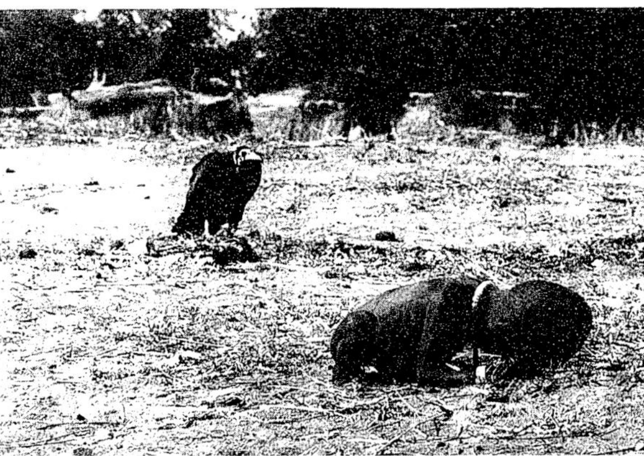

Kevin Carter

In a move meant to placate the West, the Sudanese Government is opening parts of the country's famine-stricken south to relief operations, but for some, it could be too late. A little girl, weakened from hunger, collapsed recently along the trail to a feeding center in Ayod. Nearby, a vulture waited.

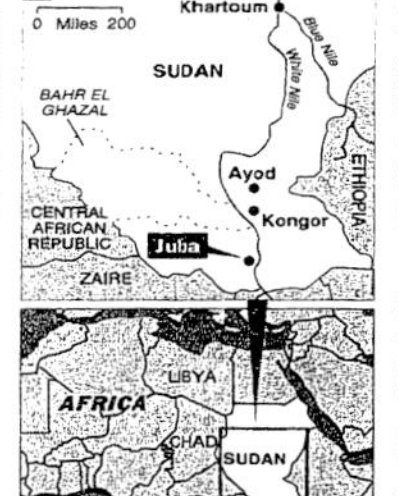

The New York Times

Over 230,000 people at Juba rely on airlifted food to survive.

Kevin Carter, *A little girl, weakened from hunger, collapsed recently along the trail to a feeding center in Ayod. Nearby, a vulture waited.* New York Times, March 16, 1993, p. A3. New York Times and Corbis

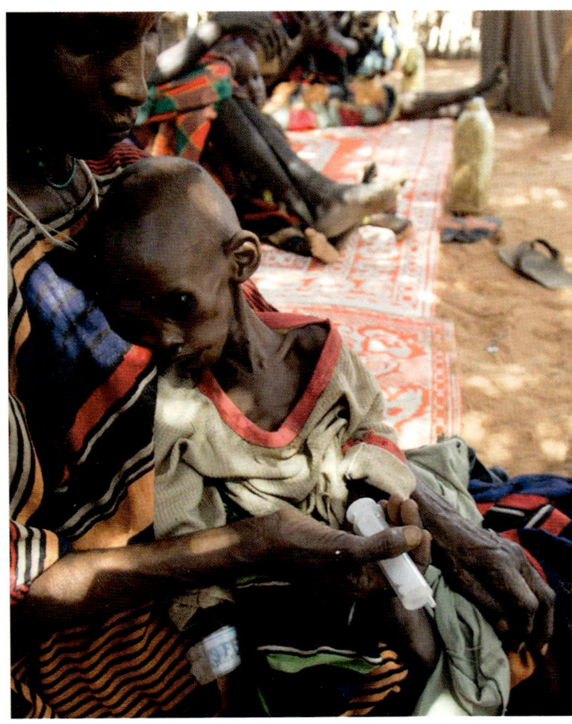

Joel Robine, *An Ethiopian mother holds her child suffering malnutrition in Gode*, 2000.
Joel Robine / AFP / Getty Images

gaping mouth. Was that child alive or dead? The answer to that question was the raison d'etre of the presentation. Geldof showed us the motion picture of the Samaritan's plot in which are gathered a horde of hollow-eyed people who stare at us with sickening desperation, pleading literally for their lives, to be saved. Then, along with pop singer Madonna, he introduced a ravishing young woman, none other than the dying child seen earlier in the arms of her mother, now healthy and whole, rescued by the nutrient-rich gruel of the humanitarian industry. We were informed that she is studying to become, of all things, an agricultural engineer in her country.

Viewing this media spectacle within the stated reason of the concert, debt relief for African nations,[22] one had the distinct impression of this woman being delivered twice, first from the clutches of starvation and death, then to the thunderous applause of the vast crowd gathered at Hyde Park in a secular crusade in which Sir Bob, in the role of miracle worker, literally brings the dead back to life before our eyes.

Documentary Heroism

Cynicism aside, Live Aid, the original musical charity event, came about because of responses to the harrowing documentary photographs and television footage of the Ethiopian famine. This makes the whole photographic set-up of the media in Africa a paradox. On the one hand, it directs our attention to serious deficits around issues of human survival; at the same time, it seems incapable of imagining any other kind of situation outside of despair. Live Aid and its myriad offspring participate in the reproduction of these photographic practices. By all counts, it was a noble act. But it is not insignificant that Geldof returned to global prominence, after a failed career as a "rock star," through the recording and concert he organized for the unfortunate famine victims. That this single event also spawned a profitable career that is part humanitarian theater, part jejune pedantry on behalf of Africa tells us something about the capacity of images to transform lives. Not least because one can notice in the staging of Live 8 a certain sense of opportunism more than obligation. To connect the photographic misery of the1984 famine to debt relief plays to the worst excesses of documentary heroism,[23] which was on full display on the screens in the park.

Looking back to the media experience of the Ethiopian famine sheds light on how we should read Carter's photograph of the Sudanese child, whose fate no one knows anything about today. (Perhaps a future concert will inform us whether he/she survived or perished, whether an enterprising white knight made it to the refugee camp in time to smite the agents of apocalypse that perpetually amplify the African dependency complex. For in the morality play in which documentary heroism participates, Africans are always at risk and white Europeans are forever there to deliver them.) It is no ordinary photograph. The skeletal hulk of the abandoned child fills the picture plane, as a corpulent vulture waits patiently in the background. Something beyond pity accompanied the experience of this image. The child came to represent more than a statistic—he/she was, literally, carrion. This devastating starkness tore at and touched the core of our humanitarian impulse. As an African, I felt a combination of shame and anger, disgust and outrage at that scandal of a picture. And it brought back haunting memories of my own experience nearly forty years earlier in the infernal refugee camps where many Biafran children were abandoned to disease, despair, and death in a brutal civil war. British photographer Don McCullin documented many scenes from the wretched ruins of the Biafran dream of self-determination. Among them are images which essayed the hollow, blank stares of pitiful children reduced to zombies by hunger. Looking at McCullin's images, I count myself lucky to have survived the harrowing experience but also to have escaped from the picturesque capture of the news reporter's autistic lens. These images raise serious issues about the nature of photography, representation, and the ethics of media reporting in Africa. Their proliferation numbs the mind, to the point of glaucoma. We stop seeing the image; the heroism of the photographer becomes paramount. More importantly, I am concerned with the violence such images do to the collective African body. Central to the questions raised by images of calamity, beyond the immediate sorrow of witnessing dreadful scenes of the emptying of African life, is the relationship between photographer and subject. This question loomed large in the reception and discussions of Carter's Sudanese child. What is the photographer's ethical responsibility to the vulnerable subject? Is a living corpse, such as the image of the Sudanese child suggests, capable of being a proper subject? Can photography itself breath life into this lifeless body in order to win it recognition as to be counted among the living? In short, can Carter's picture confer on this nameless child the status of personhood? These questions are raised here not only in relation to the image but in recognition of a broader debate directed at reaching an equilibrium between pictorial concern and violence in representation.

Problems of Anomie in Documentary Practices

Over the years, the indignant voices of Africans have grown to a crescendo, contesting the negative representations of Africa in the media. Achille Mbembe, who has frequently engaged this subject in great detail, writes about two concerns: "One is the burden of arbitrariness involved in seizing from the world and putting to death what has previously been decreed to be nothing, an empty figure. The other is the way the negated subject deprived of power, pushed even farther away, to the other side, behind the existing world, out of the world, takes on himself or herself the act of his or her own destruction and prolongs his/her own crucifixion."[24]

So what does it take for the African body to evade participation in the grotesque ceremonies of self-crucifixion, to avoid becoming a humiliated empty figure? Here is a paradox—is it possible to turn away from the kind of wrenching scenes drawn for the global public by Carter et al. of people at risk, in situations of travail and discomfort, marooned in a crepuscular indeterminacy, deprived of both agency and visibility? There are no easy answers. However, to address these questions requires an acknowledgment that pictures of African suffering are preferred by the media; stories in the *New York Times*, for example, never depict Africa or Africans in normal, ordinary situations. Today it is Darfur and Niger, tomorrow it might be the plight of slum dwellers in Nairobi.[25] These are the kinds of stories and pictures that are rewarded, the ones that condemn many a photojournalist to the vicious cycle of media martyrdom and heroism. Carter would win the Pulitzer and other accolades and awards for his "gutsy" photograph, which in turn spurred a fierce debate about the photographer's obligation to his subject. So what *is* the responsibility of the image hunter? What we see frequently is the problem of anomie in documentary photography vis-à-vis Africa. For Carter, who was born in South Africa and knew such images firsthand as picture editor of the *Mail and Guardian* in Johannesburg and as a member of the gang of four nicknamed the "Bang Bang Club,"[26] a darker emotional ravaging accompanied the making of the kind of images that turned him into a star among the elite corps of disaster and war photographers. The force was centrifugal. Unable to cope with the demands of his simultaneous celebrity and vilification, the fragile photographer was drawn into a psychological maelstrom.[27]

Seeing: Beyond Pathology

In beginning this essay thus, I wanted to force from the outset a recognition of the contradictory forms of photographic practice in Africa. I want us not so much to look away from images such as Carter's—or an eerily similar photograph shot by James Nachtwey in Baidoa, Somalia, of another child abandoned on the roadside, in a similar pose of prostration, his/her feeble wrist marked by a white tag—as to demand from them more answers than the simplistic ones to which we have become accustomed. I want us to direct attention to the multiple ways of representing African life and space, to enunciate forms of visual practice that open us up to the facts that we not only share the same space but also the same time. In other words, I am speaking about visual practices that recognize coevalness, that reach beyond the stock images that have endured until now as the iconography of the "abandoned" continent.

In light of this exhibition inquiry, how might the photographic apparatus—that is, any digital or mechanical, duplicating instrument—engage the continent's vast and complex visual world without resorting to the clichéd metaphors of the media's horror index? This inquiry is as much about photography as it is about representation. Wherever and whenever photography engages Africa, it invents a pathology of spectrality and transience. Each pathology in turn invents its own panacea: pity, infantilization, paternalism, or the reanimation of the grotesque. It could be said that photography's greatest accomplishment is the vast encyclopedia of cures that have followed each of its forays into the continent. Whether we are witnessing visual splendor or astounding civil disorder, Live Aid and other charity events will always be on the near horizon to intercede. This exhibition is not about any of that. It is not about disorder. Nor is it about the collapse of civility, nor genocidal wars. It is not a recapitulation of pathologies.

This exhibition is in part devised to ask pertinent questions about the role of images in the public narratives of the African self and spaces within a changing global image ecology. It is not centered on a specific dispute, nor is its critique simplistic. The exhibition comprises discreet, modest, and forceful propositions on how to look at Africa, how artists work with the tool of photography to trace the arc of a different social reality that is both deliberately pictorial and narrative in approach and at the same time questions the historical dependence on narratives of anomie. African artists and photographers are looking at the unfolding drama of contemporary life and experience in Africa with a fine-tuned alertness. They are examining and analyzing the dizzying processes of spatial transformation, massive transition, and social adaptation that make up the varied realities of diverse groups: urban and rural, formal and informal communities. The artists' penetrating insight provides the remarkable story of this project.

Each of the artists has either taken up a problematic or focused attention on social subjects. For instance, a number of artists explore the interstices of urban communities undergoing transformation, while others use very simple mechanisms of portraiture to spotlight the self-expression of individuals portrayed or deploy the artifice of fashion stylization to draw out values of individual identity. Overall, the works assembled here aid us in examining a different context of image making that is as African in its aesthetic intentions as in its ethical concerns. Given the prevailing, antiphotogenic gaze of these artists, the exhibition most certainly denies the viewer the violent spectacle of deprivation and depravity that has constituted the signature visual image of Africa. In fact, the works evidence a subtle yet substantive critique of such images. Not because there is no deprivation or depravity in contemporary Africa, but because the metaphors of violence and poverty cheapen our understanding of the cultural context. The paradox is that images of suffering—which function as a sort of shorthand for neither looking properly nor seeing Africans in normal human terms—do not ameliorate the disasters which they purportedly engage. On the contrary, they have compounded and skewed the photographic imperatives of a mediatized fascination with the continent's "abnormality" as the primal scene of global media's masochist pleasure, its unrelenting *horror vacui*. This is why quite often what the viewer encounters in the works produced by artists and photographers in this exhibition is a kind of antiphotogenic and antispectacular approach to making images.

Part Two

Contemporary African Art and Globalization

Part Two

Contemporary African Art and Globalization

To properly situate the large group of works presented here, one must consider the place of contemporary African art within the global context. Until the early 1990s, contemporary African artists, though not completely unknown, were relatively unfamiliar to the international public. Although African artists had been exhibiting in international venues for the better part of the post-World War II period (for instance, the South African Ernest Mancoba, who was a founding member of the avant-garde group COBRA), many of them remained marginal in the discussions and exhibitions of modern and contemporary art. These were centered in the United States and Western Europe, due partly to the Cold War,[28] and partly to certain forms of cultural nationalism that became prevalent as a consequence of the two ideological blocs. Even so, the United States and Western Europe were not the exclusive spaces for the negotiation of contemporary international art.[29] Other accounts emerged during the postwar period, albeit without the same kind of infrastructural support enjoyed by Western European and American artists.[30] These other accounts existed either in the shadow of the Euro-American network or were completely peripheral to the art historical machinery that defined the key terms of all advanced art production. Despite this, the political and social changes engendered by national liberation movements and the ideological conditions in the communist bloc profoundly affected various institutions, cultural developments, and sensibilities of postwar artistic practice.[31] As I have argued elsewhere,[32] during the tumultuous years of decolonization, African artists, along with those working in the Global South—Latin America, Asia, Australia—as well as diasporic artists in the West, were laying the groundwork for broader cultural forums which recently have fostered an incipient global artistic discourse. Much of the writing about the development of contemporary art has remained mute about the degree to which the reconfiguration of the institutions of old colonial empires has reshaped the forums of both global politics and art. We are only slowly awakening to this realization, to the sociopolitical and aesthetic dynamics that shaped the art of this period both in the communist bloc and in the Non-Aligned states.[33] The work of artists within these cultural and political spheres was characterized by socio-ideological and nationalist perspectives and has become the focus of new historiographies of mid-twentieth-century modernity that have begun to sketch a more complex topography of contemporary art. Contemporary African art emerged at the juncture of these changes in the international public sphere and civil society and participated in the evolution of what is today the global art circuit.[34]

Nevertheless, until recently it was commonplace in the reception of contemporary African art to assign to its varied and multiple practices an anomalous status within the international mainstream. It seemed that a hardened stance of inattention, coupled with intellectual timidity, would fix the work of African artists in the registers of the functional and kitsch, or authentic and inauthentic.[35] While the work of contemporary African artists has begun to be evaluated and analyzed outside of these registers,[36] much remains to be done. Different perspectives on contemporary African art have informed recent exhibitions across the world, in Africa, Europe, North America, and Japan. These exhibitions have coincided with major adjustments within the field of art history. The training of younger art historians working as specialists outside of the traditional Western focus has played a significant role in reorienting the curatorial and academic analysis of contemporary art and expanded the canon in an entirely new direction.

One reason for these changes is geopolitical in nature. As globalization spreads, it also exposes the fault lines of knowledge circuits that for such a long period remained Eurocentric. As well, important pedagogical and aesthetic issues arise that are not easily resolved by methods of evaluation traditionally used for European and American art. For one, the contexts of the global public sphere and international civil society are today radically different; they have been affected by large-scale shifts in perception and experience. Art and culture are no less affected by the structural, political, economic, cultural, and technological changes that are today driving geopolitical relationships. In the last half-century, we have witnessed the critical reorganization of the procedures of art; and the proliferation of the forms, methods, as well as the displays of contemporary art. These changes have occurred in concert with the sweeping rearrangements produced by globalization.[37] By the same token, institutions and audiences of contemporary art have had to constantly renegotiate their relationship to different forms of artistic modernity and the same for contemporary art's frames of reception.

African artists work at the nexus of these dynamic processes. Like all cultural production across the global stage today, their work is illuminated by the historical conditions which produced modernity and globalization.[38] Even if globalization portends a narrowing of the ethnocentric separation that formed part of the foundation of modern art, we must remain wary of the progressive model of development often ascribed to modernity as an occasion for the encounter with advanced artistic models. We should equally recognize that many aspects of modernity, especially colonialism, oversaw the dismantling and denigration of the artistic canons of colonized societies, and as such bears witness to the disappearance of a vital archive of modern culture. This is the universe where the artistic models of Euro-American modernity and African modernity cross. Contemporary African art emerged out of various national modern art movements that were developed in Africa during colonial and postcolonial periods.[39] These movements shared an awareness of each other's aesthetic and cultural goals.[40] The work of artists in this exhibition to some extent arose from or exists in response to the processes of independent state formation in Africa, along with the political desire to invent national cultures and identities. Contemporary African artists, like their counterparts in Asia, South America, and various diasporas, produce their work in critical dialogue with that of artists in Western Europe and North America.[41] In the wake of globalization, their works have taken on greater significance in that they open up avenues to entirely different artistic vocabularies and cultural logics, as well as underline their specific conditions of production. This in turn has produced greater attention to the language and discourse of their varied practices. As such, contemporary African art is by no means homogeneous.

The spotlight on contemporary African art today, though unprecedented, is fully merited.[42] A strong indicator of its status is the degree to which contemporary African artists have been showcased in important international exhibitions, museums, and festivals. Equally, African cities have created institutions and exhibition venues that reflect the expanding public for their work.[43] Individual artists have been subjects of monographic surveys in museums and in important international collections in Africa, the U.S., Europe, and Asia. Moreover, the academic study of African art has expanded beyond the traditional scope of historical objects. While these cannot be taken as the main index of success, they do signal the broadening intellectual and public interest in African artists' vital contributions to contemporary art. The public reception and dissemination of works by contemporary African artists; the philosophical, conceptual, formal, and cultural concerns addressed in the works; the epistemological challenges presented in the analysis of and engagement with them, all have further opened up a fertile sphere of research taken up by curators, critics, academics, and museums.

Contemporary African Art and Postcolonialism

It is not surprising, then, that much debate centers on the definition of contemporary African art. What constitutes its field of operation, identity, and language? Historically, the terms for defining the identity of African art have been generated from inside the continent.[44] These attempts have been pursued in a number of directions. One of these focuses on the parameters of cultural encounters between Africa and Europe;[45] here the concerns of artists informed by the experiences of colonization and the reception of modernism in Africa shaped part of the *aesthetic* project of modern and contemporary African art and continue to dominate the perspectives of most Western observers. Another takes up the legacy of colonialism to address the radical prioritization of African aesthetics within the discourses of postcolonialism. This is exemplified by experiments melding African forms with the materials of painterly modernism by artists such as Ben Enwonwu, Uche Okeke, Bruce Onobrakpeya, Twins Seven-Seven (all Nigeria), John N. Muafangejo (Namibia), Ibrahim El Salahi (Sudan), and Skunder Boghossian (Ethiopia), to name a few prominent examples. These readings of artistic production from the critical vantage of colonialism and postcolonialism respond to the expanded forms and new paradigms of the African artistic sphere: between artist and society, community and self, nation and citizen, culture and politics. Along with this expansion in artistic and cultural priorities, there must also be an acknowledgment of the fact that contemporary African art exists both inside and outside the continent. In fact, it is unreservedly international. This inside/outside dialectic owes much to a broad range of complex postcolonial shifts, especially the increasing participation of diasporic and expatriate African artists located in the heart of European and American art centers.[46] Consequently, the postcolonial dimension of contemporary African art encompasses recognition of the diasporic and international experiences of the artists.[47] The relationship between Africa and the Western metropolis is set in dramatic tension, producing a lively relay of arguments and counter-arguments, texts and counter-texts, to narrate the differing social temporalities (between modern and contemporary) and cultural perspectives (between African and diasporic) that are reshaping contemporary Africa.

The paths along which African art in the twentieth century has developed are obviously more complex than the episodic sequences articulated above.[48] Nevertheless, they are useful guides in the exploration of the distinct traditions that have contributed to our understanding of the artistic paradigms that fall under the rubric of modern and contemporary art in Africa, both in the specific meanings they generate and the possibilities each offers in clarifying the goals of African artists. However, this can only be a partial view, for it takes little account of the multiplicity of aesthetic systems that exist parallel to modernist and contemporary practices in Africa that are still being negotiated by the public, scholars, and historians.[49] The sequences I have offered are principally concerned with modern and contemporary art as complementary international discourses in which African art and artists have participated in shaping and have played significant roles in their continued expansion. Whatever its identity (a slippery proposition, to say the least), contemporary African art has occurred against the backdrop of historical change. And the quest to define it has been marked both by that change and by resistance to imposing a monolithic interpretation upon it.

Postcolonial Cosmopolitanism

To understand contemporary African art's resistance to a monolithic *contextual* framework is to place it at the crux of the postcolonial. It could be argued that a fundamental feature of African art today is its postcolonial identity. This identity is both local and global and has been constructed, since the nineteenth century, chiefly by urban African elites.[50] It is that identity which has called into question any essential, authentic identity that one may want attached to it. Because contemporary African art is varied and sometimes contradicts even the most stable indicators of its means and aesthetic distinctiveness, attempts to circumscribe the art of the continent inevitably run up against its dispersed practices and references, its formal and aesthetic concerns, its conceptual and historical address. The postcolonial paradigm in Africa, more than being a historical and temporal gauge by which to acquaint ourselves with political and social transformation, perhaps indicates something else: the rupture in decolonized subjectivity and how the national cultural discourse that emerged from decolonization continues to plague the conception of a singular cultural identity. In this sense, the postcolonial helps us to arrive at the cultural plurality of the continent and the inherent multiplicity of African identities. These experiences have equally shaped artistic practice. As the artists in this exhibition remind us, postcolonial identities are neither fixed geographically nor limited by ethnicity. They range widely in their geographic locations and geopolitical forma-

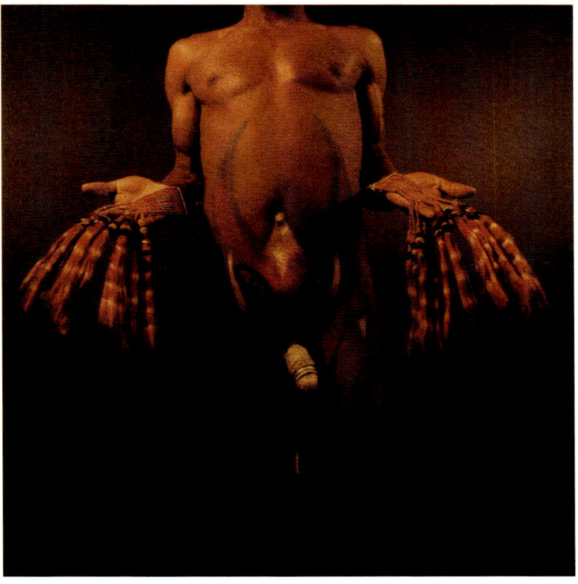

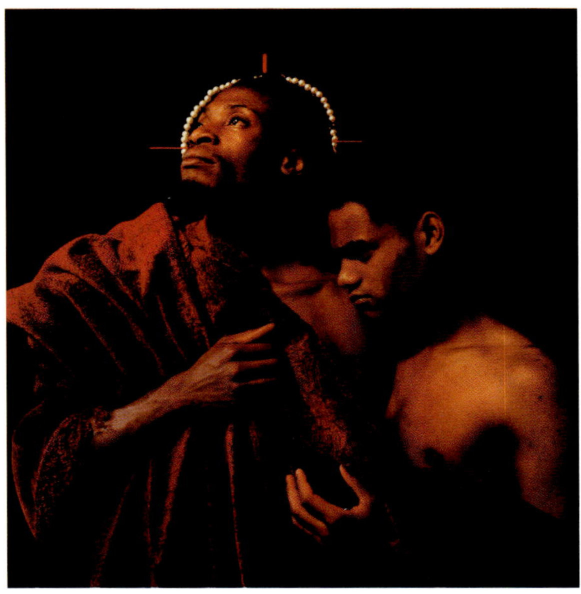

Rotimi Fani-Kayode, *Untitled*, from the series "Communion," ca. 1989. Autograph: Association of Black Photographers, London

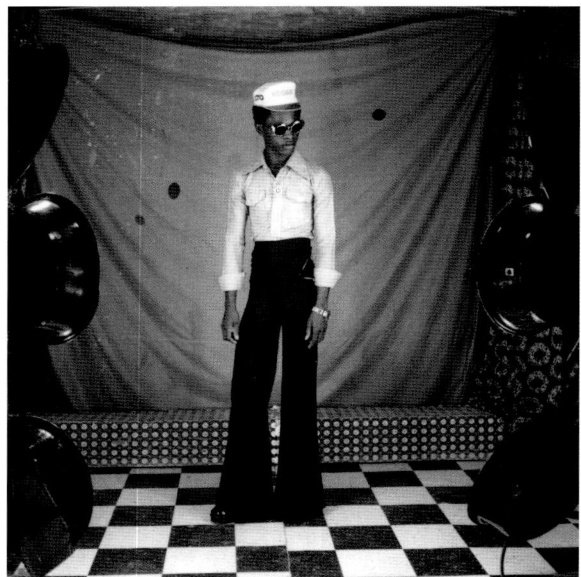

Samuel Fosso, *Untitled*, ca. 1977. Jack Shainman Gallery, New York

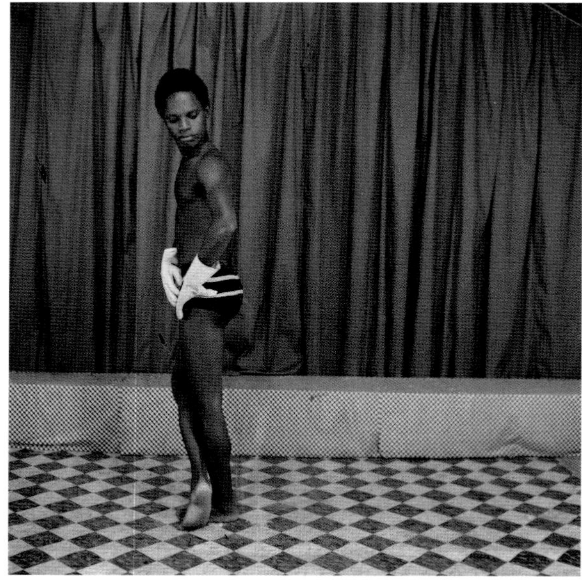

Samuel Fosso, *Untitled*, ca. 1977. Jack Shainman Gallery, New York

tions—from continental to diasporic—and are diffused through temporal networks that defy locality and self, community and nation. Whether the artists live and work in Africa or elsewhere, one essential characteristic that unites them is the cosmopolitan nature of each of their localities. I mean *cosmopolitan* in the sense of the worldview of the artists, not in the narrow sense of the urban categories usually deployed to analyze it. As such, the quest for an essential contemporary African art immediately confronts the limit placed on such an essentializing process by the multiplicity of contemporary African discursive formations. The task of *Snap Judgments*, therefore, is a dialectical one. The exhibition is keenly aware of the limitations of place (Africa) as its organizing framework. Yet it enthusiastically deploys it to give substance to the ethical positions from which the artists address their audiences, and also to foreground the multiplicity of identities, discursive formations, and itineraries each artist taps or constructs in his/her quest to map the diffused lines of contemporary global culture.

Photography in Contemporary African Art

So far I have sketched an outline of issues and questions often posed for the public understanding of contemporary African art, which has been in wide international circulation for over forty years.[51] Let us now turn to a specific aesthetic formation within that field. Photography has been a remarkably dynamic, creatively sophisticated, and artistically important component of African visual culture for over a century.[52] But the recognition of African photographers and the unique visual language they have developed has come quite late. Until recently, works of African photographers have not been examined within the history of photography or, for that matter, contemporary African art.[53] For the American public, the first major attempt to do so was *In/sight: African Photographers, 1940 to the Present*, an exhibition held at the Guggenheim Museum in 1996, for which I was a co-curator.[54] A decade later, I have again taken up the subject of photography, this time in recognition of the fact that it has become a vital tool and source of imagery for many artists. In short, a major medium in contemporary African art. While preparing the present exhibition, I was concerned with one fundamental question, namely, what was the governing rhetoric of the works in *In/sight* and how does it differ in the works created in the decade since?

While *In/sight* clearly established the centrality of photography in African visual culture, the work of the photographers who emerged from it also expanded the general history of the medium. An observer of that earlier exhibition, and many shows that came in its wake, would have noticed the preponderance of portrait photography (so-called studio photography), which encompassed the classic modernist styles seen in the work of Seydou Keïta, Malick Sidibé, Mama Casset, and Cornelius Augustt Azaglo; the conceptual, performative, and self-reflexive photography of Samuel Fosso and Rotimi Fani-Kayode; and the documentary style that has been the hallmark of South African photography.[55]

Today, a different approach rules the utilization of photography—and its correlates: video, film, and digital technology—in the practices of African artists. What is clear in this new body of work is that contemporary

African artists and photographers have responded to the expansion of photographic media in everyday life in much the same way as artists everywhere else.

Snap Judgments is conceived as a vehicle to investigate the recent trajectories in photographic practice by contemporary African artists and photographers and the analytical judgments and interpretations they bring to bear on the conditions and experiences of contemporary Africa. Naturally, there are continuities between the exhibition of a decade ago and the present one, not least because a number of artists in the first one again appear here. But the significant shift highlighted in *Snap Judgments* is the privileging of the investigative, conceptual, and archival potential of the photographic medium. Here photography has been adapted as a probing tool; it is as much a medium of witnessing as it is an analytical one. Consequently, over the last ten years, an analytical, postdocumentary photographic work oriented around the artists' heightened sense of observation has emerged more strongly.

Portraiture, Modernity, and the Dialectical Image

A distinguishing feature of the recent reception of African photographic production is the tendency to elide the boundary between modern and contemporary works. Modern African photography, exemplified by studio portraiture though by no means limited to it, tended to be highly organized formal studies of cultures and individuals in transition. Some of the images are so stylized that they recall court portraits (Keïta), while others are more casual and revel in their very quotidianness (Sidibé). The powerful Senegalese school in Dakar and Saint-Louis (Casset, Meïssa Gaye, Mix Gueye, and others); the work of the Bamako photographers (Keïta, Hamadou Bocoum, Abderramane Sakaly, and Sidibé); the politically charged works of South African photographers (Peter Magubane, Jürgen Schadeberg, David Goldblatt, Santu Mofokeng); the modernism of Sunmi Smart-Cole and J. D. Okhai Ojeikere in Nigeria; the crepuscular images of Ricardo Rangel in Mozambique; Augustt Azaglo's severe identity-card-format portraits in Côte d'Ivoire; and a number of Maghrebian photographers such as Van Leo in Cairo and Armenian-Ethiopian court photographers in Addis Ababa suggest an evolving history of modern photography in Africa.

Most modern African portrait photography constitutes an attempt at straightforward depiction of a social self, more specifically, the African self. In these portraits, beginning in the late nineteenth century, the point of view is always direct and always centered on the subject, unlike colonial photography, which usually imaged the African subject as a specimen of some exotic investigation.[56] To make this distinction between colonial images of Africans and portrayals of Africans by African photographers assists in clearing away the confusion that often attends discussions of modernity in African visual production. Such discussions tend to interpret modernity in Africa as part of the great bequest made by colonialism. This is the case only if one subscribes to the belief that "[European] colonization cohesively binds the diverse, often antagonistic, collective memories of many African cultures."[57] But, in fact colonial institutions tried to bring these antagonistic memories into a single experience of modernity by "offering and imposing the desirability of its own memory," subtending in the process the desirability of African memory whereby "[European] colonization promises a vision of progressive enrichment to the colonized."[58]

Whether or not modern African photographers intentionally constituted their work in response to colonial imagery, we must see it in light of their privileging of African memories. The portraits speak to us not just from the dichotomy of colonizer and colonized; they engage us in searching out positions of an African imaginary. At the same time, they reveal African involvement in a rich cultural exchange with more than European modernity, by drawing our attention to the deep roots of Islamic modernity in Africa. Most critics minimize this dialectical relationship between African and other modernities. But we see it very clearly in the portraits of Keïta.[59] We see it as well in the reflexive exten-

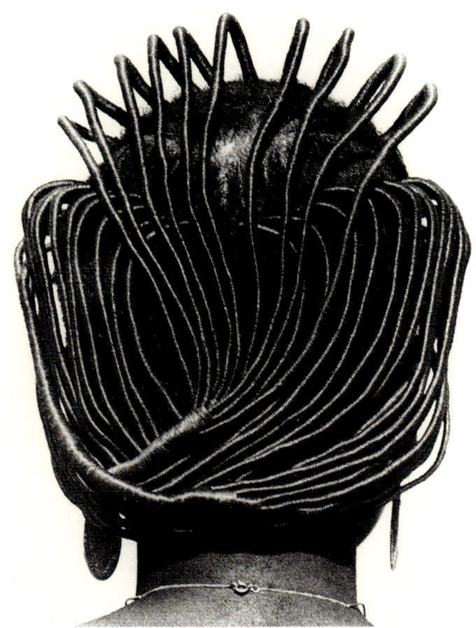

J. D. Okhai Ojeikere, *AGARACHA. This hairstyle is common among the Anambra and Imo people of Nigeria. It is an all-purpose hairstyle.* Courtesy André Magnin and the artist

sion of this dialectic in the contemporary self-portraits of Fosso and later Fani-Kayode and Oladélé Bamgboyé. In Keïta's images, a controlled, formalist approach to portraiture is often overlaid with allegorical props drawn from different cultural spaces—African, Islamic, European—to further agitate the field of photographic play. Keïta's work emerged at that moment when the colonial establishment and its various bureaucracies, institutions, and large governmental apparatus disposed toward restricting the subjectivity of Africans through the rules of *mission civilisatrice* were facing relentless resistance. This resistance aimed at the transformation and rehabilitation of African subjectivity. The thousands of men, women, and children who paraded before Keïta's camera from 1948 to 1962 represent a visual archive of this resistance and transformation. They did so with clear, unvarnished awareness of their grounding as subjects in a social milieu that is African in every sense. They were signaling and projecting their own singularity, as well as enunciating aesthetic values of African beauty previously denied them by the primitivizing apparatus of colonial ethnography. So to look at Keïta's portraits of the urban inhabitants of Bamako is to witness the near disappearance of colonial subjectivity. Critics tend to view Keïta's subjects and their petit-bourgeois attachments to Western fetish objects—cars, bicycles, motorcycles, radios, telephones, pens, among other props that made up the visual environment of his studio—as enacting through the portrait photographs their sense of inclusion in Western (read: colonial) modernity. This reading is incorrect on a number of levels.[60] First, it ignores the privileged standing of an African aesthetic in relation to fashion, stylization, gait, and pose in the representations and self-styling of the sitters.[61] Second, it disregards the exchange between African and Islamic modernity. Finally, never properly addressed is the fact that the privileging of other modes of subjectivity—ideals of beauty, concepts of leisure, the preponderance of non-European fashion—signifies a critique of how colonial subjectivity sought to replace African memories with its own. Beyond all this, and despite the intractable nature of Afro-pessimism, African visual practice has always contested the attenuated views of Africa and its collective memories. Here photography has proven a particularly rich tool in the debate

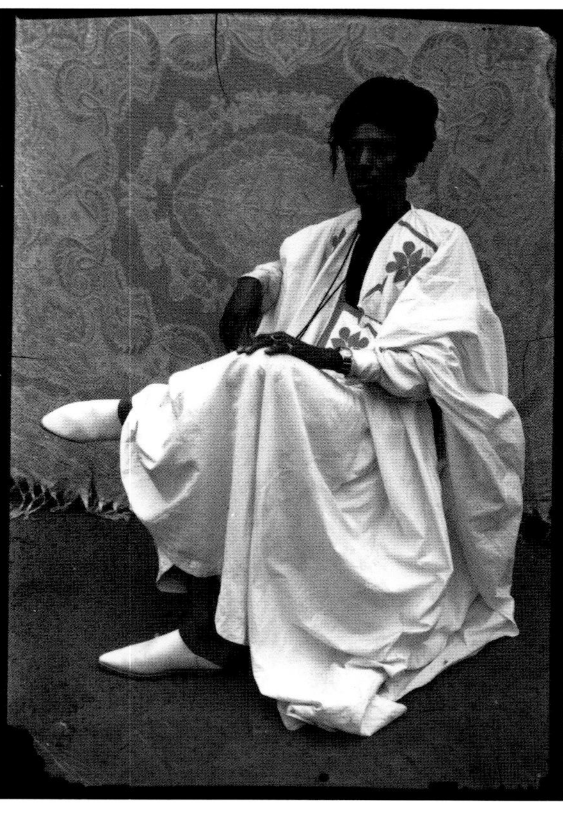

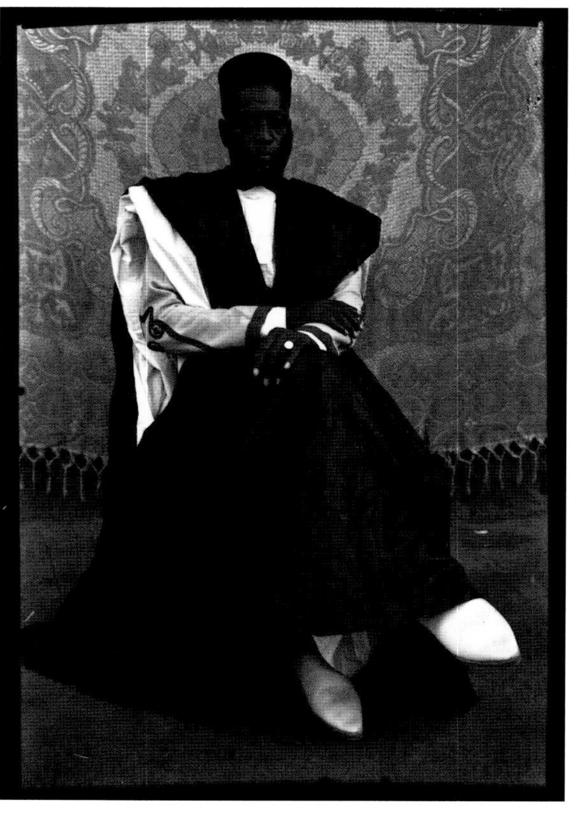

left:
Seydou Keïta, *Untitled*, ca. 1950–55. Association Seydou Keïta, Bamako; Sean Kelly Gallery, New York; JM Patras, Paris

right:
Seydou Keïta, *Untitled*, ca. 1950–55. Association Seydou Keïta, Bamako; Sean Kelly Gallery, New York; JM Patras, Paris

Part Three

The Analytical Impulse in Contemporary African Photography

Part Three

The Analytical Impulse in Contemporary African Photography

Snap Judgments proposes that the paradigmatic shift from colonial and Western documentary photography in Africa to modern and contemporary African photography is captured in the attempt by African photographers and artists to reestablish the priority of an extant African visual archive. Yet, the transformation of the languages of modern and contemporary African photography contains instances of continuity and discontinuity. These are visible in modern African photography's subtle reinscription of the identity of the African self, and in contemporary photography's move from depiction to observation. The shifts I am addressing can be explored in terms of the dialogue between the dialectical (modern) and analytical (contemporary) photographic modes of African practitioners. Sidibé's recent work captures this dynamic most succinctly, in a single corpus.

Though his work is still organized within the system of studio portraiture—the dialectical structure par excellence—he has recently employed a serial, conceptual aesthetic, particularly in his studies of the eroticism of Malian women. Unlike his documentary work of the 1960s and '70s, and studio portraits which were mainly commissions, he has shifted to a sustained analytical mode of looking that previously played little or no role in his approach to portraiture. Fosso, on the other hand, did not have to make such a leap in his work, which remains resolutely contemporary. In fact, he has expanded the simple repertoire in which he transformed his studio (after hours) into a performance theater for his self-portraits. His work today involves more complex doppelgangers.

As stated above, recent photography has become increasingly documentary—therefore reflexive—and analytical.[62] And partly because of this change in emphasis, from the individual subject to society at large, it may also appear that contemporary African photography is deliberately antagonistic to the notion that photography should be deployed principally within the register of a purely mnemonic and identity-based function. Another point to be made about younger artists and photographers is that their work deviates radically from Sidibé's, for example, in that they draw exclusively from conceptual approaches common in contemporary art at large. Consequently, the new position the artists adopt engages broader spheres of interest such as landscape, urban studies, performance, portraiture, and documentary, differing from earlier approaches used in African photography. The self-reflexive uses of portraiture in the works

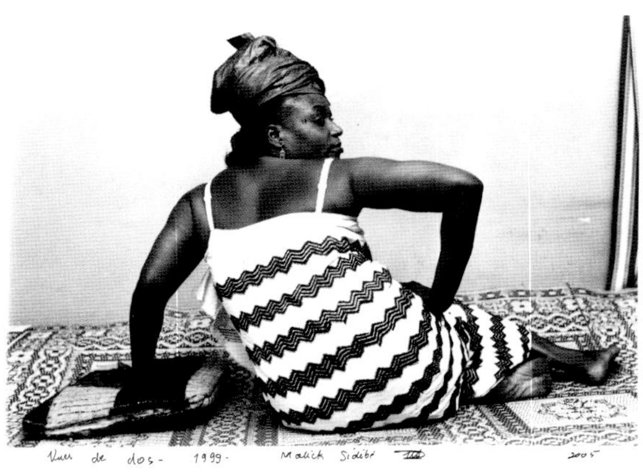

Malick Sidibé, *Vues de dos—1999*, 2005. Collection of Artur Walther

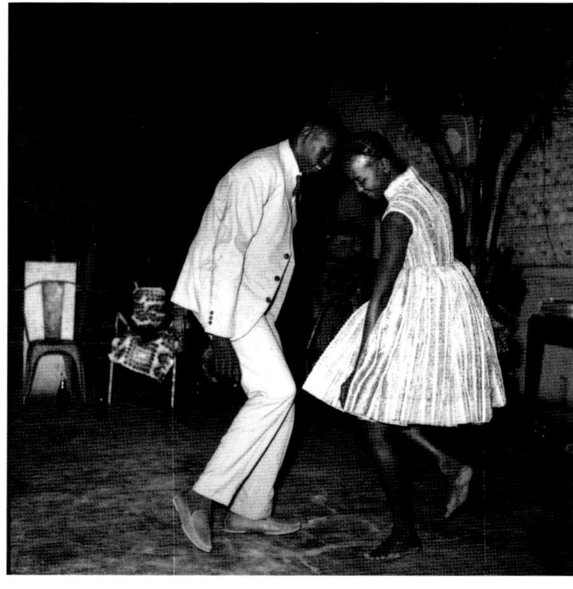

Malick Sidibé, *Christmas Eve*, 1963. International Center of Photography, New York

of Bamgboyé, Fani-Kayode, Tracey Rose, and Berni Searle extend and reroute more traditional forms to document people's conceptions of themselves and their place in society. Fosso provides the critical conceptual and historical bridge between this self-reflexive mode and earlier paradigms of studio photography, particularly in the way he uses the self-portrait as a tool for examining postcolonial identity. Here photography has been transformed into a discursive method for addressing and questioning issues of gender and sexuality (Fosso, Bamgboyé, Rotimi-Kayode) or race and gender (Rose, Searle), or gender (Angele Etoundi Essamba).

Antiphotogenic and the Eradication of the Touristic Gaze

Throughout this essay, we have been tracking the apparatus of the photographic sport, stalking its object of fascination and elements of its deformed verisimilitude. In the course of this argument, we have underlined the fact that this large apparatus and its supporting systems of production, distribution, dissemination, and mythology exist as part of the institutions of colonial modernity. We also addressed the degree to which African photographers from the late nineteenth to the latter half of the twentieth century invented a counter-imaginary, aiming through the dialectical image to oppose the anthropological machinery of colonial power. The conventions of portraiture these photographers inaugurated—as diverse as the subjects who appear in the photographs—provide the critical basis of a reverse-representation. In the wake of these developments emerged a different iconography of the African self, one at odds with that of colonial modernity. Contemporary African photography extends this dialectic. This photography focuses not just on individuals through social representation, but also on social environments, on networks of shared relations and coevalness, on the events of the self, on spatial practices. Some works are both documentary and social. Others are rooted in performance. But they are never predisposed exclusively to ideology nor do they reproduce pathology. They are fundamentally analytical. One important marker of the various approaches is the antiphotogenic lens that many of the photographers deploy. If the lens of Western photojournalism or nature photography often pictures Africa as a photogenic, exotic, intoxicating bundle of color, nature, and decay, these artists and photographers permit the viewer to see a different kind of image: Africa as a living, dynamic, changing substance. What may appear to the Western lens as photographable may not have the same appeal to a photographer living and working in West Africa.[63]

The challenge to the photogenic lens may pivot on attempts by artists to redirect the roaming lens of the touristic gaze. In short, it seeks nothing less than the eradication of that gaze. Several artists address this question of tourism and the photogenic in a number of subtle and symbolic ways. In "Chambres Maliennes" (2001–2), rather than the bustling colorful city of Bamako where he lives, Mohamed Camara focuses on the private, intimate spaces of his friends, those spaces which the lens of tourism rarely seeks or can access. Camara's work is casual. The characteristic banality of his low-tech photographs lend them the quality of a snapshot. The intimacy of the works conveys their authenticity as recordings of daily experience. This may not elevate Camara's central concern—which is about how young people like him live normal lives in Africa—to the media's attention, because there is simply no "story" there. But his images have a complicated emotional immediacy and at the same time appear utterly ambivalent about their own status. On the other hand, if Camara does not photograph his own environment in a touristic manner, he certainly approaches the cultural rituals of Europe the way an African tourist might. In the series of photographs presented in *Snap Judgments* (pages 67–69), he seems to have reversed the touristic gaze, aiming it squarely at the rituals of white Christmas through a form of performance employing the kitsch props (lights, snow, etc.) associated with it.

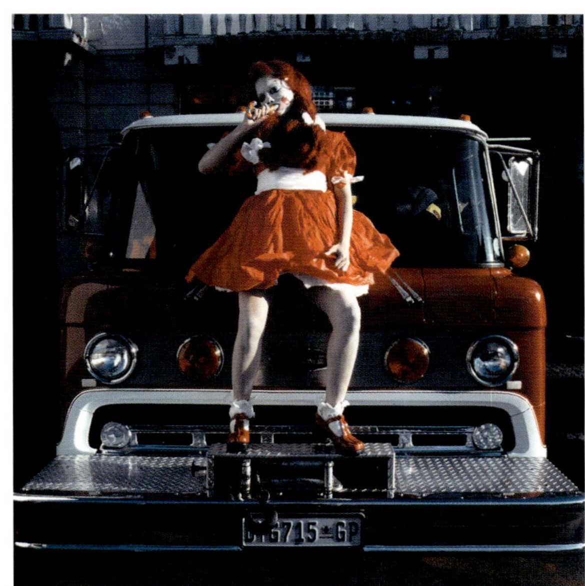

Tracey Rose, *Lolita*, 2001. Courtesy the artist and Projectile Gallery, New York

Maha Maamoun—as an artist and as a member of the Contemporary Images Collective in Cairo—has been a careful and critical interrogator of the intersection of tourism and the photogenic in her depiction of the Egyptian urban scene. The "Cairoscapes" series (2001–03) posits the fast-paced flow of the crowd, albeit as isolated and solitary figures. In the elongated horizontal format of the photographs, what is first registered is the sense of the image in motion, of bodies and gestures trapped in a freeze-frame of temporal suspension in which figuration dissolves into floral patterns (some of which may appear to the eye like designs for tablecloths or bedspreads) and the street and traffic float by like blurs and abstractions. These images project a different sensibility of the cacophonic bazaar of the African/Islamic city. Rather than focusing on the ubiquitous crowd, Maamoun's antitouristic pictures construct an imaginary domain "in which relationships between city, figure, and nature ... converge to suggest a new terrain."[64] (pages 120–123). Close inspection might infer that they are fictive, but I do not think this is the point. More important is the evident defamiliarization that indicates layers of repression subtly unpeeled and exposed. As benign as these images may appear, there is something about their mild opacity that slightly deranges the mise-en-scene.

To apprehend the touristic imagination, we need to conduct an autopsy on its images, an act which corresponds to Maamoun's reorganized beach scene. As the image suggests, tourism and travel are the establishing shots of a troubled relationship between near and far, familiar and unfamiliar, native and tourist. In the eighteenth century, the Grand Tour (which bequeathed to us the word *tourism*) was an opportunity to broaden the traveler's horizon. Ultimately, it supported a habit of consumption: to seize and possess a slice of the world. Tourism gives the traveler the illusion of worldliness, the fleeting security of cosmopolitanism. But because the touristic imagination is famished and voracious, it feeds a habit, and often makes for the manufacture of fraudulent transactions. This is especially the case with contemporary travel in the form of the packaged tour, which promises round-the-clock experience. Invented at the moment when bourgeois consciousness emerged from the development of capitalism, tourism closely follows those changes in modernity that profoundly unsettled social relations between places and peoples. With the proliferation of cameras, the touristic experience has literally expanded into surveillance. Perhaps it is possible to understand why, in so-called exotic places, tourism is a blindspot of photography. The tourist with a camera is today the ultimate figure of derision, especially in the aggressivity of his quest for images. This locates the tension proper to the wild hallucinations common to the touristic consumption of otherness. The camera grants remote access but obliterates knowledge. It deracinates all that it documents. The touristic image can be cached as a souvenir of poor pictorial judgment, because it purports to offer an innocent account of what it did not quite see.

The kind of encounter which this type of tourism implies is at the heart of how certain contemporary images of Africa have been produced and circulated. Theo Eshetu, in his pulsating, color-saturated, and hallucinatory video *Blood Is Not Freshwater* (2002), began with a return to Ethiopia, the home of his family, to make a video about himself, his father, and grandfather. The initial trip for this video then turned into the making of another one: *Trip to Mount Ziqualla* (2005). The video is divided into three contiguous images, two of which mirror the other on the flanks of the projection (pages 140–145). In the center is a cut, an image different from the mirrored flanks that functions like an anchor and divides the two repeated images on the left and right corners of the projection. This device not only stretches the narrative of the video, it also distorts its spatial and temporal pace. The result is a video that has a dense imaginative visuality and mnemonic richness. Eshetu's video exemplifies the complications that arise at the intersection of diaspora and nation, between home and exile, postcolonial and postnational identities. In his extended meditation on the annual Coptic religious pilgrimage to Mount Ziqualla, we are placed at the center of a conundrum. Is a returning son a native or outsider? Is his lens that of a visitor, a tourist absorbed in the scintillating ornamentation and serene beauty of the landscape, or is he one of the celebrants who have made this journey of faith and memory? Is there a difference between Eshetu's desire to reroot and reroute[65] himself and that of the indigenous population who have no need to be reintegrated into their own memories? If so, how does it reveal this difference? Eshetu's photographic and videographic reverse journey confounds, precisely because it allows us to question the image maker's intent without passing judgment on it. However, what changes the dynamic in Eshetu's "intimate outsider"[66] status in this quasi-ethnographic video is how he implicates himself in the narrative. He is neither distant from the scenes he depicts nor remote from the celebrants: there is a complex entanglement between Eshetu and the subjects which allows us, the viewers, to assume that he has opted for subject status as well. In fact, in the long-format version of the video, this is made explicit in the interactions between Eshetu and his grandfather, and by his constant foregrounding of the notion that, while the journey to Mount Ziqualla may be about faith to the celebrants, for him it is also about memory. Recognizing this makes possible a reading of the video and the photographs as critically posttouristic documents.

Passionate Bodies

Despite the initial use of the camera to present the view of the Other's baseness and moral debility, to merge his human traits with those of the nonhuman, the portrait photograph undermined the clinical and ideological instrumentality that beset photography the moment it touched this body. Portraiture has played a central and significant role in delineating the expressive and representational codes of modern and contemporary African photography, not least because it revealed the disjuncture between African and colonial memories. African photography transformed the instrumentality of the camera and engulfed the anthropological machine in a fiery conflagration. It registered the inscription of a figure that can no longer be subtracted from the human, excluded from the modern, or disfigured as uncivilized. The advent of postcolonialism further revealed the chasm between these memories. Postcolonialism not only rerouted the given discourse of the body politic in colonial Africa, it equally explored the cultural politics of that body after decolonization. In so doing, it illuminated the tension that demarcates cultural identity and self-representation, race and identity, gender and sexuality, masculinity and femininity. The narratives of the body and subjectivity, in the different guises in which they have appeared in recent years, obviate the primitivist codes embedded in ethnographic knowledge. If identity is understood to be underpinned by biology, it is equally underwritten by politics. The imperatives of the two always require negotiation. One can address identity in the works of the artists here by foregrounding the immediacy projected through the body's physical presence and not by some primitivist essence.

As I have been arguing, the photograph initially was a corrosive object when it touched the African body. Postcolonialism opened up another avenue by which we can explore the facts of that body in representation. Let us describe them as passionate bodies; bodies without limits, that are not circumscribed. The procedure of self-mapping in the performance-driven photographs and videos of Doa Aly is a recent example of the critical analysis artists have been pursuing about the self and gender. Aly's elegant thwarting of the body to achieve the supple pose and gesture of the ballet dancer is a rigorous test and reinvention of the docile body. In *48 Ballet Classes* (2005), Aly subjects her body to a slow process of transformation, working with a ballet master to achieve her goal (pages 70–71). Each lesson of the progression is recorded, spanning more than a month. Here the camera is a tracking instrument as well as an observant eye. This self-surgery is equally apparent in Bamgboyé's auto-erotic performances before the camera (pages 48–57). In his photographs, the camera is literally inhabited and used as a drawing tool, creating a palimpsest of forms, objects, body parts, and movement. The densely overlaid images suggest an effect of temporal and spatial derangement, a shifting away from the rationalist view of portraiture as a vehicle of disclosure. Instead, Bamgboyé's dramatic layered photographs are physical objects that project into the viewer's space, splitting the space of encounter between the concrete formation of the studio and the imaginary domain of desire and fantasy. Such series as "Arise" (1991/1997) and "Celebrate" (1994) exploit these possibilities, giving way to both a theoretically complicated representation and an aesthetically powerful set of propositions. In "Arise," the body as a physical specimen carves out a figurative, sculptural presence, while foregrounding a psychosexual tension that recalls Fani-Kayode's portfolio "Bodies of Experience" (1988).[67]

Tracey Rose, from the very inception of her career, has used photography as a companion to her explorations of identity, race, gender, and sexuality. Rose's allegories of miscegenation, sexual and racial difference, and feminist interrogations of gender are produced as *tableaux vivants* of that which is both deeply ontological and political in apartheid and post-apartheid culture. Her recent series "Lucie's Fur" (2003–04) is elliptically centered on the Eve-like figure discovered in Ethiopia and christened as the first woman (pages 58–63). At the same time, "Lucie's Fur" conflates this figure with that of the archangel Lucifer, "the condemned angel of light" who was expelled from paradise for challenging god. The series draws from and twists biblical and literary narratives and archaeological and scientific research into human origin, the discovery of sexuality, and sexual desire in the Garden of Eden. However, the story of the first man and woman has been modified in this account: rather than Adam and Eve, the couple are two black gay lovers named Adam and Yves, who may have been introduced by Rose as a commentary on homophobia. Filmed and photographed like a movie, in the studio and on location in Johannesburg, this series, by far Rose's most complex and accomplished body of work, enlarges the arena of auto-performance that has long informed her radical production. It draws from a series of surrealist tropes: dream sequences, allegory, the destabilization of the signifier, and the transformation of cultural symbols in order to deform their meaning. These *tableaux* announce the interplay between relations of gender, origin, religious belief, mythology, and fantasy.

By the same token, the fashion photographic shot, which in a sense represents another order of performance, extends the dialectical form of portraiture explored throughout this essay. Andrew Dosunmu and Nontsikelelo "Lolo" Veleko take different approaches to elucidating the depth of desire which fashion disturbs. Dosunmu's images are primarily shot for fashion magazines (pages 72–89). He is interested in the physicality of female sexuality, yet his models are not objects of his projection. In fact, unlike in most fashion photography, Dosunmu keeps fantasy at a minimum, focusing instead on his models not as characters but as subjects. There is a *verité* approach in all his work, a kind of fashion documentary that collapses the boundary between the street and the studio. And because he often works on location and uses nonprofessionals as models, Dosunmu's photographs underline the ideological conditions of the fashion system and transform our understanding of it. Veleko, on the other hand, is a scavenger of individuality, a hunter of cool and street fashion. She is entirely interested in individuals, and thus scours the streets to find the subjects of the photographic encounter (pages 90–94). She is partial to subjects who express themselves through their social camouflage, by what they wear, the manner in which they present themselves to others and to themselves. These subjects are often young, fashion-conscious, urban black South Africans living in Johannesburg. As such, we can read these pictures as both explorations and celebrations of post-apartheid identity. In these street portraits, the subjects are approached directly, frontally. Their open stances indicate a sense of ease in relation to the photographer, which might suggest to observers a form of social and ethical transaction between photographer and photographed. This is the nature of the dialectical and analytical image. The subject is never an object already predetermined, a priori, by a discourse.

Time Zones / Ruins of Memory

Contemporary African photography has so far led us to a juncture, to the point of a double negotiation. This is the divide between African and colonial memories. Today these memories return as ruins, as collapsed time zones: mementos of disturbed relations, for colonial subjectivity may never be completely vanquished. Even if decolonization proposed a liberation from colonial subjectivity toward "African modes of self writing,"[68] it was never, in any case, a complete rupture. Artists such as Allan deSouza, Zarina Bhimji, Otobong Nkanga, Fatou Kandé Senghor, Kay Hassan, Moshekwa Langa, and Yto Barrada have drawn from this tension, fashioning works that investigate those disturbed relations. In their individual works, a careful forensic approach searches through the remainders of the colonial and postcolonial past to question the emancipatory philosophy and utopianism of decolonization. Each of their projects in this exhibition takes up an archaeology of institutional, personal, social, and economic space which leads us to the edge of disenchantment and ennui.

Allan deSouza's series "The Lost Pictures" (2004) is a special case in point (pages 174–183). The source of these images is the family album, that technological archive which, since the invention of photography, has never ceased confronting us with death, with disappearance, with the apparition of life. The images in "The Lost Pictures" were summoned on such an occasion: the death of the artist's mother. It was as if something that held him tethered to the flimsiest connection had broken, setting him adrift on "a feeling of an undoing, of dislocation in time, in place, as well as memory and imagination."[69] But what led to these feelings, beyond the grief we experience upon loss of a close family member? It was the rediscovery of an archive, the family archive. Derrida, examining Freud's archive, tells us a story of Freud's receipt of the gift of his lineage when his father gave him a torah that had previously belonged to Freud's grandfather. The gift had come leather-bound: a new binding ordered by his father. It is as if the gift were presented with new skin, an opening toward identity. Derrida writes that the archive as a "science, in its very movement, can only consist in a transformation of the techniques of archivization, of printing, of inscription, of reproduction, of formalization, of ciphering, and of translating marks."[70]

The nine photographs that make up "The Lost Pictures" succinctly represent the procedures in Derrida's description of the archival imperative. The images are worn and eaten around the edges, as if by a biting melancholic fervor. This was achieved by subjecting them first to a slow process of accretion, then decay, erasure, evanescence, and reproduction. DeSouza began by collecting printed images of slides shot by his father in the mid-1960s in Nairobi, Kenya (before the family's emigration to England and the ensuing scattering that drove his mother to Portugal). These consist of pictures of Allan and his siblings, mother, and the entire family in various contexts (on the beach, sidewalk, visiting a railway exhibition). By taping the printed slides on heavily trafficked areas (the bathroom sink, shower, kitchen counter) around his house in Los Angeles, he invested them with the power of both fetish and talisman, even as he deliberately destroyed them, letting the leavings, dust, and acid of daily existence settle on them and wear them away. He lived with the images, literally, drawing from them a kind of sustenance, and at the same time subjecting them to a punishing disregard, as if wrestling with his own past. This past is entangled in a web of mnemonic, geographical, imaginary, and phantasmatic narratives. The images open up deSouza's meditation on the loss of his mother and the rupture of familial bonds, and therefore can be understood as an expression of mourning.[71] But this loss, while looming large over the expansive field of the artist's memory, also enunciates his ambivalence toward the idea of a fixed home, of a place in the world that can be returned to physically. In this way, deSouza directs us toward that malady of modern existence: exile, dias pora, dislocation; to the confused itinerary of Indian diasporic communities, from South Asia to East Africa, Europe, and the United States, such has been the trajectory of the deSouza family.

Like deSouza, Zarina Bhimji is a member of the diasporic Indian community of East Africa, many of whom followed colonial trade as migrant labor, arriving on the continent at the end of the nineteenth century. Her family, who settled in Uganda and witnessed the decolonization process and independence in 1962, were expelled from the country along with other Asians by the regime of Idi Amin in 1972.[72] The expulsion marks another juncture in the series of uprootings and displacements that have remained palpable for all contemporary subjects. Again like deSouza, Bhimji's return to Uganda was precipitated by the death of her father. But unlike him, her intent is not to blunt memory but to rouse it. Interspersing images of architecture, landscape, and objects, the photographs are vivid documentary records—from prison interiors to the ruins of the Entebbe airport—showing the unfinished aspects of her Ugandan past (pages 156–159). At the same time, they defy the documentary reflex, for they are neither news nor purely information, made to be viewed as evidence. Embedded deep within the reflective surface of the images is the kind of disturbance that is almost imperceptible to the eye unless it is directed. But, if these works are intimately connected to death, are they to be read then as works of mourning?[73] What is the object/subject of mourning: The disappeared world of the Asian community? Or their disconnection from a land, a home? Bhimji's work forces the viewer to interrogate the assumptions of documentary. Her work is located in the interstices of questions concerned with memory and in the archival reproduction of the history connected to that memory. She wants her archaeology of the Ugandan past—which she has been exploring since 1998 through film and photography—to function as historical reckoning, where "history serves the present" because, according to her, "what is not recorded does not exist."[74] The photographs in this exhibition draw from the twin legacies of colonialism and the unfulfilled promise of the postcolonial moment to further animate the photographic discourse of African modernity. Bhimji's intent is one of insistence, to carve into the withered tree a trace of her own account, to inscribe the memory and violence of expulsion, and to recuperate, even if fleetingly, a gesture of homecoming.

In a different register, Zwelethu Mthethwa's magisterial rendition of landscape and the alienation of labor in his sugar cane series ("Untitled," 2003) strikes a critical balance between portraiture and landscape (pages 186–195). It clearly draws from Dutch genre painting, in which everyday life is represented with little heroic fanfare. Despite the seemingly quotidian quality of Mthethwa's portraits, it is obvious that, though the formal style of the work has art historical precedents, it is not about the ordinary life of workers in the field. His take on landscape, portraiture, and social class is reminiscent of Thomas Gainsborough's famous eighteenth-century painting *Mr and Mrs Andrews* (1750), which belongs to a genre known as the "conversation piece." The painting depicts the Andrews estate with the owners inserted in it. The typical English landscape painting of the eighteenth century was connected to the social representation of aristocracy and the landed gentry. The portraits often included inside the landscape are of a piece not only with the representation but the actuality of their ownership and therefore were expressive of the portrait subjects' social stature. It is important to make this distinction because Mthethwa's portrait of the cane workers inverts the moral codes (work ethic) and the process of identification (social stature) respectively associated with Dutch and English genre painting. On the contrary, his is an interrogation of a political landscape and its supporting economic system; namely, the imbrication of global capitalism in the post-apartheid landscape. These men who stare at us like medieval warriors, dressed in the field worker's garb, holding on to their primitive machetes, appear before us in regal defiance of their solitary fate as alienated labor, trapped in servitude to multinational capitalism. In a more recent series, Mthethwa focused on the mining industry in South Africa. As in previous works, such as the portraits of displaced workers living in "informal settlements" (née shantytowns) and the sugar cane series, Mthethwa, like August Sander, is developing a kind of photographic typology, often placing his subjects in their own surroundings. This approach has less to do with the dramatic spectacle of the ramshackle environments in which his subjects live and more with applying a stringent realism to his pictures. This realism requires a rendering of the subjects in their own environments, not the ones they would have wished for, but the actuality of their circumstances, the dignity of their grounding in their own space. Yet the aim is not to achieve some fictional authenticity. In this sense, the sugar cane series is especially apposite, because in it Mthethwa addresses the very instability of portraiture and identity.

The increased adoption of photography as a mode of working and method of analysis converges at the point where Western documentary and photojournalistic practices have always been dominant. It would appear from research to date that nineteenth-century African photography was initially uninterested in the recording or documentation of the African landscape. This lacuna is surprising. Excepting the work of David Goldblatt, the absence of landscape as a subject of historical and pictorial interest has not been remedied in modern and contemporary art. However, recently a number of artists have taken on the task of reinvesting landscape with a particular sense of urgent and historical sensitivity. In such works, landscape serves as a vehicle for understanding trauma or social alienation. Otobong Nkanga's work is resolutely centered in the postcolonial moment. Her recent ongoing projects "Emptied Remains" (2004–05) and "Things have fallen" (2004–05) are photographic analyses of the psychological and phenomenological experience of land and landscape (pages 160–165). In the former, Nkanga is interested in the spatial, physical attributes of the built environment, in the forms, objects, and other embedded structures that define the relationship between nature and culture. In the latter, she trawls the Nigerian, Dutch, and German countryside to record the convergence of the ruin and the picturesque, picturing the landscape as a series of disturbed, interrupted movements of development and stasis. These emptied remains address the collapse of time and space, opening them up within the mnemonic framework of loss, mourning, and melancholy.

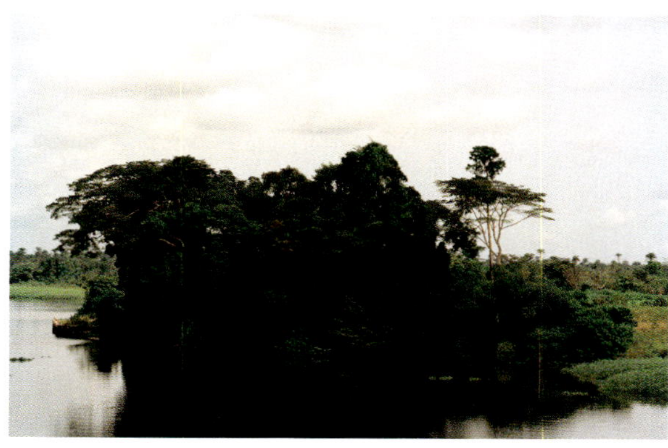

Otobong Nkanga, *Things have fallen I*, 2004–05
Courtesy the artist

If Nkanga photographs around loss and soft-edged dystopias, around remains and absences, addressing disturbances where nature struggles with human development, Moshekwa Langa, in his "Untitled" (2005) photographs, illuminates sites of recovery and recollection (pages 258–265). Langa's silent photographs record the wounds of absence to memory. His focus is on domestic space and the accoutrements that dot its interior and exterior spaces. Each of these images suggests and projects the fundamental relationship between what Avishai Margalit calls the "ethics of memory"[75] and a palpability that makes place and space more than an illusion or fantasy, hence the necessity of transforming the fatal ennui often associated with memory. Photographed over a brief vacation in the Northern Province, in a rural area of South Africa where he grew up, these images of domestic scenes and still lifes are simple mementos that paradoxically efface the author's relationship to place, but at the same time reestablish the priority and necessity of a distance from one's own memories. There is no mark of homecoming in these light-filled, poetic essays on time and longing, where distance imperils connection, leading to Paul Gilroy's "postcolonial melancholia."[76]

Like Langa's enigmatic vacant sites, Nkanga's emptied remains, Bhimji's haunted landscapes, and deSouza's erased pictures, Fatou Kandé Senghor, in her work *Palais de Justice*, opens up another consideration of postcolonial melancholia (pages 152–155). The series of photographs and accompanying video, called *Room 12*, shot in the ruins of the Palais de Justice, examine a farcical piece of colonial architecture within the postcolonial present of Senegal. A fake Neoclassical structure set in a ring of similar buildings (including the presidential palace and national assembly), the Palais de Justice mimics the elusive grandeur of French colonialism in Africa. It is especially apt that this particular building, structurally unstable and now abandoned, served as a space for the administration of justice—with its various courts—and denial of the same in the prison cells that dot its interior. Senghor's archaeology of the Palais de Justice reveals its utter inappropriateness within the national ideology of the Senegalese, a Potemkin structure that stands as a monument to French colonialism. As Senghor shows in the forty-eight photographs, this is the ground in which to explore the memory now hidden behind the curve of a vanishing colonial fantasy.

Not every instance in which the artists explore memory collapses into melancholia. Lamia Naji's work is vitally concerned with foregrounding the spaces and rituals of her native Morocco. In the ironically titled *Couleurs Primaires* (2005), Naji blends a noir sensibility and a poetic documentary style in a series of black-and-white photographs recording a Muslim feast and spiritual ritual (pages 132–139). Using stop-motion and intercutting techniques, she transformed the photographic stills into a fast-paced energetic video, whose staccato editing format gives the projected image a sense of frenzy. Photographed both close up and from a distance—including aerial shots—*Couleurs Primaires* offers glimpses of architecture, crowds, and solitary figures of celebrants in rapture or in various states of celebration. Rather than working with the false opposition between tradition and modernity, Naji (in collaboration with a Spanish composer) has wed the syncopation of Gnawa music to the abbreviated computer-driven beats of urban trance tracks. In this hybridization, Naji appears to aim at exploring the combined spiritual and social dimensions of Sufism and contemporary youth culture. Her sonic and visual elaborations of the mysticism of Sufism in Gnawa music and contemporary trance compositions point to the intersection of religious and secular subjectivity, tradition and modernity in the contemporary experiences of Morocco, while extending its reach beyond the borders of the Muslim world. Here it is not a question of separate time zones but a relation of temporal structures that is the fundamental subject of the work.

There is visual pleasure in the allegories of desire and excess that define the Orientalist kitsch of Lara Baladi's work. Baladi rarely uses the camera in the traditional sense; instead she works like an archaeologist. But rather than excavate, she accumulates, samples, and plunders the vast digital archive (television and cell phone images, Japanese *manga*, digital files from the Internet and other file-sharing sources) and analogue files that exist today in such profusion. She expropriates images from the relentless traffic of photographic and pictographic media and Internet industry and remixes them to form a new pictorial content (pages 124–131). Consequently, her work contains an element of compositional frenzy in which multiple images, cultural settings, symbols of sentimentality, stereotypes, sexuality, gender, identity, vulgarity, and excess are intermingled and collapsed.

Chronicles of the City

A large section of *Snap Judgments* brings together studies of urban sites, as narratives and chronicles of the city. Each project addresses modes of urban living and the changes that shape the postcolonial metropolis. Depth of Field (DOF), a loose collective of six photographers residing in Lagos, Nigeria, adopts the attitude of a social geographer to investigate the layers of living arrangements in which informality and formality converge. Each of DOF's works, which reveal an increasingly documentary practice, is developed based on themes that emerge from the group's weekly meetings. From these meetings assignments are drawn by individual members who then work autonomously to develop an essay. At the conclusion of the assignment, the members meet again to discuss and analyze their output, as well as the photographic value of the work, its social and artistic relevance. Since its founding, Depth of Field has generally focused on examining urban narratives around Lagos, the vast megalopolis, searching for the city's identity within its contours and meandering neighborhoods. To the unstudied eye, the pictures appear impressionistic, like casual tourist snapshots, as if taken on the fly (pages 334–349). But this is because the methodology of documentation is more like a digest than a purely formal study. The huge compendium of images DOF has built so far has the quality of a wide-ranging and interpretive archive. No one picture can capture the vitality and multiplicity of the city.[77] Each image contains a story and each story incubates another one. This archive is built around exploration of the most recognizable physical, social, and economic features of Lagos, some of which take on an almost iconic quality—its bus ranks, markets, night life on the beach, churches, traffic, street trading, its expanding skyline. While the images may lend themselves to the genre of touristic myth, they are anything but, since one intention of the group is to detach their approach from the picturesque study that has made Lagos the latest photographic cliché of the third world city.

Cairo is the context of Randa Shaath's recent photographic investigation. Shaath has worked as a photojournalist for *Al Ahram Weekly* covering diverse subjects and issues across Egypt. Over the last decade, however, she has turned her attention to the cultural milieu of the Cairene artistic community, documenting its intimate environments and making portraits of actors, dancers, musicians, theater professionals, filmmakers, writers, and artists. The profoundly cosmopolitan character of the Islamic world's great intellectual and cultural crossroads gradually unfolds in Shaath's portraits. In a related but socially divergent body of work, Shaath photographed the city's architectural spaces. But rather than the classic images of monumental architecture, wide boulevards, chic neighborhoods, and middle-class haunts, she has turned her lens on another part of the city, one that is almost invisible from the street, but nonetheless comprised of a massive community of informal and perhaps illegal homes constructed on the rooftops of Cairo's highrise buildings (pages 290–299). These concealed arboreal dwellings essentially constitute a kind of "other" city. Shaath's photographic view is not panoramic. Her pictures are discreet compositions of parts and wholes, of domestic and communal spaces. There is something oneiric in these images, not least because some of the nocturnal ones lend the entire constructivist ensemble a poetic quality that belies the precariousness of the structures which are contrasted against the solidity of the buildings dotting the jagged skyline. Yet, despite their makeshift character, there is a sense of permanence to this ur-city. I recall the solitary silence I once experienced while visiting an artist living in a small two-room flat on top of one of these buildings. Nothing about the setting appeared transitory. It was home. Shaath conveys this sense of permanence by focusing not only on the architecture but the active life of the inhabitants. Her aerial shots taken from rooftops across the city reveal the creative adaptation that Cairo's urban inhabitants have made out of their circumstances. The images unfold another reality of the city invisible from street level, showing us a new kind of urbanism, a spectacular rethinking of the rooftop as a platform of new urban community.

Hala Elkoussy's "Peripherals" (2004) provides a counterpoint to Shaath's alternate reading of Cairo, a dense city teeming with life and subjectivities. Rather than the urban core, "Peripherals" focuses on the codes of a second wave of modernity and modernization that is rapidly changing the relationship between center and periphery, fracturing the contained balance between formality and informality that characterizes a new urbanism with a distancing, sterile, vaguely modern architecture sprouting on the edge. Elkoussy insists that this group of images not function like fetishized, tastefully framed commodity objects. Staged as mock tourist wallpaper, she envisions their presentation much like a backdrop, an urban mise-en-scene (pages 328–332). She explores the underlying vulgarity of images such as these, which project fantasies of place without revealing the fictions nestled within them. Here the wallpaper suggests certain kitschy elements of the tourist posters which invite an illusion bigger and more saturated than the reality they claims to represent. Elkoussy photographs these new urban developments, many of which remain unfinished or are already abandoned, to unmask the contradiction between the desire for Western modernity and the resolute attempt to include a vernacular modernity in the future of the city. At the core of this series of images is a subtle critical stance toward the fever of expansion and modernization that has overtaken most of the developing world.

The city as exploding megalopolis is not the locus of Yto Barrada's photographic and filmic concern, rather it is its emptying, its slow evisceration and asphyxiation. Barrada's ongoing project "A Life Full of Holes: The Strait Project," begun in 1998, is a critical meditation on migrancy, immigration, asylum, labor, and the illicit business of human trafficking centered in the Strait of Gibraltar, the narrow causeway linking Morocco and Spain, Africa and Europe (pages 96–105). But more than economic determinism drives this investigation. The riskiness of attempts to cross the strait is succinctly captured in Barrada's examination of the root meanings of the word *strait*, which in French and Arabic translations "combine[s] the sense of narrowness and distress."[78] As thousands of young men and women, without opportunity in the bleak economic conditions produced by globalization in the South, place themselves on the precarious threshold of illegality, becoming clandestinis, facing deportation or lengthy detention in asylum camps throughout Europe, their desperation is unfolding a catastrophic human rights problem. The plight of these "economic immigrants" and the ensuing political and ethical tensions illuminate the core idea to which this project is addressed, namely the biopolitical issue of the refugee problem. Refugees have become the limit figures of the new millennium. And the fact that the refugee problem is framed within an economic rationale exposes the philosophical and juridical ambiguity that surrounds the exclusion of North African immigration from the universal legal protections generally accorded refugees and people in distress. Barrada's project hinges on this aporia. She pursues the question of violence inherent in the risk of entrusting one's life, hopes, and dreams to the ability to reach the other place, to not touch the bottom of the sea but to reach the other shore. She wants to puncture the silence that surrounds the discussion of the daily tragedies of immigration: "I try to expose the metonymic character of the Strait through a series of images that reveal the tension—that restlessly animates the streets of my hometown—between its allegorical nature and immediate, harsh reality. My work attempts in part, to exorcise the unspoken violence of other people's departures. I, too, left Tangier, for more than ten years; by moving back, I have placed myself amidst the violence of homecoming. There are no *flâneurs* here, and no innocent bystanders."[79] Poetic, photographically dense, intellectually powerful, the elliptical narratives and methodological precision of "The Strait Project" are the photographic equivalent of a surgical scalpel, used to slice open the belly of an open secret, to lay it bare and force a confrontation with one of the biggest problems of the twenty-first century: the refugee.

Shifts in urban subjectivity, questions of mobility and migration, are recurring motifs in the work of Kay Hassan and Guy Tillim. Like the strait in Morocco, the cities of South Africa have become new and complex spaces in which African social agency and sense of hospitality are currently being tested. Since the end of apartheid, the relatively modern and affluent economy, sophisticated amenities, services, and Western efficiency of South Africa have attracted new immigrants from other African countries seeking opportunity. This flood of immigrants has opened a debate on access to the country and exposed a painful conflict at the root of which cities like Johannesburg have to renegotiate old issues of inclusion and exclusion, involving social classes, racial groups, and communities. Under apartheid, deplorable living conditions, brutal evictions, and spatial marginalization and invisibility were the standard tools of social deracination employed by the paranoiac state security apparatus. The city was off-limits to entire categories of people, and therefore served in its organization a repressive function.

To understand the projects by Tillim and Hassan for this exhibition requires a renewed acquaintance with apartheid's social engineering, but also how the terms of urban existence have been turned on their head with the frightening influx of people seeking jobs,

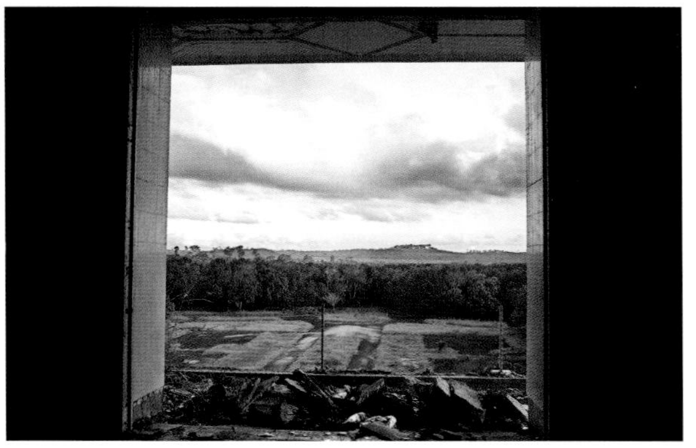

Guy Tillim, *Reception room at Mobutu's looted palace at Gbadolite*, 2002–3. Courtesy the artist and Michael Stevenson Gallery, Cape Town

housing, and access. Tillim's "Jo'burg" series (2004) is located at the epicenter of the city's unique modernist downtown, which within ten years was transformed from a pretense as a cosmopolitan neighborhood inhabited by whites into a ghetto now populated mostly by blacks, immigrants, and masses of the urban poor. This section of the city represents an epic of deliberate neglect and abandonment, forcing the inhabitants to live in a kind of survivalist archipelago with little official recognition. Tillim's work on this part of the city is a sustained essay on post-apartheid Johannesburg (pages 314–327). There is a sense of erased distance between photographer and photographed. Yet this proximity does not seem to trouble the relations of power between Tillim and the nearly incarcerated denizens of his recordings. With its gritty realism and disturbing ennui, the images that comprise this body of work (produced over the course of five months when Tillim moved into one of the grungy tenements that make up the sprawling complex of highrises in the city's downtown) expose the fault lines of an oncoming battle between speculative real estate and tenancy rights. Sometimes the scenes are photographed the way a photojournalist would (which is what Tillim has been for two decades), as battlegrounds between competing moral and political systems. In others, the images are shot from angles that blur the line between voyeurism and pictorialism. Yet this series offers a clear vantage into the unique spatial changes that are occurring everywhere as new populations enter into settled communities and bring with them their own claims to space and identity.

A recurring issue in the work of Kay Hassan centers around questions of labor, migration, and sovereignty. Hassan has worked in diverse media—photography, film, video—and until recently was known chiefly for the large-scale installations of paper collages he made in the mid-1990s. The new work presented in *Snap Judgments* incorporates found images, Hassan's growing archive of discarded Polaroid negatives taken by self-employed street photographers (pages 148–151). He collects these negatives by the hundreds, seeing in them another form of portraiture. Unlike deSouza's "Lost Pictures," Hassan's could be seen as engendering a form of recovery, though the images are still very much situated between found and lost. These images, in which subjects share part of the four-panel negative, are remnants of documentation photographs that migrants require in order to procure identity cards. Continuing his work on apartheid's topographical grid and its legislation of access to the city, its laws of spatial exclusion, its transformation into a zone that lies between legality and illegality—a separation marked by the pernicious mechanism of the *dompas* (identity books required of all black Africans)—Hassan obliquely speculates, in his assessment of the growing demand for identity cards, on an emerging order of bureaucratic control over urban citizens. Over the last several years, he has continuously visited the offices of the South African Home Affairs, where internal and foreign migrants come to seek papers, searching for a legal framework in which to reinvent themselves and thereby secure a space in the city.

James Muriuki, Sada Tangara, Boubacar Touré Mandémory, Michael Tsegaye, and Mamadou Gomis also study the shifting context of the city between formal and informal, official and unofficial narratives of urban life, architecture, public transport, and the fleeting presences that inhabit the postcolonial city. Tangara's "Le grand sommeil" [The Big Sleep], 1998–2003) is a disturbing essay on the nocturnal living arrangements of street children in Dakar (pages 226–235). Himself a former street child, his photographs are taken at close-up, revealing the vulnerability of the young boys, who move in packs and sleep in clusters, huddled together in street corners, abandoned cars, and makeshift crevices. This is an empathetic view into the intractable problems of postcolonial urban life. In the same vein of photographic archaeology, Mamadou Gomis presents yet a different view of Dakar. Like Sylvia Plachy in New York's *Village Voice*, he employs the pages of the independent newspaper *Le Journal* to produce a deceptively simple series of urban stories, teasing out the division between *le quartier* and *centre de ville*, and foregrounding through his pictorial testimonies the changing cycle of daily experience in Dakar (pages 236–245). His work is perhaps the most methodical example of an ongoing chronicle, a shifting, dispersed group of images that never consolidate into a typology. The growing archive of images, which appear six days a week, is classic photojournalism. But it also constitutes both an iteration of a new form of self-writing and a view of the role of images in the development of African public narratives.

Over the last two years, James Muriuki has documented a range of economic and cultural scenes around Nairobi. Because the city is the gateway to the safari and vacation economy of Kenya, he is interested in the transitional spaces occupied by Kenyans. In the past, he produced a series of performance-based images of himself in his small apartment. These images were always taken after hours, upon return from work. The apartment functioned as a transitional space, between work, the street, and home, both a place of refuge and a vessel for experimentation with a different structure of being and contemporary identity. Likewise, his recent project is focused on another transitional space, the zone made up of bus terminals, taxi ranks, and other modes of transportation on which the majority of the city's inhabitants and workers depend (pages 300–303). This recent body of work is composed of cinematic digital images photographed at night, at the point when the massive labor force that commutes daily into the center of Nairobi begins its exodus to the outlying towns on the margins of the city. Muriuki embeds himself like a phantom in the midst of the commuters or at a slight distance from them, focusing on the transitional relationship between himself, his subjects, and the city. The juxtaposition of the vibrant and colorful neon-rigged buses against the soft, glowing Oz-like lights of Nairobi's sparkling towers creates a contrast of forms that is at once exuberant and mysterious.

Most of the artists in this exhibition have made a shift to photography from other media such as painting. To be sure, photography has become the common tool of contemporary art. Michael Tsegaye, a former painter, sees in photography a new opportunity to compose a painterly investigation of the intimate private spaces of homes in the old quarters of Addis Ababa, as well as a lyrical interpretation of the languorous flow of the city at large (pages 258–265). His photography has a distinct compositional formality, and is organized the way a painter would work on isolated effects within an overall frame. The resulting images are dense and layered with material, forms, color, and chiaroscuro, careful translations of mood and detachment, light and shadow. The direct sense of seeing recorded in these spaces is ultimately not documentary. Rather, it draws largely from tropes of painterly modernism, which distinguishes

Tsegaye's work from the hard-edged urban analysis that is to be found in other works in the exhibition.

Boubacar Touré Mandémory, a veteran reporter based in Dakar, photographs with an aggressive and desensitizing lens (pages 304–313). The weird angles of his compositions invest ordinary scenes of fleeting urban life with a surreal sense of disturbance. As with his angles, so his sense of color, timing, and detachment. The quirky movement of Mandémory's method calls on viewers to mimic his angle of vision, to see the whirling world, the vertiginous motion of the street at the same point of contact as the photographer. These are motion pictures, in a literal sense. All forms in Mandémory's work are in motion, disenchanted, agitated, restless, torn from their immediate documentary referent. These are photographs of a different kind of substance: both psychic and corporeal, haptic and retinal, real and derealized.

Jo Ractliffe, one of the most accomplished and underrated photographers of her generation, continues to experiment with multiple modes of picture making. From her earliest work in the mid-1980s to her current images (pages 274–289), each of her projects can be seen as little dramas in which the subjectivity of the artist is fully registered in the resulting work. The conceptual premise of Ractliffe's work is always in her attempt to grapple with and undermine the apparatus, to use the vulnerability of the technology to her advantage. In a now classic work, *Shooting Diana* (1995), she employed a plastic Diana camera to shoot haunting scenes of urban decrepitude. And in another, *Vlakplaas* (1999), she used a toy camera to visit a landscape of a horrific apartheid crime, producing a continuous strip of uninterrupted images as if the camera were performing a slow pan across the landscape. We all remember Walter Benjamin's insight about Atget's photographs resembling crime scenes. This work, as well as the photographs in the exhibition, are shot like a drive-by-shooting, literally through the scene of a crime, from the point of view of a traveler moving through and between moments of analysis and documentation. And again, the painterly, vertiginous spaces Ractliffe achieves here are accomplished with a dismantled and reconfigured toy camera, creating a fuzzy filmstrip effect of forms, structures, and street scenes.

Rather than crisis, Romuald Hazoumé and Zohra Bensemra each approach their photographic targets as witnesses to an unfolding but constantly changing drama, the making of possibility in cities ravaged by economic malaise and political violence. Both artists eschew the paradigm of victim photography common in contemporary photojournalism. Rather, they use their knowledge of the cities in their respective countries (Benin and Algeria) as guides to document the transformations taking place within each context. Hazoumé's take on the lucrative business of petrol smuggling by small-time traders shuttling between towns that line the borders of Benin and Nigeria is as lyrical as it is dispassionate (pages 246–249). Working in the same manner he has employed as a sculptor, Hazoumé records, like sculptural propositions, the precarious but formally alluring plastic vessels used by the smugglers to ferry their contraband liquid. His compositions assume the quality of small monuments. He exploits the formal qualities of the devices—tied to motorcycles, on bicycles, or lugged on top of the head—to create images of balletic grace. Bensemra, on the other hand, works from the perspective of an implicated photojournalist in her lengthy documentation of the violence precipitated by the civil war in her native Algeria, emphasizing the everyday lives and experiences of women against the backdrop of political bloodshed (pages 250–255). A photographer for Reuters, Bensemra, in the images she has made around Algerian cities, particularly Algiers, permits herself to lose the vaunted neutrality photojournalists are supposed to bring to their assignment: "I am not suffering from acute patriotism, nor from excessive professionalism. It is just that my heart is suffused with love for my country. My life is shaped by its joys, its disappointments, its fortunes and misfortunes. I have constantly had to a fight with myself to remain neutral in my work, to be but an eyewitness."[80] She not only underscores the way her work implicates her, she also wants to use it to address what are for her the most pressing questions, as an Algerian and a woman living between two kinds of violation. Her work on Algeria is meant "to explain my relationship with my country—to talk about *my* Algeria. It was intended to show that it is difficult to remain neutral when it is one's very flesh that is being slashed. The goal was also to say that Algeria, in the same way as a woman who is marginalized because she is different from others, is striving to find a solution to its problems, on its own. The country is learning to be strong and to weather all sorts of storms."[81]

The photographs of Omar D. (Daoud) consist of close-up portraits of Algerians that dwell on the existential attributes of the subject's face (pages 112–118). The portraits are not studies of character and do not so much objectify the sitters as underline the traumatic experiences that are permanently etched on their faces.

The faces, then, become landscapes, or atlases of events that have shaped the contours of the individual but, paradoxically, do not quite divulge the emotional disturbance that threatens to burst the surface. A particularly charged portrait shows the face of a young blind man whose eyes seem to have been violently removed. Of all the portraits (including those of men and women with ancient wrinkled faces), this image is the most direct, the one that seeks a correlation between an event and its distillation in an individual. Omar D.'s portraits are therefore not isolated from the cultural environment. They are not autonomous images of individuality. They may be read as ciphers of social trauma, in environments that lie at the intersection of public and private space, and as indictments of the spectacular conflict that has riven the nation: between secularists and fundamentalists, nationalism and religious insurgency.

In all the changes occurring in Africa today, the foregoing should be taken as sign posts for understanding the photographic event as such, whether as an indexical trace or documentary account, but always as an instance for enacting a new position in the map of contemporary Africa within global culture. Toward this end, inhabitants of African cities have not remained just another specimen of photographic speculation on the limits of existence, the withering away of life from the ravages of industrial-scale diseases. The individuals have become subjects literally bearing witness to their own existence, counteracting the constant reports about their imminent disappearance. In Luis Basto's work, portraiture is the means used to signal this desire. However, Basto's images produce a subtle agitation in the images of the photographed individuals shown looking directly at the camera (pages 106–110). Taciturn and enigmatic, the portrayed look into the camera with a sort of placid detachment or mild disregard. The frontal directness of Basto's documentary portraits of ordinary people on the streets of Maputo illuminate the boundary between the photographer and the photographed, extending his exploration of subjects and their everyday environments into a space of ethical negotiation.

Infernal Machines and Institutions of Modernity

Another area of concern takes up the question of secular institutions of modernity such as the museum, prison, and factory. Hentie van der Merwe's "Trappings" (2002–03) is comprised of photographs of starched, formal military uniforms confined in the Museum of Military History in Cape Town, which unfold a spectral shadow that overhangs South Africa's transition from apartheid to post-apartheid democracy, from colonial to postcolonial institutions (pages 166–173). Photographed in a soft, slightly unfocused manner, van der Merwe's hazy photographs of empty suits hover before the viewer like apparitions, suggesting both surrogate bodies and the erased corporeality of masculine sexuality. The ceremonial pageantry of the military's sense of *espirit de corps* gives way to the seedy violence of its machinery, its system of apartheid repression. Here the array of types and ranks comprise a collective portrait of the institution.

If the military is an institution of discipline and restraint, the prison represents the obverse: the space of the disciplined. Like the clinical vitrines in which van der Merwe's ceremonial uniforms are incarcerated, the prison stands for the brutal reality of human incarceration and denial of freedom, a despairing and dispiriting infernal machine. Mikhael Subotzky's "Die Vier Hoeke" (2004–05) is a sober and at times aesthetically paradoxical documentary project (pages 206–224). The detailed examination of the prison complex is analytically powerful and at the same time calls attention, through the panoramic sweep of the camera, to the dreadful spectacle of the panoptic society, its regulative mechanisms, its hellish scenes of trauma, its disembodiment of the human character. Witness, for instance, the grotesque autopsy scene of a young prisoner who immolated himself in his cell, or the humiliation that accompanies the strip-search of prisoners. In this body of work, which grew out of his BFA thesis at the University of Cape Town, Subotzky's picturing of the Pollsmoor and Voorberg prison complexes outside Cape Town and the groups and gangs that make up their tight-knit communities opens up those spaces concealed from public scrutiny to reveal them as sites of infamy. The pictures are documents of an infernal encounter, a descent into a netherworld of forgotten men who live out their lives in conditions of daily humiliation, rituals of masculinity, psychosexual tension, camaraderie, racial antagonism, and the search for justice.

Like the prison, the factory depersonalizes and eviscerates, radically disembodying and methodically stripping the worker down to a statistic. The factory serves a repressive function of instrumental efficiency. It represents a regulative and disciplinary space in which the personality of men and women are organized according to the logic of hierarchization: between the factory foreman and worker, man and machine, personhood and its absence. If the prison evokes, according to Michel Foucault, scenes of discipline and punish, the factory as one of the most important inventions of modernity is not far behind. In it, the worth of a person is calculated according to the iron law of industrial science: on profit. It is all this and more that Ali Chraïbi, in his investigation of the factory, has sought to illuminate (pages 196–205). However, it is not the factory as an isolating, overwhelming machine that he has recorded, but the very human scale of industrial production. Consequently, in his extended documentation, the machine is relegated to the background, while the workers occupy the central space of the photographic inquiry. Mingling the empathy of portraiture and the detachment directed at picturing machines, Chraïbi, like Subotzky, permits the viewer no programmatic ordering of industrial production. The men look out of the frames and at the viewer. And here we can look back in a gesture of reciprocity, in a double articulation of identification and subjectification.

The photographic projects described here represent experiments and therefore new initiatives in the artistic exploration of different dimensions of the African imaginary and African spaces. The selection of works for *Snap Judgments* was guided by a desire to highlight what, in my view, constitutes a new position in the expanding lexicon of contemporary African art. The emphasis in this case is on works and ideas that maintain a rigorous analytical perspective in photographic examinations of Africa in the twenty-first century. Most of the works (with the exception of Bamgboyé's "Arise") were produced within the last five years, and many others were made in the last year or commissioned specifically for the exhibition. In laying out my reasons for selecting these works and artists, I should like to say that my perspective is to be read as insistently partial, yet it should also be understood as a declaration of direction without a fixed horizon.

The key task of *Snap Judgments* is to create a space for critical conversation between the artists and their ideas, to reveal their intersections and to illuminate the context and conditions of production that make up the space of contemporary African photography and artistic practices. In *Snap Judgments*, this conversation has enabled an elaboration of the conceptual methods that drive the procedures of the artists. While none of the artists explicitly address the terrain of Afro-pessimism, there is little doubt that their works register a subtle deviation from its pathology, and the dystopia associated with it. This could be understood as a repudiation of Afro-pessimism's obsession with obsolescence and entropy common to the media's view of Africa. The artists and photographers whose works are collected under the rubric of this exhibition are active in their response to the conditions of modernity and globalization and the impact each has had on African experience. But they are not inventing new fictions and mythologies. Rather, they are formulating new visions of the African present in all its heterogeneity and multiplicity: with neither heroes nor villains. The African worldview presented in this crop of images is not total. Neither is it always explicitly referential. These are pictures, to be sure, but also systems of meaning, ways of confounding and interrogating historical certitudes of the truth of the photographic mark, and of the exhibition's principal subject: the African postcolonial condition.

Okwui Enwezor

Notes

1 See Léopold Sédar Senghor, *Négritude et humanisme* (Paris: Seuil, 1964). The Negritude movement, especially the version adopted by one of its principal founders, the philosopher, poet, and statesman Léopold Sédar Senghor, could be reread today as an attempt to restage colonial pessimism about Africa. But while Senghor's theory of Negritude may have unwittingly perpetuated certain prejudices about Africa by articulating the difference between Africa and Europe as the opposition between feeling (Africa) and reason (European), he was primarily vested in delineating an African ethic of which Africans should and could be proud, even if some of the values were anathema to how modern Africans actually thought of themselves.

2 For critical responses to Afro-pessimism, see Chinua Achebe, *Hopes and Impediments: Selected Essays* (New York: Anchor Books, 1988) and *Home and Exile* (Oxford: Oxford University Press, 2000), especially the essay "An Image of Africa: Racism in Conrad's *Heart of Darkness*," pp. 1–20; see also Ngugi wa Thiong'o, *Decolonising the Mind: The Politics of Language in African Literature* (London and Nairobi: James Currey/Heinemann, 1986), and, most famously, Frantz Fanon, *Black Skin, White Masks* (New York: Grove Press, 1967).

3 See Manthia Diawara, *In Search of Africa* (Cambridge, MA: Harvard University Press, 1998); Kwame Anthony Appiah, *In My Father's House: Africa in the Philosophy of Culture* (New York: Oxford University Press, 1992); Achille Mbembe, *On the Postcolony* (Berkeley: University of California Press, 2001).

4 See V. Y. Mudimbe, *The Invention of Africa: Gnosis, Philosophy, and the Order of Knowledge* (Bloomington: Indiana University Press, 1988) and *The Idea of Africa* (Bloomington: Indiana University Press, 1994).

5 In 1931, the French ethnographer and Surrealist Michel Leiris embarked on a long trip as the secretary of the Dakar-Djibouti *expedition* (my italics). What resulted was not just the collection of objects and other material plundered from Africa through the course of the *expedition*, but a book, *L'Afrique fantôme* (1934), comprised of Leiris's work during the trip. The tradition of writing and conjuring Africa from which Leiris's book emerged is long and distinguished. Joseph Conrad's *Heart of Darkness* belongs to this tradition, as does Arthur Rimbaud's retirement to Abyssinia (Ethiopia) and André Gide's *Voyage au Congo* (1927) and *Retour du Tchad* (1928). The point is that a long literature by eminent figures makes up the intellectual and visual imaginary of our exploration of Afro-pessimism.

6 In a recent edition of CNN, I saw an advertisement produced by the Nigerian Tourist Board flash across the screen touting the beauty of the people, the cultural dynamism of the cities, and the natural landscape. South Africa has used various contexts to promote itself to the world. No doubt, many African countries know the damage done their self-image and should engage the negative representations that have proved problematic to their conception of themselves.

7 See Roland Barthes, *Mythologies* (New York: Noonday Press, 1972). The study which Barthes initiated in this book is partly based on the specific examples of certain phenomena of postwar mass culture and popular entertainment, but guiding this examination is the attempt to understand how myth is rooted in language. In "Myth Today," a section of this fascinating book, Barthes defined myth as "a type of speech"; the conditions of this speech are what give it utility, in other words "as a system of communication, that it is a message." He calls this message: signification, a way to communicate a message about something as basic as a car to the description of the cultural effect it has on the public perception of transportation. Consider, then, the nature of the myth embedded within the message of Afro-pessimism, and the manner in which it amplifies what is quite secondary to the African condition and we can understand the powerful and affective nature of myth, being as it is a translation of something quite apart from its actual content.

8 Walter Benjamin, "Little History of Photography," in *Selected Writings: Volume 2, 1927–1934*, edited by Michael W. Jennings et al. (Cambridge, Mass.: Belknap Press, 1999).

9 A good example in this exhibition is the daily photograph published by Mamadou Gomis in the Dakar-based newspaper *Le Journal*.

10 Compare, for instance, Gomis's photographs to the examples in the September 2005 *National Geographic* special issue on Africa.

11 Leni Riefenstahl's book *Nuba* (1972) is one of the great examples of this photographic discourse. See also the photographic industry Carol Beckwith and Angela Fisher have built around the powerful visual seductiveness of "tribal" African ceremonies.

12 Johannes Fabian, *Time and the Other: How Anthropology Makes Its Object* (New York: Columbia University Press, 1983), pp. 111–12.

13 Ibid., p. 38.

14 Ibid., p. 30.

15 See Giorgio Agamben, *The Open: Man and Animal* (Stanford: Stanford University Press, 2004).

16 I use *archive* here in the sense employed by Jacques Derrida in which relation to knowledge and authority is placed at the service of an interpretive, institutionalized function. Derrida noted that "A science of the archive must include the theory of this institutionalization, that is to say, the theory both of the law which begins by inscribing itself there and the right which authorizes it." *Archive Fever: A Freudian Impression* (Chicago: University of Chicago Press, 1996), p. 4.

17 Over the course of two weeks, as this essay was in progress, I randomly followed stories and images of Africa in my current hometown's newspaper, the *New York Times*. Each day a new story appeared about Africa, either as text or image. On Sunday, October, 23, 2005, Nicholas Kristof, writing on the Op-Ed page, had this to say about his visit to a hospital in Zinder, Niger: "When I walked into the maternity hospital here, I wished President Bush was with me. A 37-year-old woman was lying on a stretcher, groaning from labor pains and wracked by convulsions. She was losing her eyesight and seemed about to slip into a coma from eclampsia, a complication of pregnancy that kills 50,000 women a year in the developing world. Beneath her, cockroaches skittered across the floor." On November 1, a story about deforestation in Malawi was published by Michael Wines, along with a black-and-white photograph by Jeffrey Barbee on page A3, showing a group of people seemingly logging wood for firewood; in the same edition, the oil giant ExxonMobil ran an advertisement about malaria in a nameless African country with a color photograph of a group of school children looking directly at the reader. On November 2, a front-page story by Michael Wines with the headline "Drought Deepens Poverty, Starving More Africans" was accompanied by a color photograph by Jeffrey Barbee of a group of men buying corn from a shopkeeper. The emphasis of the stories makes all the more clear how readers ought to understand Africa and what makes for a compelling narrative about this vast continent.

18 See Susan Sontag, *Regarding the Pain of Others* (New York: Farrar, Straus & Giroux, 2003), for an extensive analysis of the relationship between photography and humanitarianism.

19 On November 6, 2005, the *New York Times* published an extensive story on prison conditions in Africa. What makes this article fascinating is how the accompanying images by Joao Silva completely overshadowed the dire conditions under which the prison inmates live. The online version of the story included a slide version of the arresting

images, many of which, as photographs, are indeed stunning.

20 Mbembe, *On the Postcolony*, p. 176.

21 Ibid.

22 The rock star Bono, lead singer of the Irish band U2, has since supplanted Geldof as patron saint of African debt relief and the antipoverty campaign.

23 Paris-based Brazilian photographer Sebastião Salgado is today the undisputed master of documentary heroism. The saturated dark and silvery tones of his print monumentalize misery and turn terrible images of suffering into carefully executed pietas, as if the struggle within the photographer's imagination is to both render the reality and transcend that reality in the name of art. A good contrast to the kind of documentary heroism often found in works such as Salgado's and even those of Gilles Peress can be observed in the work of Kenyan/American photographer Fazal Sheikh, whose practice involves making photographs in disaster areas as the first signs of normalcy begin to creep back into the lives of traumatized populations such as refugees.

24 Mbembe, *On the Postcolony*, pp. 173–74.

25 CNN has recently been advertising its new anchor Anderson Cooper as a rising star of reporting from such disaster zones as Niger, Rwanda, and New Orleans.

26 The Bang Bang Club was comprised of Carter, Joao Silva, Ken Oosterbroek, and Greg Marinovich. Silva and Marinovich, the surviving members of this unofficial club, continue to contribute reportage to newspapers and magazines all over the world. They also recently published a memoir of the group.

27 At the height of the firestorm ignited by the publication of the photograph in which many questioned the photographer's motives and condemned his detachment from the child, Carter, who was already suffering from depression and stress, committed suicide.

28 See Serge Guilbaut, *How New York Stole the Idea of Modern Art: Abstract Expressionism, Freedom, and the Cold War* (Chicago: University of Chicago Press, 1983).

29 In the 1960s and all through the '80s, many African artists and filmmakers, notably Sembène Ousmane and Abderrahmane Sissako, trained in the academies of the communist bloc in the Soviet Union and Cuba. Many exhibited their work throughout much of Eastern Europe, as well as in countries of the Non-Aligned Movement.

30 For example, in Nigeria a lively scene of contemporary art and writing was organized by the Mbari Club in Ibadan in the late 1950s.

31 See Geeta Kapur's excellent book *When Was Modernism: Essays on Contemporary Cultural Practice in India* (New Delhi: Tulika, 2000) on the development of Indian modern art and the relationship between vanguard artistic propositions and progressive political movements.

32 See Okwui Enwezor, ed., *The Short Century: Independence and Liberation Movements in Africa, 1945–1994* (Munich: Prestel, 2001).

33 The 1955 meeting of the Non-Aligned states held in Bandung, Indonesia, under the auspices of Sukarno was a dialectical political response to the bipolar division that characterized the capitalist and communist dichotomy that shaped much of the Cold War. The Bandung Conference marked a watershed moment in its radical response to American and Soviet hegemony and articulated an alternative perspective of twentieth-century modernity that remains a model of balance, solidarity against aggression, and support of the right of self-determination. Artists and writers were immensely influenced by the propositions of nonhegemonic international relations spelled out by the Non-Aligned states. In attendance during this historic conference were Tito (Yugoslavia), Nasser (Egypt), Nkrumah (Ghana), and Nehru (India). See Richard Wright, *The Color Curtain: A Report on the Bandung Conference* (Cleveland: World Pub. Co., 1956).

34 See Chika Okeke's careful analysis of contemporary Nigerian art: "Nigerian Art in the Independence Decade, 1957–1967," Ph.D. diss., Emory University, 2004; see also Clémentine Deliss, ed., *Seven Stories About Modern Art in Africa* (New York: Flammarion, 1995). Rasheed Araeen's *Third Text* remains one of the most vital intellectual platforms where a counter-theory of the contemporary has been developed. The journal not only exemplified this theoretical position in its name, it did so in recognition that the struggle is as much a cultural as ideological and historical issue.

35 In spite of his best efforts and intentions, Jean-Hubert Martin's *Magiciens de la terre* (1989) created an impression of a hierarchy of artistic forms within which the work of contemporary African artists could be understood; this hierarchy encompassed two tracks of practice, one authentic (meaning developed outside any influence of Western academic style and therefore more properly African) and the other inauthentic (based on a Western academic style that was read as largely derivative). It may appear too late in the day to reprise these arguments, but I do so here in light of the critical amnesia that tends to accompany exhibition surveys such as the present one.

36 Certainly seeing the work of Yinka Shonibare (Nigeria), Malick Sidibé (Mali), William Kentridge (South Africa), and Chéri Samba (Republic of Congo) in the reinstalled permanent exhibition galleries of the Museum of Modern Art, New York, seems like a reflection on and acknowledgment by the museum's curators of the expanded spaces of contemporary art. In fact, this reinstallation, organized by Klaus Biesenbach, seems to me one of the most comprehensive attempts yet by a major museum to look at contemporary art through a decidedly global lens. Other artists in the galleries include Marina Abramovic (Serbia), Ilya and Emilia Kabakov (Russia), and Waltercio Caldas (Brazil), among others.

37 Notwithstanding the complaints of many New York critics, the spread of biennials has had a salutary effect on access to works by artists who live and work in places other than the Western world. It has also opened curators, museums, and historians to new possibilities of artistic production.

38 It is worth emphasizing that colonialism and imperialism cannot be dissociated from the projects that led to the rise of modernity and globalization. Each of these come together in the far-reaching study of the development of capitalism that encapsulates what the eminent historian Fernand Braudel called the *longue duree* in his three-volume study *Civilization and Capitalism, 15th–18th Century* (Berkeley: University of California Press, 1992).

39 *Seven Stories About Modern Art in Africa*, an exhibition organized by the Whitechapel Art Gallery in London in 1995, explored the vital link between modern African art, artists, and institutions of postcolonial nationalism under which many artists sought to develop autonomy from Western artistic practices.

40 See Elizabeth Harney, *In Senghor's Shadow: Art, Politics, and the Avant-Garde in Senegal, 1960–1995* (Durham: Duke University Press, 2004). Harney's book is an excellent and significant example of the new art history that has recently begun to address the distinct discursive, intellectual, and political developments instrumental to the emerging scholarship that shaped both modern and contemporary art in a broad sense, but also Africa in particular.

41 It is noteworthy that, despite the recent integration of Eastern European countries into the European Union, the art scenes of Western and Eastern Europe remain largely separated, though increasingly many artists from the East are being recognized in the more developed economies of the West.

42 Simon Njami's very successful and dynamic exhibition of contemporary African art, *Africa Remix*, which has been touring European venues such as the Museum Kunst Palast, Düsseldorf, Hayward Gallery, London, Centre Pompidou, Paris, and Mori Art Museum, Tokyo, is a great recent example; another is *Fault Lines: Contemporary African Art and Shifting Landscapes*, curated by Gilane Tawadros for the Venice Biennale in 2003.

43 The development of new spaces of reception for contemporary art in Africa has been central to the expansion and critical positioning of

the work of African artists both within and outside the continent. Institutions such as the Cairo and Dakar biennials, the Bamako Photography Biennial, Cape Town Month of Photography, and, before it closed, the Johannesburg Biennial have been central to animating a critical discursive space for understanding the role of photography in the changing views of African art.

44 The body of writing generated by African artists in the first half of the twentieth century has been essential to the historical projects concerned with addressing questions of modern and contemporary art in Africa. Critical essays such as Aina Onabolu's "Discourse on Art," published in pamphlet form in 1920 in Lagos, as well as manifestos by varying groups in Egypt, South Africa, and Nigeria, are part of this trajectory. The various schools of art within which academic practices were developed spawned several distinct positions—particularly in the 1950s—upon which modern and contemporary art has been elaborated in African countries. Some of the prominent ones include the École de Dakar in Senegal; the Uli art movement in Nsukka, Nigeria; the Crystalist artists of the Khartoum School in Sudan; the Oshogbo artists of Nigeria; and the Polly Street Art Centre in Johannesburg. All developed distinct artistic paradigms that remain important benchmarks in their respective countries.

45 The writings of expatriate European historians such as William Fagg, Ulli Beier, Kenneth Murray, Margaret Trowell, Pierre Delafosse, and Frank McEwen represent some of the scholarship that can be summed up as "encounter" historiography.

46 The first great attempt to fully address the diasporic question in cultural terms was the the First World Festival of Negro Arts, organized under the patronage of the Senegalese president, poet, and philosopher Léopold Sédar Senghor in 1966 in Dakar. The festival spanned the broad aesthetic and cultural connections between African artists and artists of African descent from Europe, the Caribbean, South America, the United States, and Canada. Recent exhibitions in the U.S. and Europe have explored the dimension of diasporic and expatriate practices of African artists: *A Fiction of Authenticity: Contemporary Africa Abroad*, curated by Shannon Fitzgerald and Tumelo Mosaka at the Contemporary Art Museum, St. Louis, and *Looking Both Ways: Art of the Contemporary African Diaspora*, curated by Laurie Ann Farrell at the Museum for African Art, New York. Salah Hassan and Olu Oguibe's *Authentic / Ex-centric* inaugurated the first African pavilion at the Venice Biennale in 2001 with artists from Africa and the diaspora. Hassan continued exploring this link at the Dakar Biennial in 2004 with three diasporic artists: David Hammons, Pamela Zee, and María Magdalena Campos-Pons.

47 See recent monographs on the works of the Nigerian painter Uzo Egonu, Senegalese painter Iba Ndiaye, Gerard Sekoto, and Ernest Mancoba: Olu Oguibe, *Uzo Egonu: An African Artist in the West* (London: Kala Press, 1995); Okwui Enwezor and Franz-W. Kaiser, *Iba Ndiaye: Peintre entre continents* (Paris: A. Biro, 2002); N. Chabani Manganyi, *A Black Man Called Sekoto* (Johannesburg: Witwatersrand University Press, 1996); Elza Miles, *Lifeline Out of Africa: The Art of Ernest Mancoba* (Cape Town: Human & Rousseau, 1994).

48 Spheres of contemporary African art can be further delineated to accommodate the vast and aesthetically vigorous practices of vernacular artists, commercial artists, artisans, and craft producers.

49 A wonderful example of the intertextual possibilities of the visual and iconographic exploration between traditional African forms and contemporary uses of those forms is provided by the Nsukka group of artists who, in the 1970s and '80s, devoted their research to applying the aesthetic forms of traditional Igbo women, the mural form of Uli, to new contemporary painting and sculptural inventions. While many of these dialectical paintings and sculptures have not been entirely successful, often appearing merely a stylistic hybrid of the magnificent open compositions of the Uli, they have nevertheless injected an important theoretical and aesthetic reconsideration of the positions being developed by African artists independent of any international artistic style. See Simon Ottenberg, *New Traditions from Nigeria: Seven Artists of the Nsukka Group* (Washington, DC: Smithsonian Institution Press in association with the National Museum of African Art, 1997).

50 After decolonization, most of these elites, which comprise the main actors within the political, economic, and cultural class of the postcolonial state, were derisively labeled a comprador class by 1970s Marxist critics.

51 Ulli Beier's 1969 exhibition *Contemporary African Art* at Camden Arts Centre, London, marked one of the first instances in which contemporary African art as such was curated with the express intention of exploring its international position and scope. See the accompanying catalogue, *Contemporary African Art* (London: Studio International, 1970). It was also the first concerted attempt to bring together the most significant work by East, West, North and Southern African artists under the rubric of one exhibition. With over ninety artists, the scope and ambition of this exhibition remain unprecedented.

52 There has been historical confusion as to when photography became entrenched as an artistic form within contemporary African art. One problem of art history is the interpretation of art through chronology, through attempts to pinpoint the moment when an important shift occurred in artistic development. Because limited research has so far been undertaken with regard to how frequently photography has been included in contemporary African art exhibitions, there has been the erroneous perception that it first occurred in the 1991 exhibition *Africa Explores*, organized by the Center for African Art in New York. One can make the argument that the studio represents a kind of informal exhibition space, and therefore offers the foundational instance for public participation in photographic exhibitions in that the public (whether or not as clients) have always visited these studios to see the newest styles each photographer was producing. However, in the more formal terms which art history tends to privilege, we can certainly indicate that as early as 1960, photography has been a part of contemporary African art. The Nigerian photographer Dotun Okunbanjo (b. 1928), who studied at the Ealing School of Photography in London (1957–60), had his first exhibition in London in 1960 titled *Black and White Studies*. A review of it, with several full-page illustrations, was published in *West African Review* 31, no. 392 (July 1960). Upon his return to Nigeria, Okunbanjo organized the First International Photographic Exhibition in Lagos in 1961, and exhibited his own work in a group exhibition, *Some Nigerian Artists*, at Mbari Gallery, Ibadan, in 1962.

53 For example, when the work of the great Malian portrait photographer Seydou Keïta was presented in New York in *Africa Explores*, an exhibition organized in 1991 by Susan Vogel at the Center for African Art, the prints displayed in the exhibition were designated as the work of an unknown photographer, even though Keïta's stamp was clearly visible in the published prints in the catalogue. It is hard to fathom the reason for this omission of the photographer's name and hence the invalidation of his authorship. One answer may lie in the challenge photographic practices by Africans presented to the Western museum's interest in seeing African art as the work of anonymous authors. The question raised by the exhibition therefore is not only about the proper place of photography within African visual history, but, most importantly, about the relationship between artistic practice and authorship as conventionally understood in Western terms. See Susan Vogel, *Africa Explores: 20th Century African Art* (New York: Center for African Art, 1991), pp. 160–61.

54 Before this, a number of exhibitions in Europe and most notably the 1994 Bamako Biennial, had begun a concerted examination of photographic practices in Africa. Exhibitions such as *Self Evident* (1995) at Ikon Gallery, Birmingham, repositioned the work of African photographers within the terms of contemporary exhibition practices. A seminal moment in this contemporary formation is the founding of the photographic agency/collective Autograph Association of Black

Photographers in London in 1986 under the leadership of the Nigerian artist Rotimi Fani-Kayode, who went on to produce some of the most important photographic works to be made in England in the last twenty-five years.

55 Because of the depredations of apartheid, the documentary style became the dominant photographic genre in South Africa. Photography was consistently used in the service of news reportage and in the ideological struggle between the apartheid state and its opponents.

56 See Okwui Enwezor, "Life and Afterlife in Benin: Photography in the Service of Ethnographic Realism," in *Life & Afterlife in Benin*, edited by Alex Van Gelder (London: Phaidon, 2005), pp. 6–15; see also Michael Stevenson and Michael Graham-Stewart, *Surviving the Lens: Photographic Studies of South and East African People, 1870–1920* (Vlaeberg, South Africa: Fernwood Press, 2001).

57 Mudimbe, *The Idea of Africa*, p. 129.

58 Ibid.

59 For an excellent interpretation of Keïta's portraiture, see Elizabeth Bigham, "Issues of Authorship in the Portrait Photographs of Seydou Keïta," *African Arts* 32, no. 1 (Spring 1999), pp. 56–67.

60 See Manthia Diawara, "Talk of the Town," *Artforum* 36, no. 6 (February 1998), pp. 64–72; and André Magnin, *Seydou Keïta* (Zürich: Scalo, 1997).

61 See Michelle Lamunière, *You Look Beautiful Like That: The Portrait Photographs of Seydou Keïta and Malick Sidibé* (Cambridge, MA: Harvard University Art Museums; New Haven: Yale University Press, 2001).

62 My use of the term *documentary* here for the work of artists and photographers under discussion is limited to the conceptual frame of the term as a tool of documentation and analysis, as a method of foregrounding a field and object of investigation, rather than the general understanding of documentary as a style of journalism for presenting facts.

63 Alioune Bâ, a photographer based in Bamako, made this point in conversation with me during my visit to Mali in summer 2005. When asked why he and other Malian photographers seem uninterested in exploring the colorful images that make up the vibrant street culture of Bamako, he responded that they did not find such images beautiful or noteworthy, that they, in fact, try to avoid any kind of representation that might appeal to Western curators and could therefore isolate or limit the range of the photographers' interests. Moreover, it would be absurd, he stated, to photograph this kind of image because it is a readymade cliché available on postcards. He added that many photographers have chosen to photograph fragments of nonrecognizable objects or make what may appear to some eyes as hackneyed lyrical compositions as a way of resisting the photogenic object or subject. Above all, these photographers did not want to become another Keïta or Sidibé. Bâ's candor would be echoed by Boubacar Mandémory in Dakar and a host of other artists and photographers throughout my travel. Their observations opened for me a new insight into the discursive framework in which the photographers have grounded their work.

64 Artist's statement.

65 I use the notions of rooting and routing in the sense employed by James Clifford as occasions for thinking about place and displacement, as moments of grounding and diaspora. See James Clifford, *Routes: Travel and Translation in the Late Twentieth Century* (Cambridge, MA: Harvard University Press, 1997).

66 This phrase has been used by Susan Vogel to describe the legitimacy of the outsider perspective of ethnographic knowledge of non-Western cultures. She suggests that an intimate outsider is one who has gained the trust of the community, who, although an outsider, is often received as a member or confidant of the community being studied. There is obviously an ethical issue surrounding the ethnographer's self-identification with the Other in this way, which raises afresh the critical issue of photographic study of other cultures where negotiation of knowledge is as much about access as about privilege and power. See Vogel, *Africa Explores*.

67 See Mark Sealy and Jean Loup Pivin, eds., *Rotimi Fani-Kayodé & Alex Hirst* (Paris: Revue Noire, 1996).

68 See Achille Mbembe, "African Modes of Self-Writing," *Public Culture* 14, no. 1 (Winter 2002), pp. 239–73.

69 Allan deSouza, "Recovering Vision," in *Allan deSouza: The Lost Pictures* (New York: Talwar Gallery, 2005).

70 Derrida, *Archive Fever*, p. 15.

71 See Freud's essay, "Mourning and Melancholia," in *The Standard Edition of the Complete Psychological Works of Sigmund Freud*, vol. 14 (London: Hogarth, 1957).

72 Willy Mukasa, reporting about the expulsion order of President Idi Amin in Uganda, *Argus*, August 10, 1972, wrote: "Asians holding British passports and nationals of India, Pakistan and Bangladesh—except those in essential occupations will have to leave Uganda within three months. This final order came yesterday from the president, General Idi Amin, who told a press conference at the command Port, Kampala that he had signed a decree to this effect, which came into force from August 9."

73 See Jacques Derrida, *The Work of Mourning* (Chicago: University of Chicago Press, 2001).

74 Zarina Bhimji, artist's proposal for the film *Out of Blue* for documenta 11 (2001).

75 See Avishai Margalit, *Ethics of Memory* (Cambridge, MA: Harvard University Press, 2002).

76 See Paul Gilroy, *Postcolonial Melancholia* (New York: Columbia University Press, 2004).

77 See Rem Koolhaas, "Fragments of a Lecture on Lagos," in *Under Siege: Four African Cities*, edited by Okwui Enwezor et al. (Ostfildern-Ruit: Hatje Cantz, 2002), and Rem Koolhaas et al., *Lagos Handbook, or, A Brief Description of What May Be the Most Radical Urban Condition on the Planet* (Cambridge, MA: Harvard University Graduate School of Design, 2000).

78 Yto Barrada, *A Life Full of Holes: The Strait Project* (London: Autograph, 2005), p. 56.

79 Ibid. p. 4.

80 Artist's statement sent to the author.

81 Ibid.

Oladélé Ajiboyé Bamgboyé

Tracey Rose

Mohamed Camara

Doa Aly

Andrew Dosunmu

Nontsikelelo “Lolo” Veleko

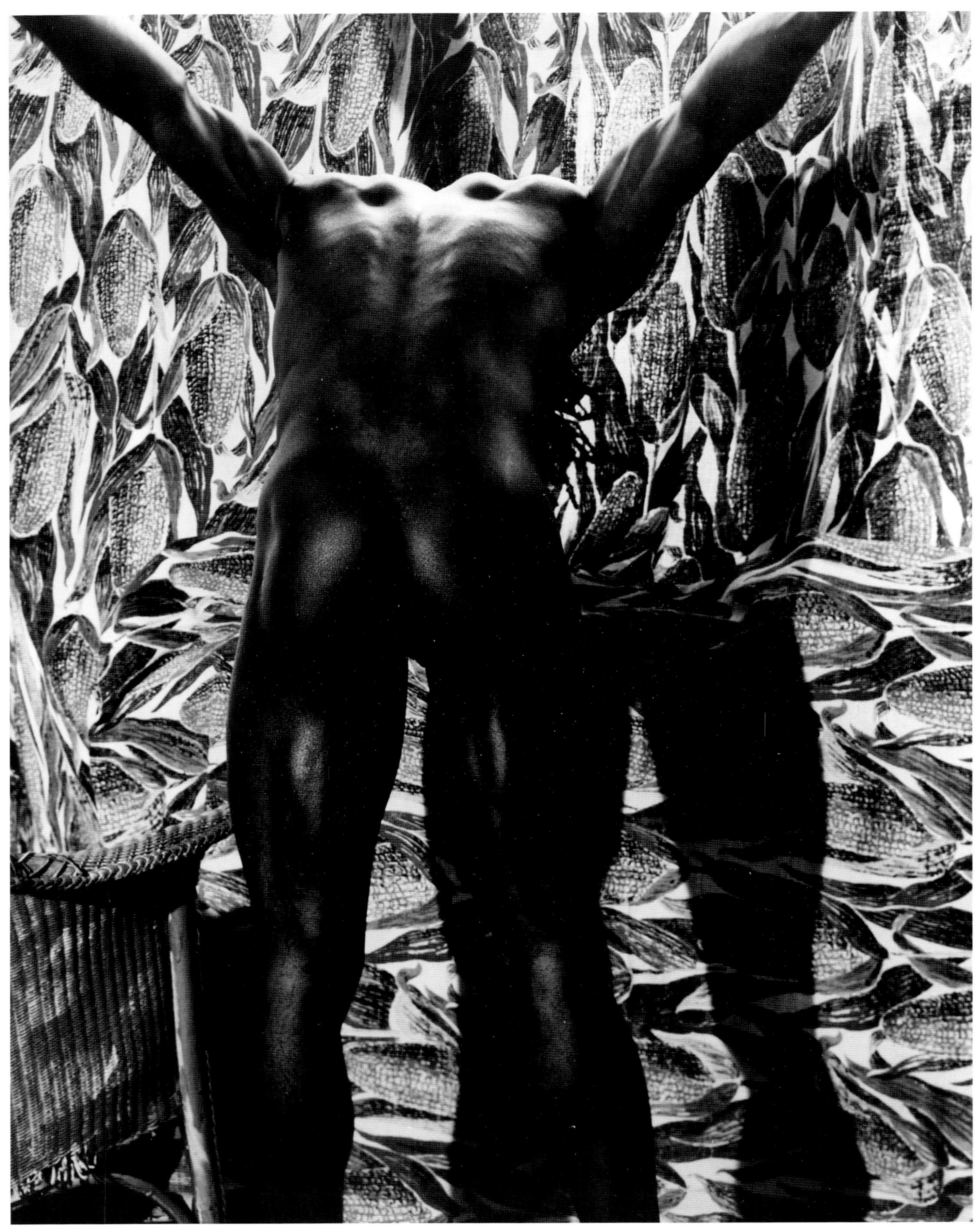

Arise I and II, 1991/1997
Diptych, two gelatin silver prints, each 75 x 50 in. (190.5 x 127 cm)
Courtesy the artist and Thomas Erben Gallery, New York

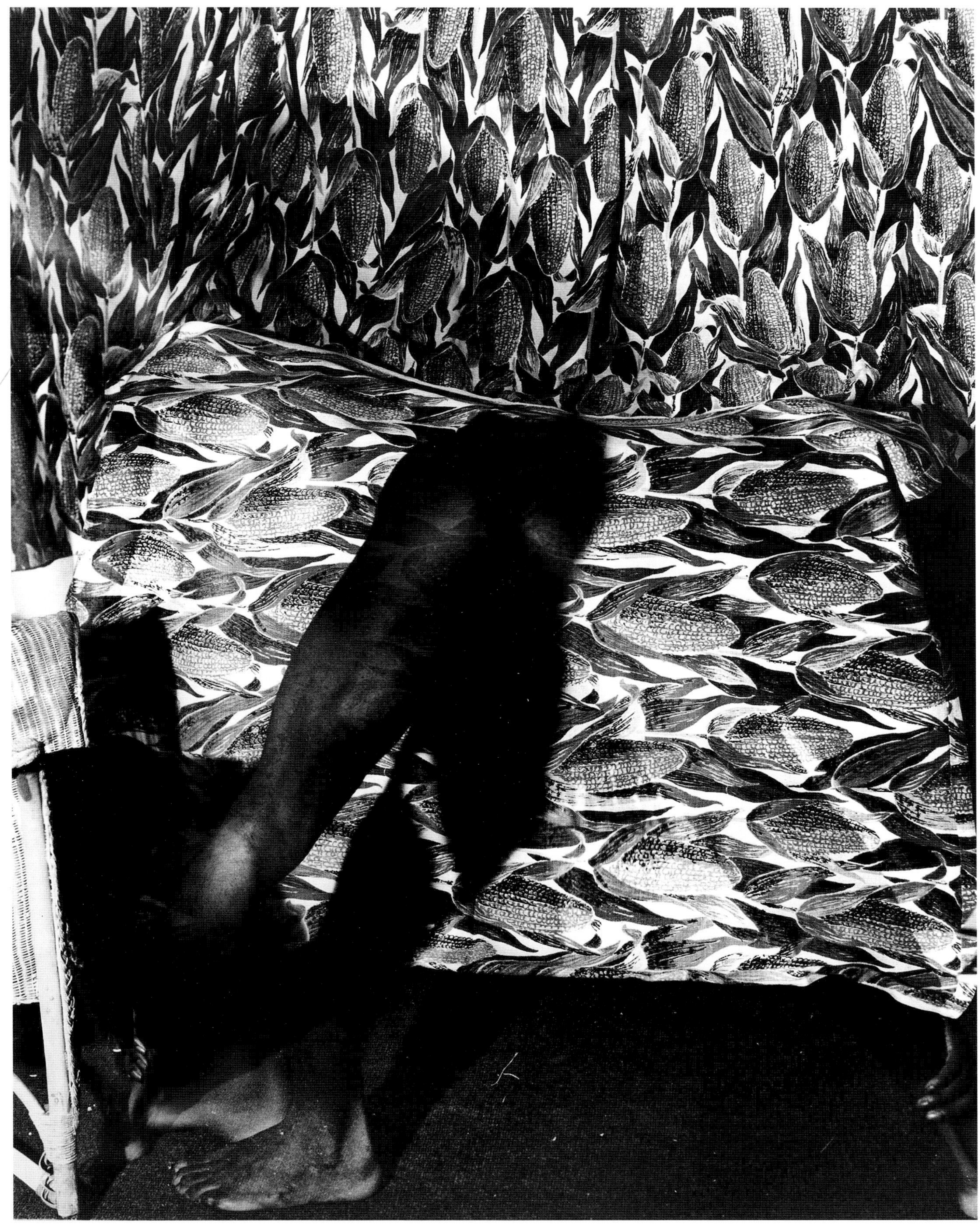

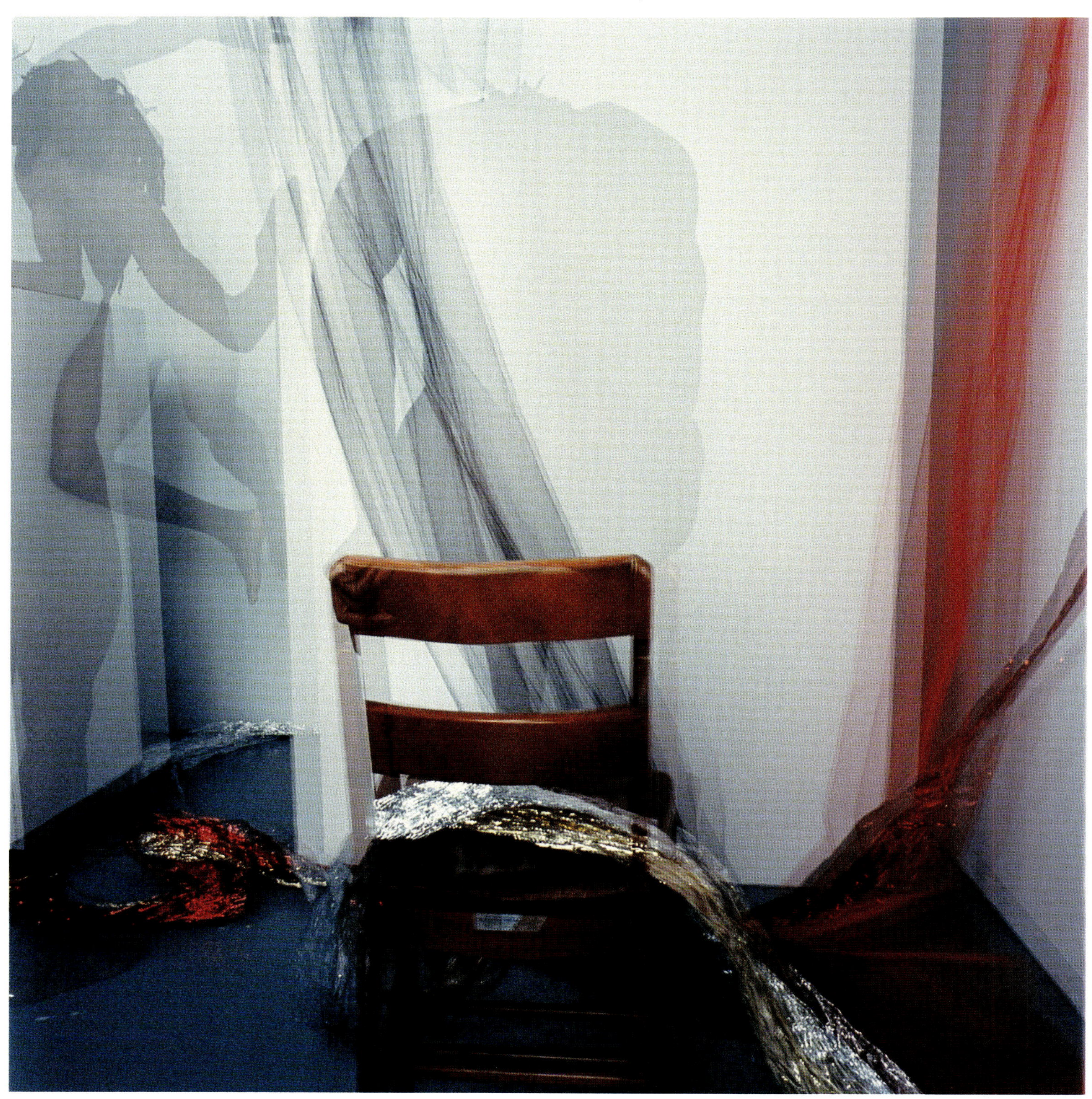

Celebrate No. 1, 1994
Chromogenic print, 16.25 x 16 in. (41.3 x 40.6 cm)
Courtesy the artist and Thomas Erben Gallery, New York

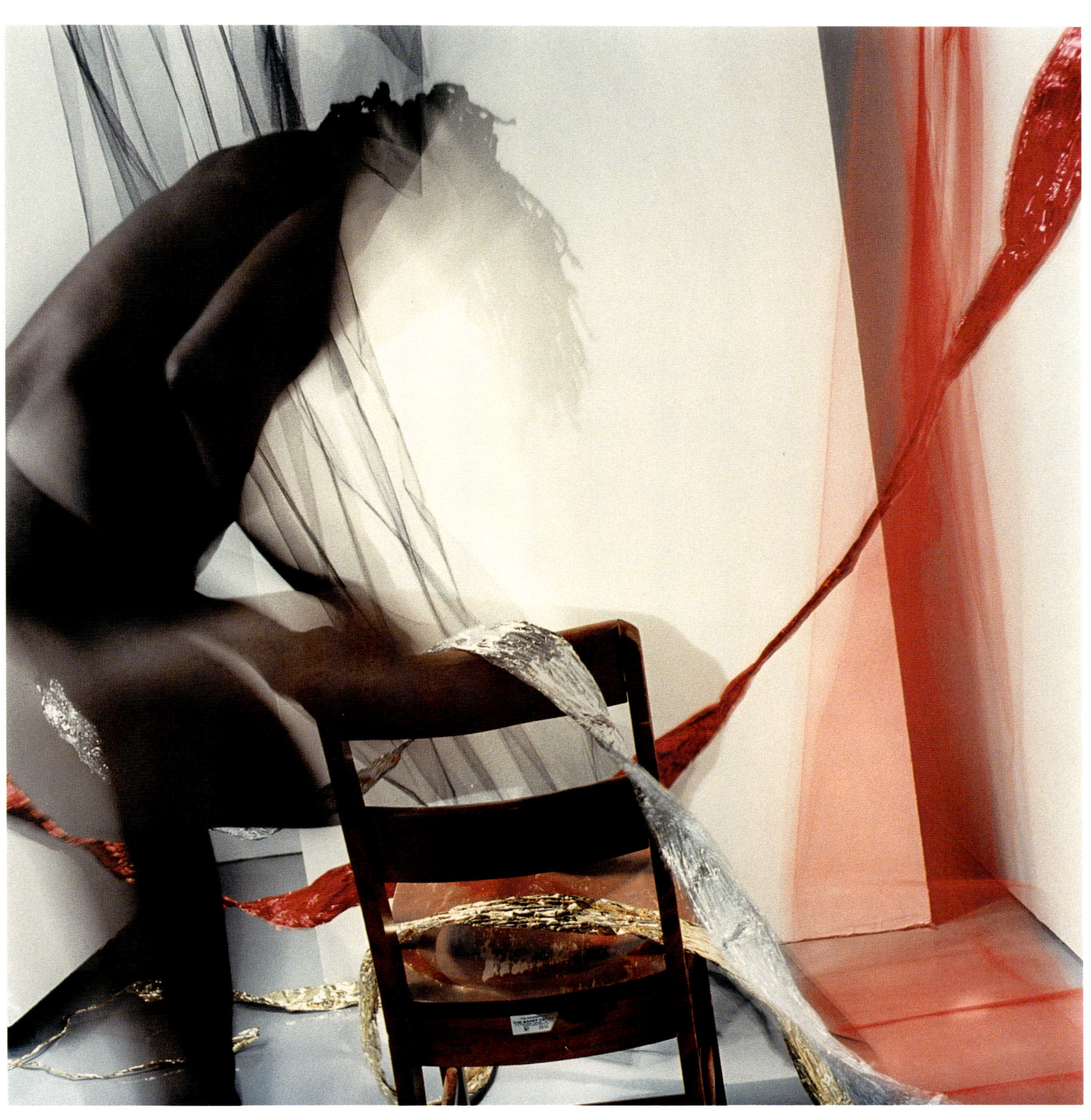

Celebrate No. 2, 1994
Chromogenic print, 16.25 x 16 in. (41.3 x 40.6 cm)
Courtesy the artist and Thomas Erben Gallery, New York

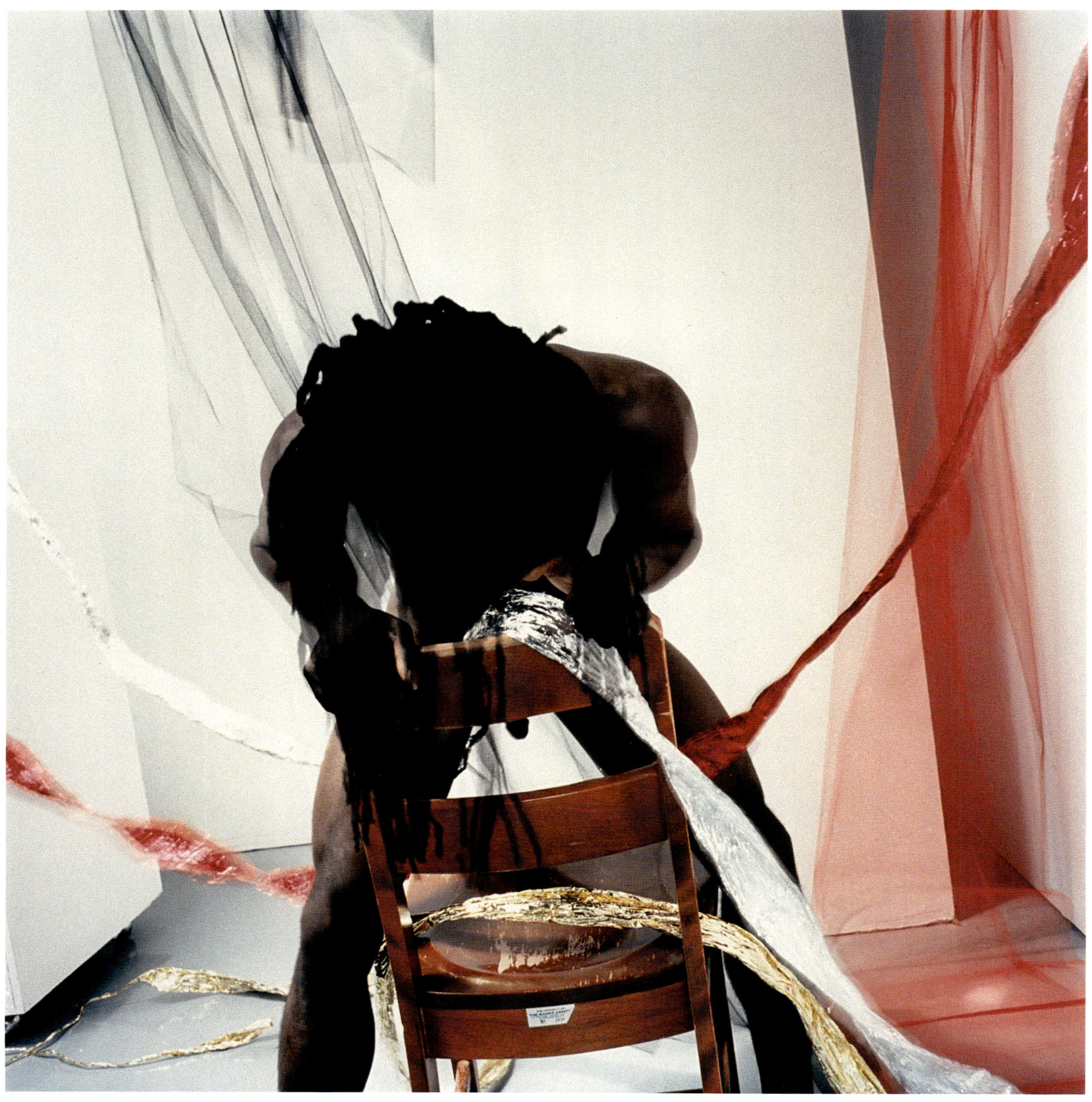

Celebrate No. 3, 1994
Chromogenic print, 16.25 x 16 in. (41.3 x 40.6 cm)
Courtesy the artist and Thomas Erben Gallery, New York

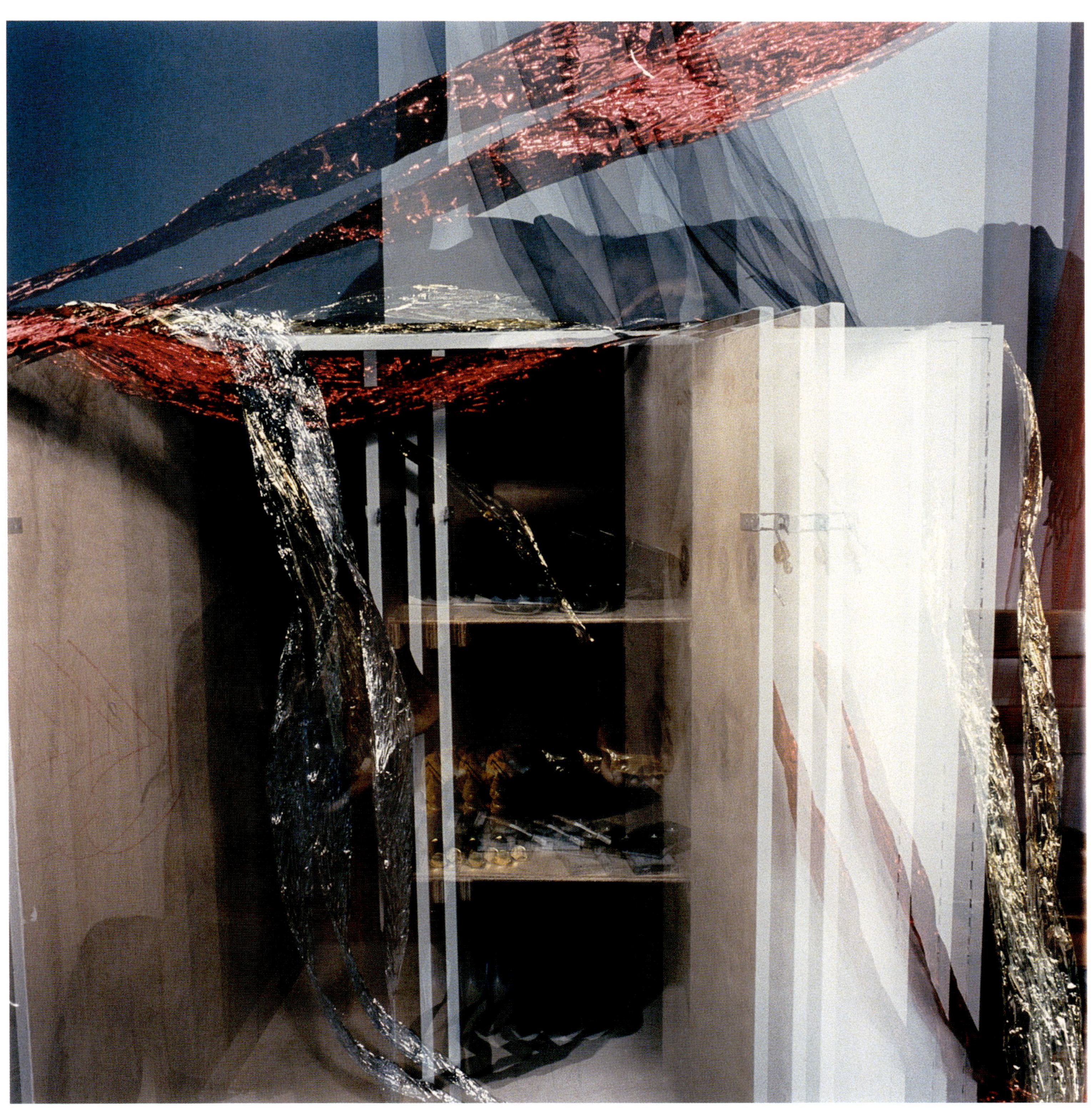

Celebrate No. 4, 1994
Chromogenic print, 16.25 x 16 in. (41.3 x 40.6 cm)
Courtesy the artist and Thomas Erben Gallery, New York

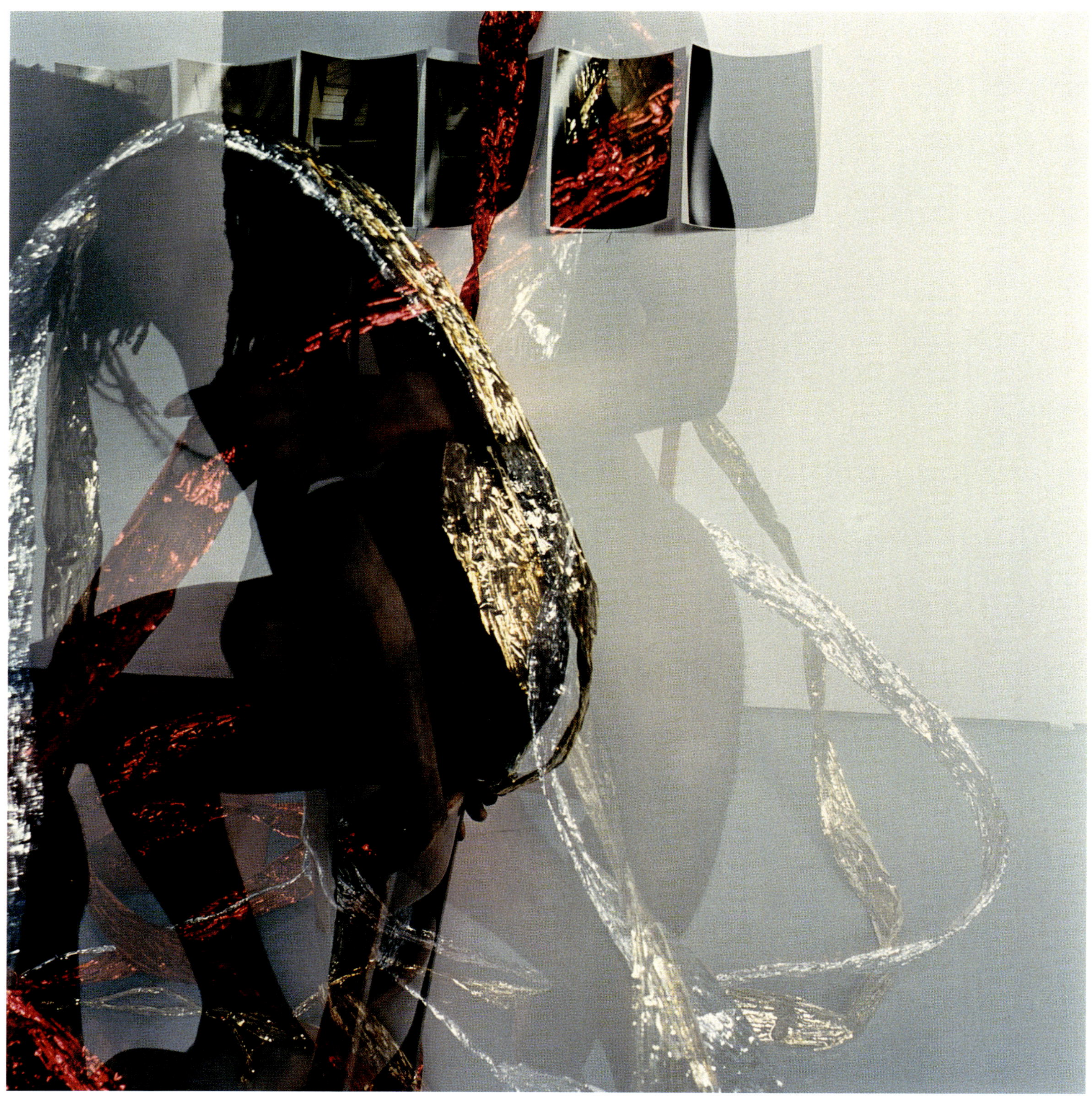

Celebrate No. 5, 1994
Chromogenic print, 16.25 x 16 in. (41.3 x 40.6 cm)
Courtesy the artist and Thomas Erben Gallery, New York

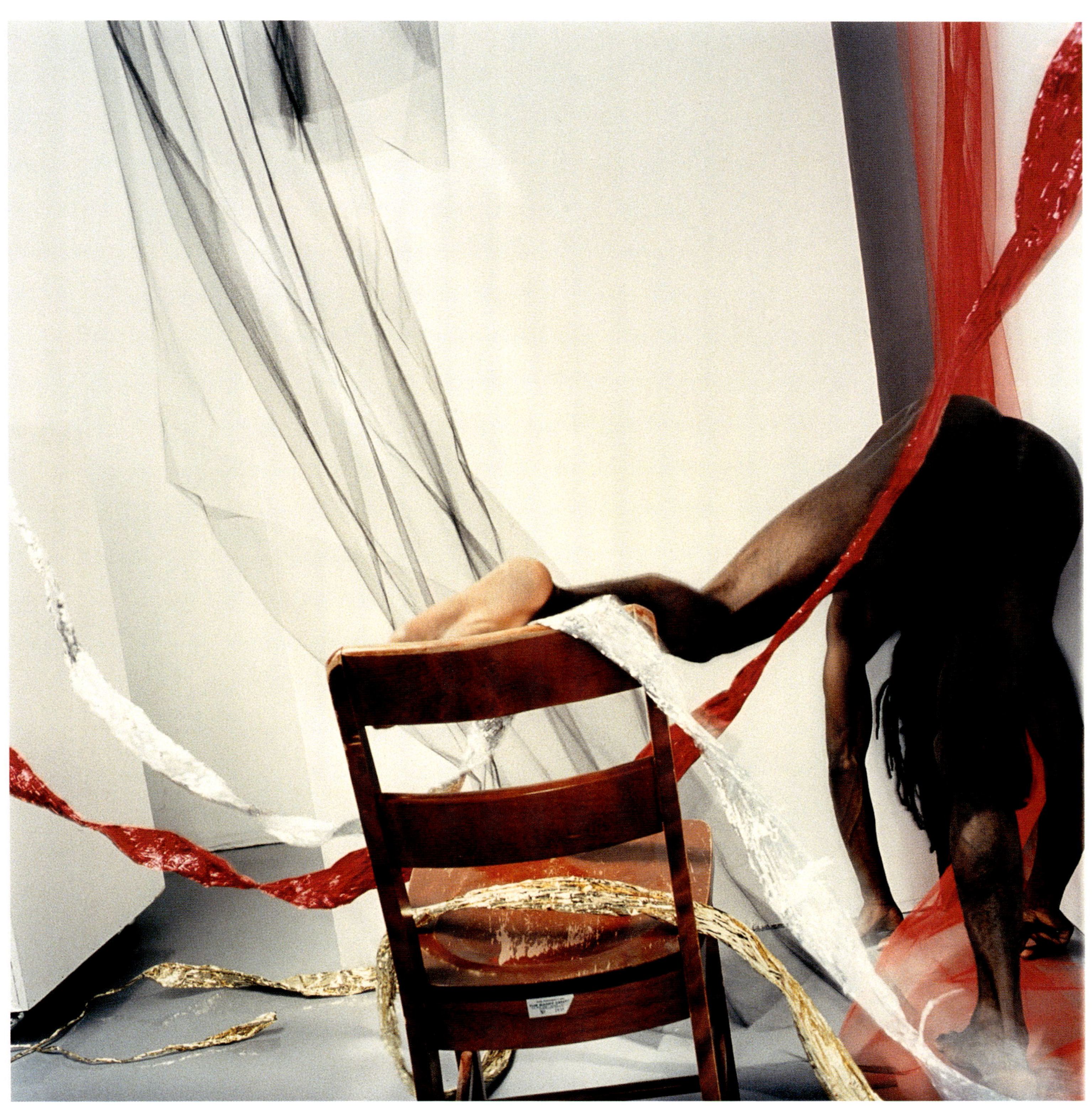

Celebrate No. 6, 1994
Chromogenic print, 16.25 x 16 in. (41.3 x 40.6 cm)
Courtesy the artist and Thomas Erben Gallery, New York

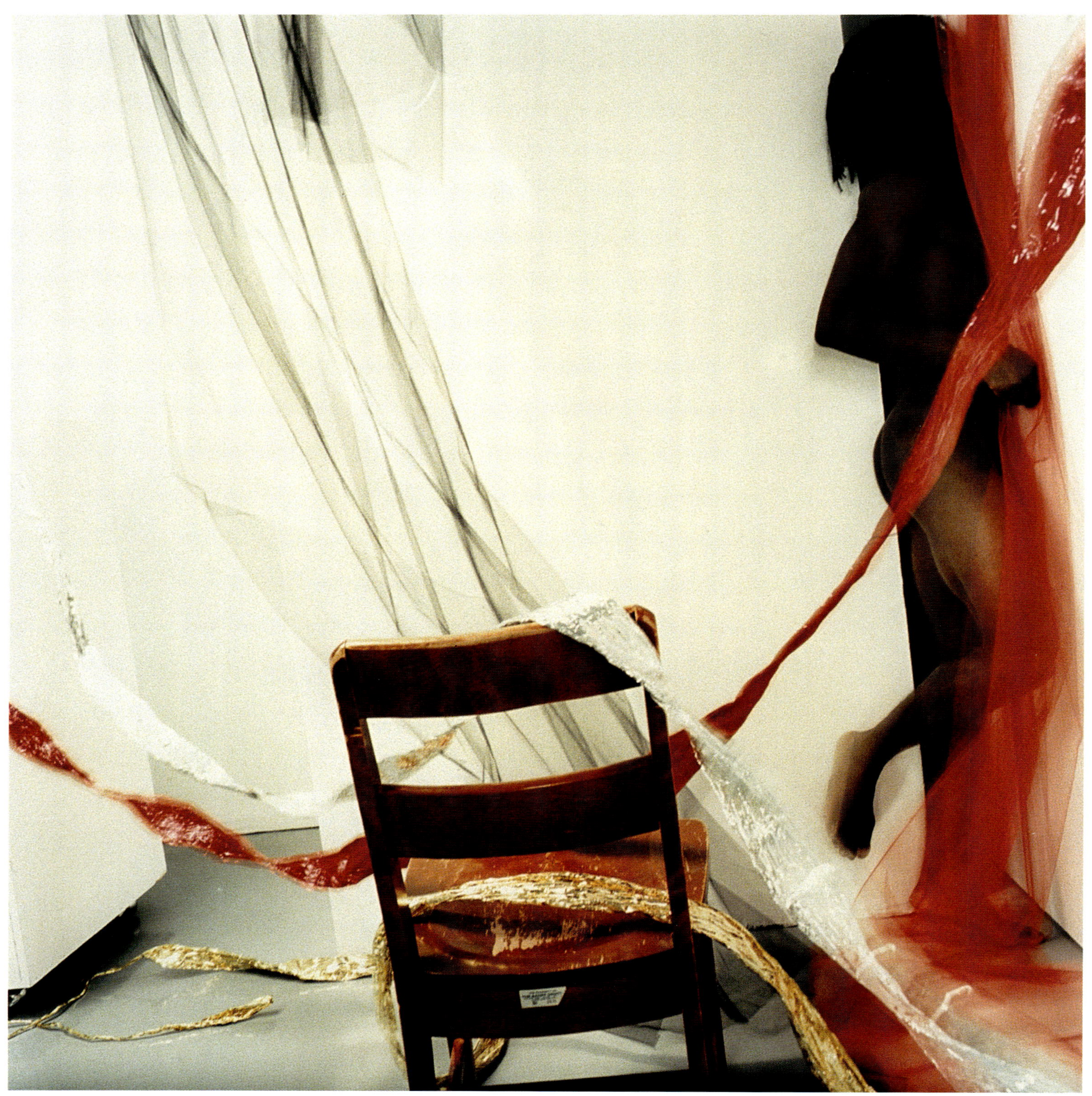

Celebrate No. 7, 1994
Chromogenic print, 16.25 x 16 in. (41.3 x 40.6 cm)
Courtesy the artist and Thomas Erben Gallery, New York

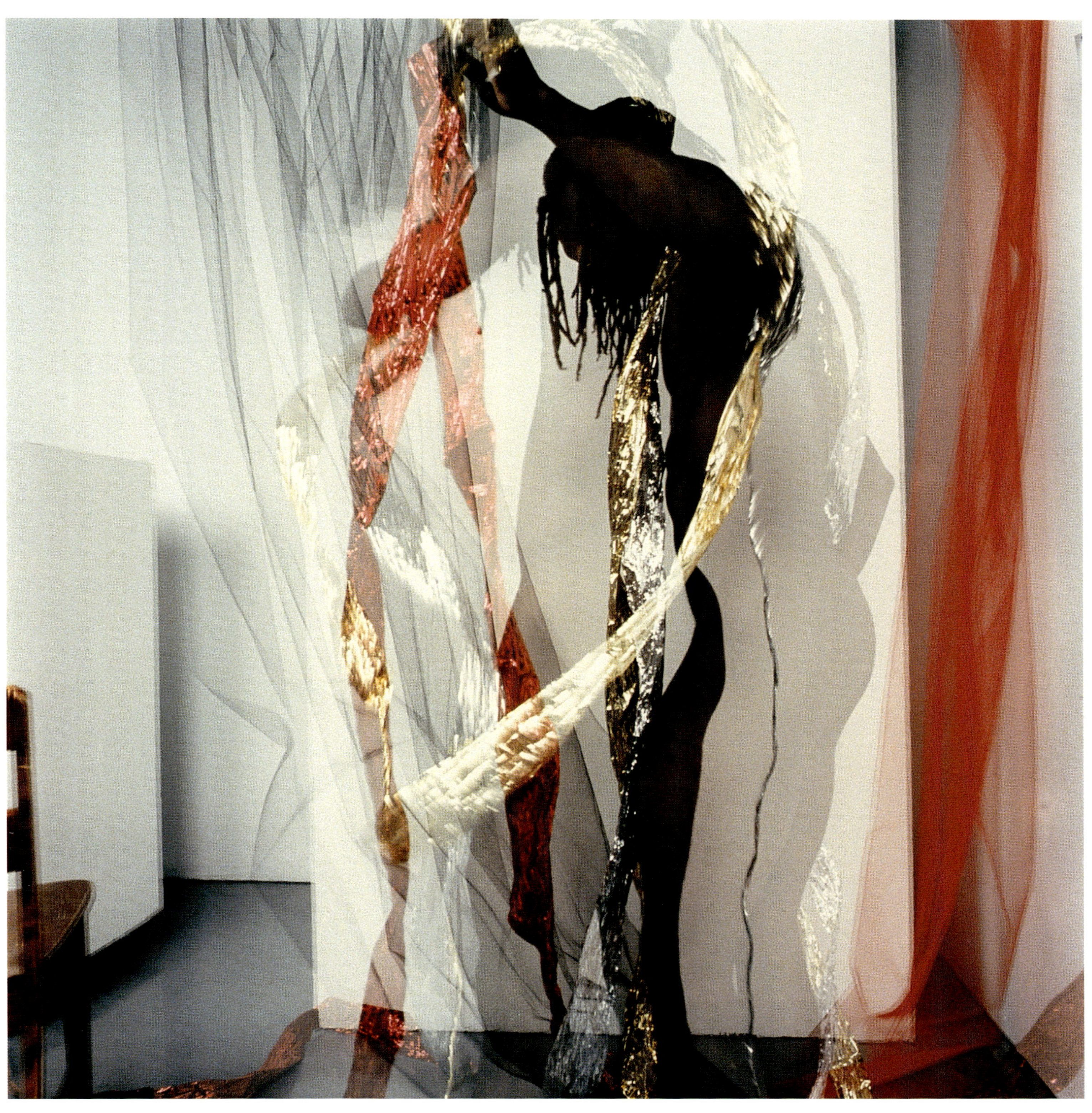

Celebrate No. 8, 1994
Chromogenic print, 16.25 x 16 in. (41.3 x 40.6 cm)
Courtesy the artist and Thomas Erben Gallery, New York

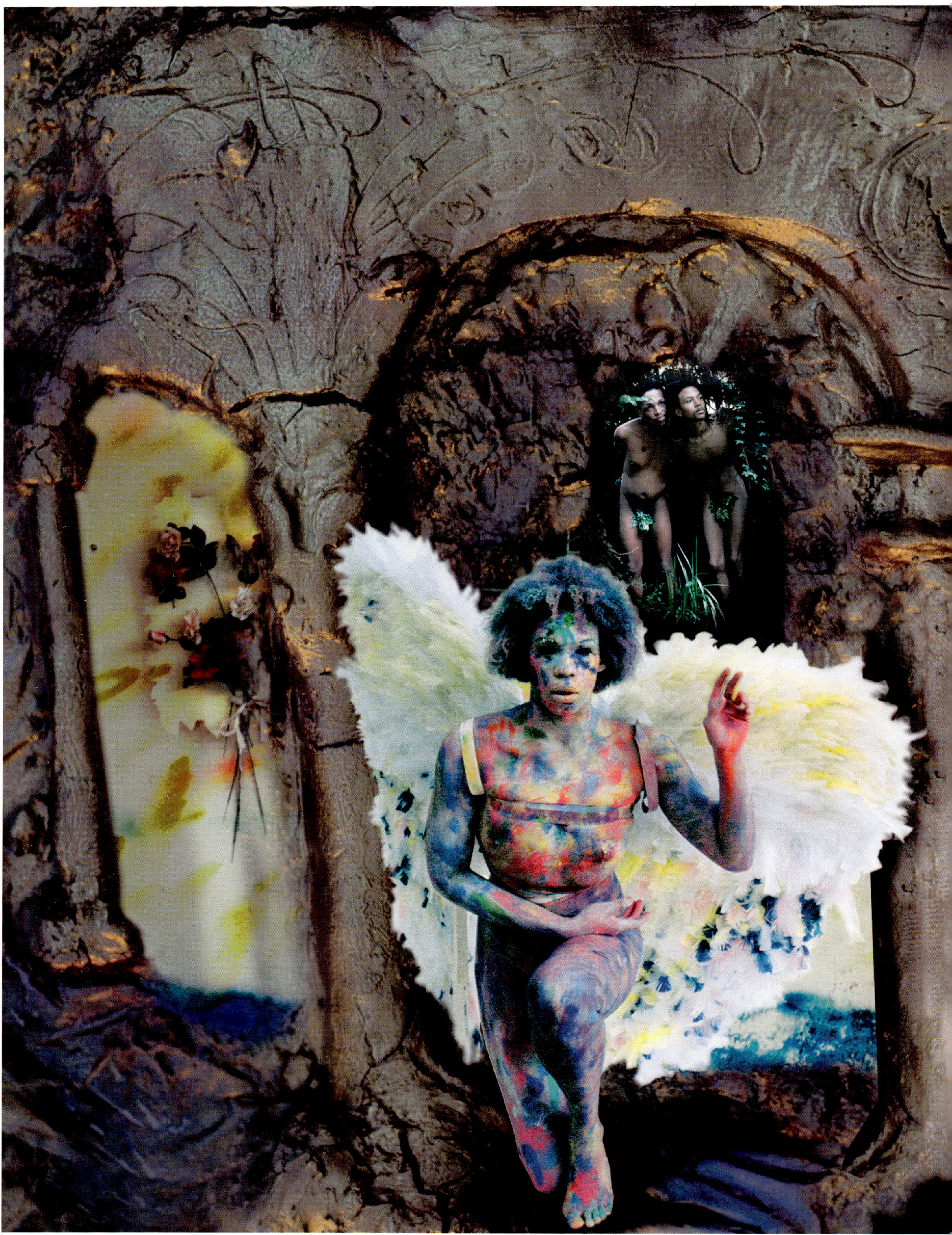

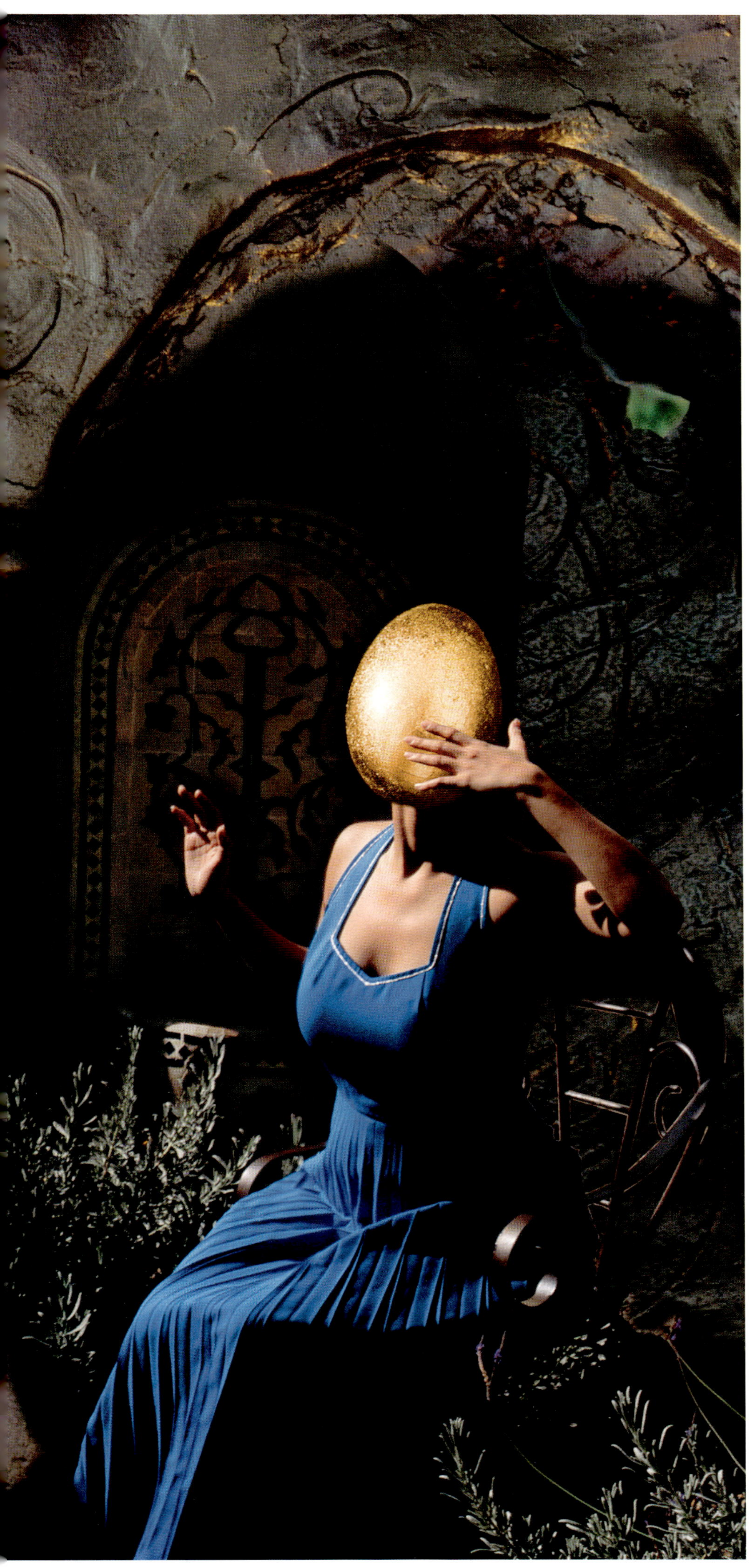

Lucie's Fur Version 1:1:1—L'Annunciazione (After Fra Angelico) c. 1434–2003, 2003
Lambda photograph, 48.4 x 61 in. (122.9 x 154.9 cm)
Courtesy the artist and The Project, New York

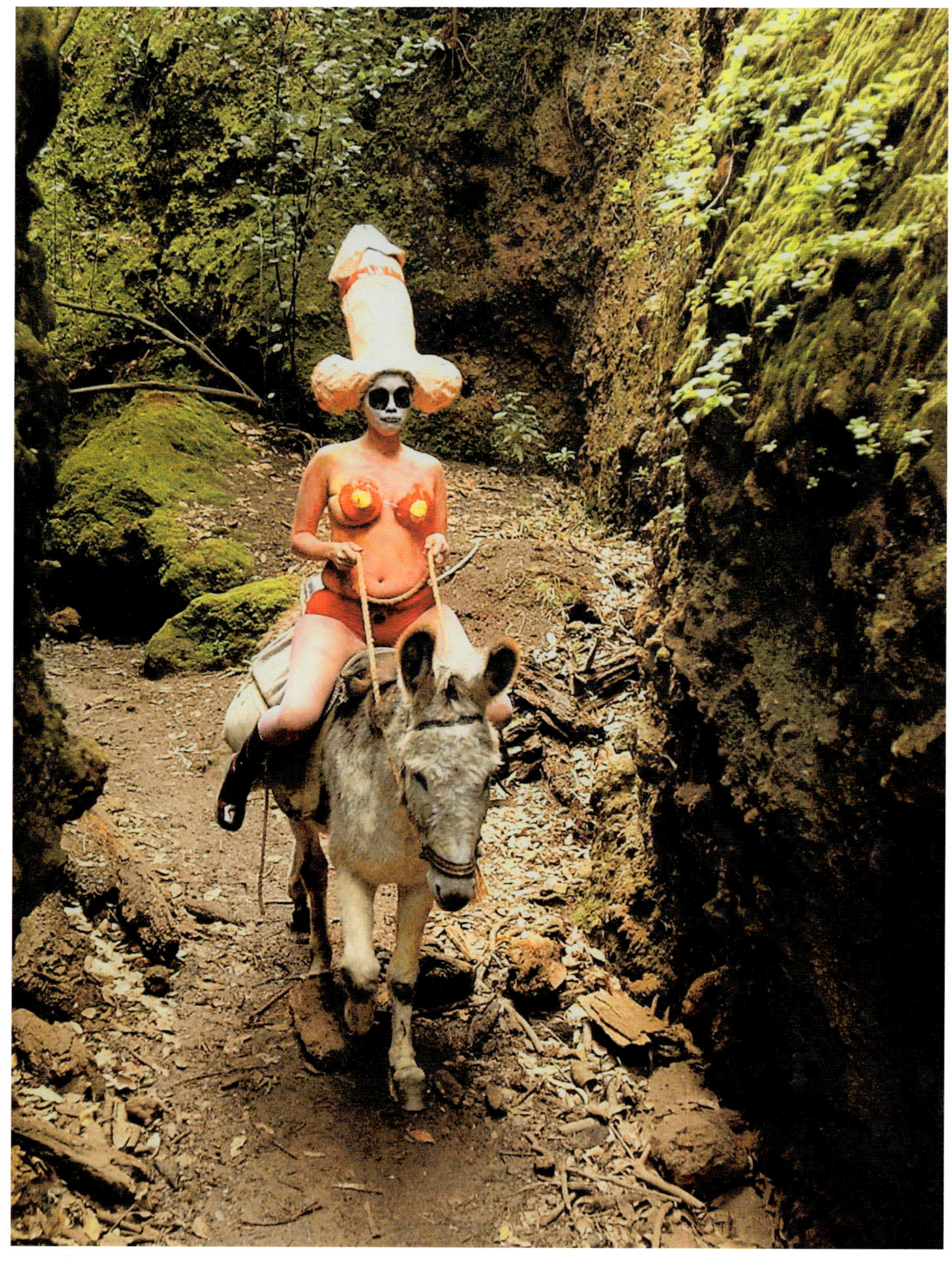

The Prelude: The Garden Path, 2004
Iris print, 58.3 x 40.2 in. (148 x 102 cm)
Courtesy the artist and The Project, New York

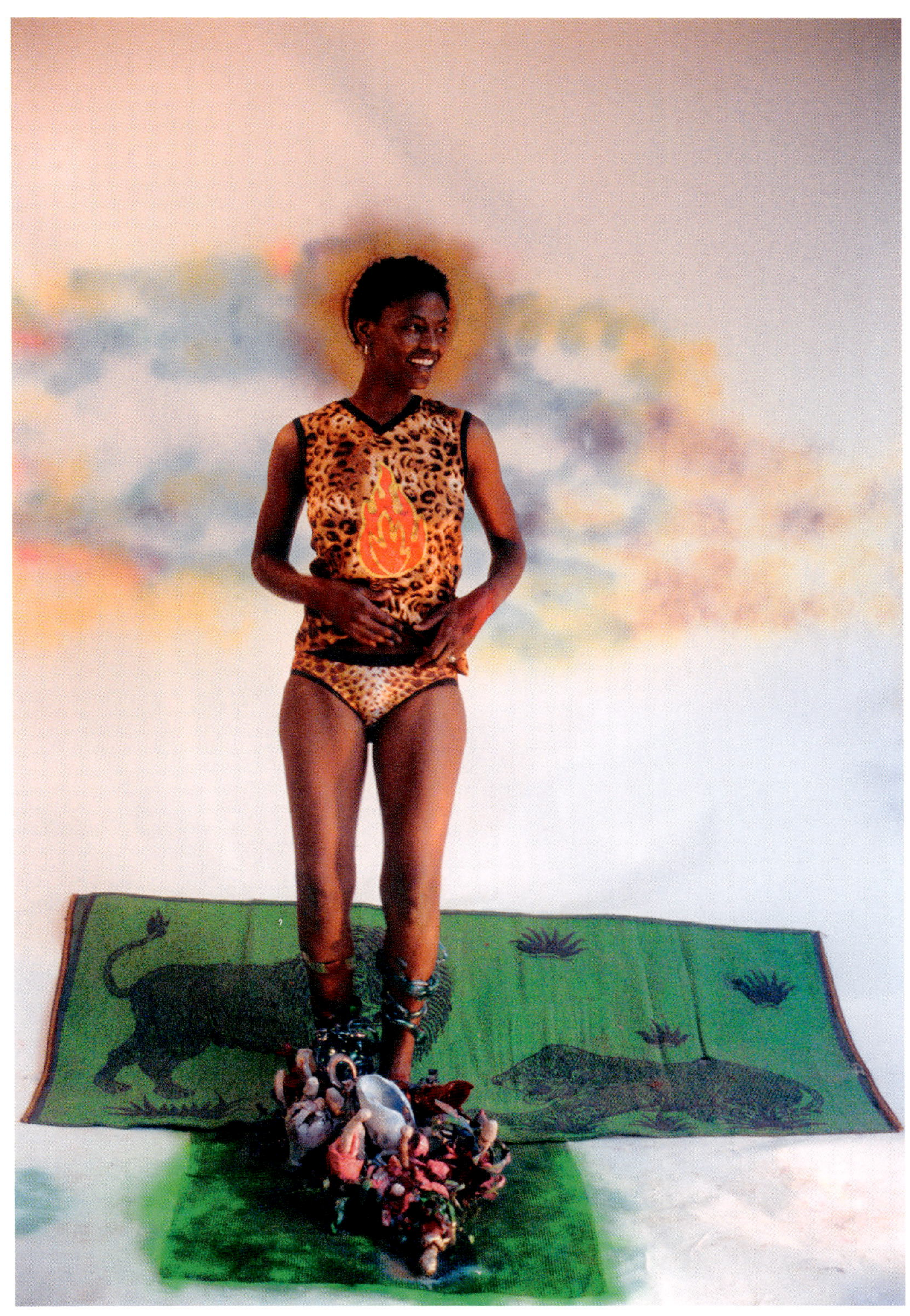

Lucie's Fur Version 1:1:1—La Messie, 2003
Lambda photograph, 58.3 x 40.2 in. (148 x 102 cm)
Courtesy the artist and The Project, New York

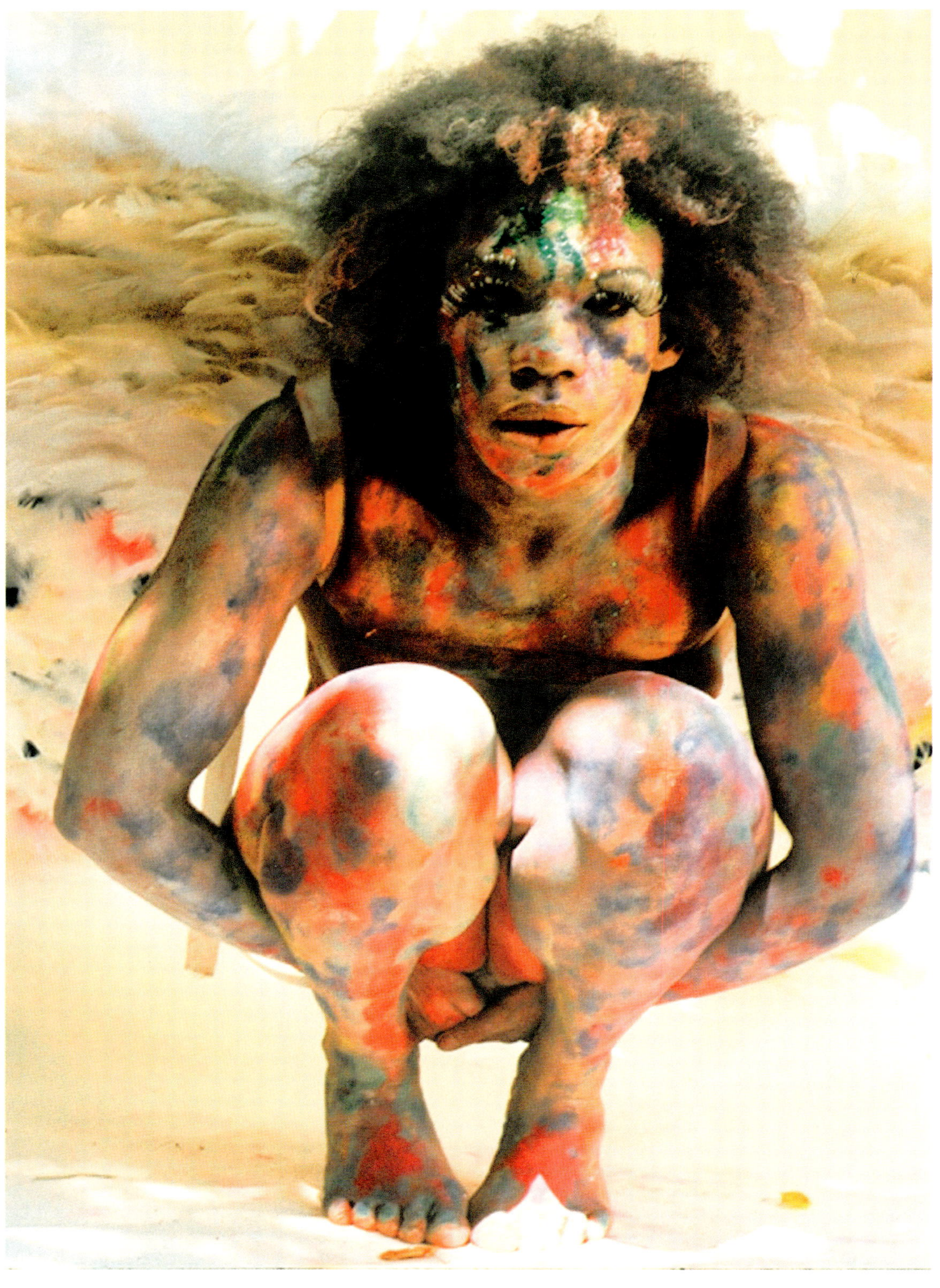

Lucie's Fur Version 1:1:1—The Messenger, 2003
Lambda photograph, 31.5 x 23.6 in. (80 x 60 cm)
Courtesy the artist and The Project, New York

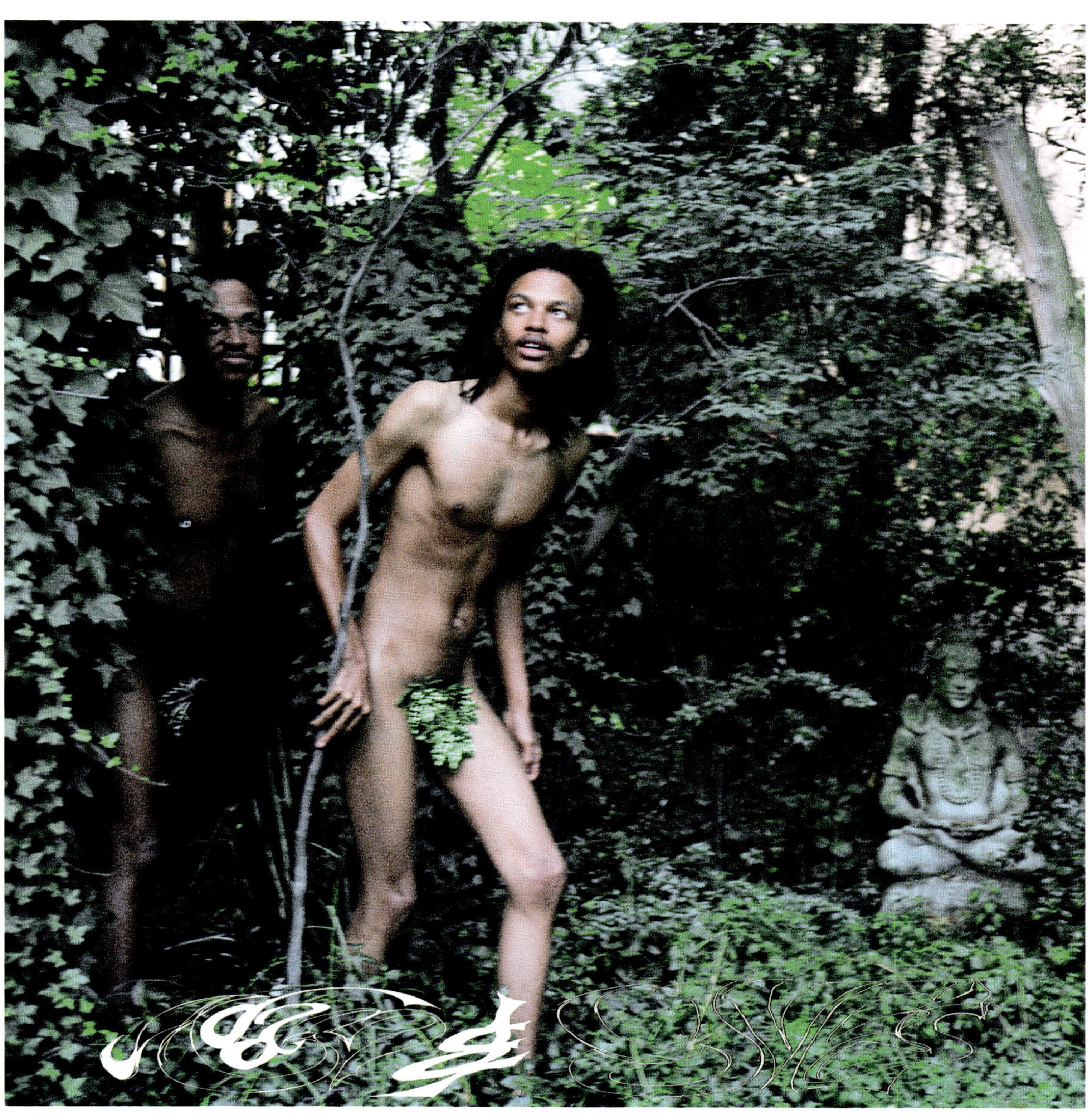

Lucie's Fur Version 1:1:1 - Adam and Yves, 2003
Lambda photograph, 32.3 x 32.3 inches (82 x 82 cm)
Courtesy the artist and The Project, New York

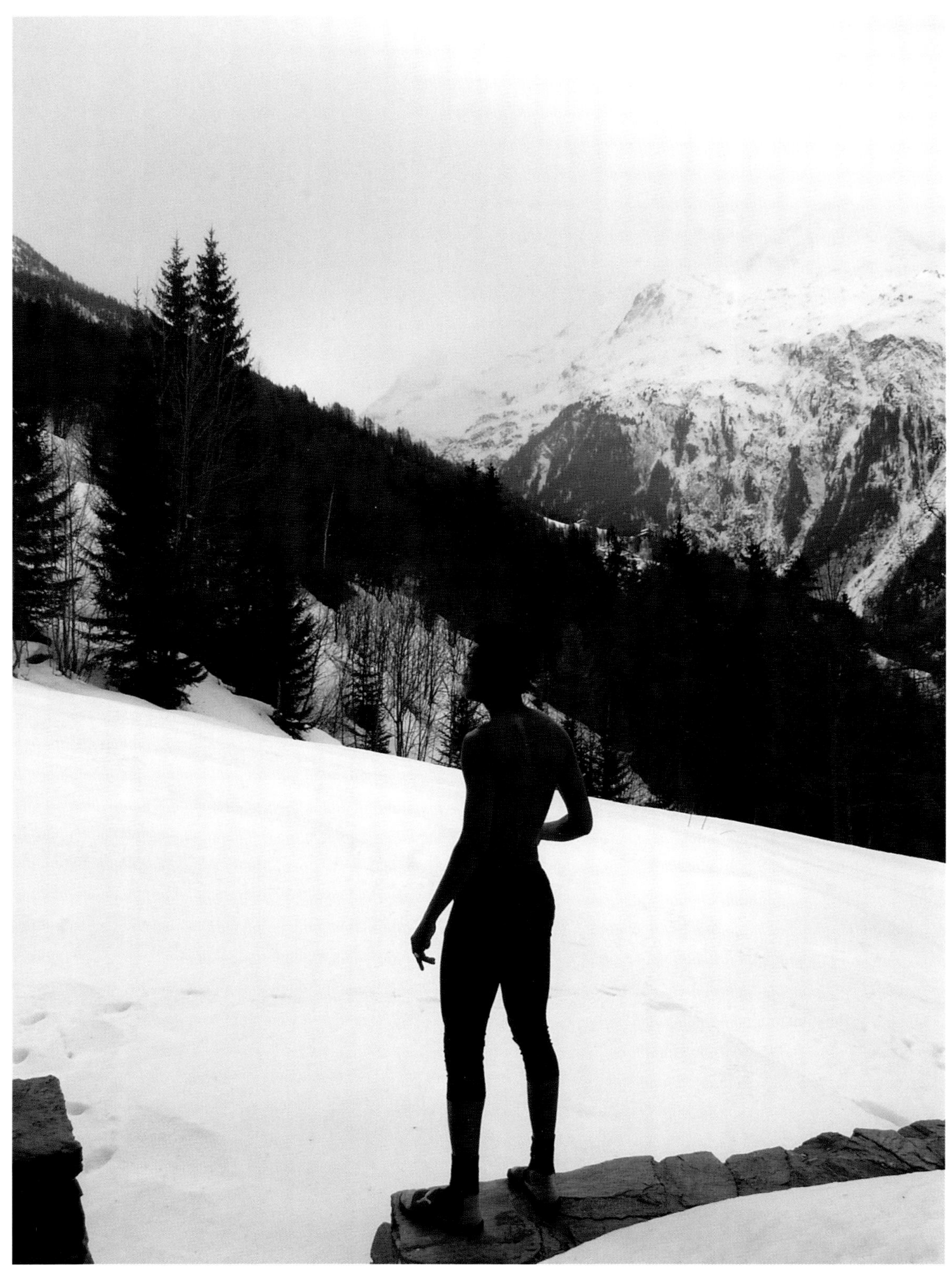

Cactus de Sibérie 1: Mohamed à la montagne: le cactus de Sibérie!
[Mohamed in the mountains: the cactus of Siberia!], 2001–02
Chromogenic print, 11 x 14.7 in. (27.9 x 37.3 cm)
Courtesy the artist and Galerie Pierre Brullé, Paris

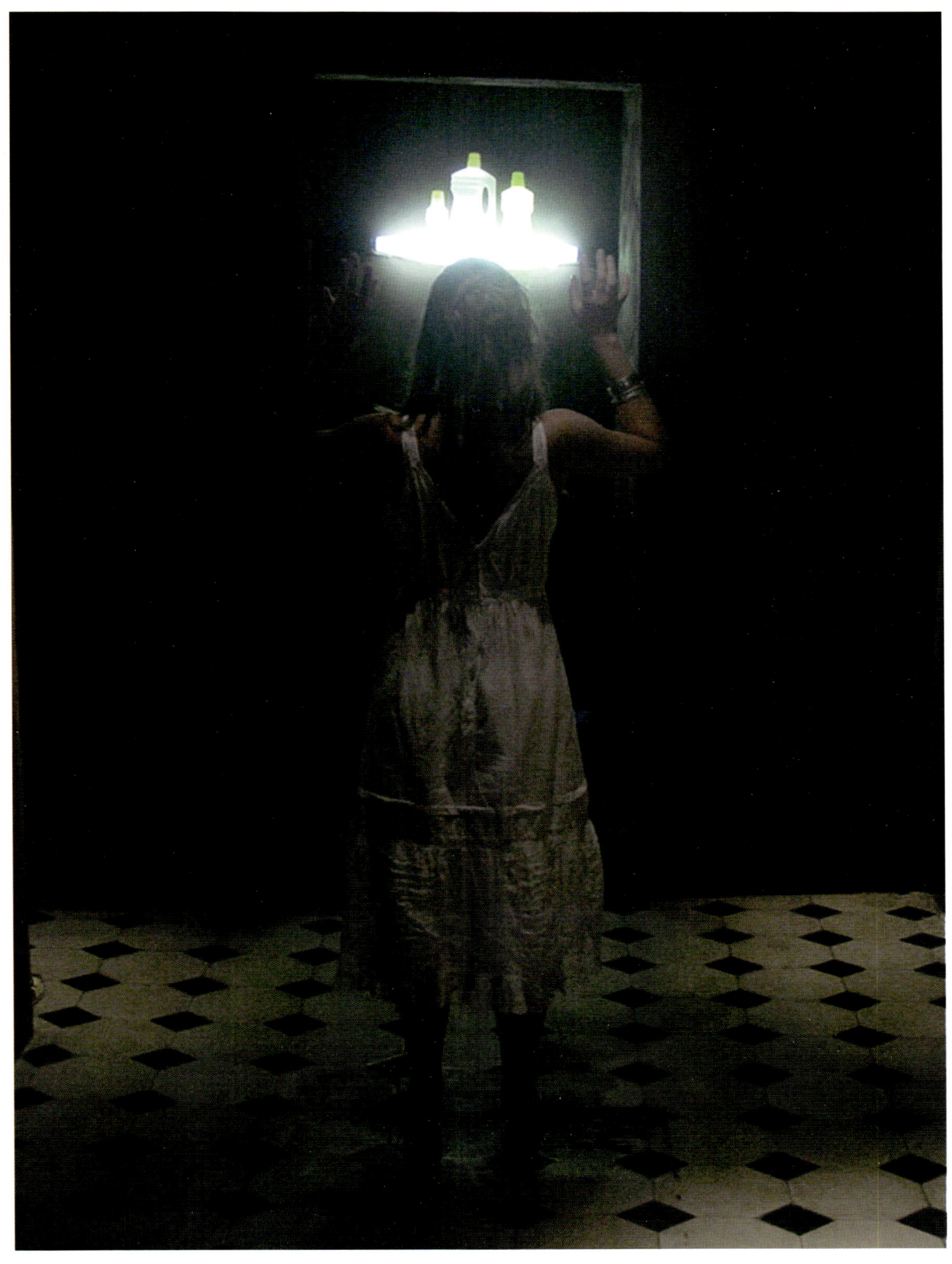

Nora 4: Même la marchande de sable fait sa corvée d'eau avant de m'endormir
[Even the sandgirl makes her water before lulling me to sleep.], 2001–02
Chromogenic print, 11 x 14.7 in. (27.9 x 37.3 cm)
Courtesy the artist and Galerie Pierre Brullé, Paris

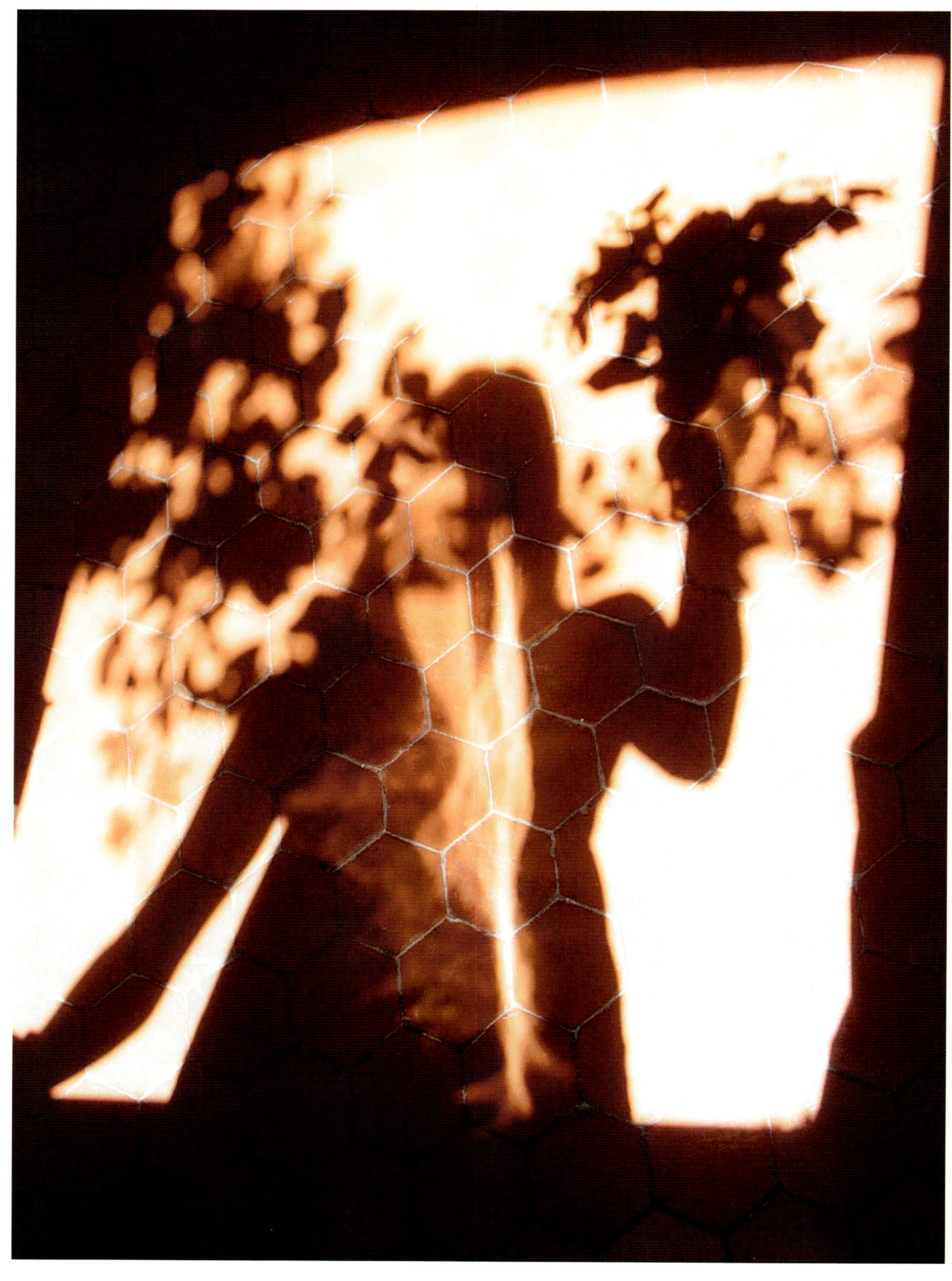

Nora 2: Quand j'ai éternué elle a disparu
[When I sneezed she disappeared.], 2001–02
Chromogenic print, 14.7 x 11 in. (37.3 x 27.9 cm)
Courtesy the artist and Galerie Pierre Brullé, Paris

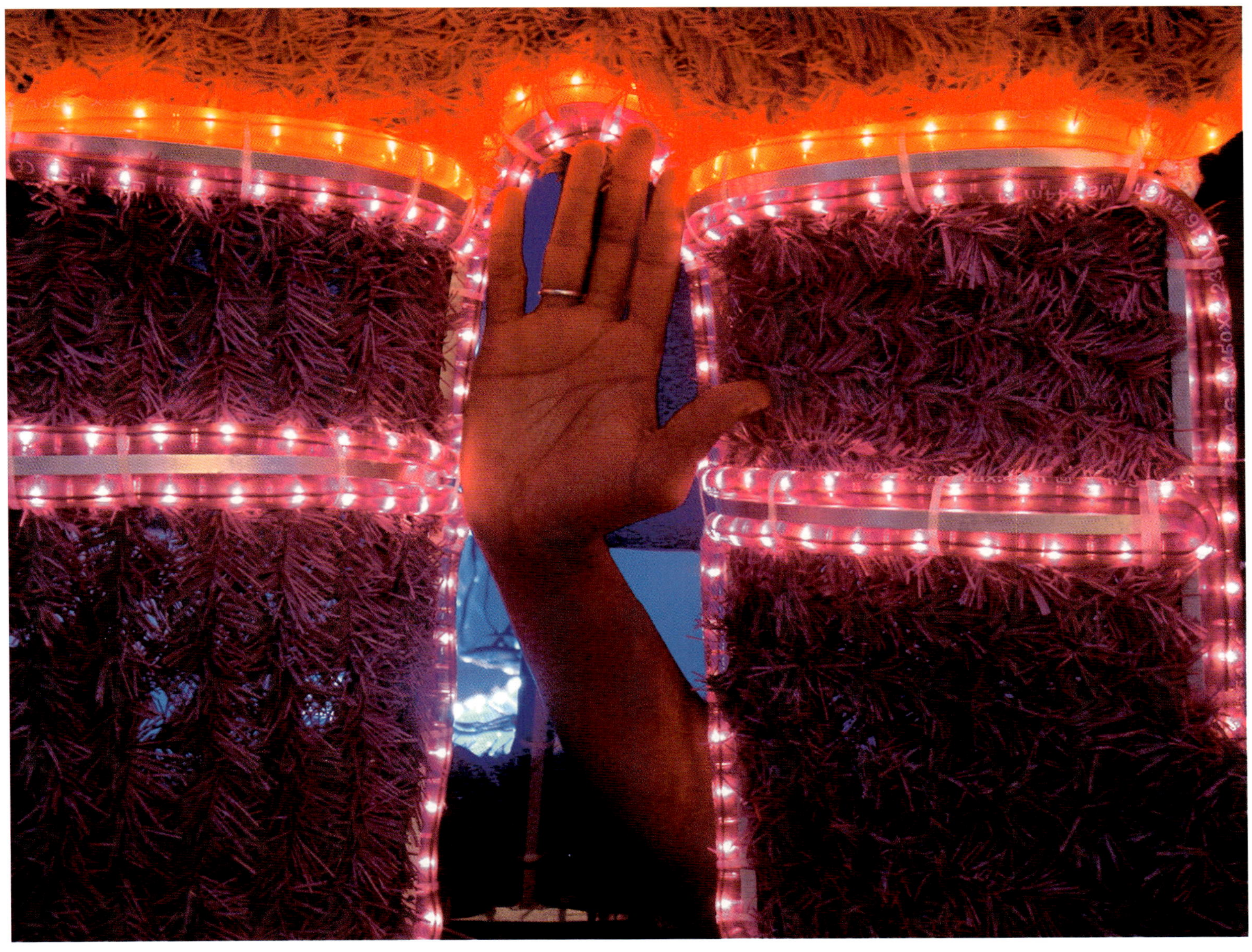

Cactus de Noël 5: Merci la Chance de me suivre dans mes rêves
[Thank you, Lady Luck, for following me in my dreams.], 2001–02
Chromogenic print, 11 x 14.7 in. (27.9 x 37.3 cm)
Courtesy the artist and Galerie Pierre Brullé, Paris

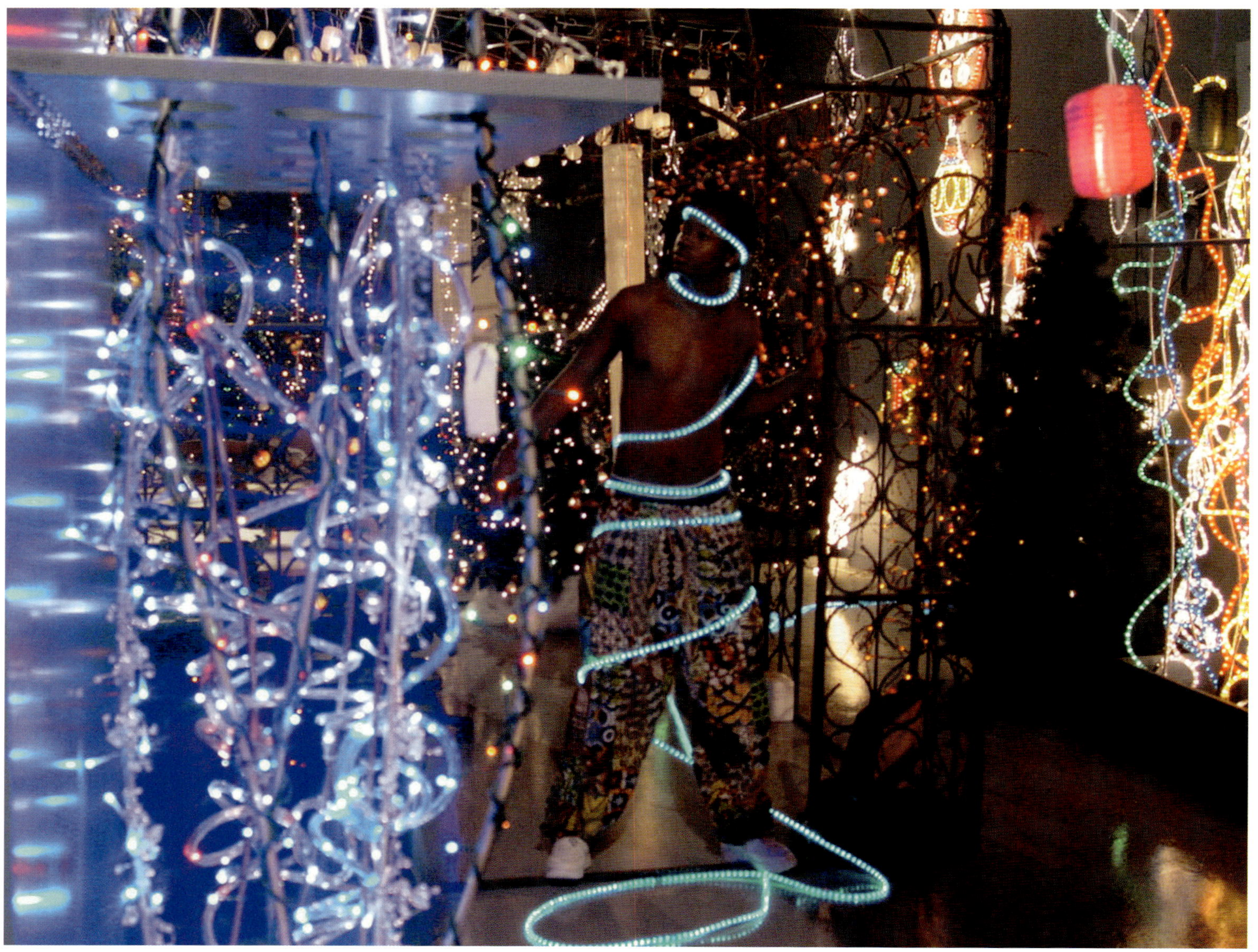

Cactus de Noël 3: Au secours Blachère, Tarzan s'est pris dans ses lianes!
[Help! help! Mr. Blachère. Tarzan got caught in his lianas!], 2001–02
Chromogenic print, 11 x 14.7 in. (27.9 x 37.3 cm)
Courtesy the artist and Galerie Pierre Brullé, Paris

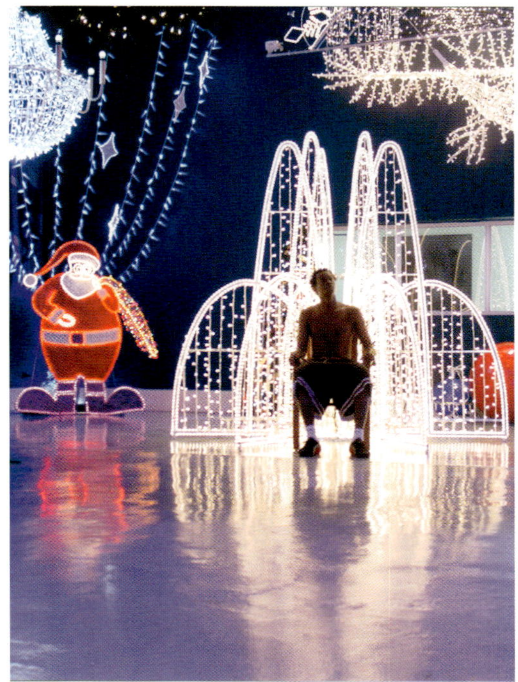

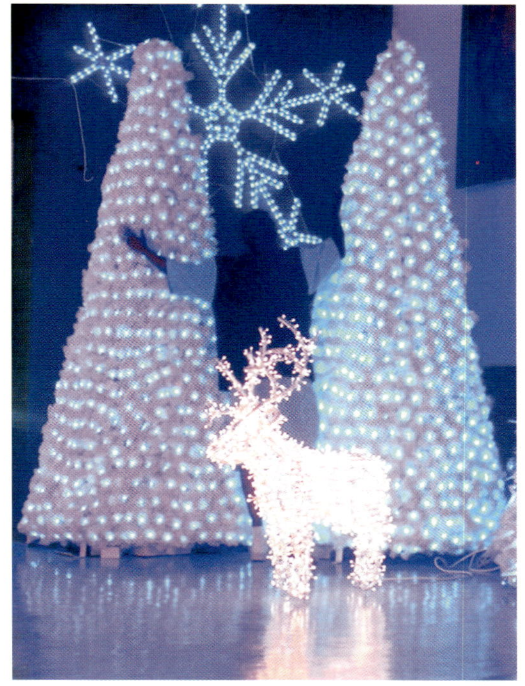

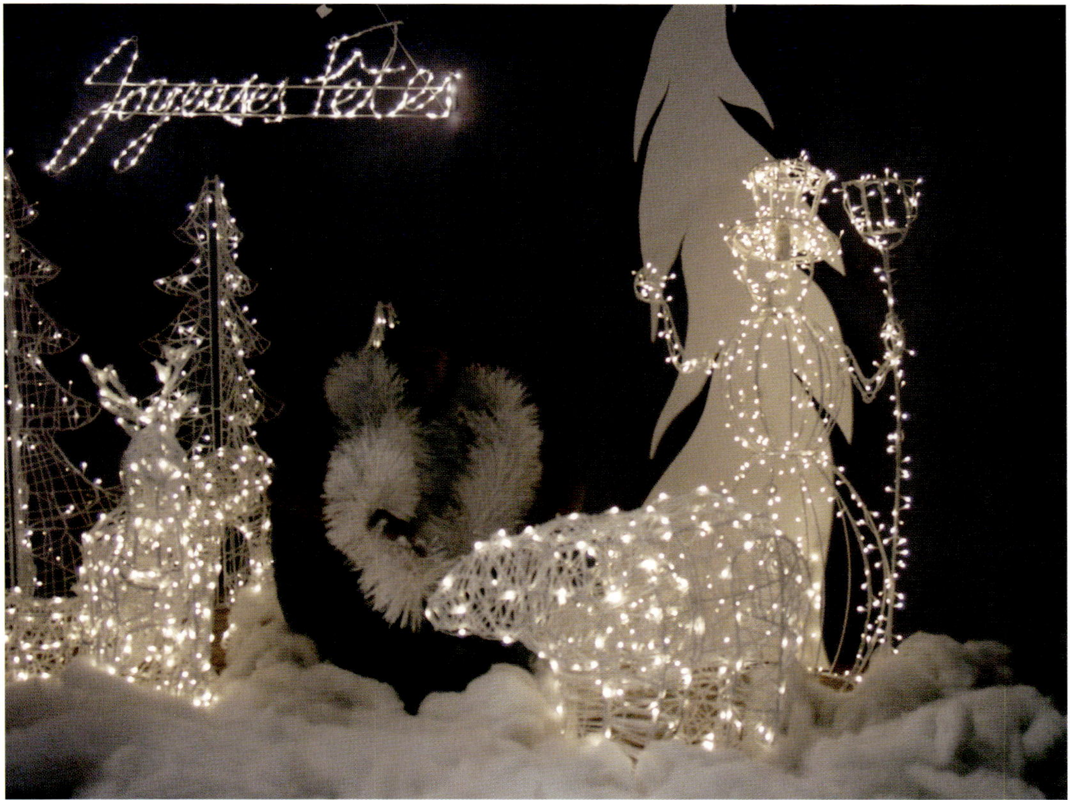

Top left:
Cactus de Noël 2: Quand je prendrai la place du Père Noël, tu verras.
[When I take the place of Santa Claus, you will see.], 2001–02
Chromogenic print, 11 x 14.7 in. (27.9 x 37.3 cm)

Top right:
Cactus de Noël 4: Il est où mon cerf? [Where is my stag?], 2001–02
Chromogenic print, 11 x 14.7 in. (27.9 x 37.3 cm)

Bottom:
Cactus de Noël 1: Dans mes rêves à Bamako c'était Noël.
[In my dreams in Bamako it was Christmas.], 2001–02
Chromogenic print, 11 x 14.7 in. (27.9 x 37.3 cm)

All courtesy the artist and Galerie Pierre Brullé, Paris

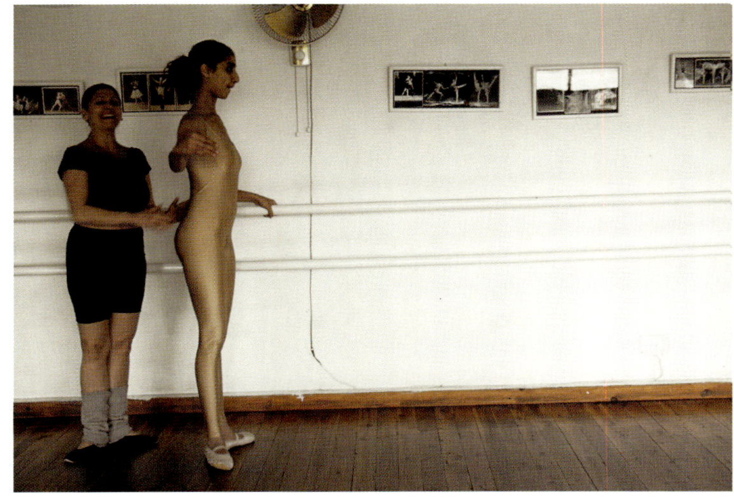
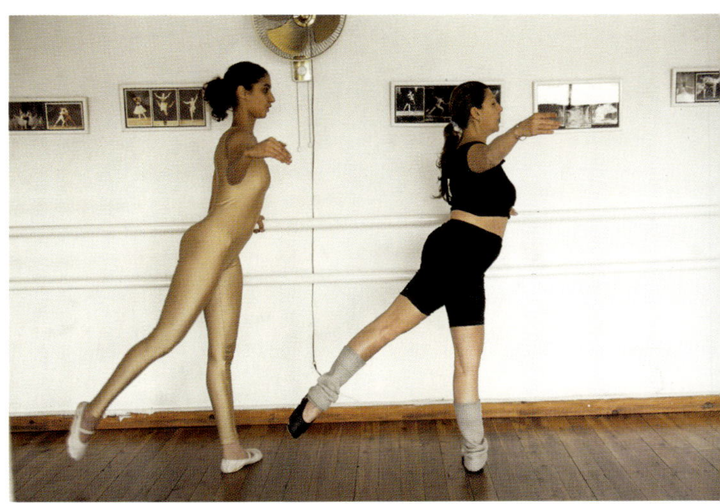
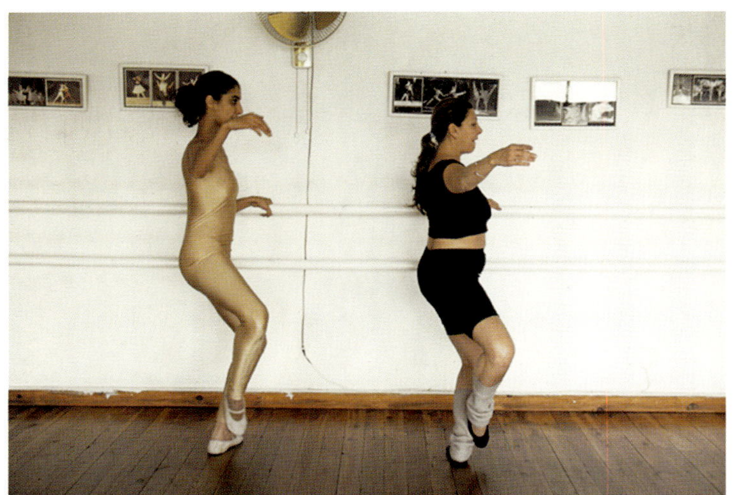
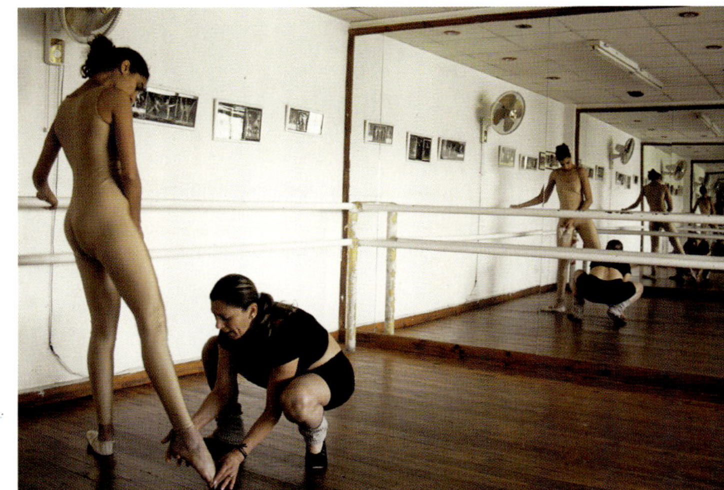
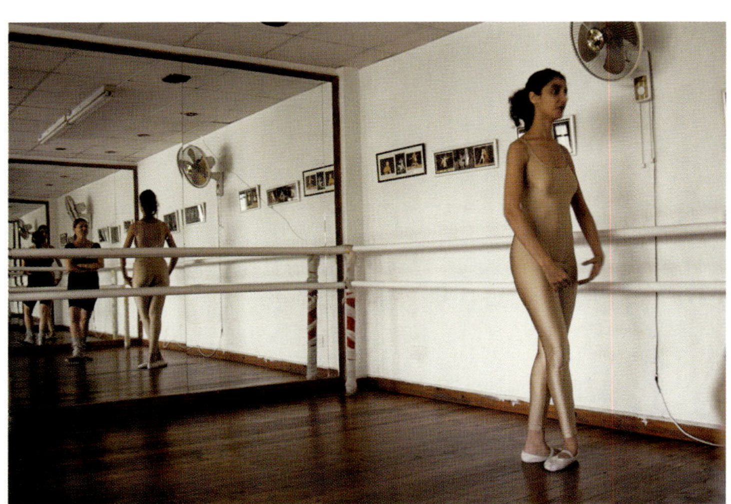
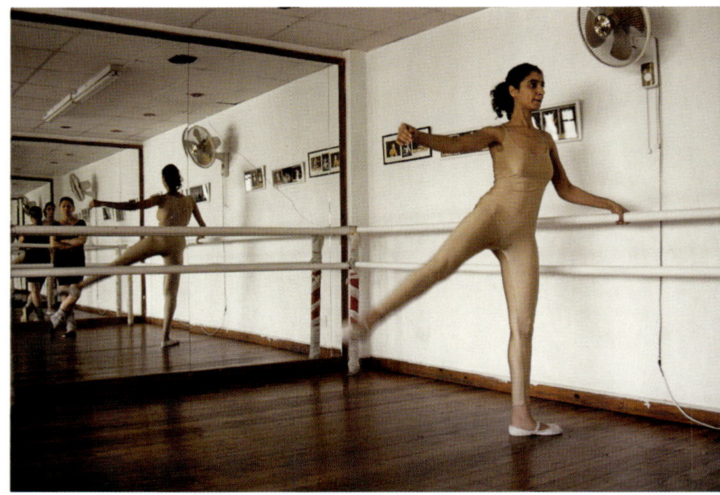
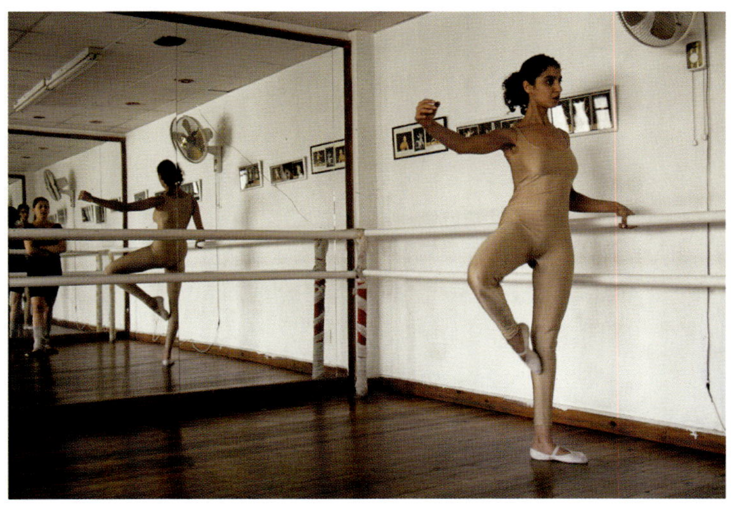
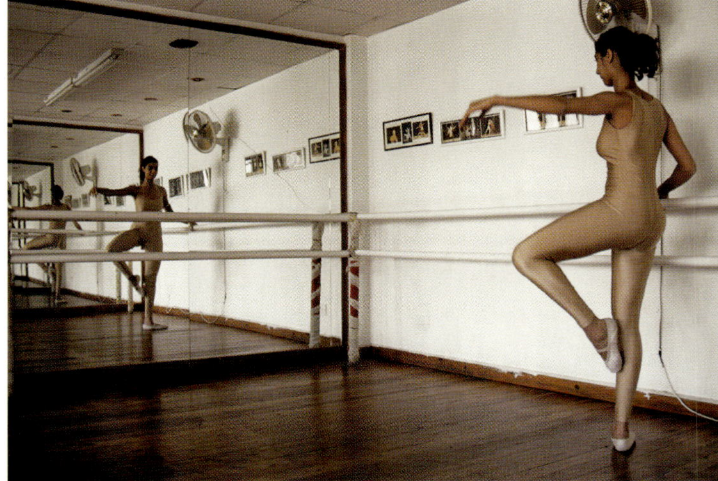

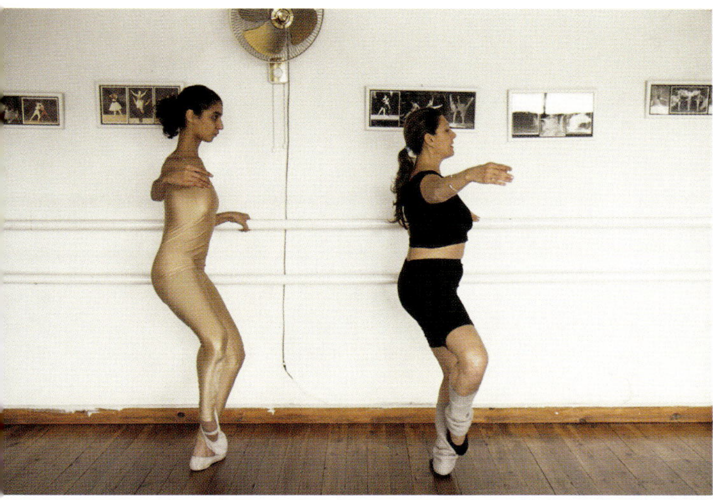
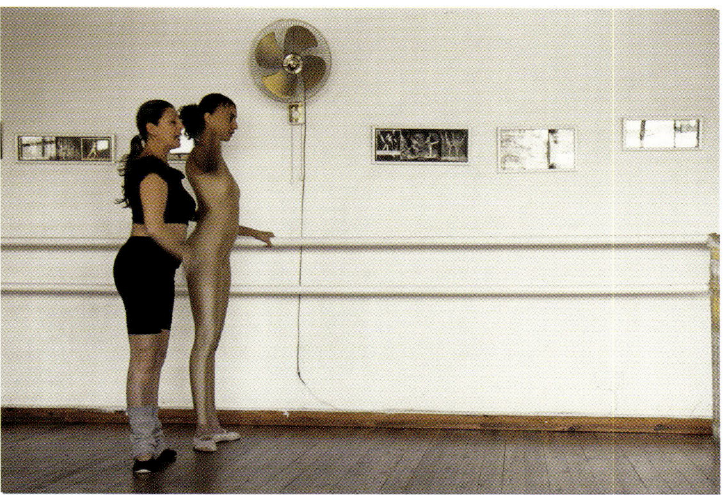
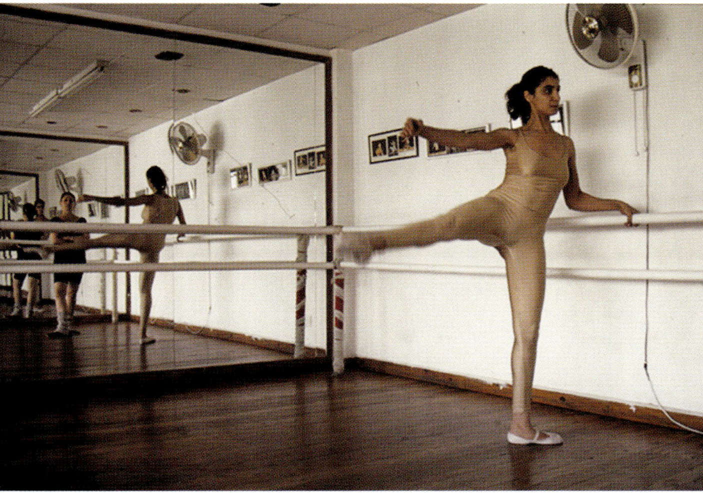
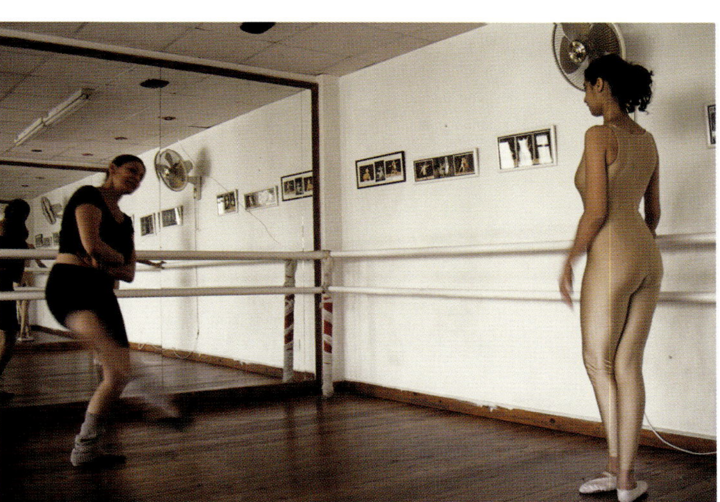
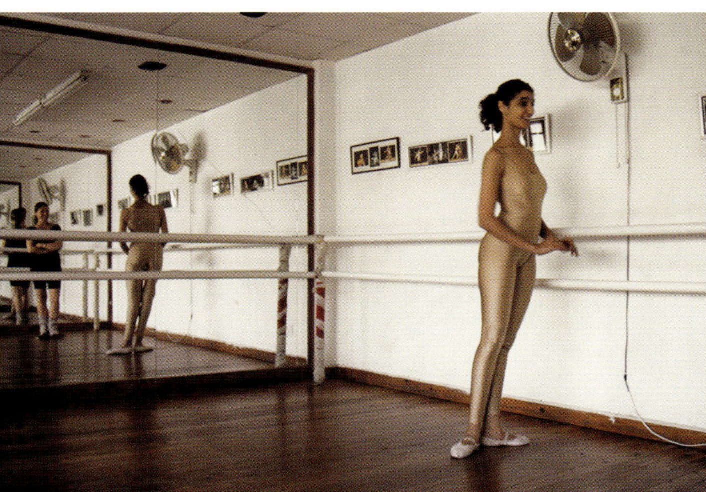
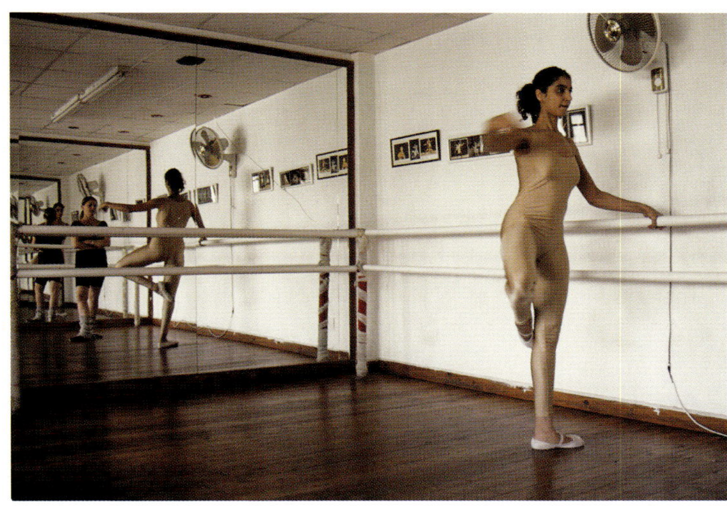
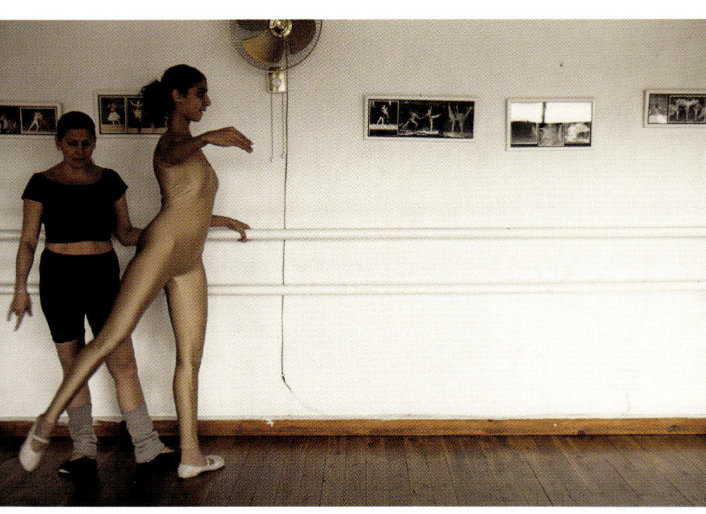
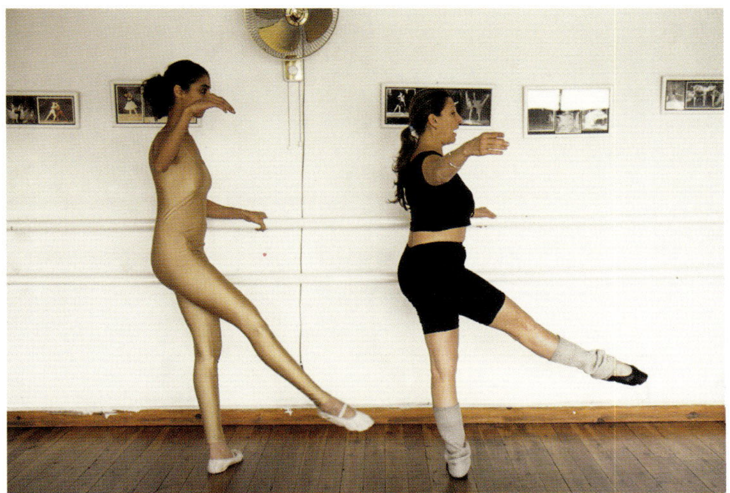

40 Ballet Classes, 2005
Installation of 48 chromogenic prints (each 8 x 10 in. [20.3 x 25.4 cm]) and 4 DVD monitors
Courtesy the artist and Townhouse Gallery, Cairo

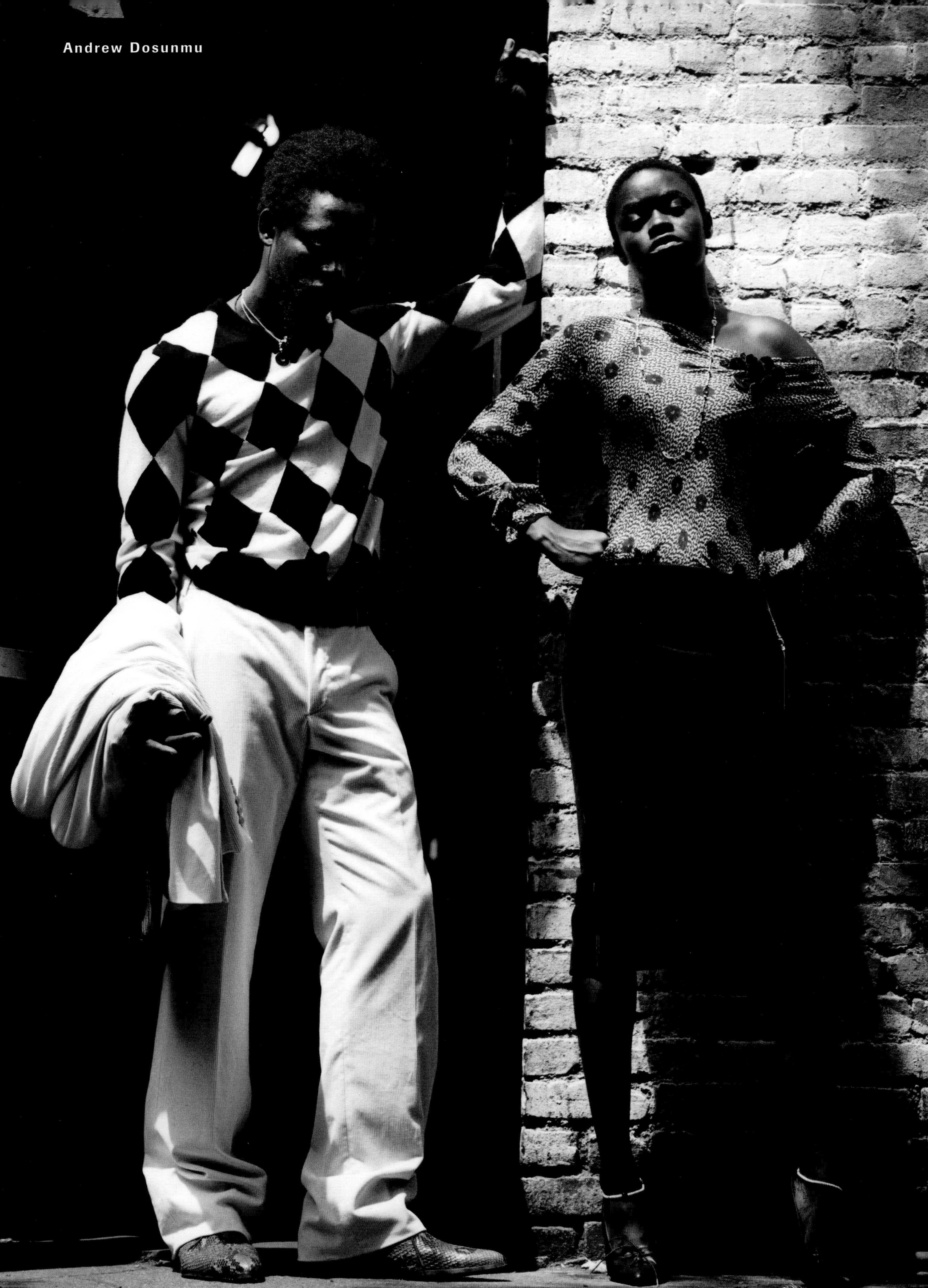

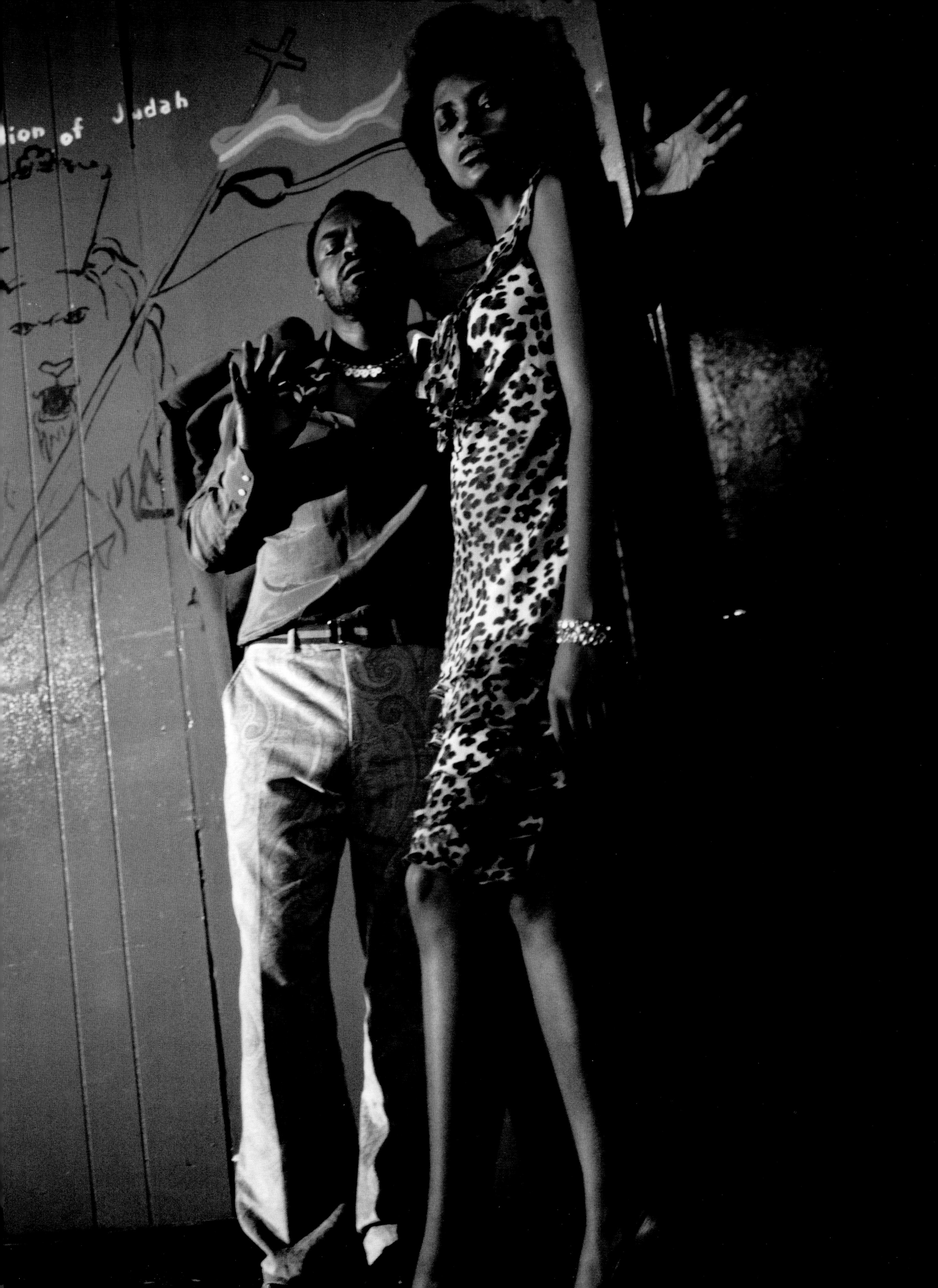
ion of Judah

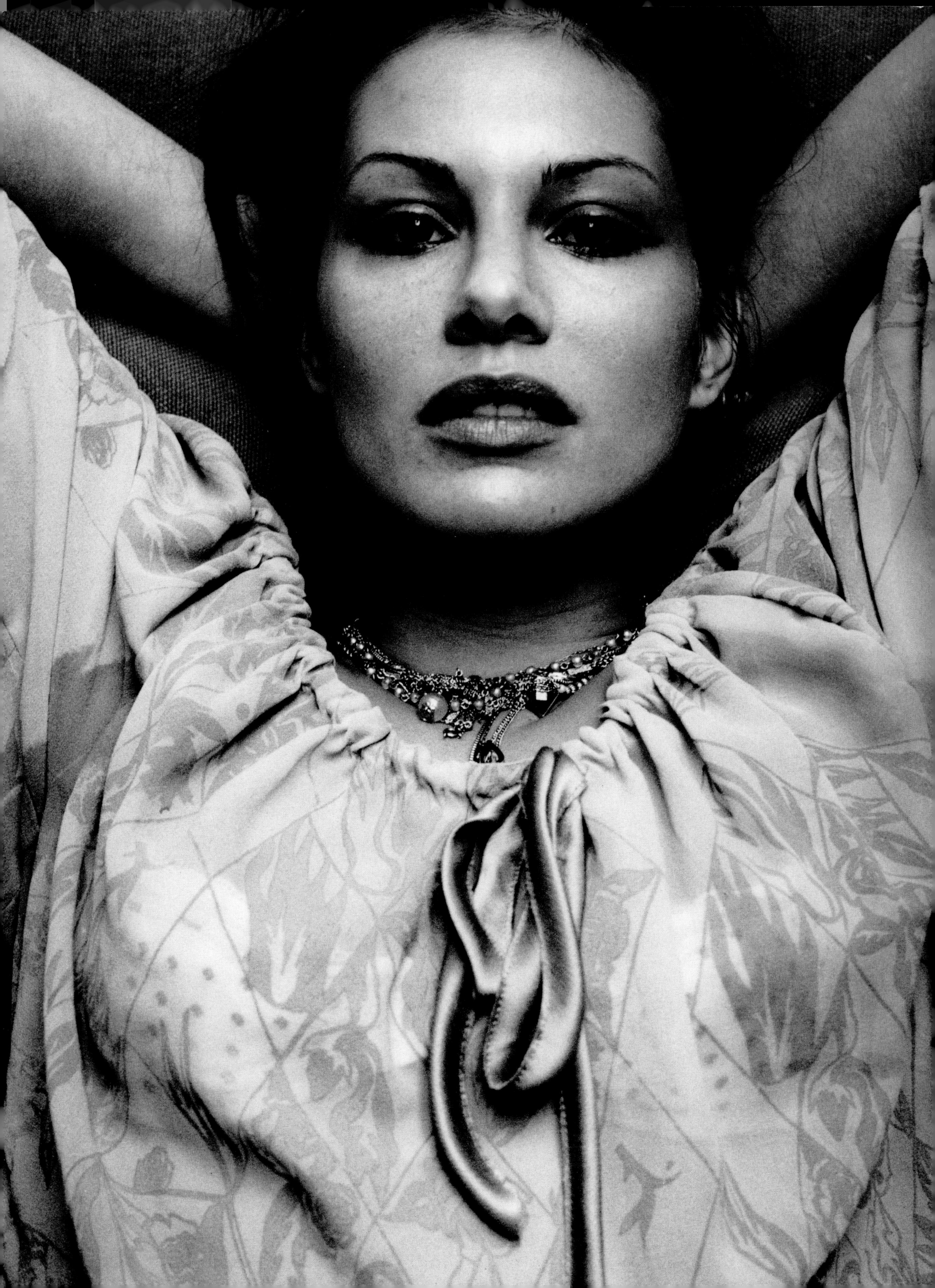

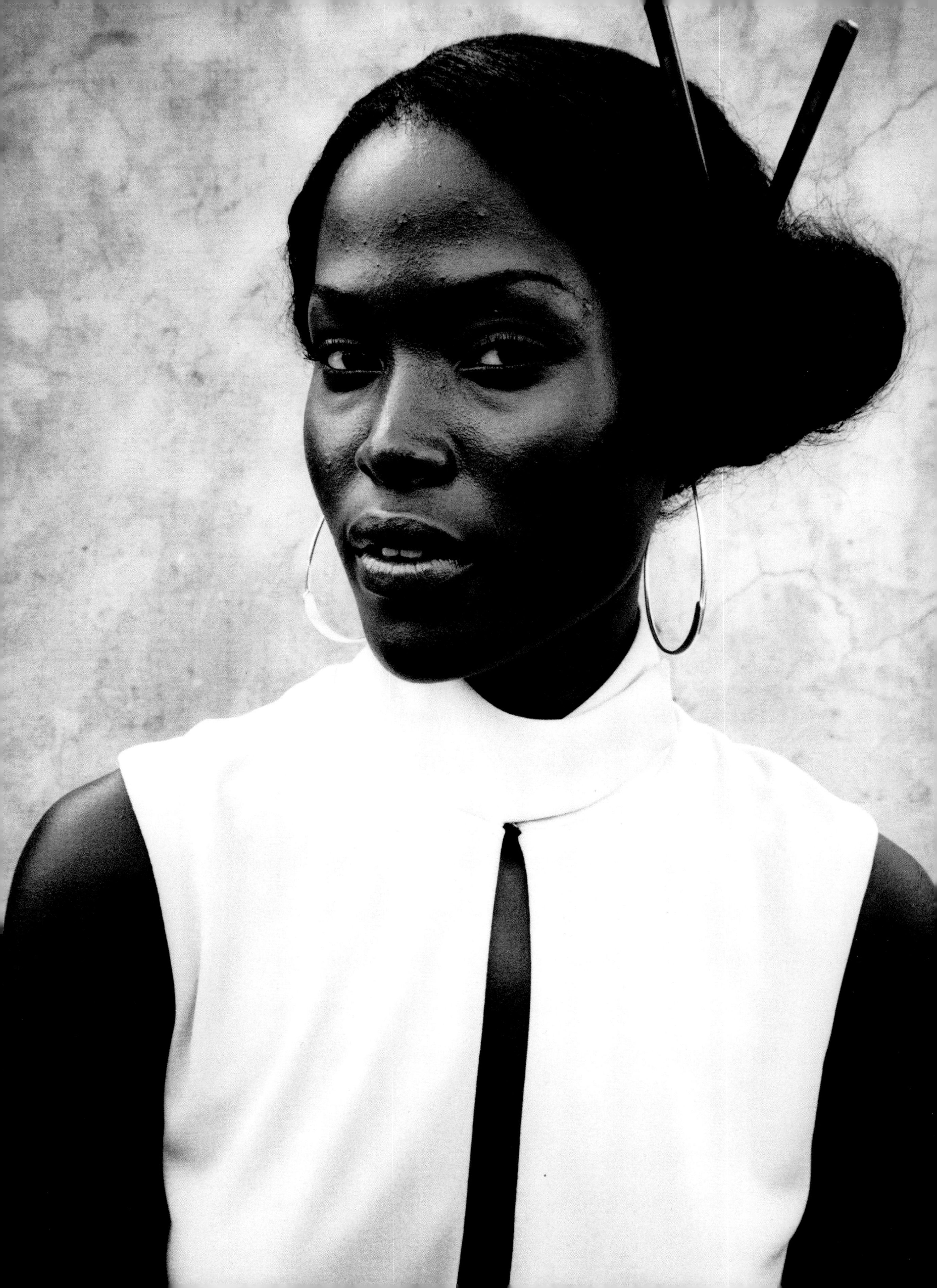

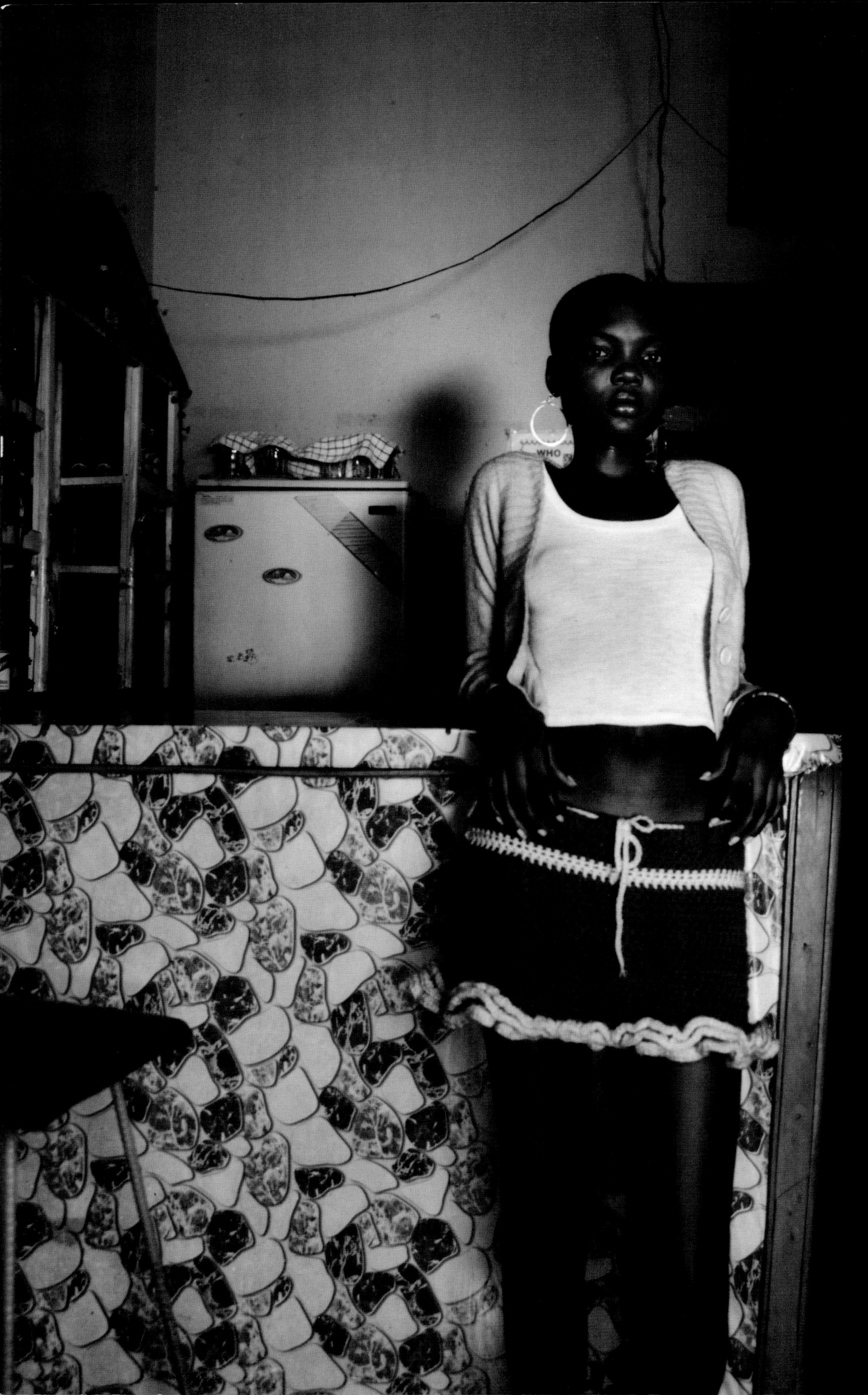
WHO

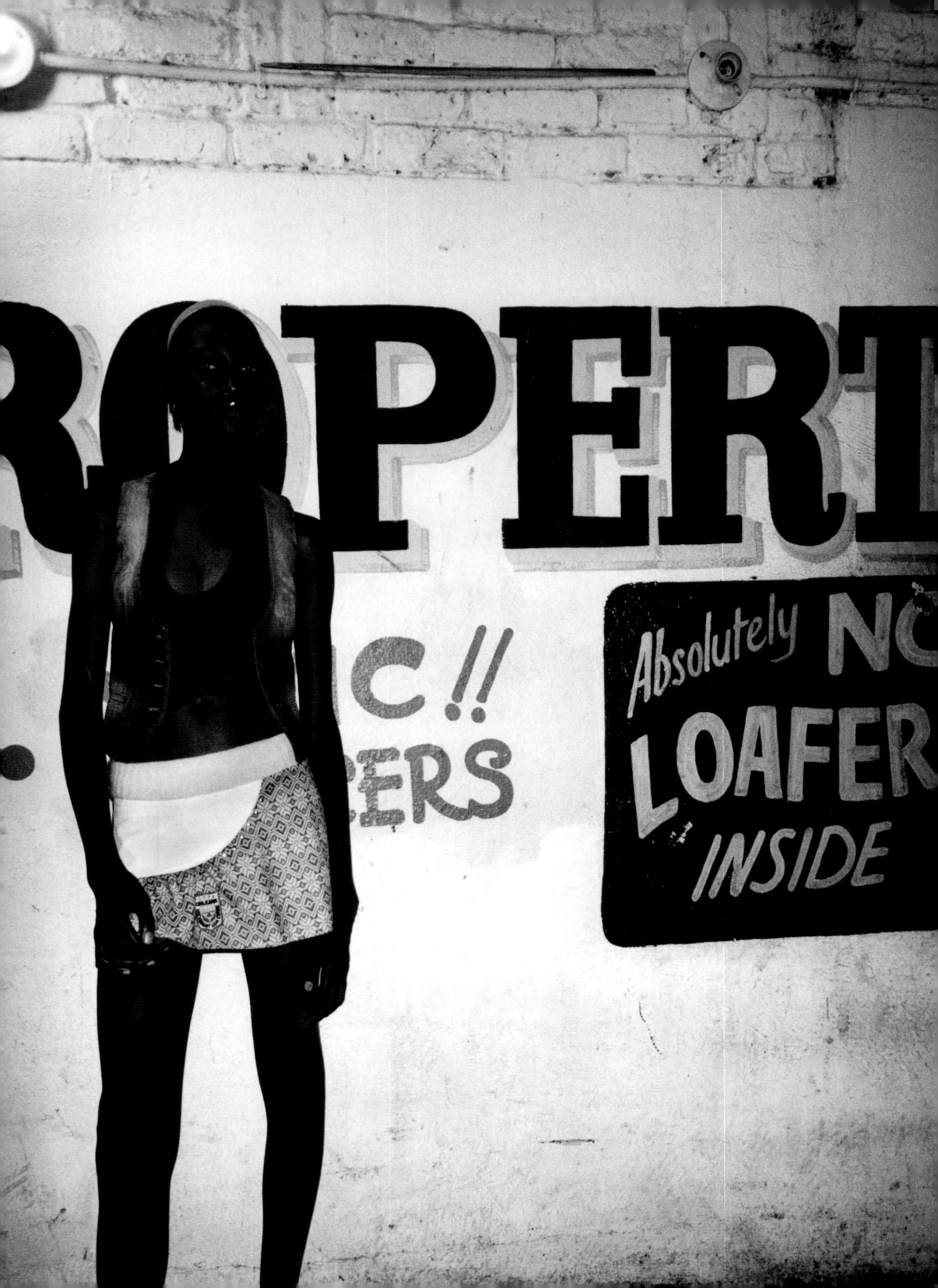

ROPERT
Absolutely NO
LOAFER
INSIDE

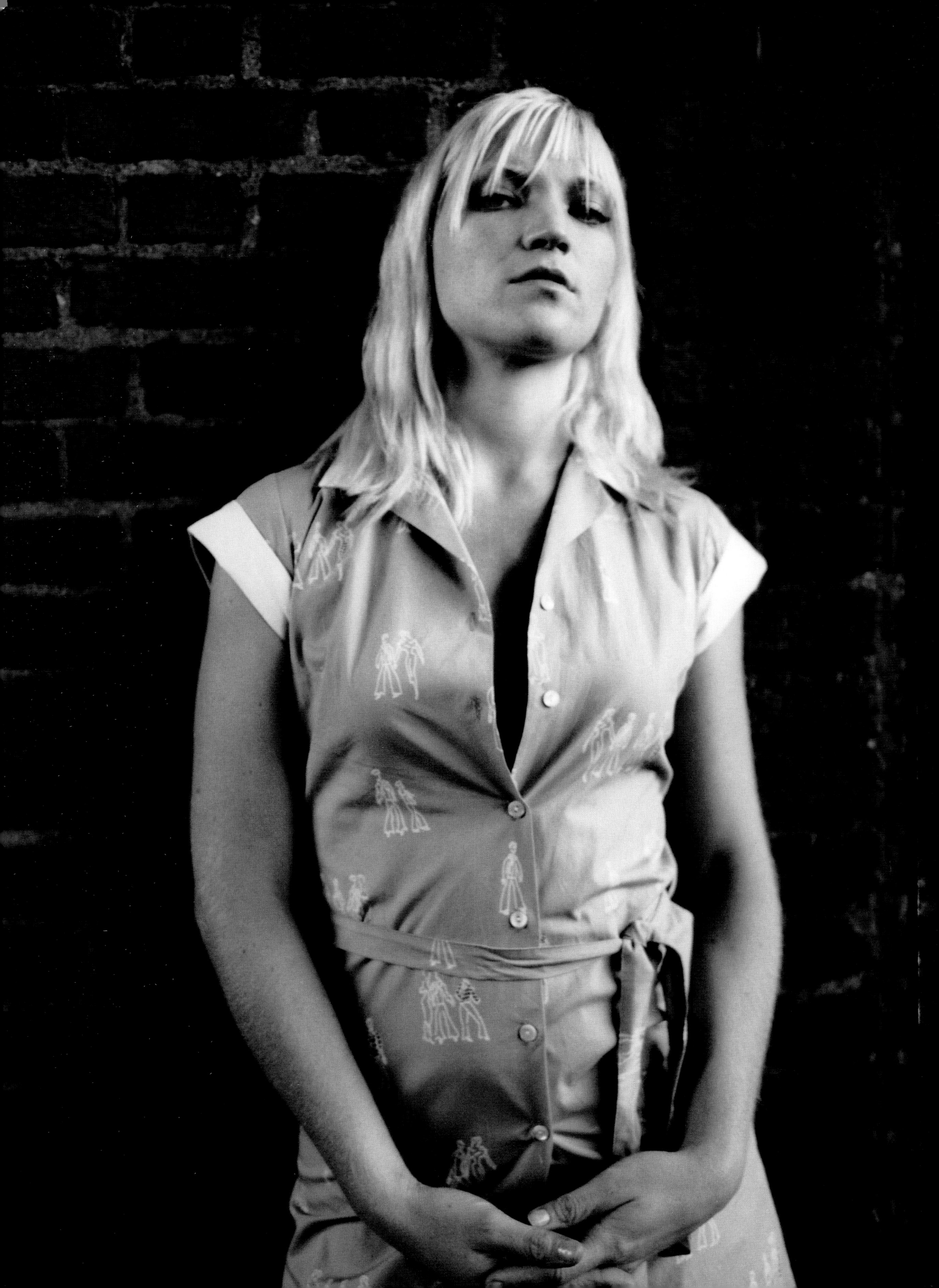

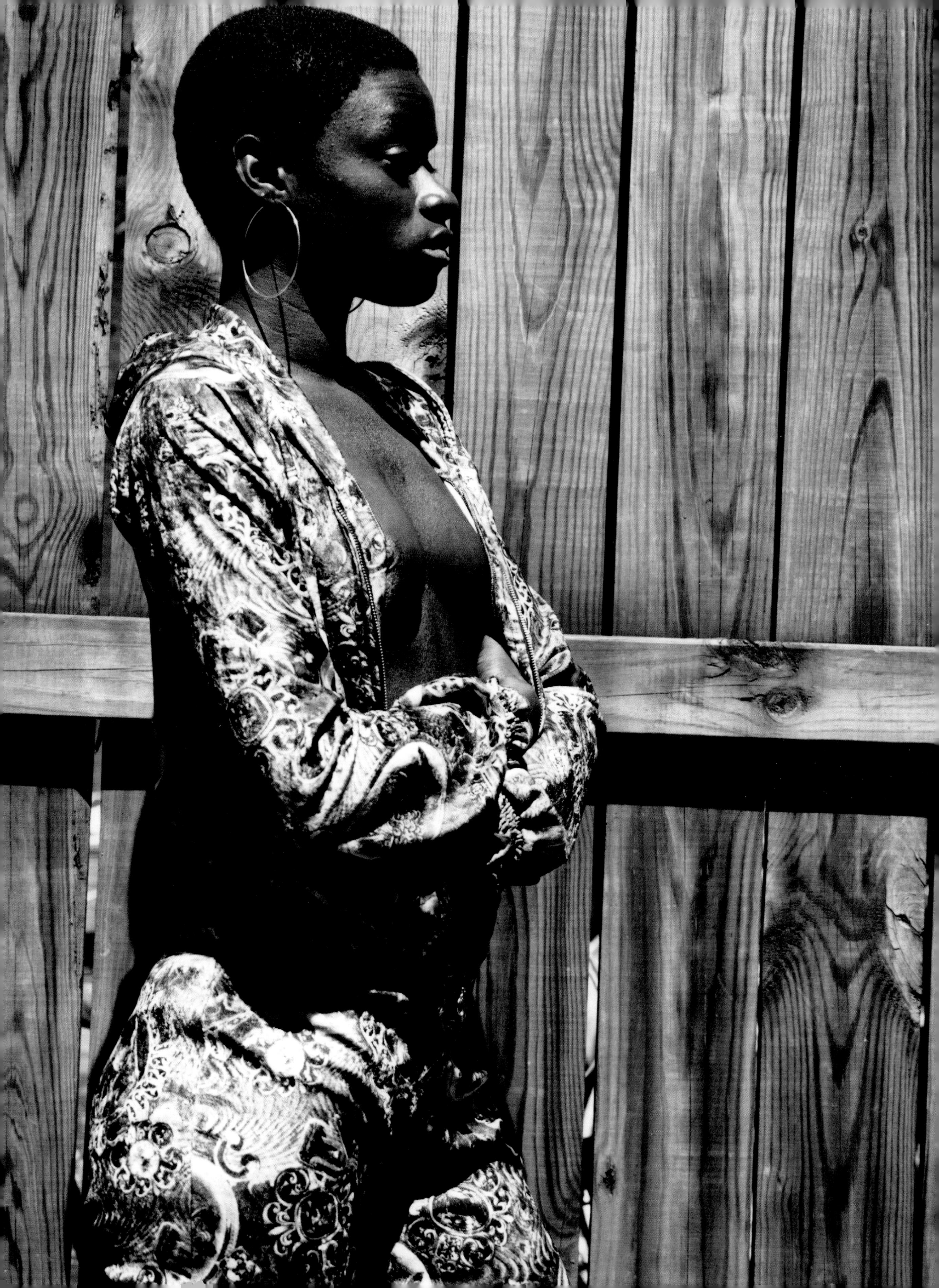

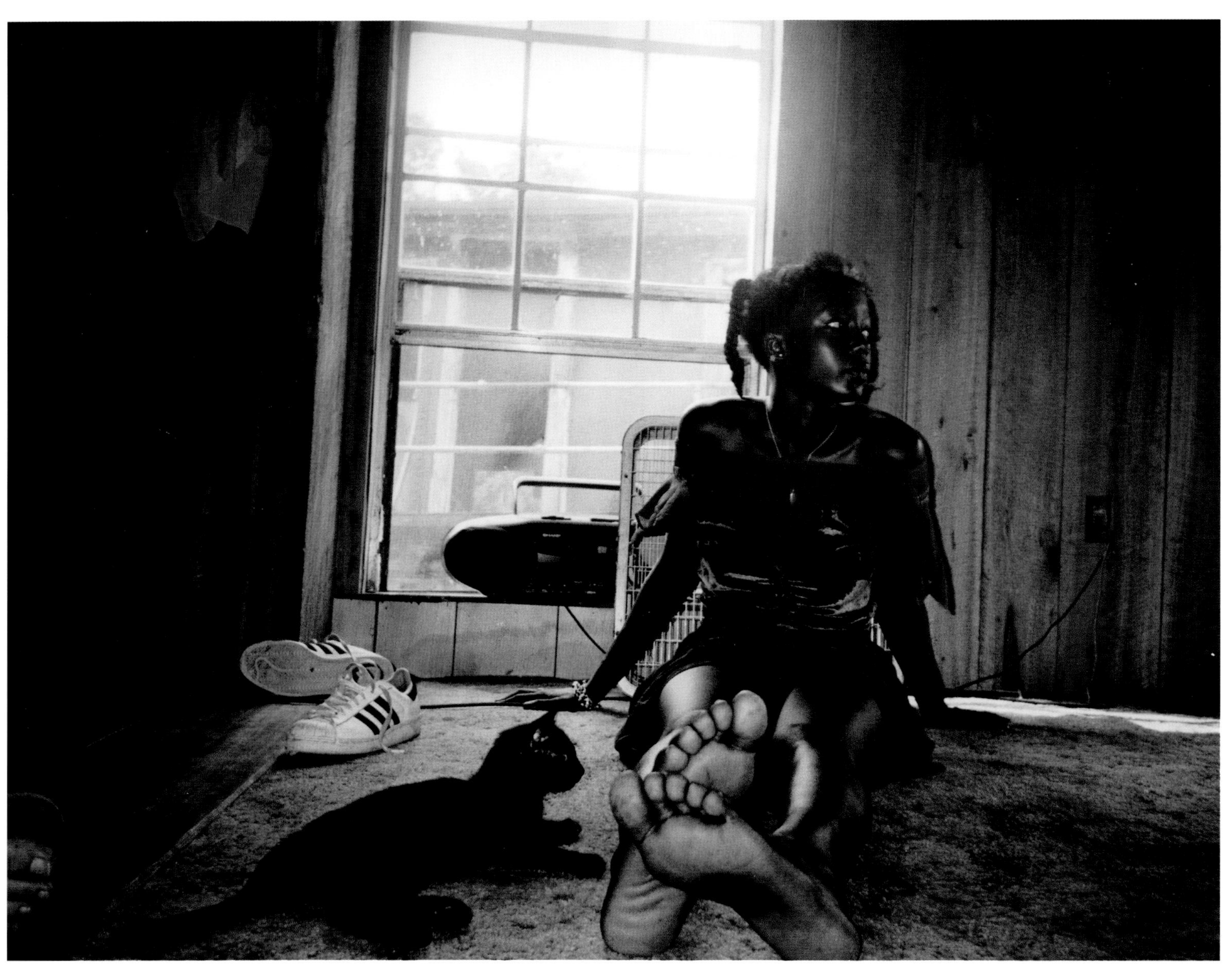

Previous spreads:
Untitled fashion photograph, 2005
Gelatin silver print, dimensions variable
Courtesy the artist

Untitled fashion photograph, 2005
Gelatin silver print, dimensions variable
Courtesy the artist

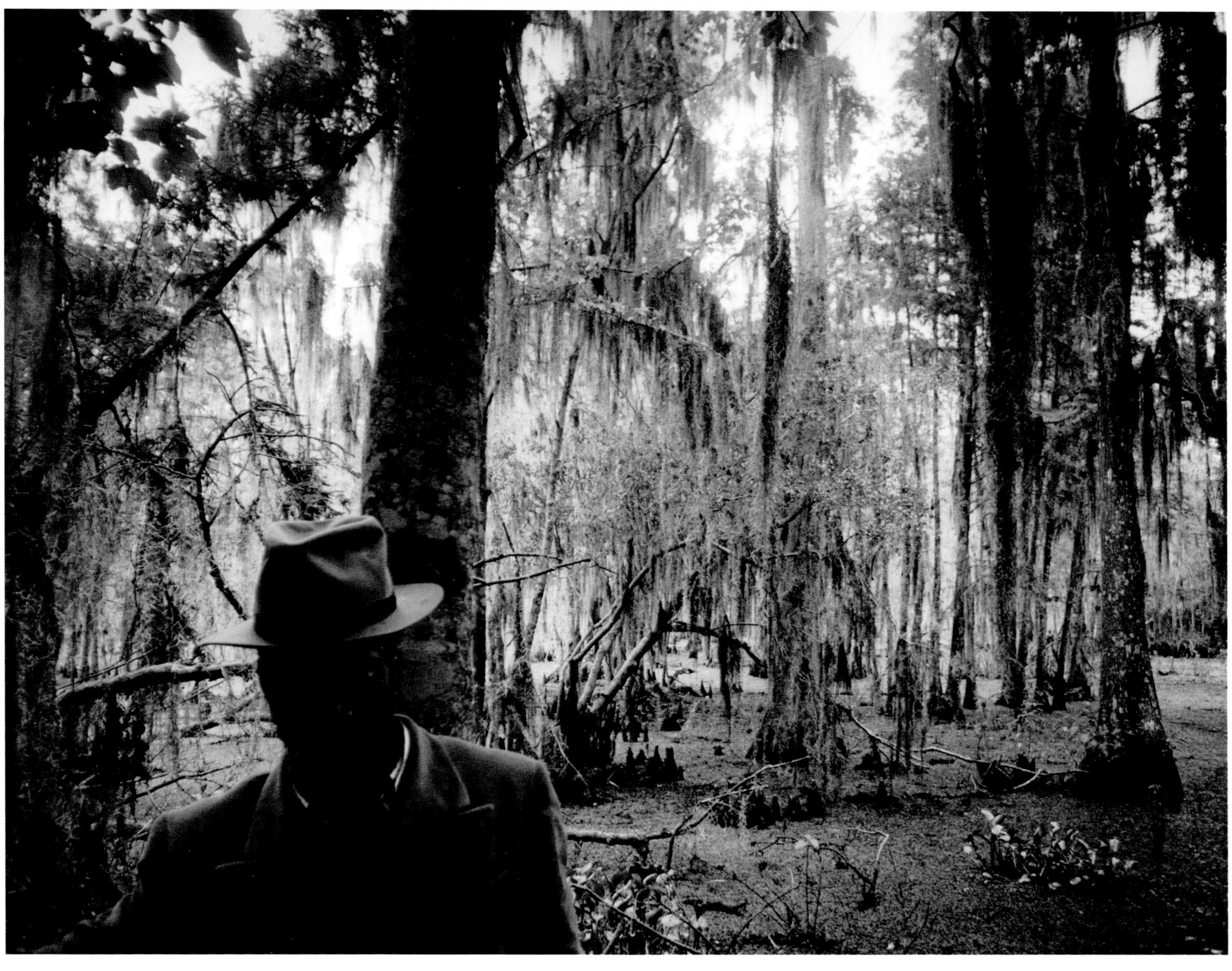

Untitled fashion photograph, 2005
Gelatin silver print, dimensions variable
Courtesy the artist

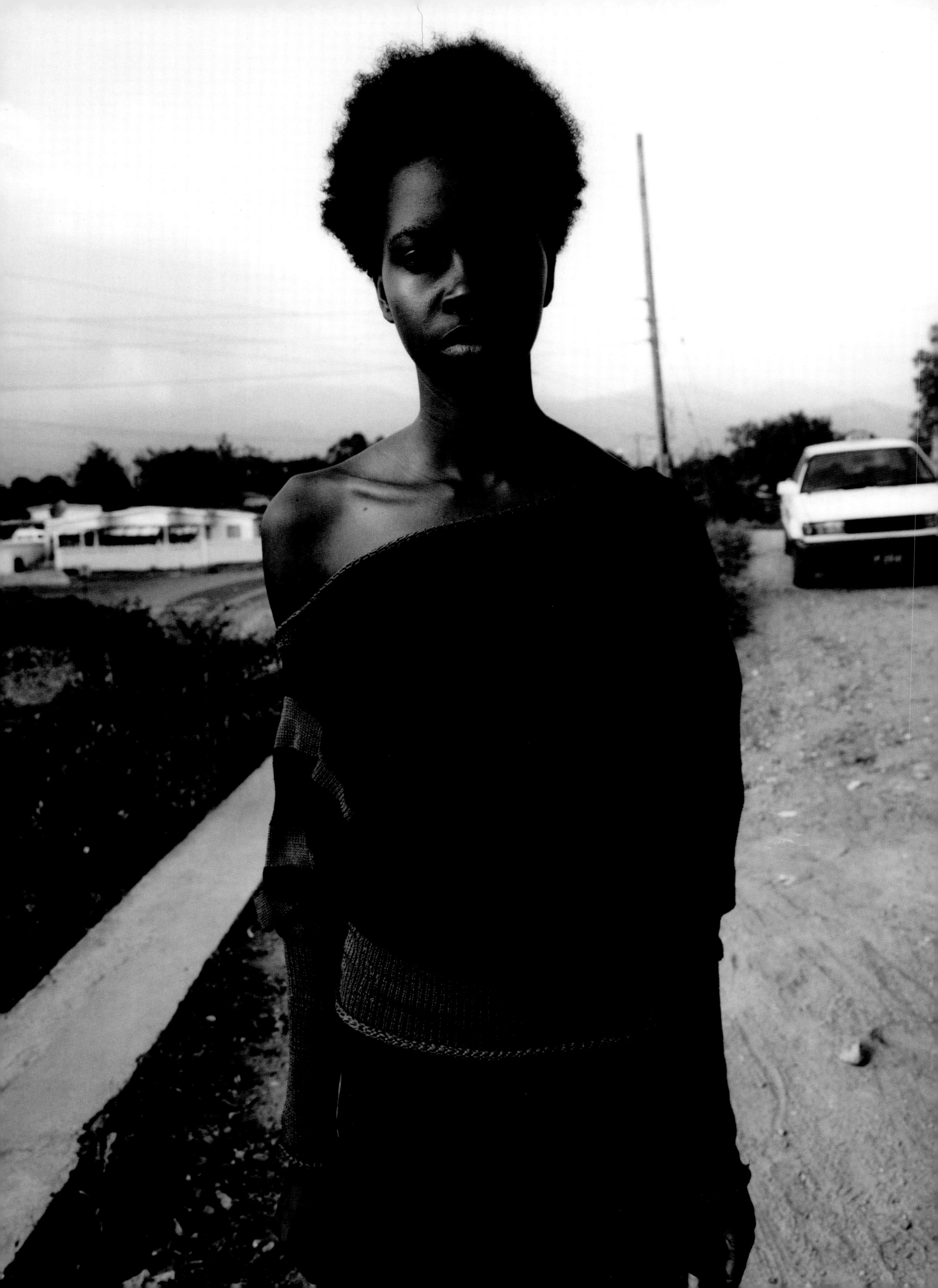

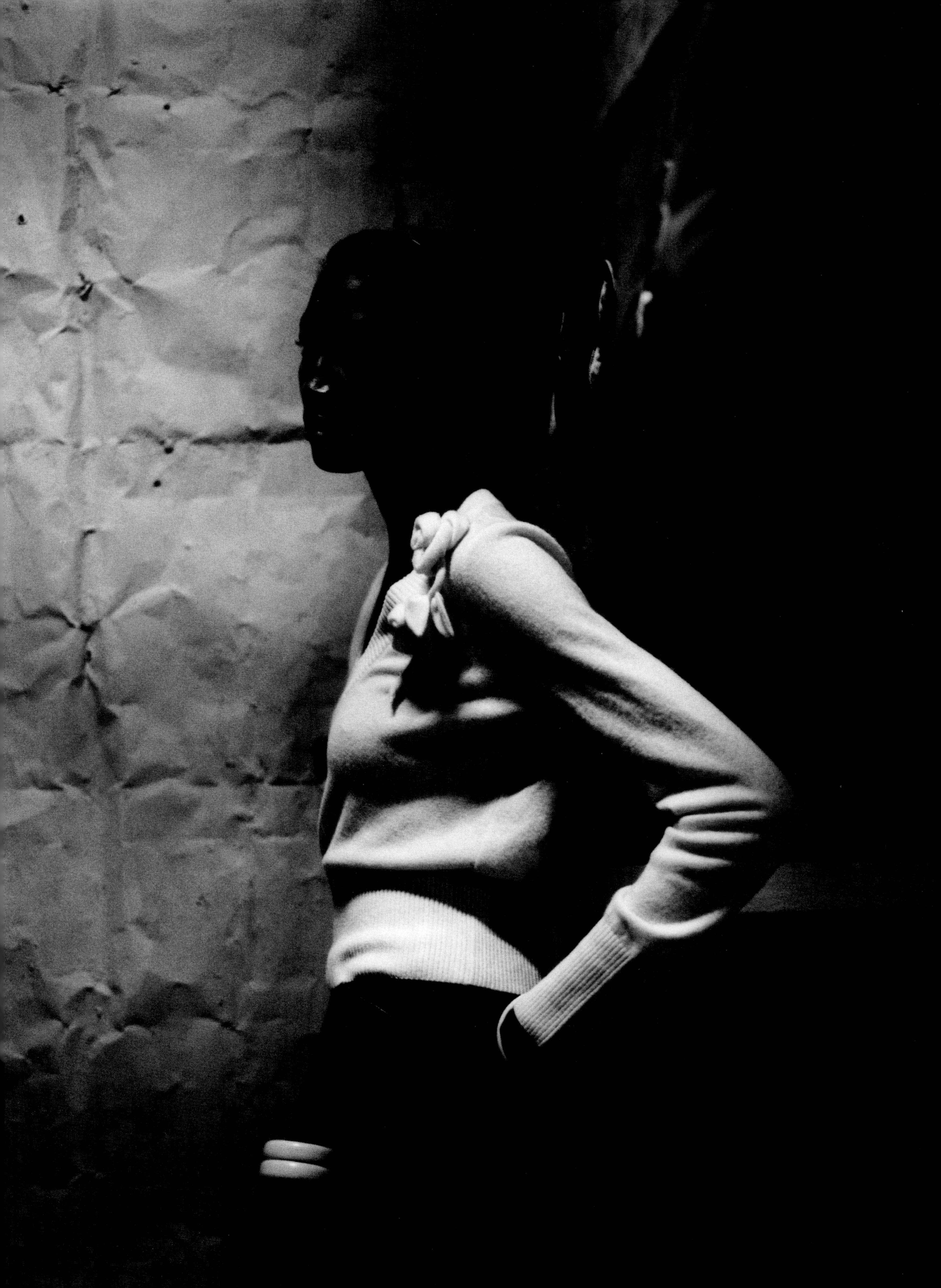

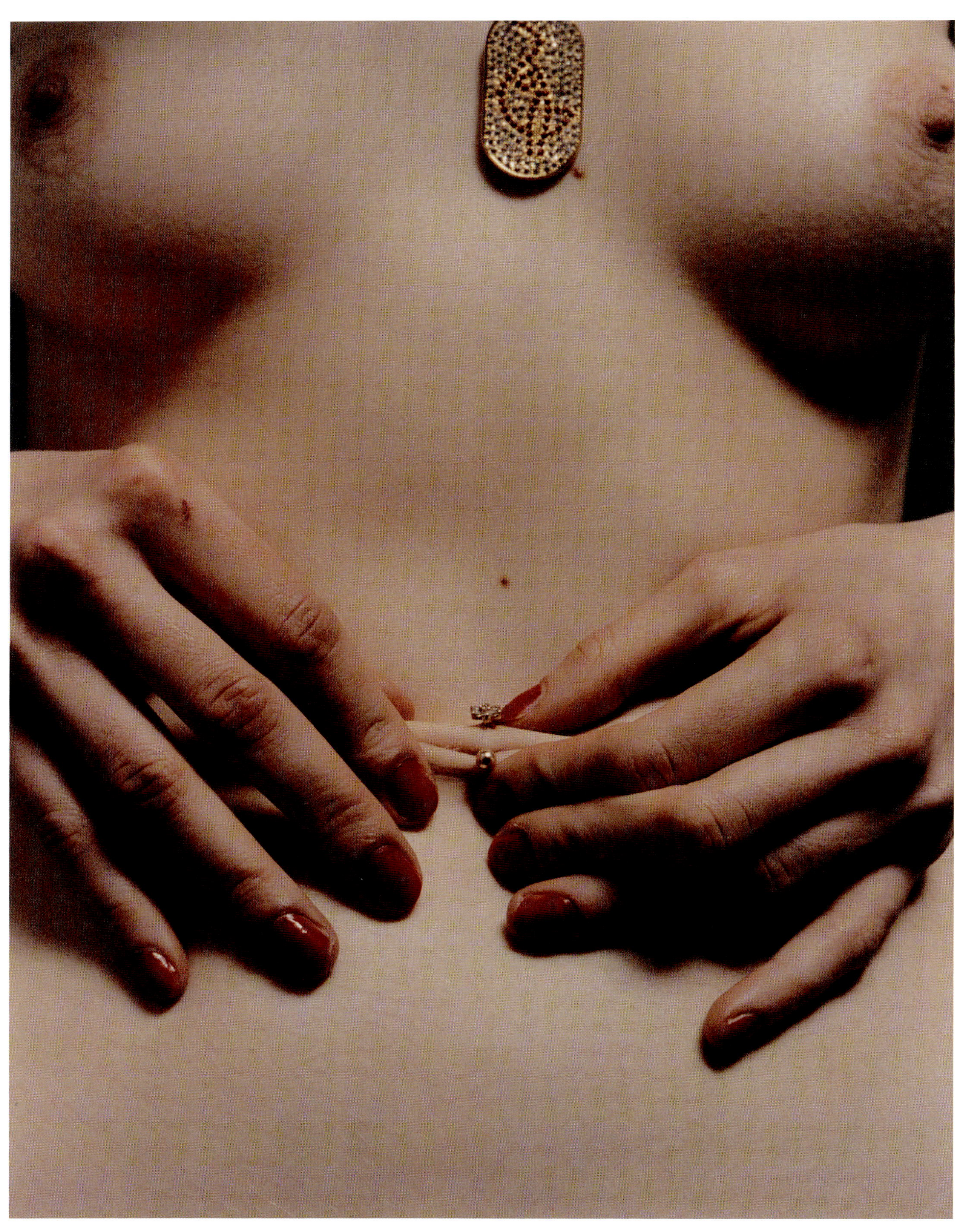

Previous spread:
Untitled fashion photograph, 2005
Gelatin silver print, dimensions variable
Courtesy the artist

Untitled fashion photograph, 2005
Chromogenic print, dimensions variable
Courtesy the artist

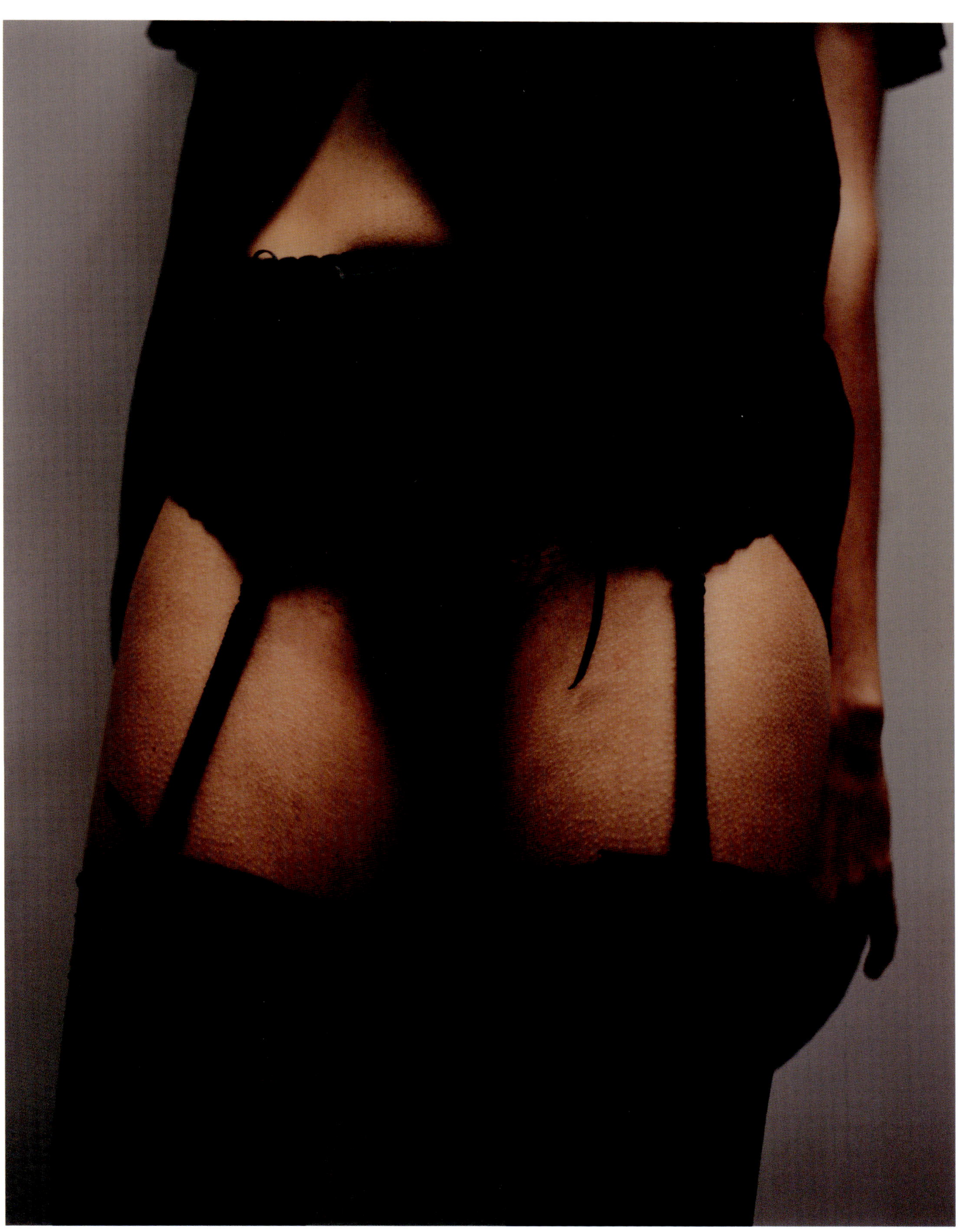

Untitled fashion photograph, 2005
Chromogenic print, dimensions variable
Courtesy the artist

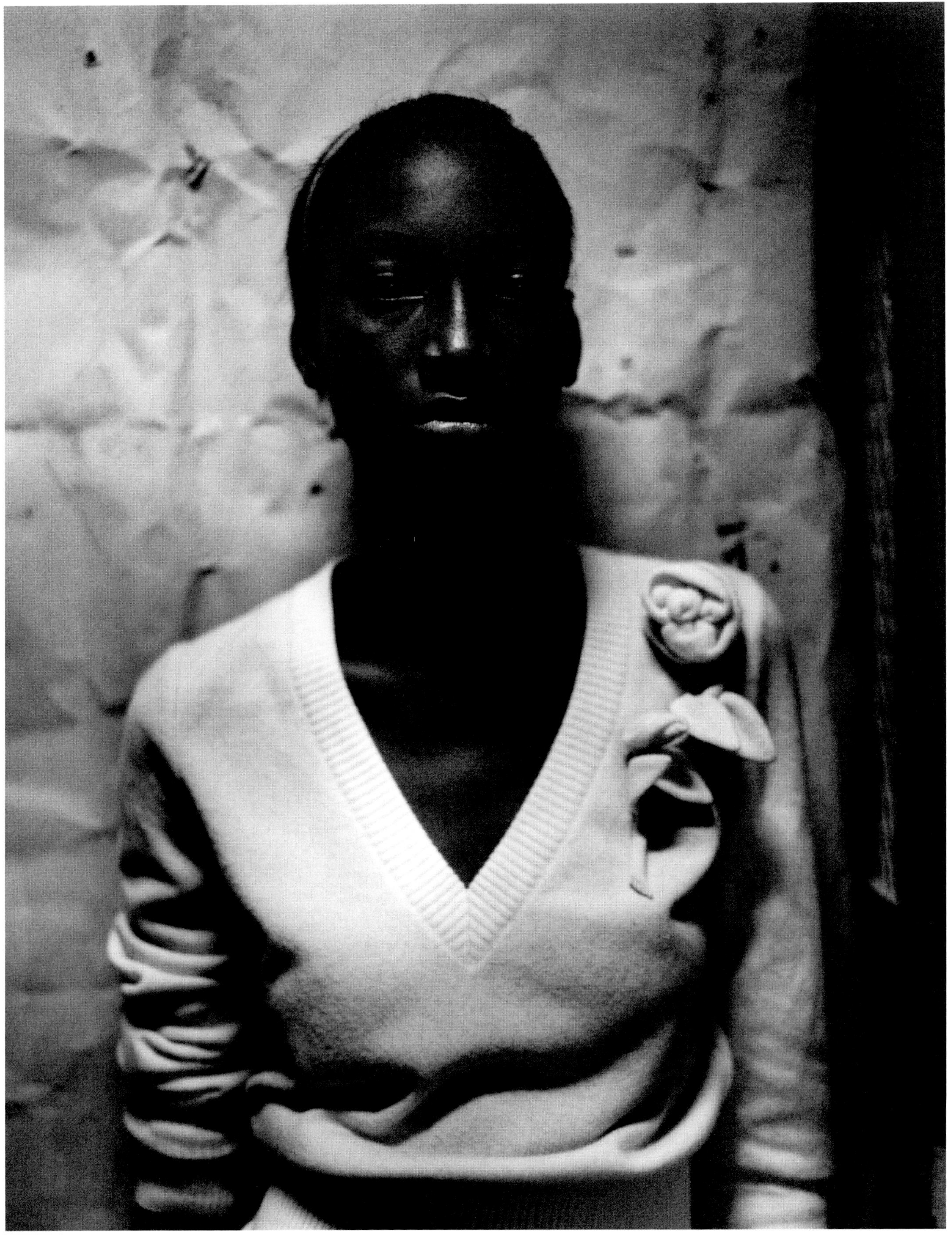

Untitled fashion photograph, 2005
Gelatin silver print, dimensions variable
Courtesy the artist

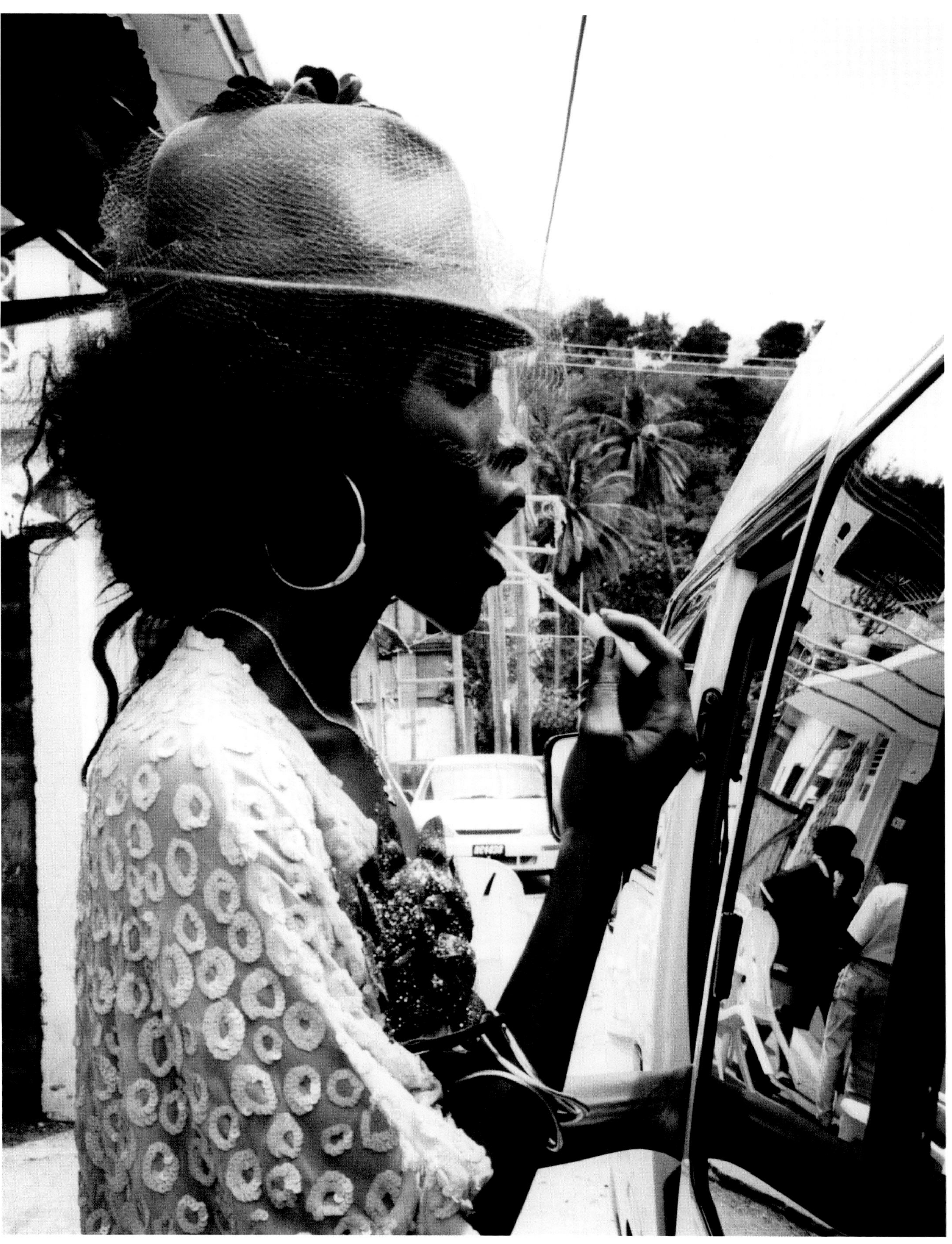

Untitled fashion photograph, 2005
Gelatin silver print, dimensions variable
Courtesy the artist

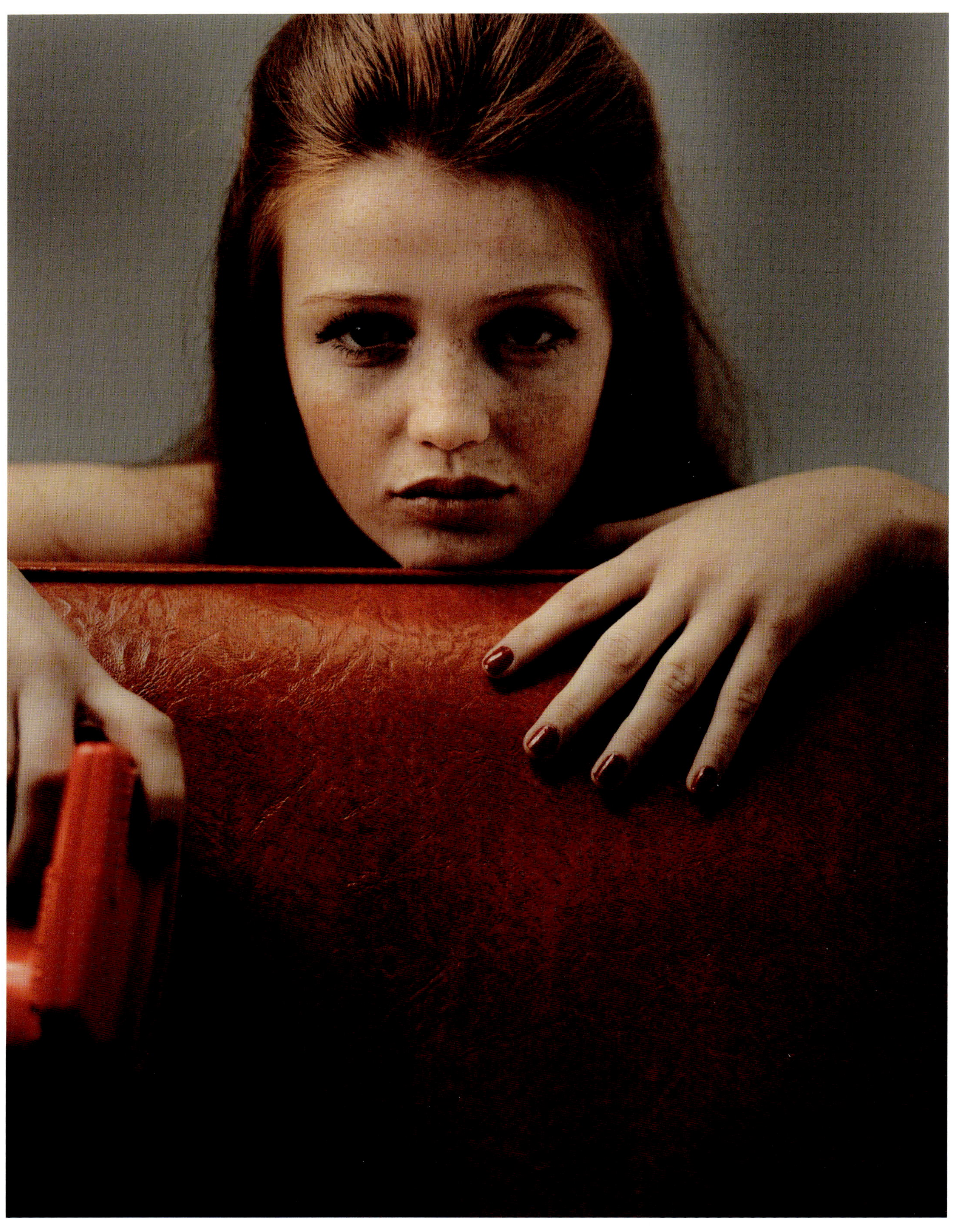

Untitled fashion photograph, 2005
Chromogenic print, dimensions variable
Courtesy the artist

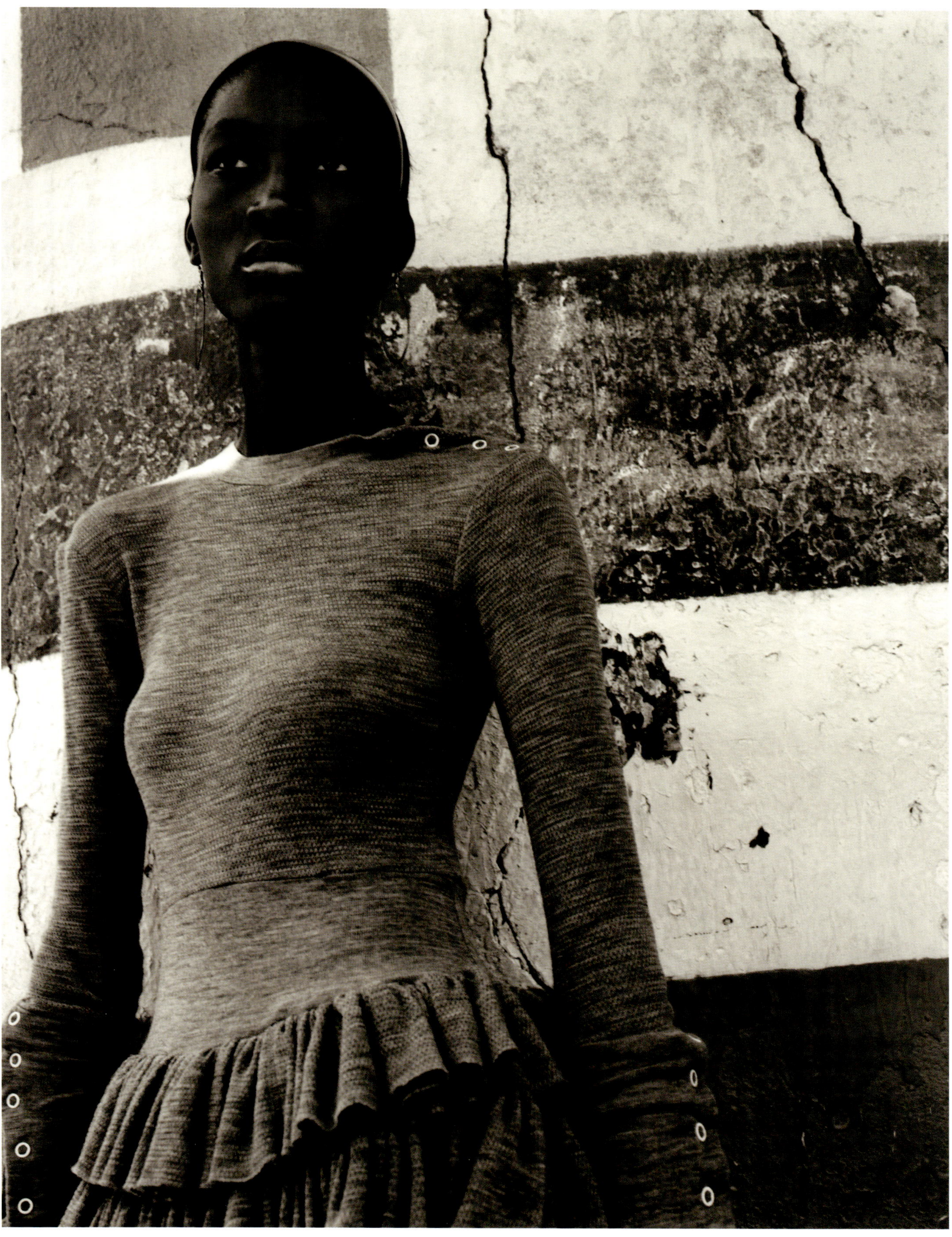

Untitled fashion photograph, 2005
Gelatin silver print, dimensions variable
Courtesy the artist

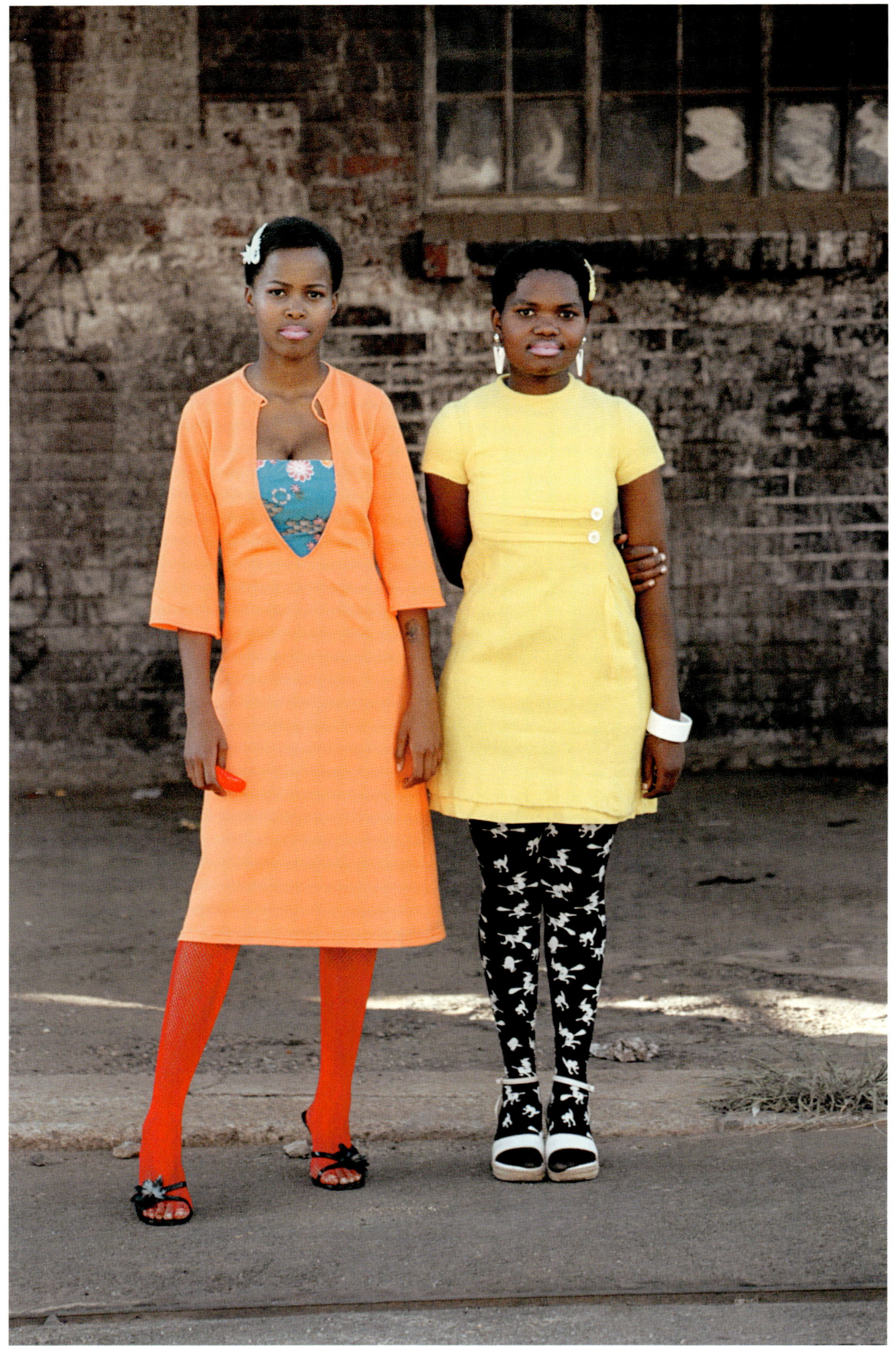

Cindy & Nonkululeko, 2004
Pigment print on paper, 8 x 12 in. (20.3 x 30.5 cm)
Courtesy the artist, International Center of Photography, New York

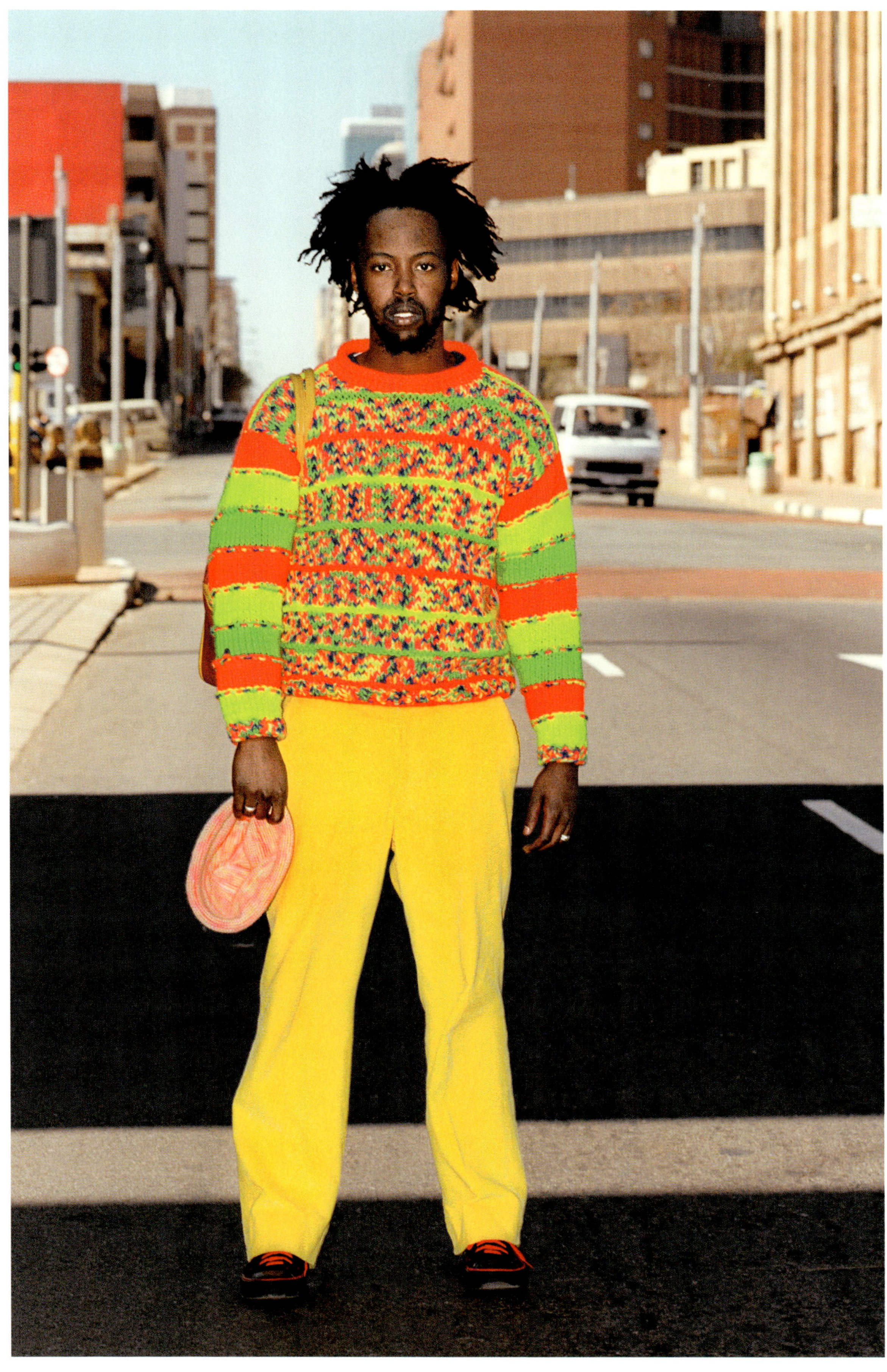

Hloni, 2004
Pigment print on paper, 8 x 12 in. (20.3 x 30.5 cm)
Courtesy the artist, International Center of Photography, New York

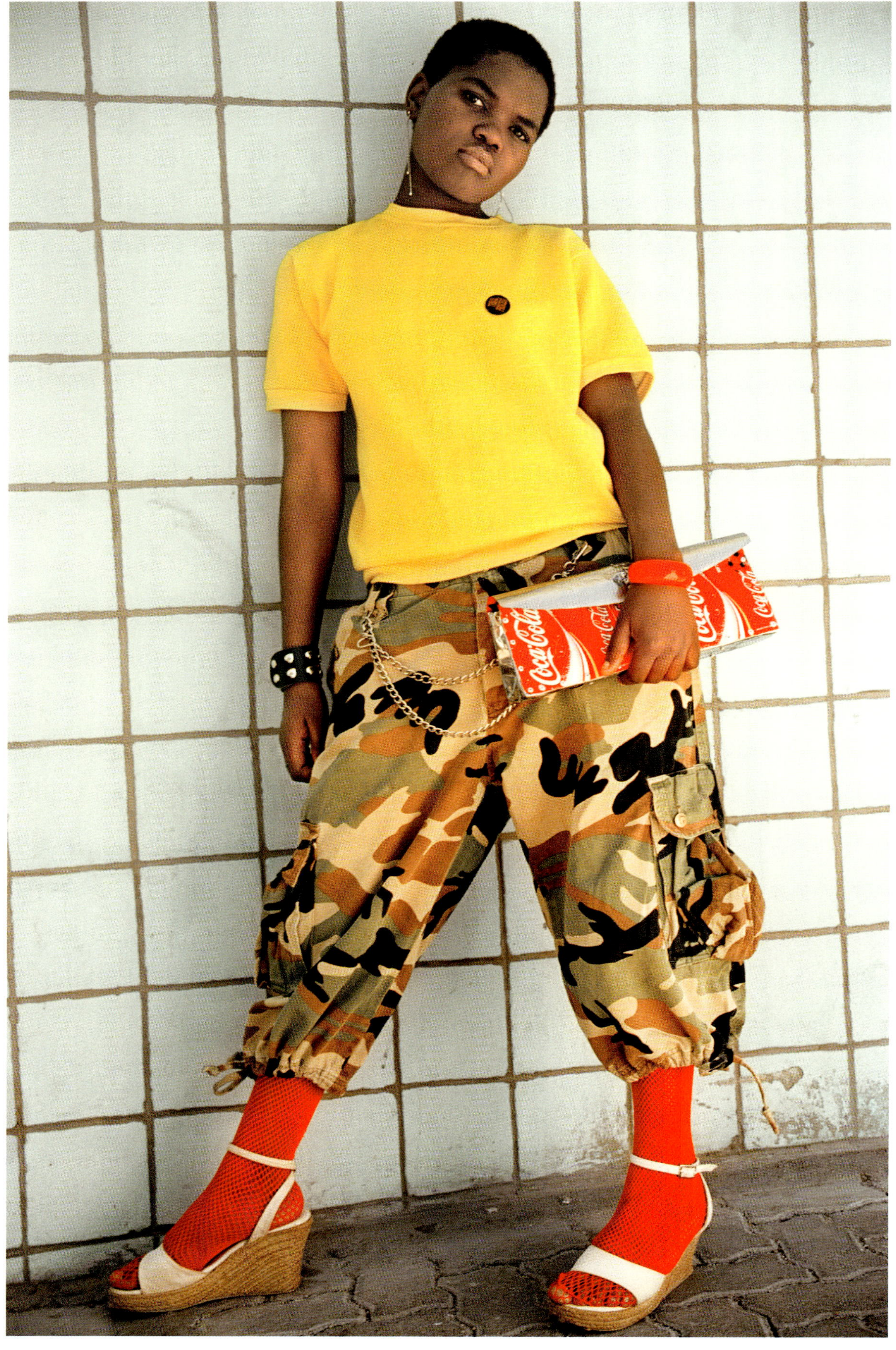

Nonkululeko, 2004
Pigment print on paper, 8 x 12 in. (20.3 x 30.5 cm)
Courtesy the artist, International Center of Photography, New York

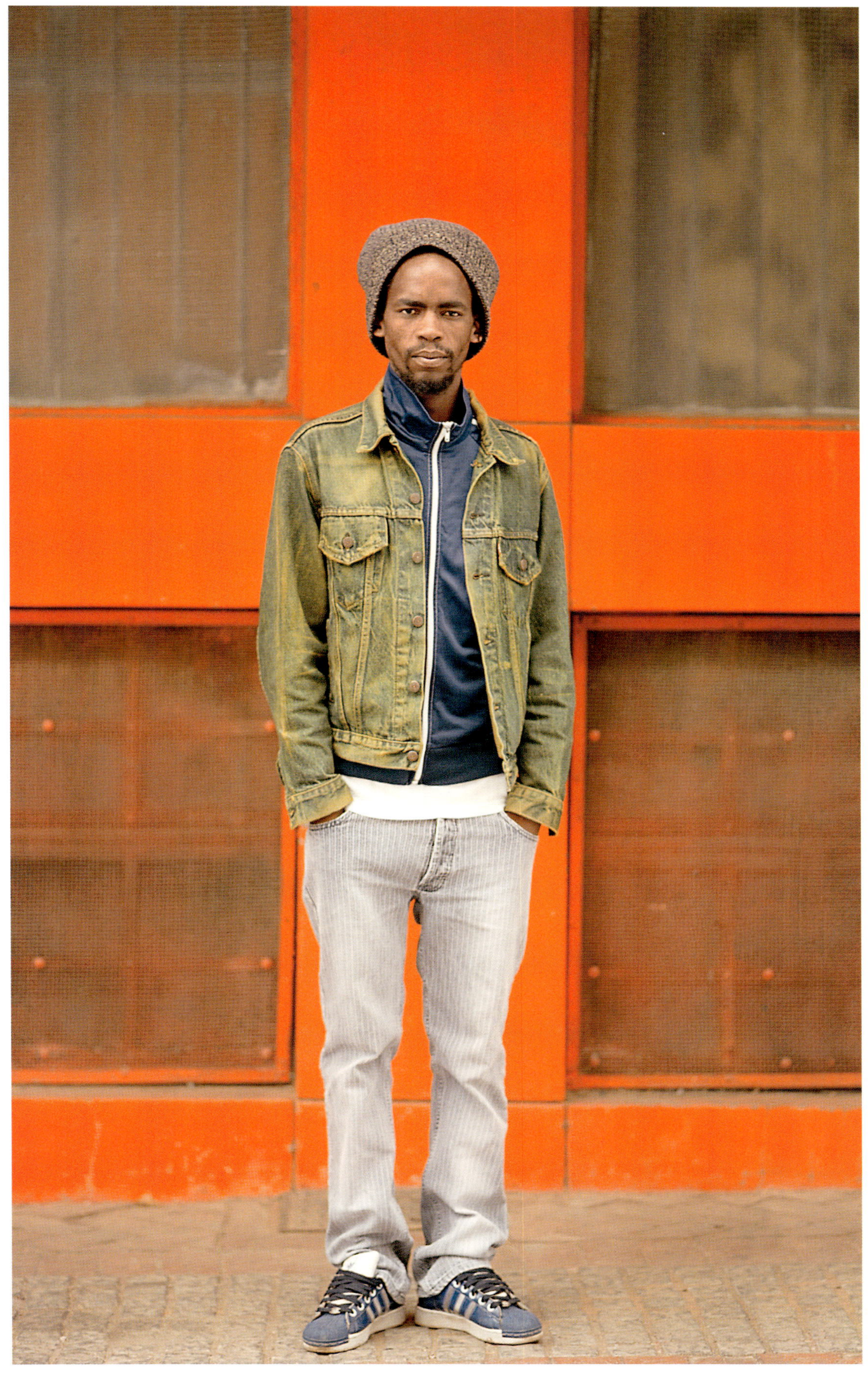

Thato J, 2004
Pigment print on paper, 8 x 12 in. (20.3 x 30.5 cm)
Courtesy the artist, International Center of Photography, New York

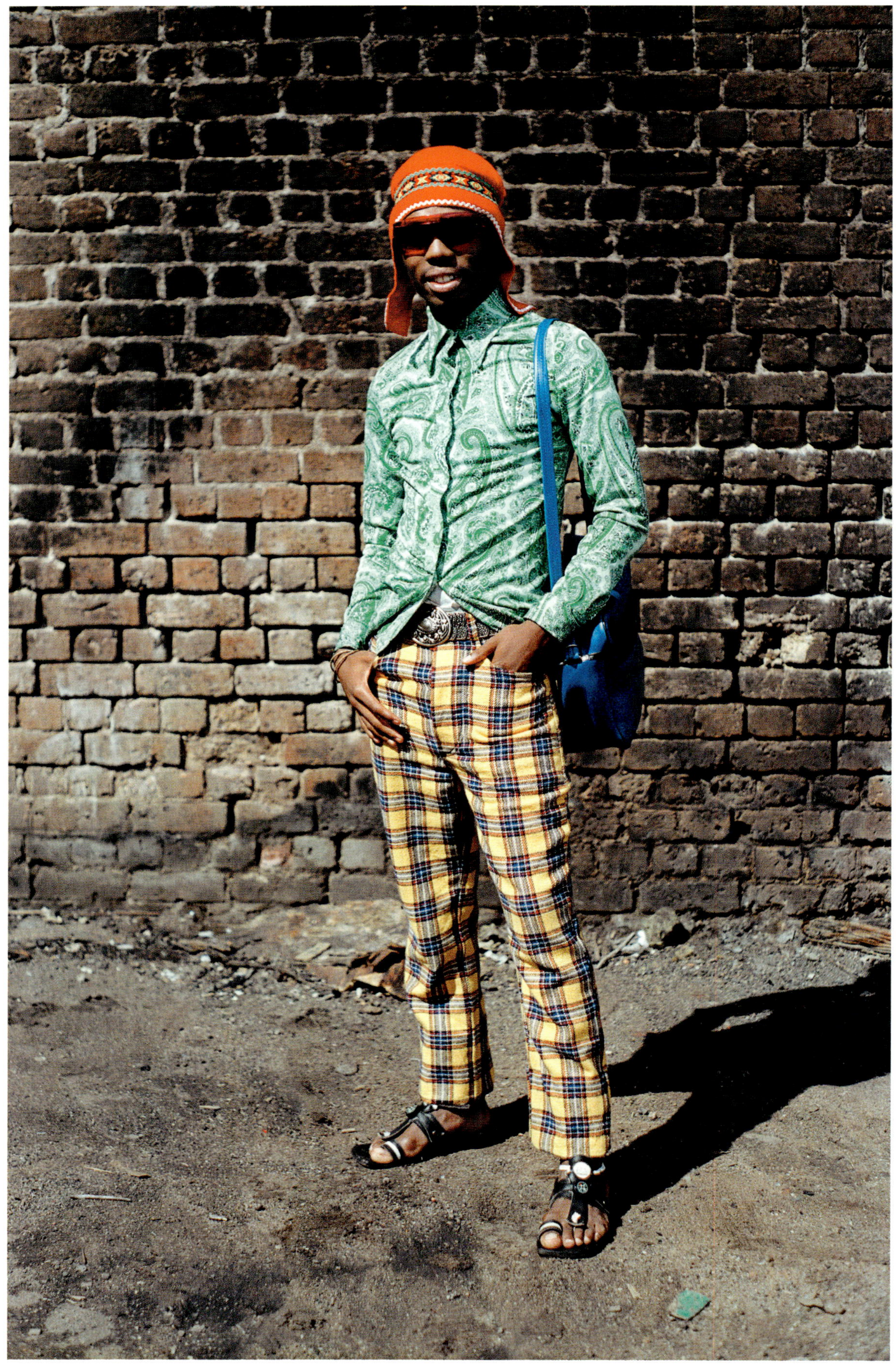

Thulani, 2004
Pigment print on paper, 8 x 12 in. (20.3 x 30.5 cm)
Courtesy the artist, International Center of Photography, New York

Yto Barrada

Luis Basto

Omar D. (Daoud)

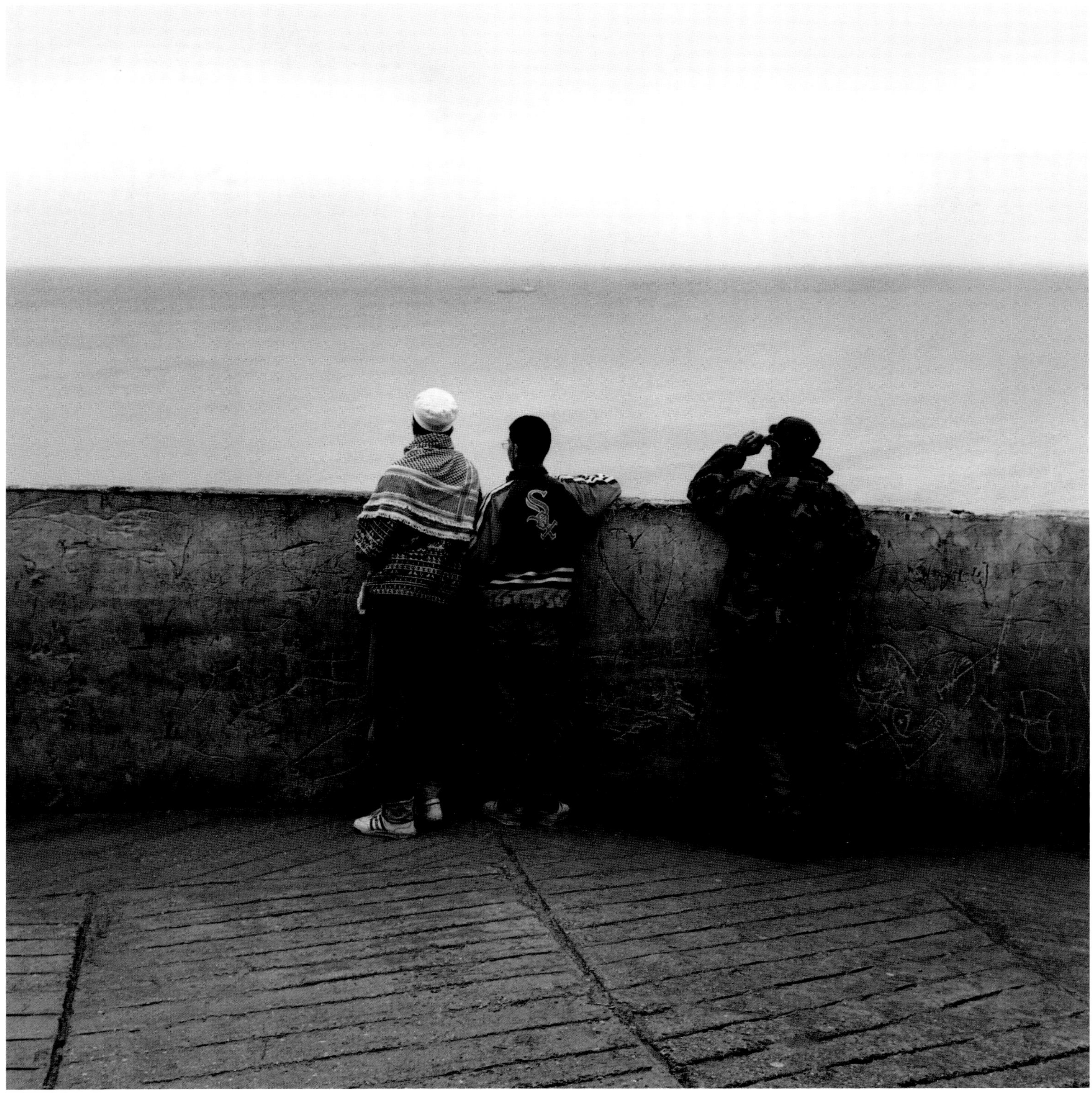

Belvédère 1—Tangier 2003, from the series
"A Life Full of Holes: The Strait Project," 1998–2004
Gelatin silver print, 22.8 x 19.5 in. (58 x 49.5 cm)
Courtesy the artist and Galerie Polaris, Paris

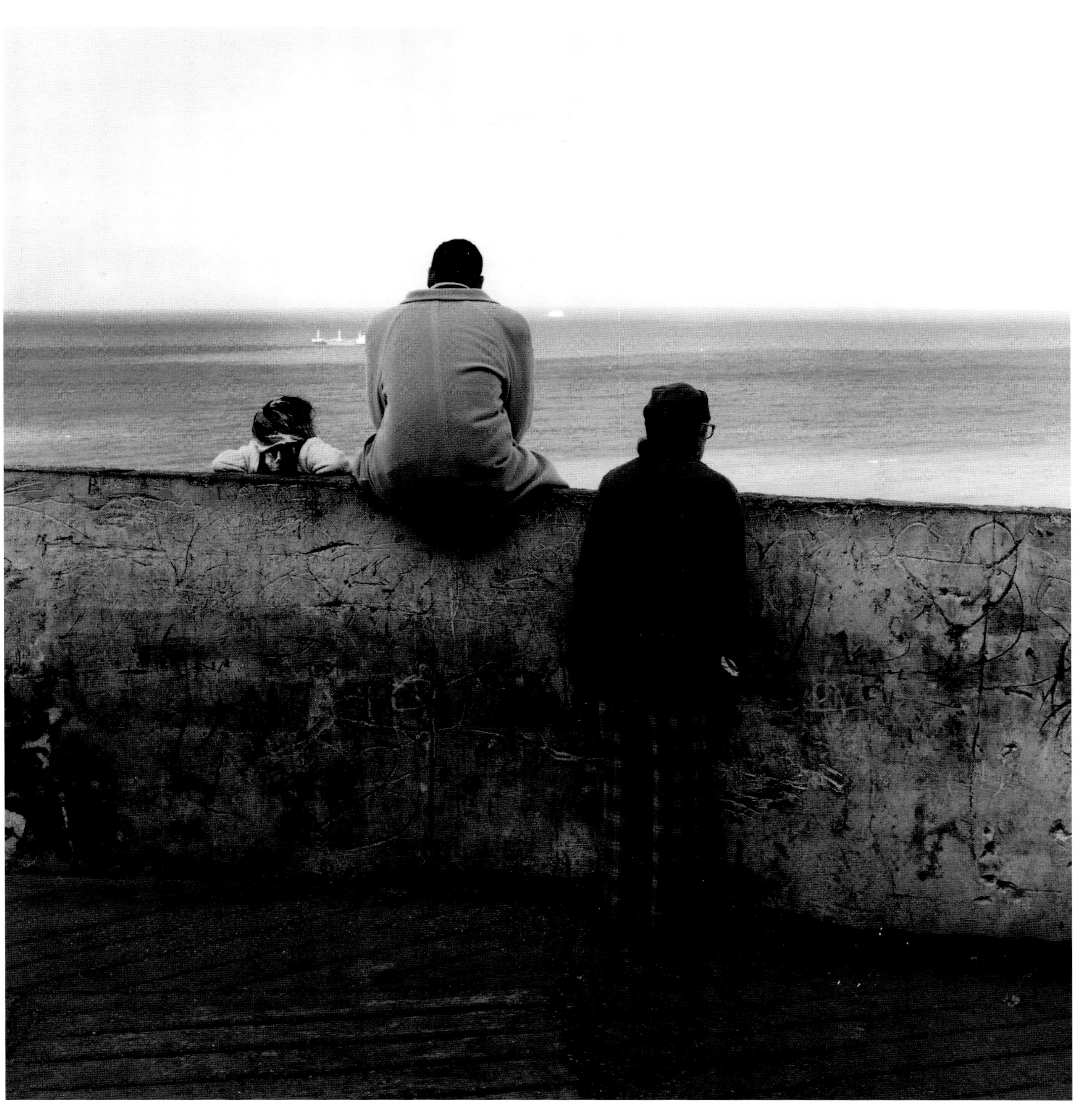

Belvédère 2—Tangier 2003, from the series
"A Life Full of Holes: The Strait Project," 1998–2004
Gelatin silver print, 22.8 x 19.5 in. (58 x 49.5 cm)
Courtesy the artist and Galerie Polaris, Paris

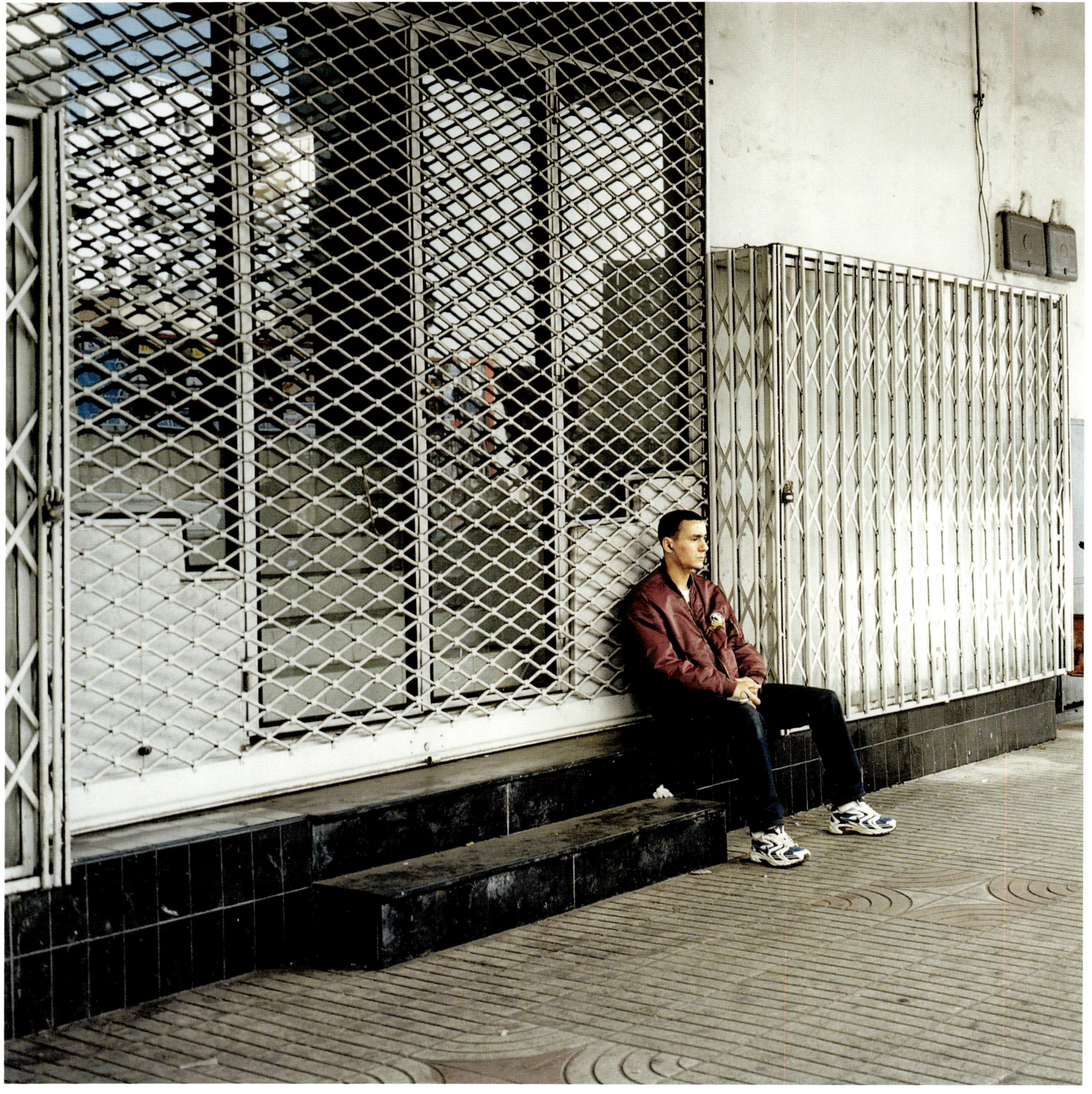

Man Sitting—Boulevard Mohamed V, Casablanca 2001, from
the series "A Life Full of Holes: The Strait Project," 1998–2004
Chromogenic print, 31.5 x 31.5 in. (80 x 80 cm)
Courtesy the artist and Galerie Polaris, Paris

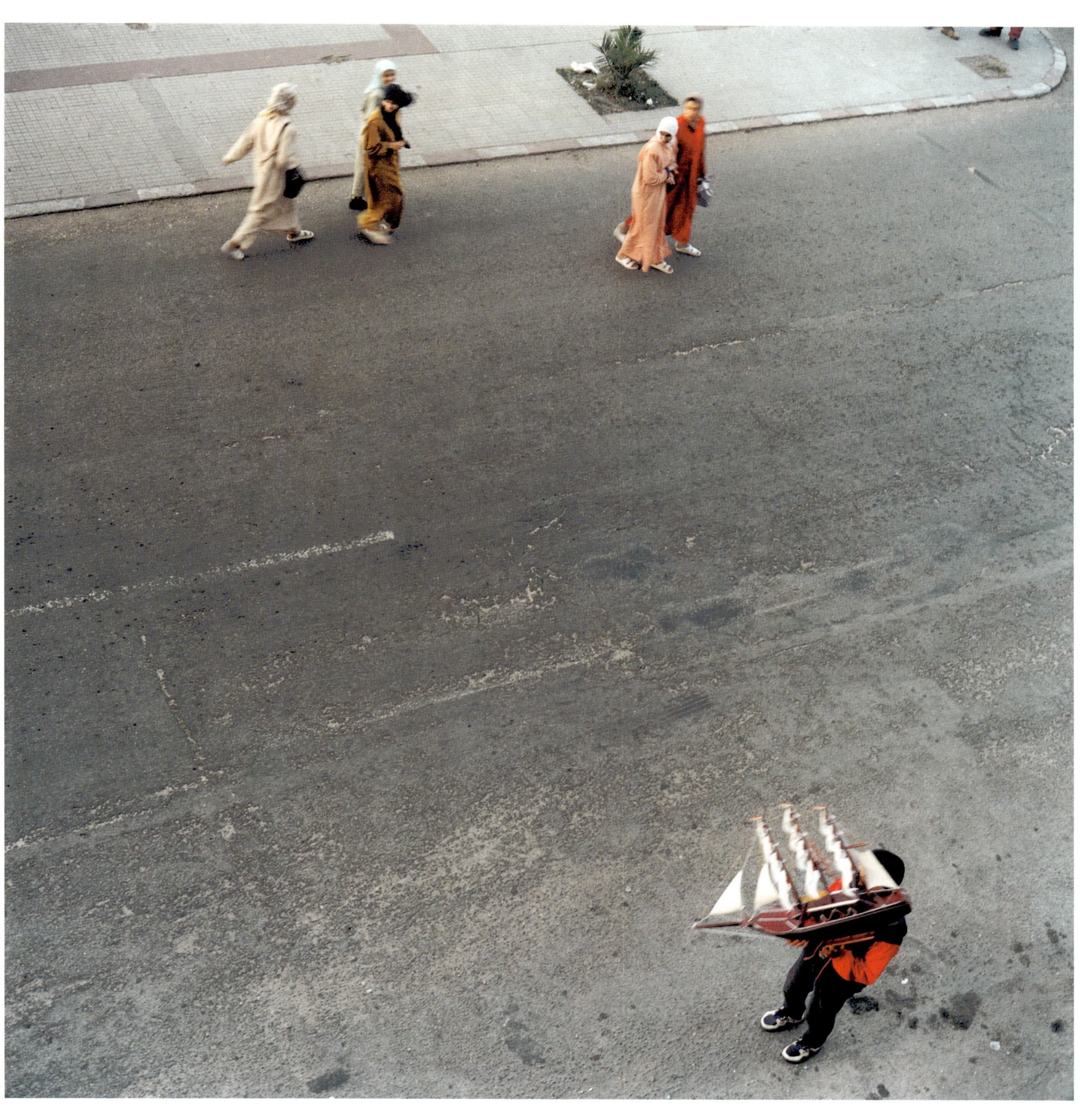

Le Détroit—Avenue d'Espagne—Tangier 2000, from
the series "A Life Full of Holes: The Strait Project," 1998–2004
Chromogenic print, 23.6 x 23.6 in. (60 x 60 cm)
Courtesy the artist and Galerie Polaris, Paris

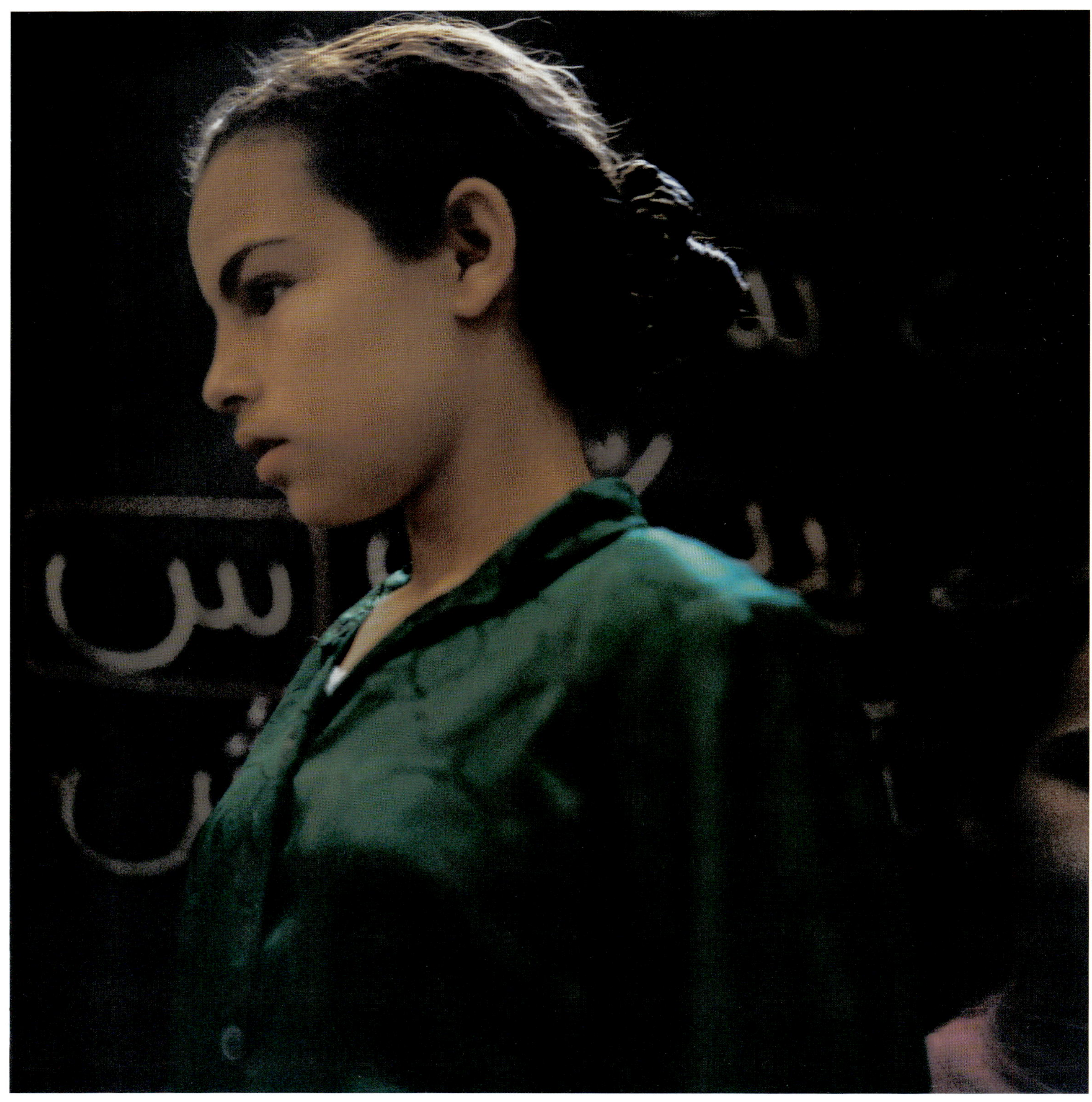

Meriem—A spelling class at the Darna day centre for street children—Tangier 1999
from the series "A Life Full of Holes: The Strait Project," 1998–2004
Chromogenic print, 29.1 x 29.1 in. (74 x 74 cm)
Courtesy the artist and Galerie Polaris, Paris

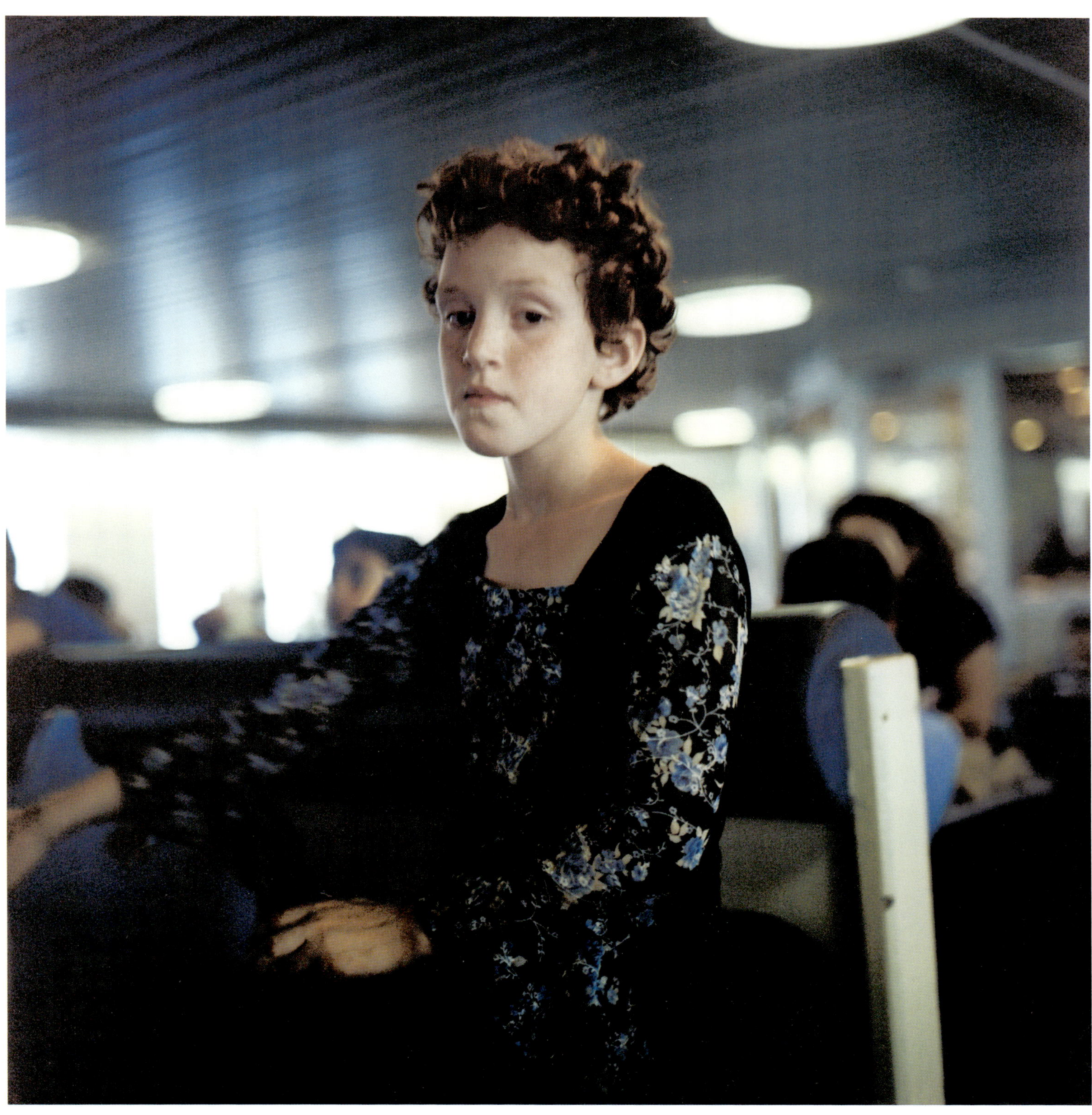

Girl with red hair—Ferry from Algeciras to Tangier—2002,
from the series "A Life Full of Holes: The Strait Project," 1998–2004
Chromogenic print, 31.5 x 31.5 in. (80 x 80 cm)
Courtesy the artist and Galerie Polaris, Paris

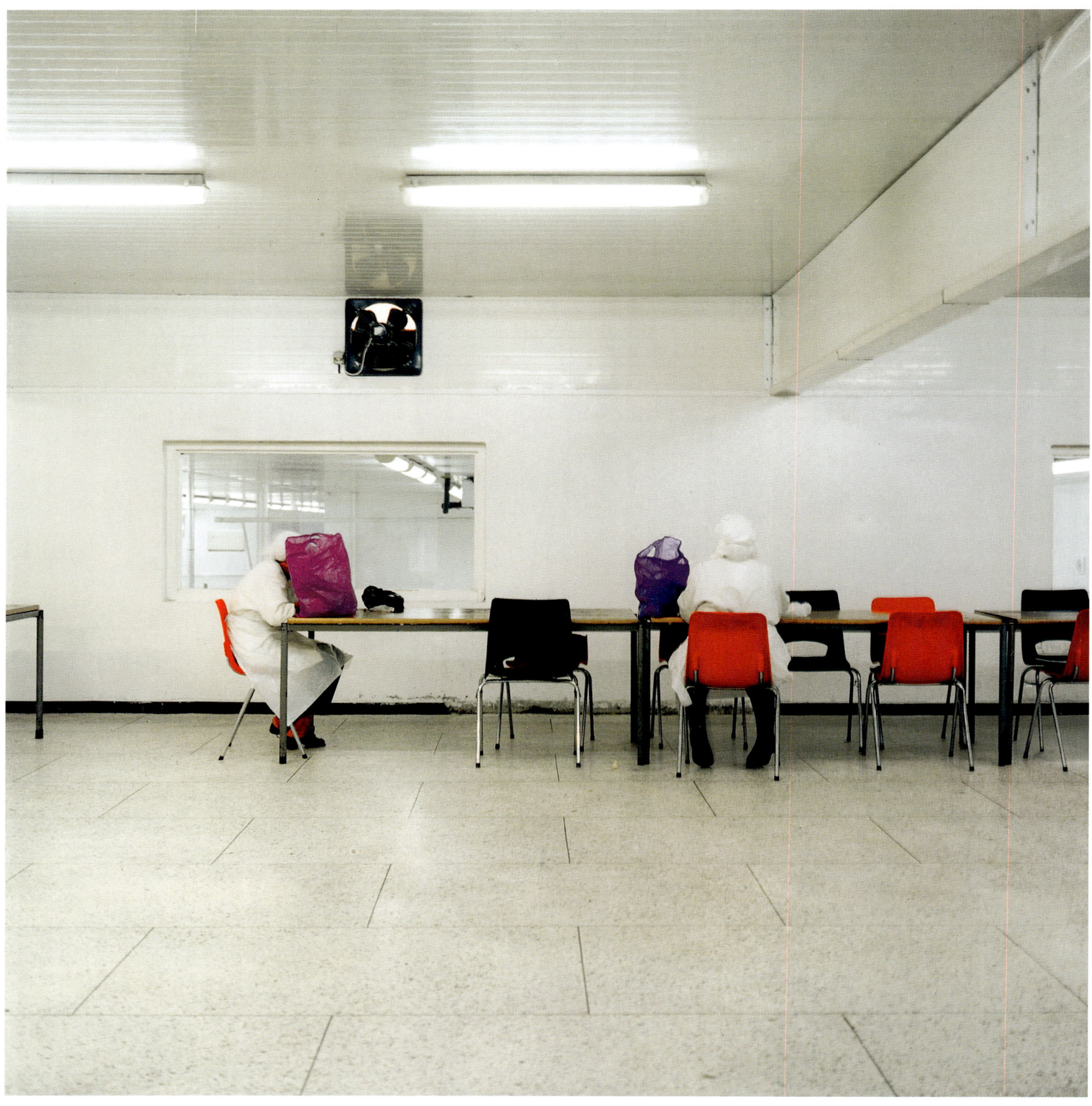

Factory 2—Canteen—Tangier 1998
from the series "A Life Full of Holes: The Strait Project," 1998–2004
Chromogenic print, 40.6 x 40.6 in. (103 x 103 cm)
Courtesy the artist and Galerie Polaris, Paris

Marks left by a football—Tangier 2002,
from the series "A Life Full of Holes: The Strait Project," 1998–2004
Chromogenic print, 31.5 x 31.5 in. (80 x 80 cm)
Courtesy the artist and Galerie Polaris, Paris

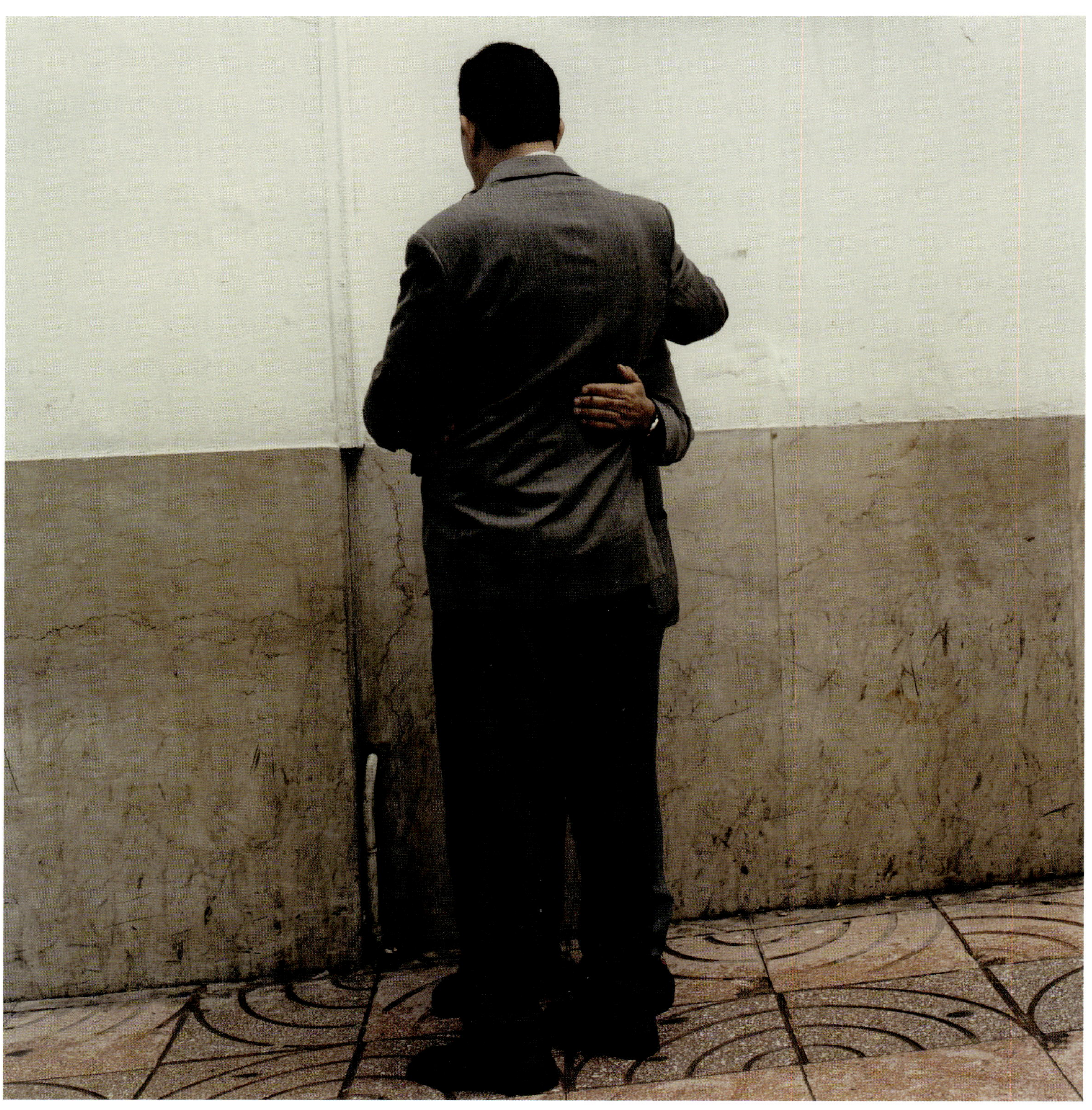

Rue de la Liberté—Tangier 2000
from the series "A Life Full of Holes: The Strait Project," 1998–2004
Chromogenic print, 49.2 x 49.2 in. (125 x 125 cm)
Courtesy the artist and Galerie Polaris, Paris

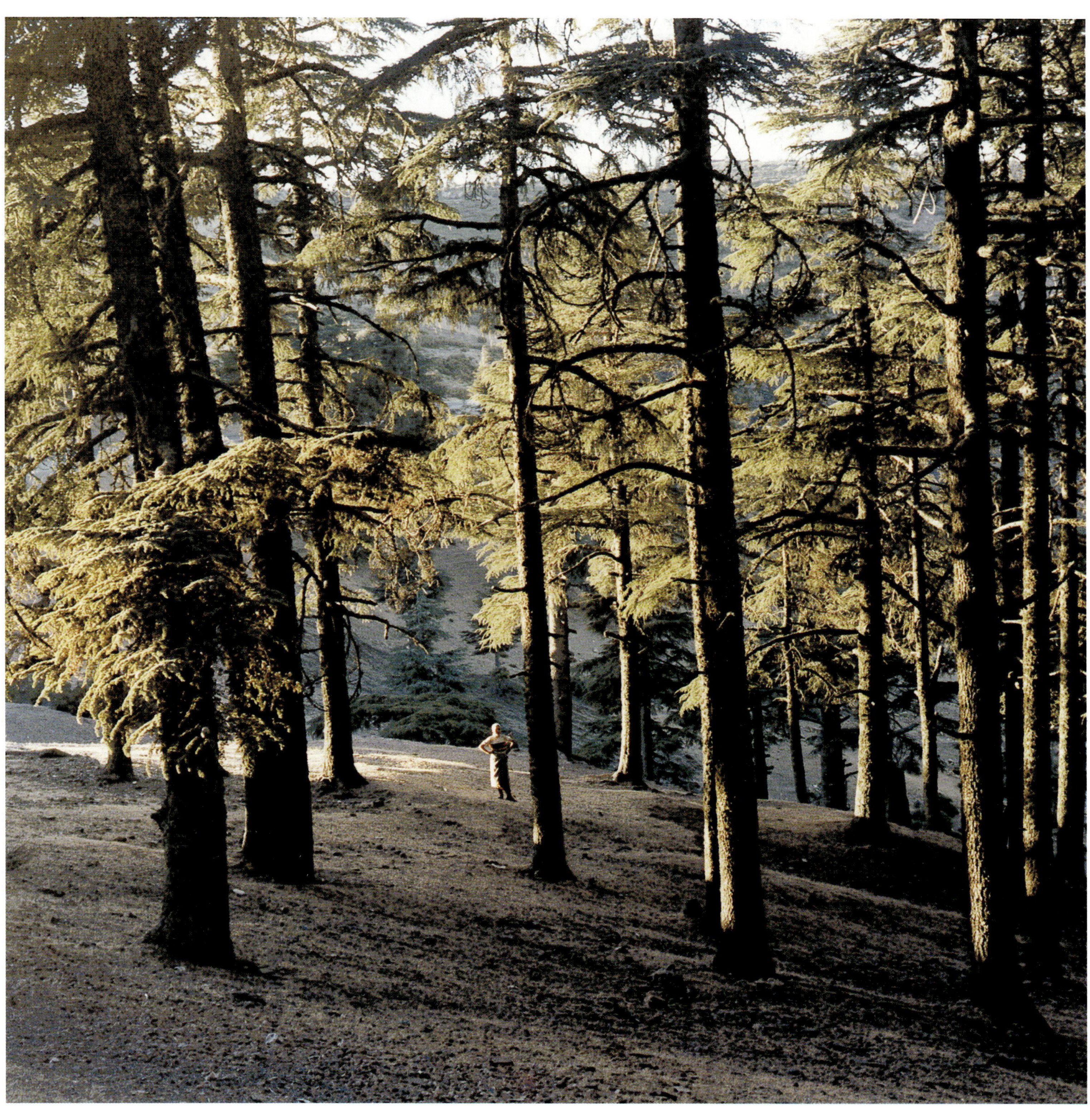

Issagen—A cedar forest in the Rif mountains—2002,
from the series "A Life Full of Holes: The Strait Project," 1998–2004
Chromogenic print, 31.5 x 31.5 in. (80 x 80 cm)
Courtesy the artist and Galerie Polaris, Paris

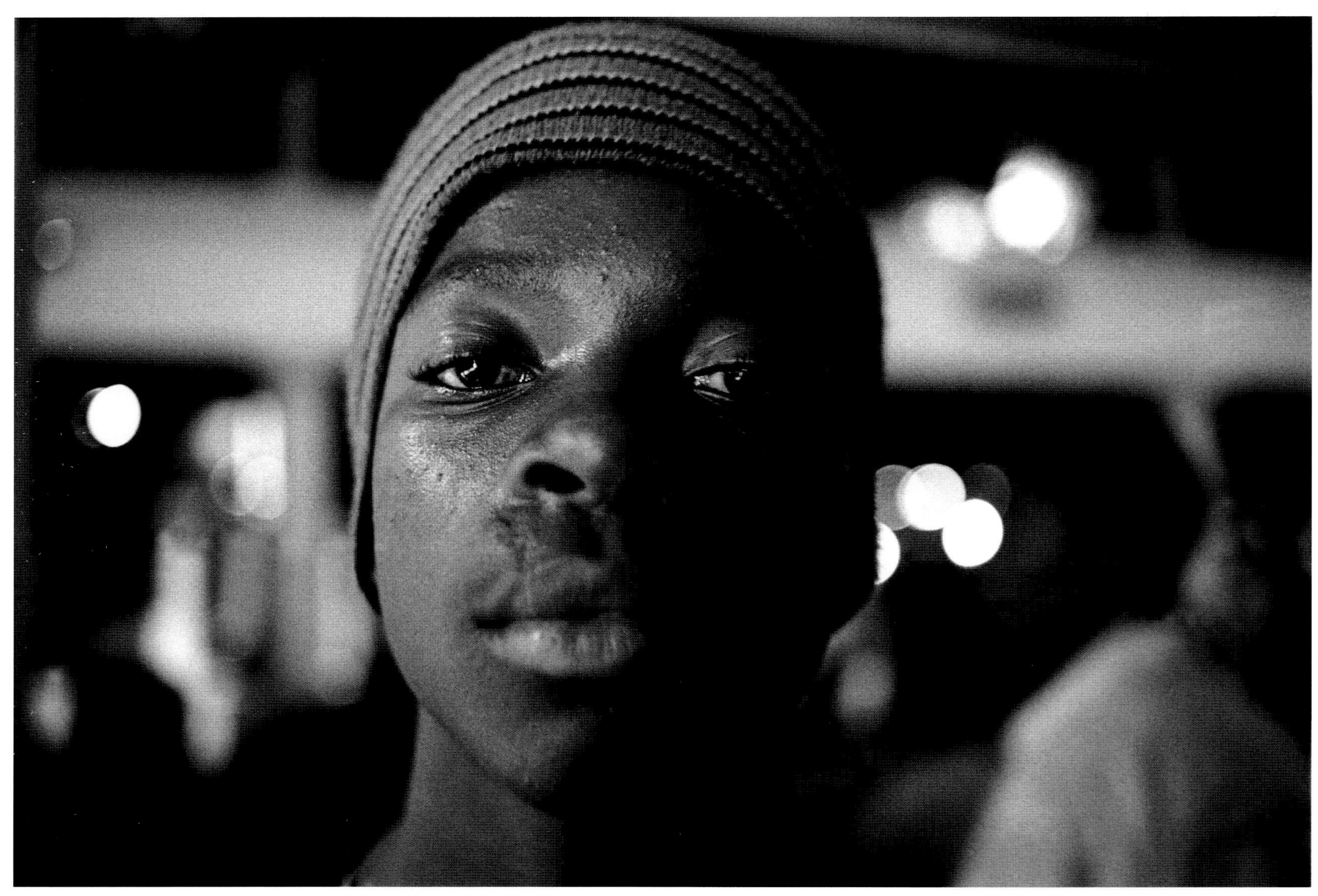

Feira Popular de Maputo, 2005
Fiber-based photographic print, 13.8 x 19.3 in. (35 x 49 cm)
Courtesy the artist

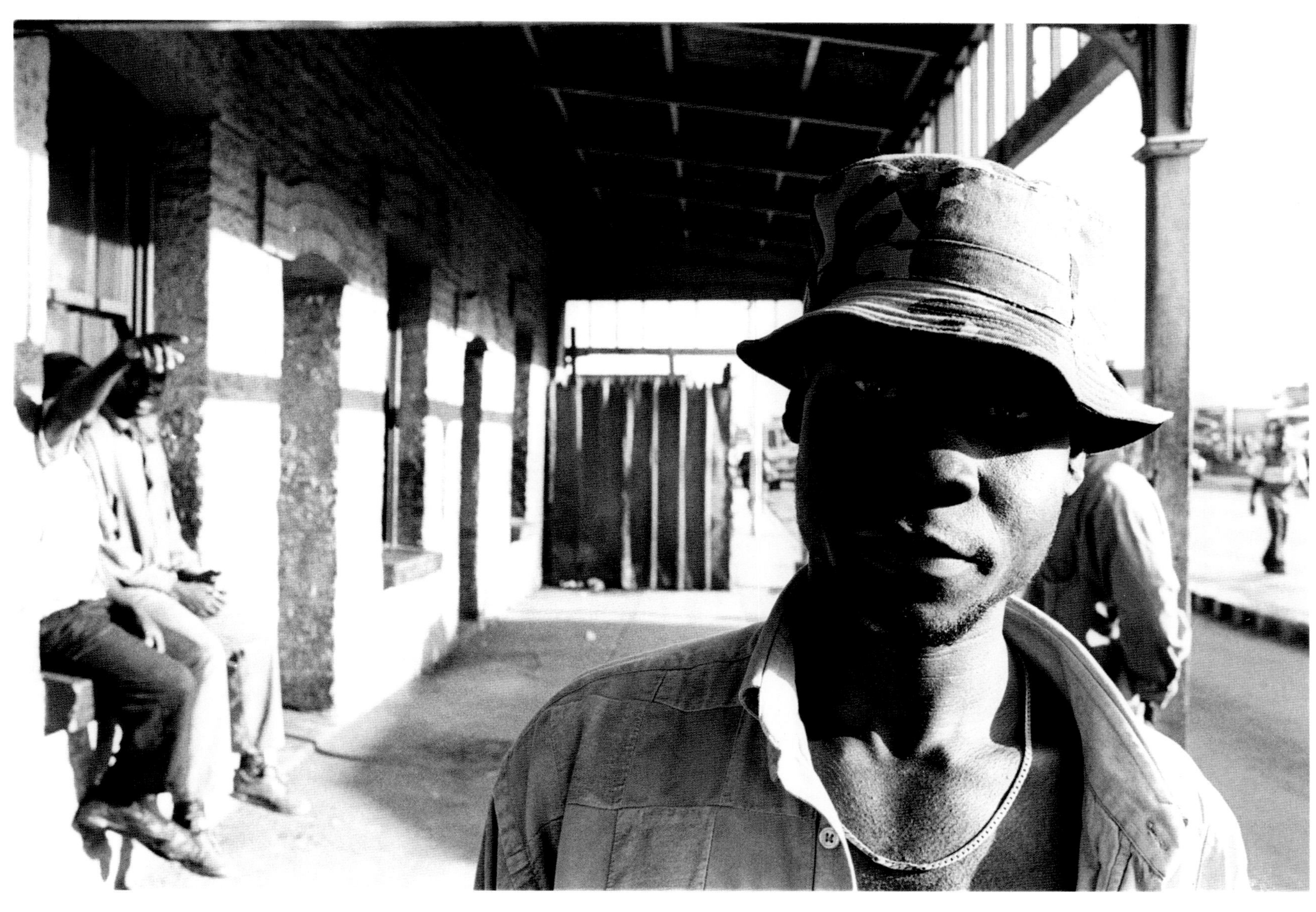

Bus Stop, Old Harare, 2001
Fiber-based photographic print, 13.8 x 19.3 in. (35 x 49 cm)
Courtesy the artist

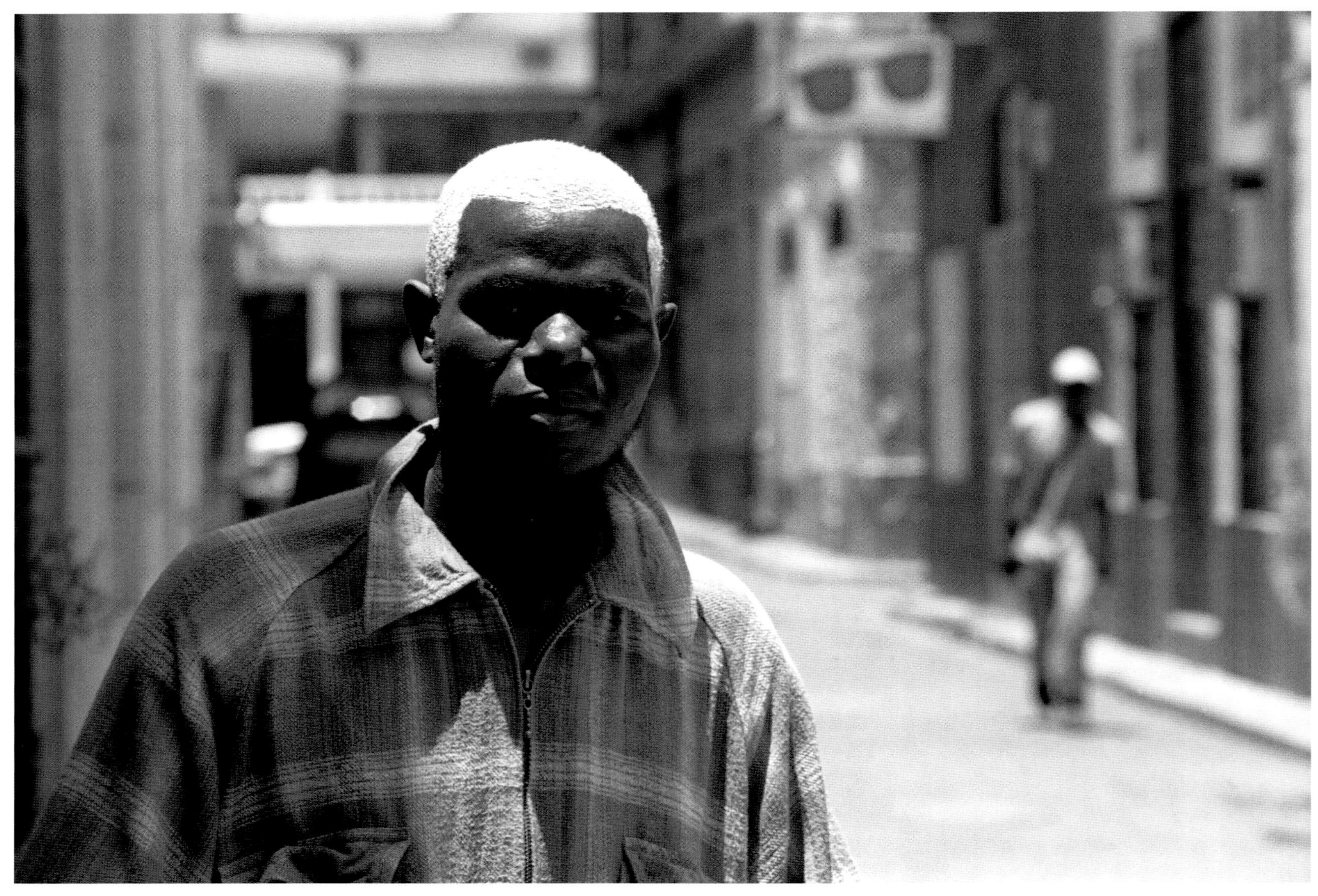

G.G. Down Town, Maputo, 2005
Fiber-based photographic print, 13.8 x 19.3 in. (35 x 49 cm)
Courtesy the artist

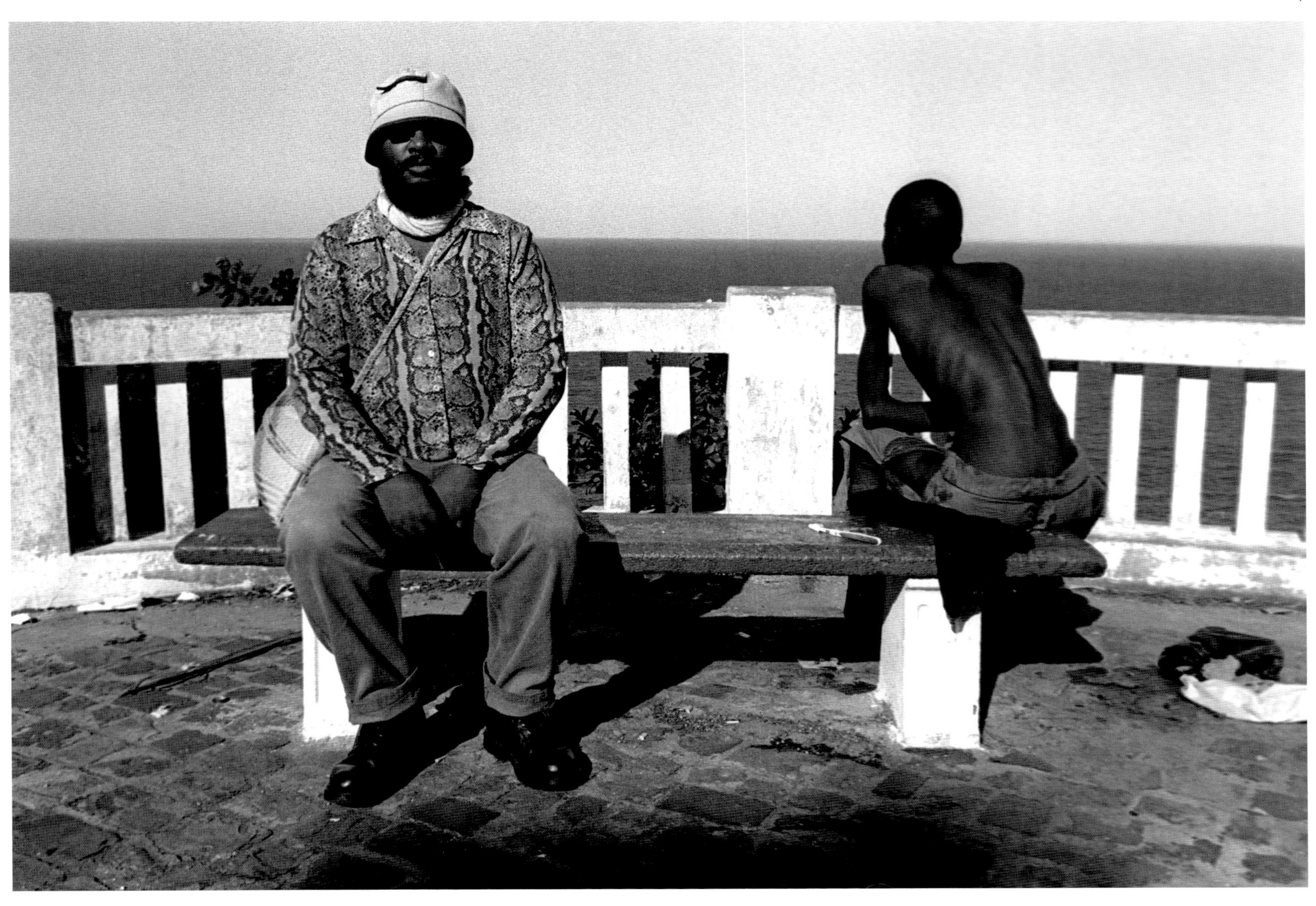

Rashid, Maputo, 2004
Fiber-based photographic print, 13.7 x 19.3 in. 13.8 x 19.3 in. (35 x 49 cm)
Courtesy the artist

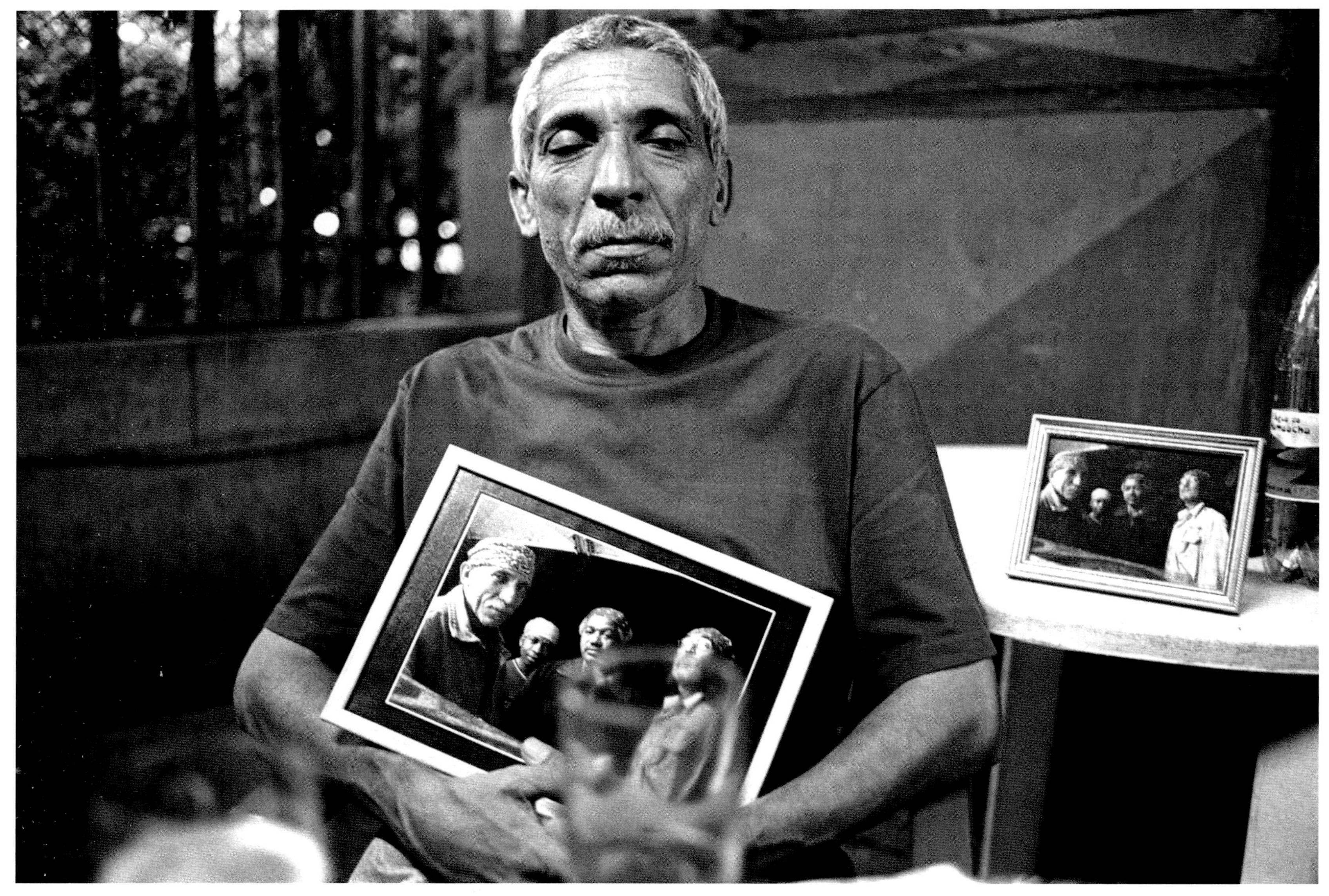

Isidine (The Green Man), Maputo, 2004
Fiber-based photographic print, 13.8 x 19.3 in. (35 x 49 cm)
Courtesy the artist

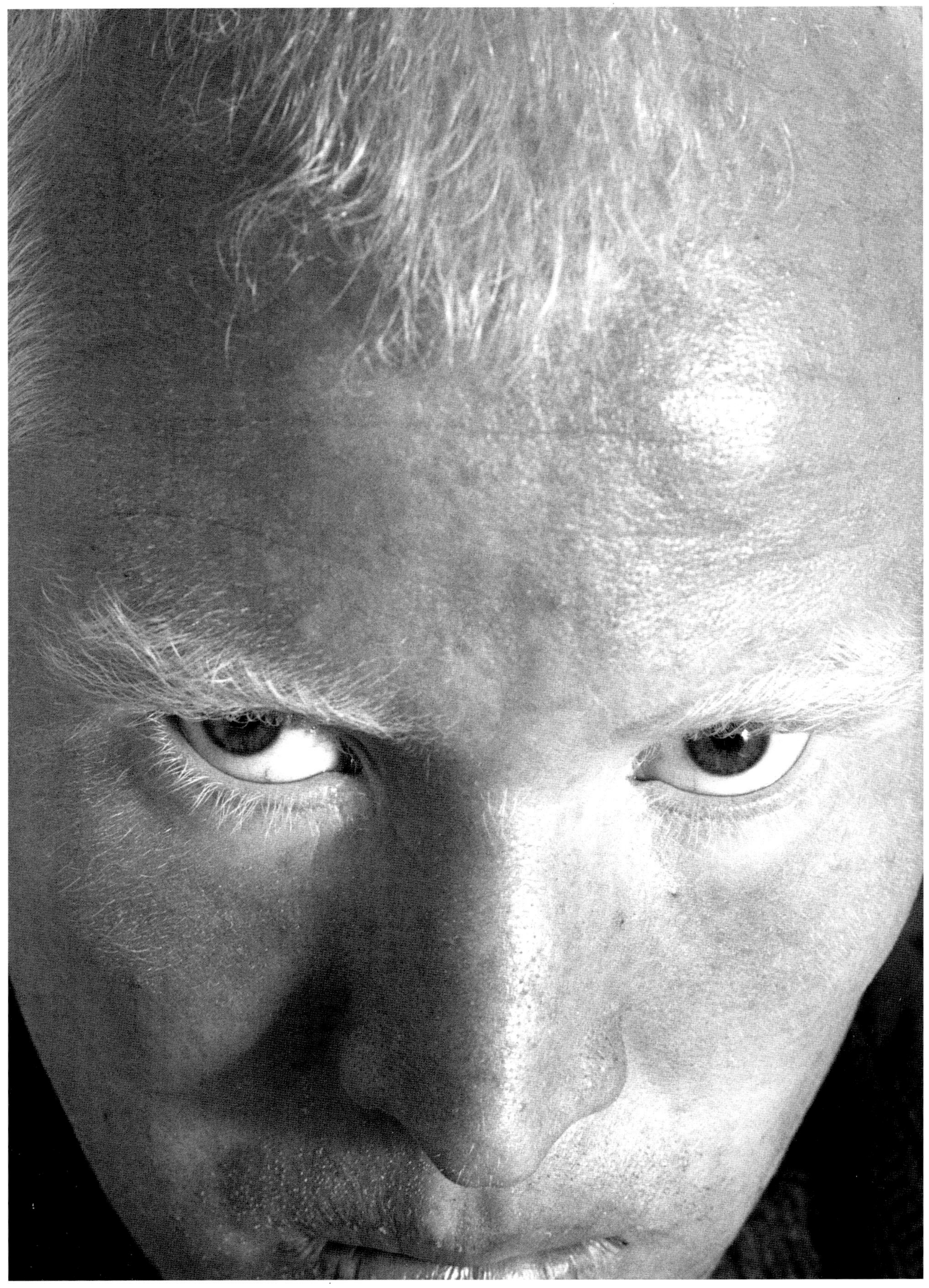

Untitled, 1998–2005
Gelatin silver print, 12.5 x 17.6 in. (31.8 x 44.7 cm)
Courtesy the artist

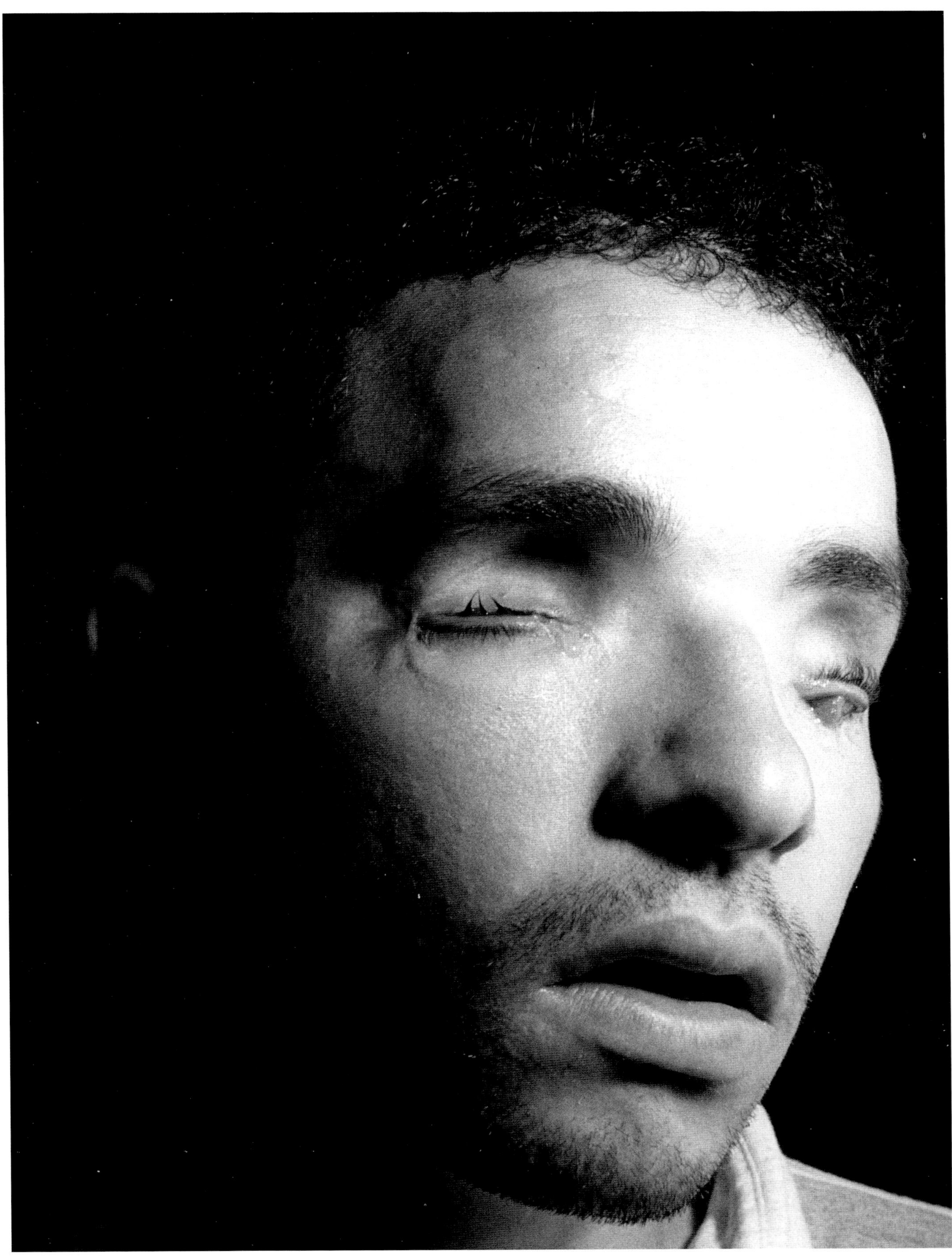

Untitled, 1998–2005
Gelatin silver print, 12.5 x 17.6 in. (31.8 x 44.7 cm)
Courtesy the artist

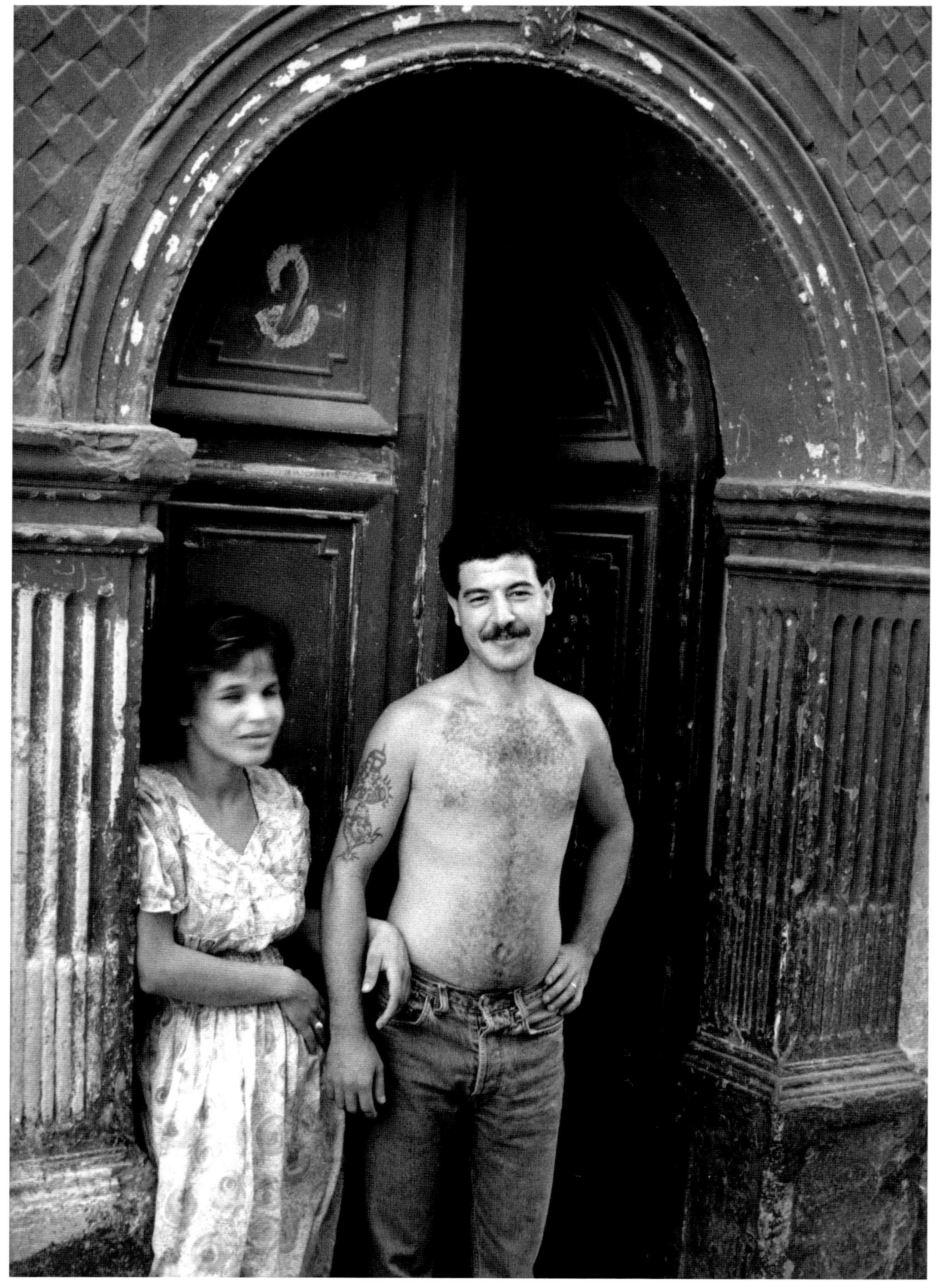

Untitled, 1998–2005
Gelatin silver print, 12.5 x 17.6 in. (31.8 x 44.7 cm)
Courtesy the artist

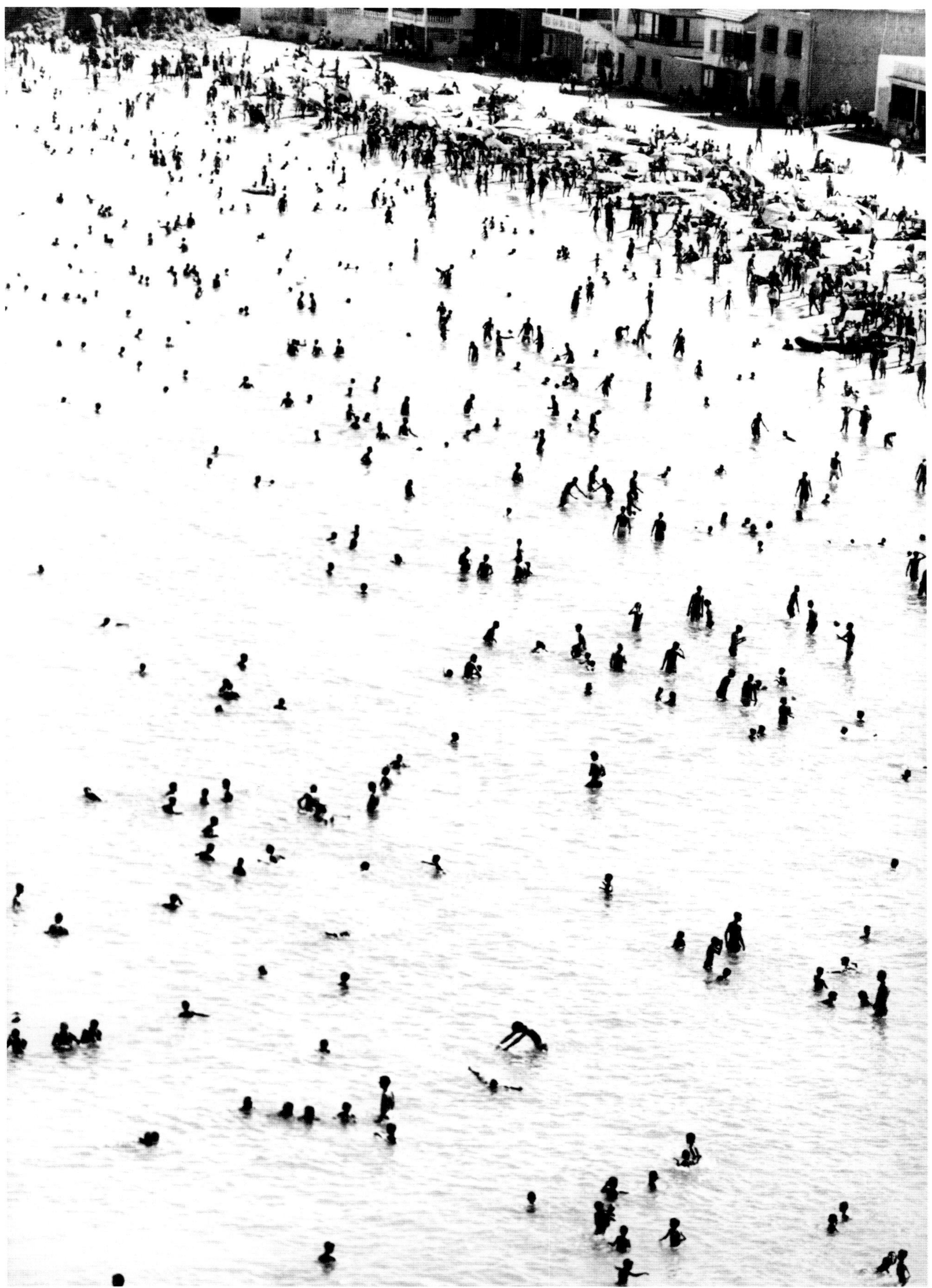

Untitled, 1998–2005
Gelatin silver print, 12.5 x 17.6 in. (31.8 x 44.7 cm)
Courtesy the artist

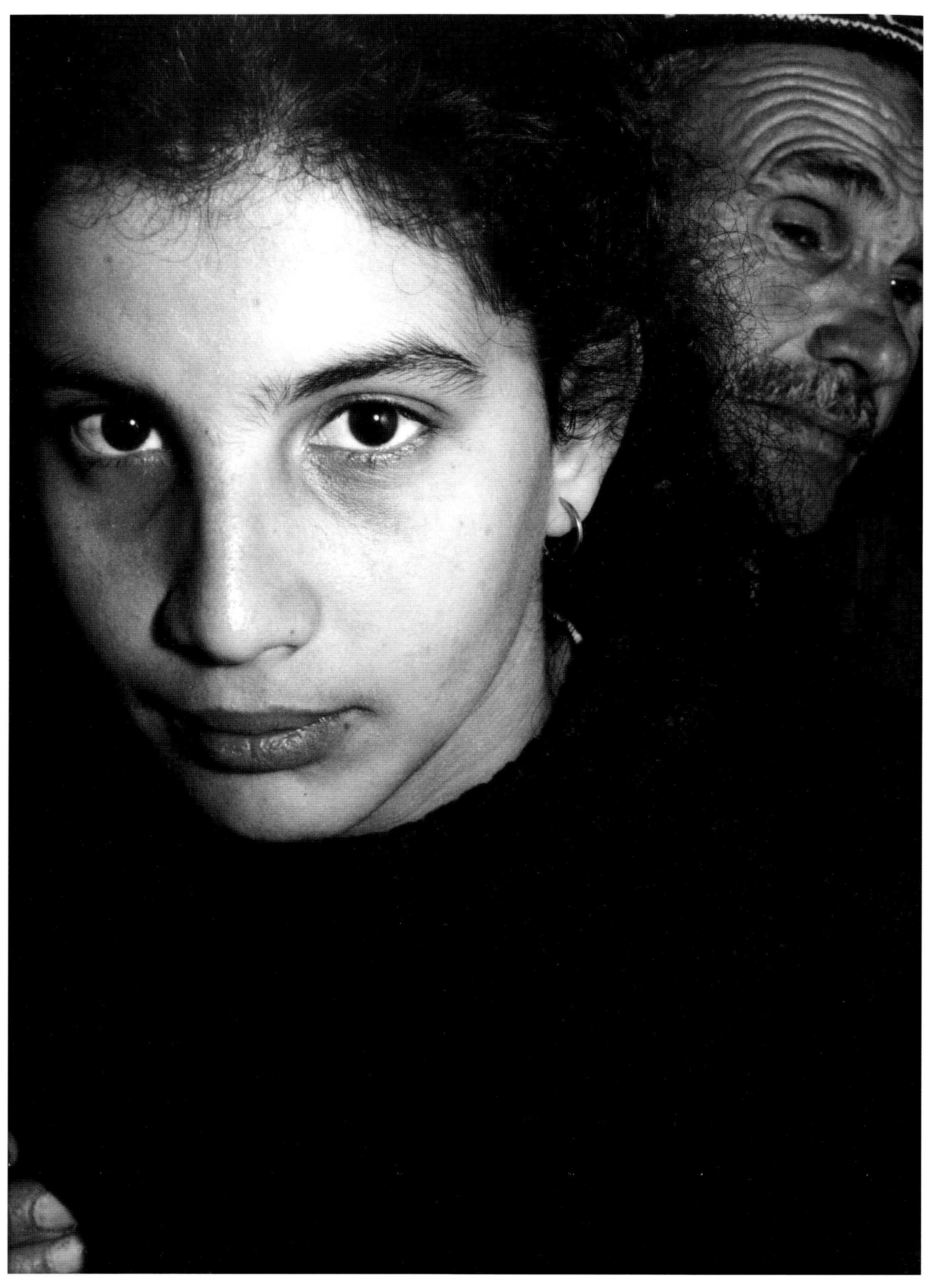

Untitled, 1998–2005
Gelatin silver print, 12.5 x 17.6 in. (31.8 x 44.7 cm)
Courtesy the artist

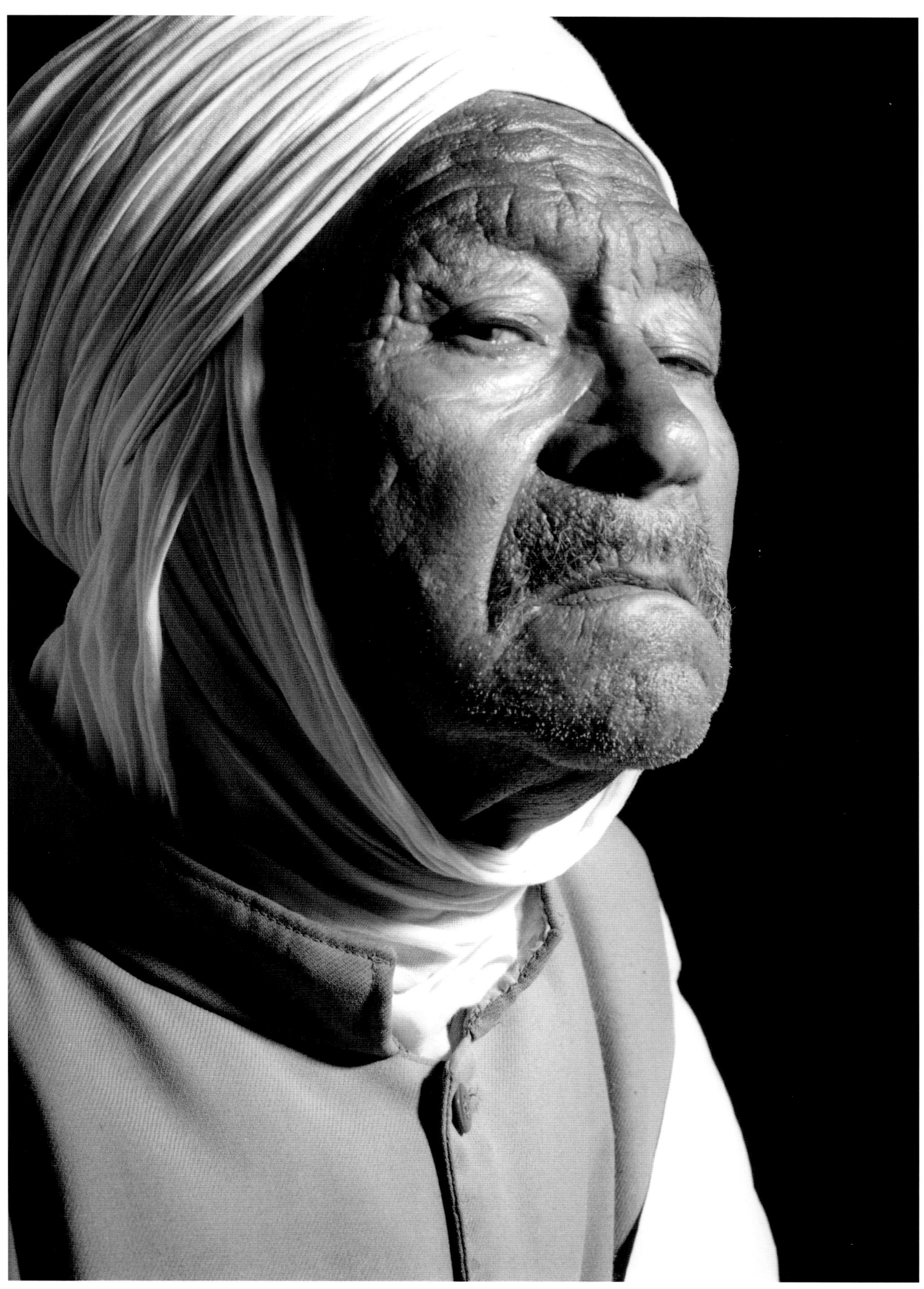

Untitled, 1998–2005
Gelatin silver print, 12.5 x 17.6 in. (31.8 x 44.7 cm)
Courtesy the artist

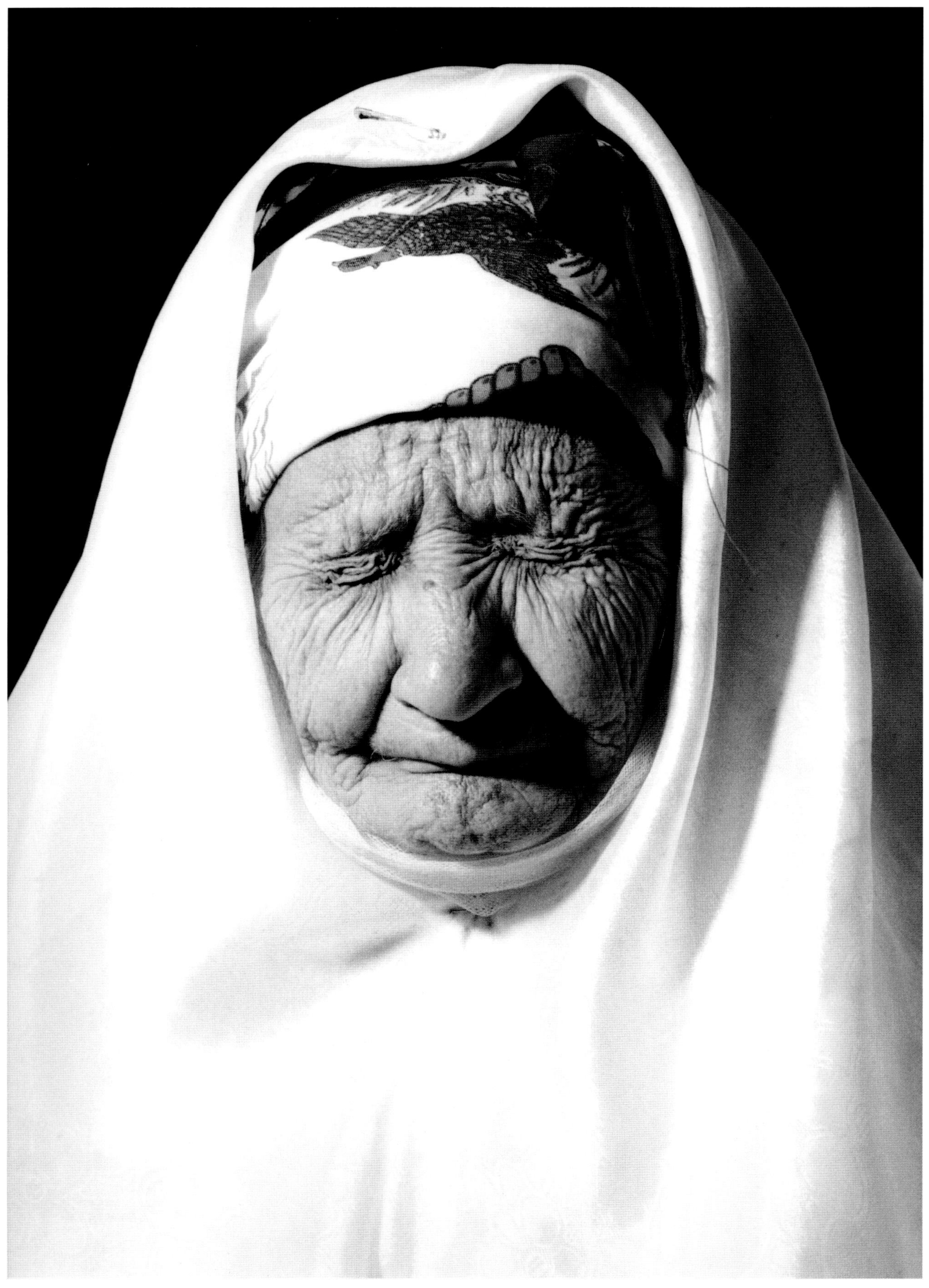

Untitled, 1998–2005
Gelatin silver print, 12.5 x 17.6 in. (31.8 x 44.7 cm)
Courtesy the artist

Maha Maamoun

Lara Baladi

Lamia Naji

Theo Eshetu

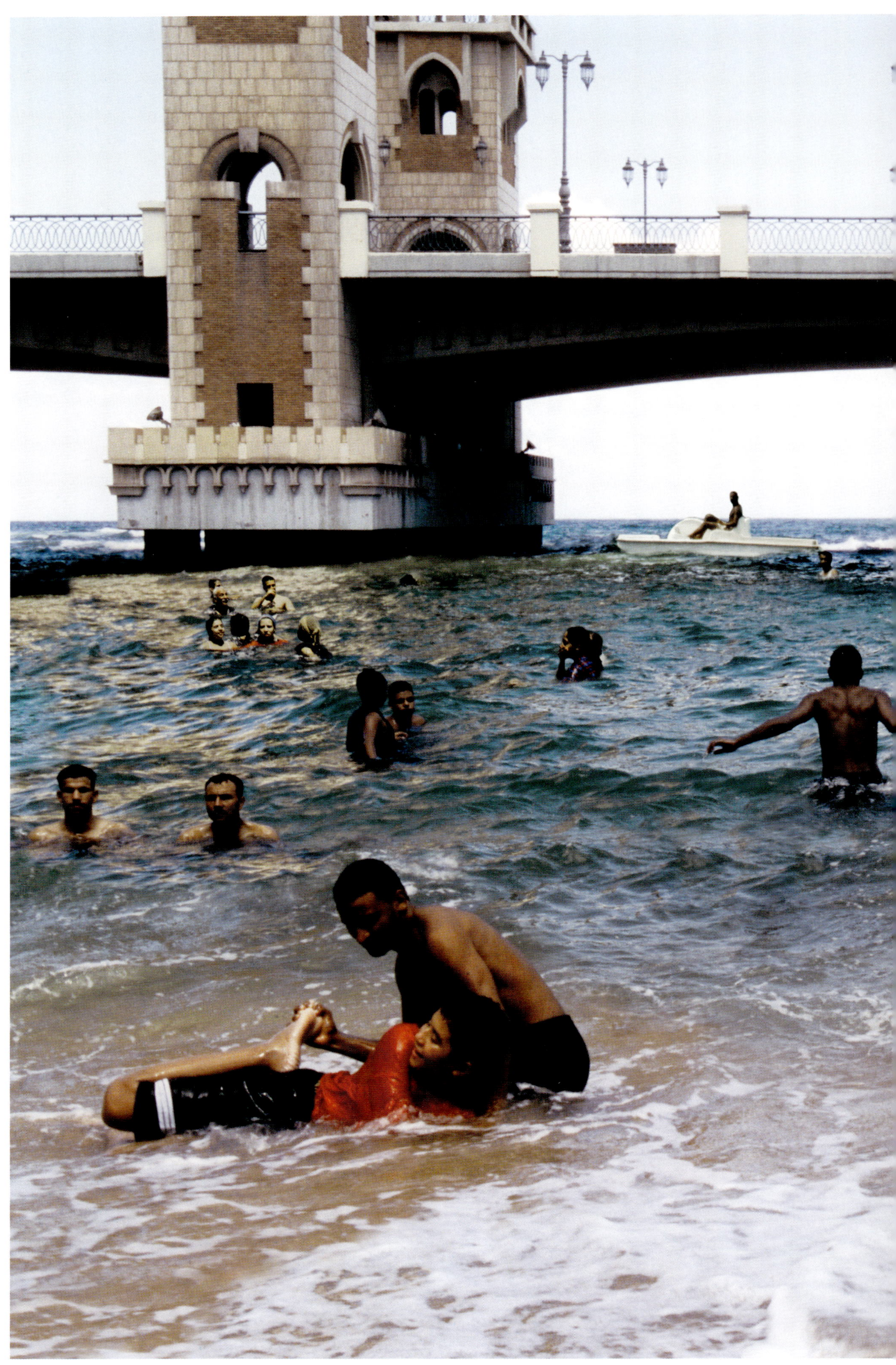

The Beach, from the series
"Domestic Tourism," 2005
Chromogenic print
19.7 x 29.5 in. (50 x 75 cm)
Courtesy the artist and
Townhouse Gallery, Cairo

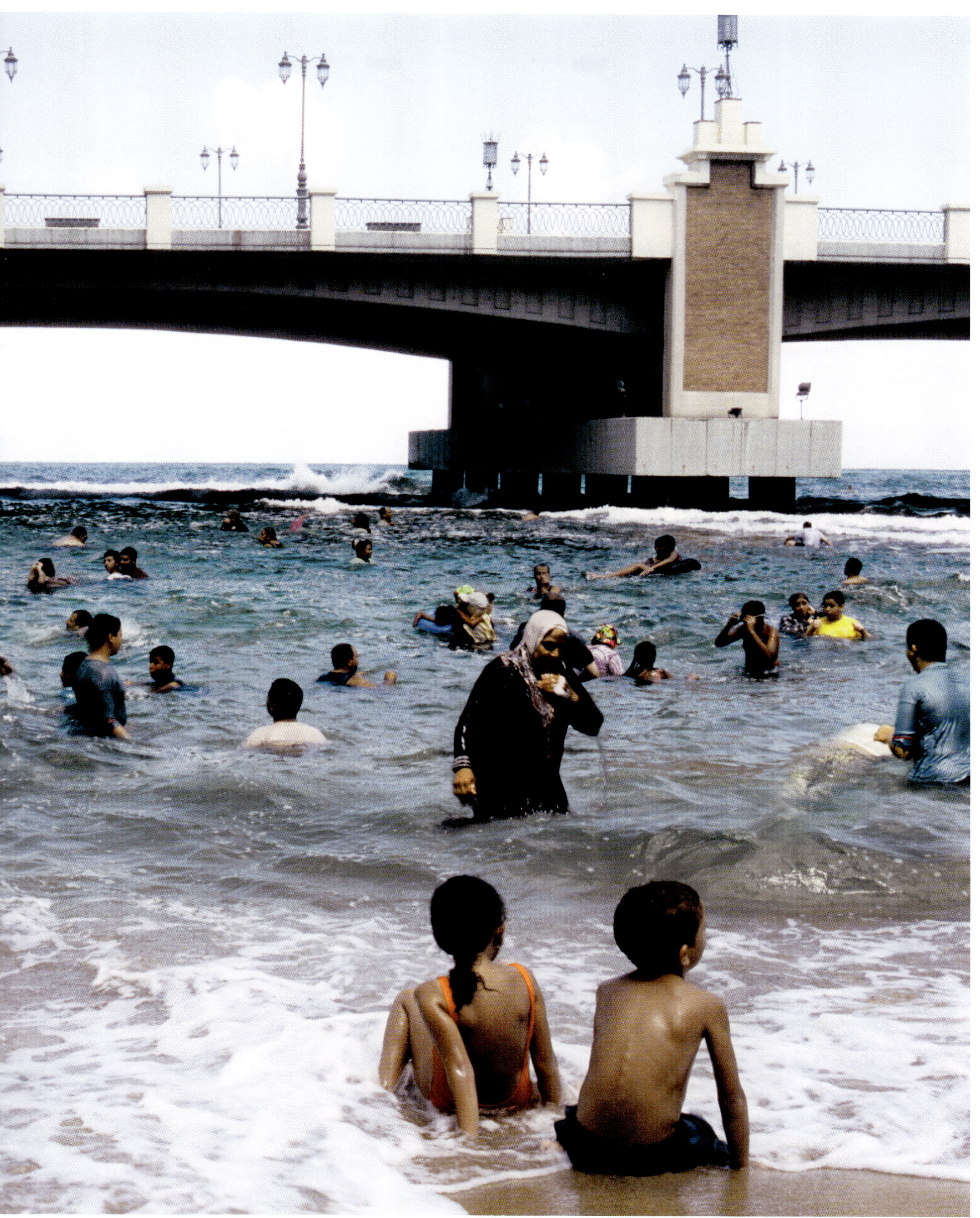

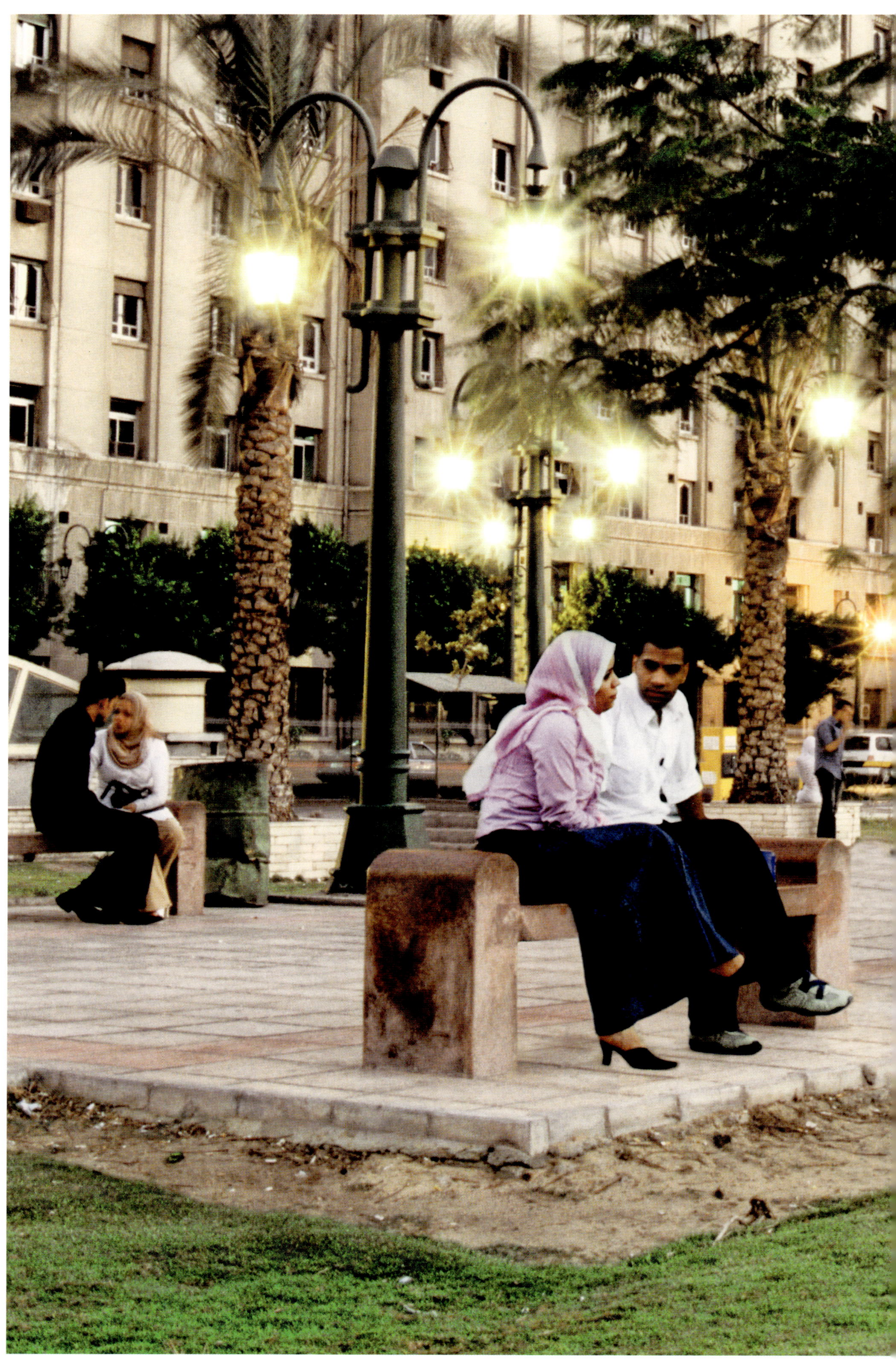

The Park, from the series "Domestic Tourism," 2005
Chromogenic print
19.7 x 29.5 in. (50 x 75 cm)
Courtesy the artist and Townhouse Gallery, Cairo

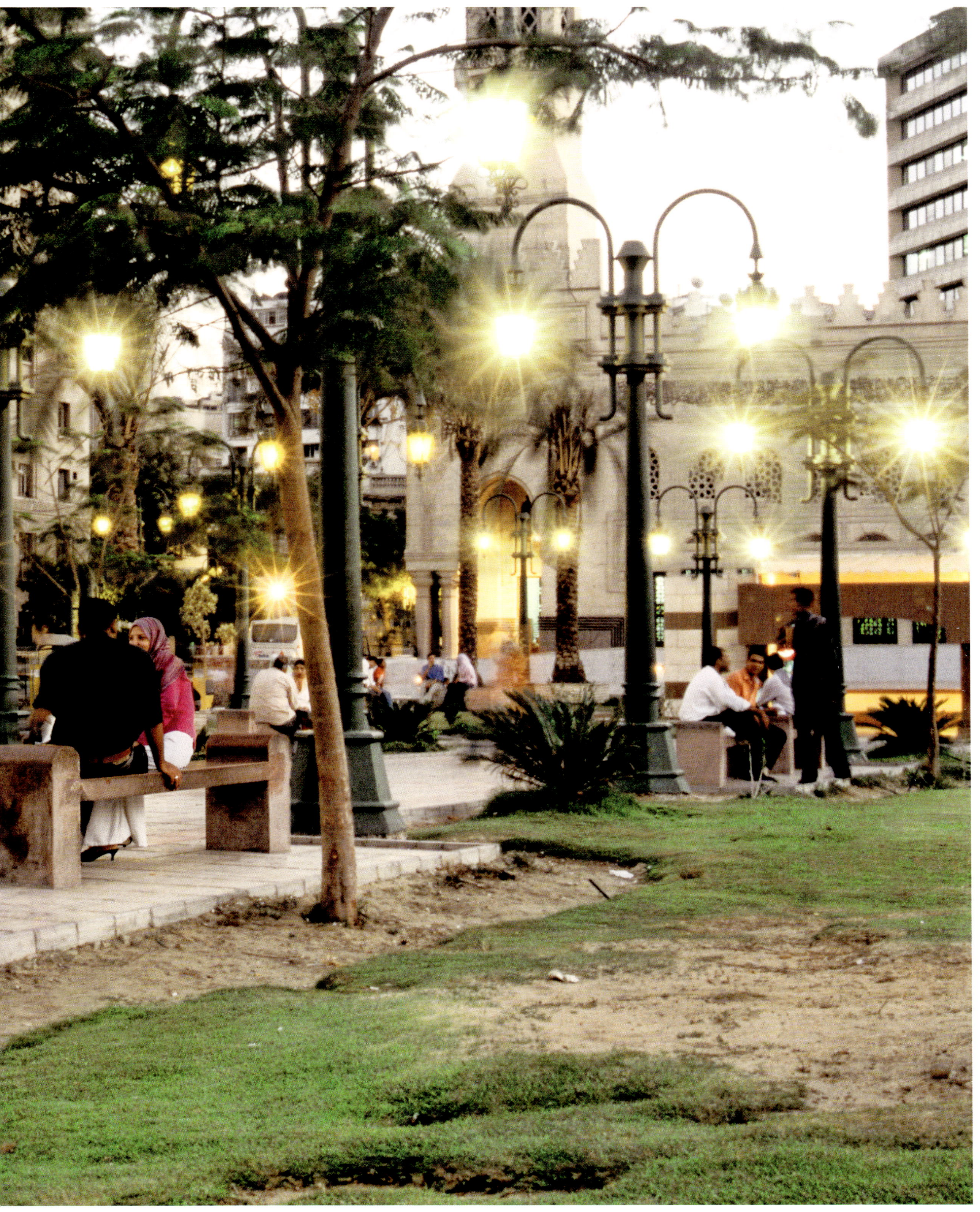

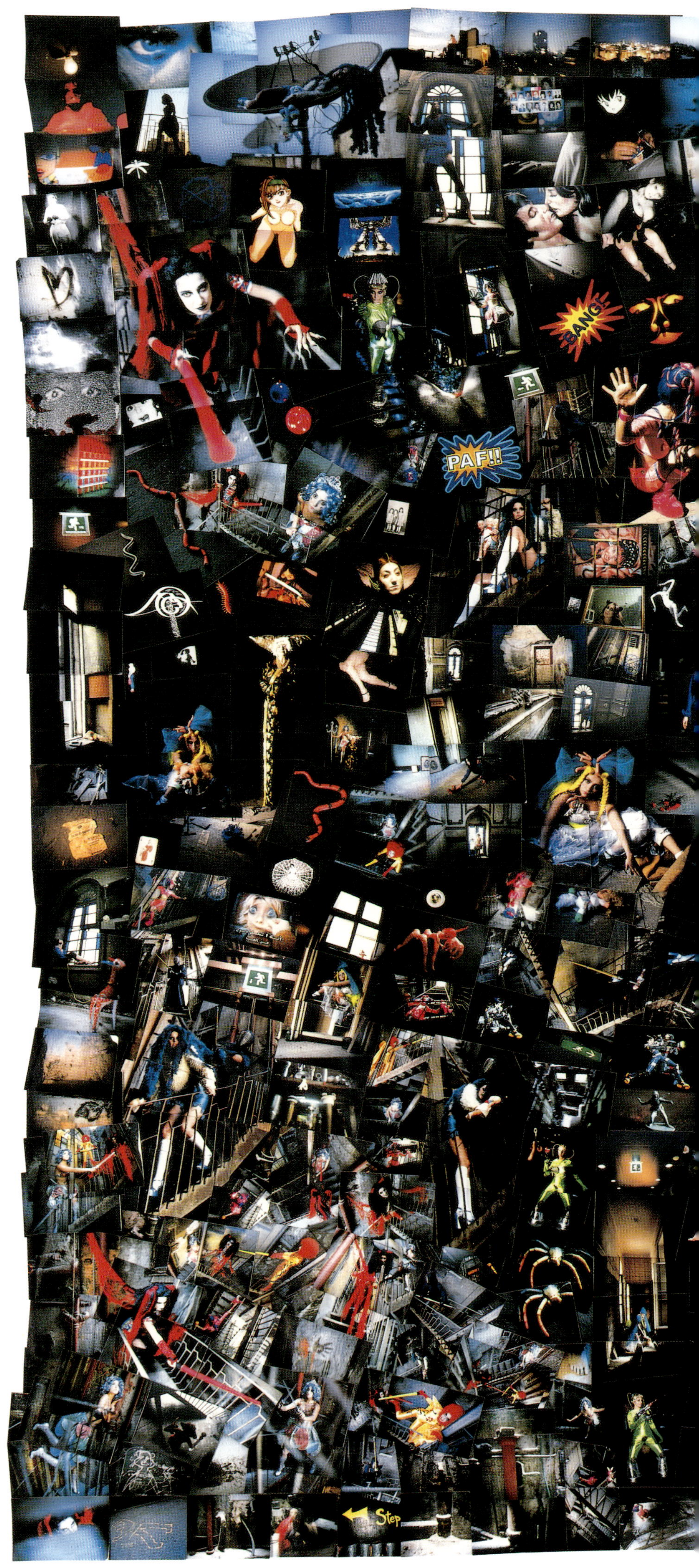

Sandouk el Dounia (The World in a Box), 2001
Photographic color prints, 118.1 x 94.5 in. (300 x 240 cm)
Courtesy the artist

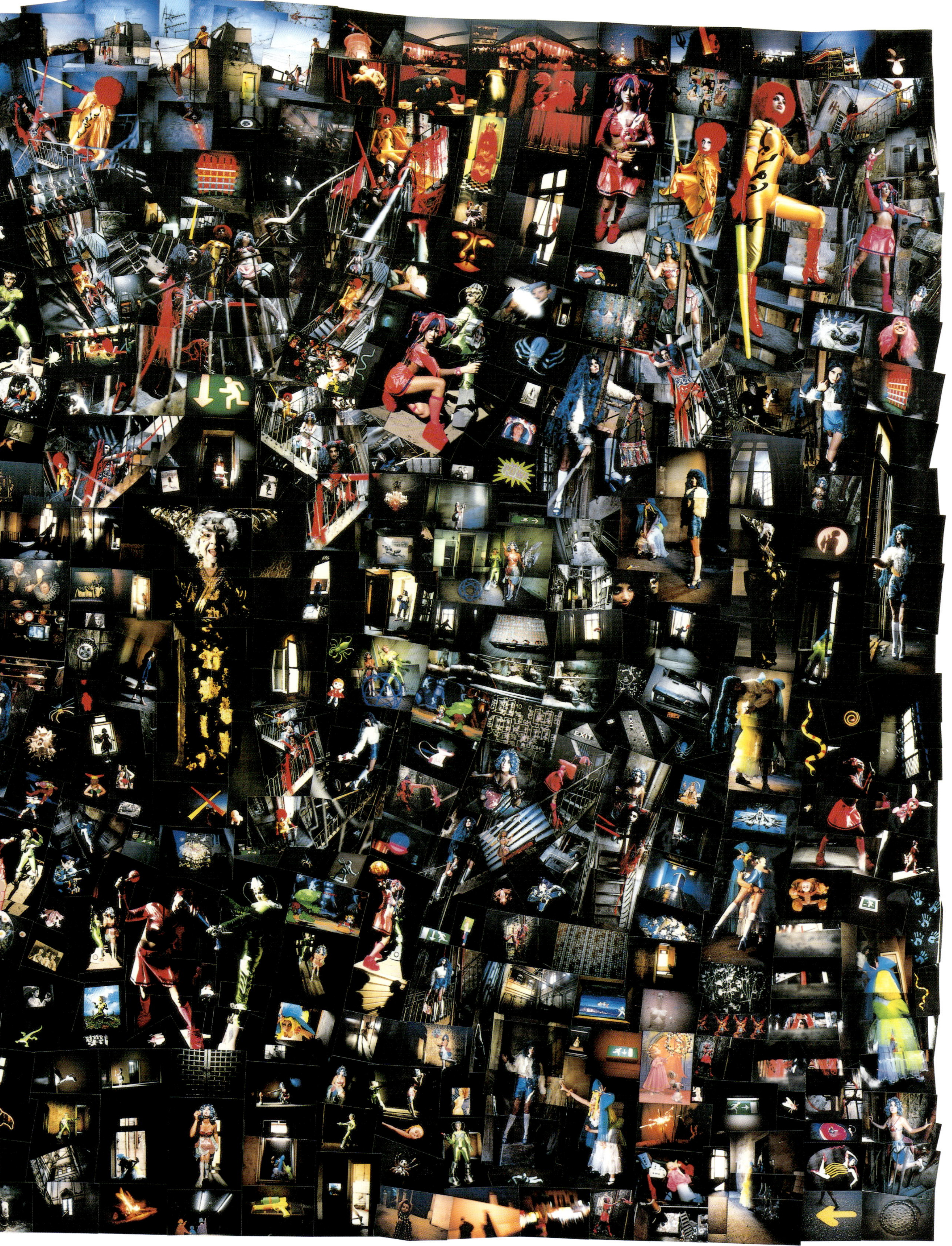

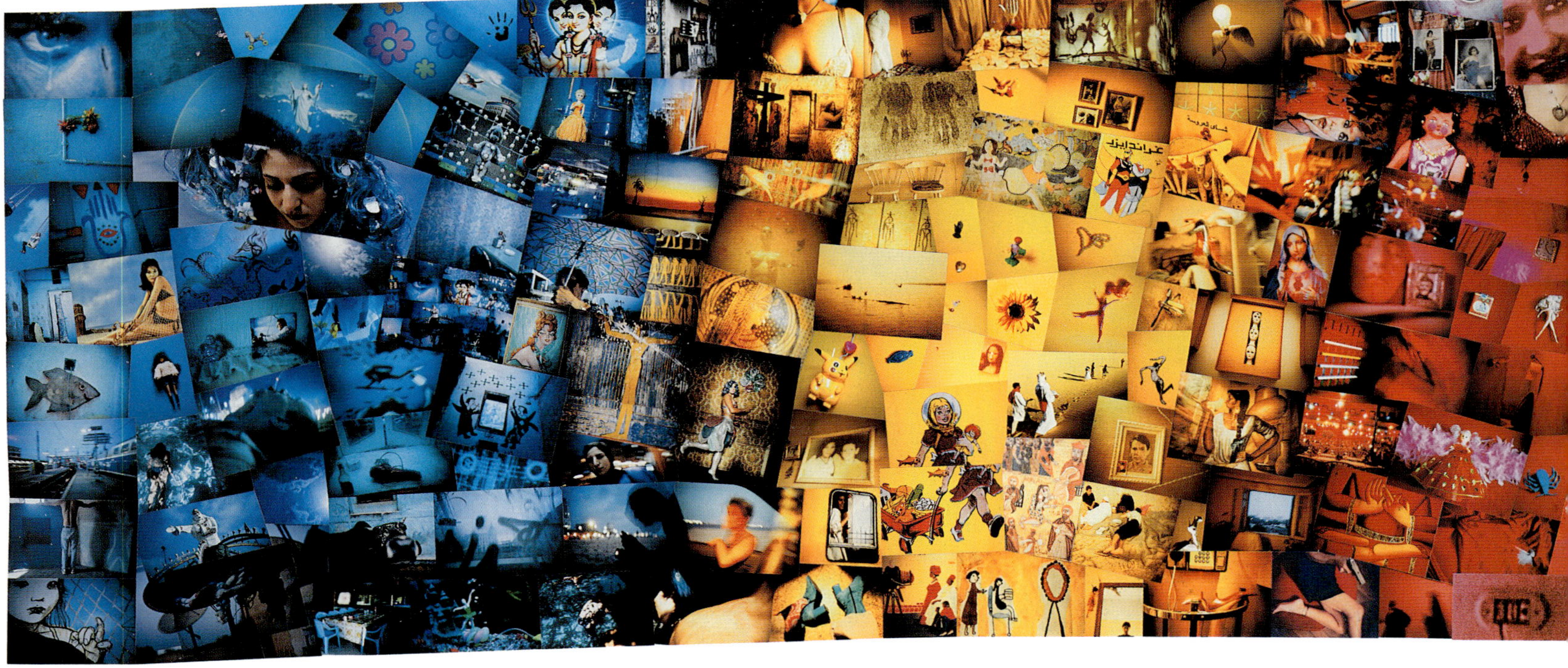

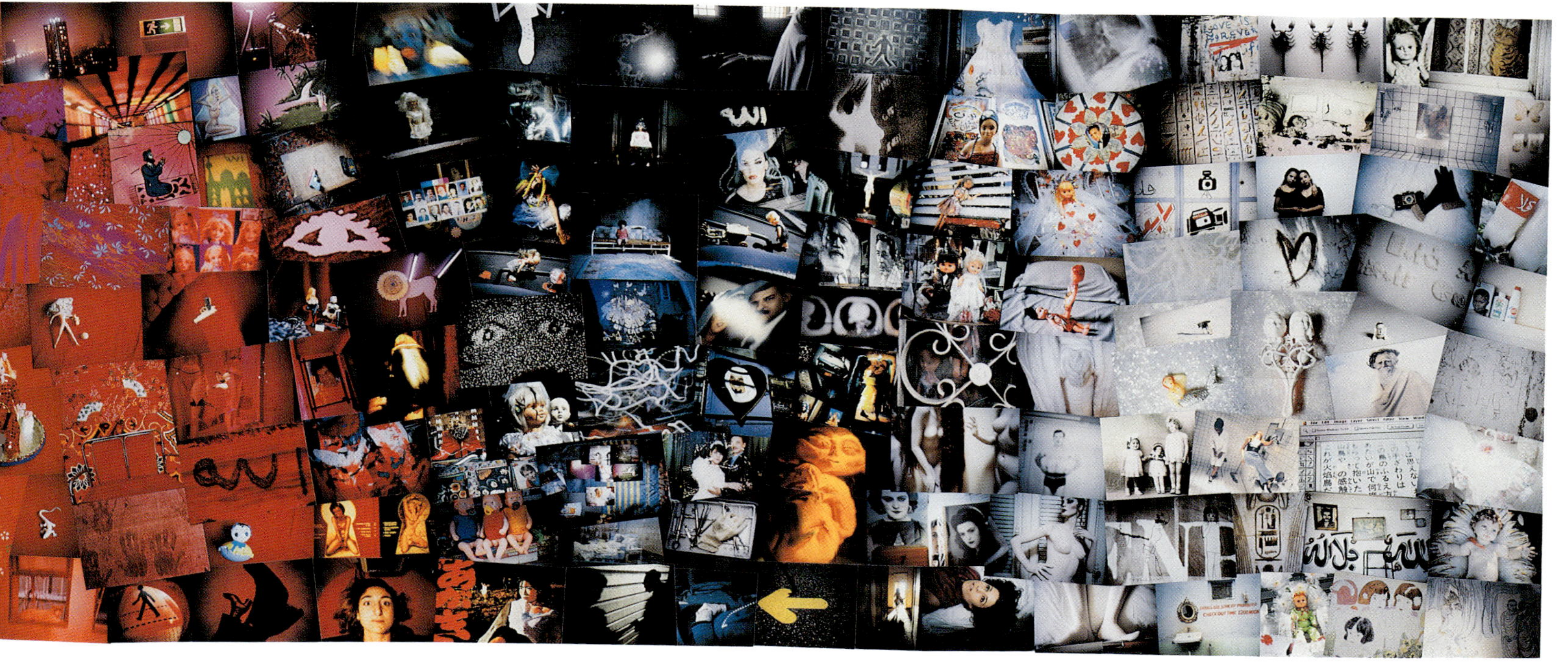

Nawara, 2001
Photographic color prints, 143.7 x 29.5 in. (365 x 75 cm)
Collection Stage Holding, courtesy the artist

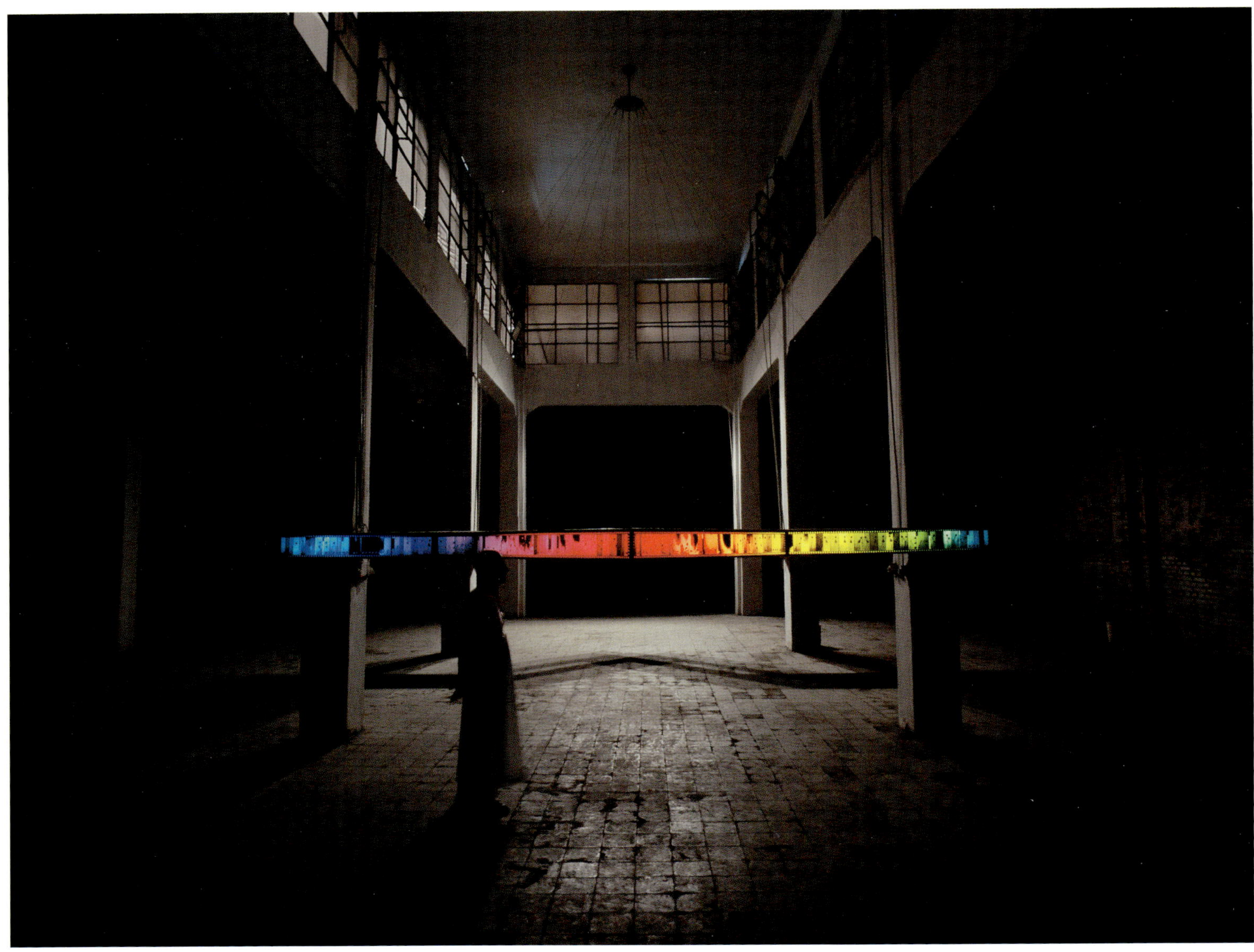

Al Fanous el Sehry (The Magic Lantern), 2002
Sixteen light boxes with acetate prints in shape of Islamic star
each 70.9 x 9.8 x 8.7 in. (180 x 25 x 22 cm); circumference 95.1 ft. (29 m)
Courtesy the artist and Townhouse Gallery, Cairo

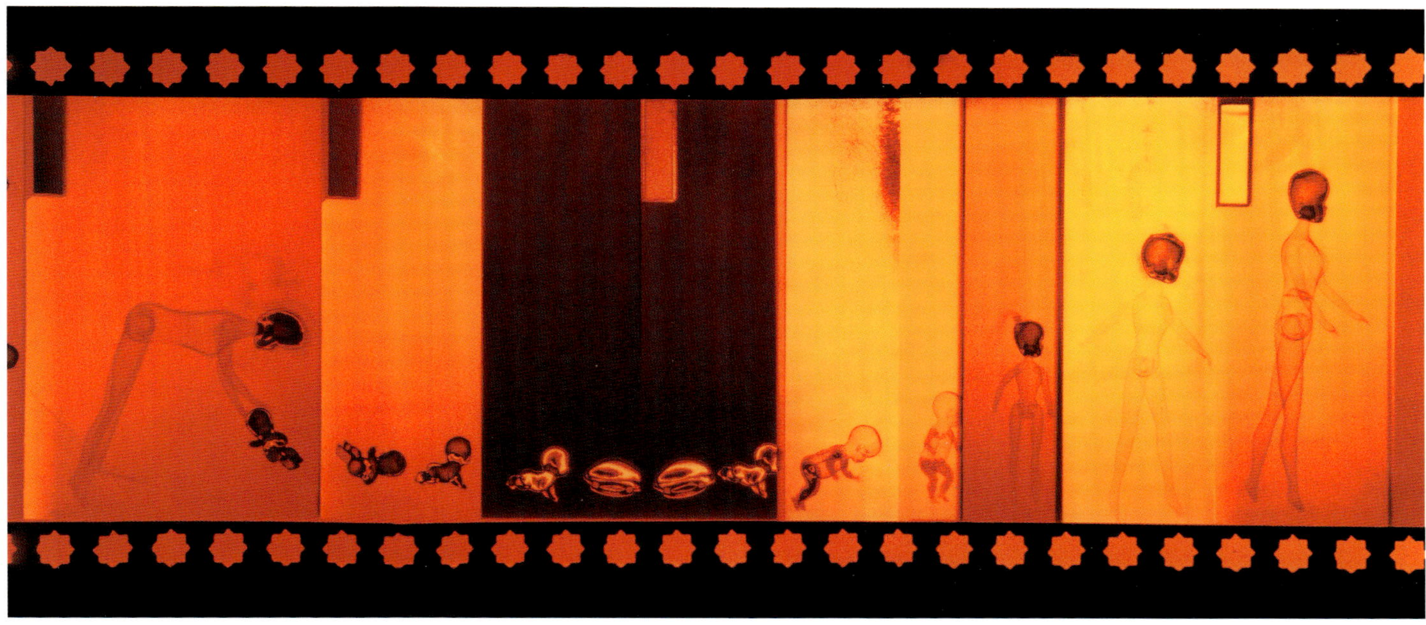

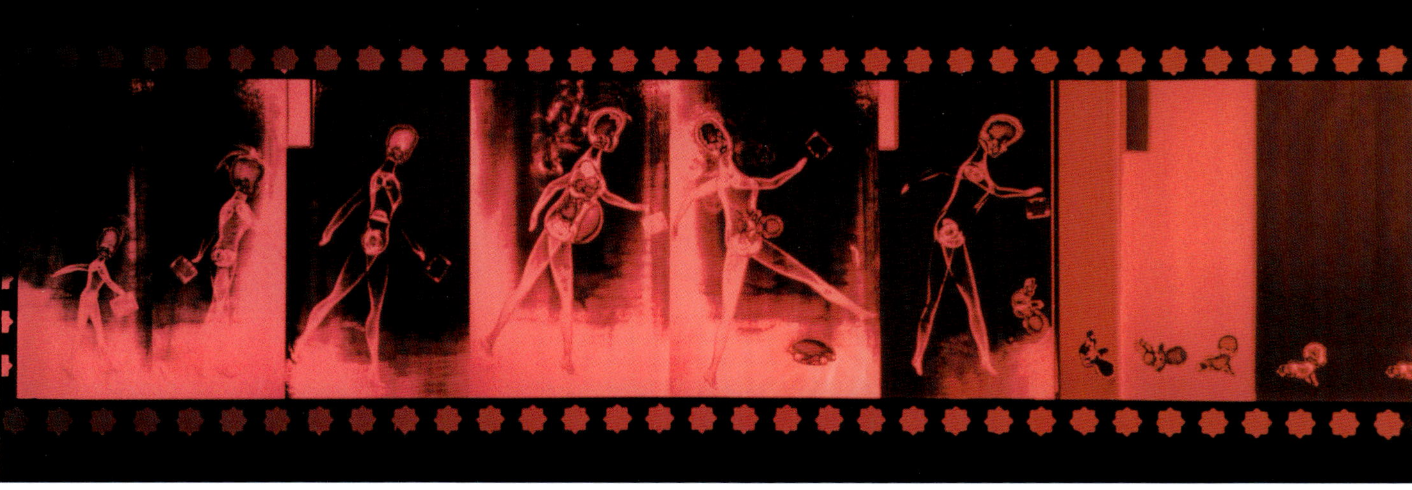

Al Fanous el Sehry (The Magic Lantern), 2002
Sixteen light boxes with acetate prints in shape of Islamic star
each 70.9 x 9.8 x 8.7 in. (180 x 25 x 22 cm); circumference 95.1 ft. (29 m)
Courtesy the artist and Townhouse Gallery, Cairo

Top:
Detail: *strip 1*

Bottom:
Detail: *strip 3*

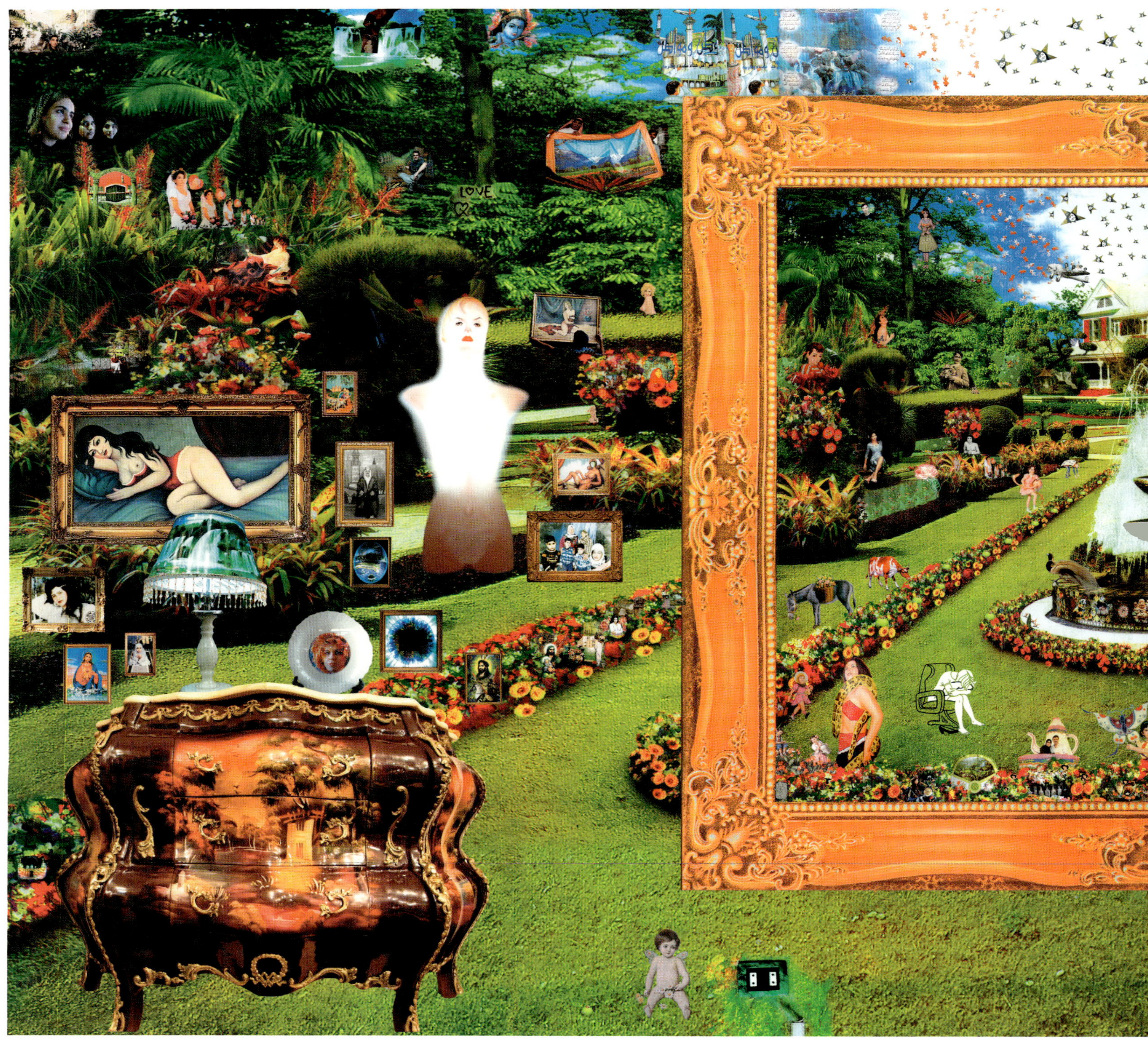
LOVE

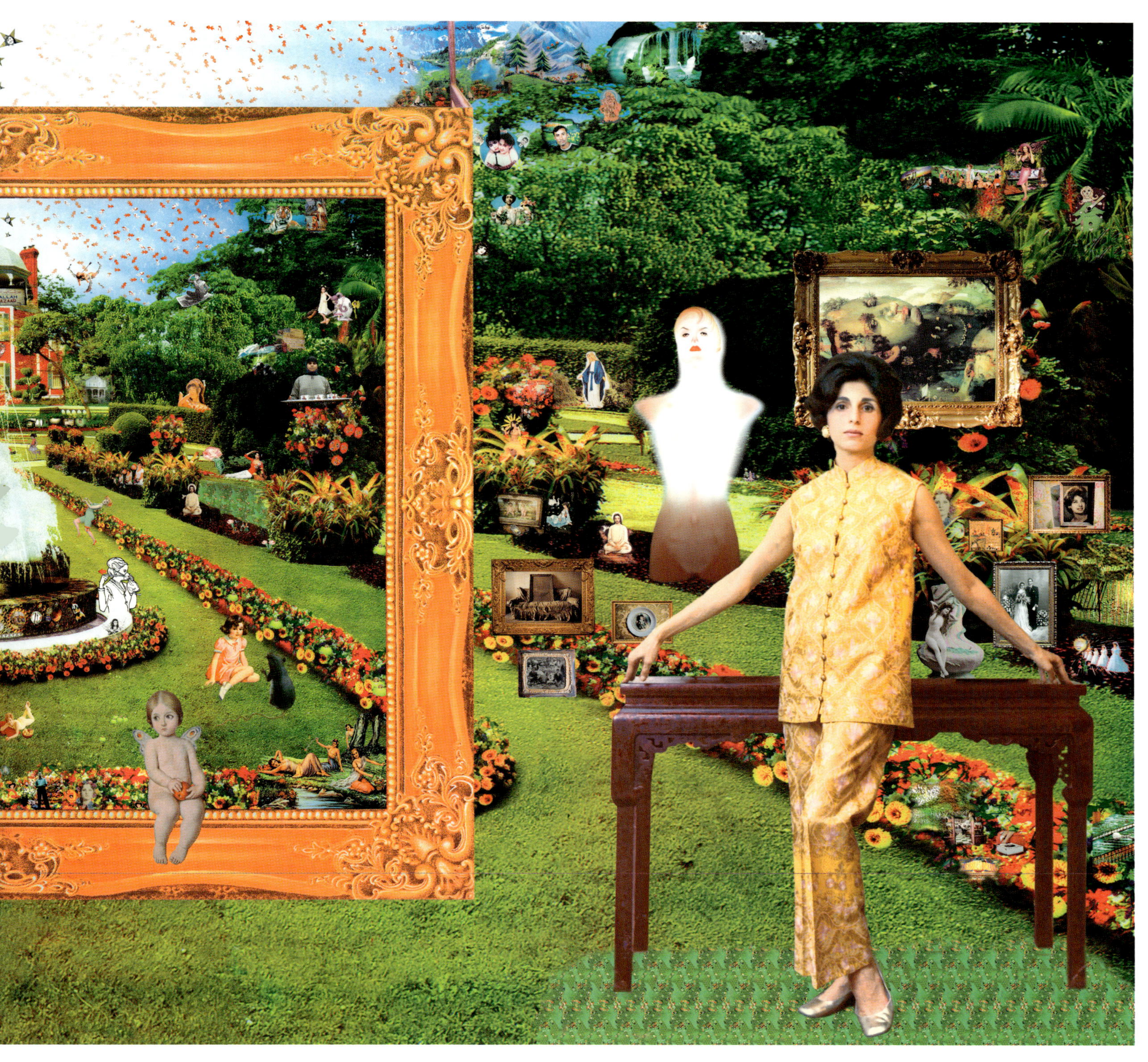

Perfumes & Bazaar, 2005
Photographic montage, pigment print on self-adhesive vinyl and duratrans print for light box, 94 x 212 in. (239 x 539 cm)
Technical production and printing, Factum Arte, Madrid
Courtesy the artist

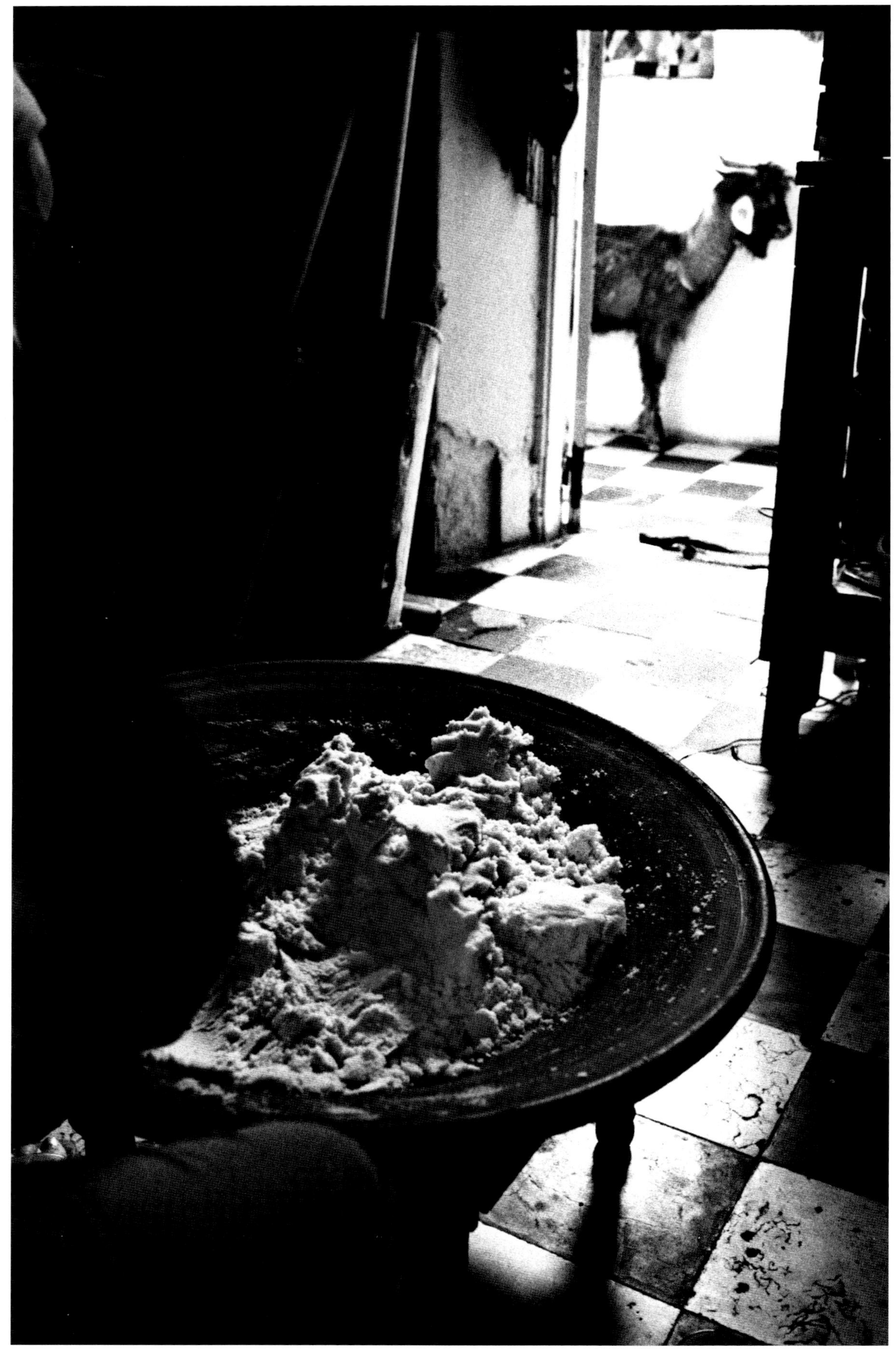

Couleurs Primaires, 2005
Still from DVD
Courtesy the artist and Galería Rafael Pérez Hernando, Madrid

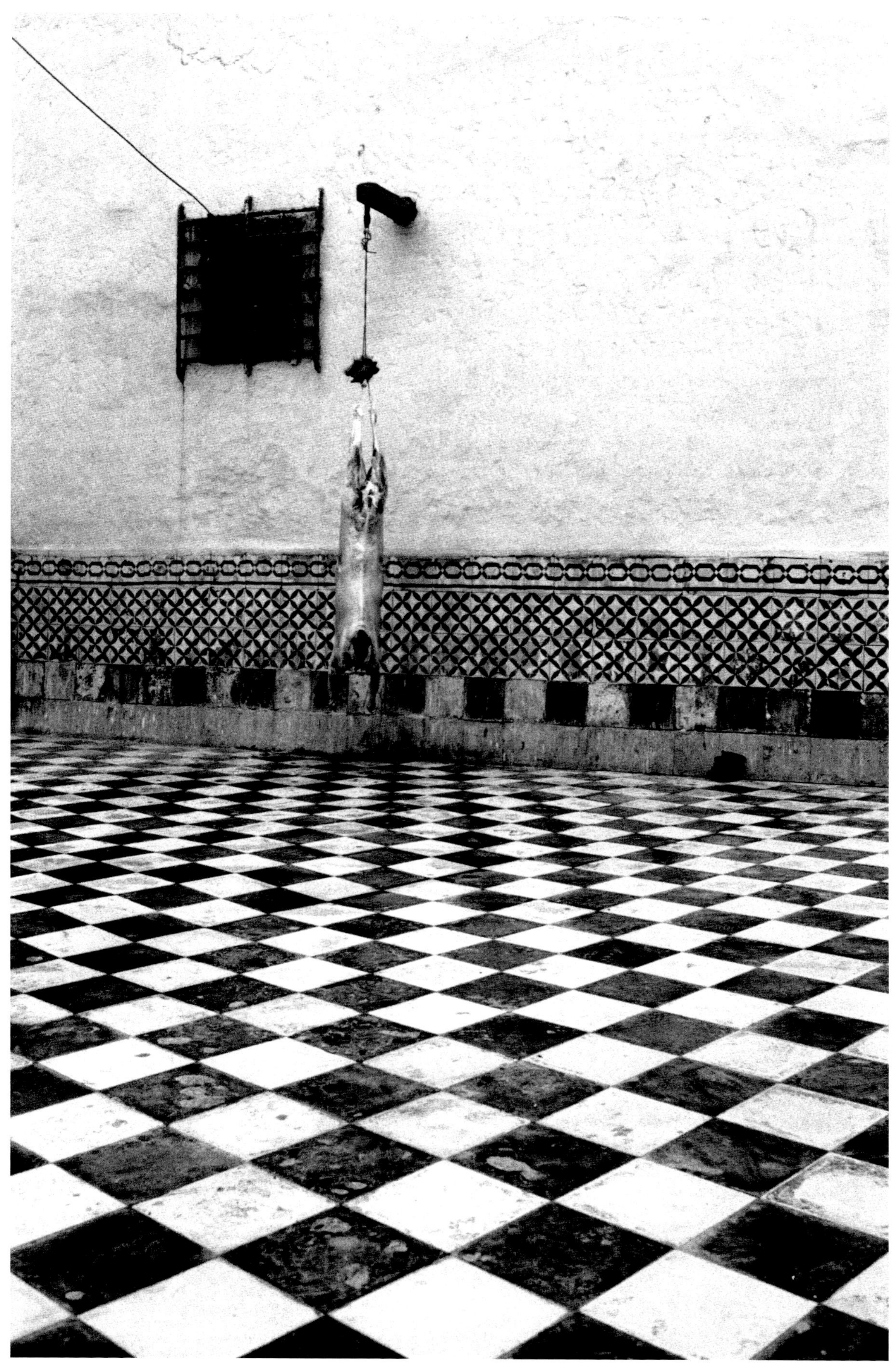

Couleurs Primaires, 2005
Still from DVD
Courtesy the artist and Galería Rafael Pérez Hernando, Madrid

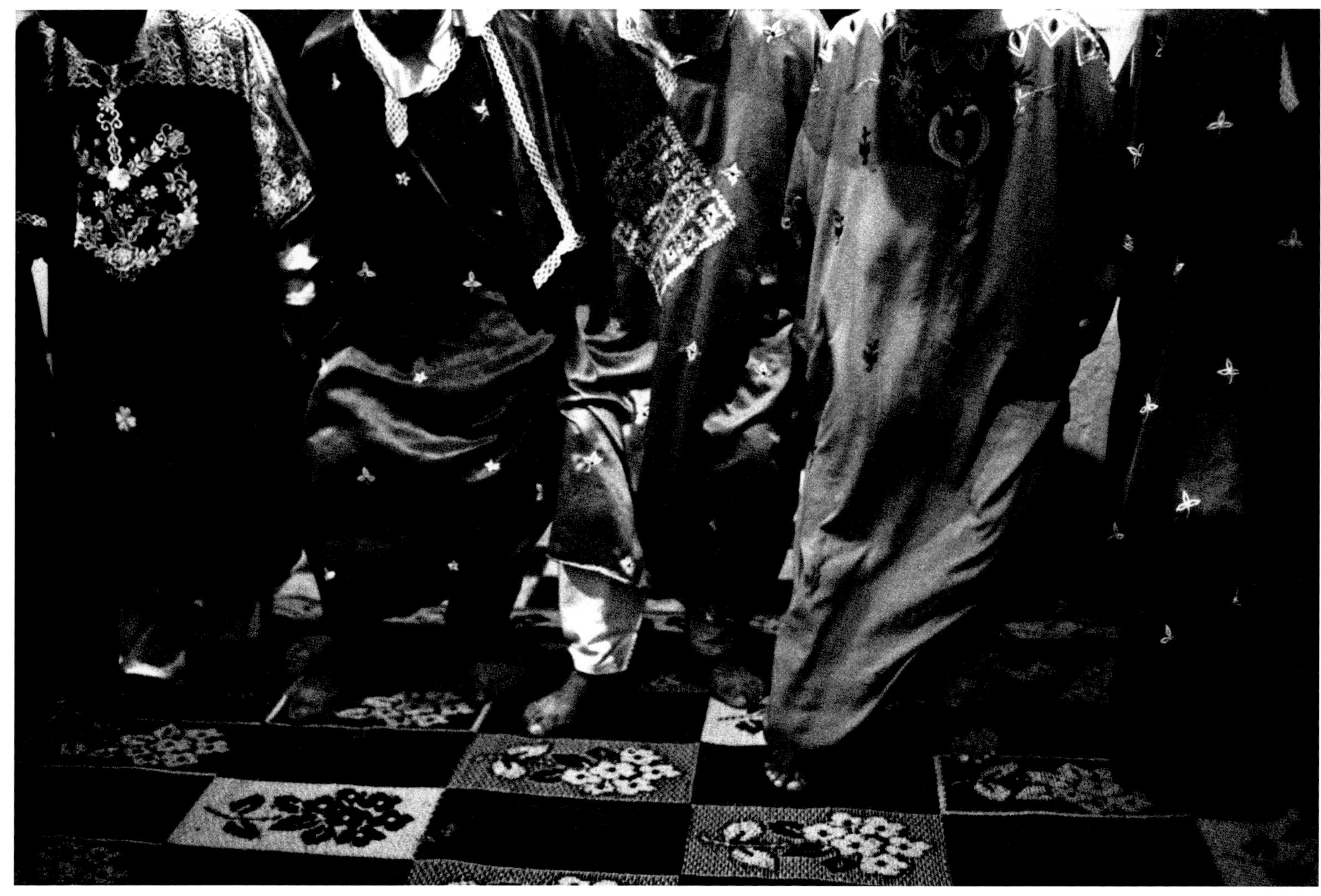

Couleurs Primaires, 2005
Still from DVD
Courtesy the artist and Galería Rafael Pérez Hernando, Madrid

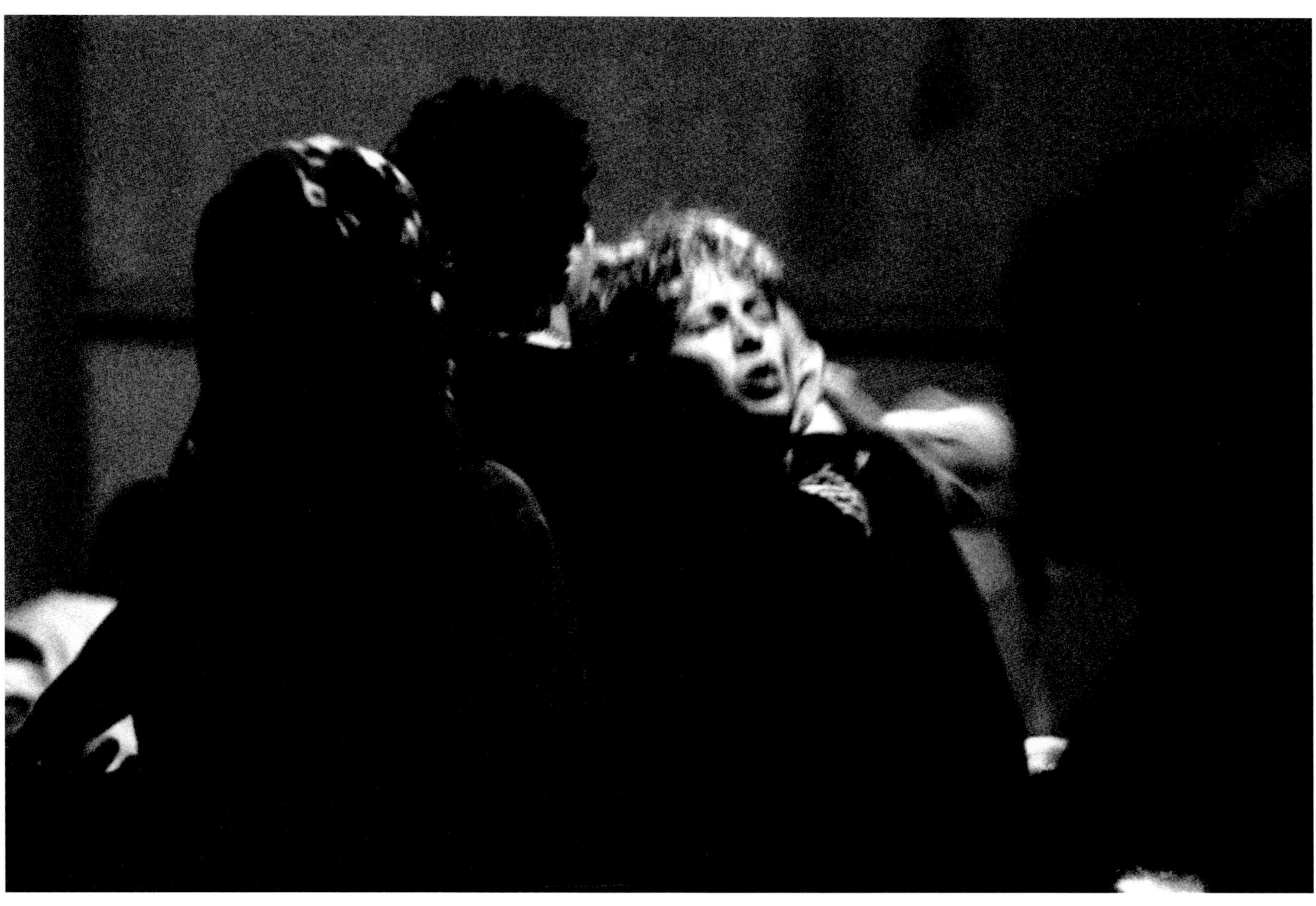

Couleurs Primaires, 2005
Still from DVD
Courtesy the artist and Galería Rafael Pérez Hernando, Madrid

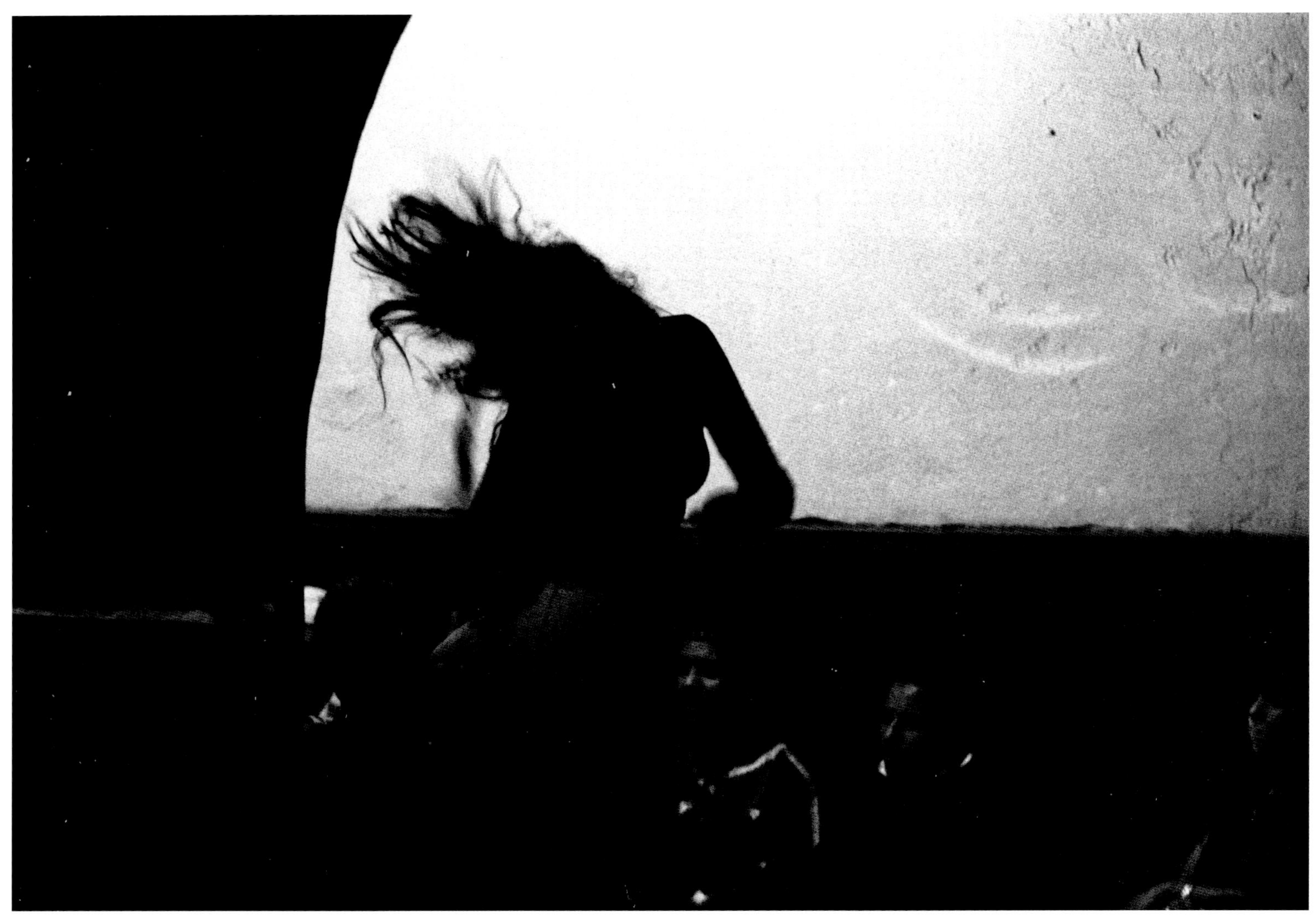

Couleurs Primaires, 2005
Still from DVD
Courtesy the artist and Galería Rafael Pérez Hernando, Madrid

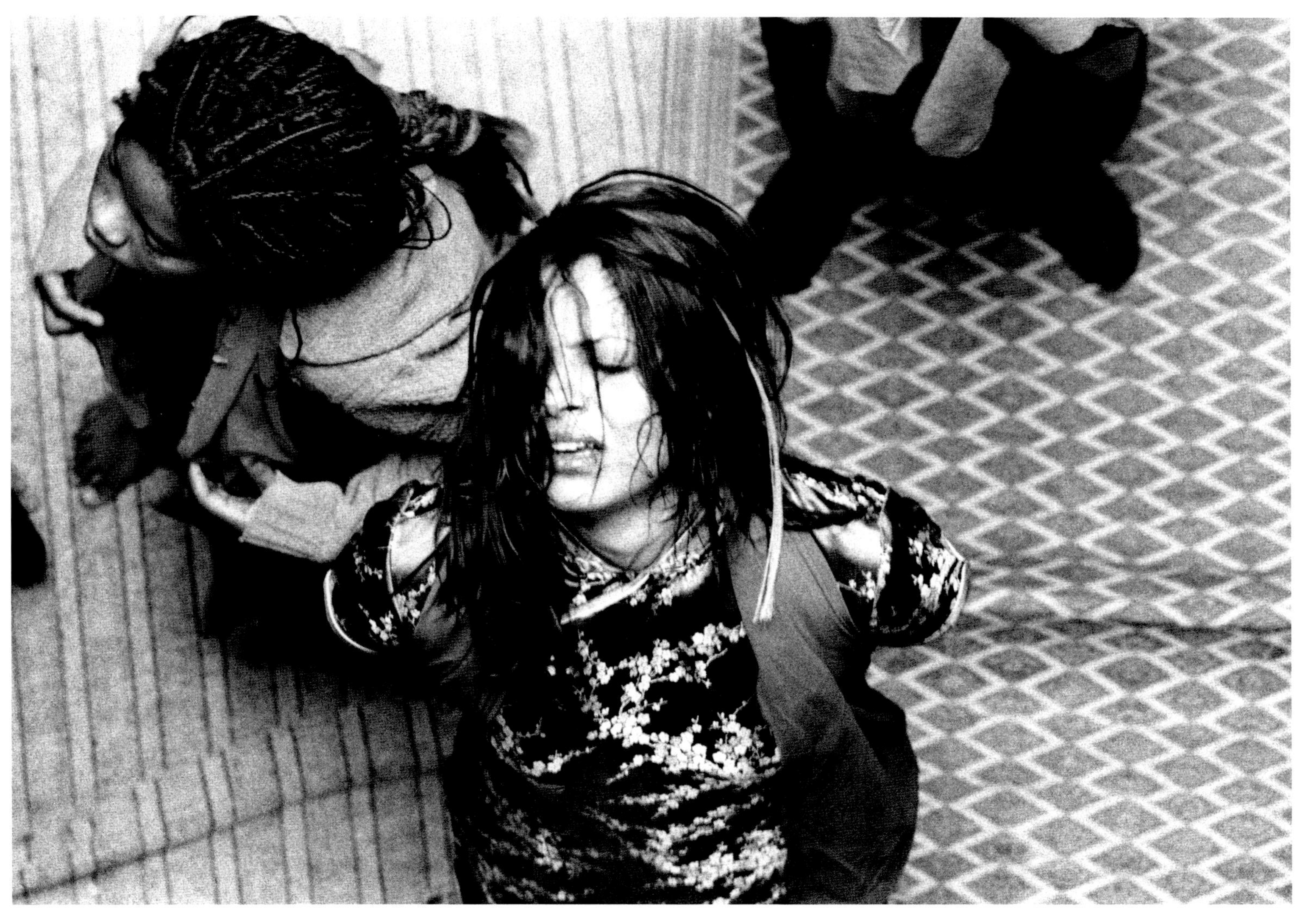

Couleurs Primaires, 2005
Still from DVD
Courtesy the artist and Galería Rafael Pérez Hernando, Madrid

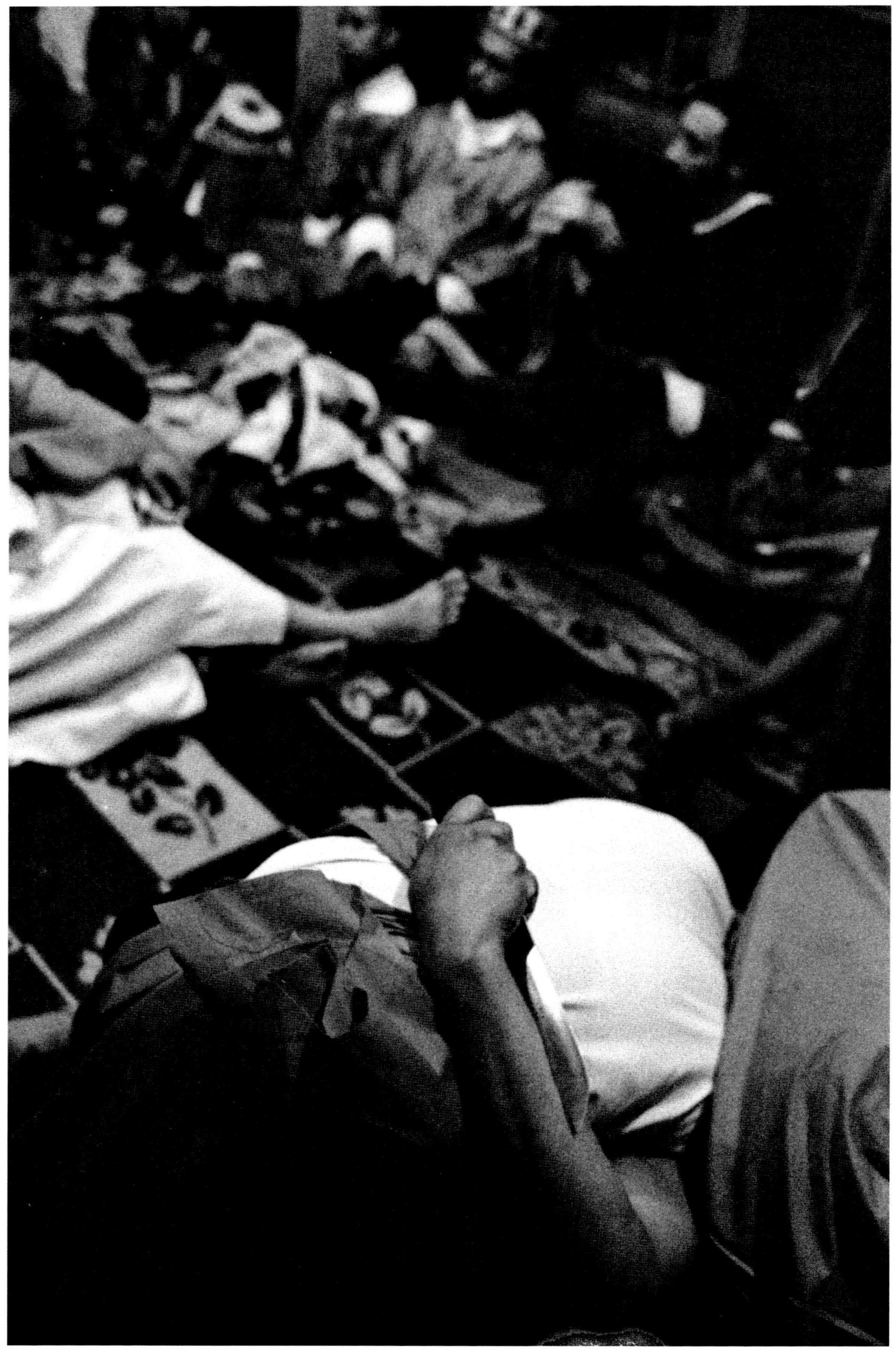

Couleurs Primaires, 2005
Still from DVD
Courtesy the artist and Galería Rafael Pérez Hernando, Madrid

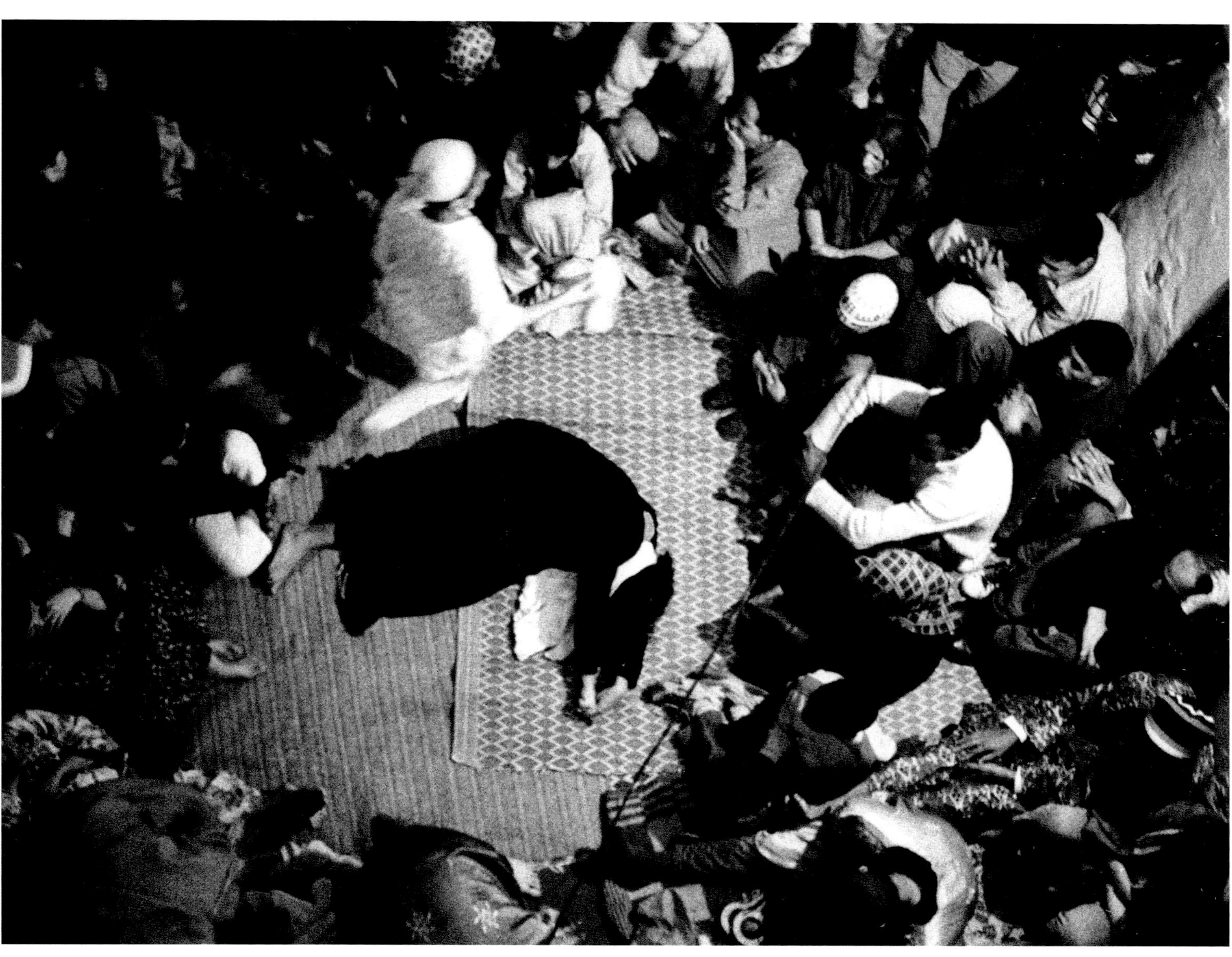

Couleurs Primaires, 2005
Still from DVD
Courtesy the artist and Galería Rafael Pérez Hernando, Madrid

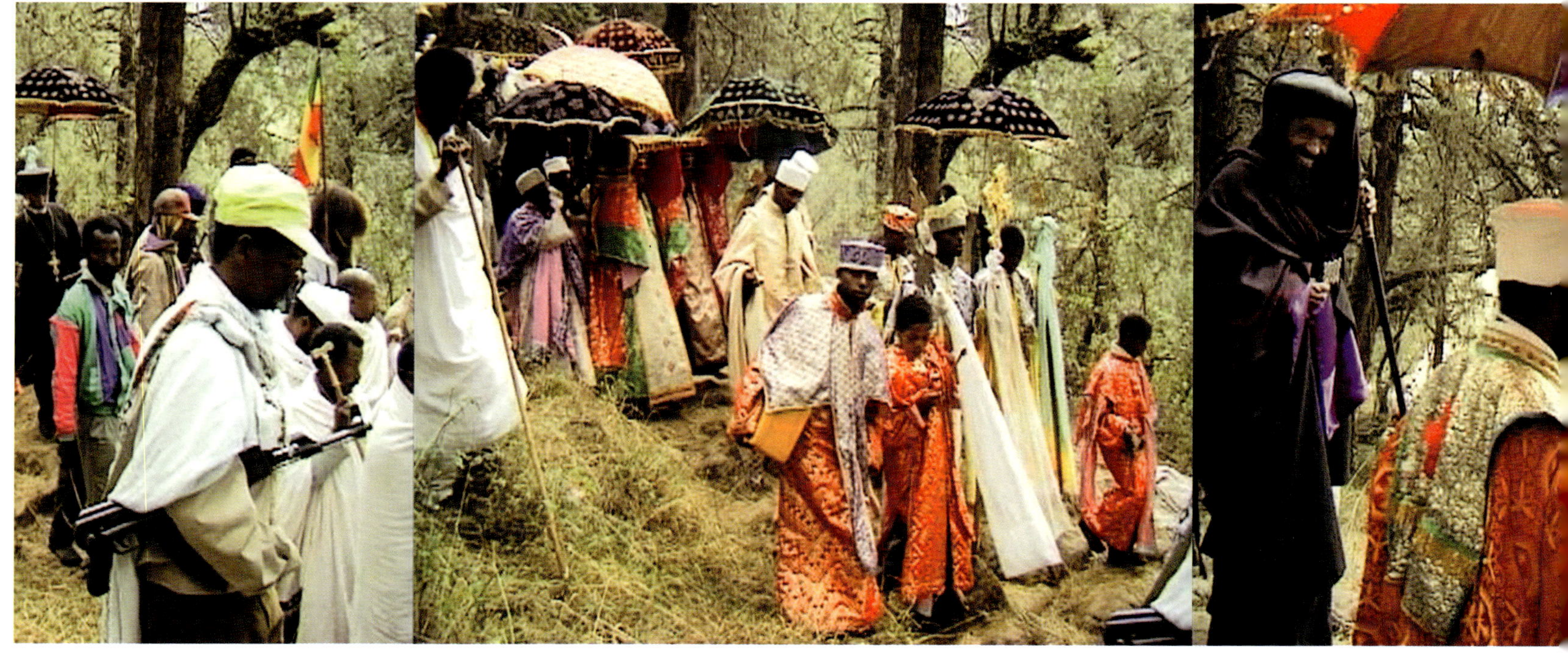

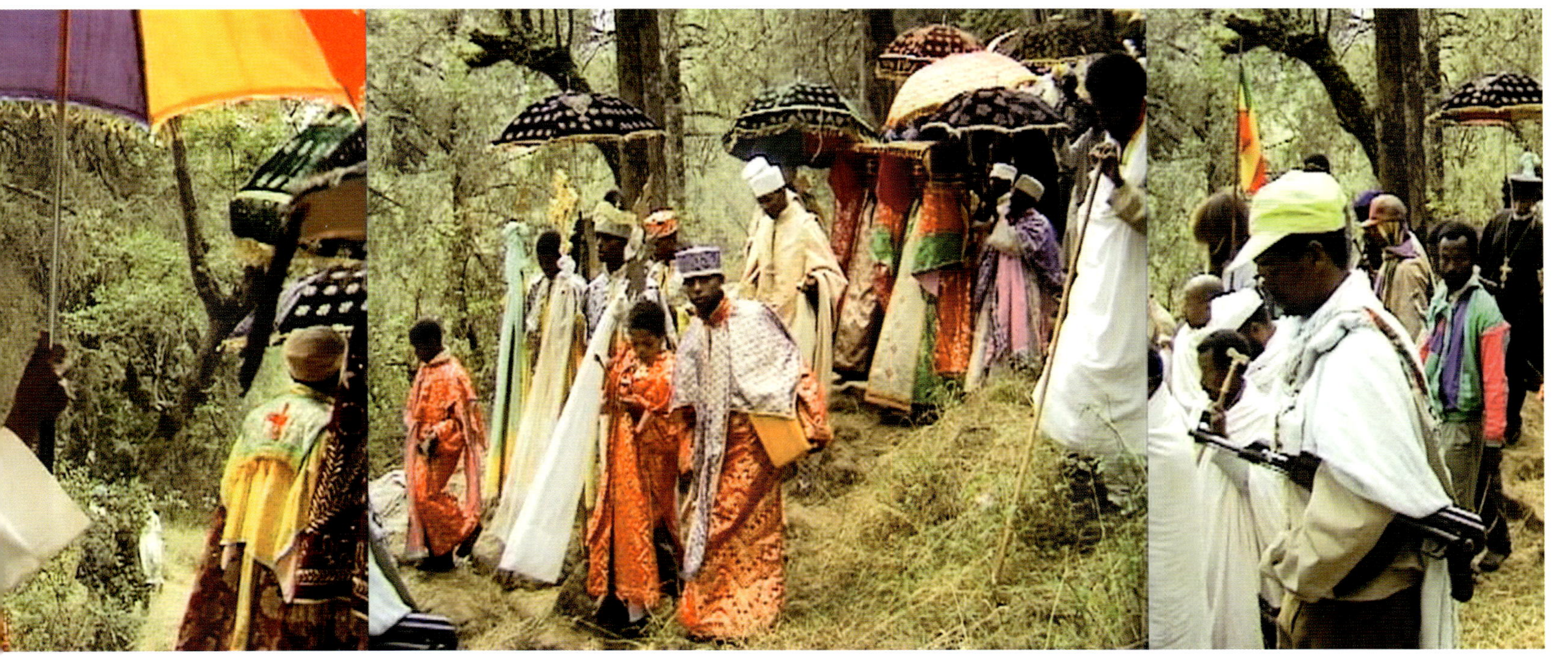

Passage (Version 2), from *Trip to Mount Ziqualla*, 2005
Inkjet print, 15.75 x 106.3 in. (40 x 270 cm)
Courtesy the artist

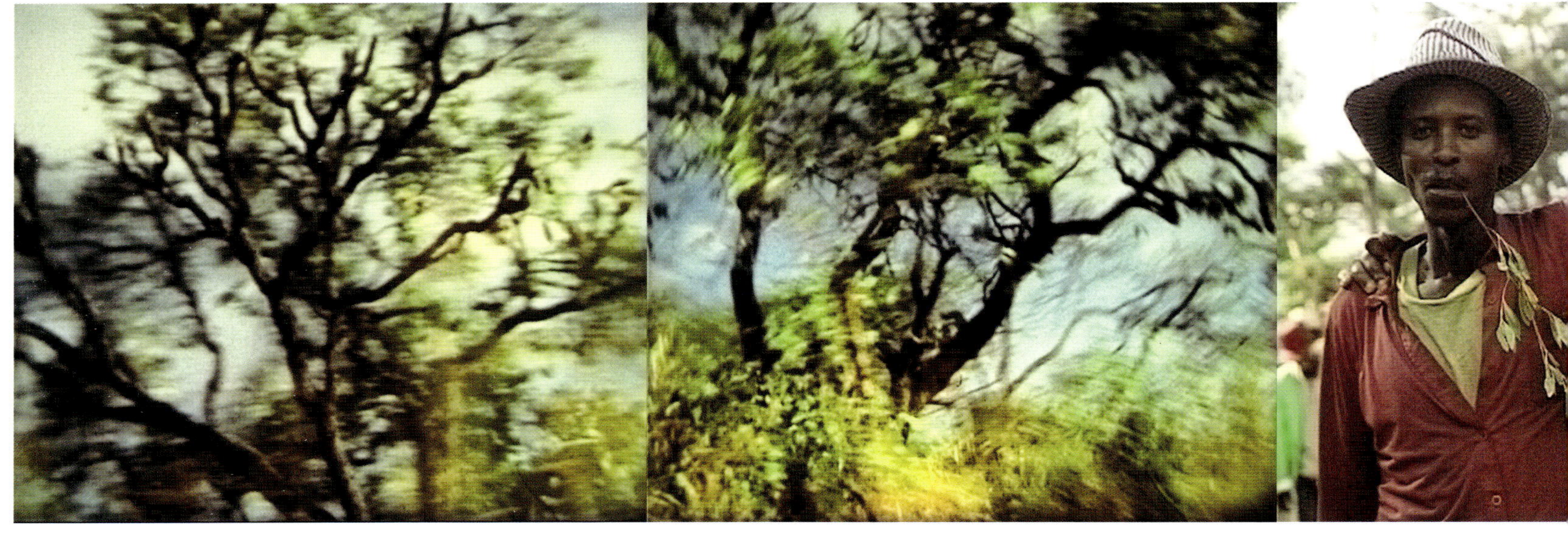

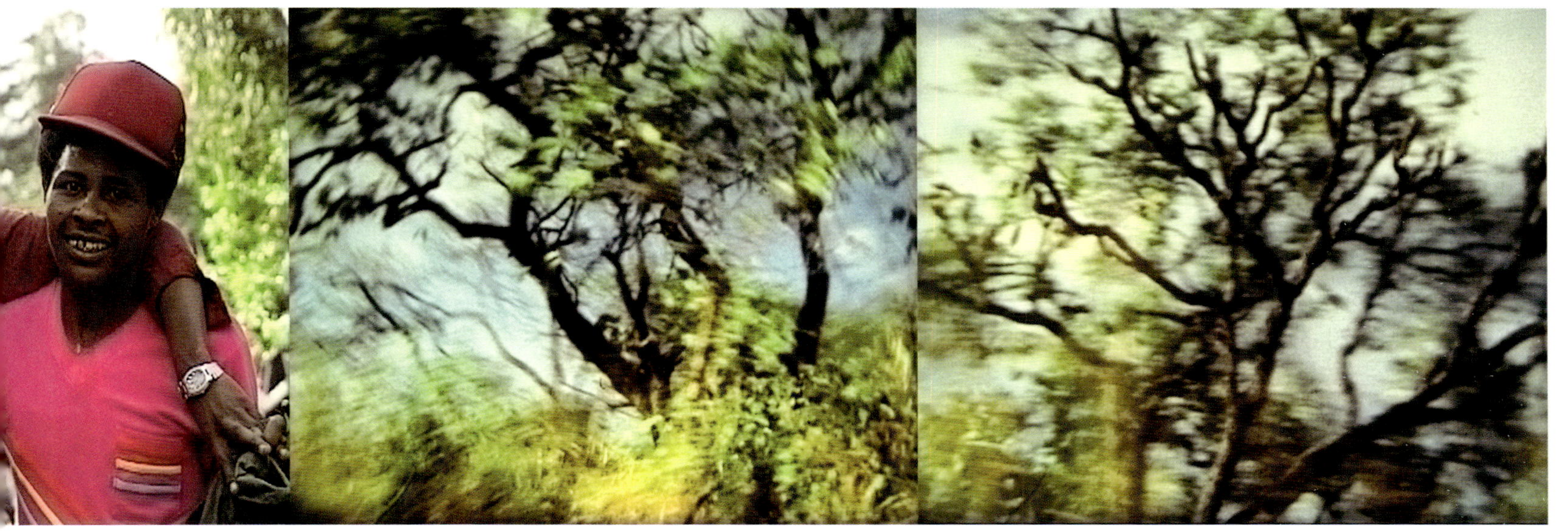

Wild Trees, from *Trip to Mount Ziqualla*, 2005
Inkjet print, 15.75 x 106.3 in. (40 x 270 cm)
Courtesy the artist

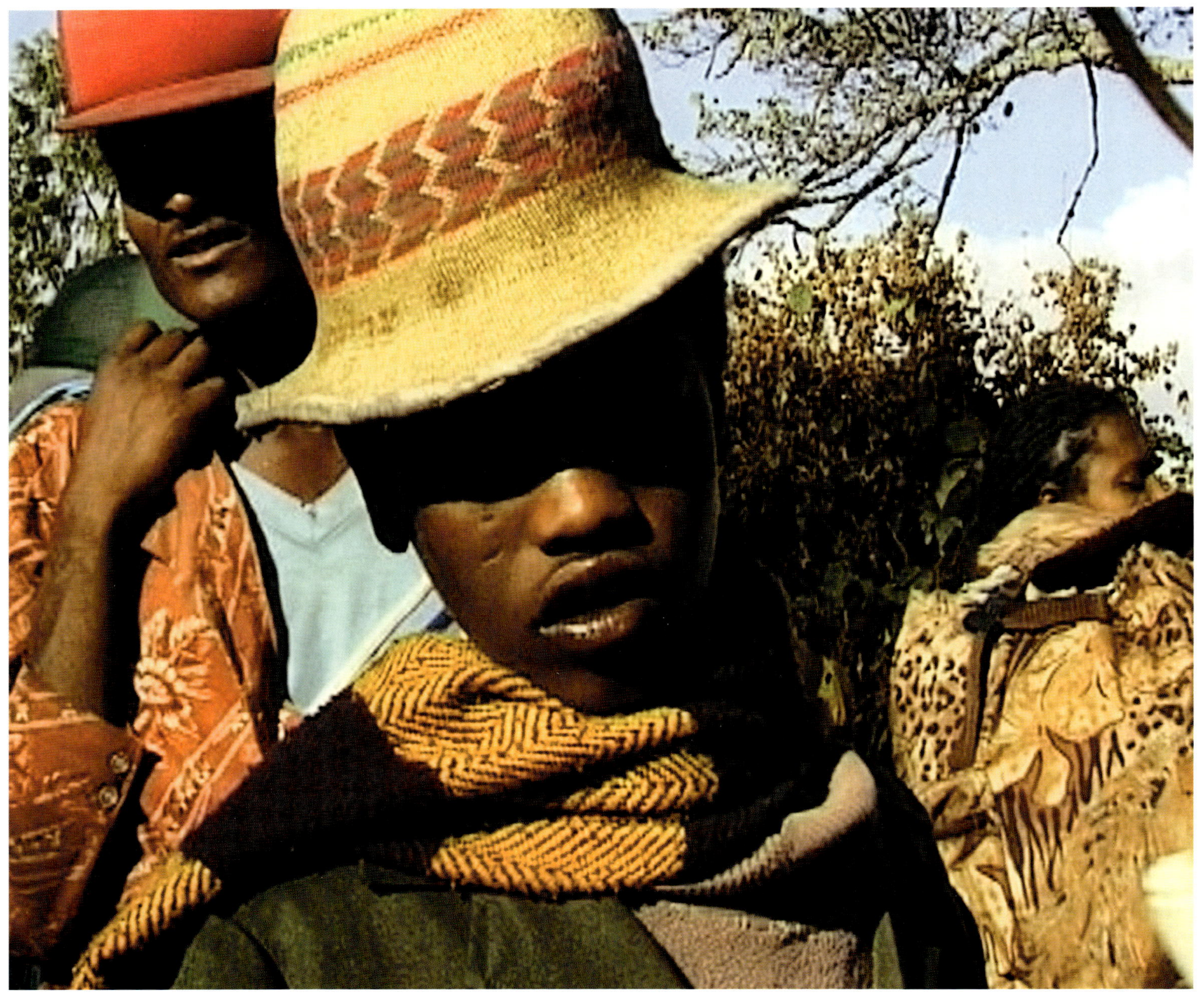

Girl, from *Trip to Mount Ziqualla*, 2005
Still from video
Courtesy the artist

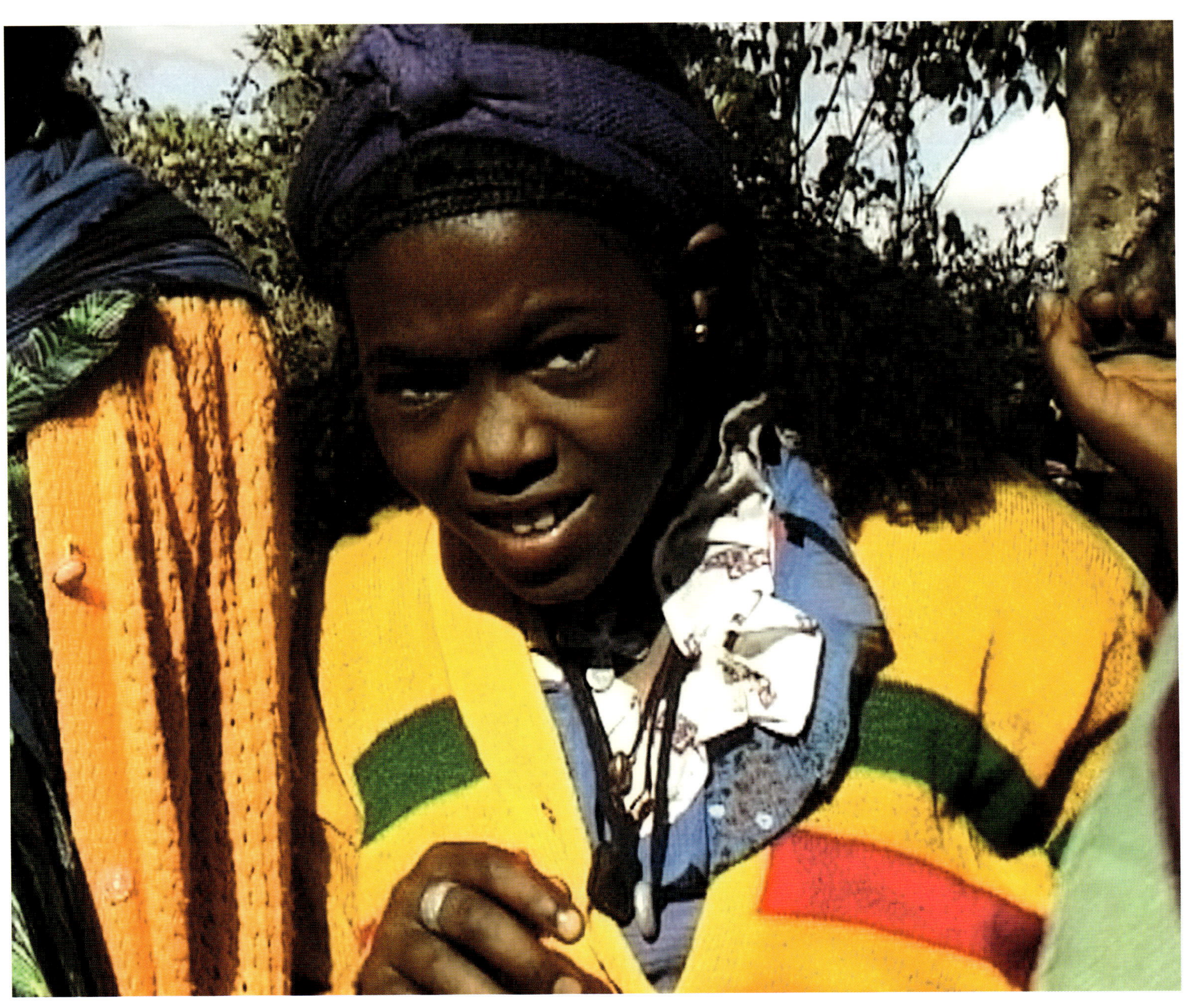

Boy, from *Trip to Mount Ziqualla*, 2005
Still from video
Courtesy the artist

Kay Hassan

Fatou Kandé Senghor

Zarina Bhimji

Otobong Nkanga

Hentje van der Merwe

Allan deSouza

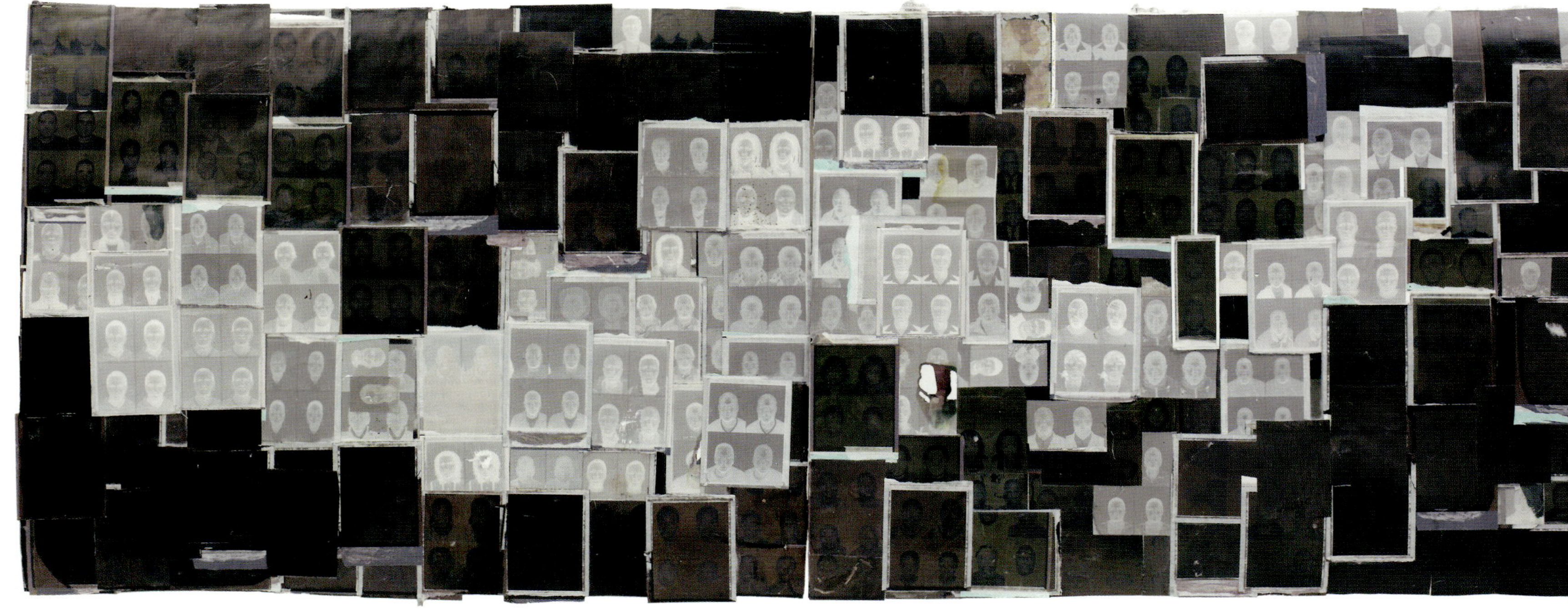

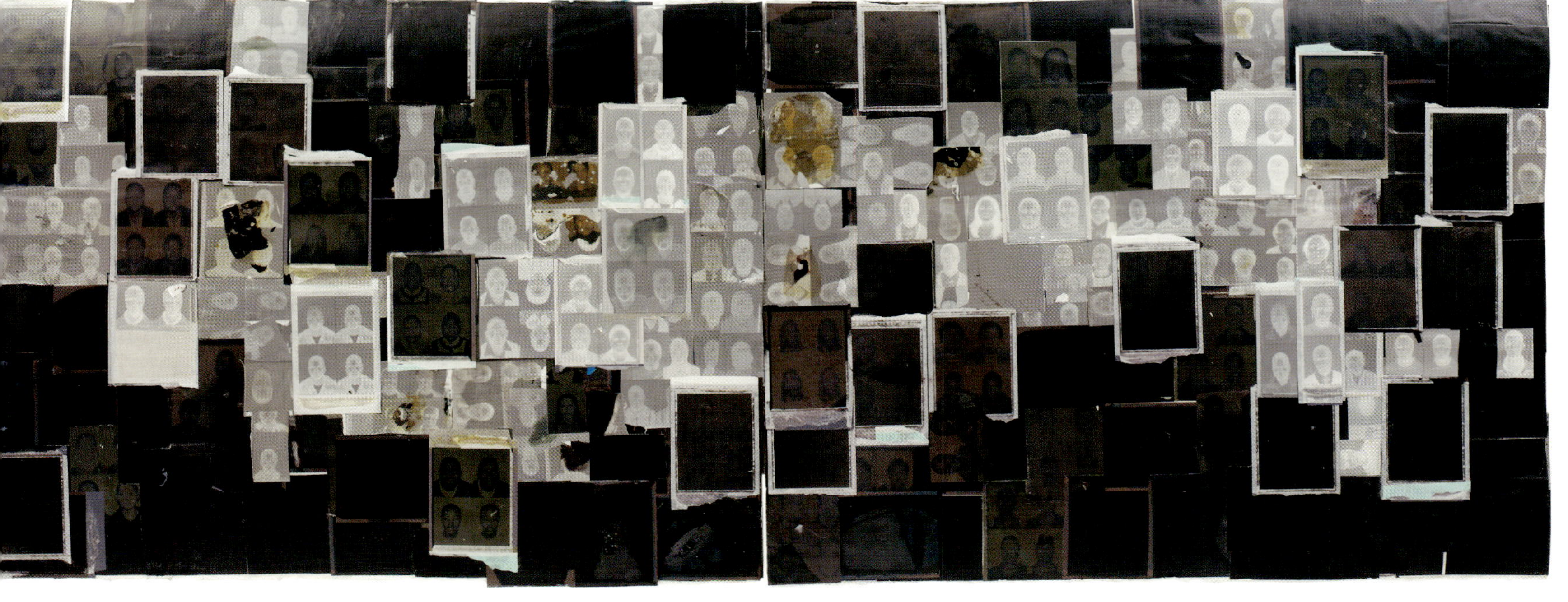

Negatives 1–6, 2006
Installation, 6 pieces, each 22.4 x 29.9 in. (57 x 76 cm)
Courtesy the artist

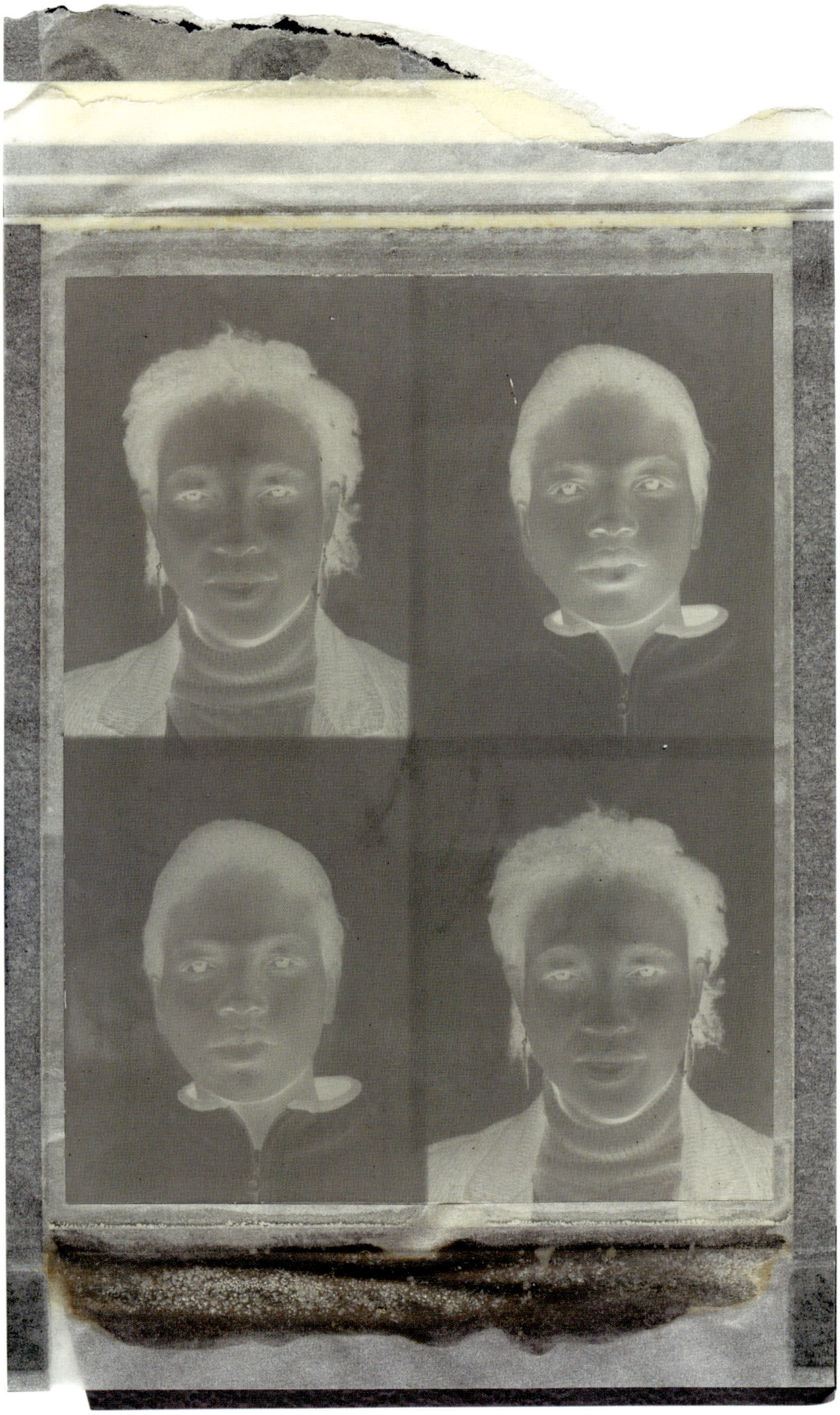

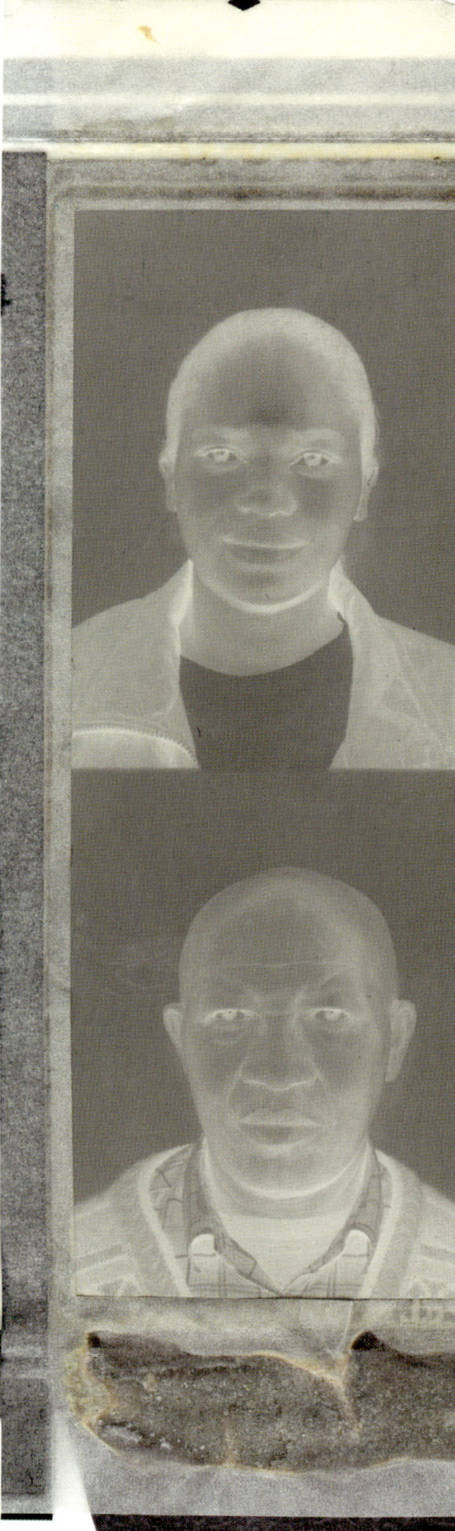

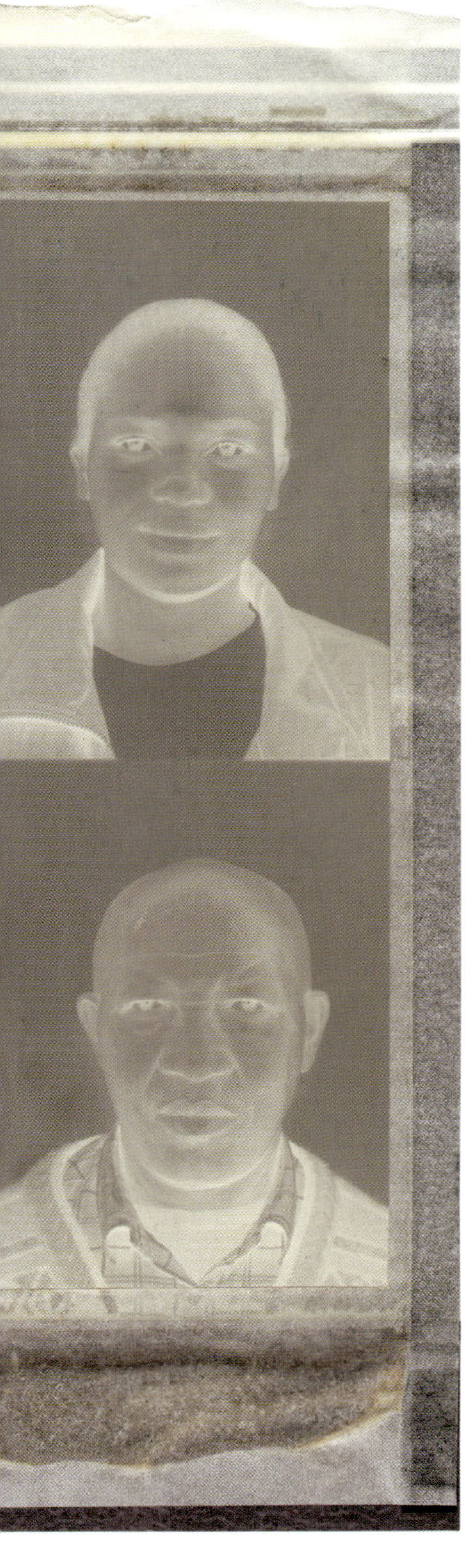

Negatives 1–6 (details), 2006
Installation, 6 pieces, each 22.4 x 29.9 in. (57 x 76 cm)
Courtesy the artist

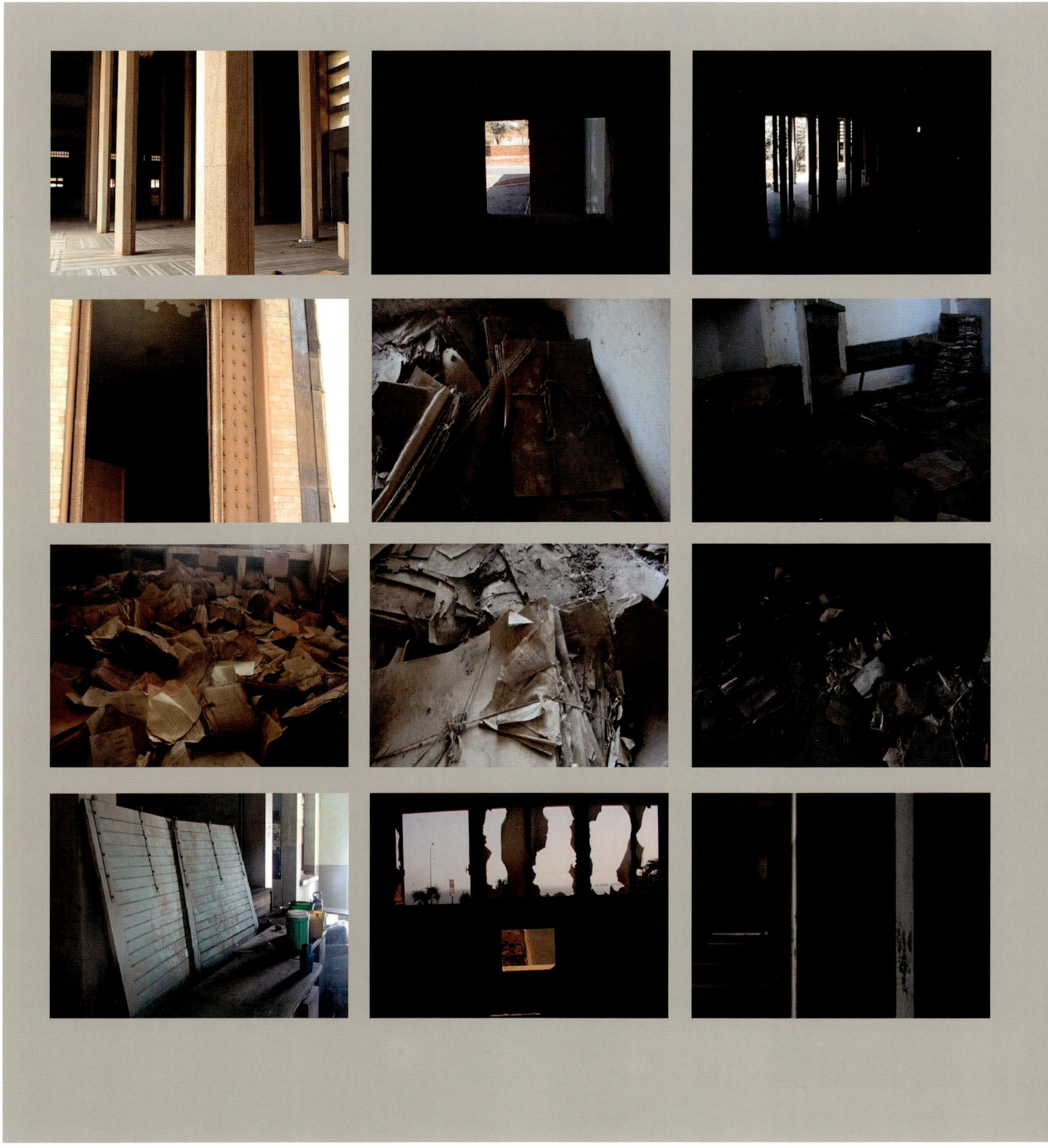

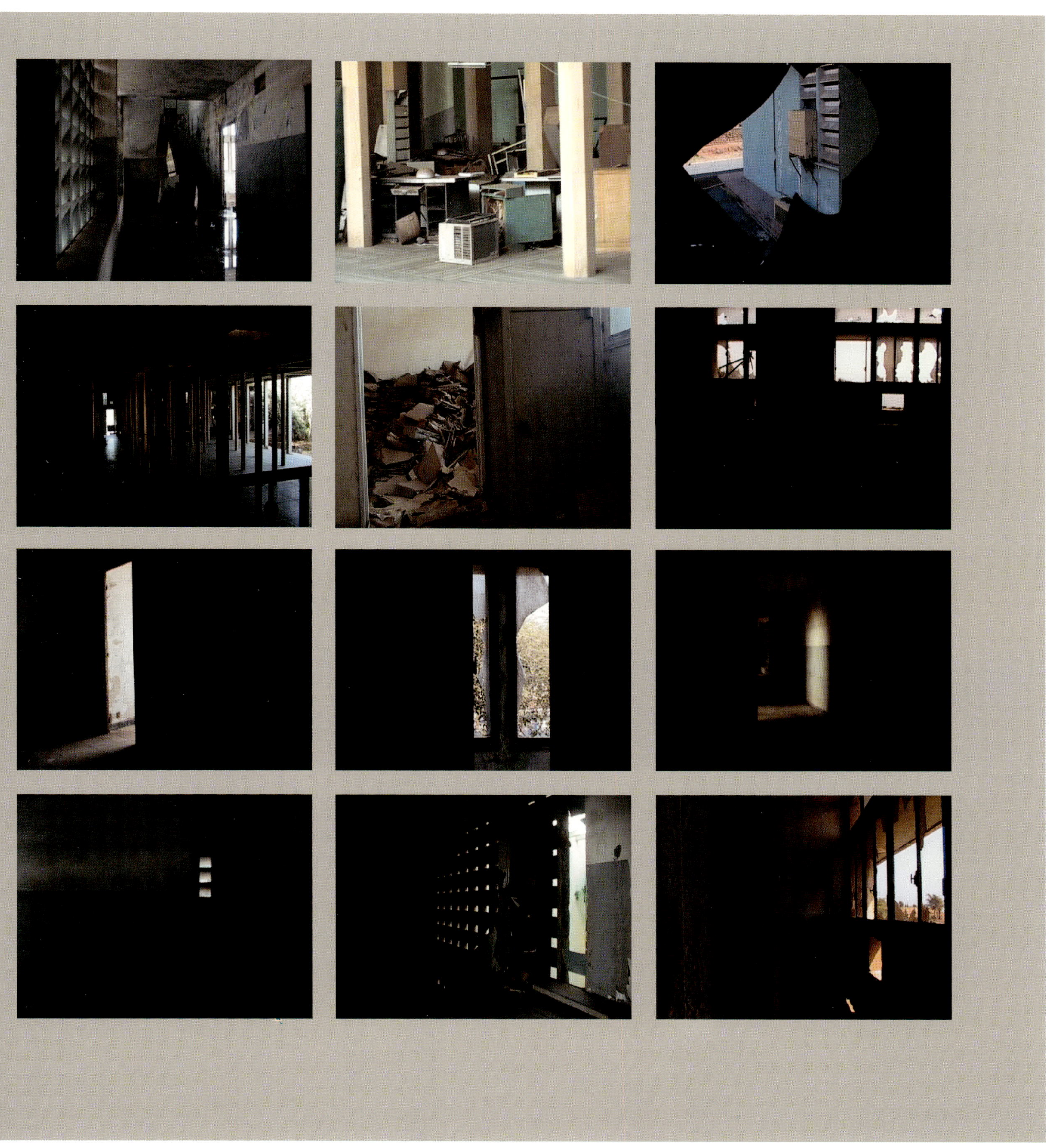

Palais de Justice, 2005
48 transparencies on light table, each 4 x 5 in. (10.2 x 12.7 cm)
Courtesy the artist

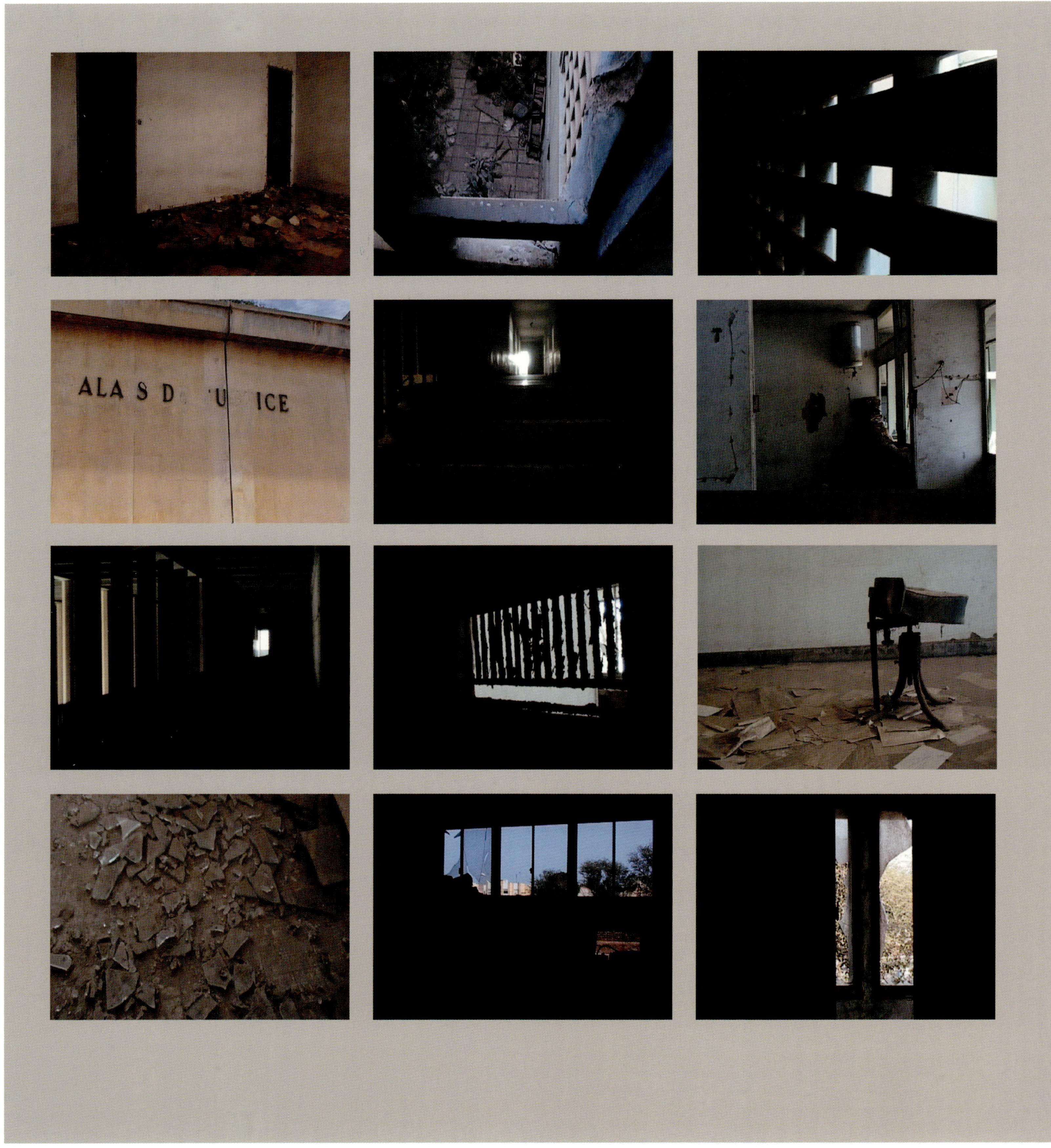
ALA S D U ICE

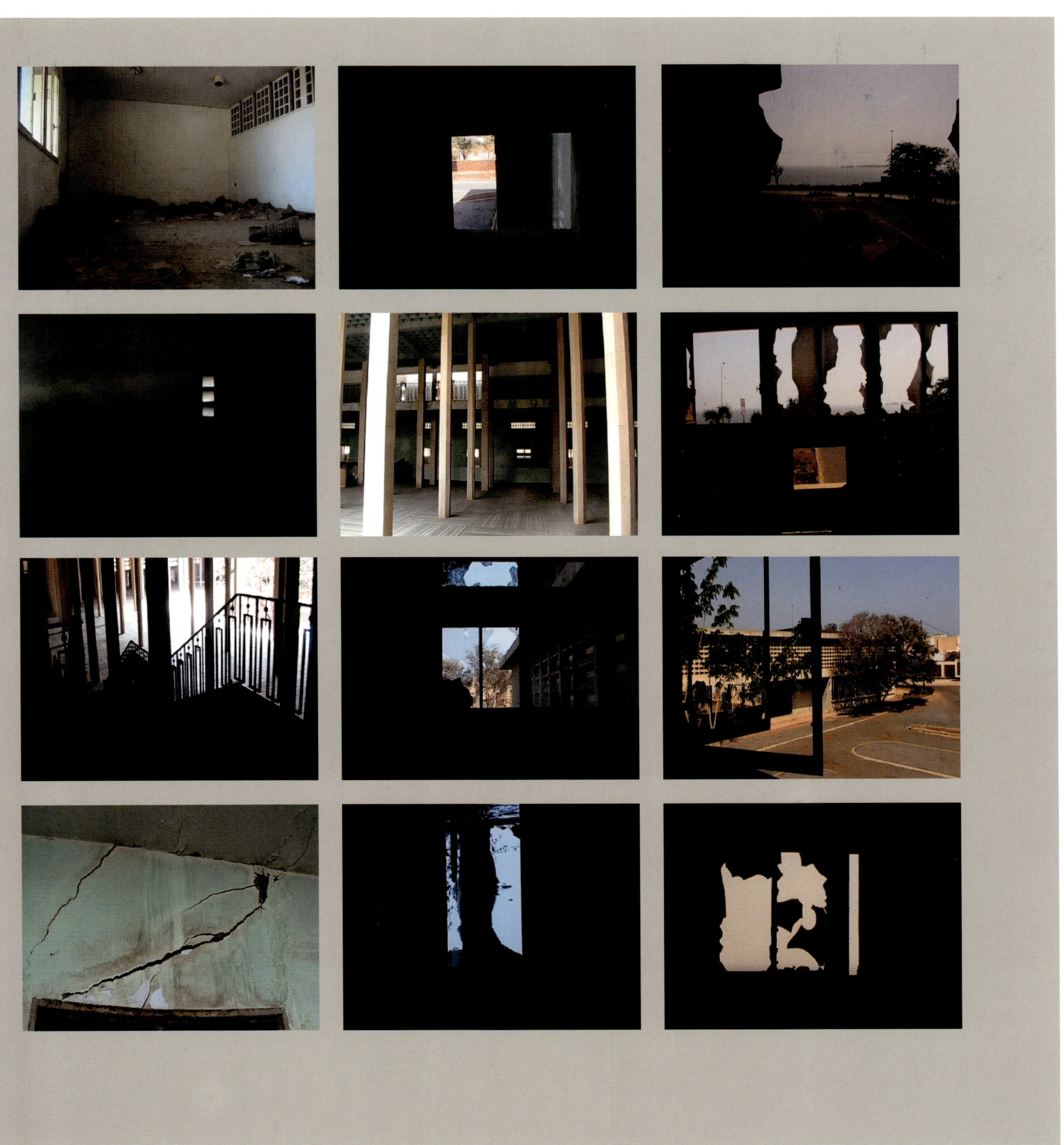

Palais de Justice, 2005
48 transparencies on light table, each 4 x 5 in. (10.2 x 12.7 cm)
Courtesy the artist

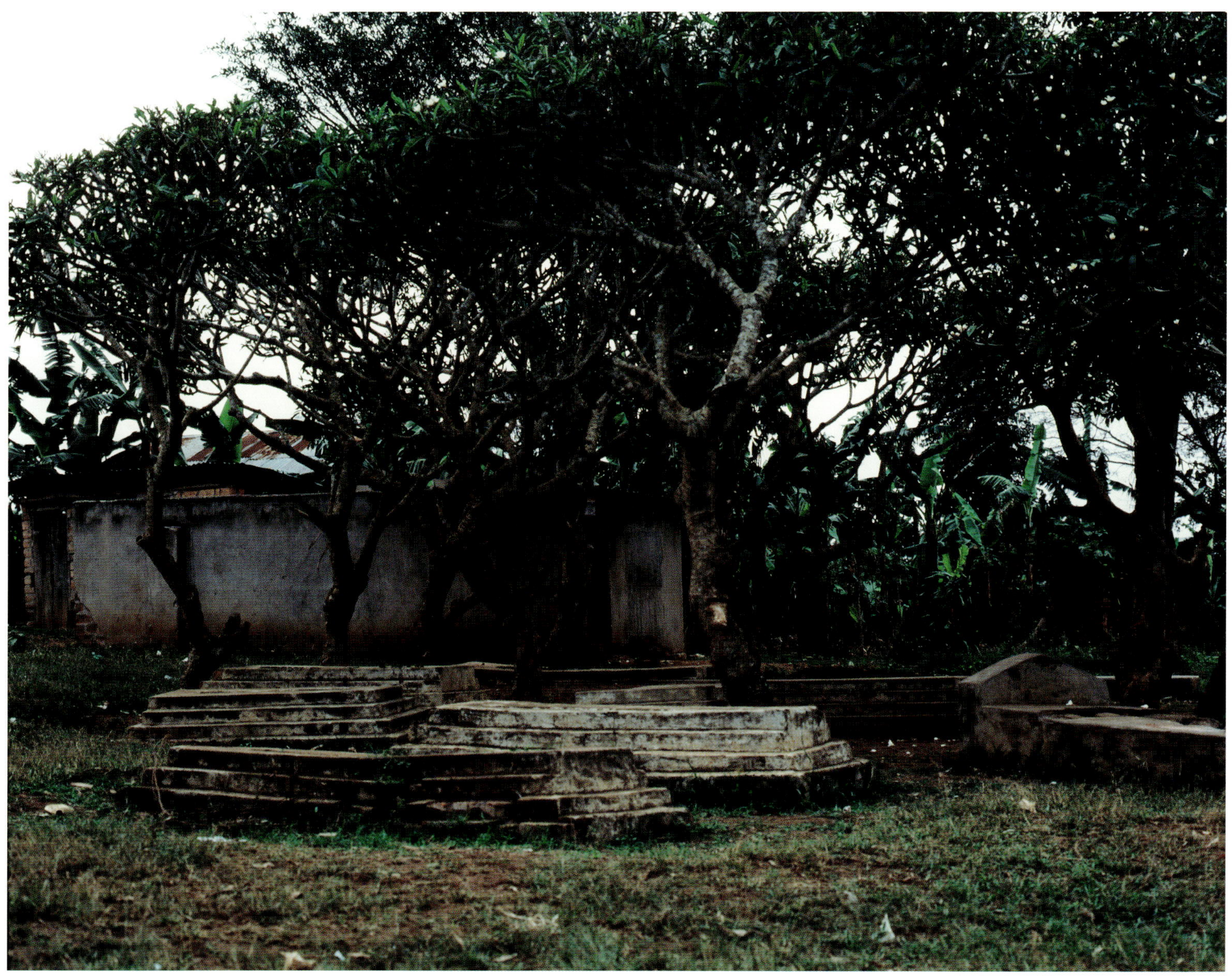

Untitled (Uganda), 2002
Chromogenic print, 51.2 x 66.9 in. (130 x 170 cm)
Courtesy ARS, New York

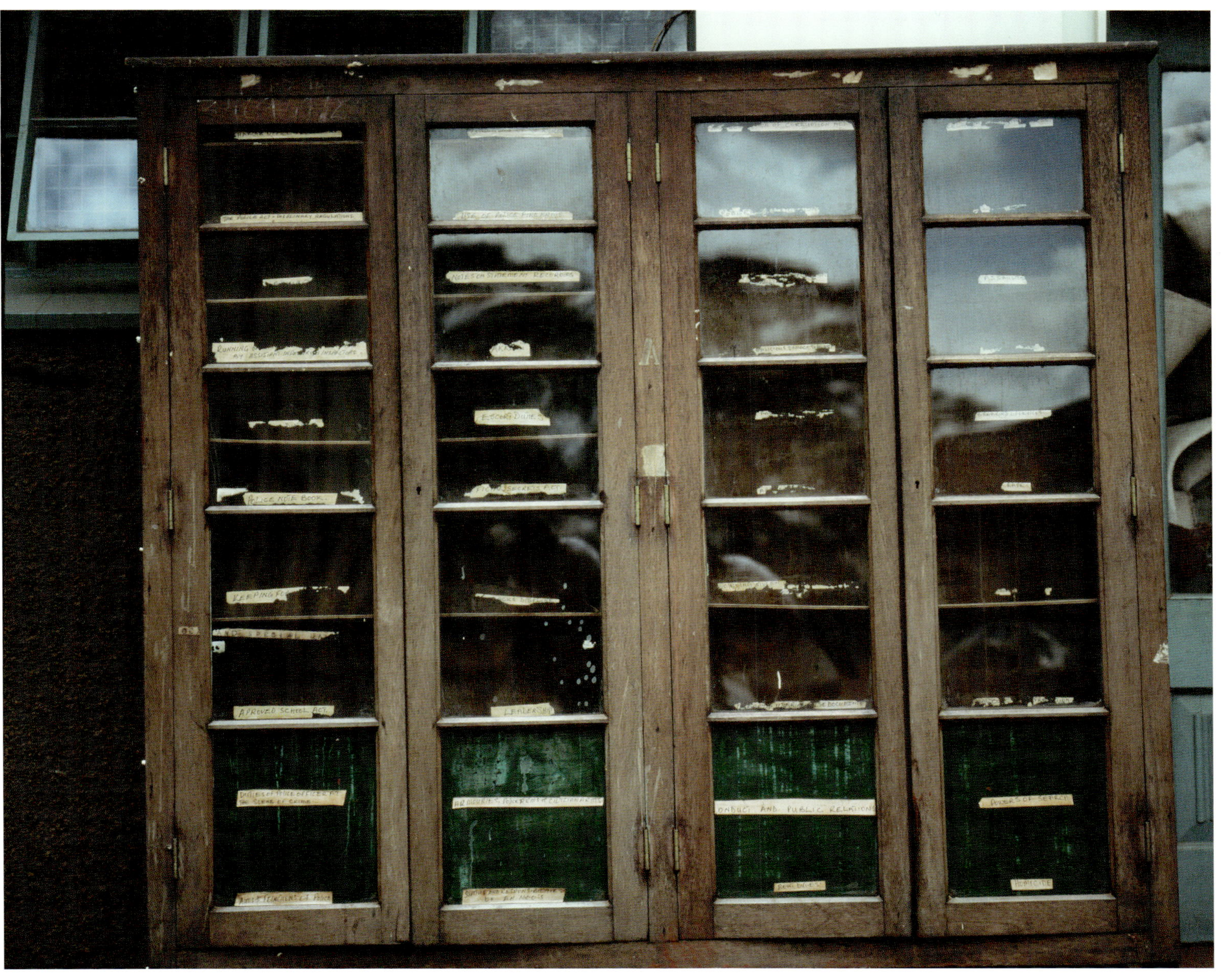

Untitled (Uganda), 2002
Chromogenic print, 51.2 x 66.9 in. (130 x 170 cm)
Courtesy ARS, New York

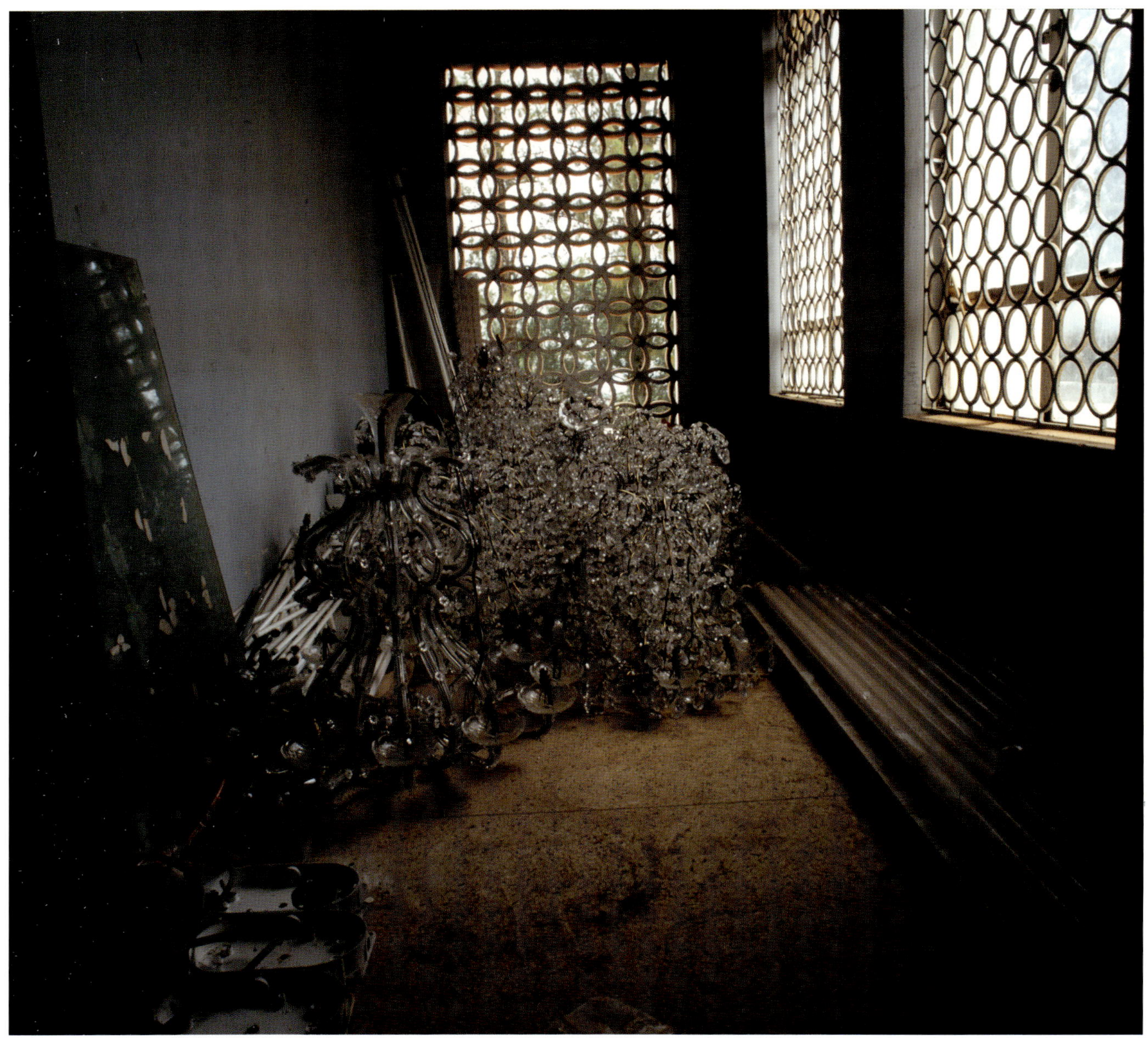

Untitled (Uganda), 2002
Chromogenic print, 51.2 x 66.9 in. (130 x 170 cm)
Courtesy ARS, New York

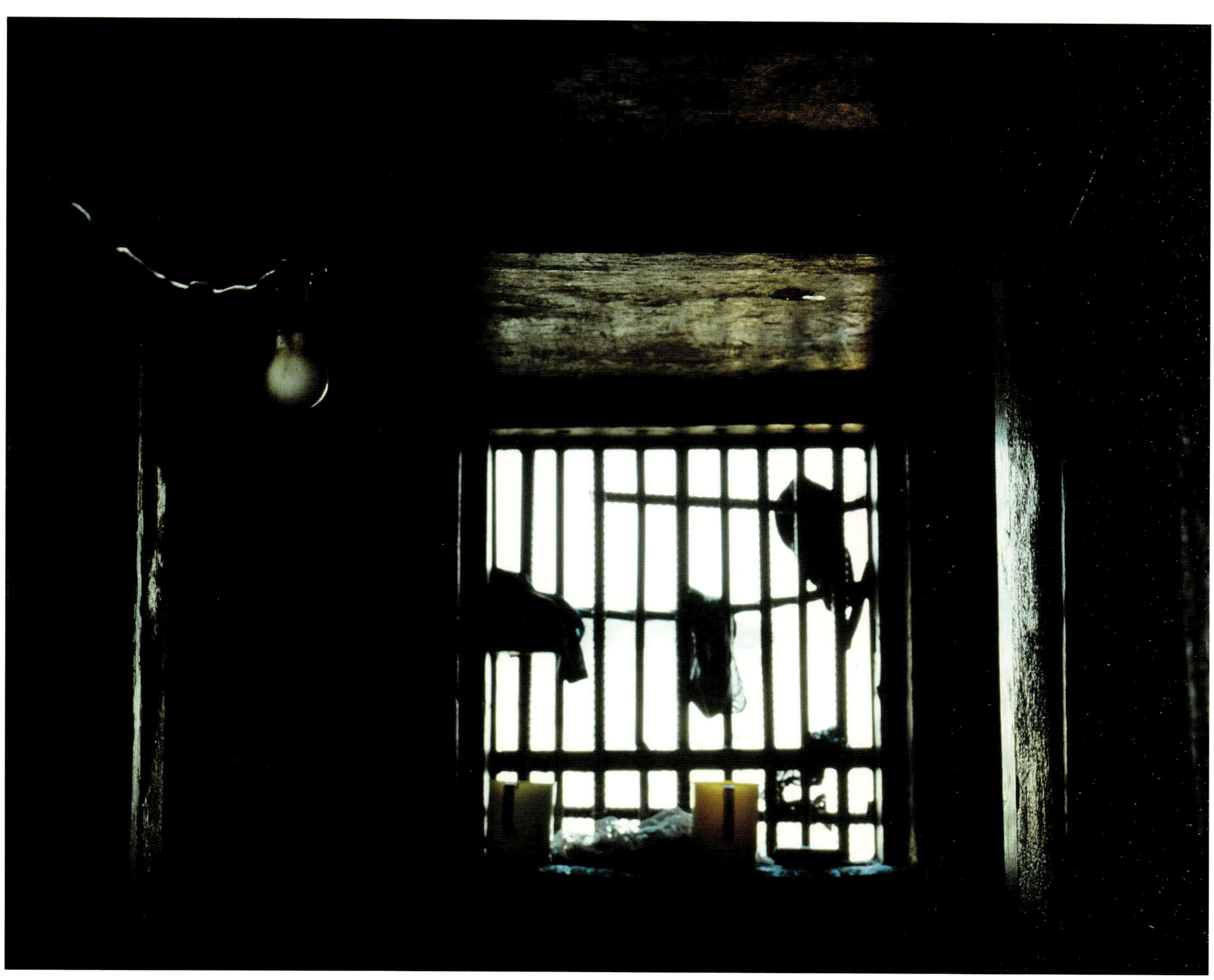

Untitled (Uganda), 2002
Chromogenic print, 51.2 x 66.9 in. (130 x 170 cm)
Courtesy ARS, New York

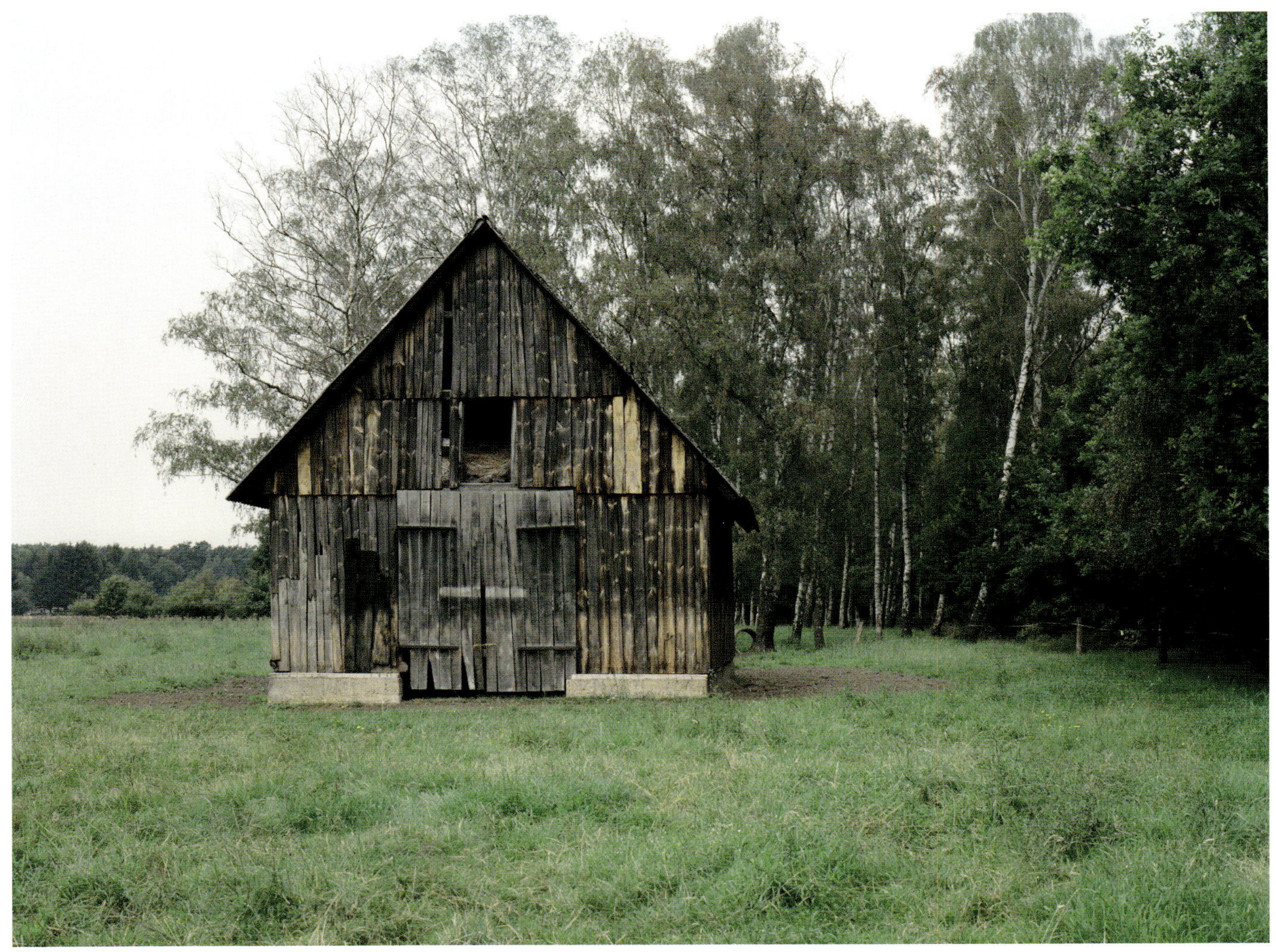

Emptied Remains: Barn, Hertel–Rutenmühle, 2004
Chromogenic print, 34.25 x 45.7 in. (87 x 116 cm)
Courtesy the artist and Leader+, Kunstverein & Stiftung Springhornhof, Neuenkirchen, Germany

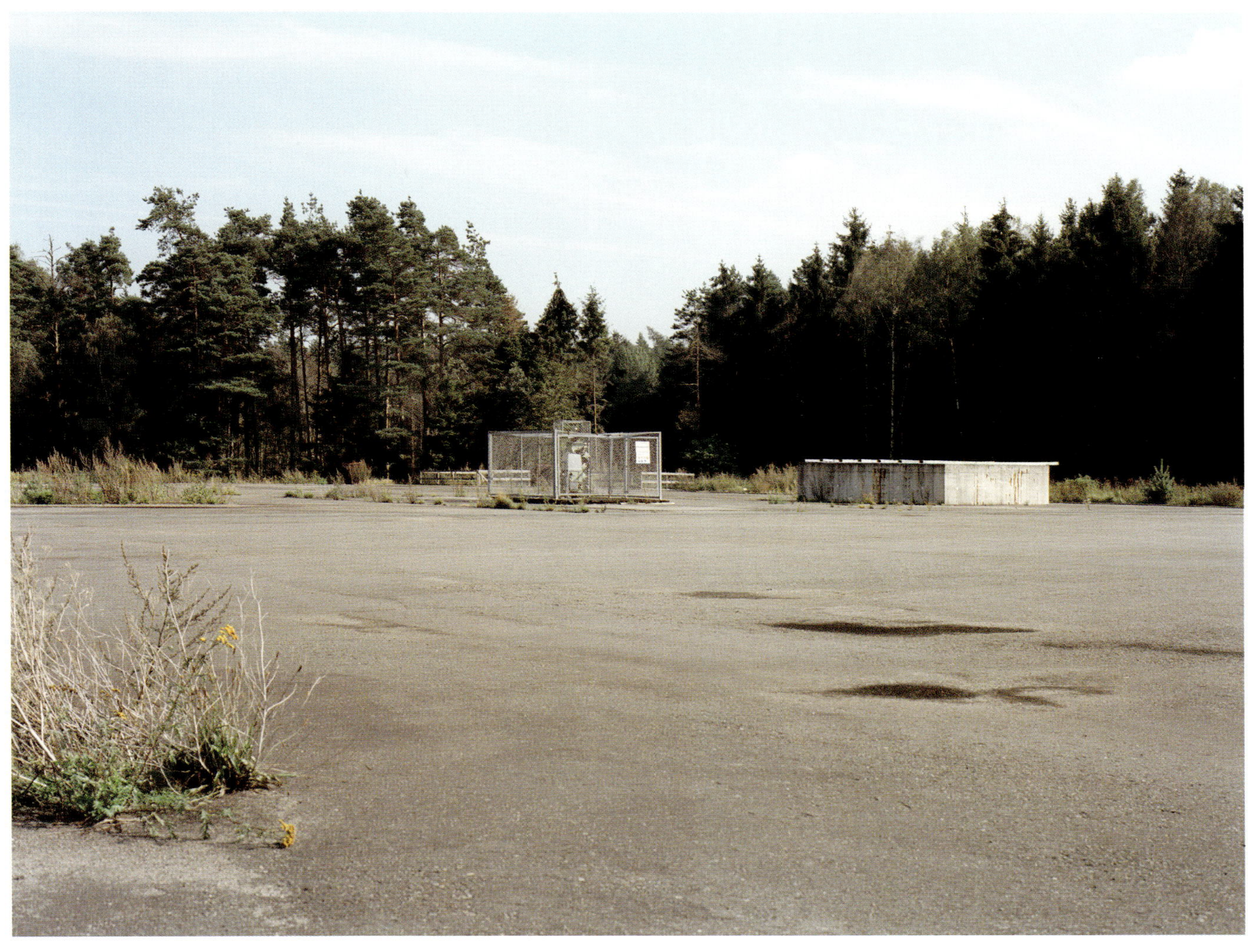

Things have fallen III, 2004–05
Chromogenic print, 23.6 x 35.4 in. (60 x 90 cm)
Courtesy the artist

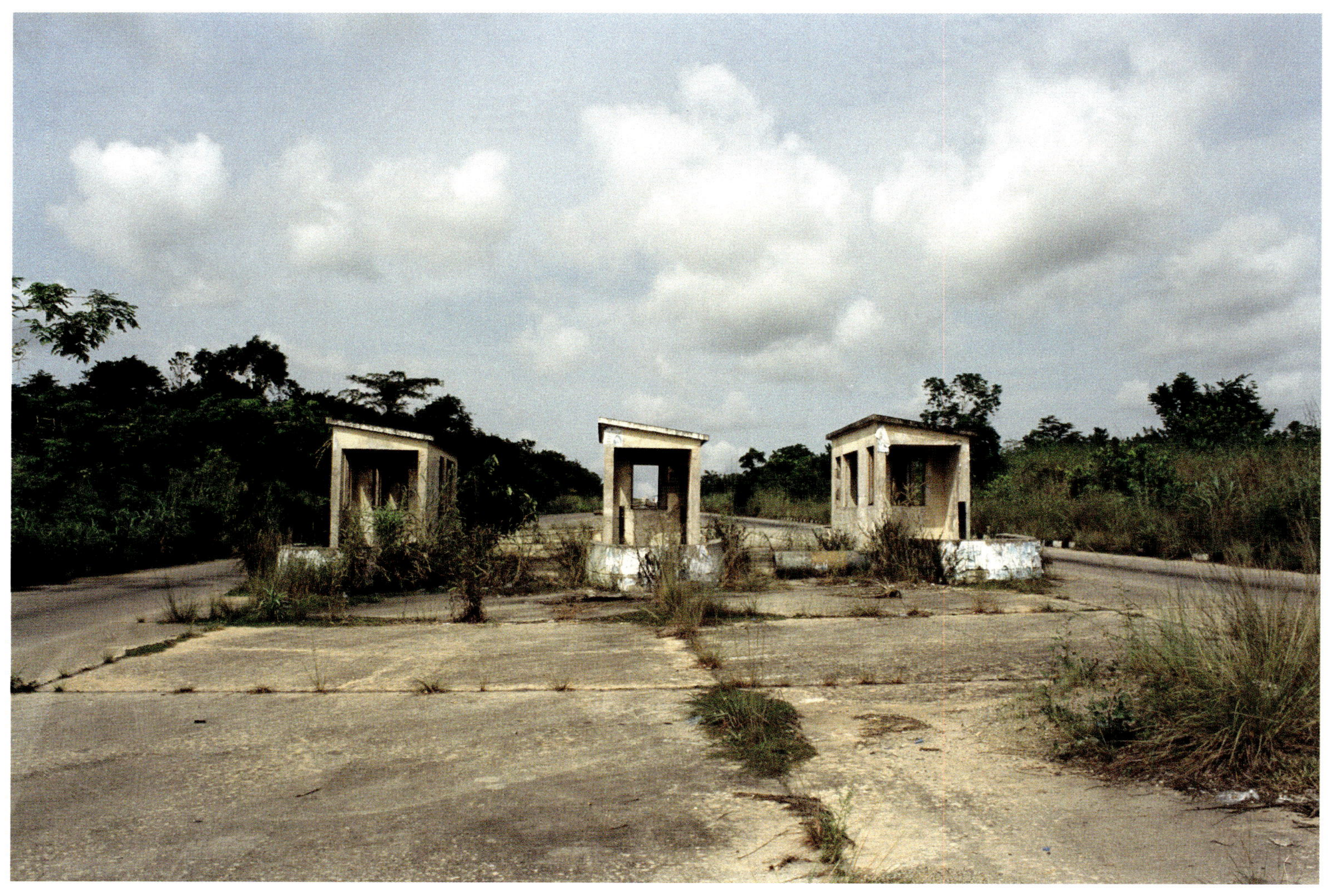

Emptied Remains: Check point, 2004–05
Chromogenic print, 23.6 x 35.4 in. (60 x 90 cm)
Courtesy the artist

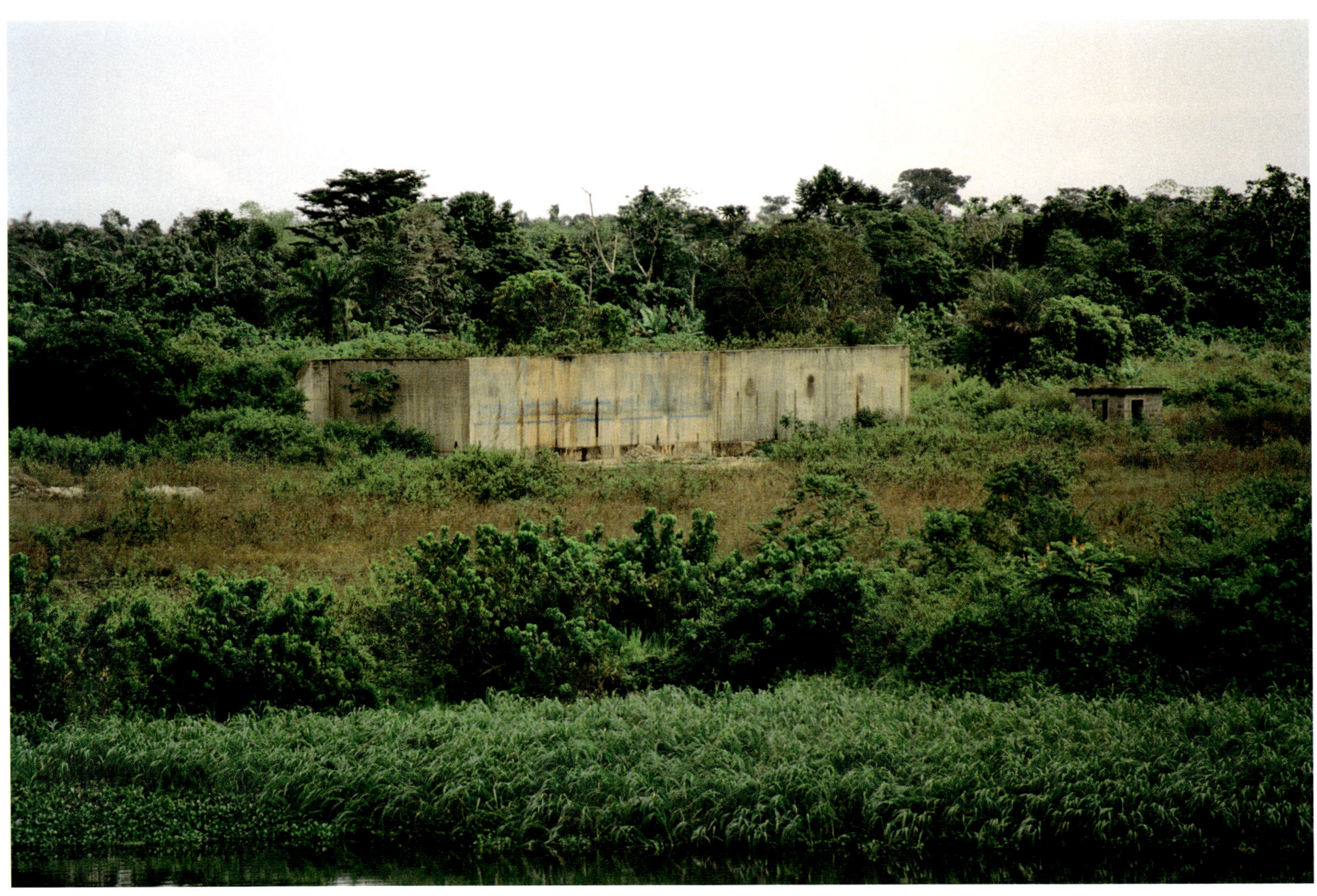

Emptied Remains: Gas field vestige, Wisselshorst, 2004–05
Chromogenic print, 34.25 x 45.7 in. (87 x 116 cm)
Courtesy the artist and Leader+, Kunstverein & Stiftung Springhornhof, Neuenkirchen, Germany

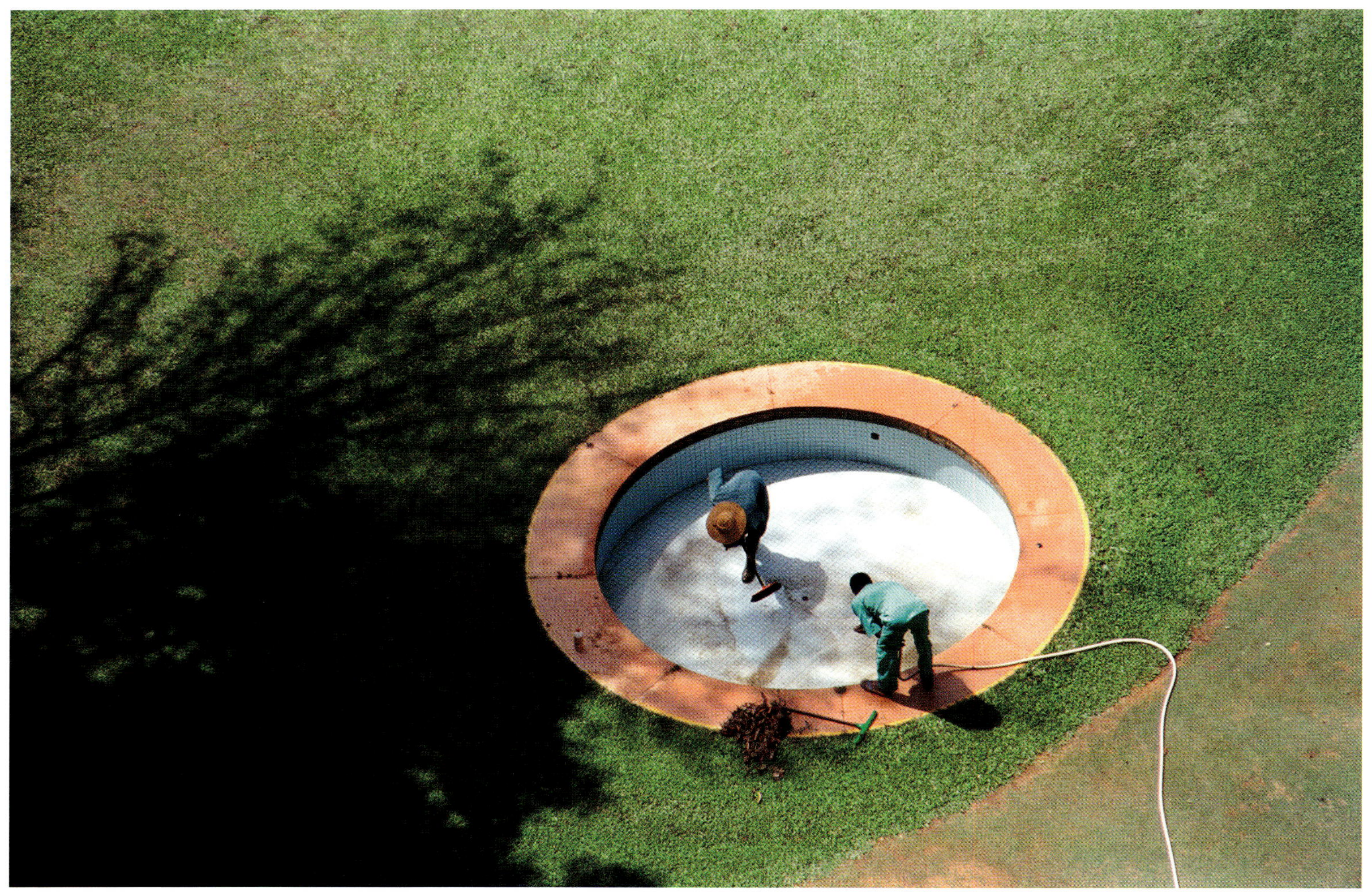

Workmen in pool 1, 2005
Chromogenic print, 23.6 x 35.4 in. (60 x 90 cm)
Courtesy the artist

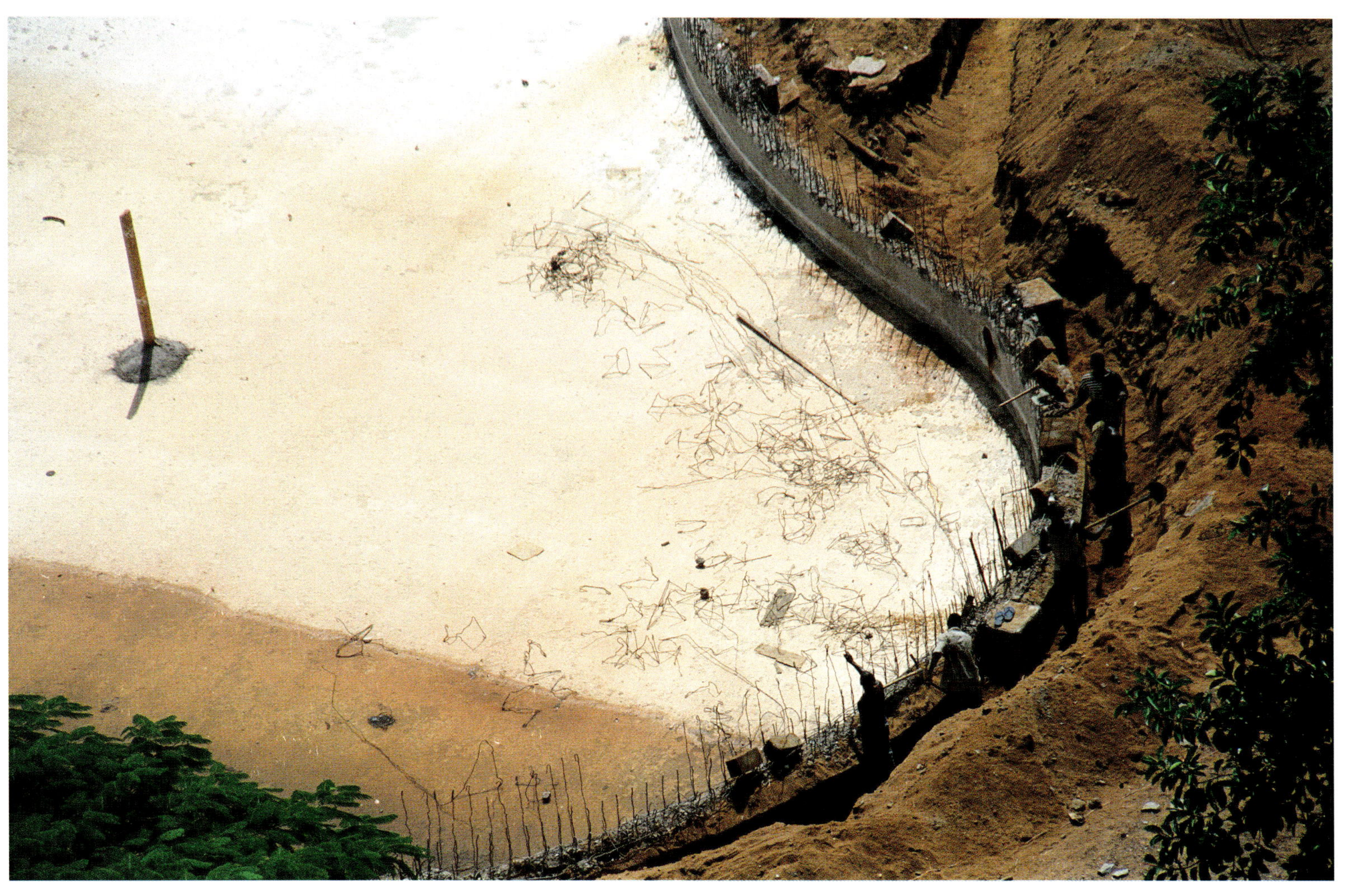

Working men II, 2005
Chromogenic print, 23.6 x 35.4 in. (60 x 90 cm)
Courtesy the artist

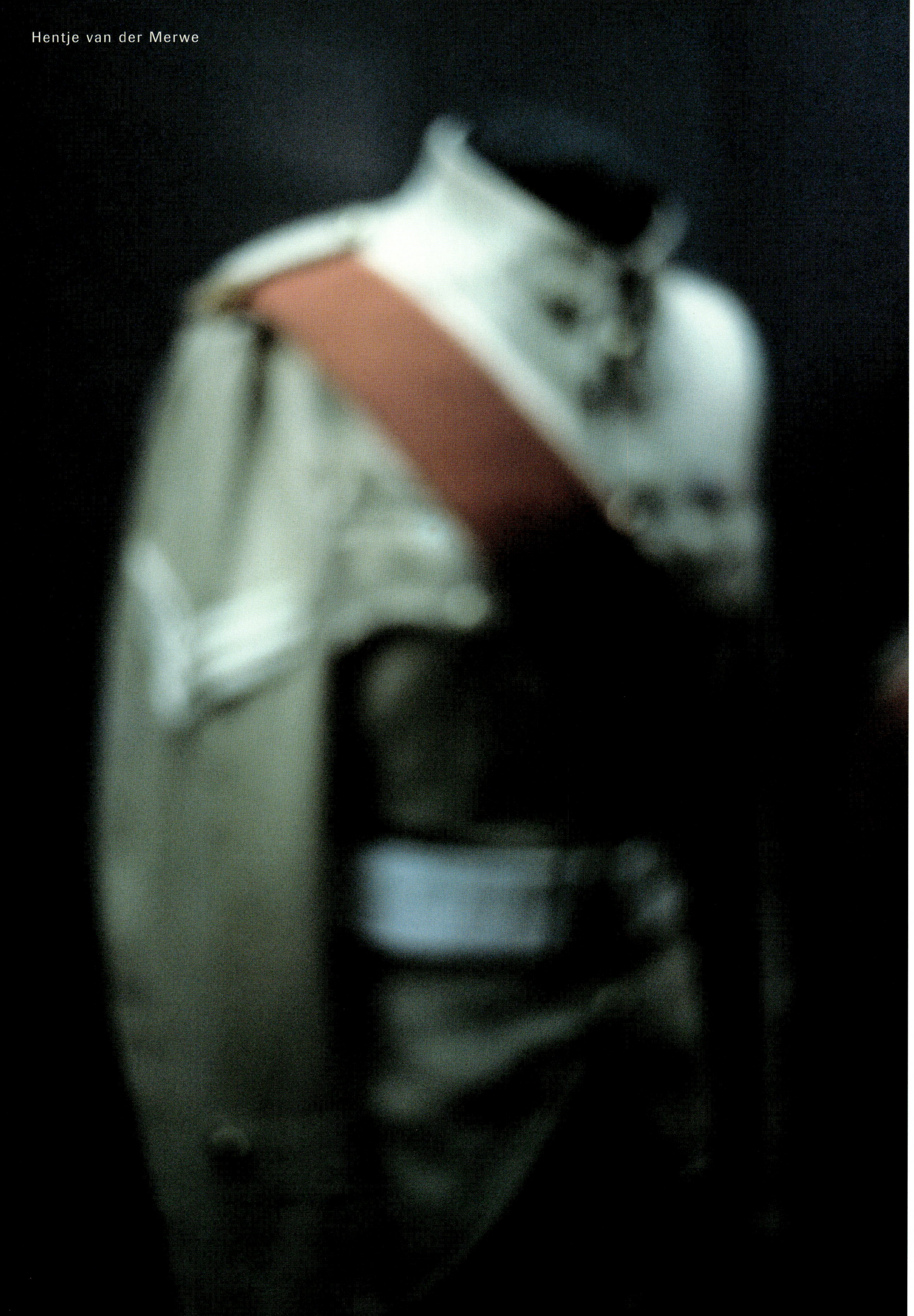

Hentje van der Merwe

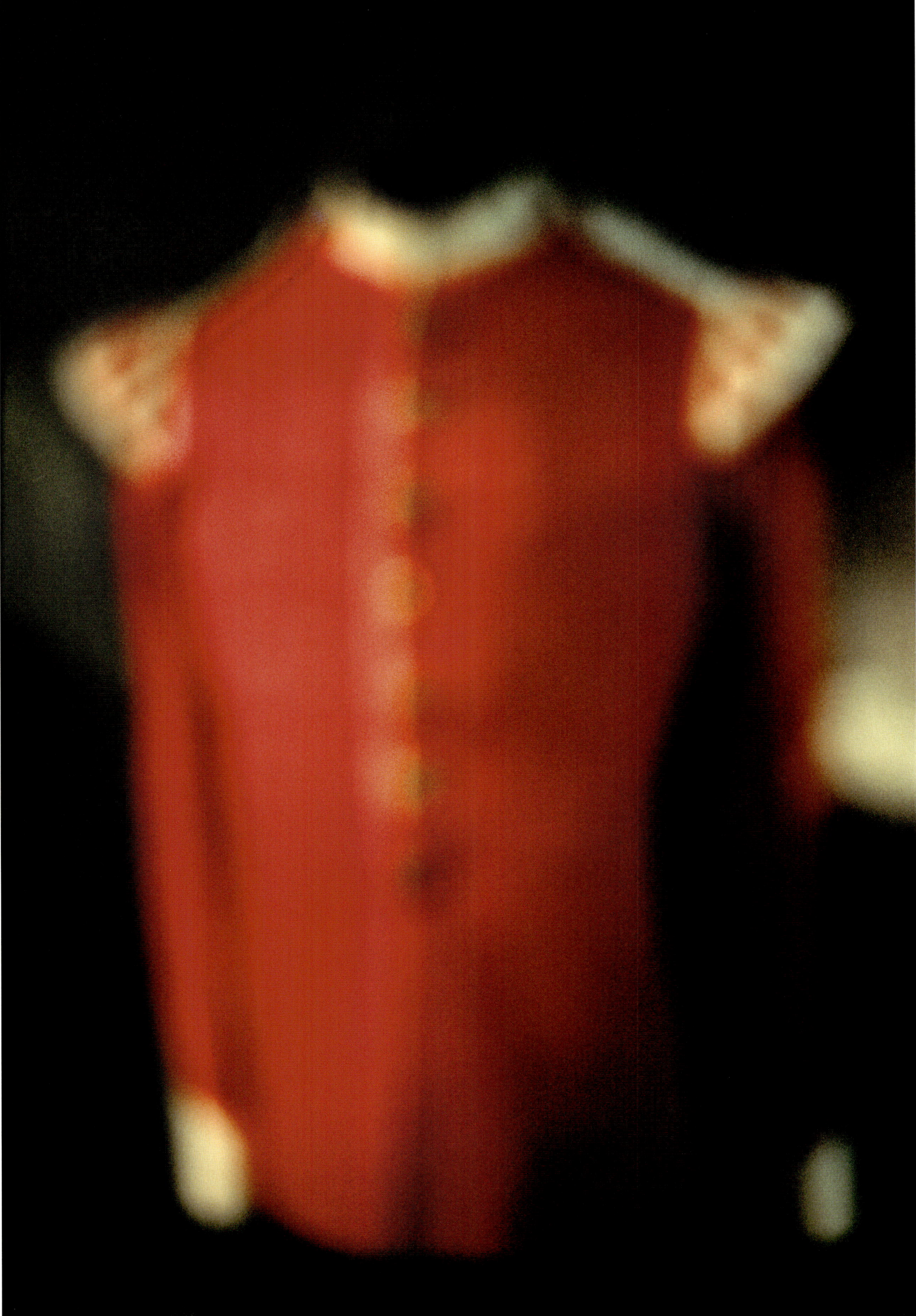

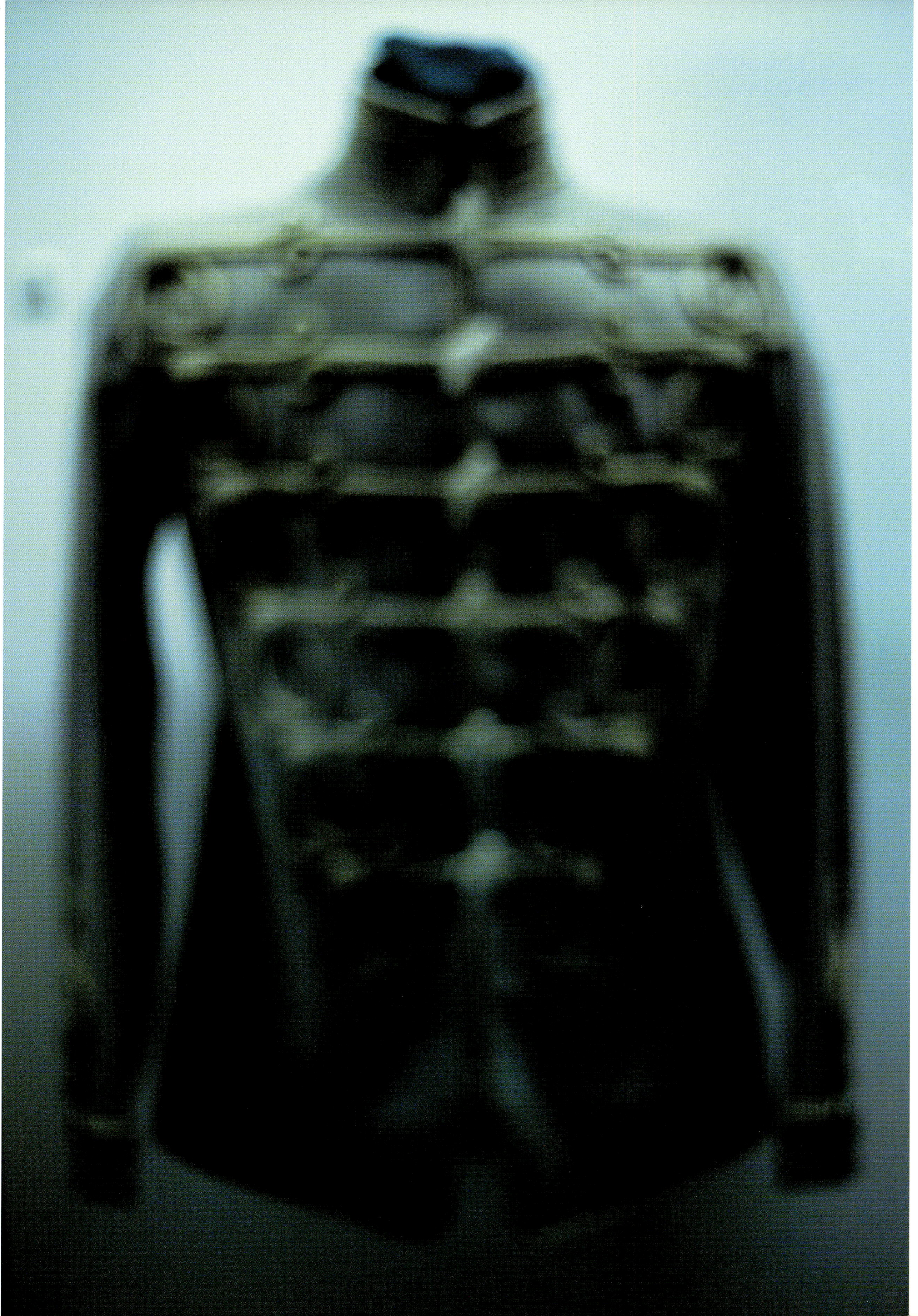

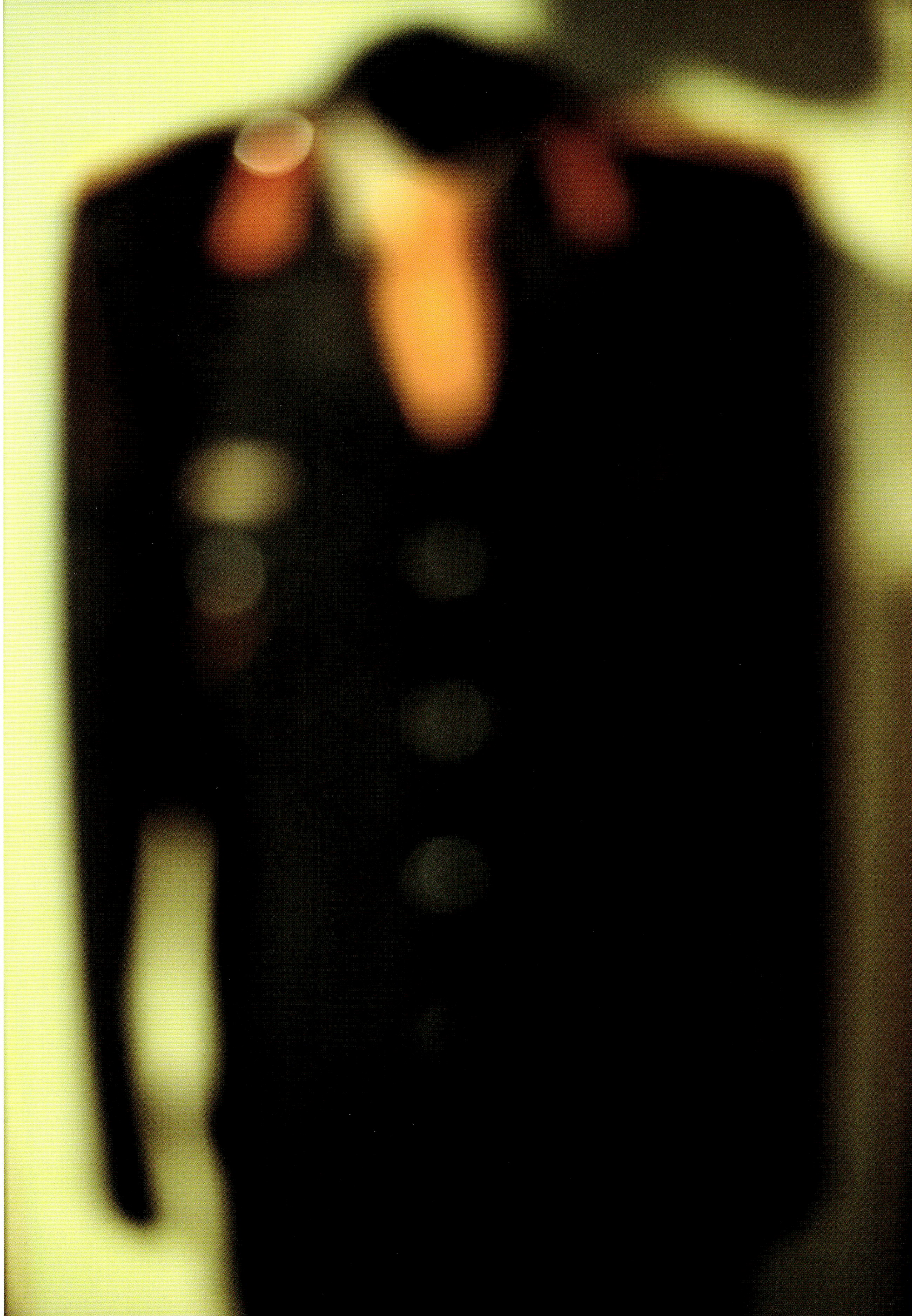

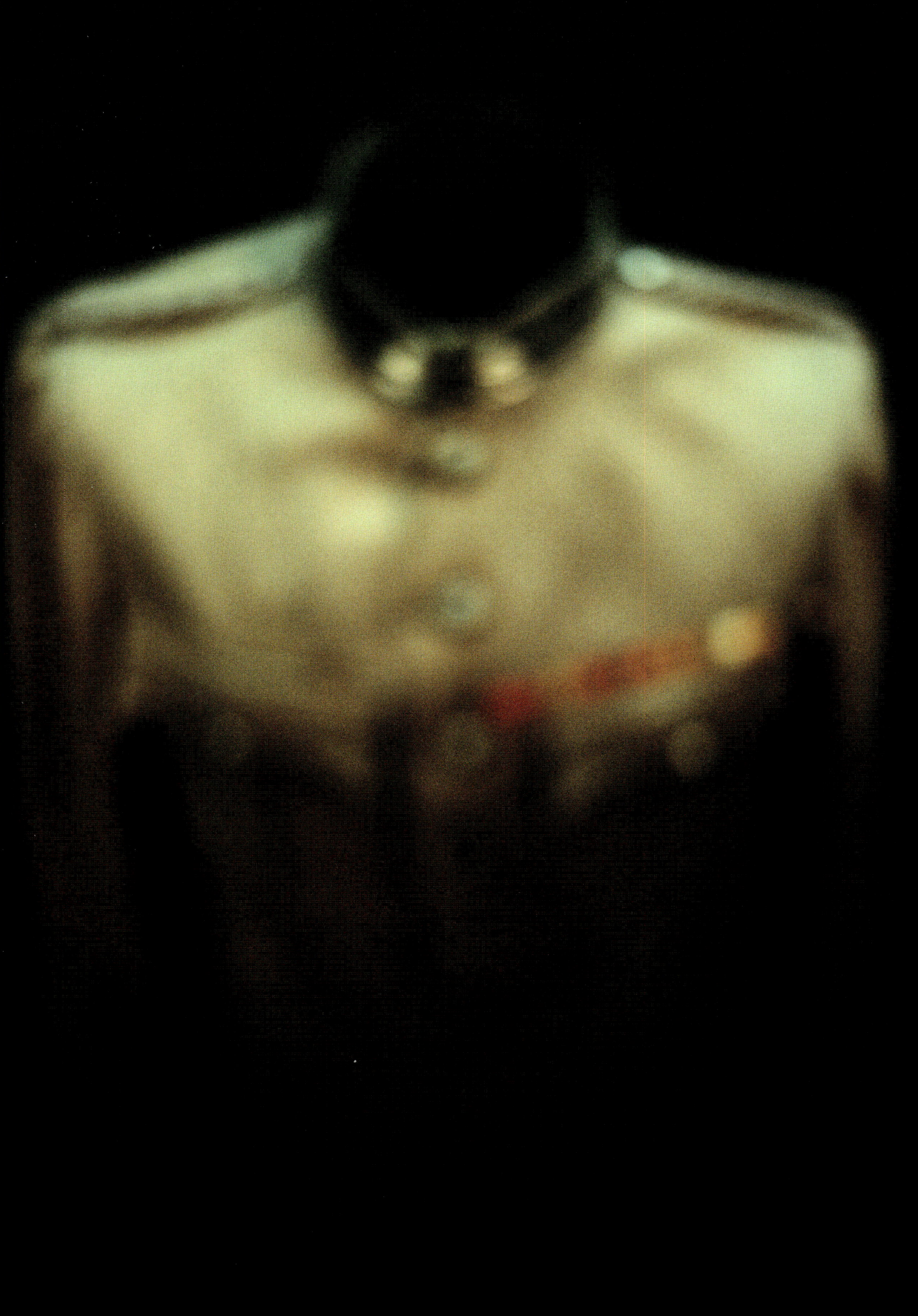

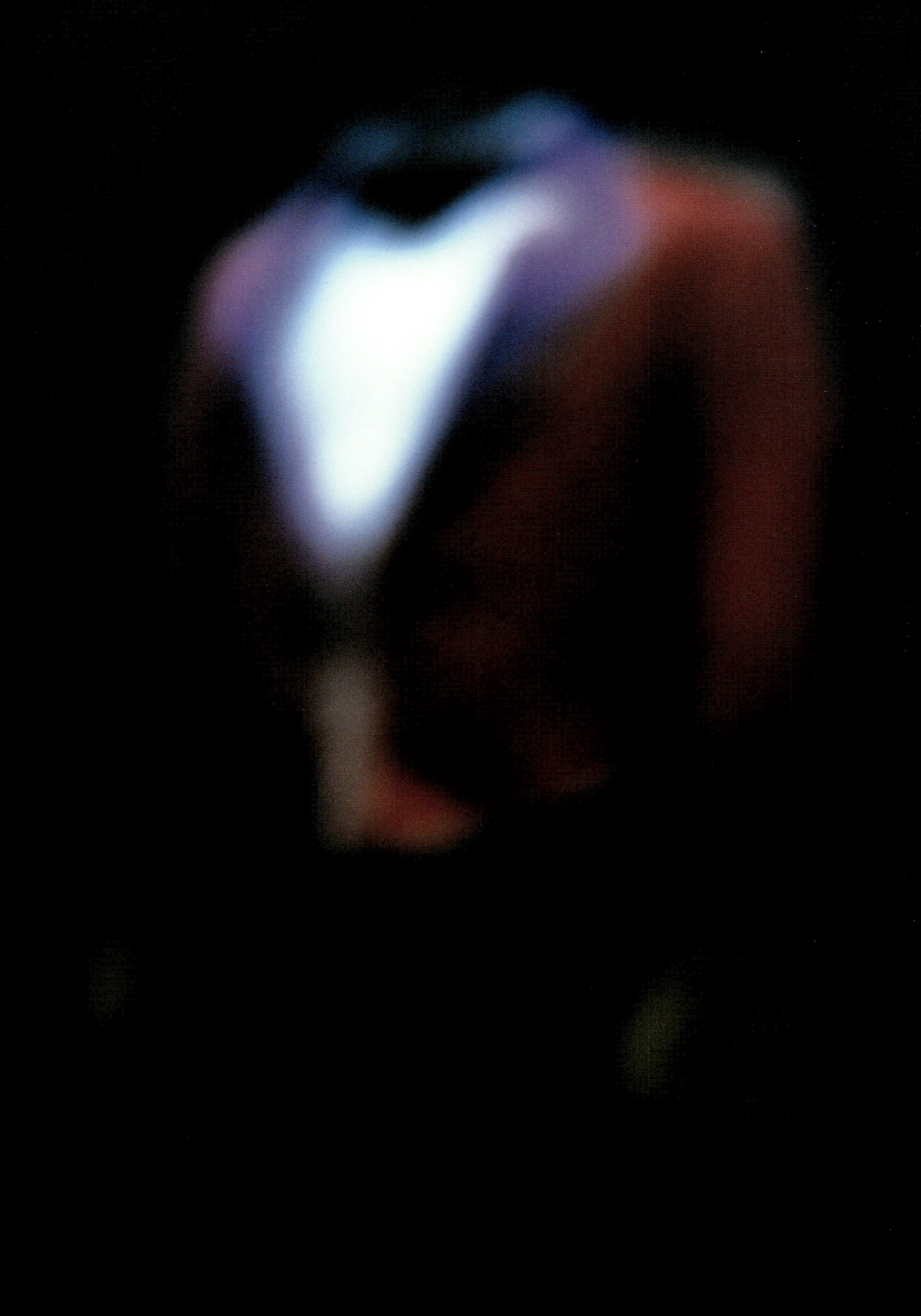

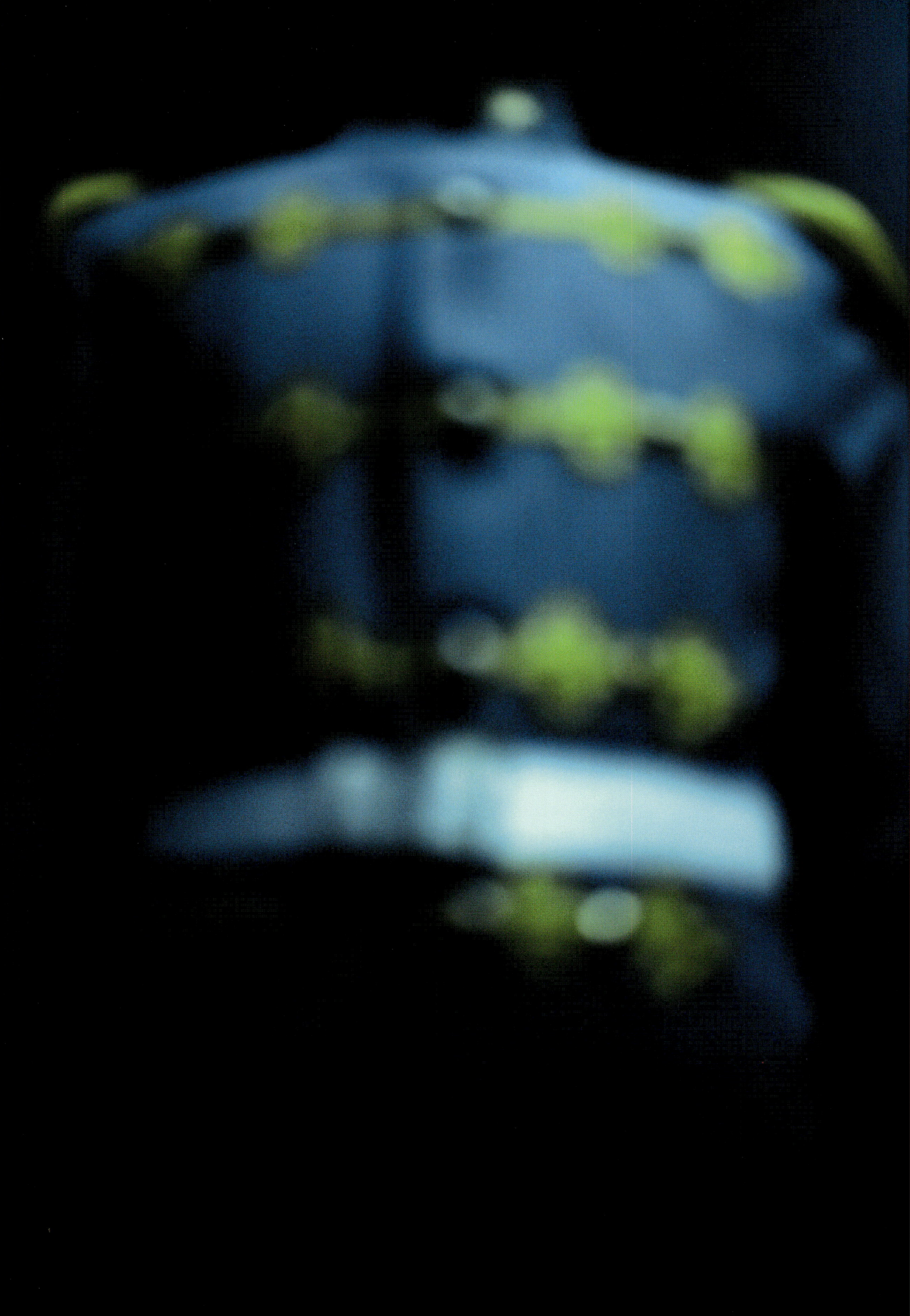

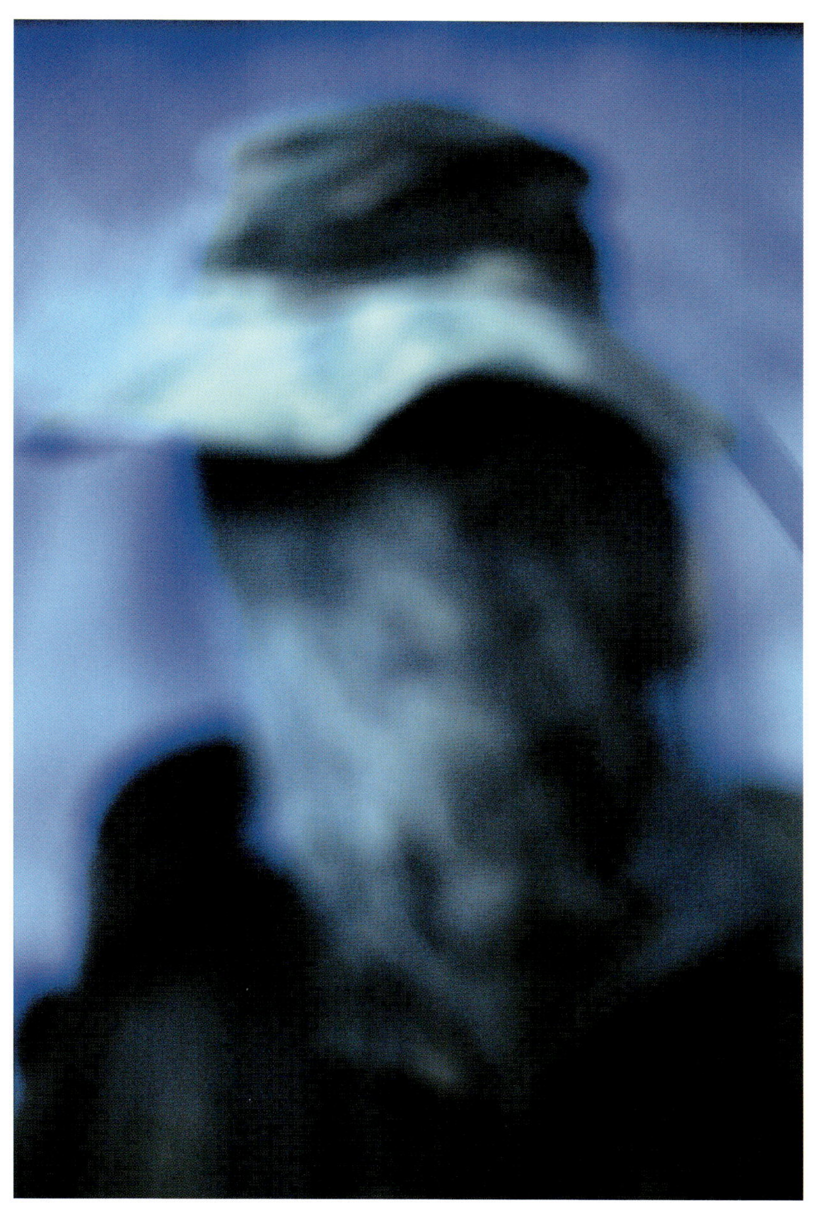

Previous Spreads:
Transvaal Scottish (8th Infantry) Sergeant (1945–1951);
Cape Mounted Rifles (Dukes), Bandsman (1913–1926);
Transvaal Horse Artillery (Colonial), Officer (1903–1913);
Parade Uniform (1967–1990);
WW I Service Jacket, Lieutenant;
Cape Town Highlanders, Officer (1921–1958);
State President's Guard (Formed 1967–Deactivated 1990), Riflemen

Top:
TA member of 32 Battalion Reconnaissance Wing

All from the series "Trappings," 2002–03
Photo-installation, 70.9 x 47.2 in. (180 x 120 cm)
Courtesy the artist

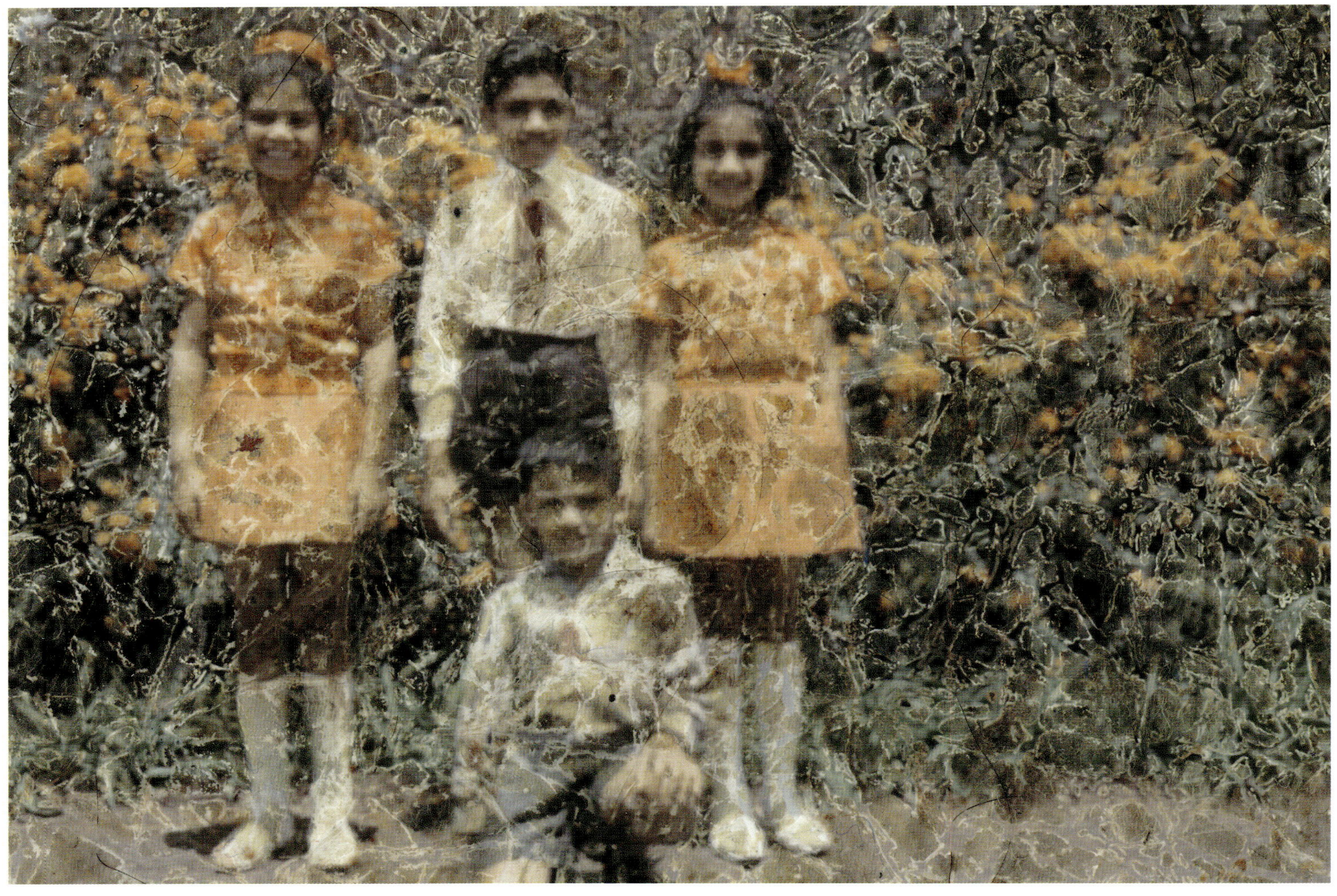

Arbor, from the series "The Lost Pictures," 2004
Chromogenic print, 40 x 60 in. (101.6 x 152.4 cm)
Courtesy the artist and Talwar Gallery, New York

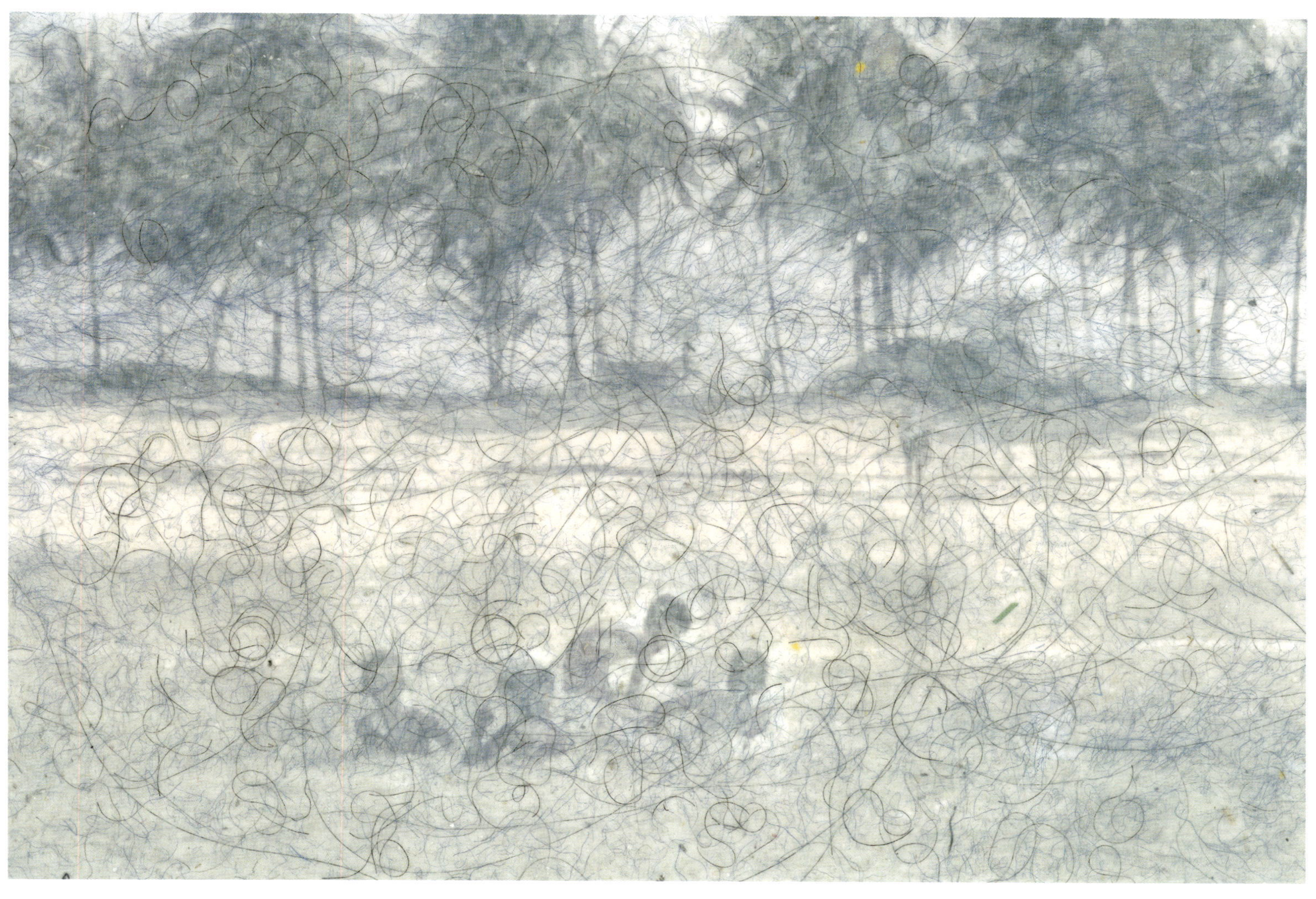

Beach, from the series "The Lost Pictures," 2004
Chromogenic print, 40 x 60 in. (101.6 x 152.4 cm)
Courtesy the artist and Talwar Gallery, New York

Bike, from the series "The Lost Pictures," 2004
Chromogenic print, 40 x 60 in. (101.6 x 152.4 cm)
Courtesy the artist and Talwar Gallery, New York

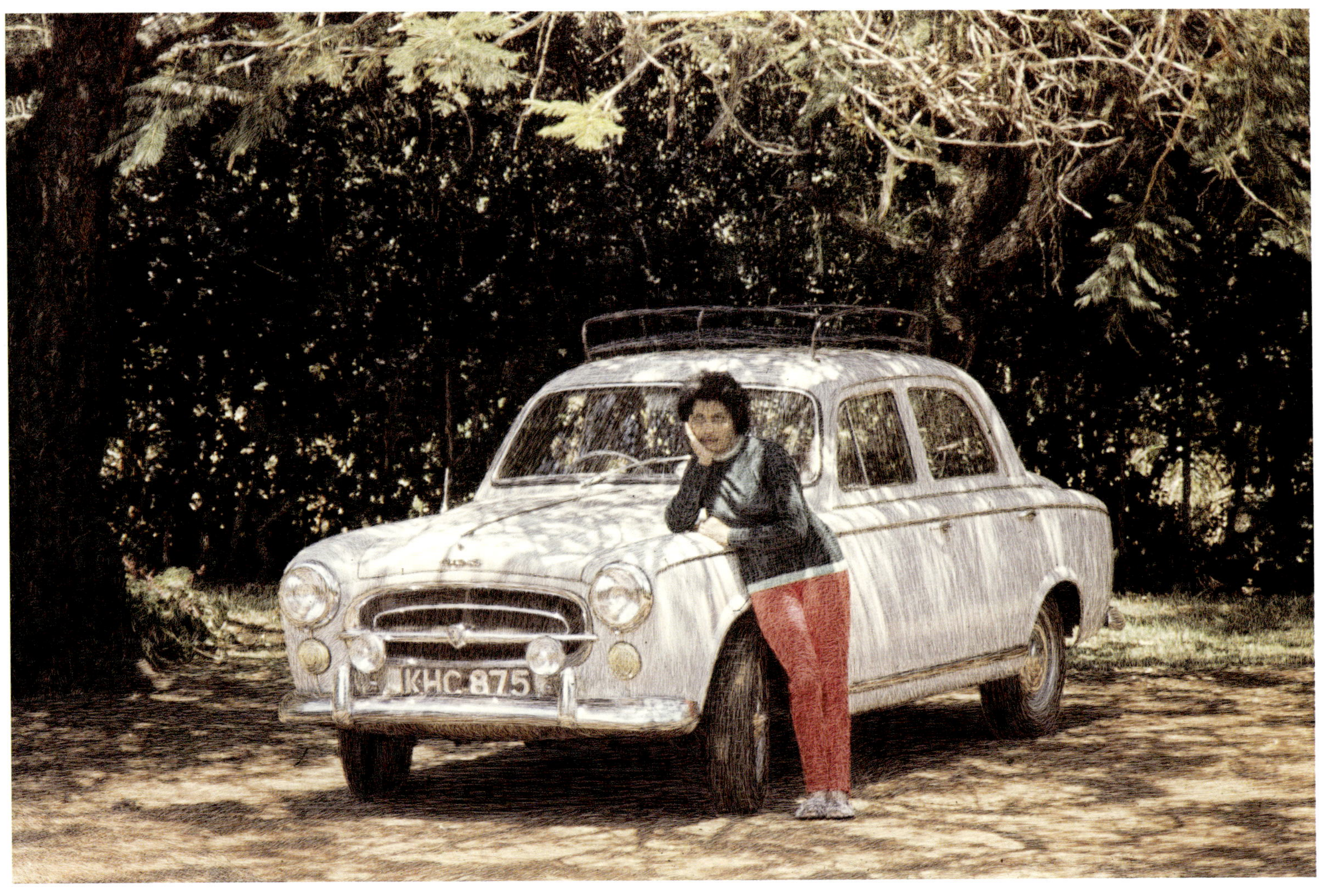

Car, from the series "The Lost Pictures," 2004
Chromogenic print, 40 x 60 in. (101.6 x 152.4 cm)
Courtesy the artist and Talwar Gallery, New York

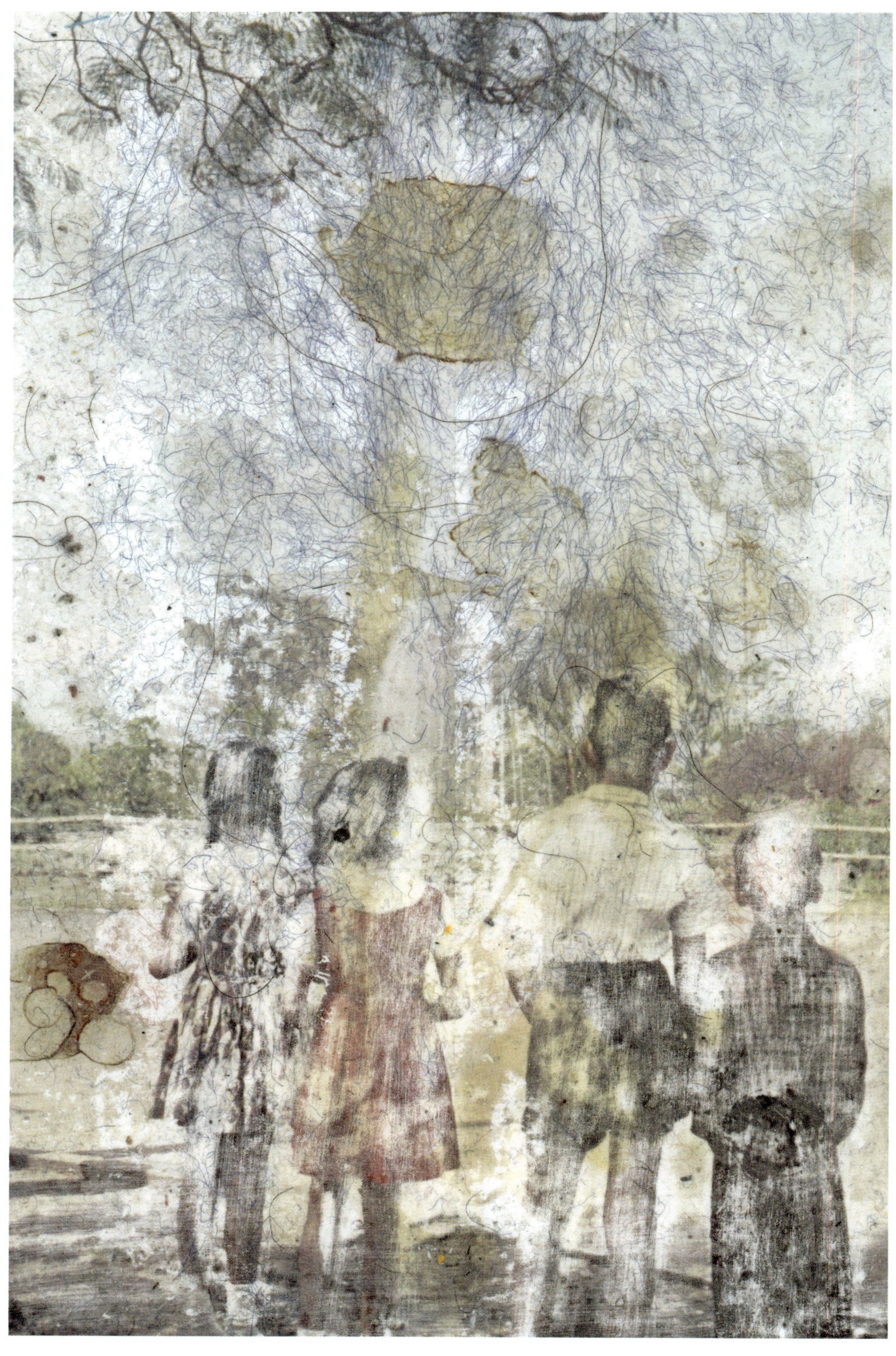

Fountain, from the series "The Lost Pictures," 2004
Chromogenic print, 60 x 40 in. (152.4 x 101.6 cm)
Courtesy the artist and Talwar Gallery, New York

Harambee!, from the series "The Lost Pictures," 2004
Chromogenic print, 40 x 60 in. (101.6 x 152.4 cm)
Courtesy the artist and Talwar Gallery, New York

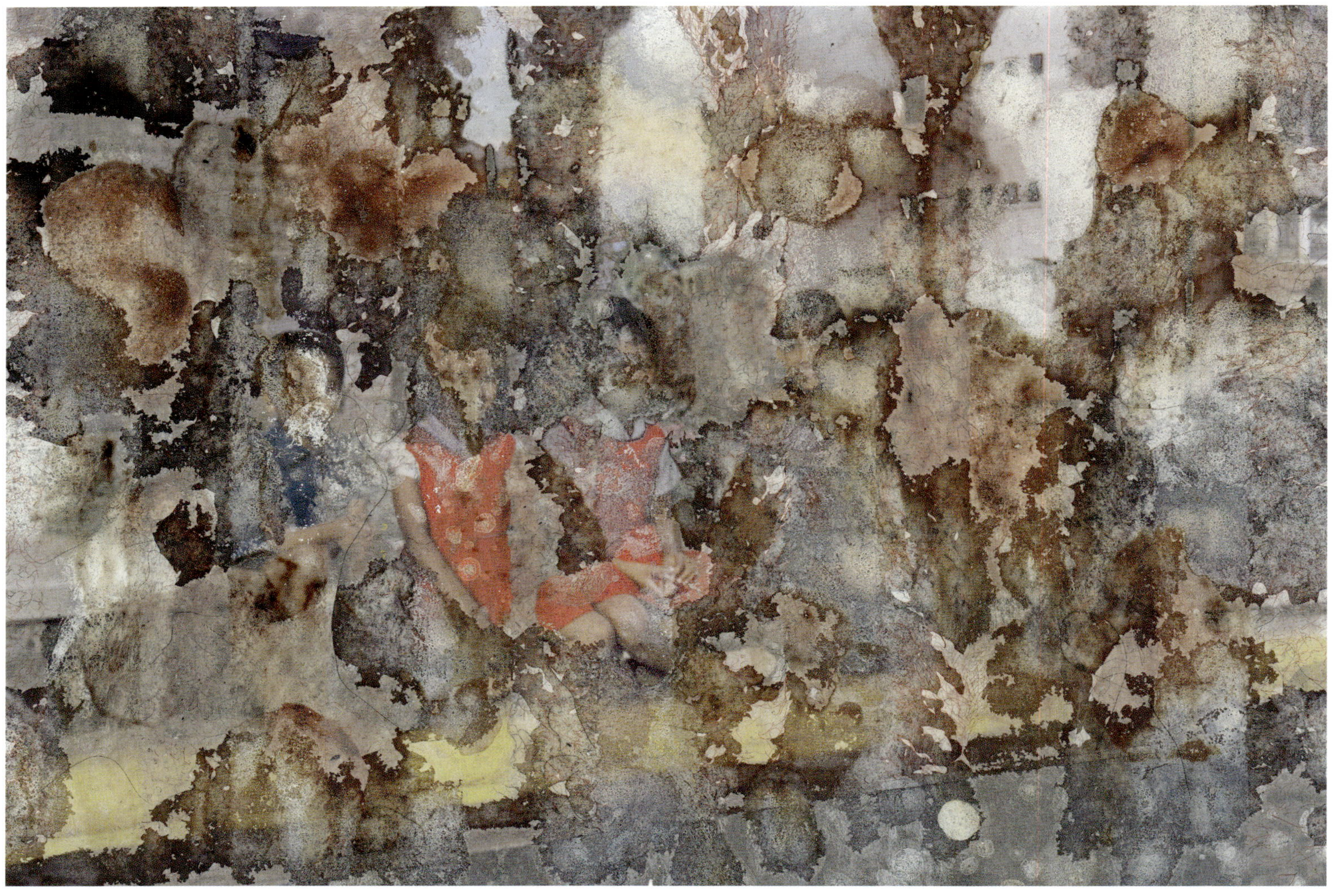

Lechko, from the series "The Lost Pictures," 2004
Chromogenic print, 40 x 60 in. (101.6 x 152.4 cm)
Courtesy the artist and Talwar Gallery, New York

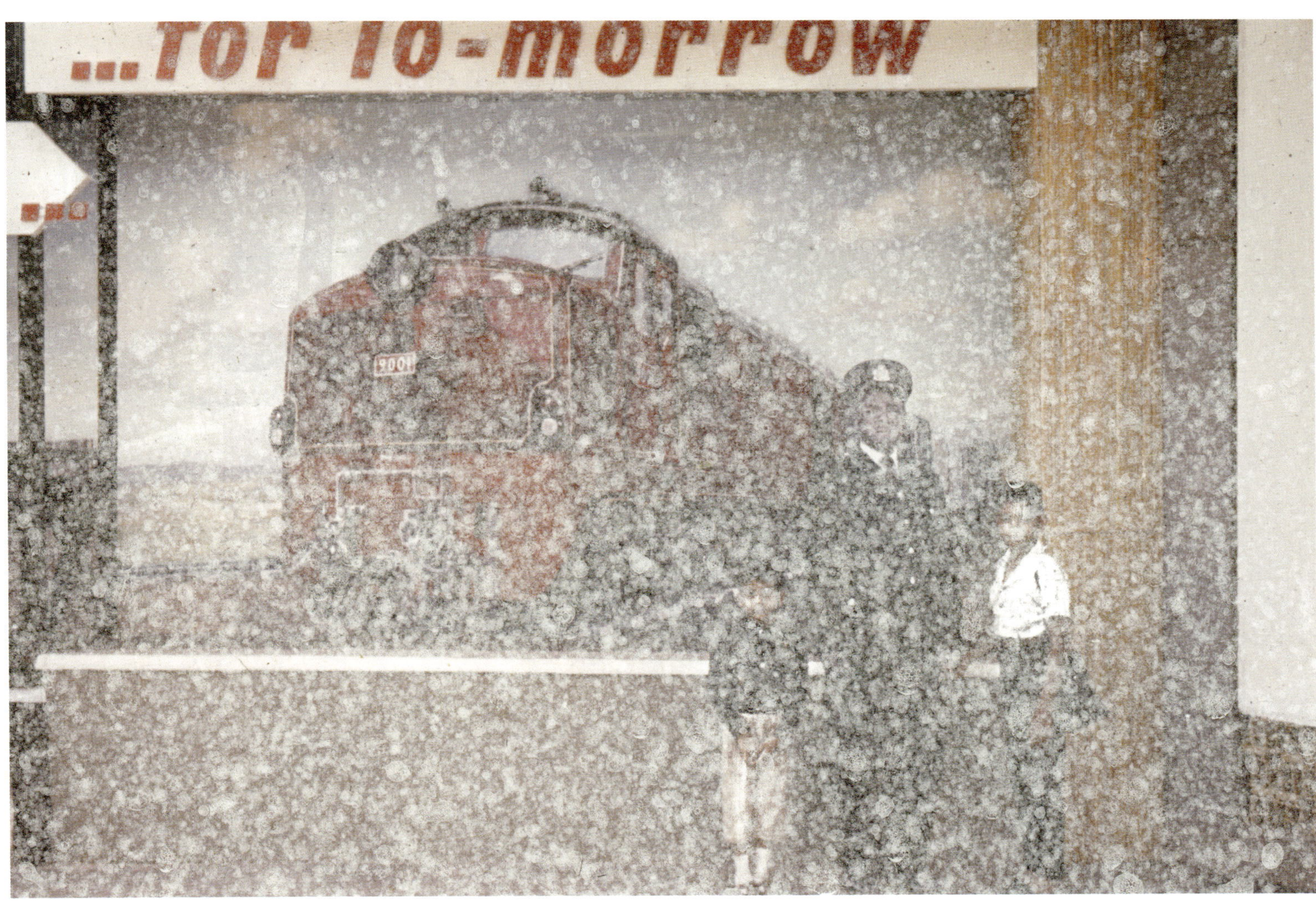

Tomorrow, from the series "The Lost Pictures," 2004
Chromogenic print, 40 x 60 in. (101.6 x 152.4 cm)
Courtesy the artist and Talwar Gallery, New York

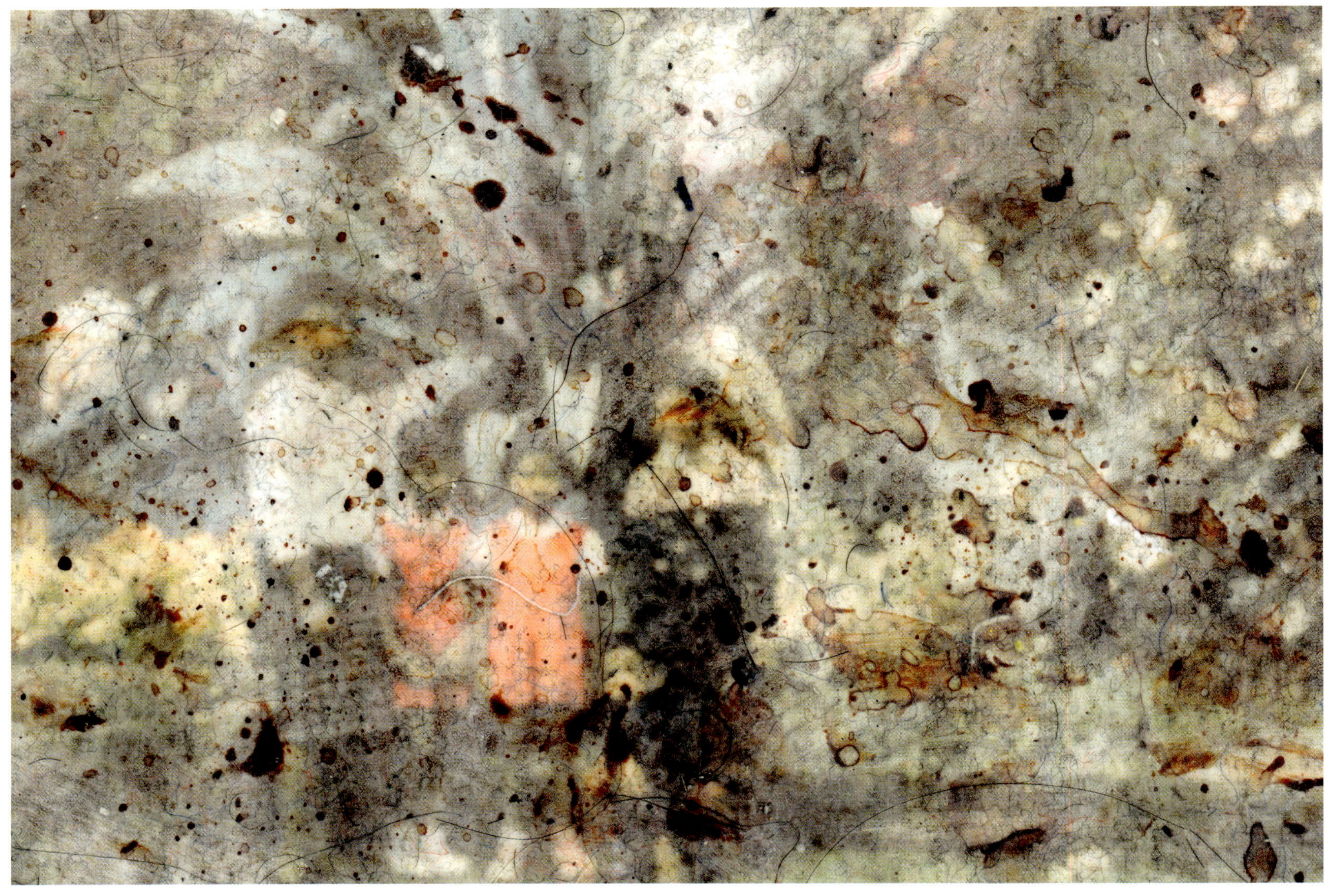

Spray, from the series "The Lost Pictures," 2004
Chromogenic print, 40 x 60 in. (101.6 x 152.4 cm)
Courtesy the artist and Talwar Gallery, New York

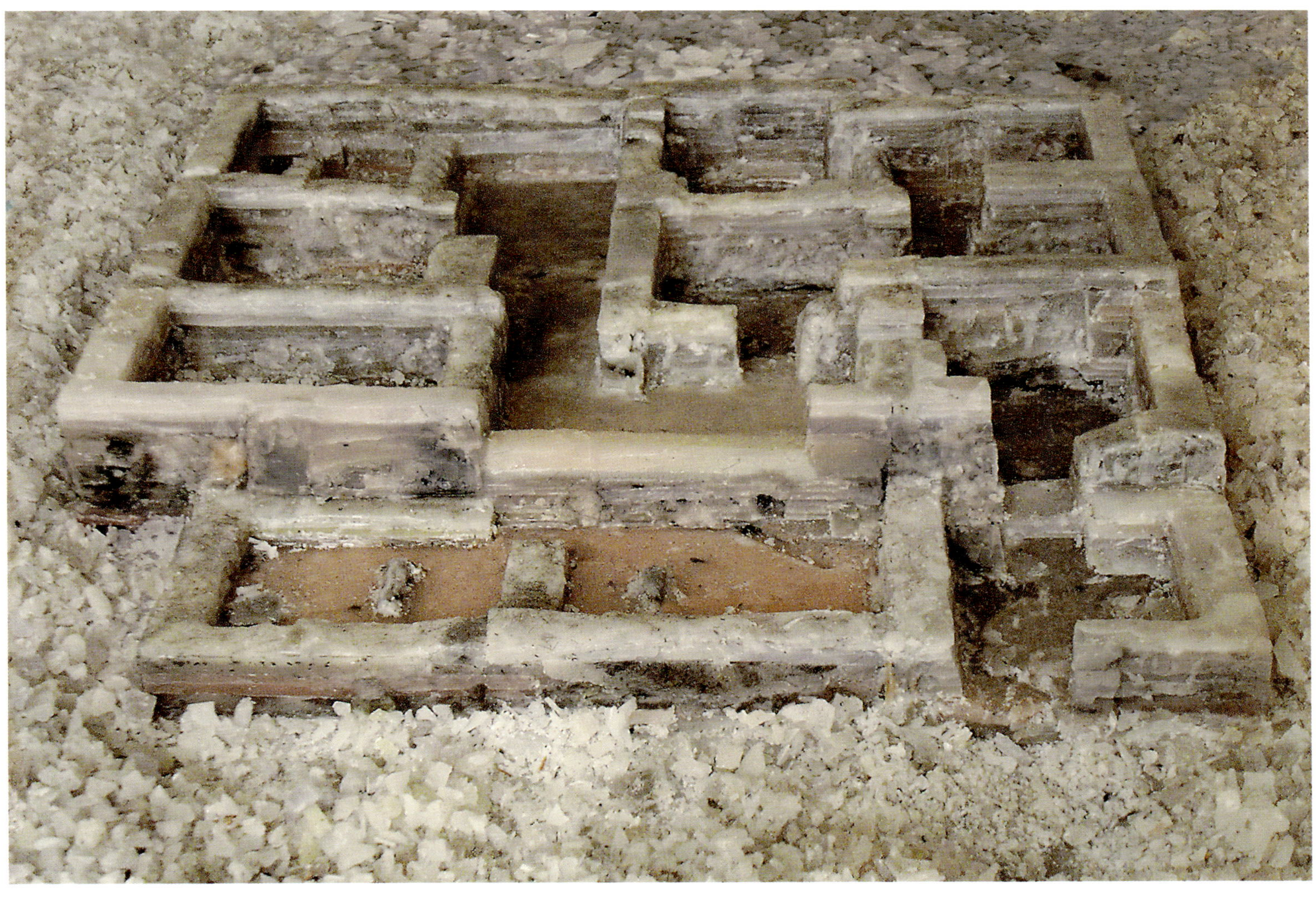

House, 2004
Mixed media, 32 x 48 x 4 in. (81.3 x 121.9 x 10.2 cm)
Courtesy the artist and Talwar Gallery, New York

Zwelethu Mthethwa

Ali Chraïbi

Mikhael Subotzky

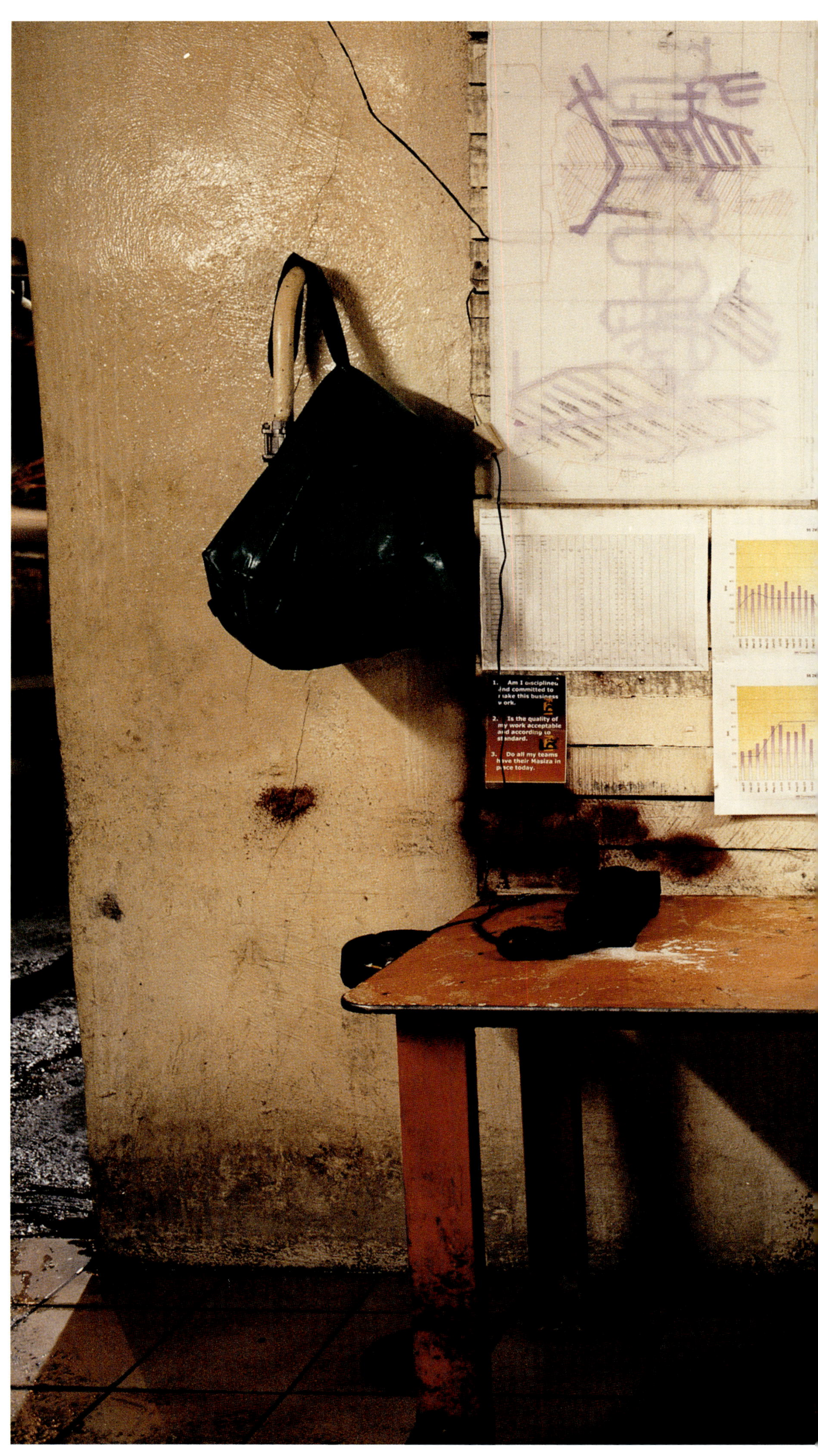

Untitled, 2005
Chromogenic print
49 x 76.75 in. (124.5 x 195 cm)
Courtesy the artist and
Jack Shainman Gallery, New York

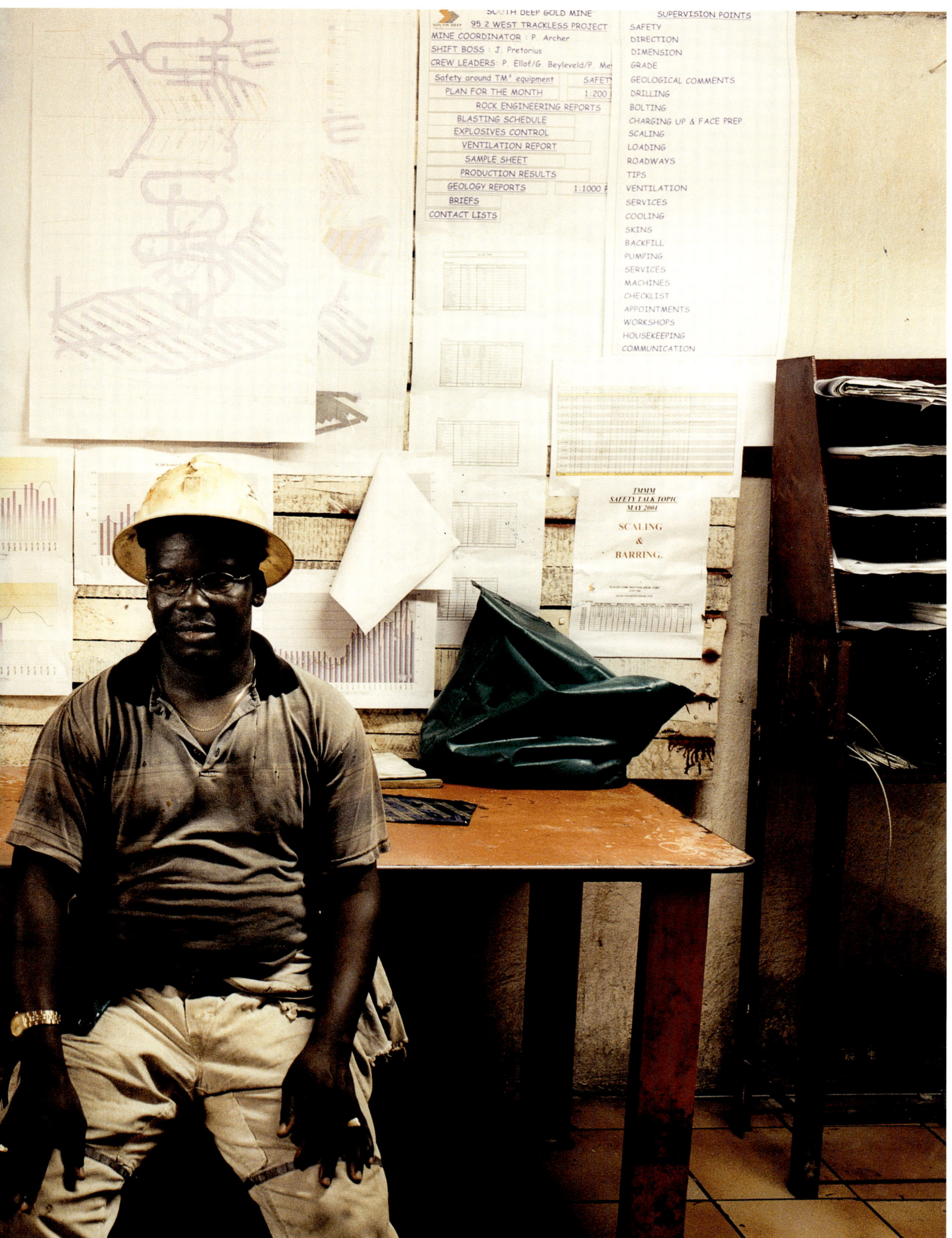

DEEP GOLD MINE
95 2 WEST TRACKLESS PROJECT
MINE COORDINATOR : P. Archer
SHIFT BOSS : J. Pretorius
Safety around TM³ equipment
PLAN FOR THE MONTH
ROCK ENGINEERING REPORTS
BLASTING SCHEDULE
EXPLOSIVES CONTROL
VENTILATION REPORT
SAMPLE SHEET
PRODUCTION RESULTS
GEOLOGY REPORTS
BRIEFS
CONTACT LISTS
SUPERVISION POINTS
SAFETY
DIRECTION
DIMENSION
GRADE
GEOLOGICAL COMMENTS
DRILLING
BOLTING
CHARGING UP & FACE PREP.
SCALING
LOADING
ROADWAYS
TIPS
VENTILATION
SERVICES
COOLING
SKINS
BACKFILL
PUMPING
SERVICES
MACHINES
CHECKLIST
APPOINTMENTS
WORKSHOPS
HOUSEKEEPING
COMMUNICATION
TMMM
SAFETY TALK TOPIC
MAY 2004
SCALING
&
BARRING.

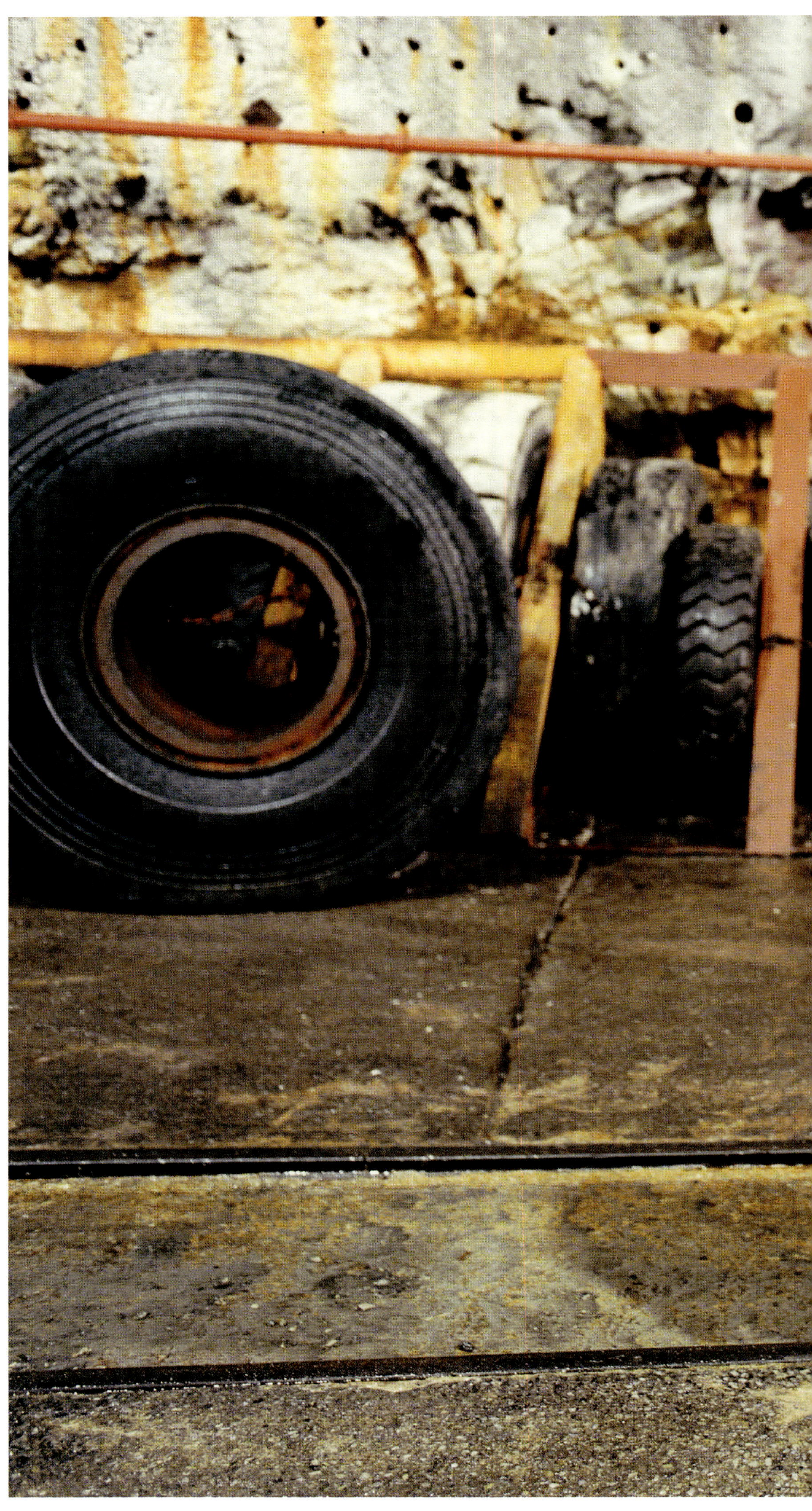

Untitled, 2005
Chromogenic print
49 x 76.75 in. (124.5 x 195 cm)
Courtesy the artist and
Jack Shainman Gallery, New York

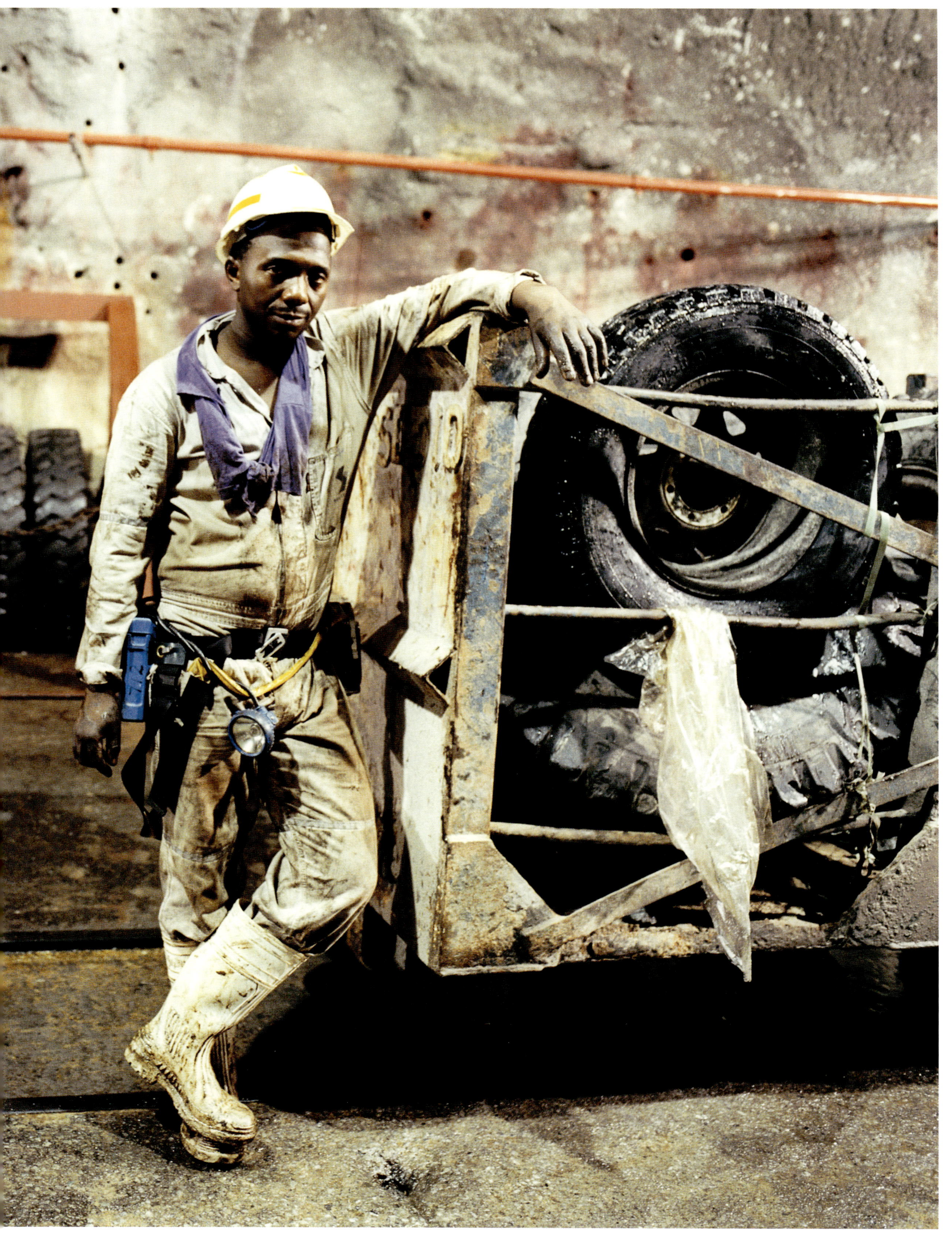

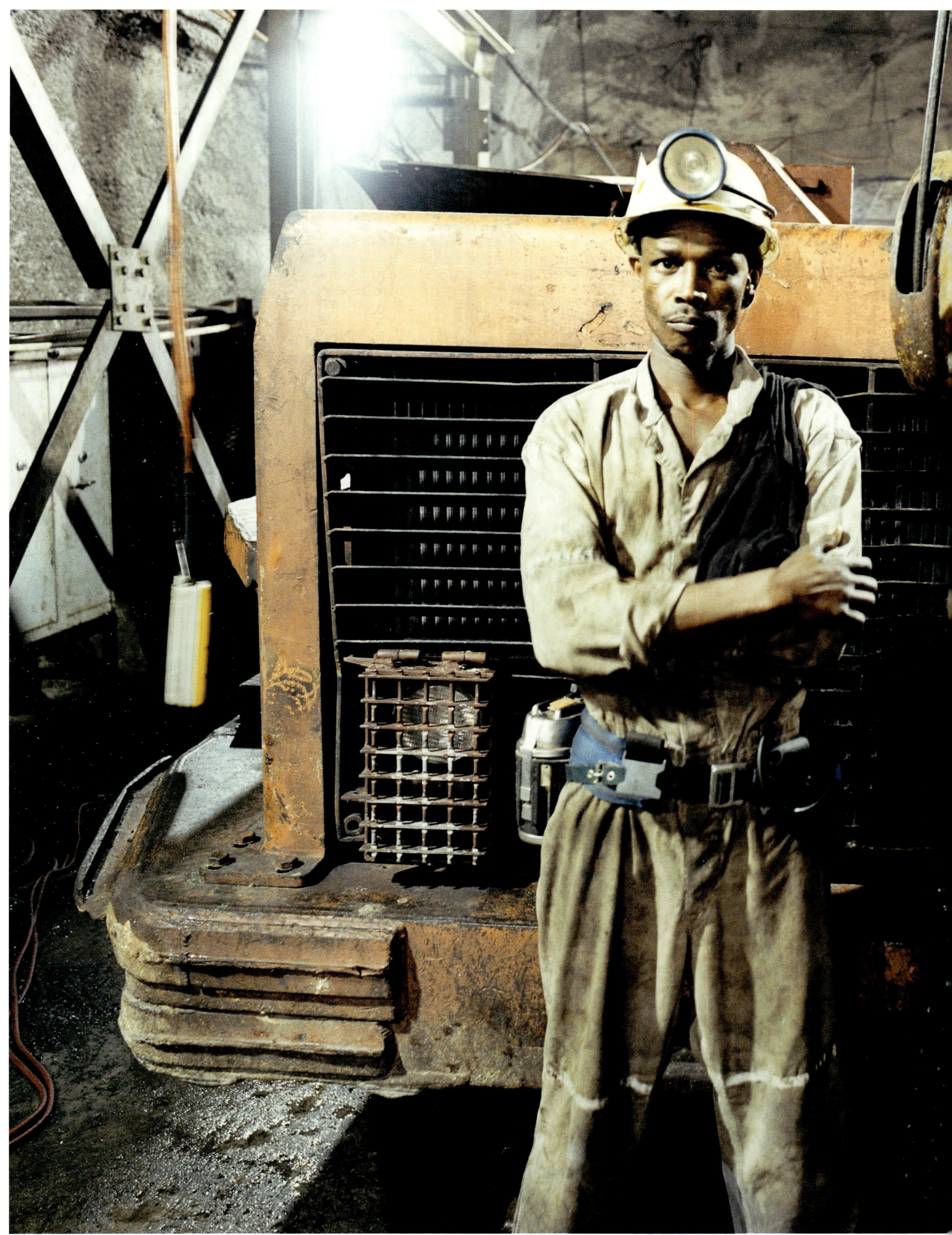

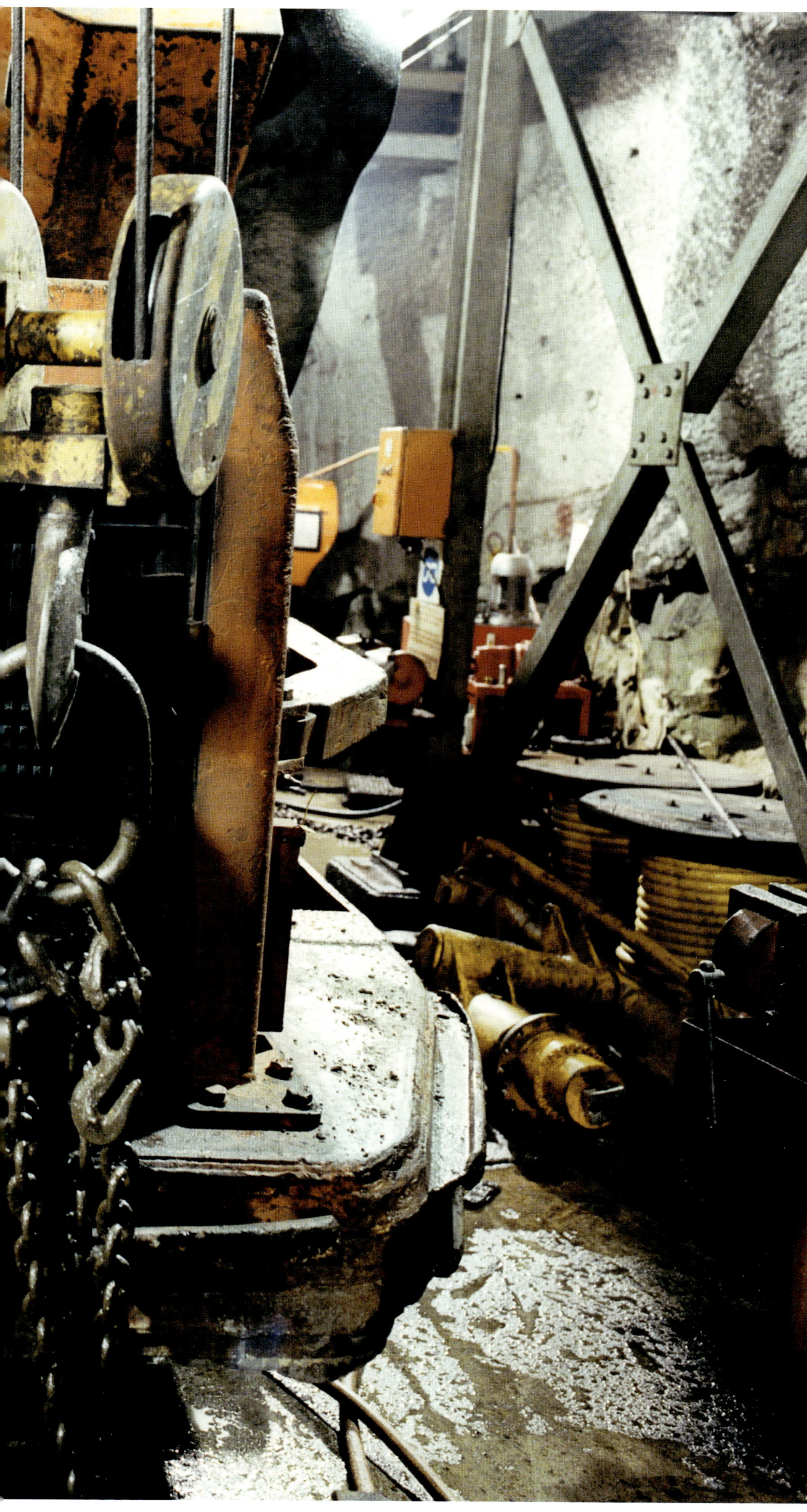

Untitled, 2005
Chromogenic print
49 x 76.75 in. (124.5 x 195 cm)
Courtesy the artist and
Jack Shainman Gallery, New York

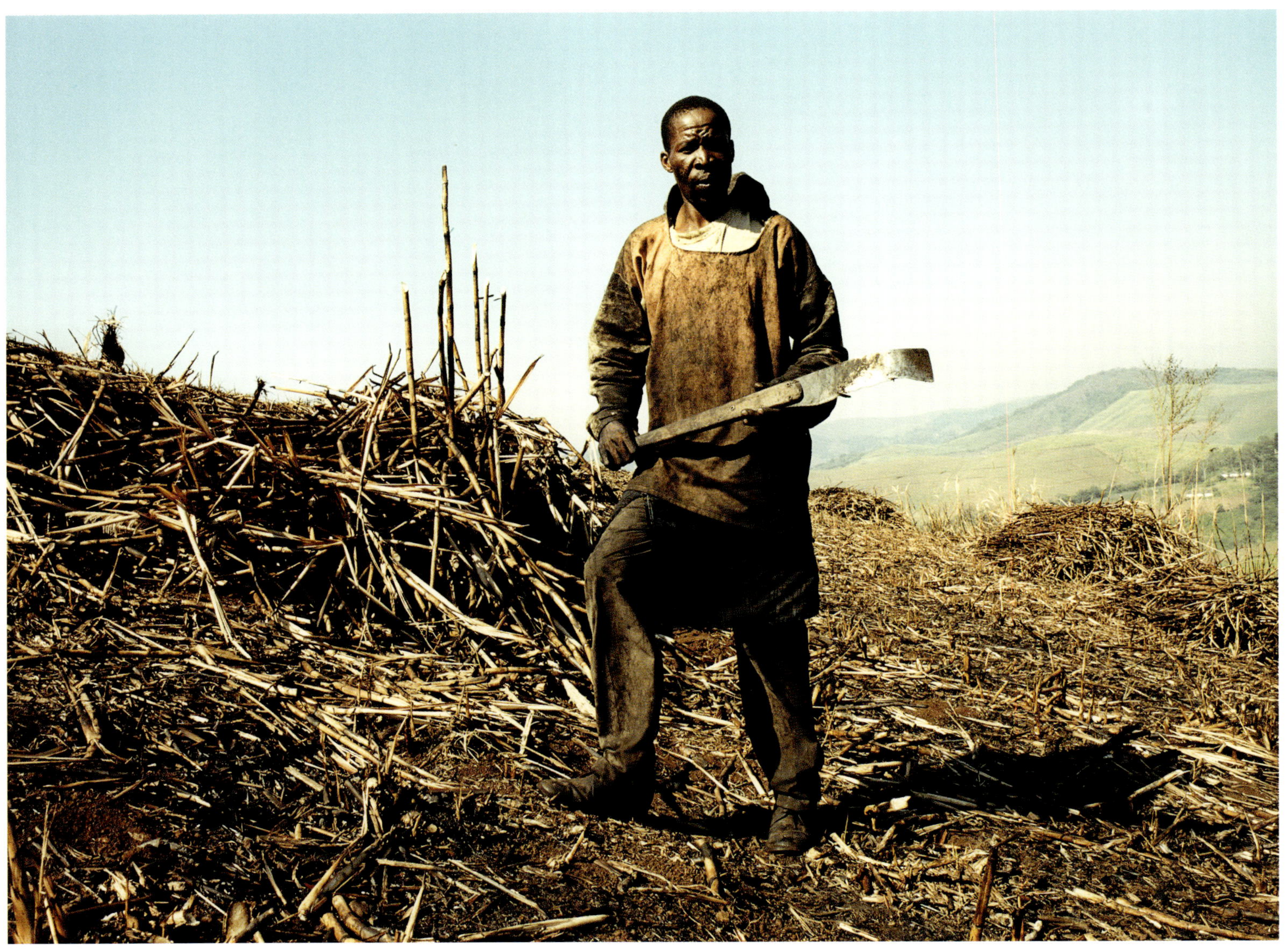

Untitled, 2003
Chromogenic print, 59 x 76 in. (149.9 x 193 cm)
Courtesy the artist and Jack Shainman Gallery, New York

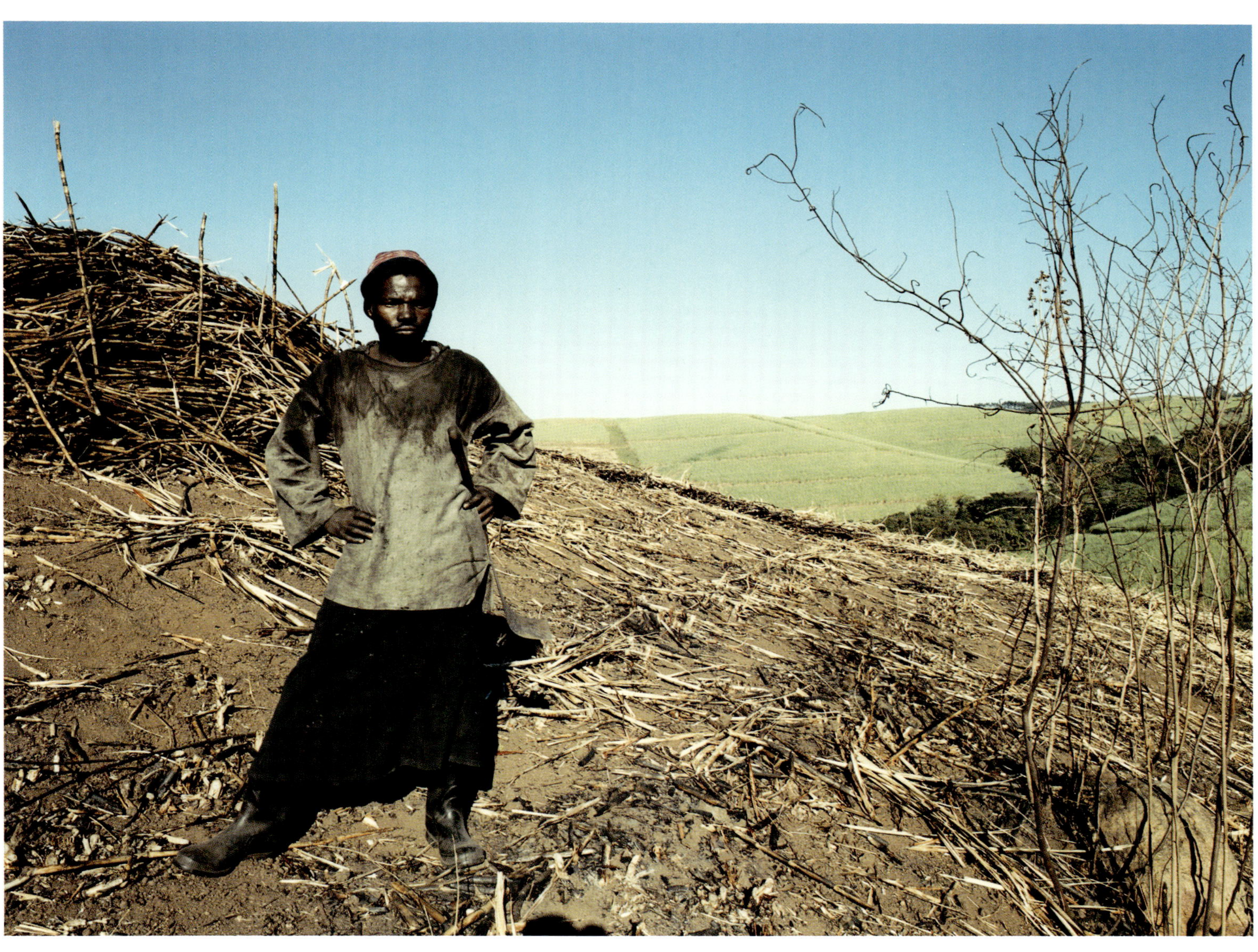

Untitled, 2003
Chromogenic print, 59 x 76 in. (149.9 x 193 cm)
Courtesy the artist and Jack Shainman Gallery, New York

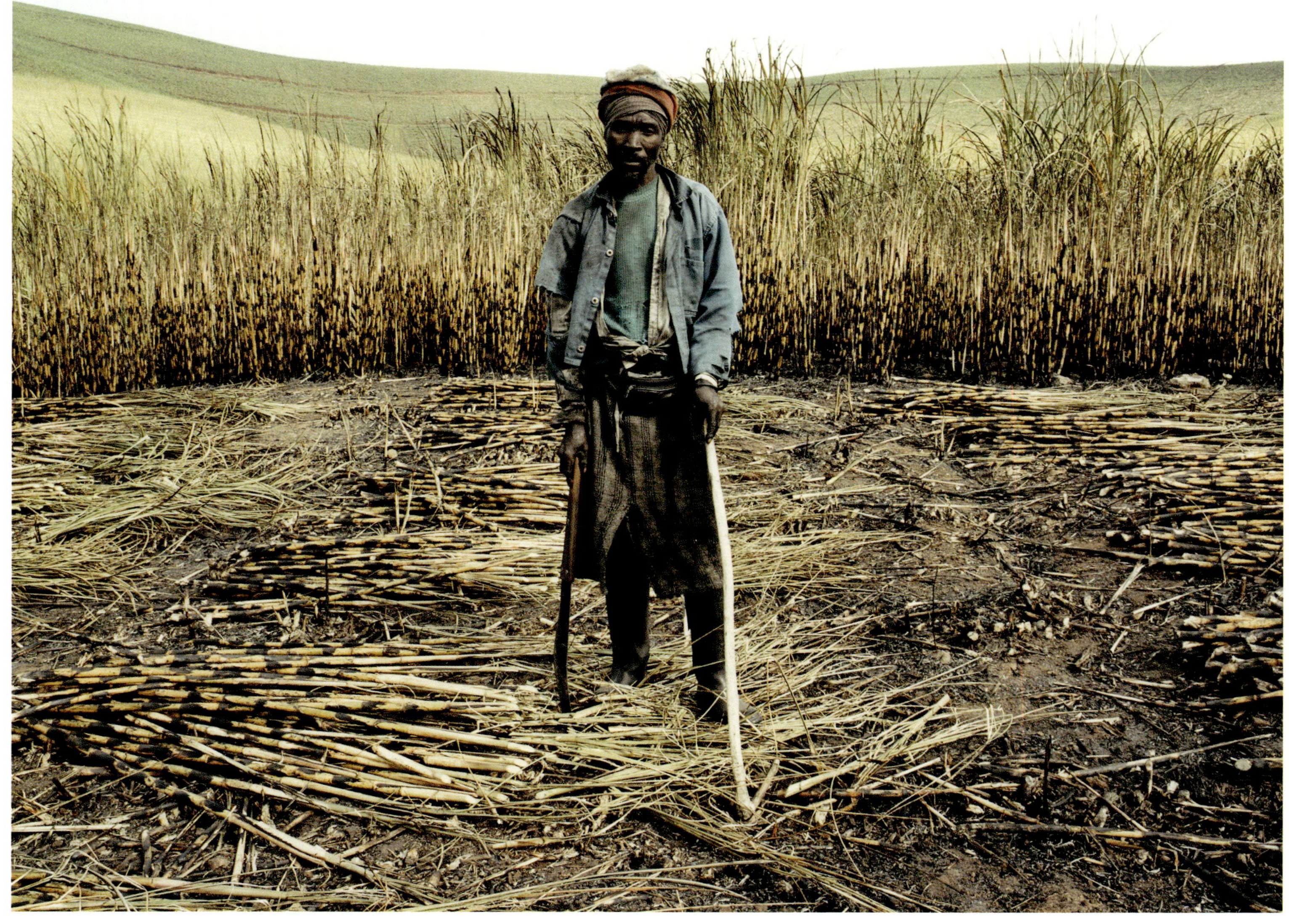

Untitled, 2003
Chromogenic print, 59 x 76 in. (149.9 x 193 cm)
Courtesy the artist and Jack Shainman Gallery, New York

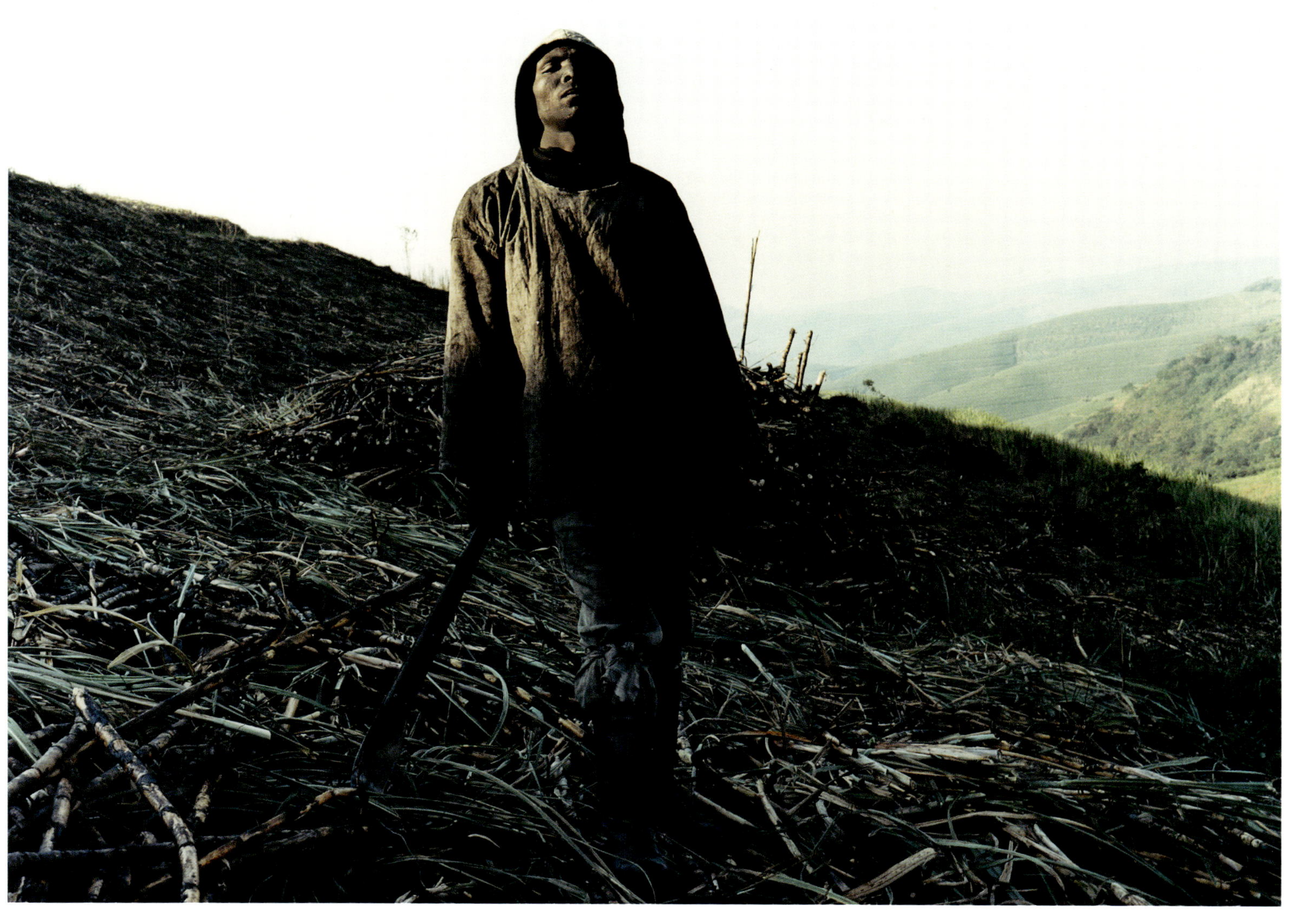

Untitled, 2003
Chromogenic print, 59 x 76 in. (149.9 x 193 cm)
Courtesy the artist and Jack Shainman Gallery, New York

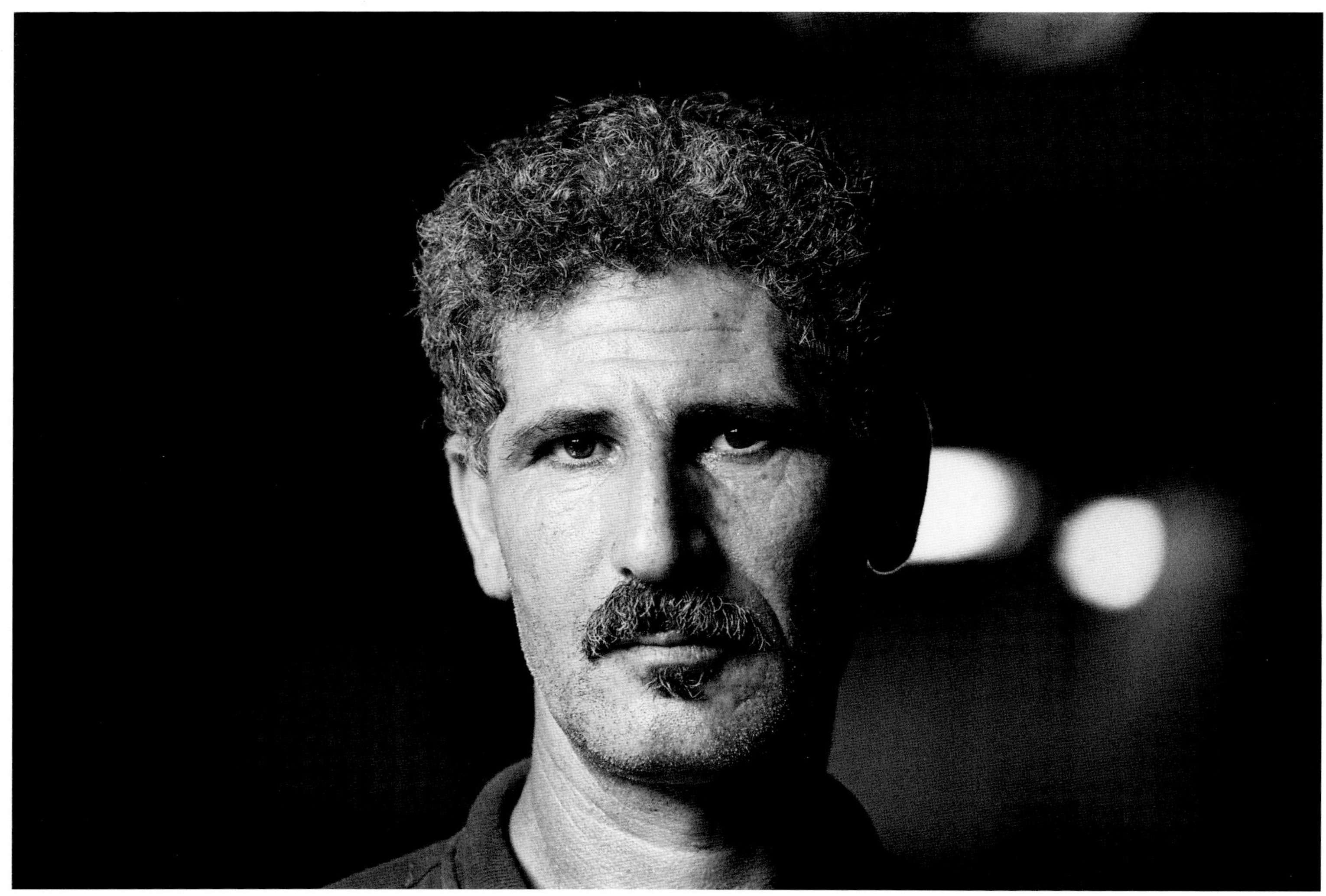

Untitled, from the series "Modern Times," 1998
Gelatin silver print, 12.6 x 17.7 in. (32 x 45 cm)
Courtesy the artist

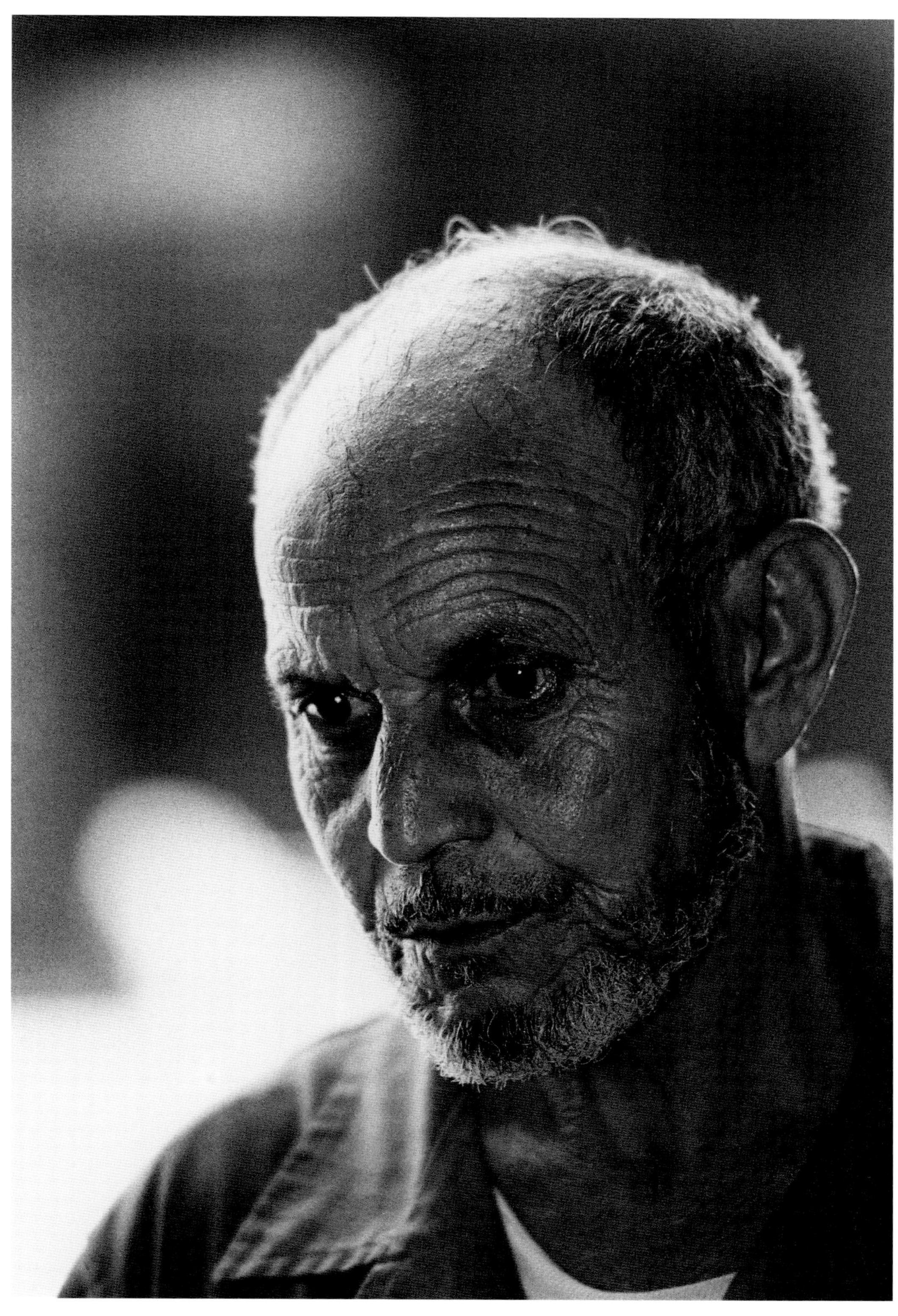

Untitled, from the series "Modern Times," 1998
Gelatin silver print, 17.7 x 12.6 in. (45 x 32 cm)
Courtesy the artist

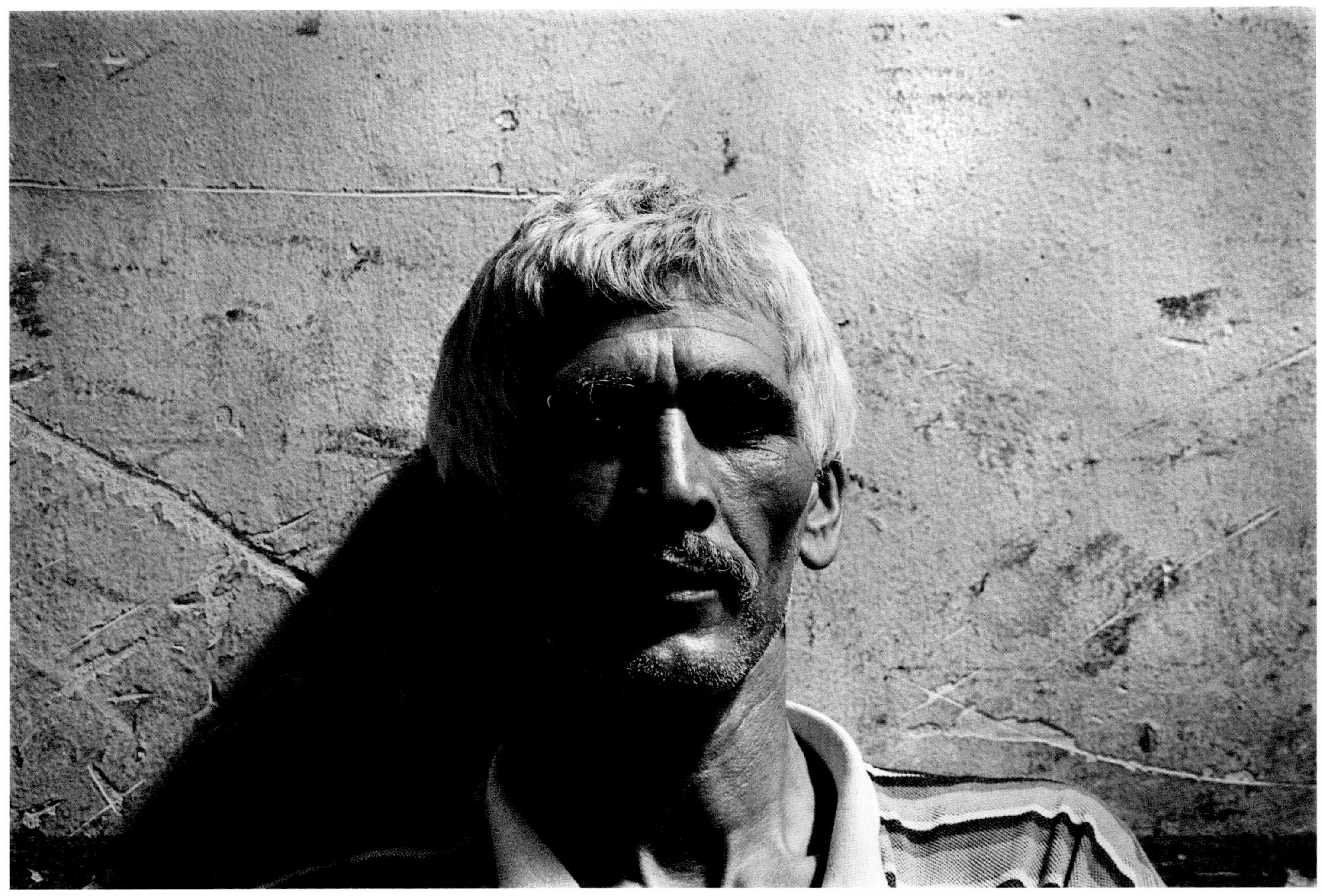

Untitled, from the series "Modern Times," 1998
Gelatin silver print, 12.6 x 17.7 in. (32 x 45 cm)
Courtesy the artist

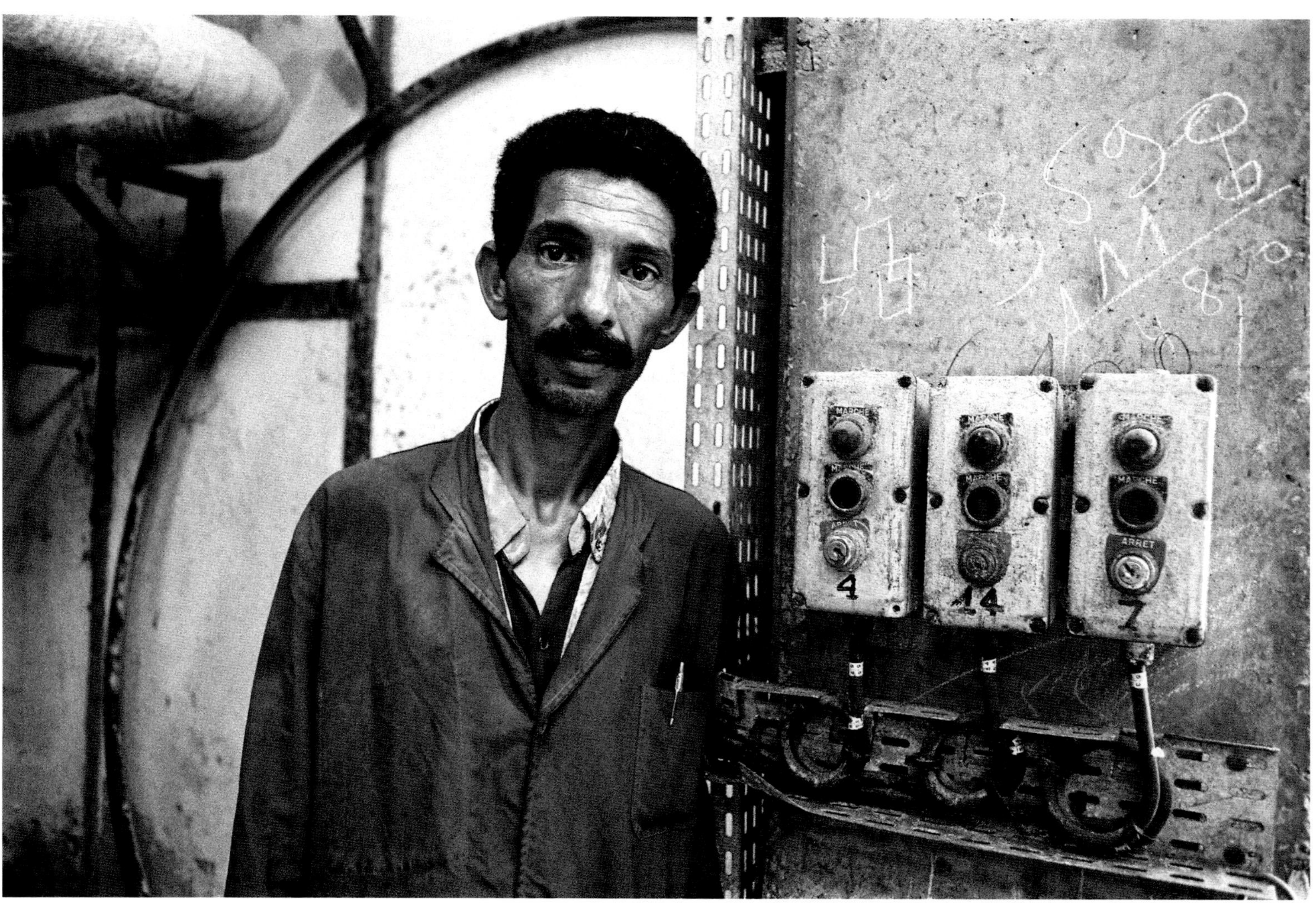

Untitled, from the series "Modern Times," 1998
Gelatin silver print, 12.6 x 17.7 in. (32 x 45 cm)
Courtesy the artist

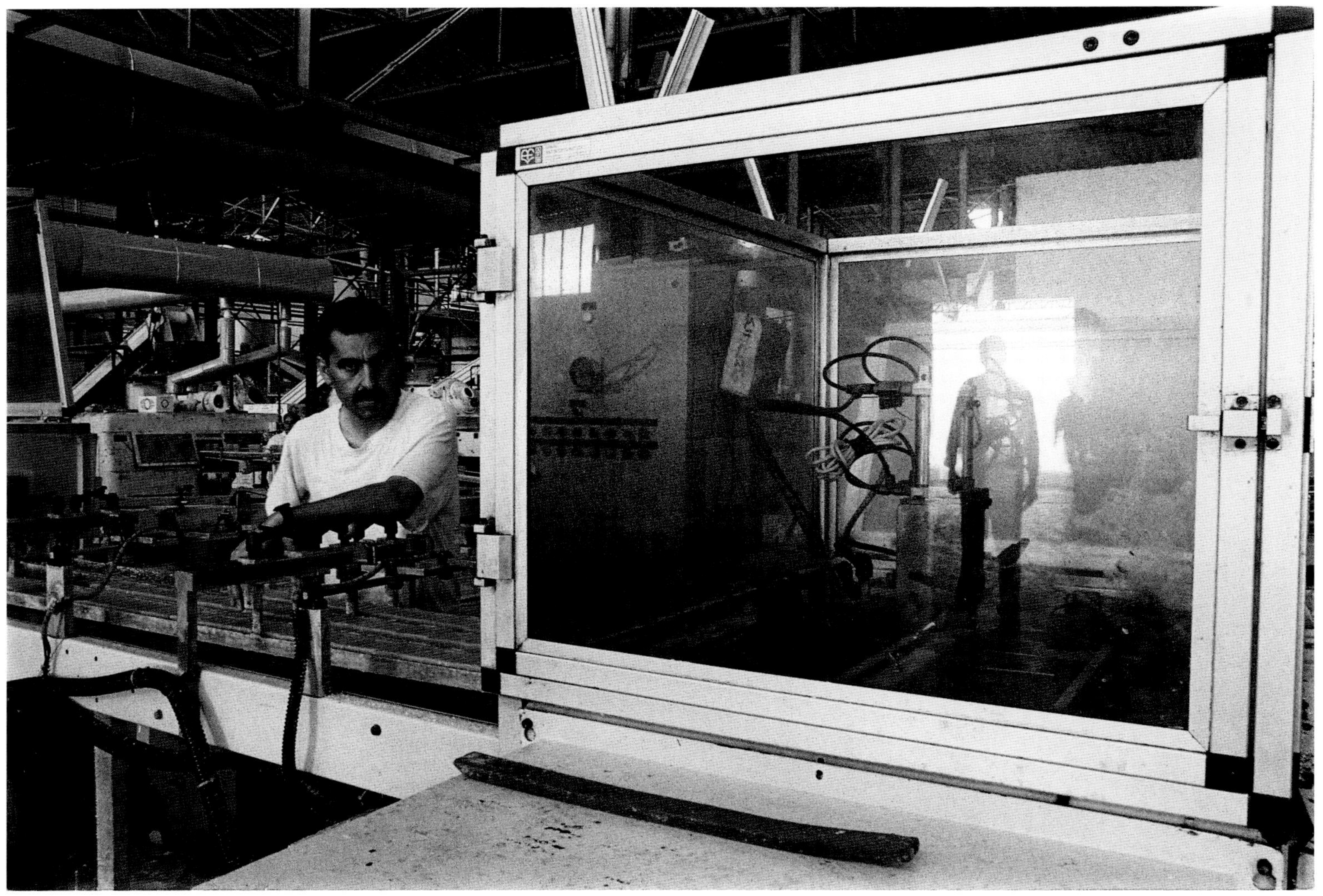

Untitled, from the series "Modern Times," 1998
Gelatin silver print, 12.6 x 17.7 in. (32 x 45 cm)
Courtesy the artist

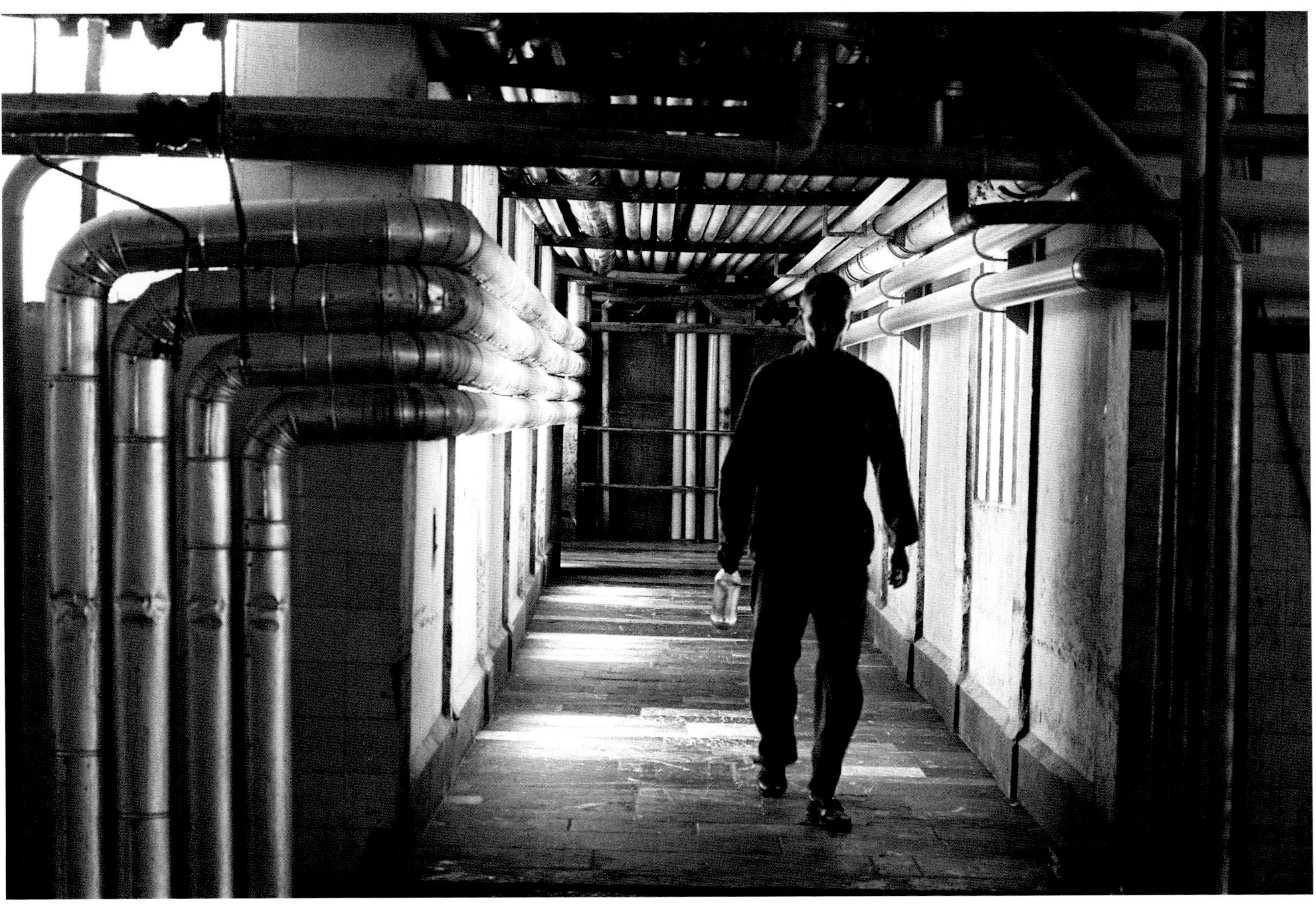

Untitled, from the series "Modern Times," 1998
Gelatin silver print, 12.6 x 17.7 in. (32 x 45 cm)
Courtesy the artist

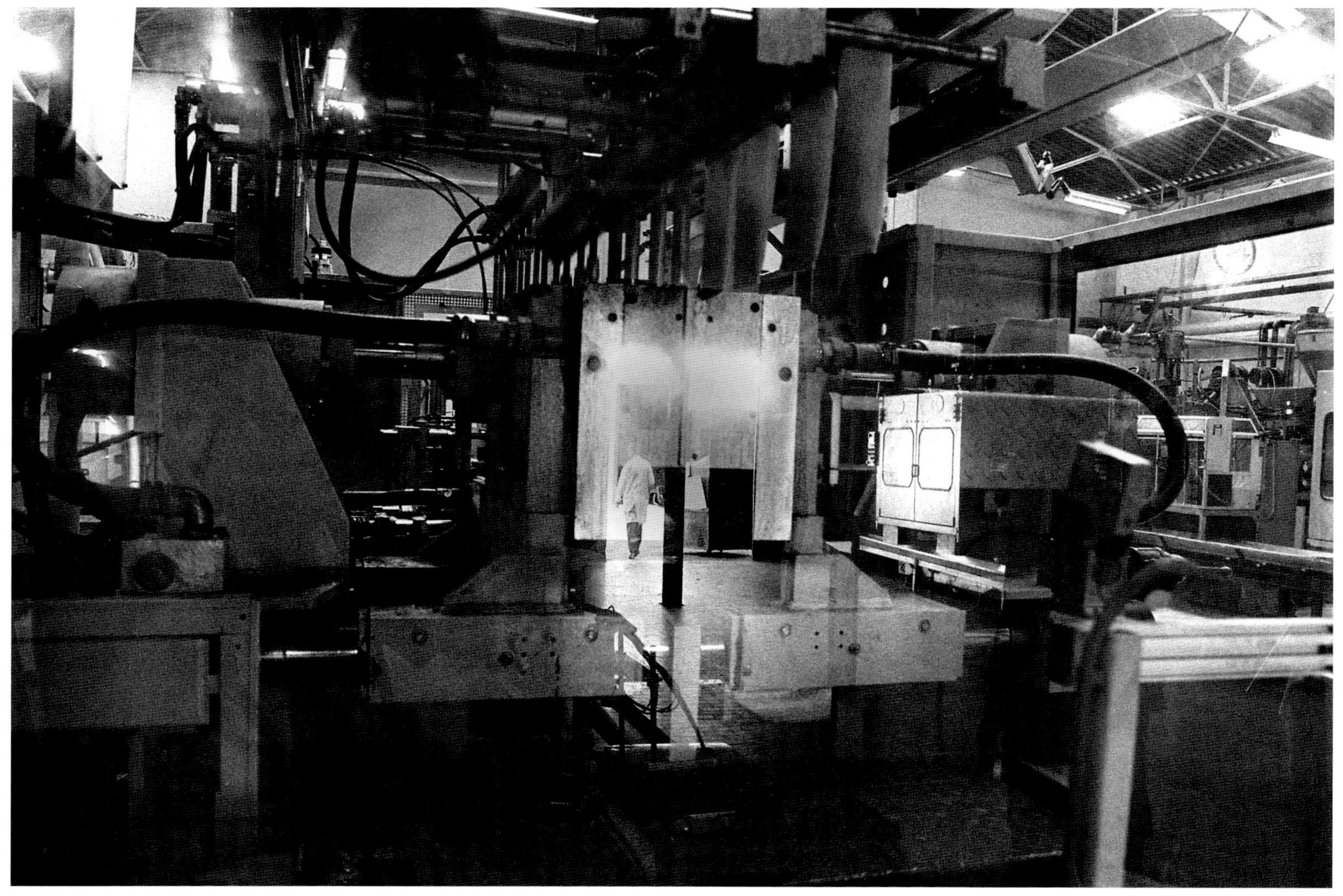

Untitled, from the series "Modern Times," 1998
Gelatin silver print, 12.6 x 17.7 in. (32 x 45 cm)
Courtesy the artist

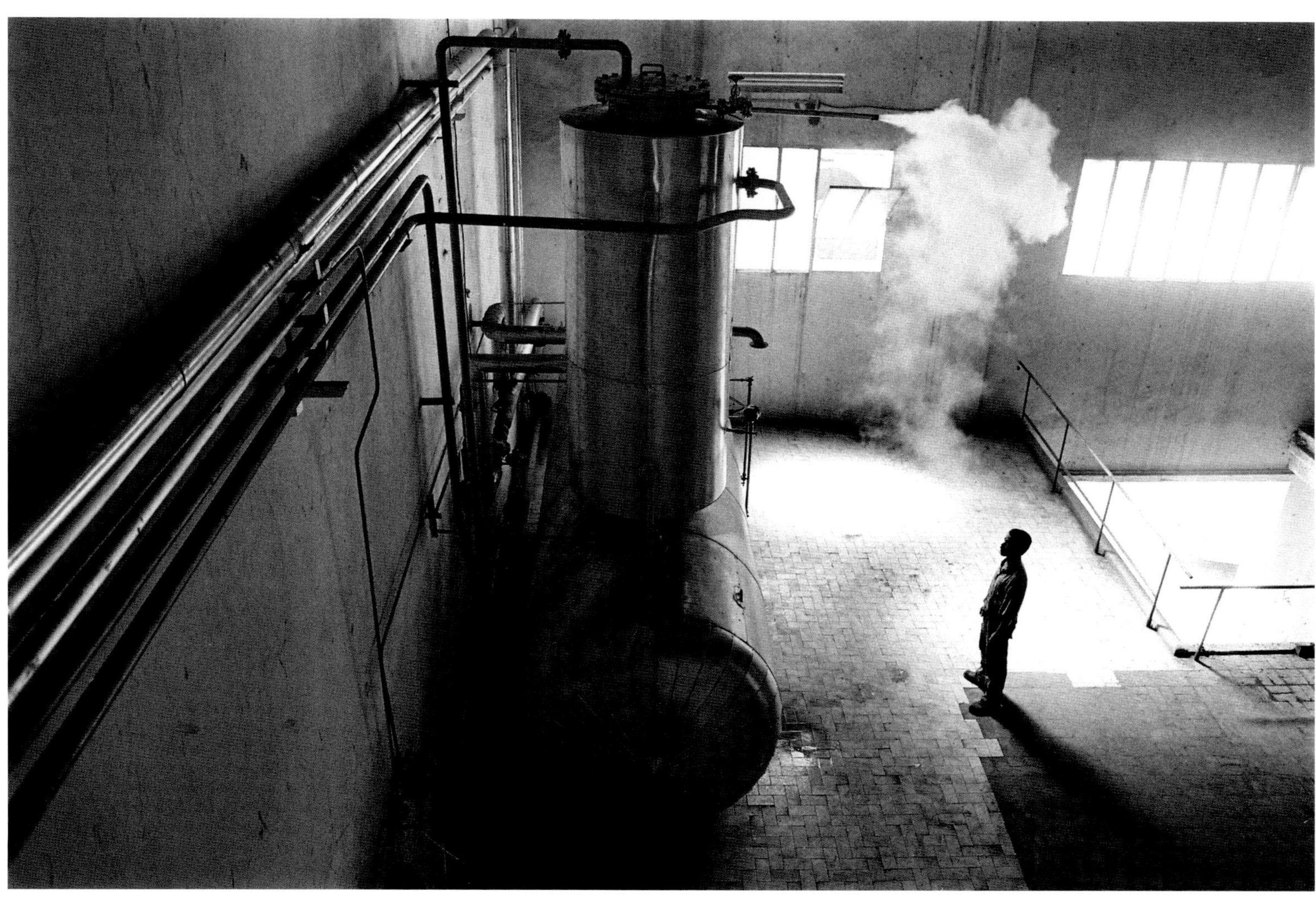

Untitled, from the series "Modern Times," 1998
Gelatin silver print, 12.6 x 17.7 in. (32 x 45 cm)
Courtesy the artist

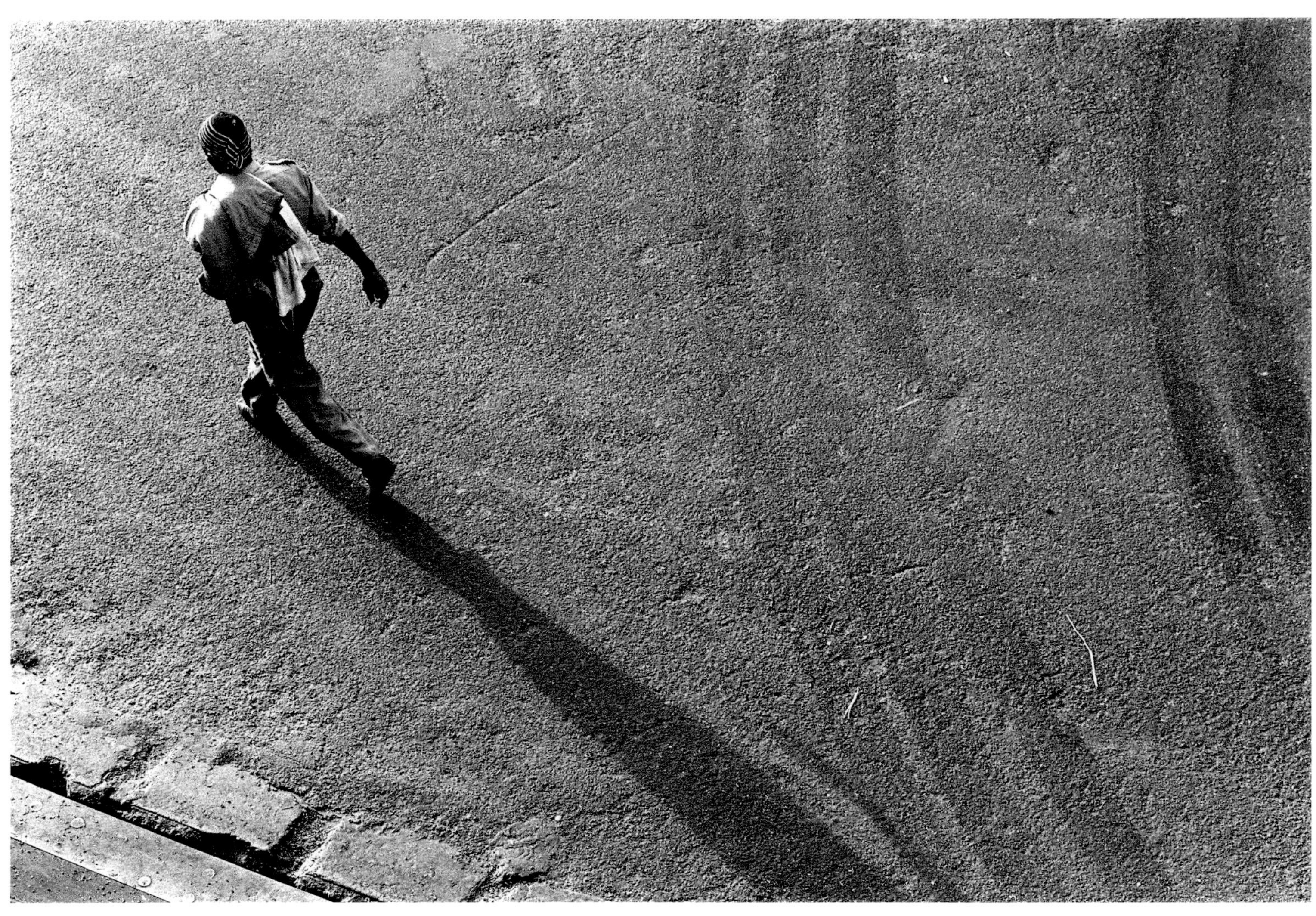

Untitled, from the series "Modern Times," 1998
Gelatin silver print, 12.6 x 17.7 in. (32 x 45 cm)
Courtesy the artist

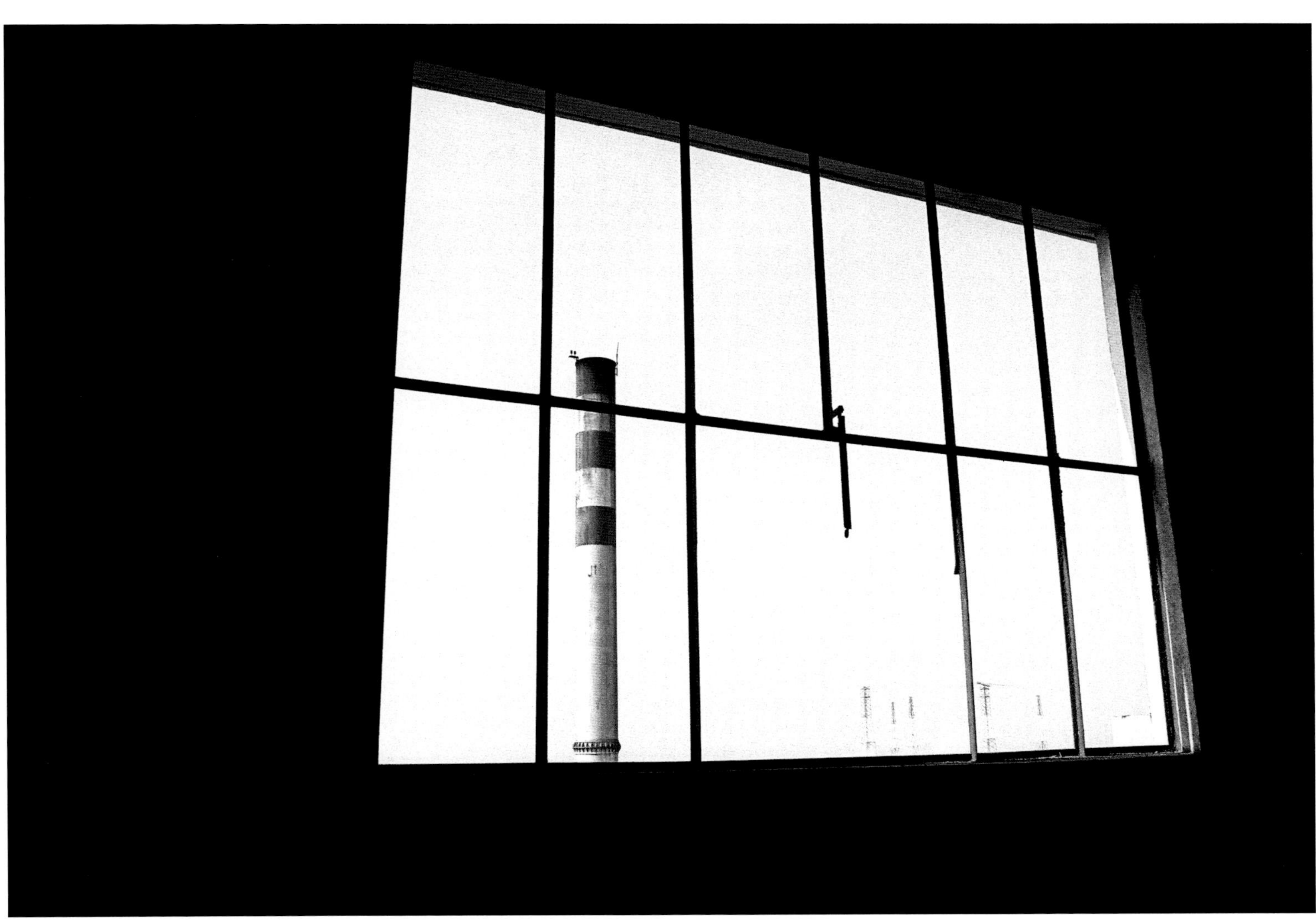

Untitled, from the series "Modern Times," 1998
Gelatin silver print, 12.6 x 17.7 in. (32 x 45 cm)
Courtesy the artist

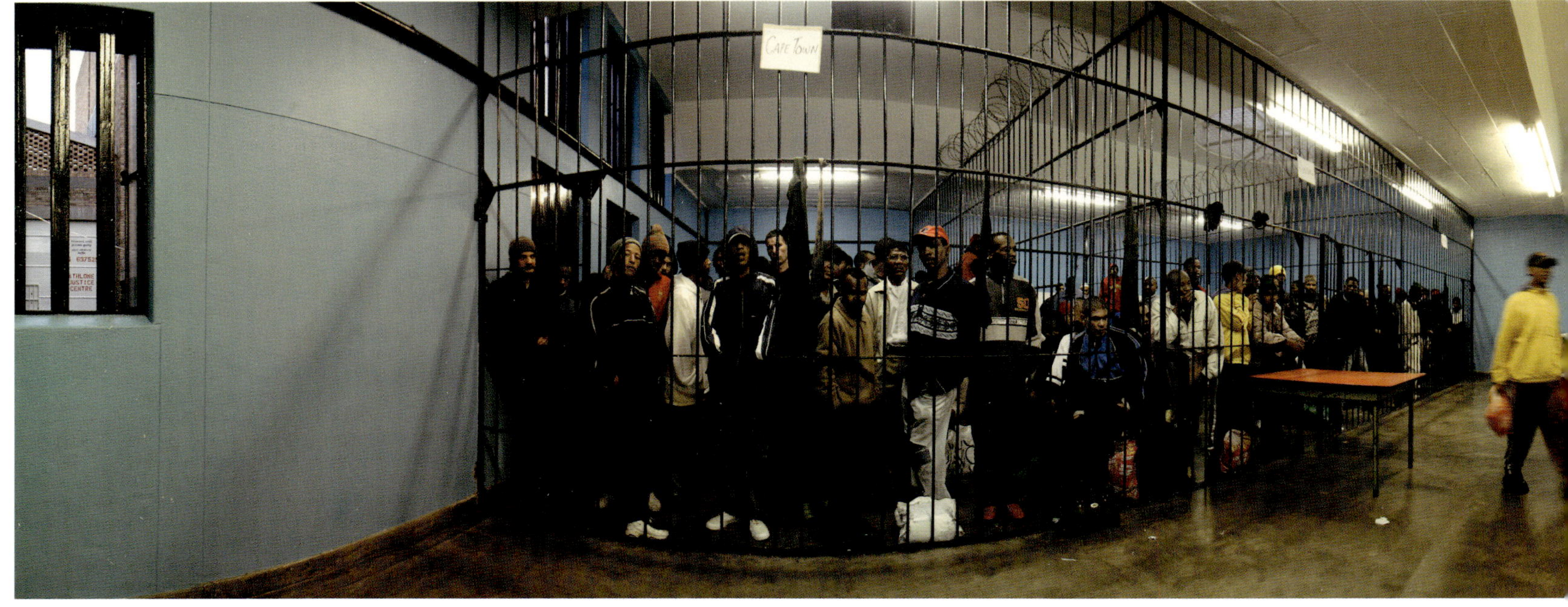
CAPE TOWN

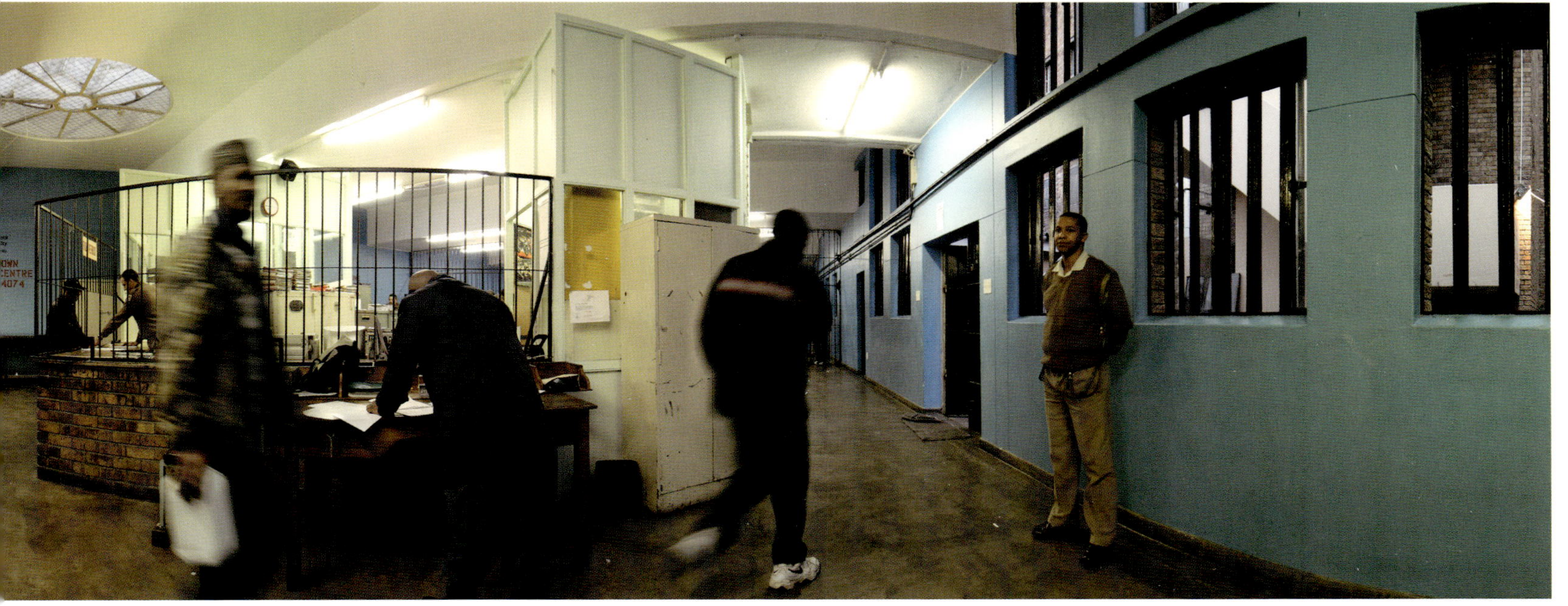

'Reception,' Pollsmoor Maximum Security Prison, from the series "Die Vier Hoeke" (The Four Corners), 2004–05
Pigment print on paper, 22 x 92 in. (55.9 x 233.7 cm)
Courtesy the artist and Goodman Gallery, Johannesburg, Collection of Artur Walther

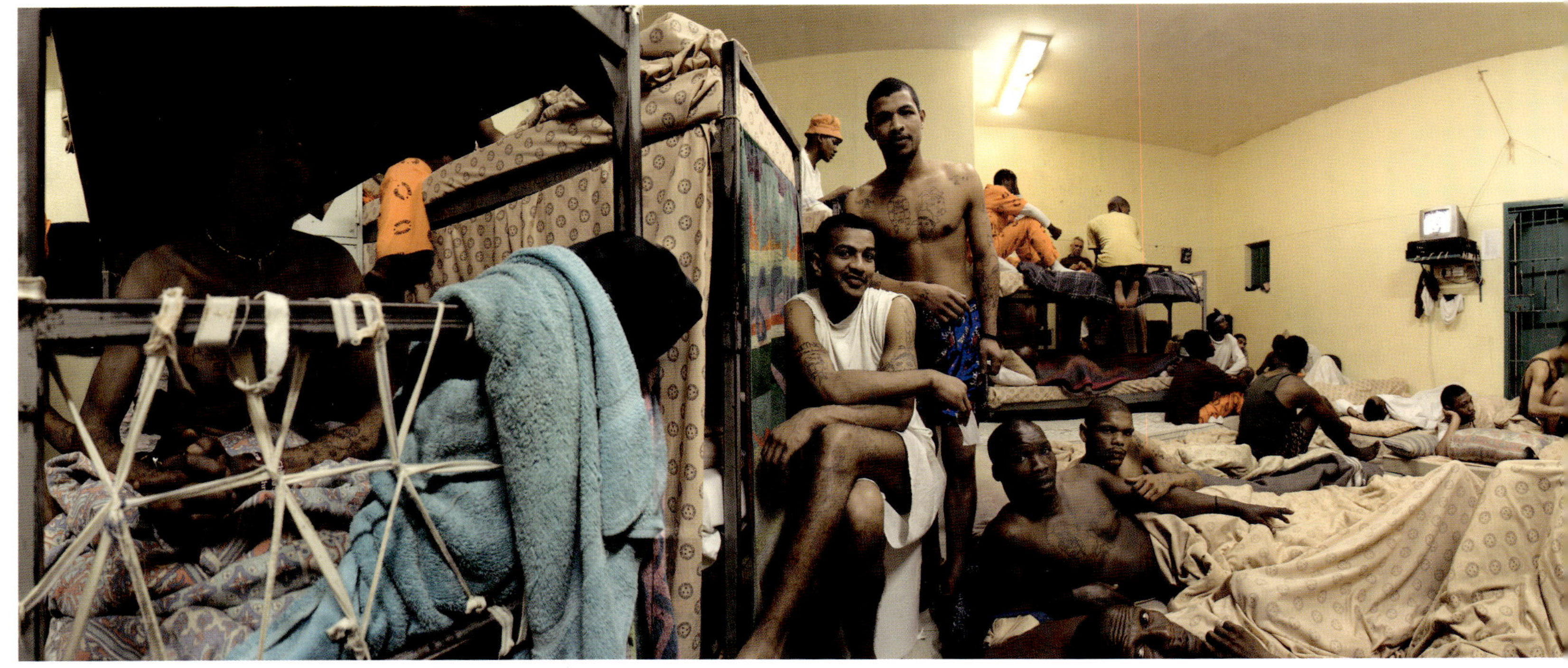

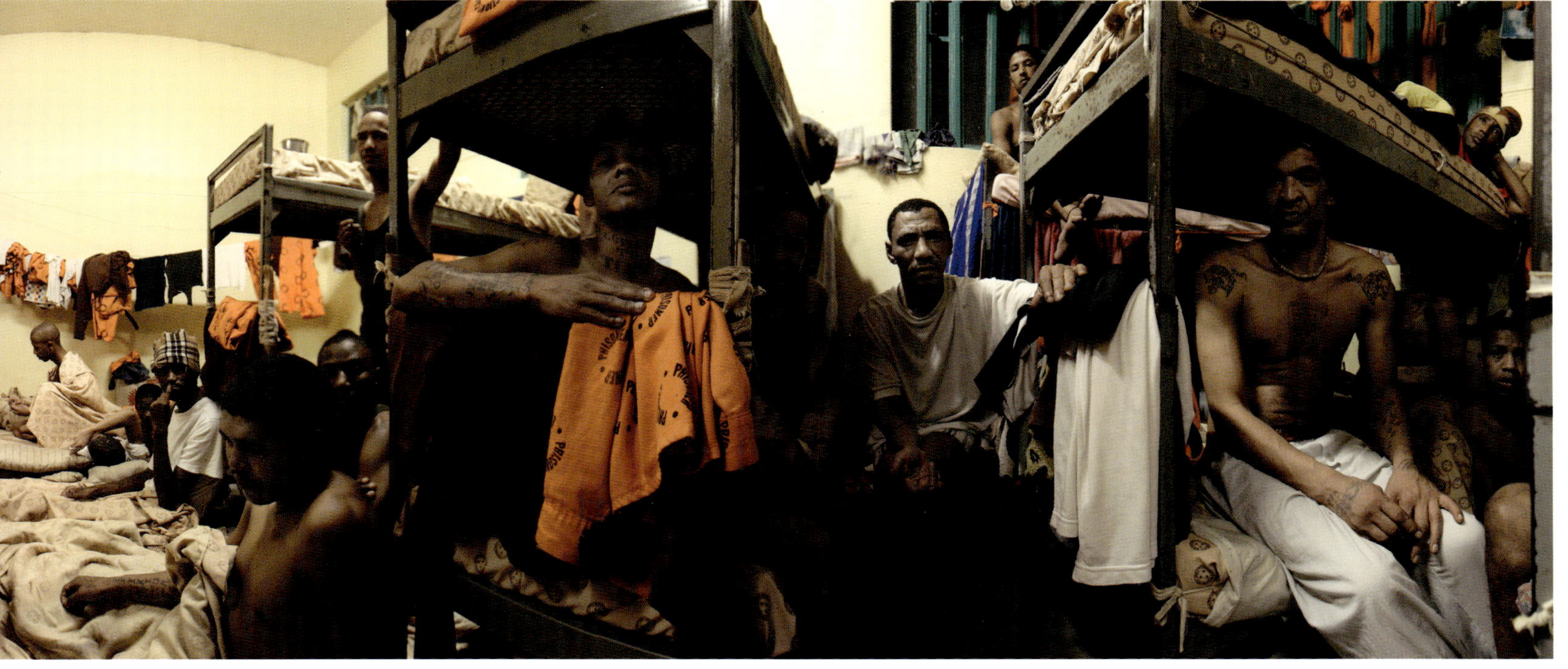

Cell 508b, A Section, Pollsmoor Maximum Security Prison, from the series "Die Vier Hoeke" (The Four Corners), 2004–05
Pigment print on paper, 22 x 92 in. (55.9 x 233.7 cm)
Courtesy the artist and Goodman Gallery, Johannesburg, Collection of Artur Walther

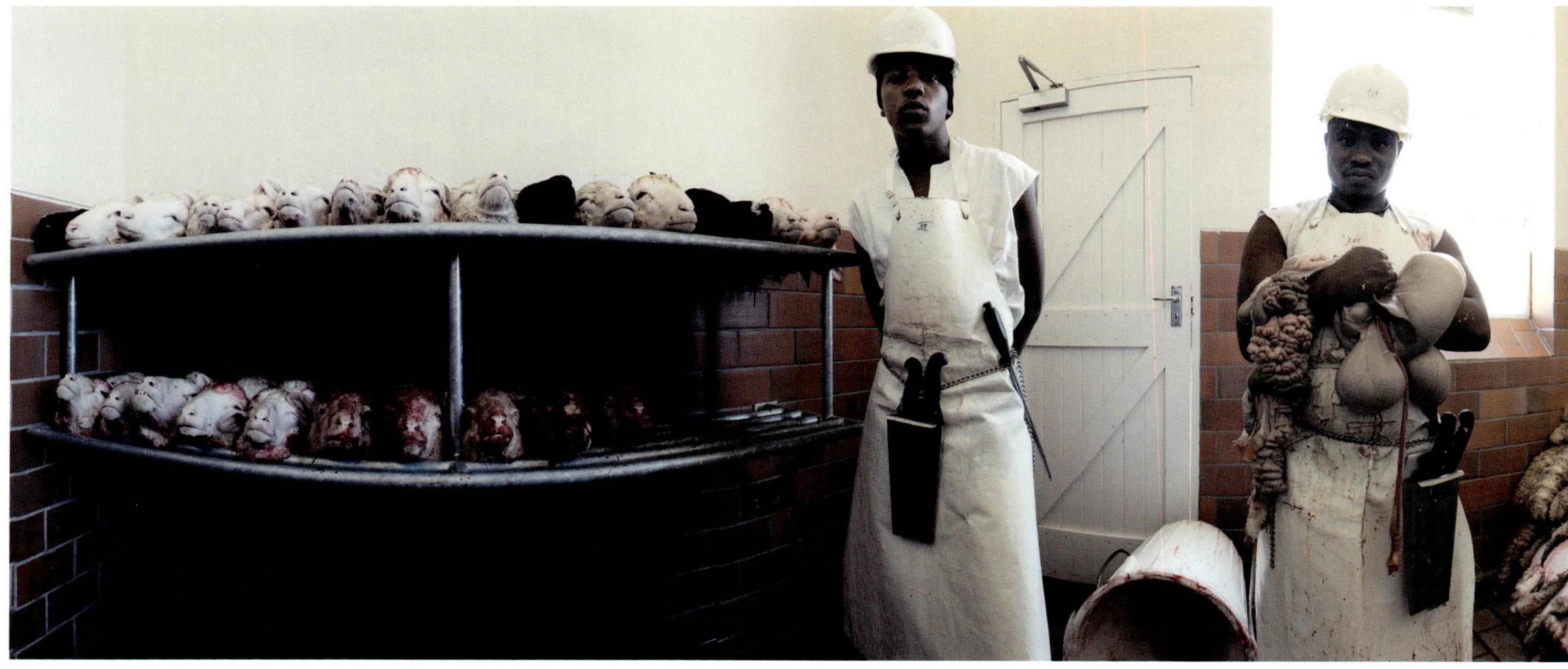

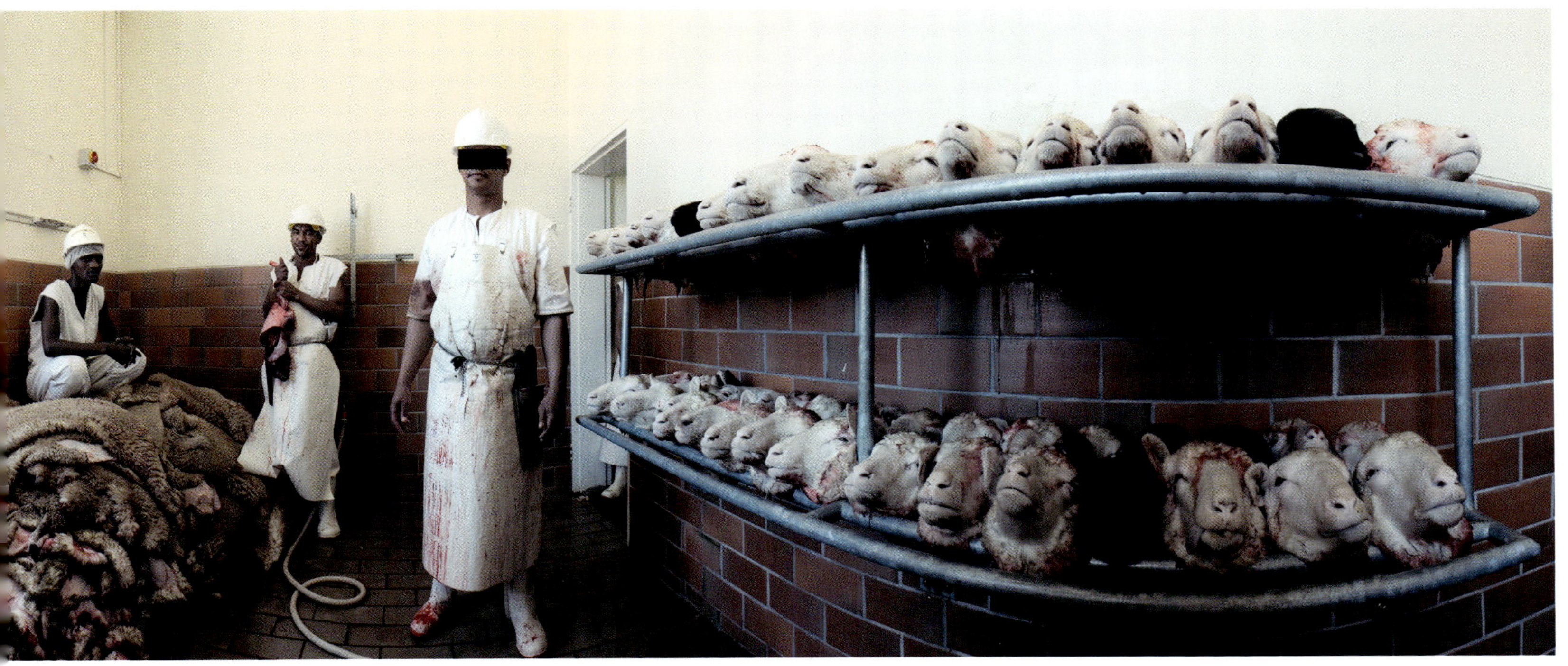

Abbatoir, Voorberg Prison, from the series "Die Vier Hoeke" (The Four Corners), 2004–05
Pigment print on paper, 22 x 92 in. (55.9 x 233.7 cm)
Courtesy the artist and Goodman Gallery, Johannesburg, Collection of Artur Walther

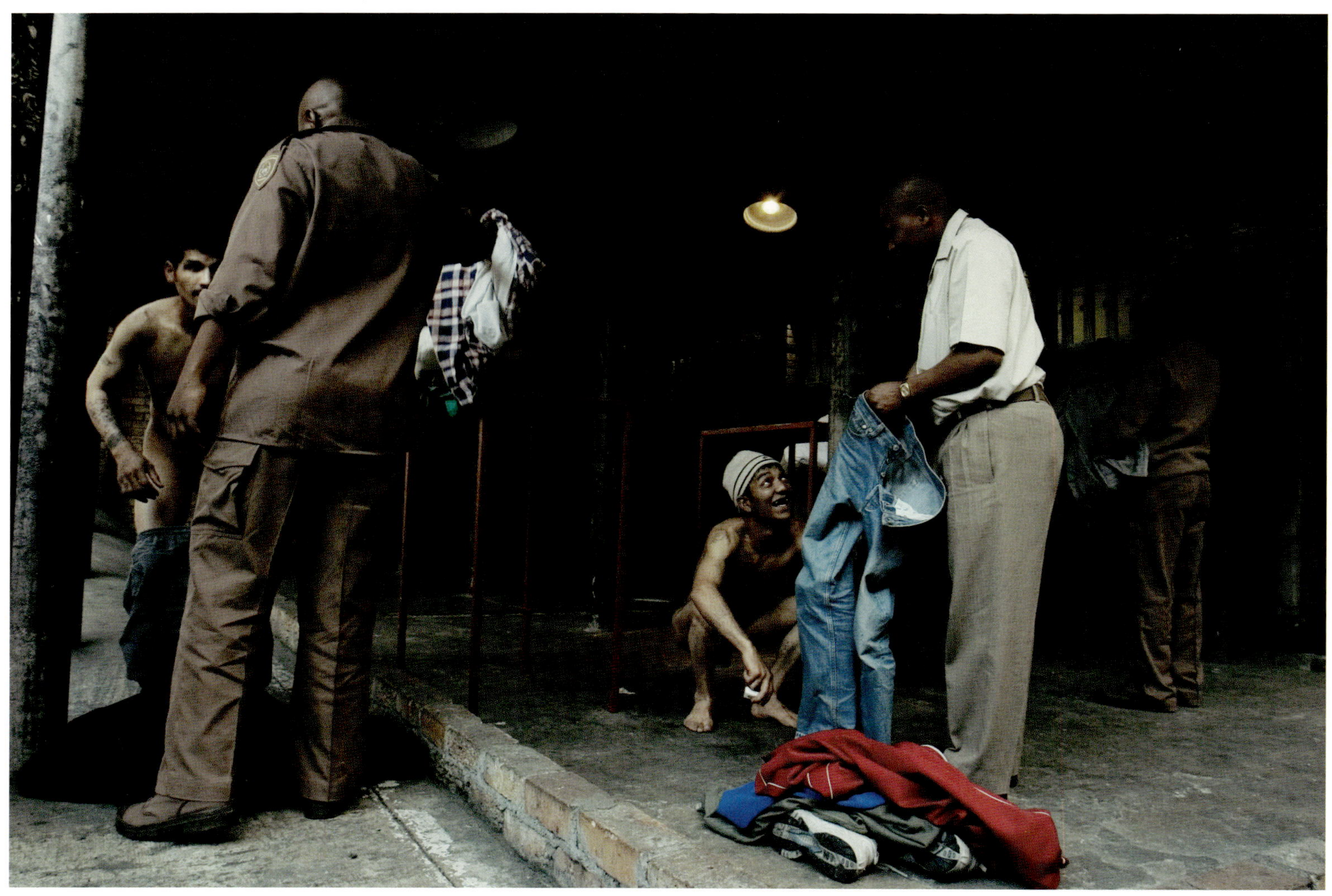

Strip Search, Pollsmoor Maximum Security Prison
from the series "Die Vier Hoeke" (The Four Corners), 2004–05
Pigment print on paper, 22 x 30.75 in. (55.9 x 78.1 cm)
Courtesy the artist and Goodman Gallery, Johannesburg

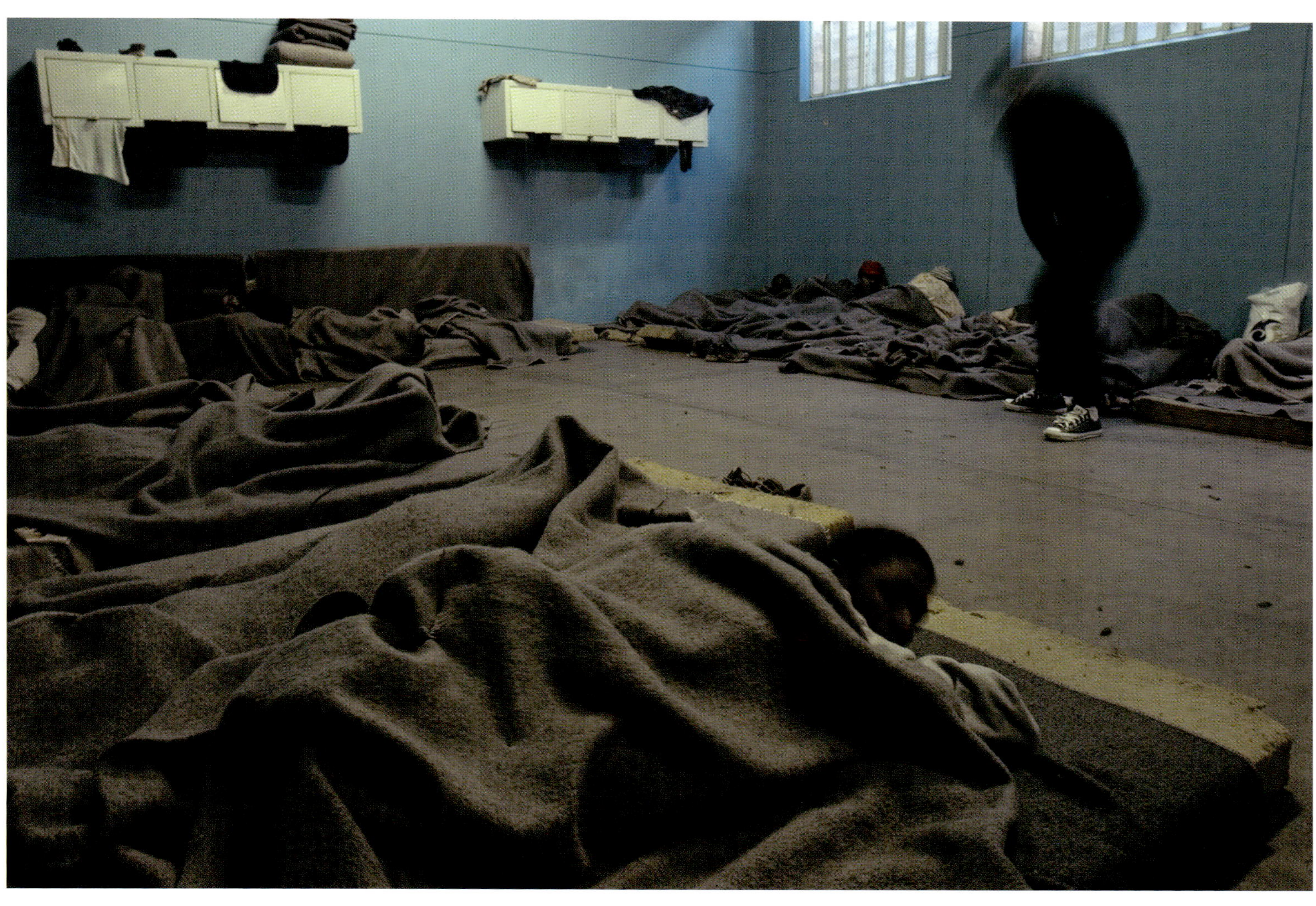

Hof Cell, Pollsmoor Maximum Security Prison,
from the series "Die Vier Hoeke" (The Four Corners), 2004–05
Pigment print on paper, 22 x 30.75 in. (55.9 x 78.1 cm)
Courtesy the artist and Goodman Gallery, Johannesburg

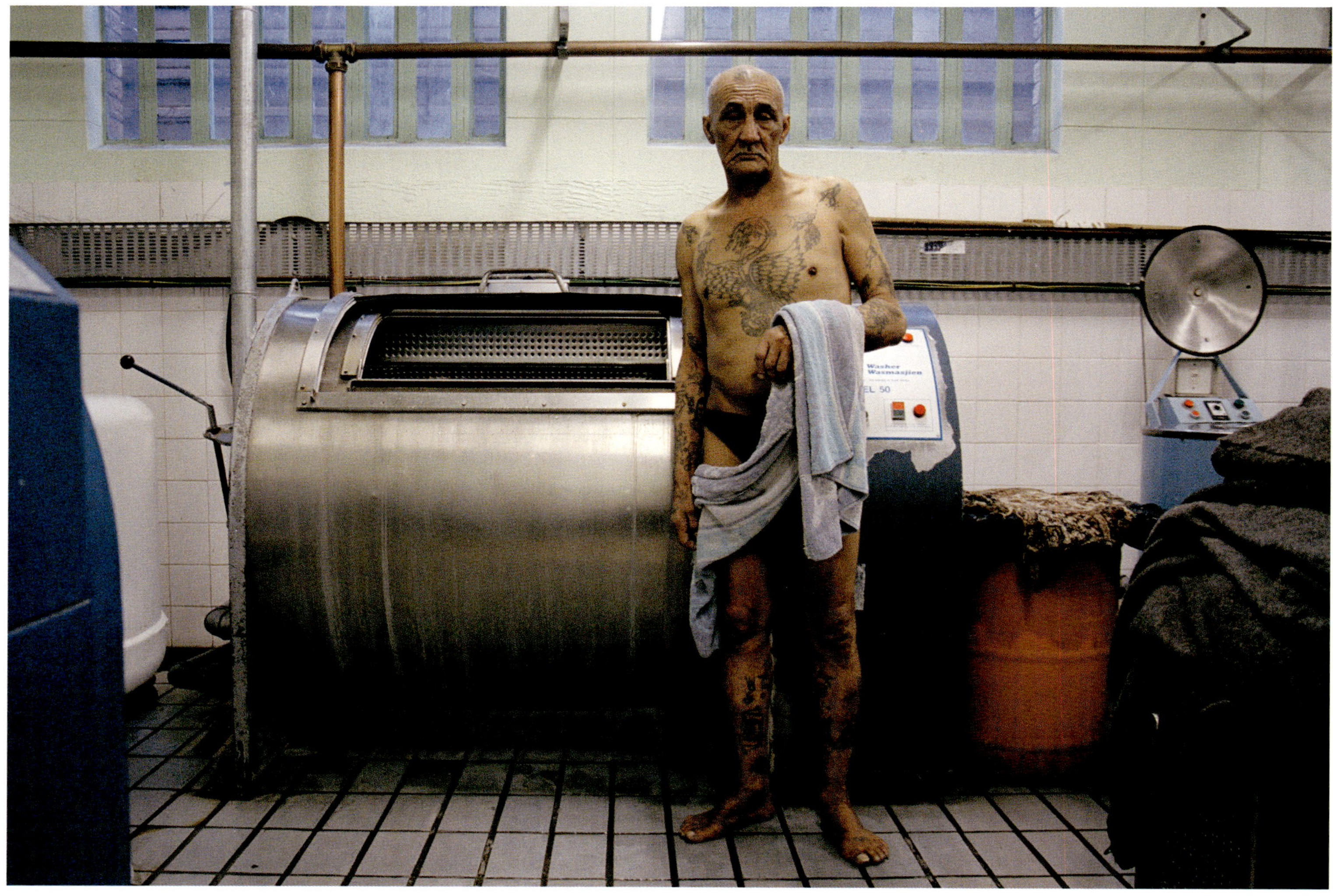

Johny Fortune, Pollsmoor Maximum Security Prison,
from the series "Die Vier Hoeke" (The Four Corners), 2004–05
Pigment print on paper, 22 x 30.75 in. (55.9 x 78.1 cm)
Courtesy the artist and Goodman Gallery, Johannesburg

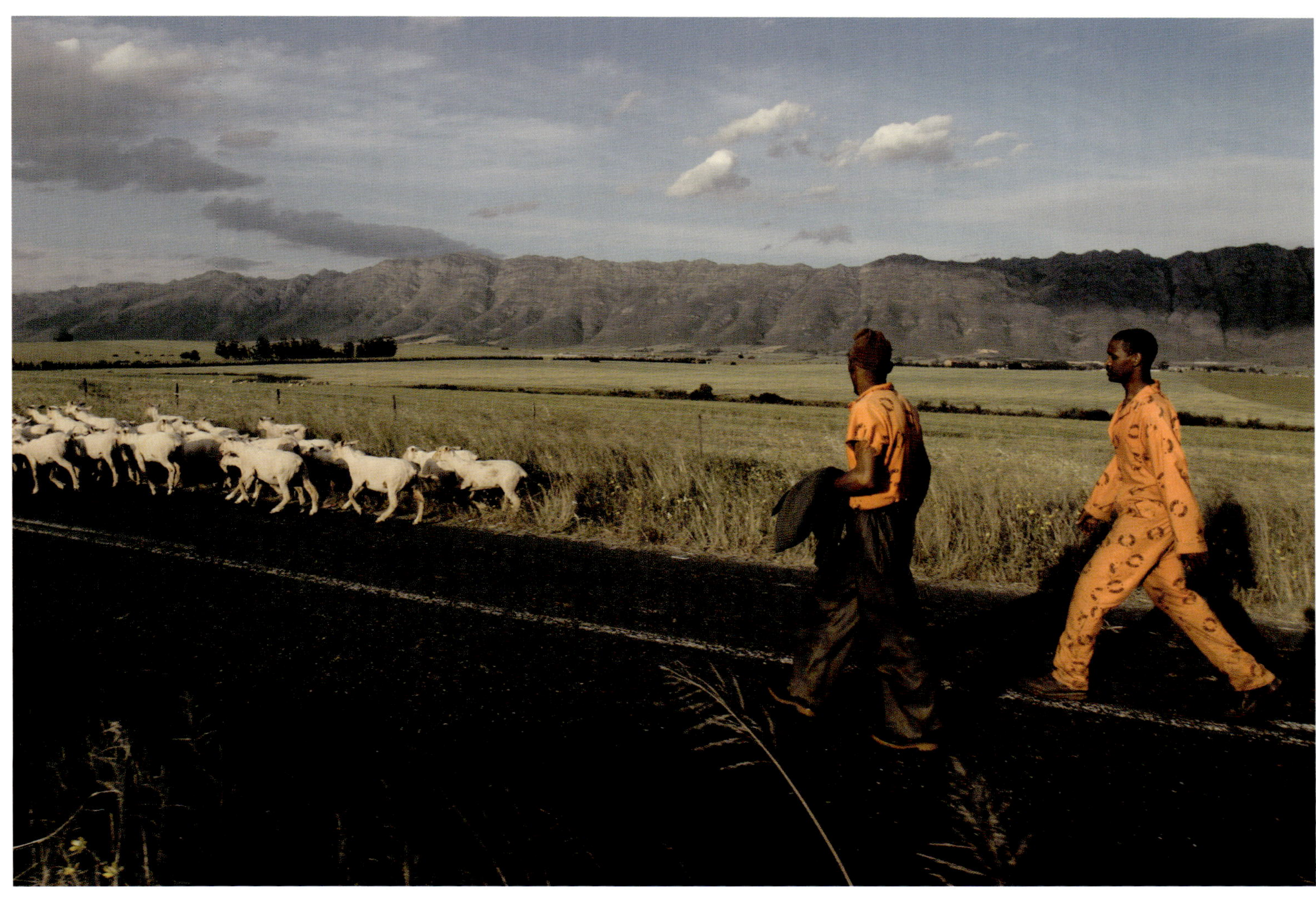

Prisoners, Voorberg Prison,
from the series "Die Vier Hoeke" (The Four Corners), 2004–05
Pigment print on paper, 22 x 30.75 in. (55.9 x 78.1 cm)
Courtesy the artist and Goodman Gallery, Johannesburg

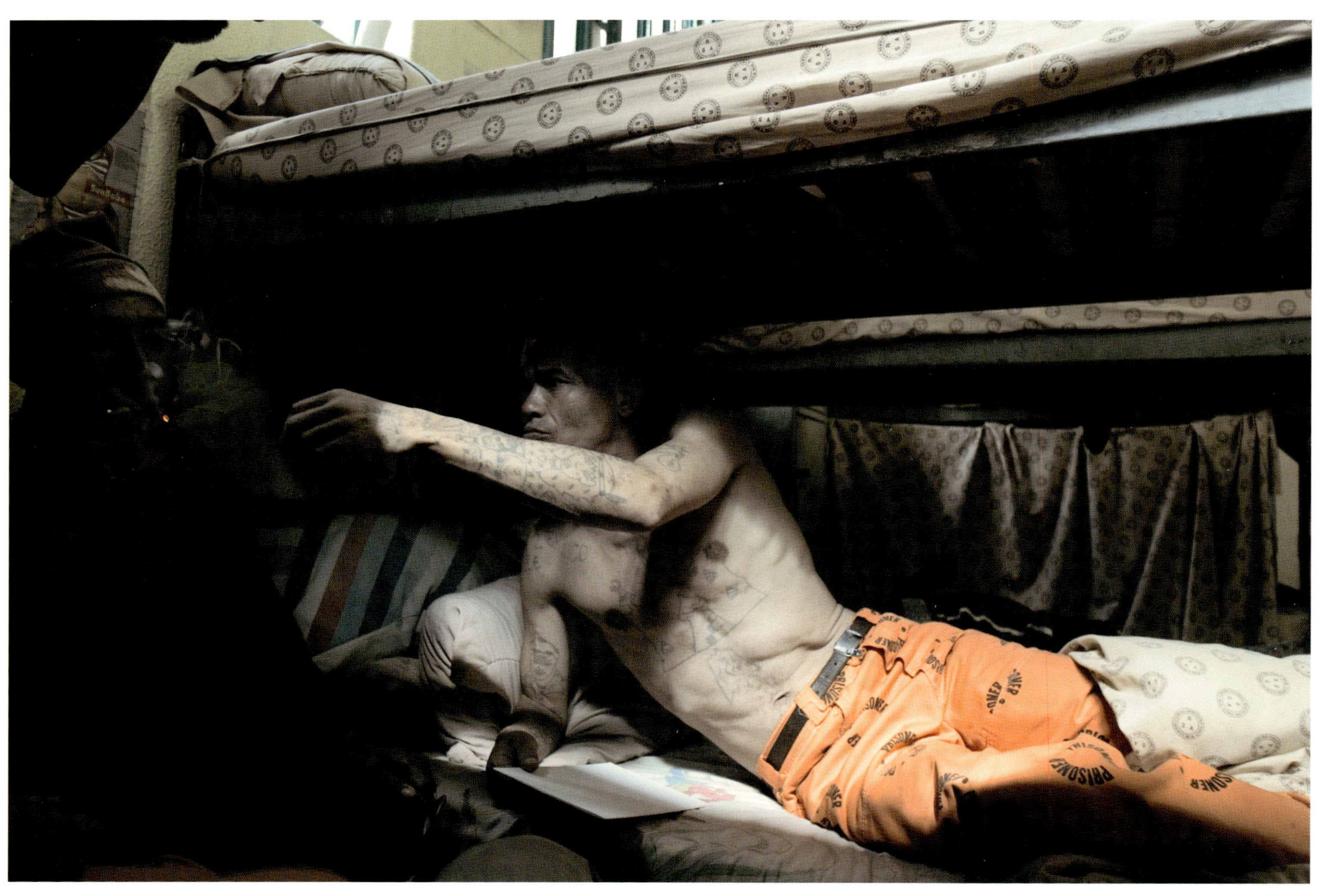

Marc, Pollsmoor Maximum Security Prison,
from the series "Die Vier Hoeke" (The Four Corners), 2004–05
Pigment print on paper, 22 x 30.75 in. (55.9 x 78.1 cm)
Courtesy the artist and Goodman Gallery, Johannesburg

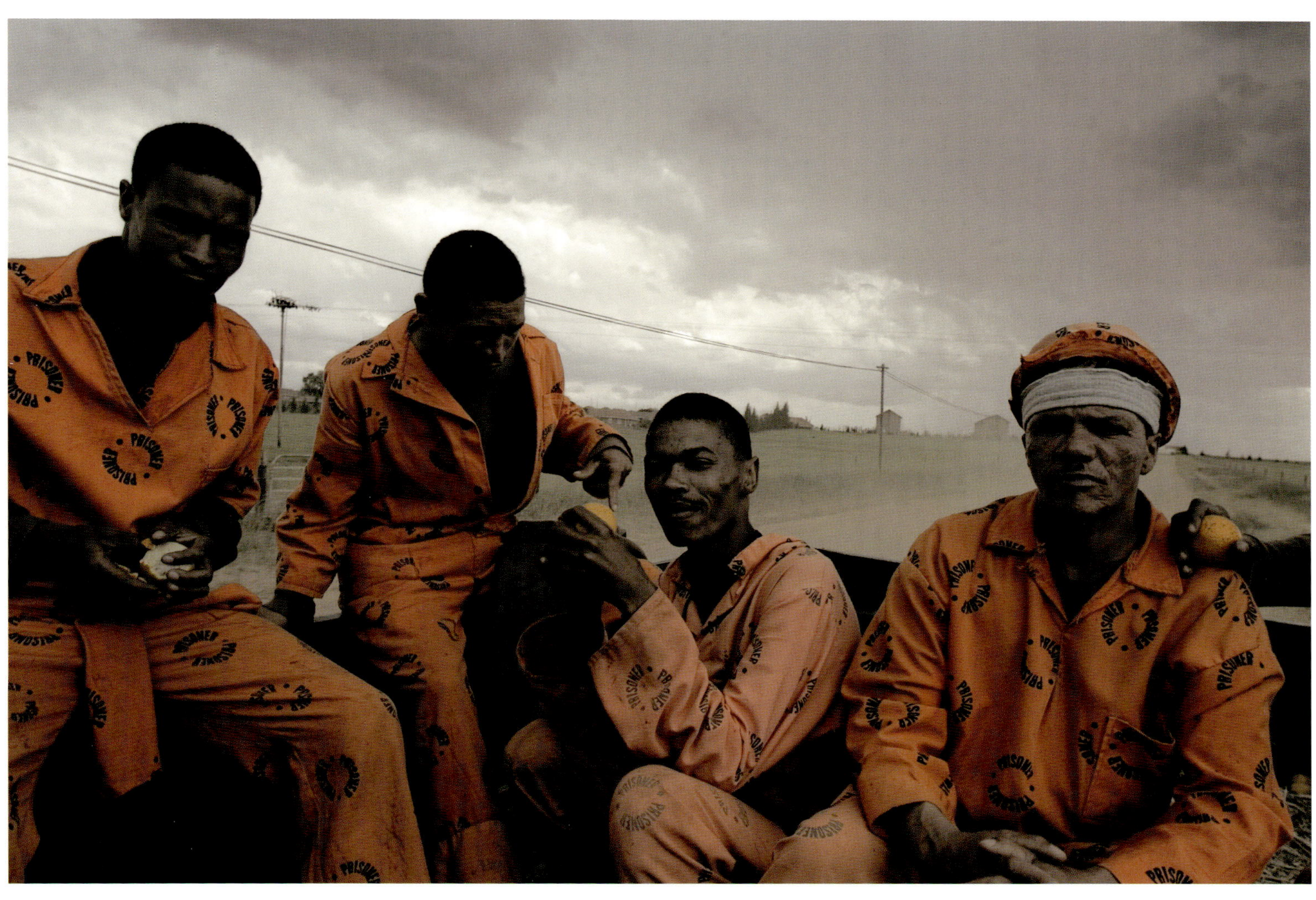

Prisoners, Voorberg Prison,
from the series "Die Vier Hoeke" (The Four Corners), 2004–05
Pigment print on paper, 22 x 30.75 in. (55.9 x 78.1 cm)
Courtesy the artist and Goodman Gallery, Johannesburg

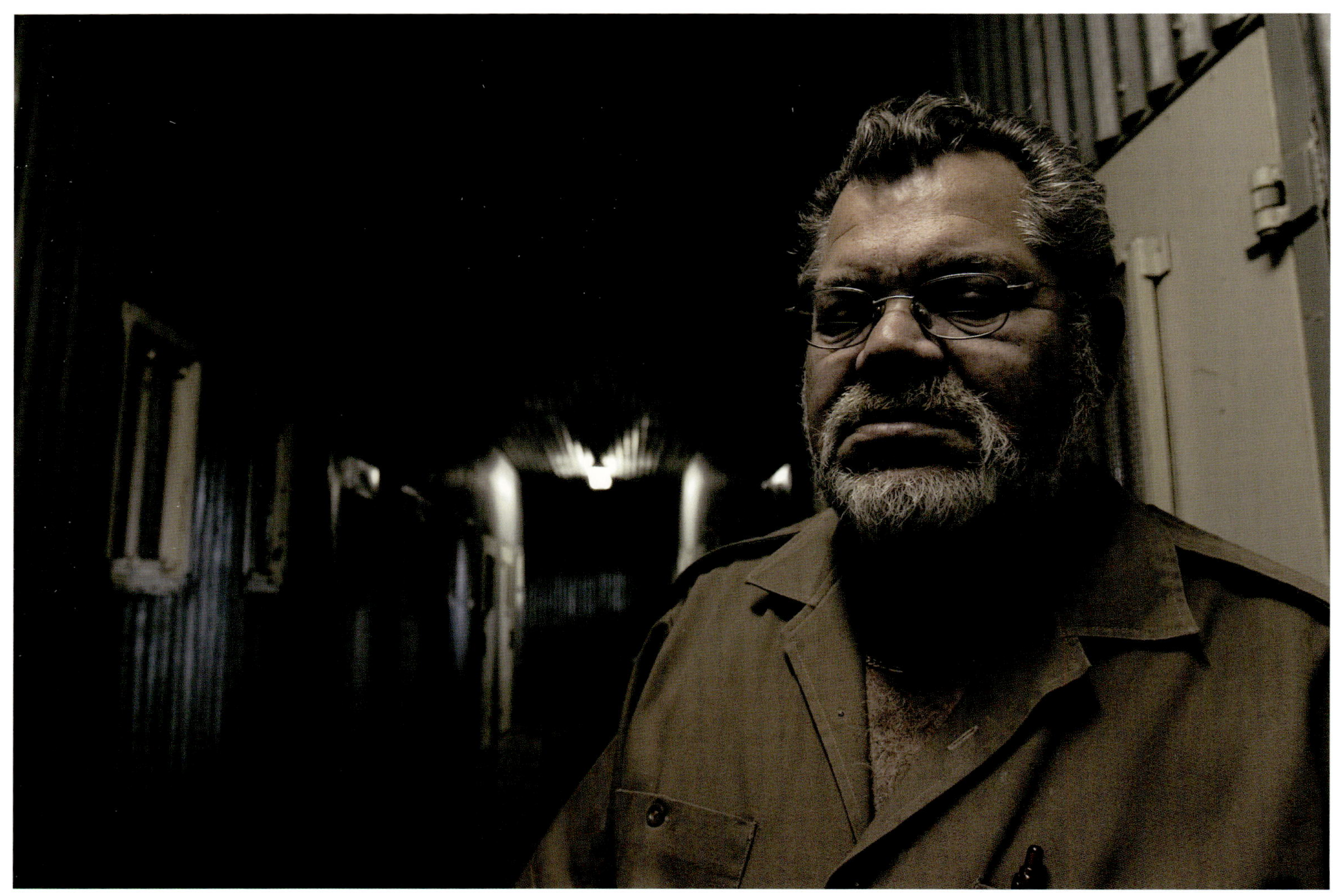

Flynn, Voorberg Prison,
from the series "Die Vier Hoeke" (The Four Corners), 2004–05
Pigment print on paper, 22 x 30.75 in. (55.9 x 78.1 cm)
Courtesy the artist and Goodman Gallery, Johannesburg

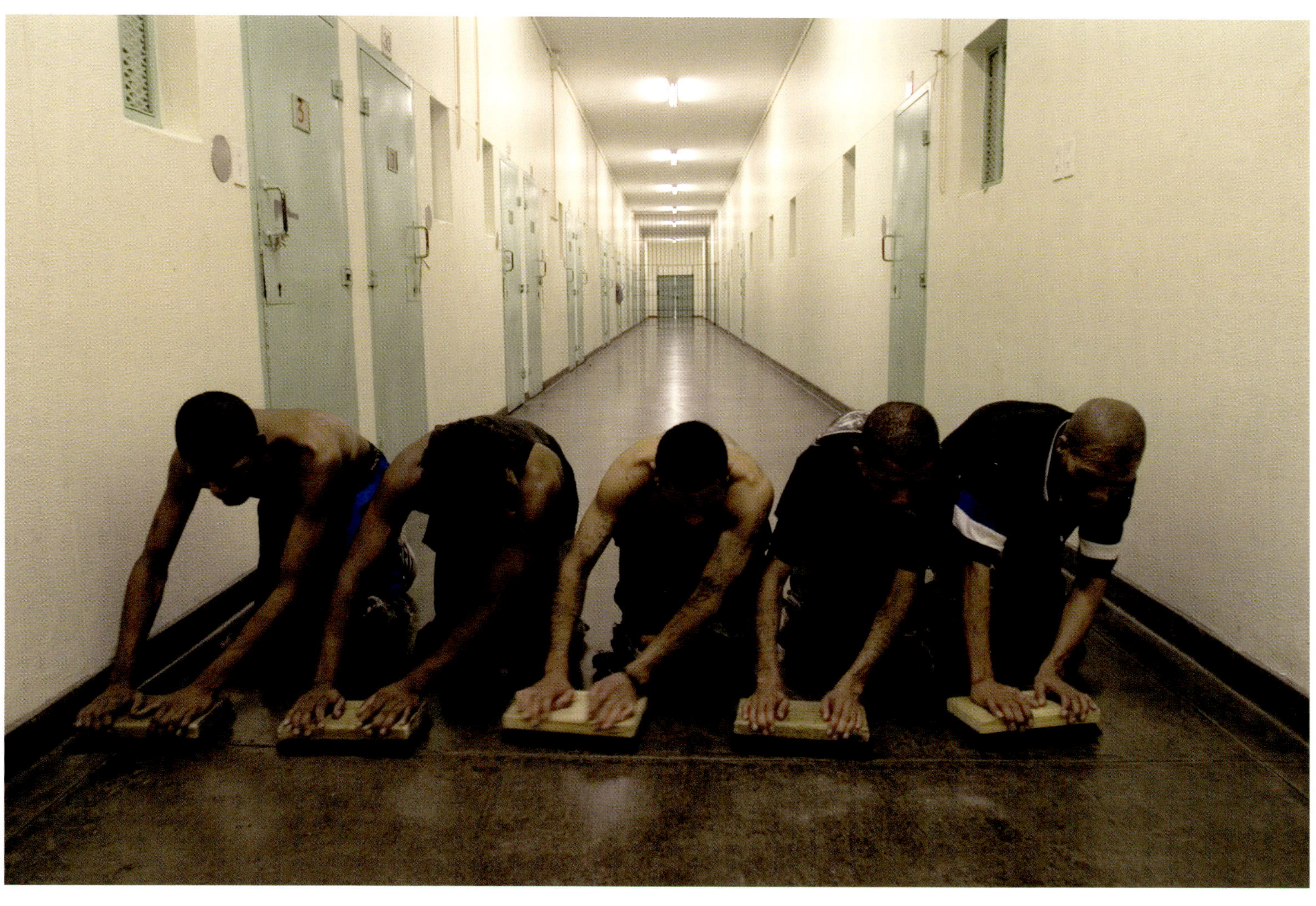

Pasvang, Pollsmoor Maximum Security Prison,
from the series "Die Vier Hoeke" (The Four Corners) 2004–05
Pigment print on paper, 22 x 30.75 in. (55.9 x 78.1 cm)
Courtesy the artist and Goodman Gallery, Johannesburg

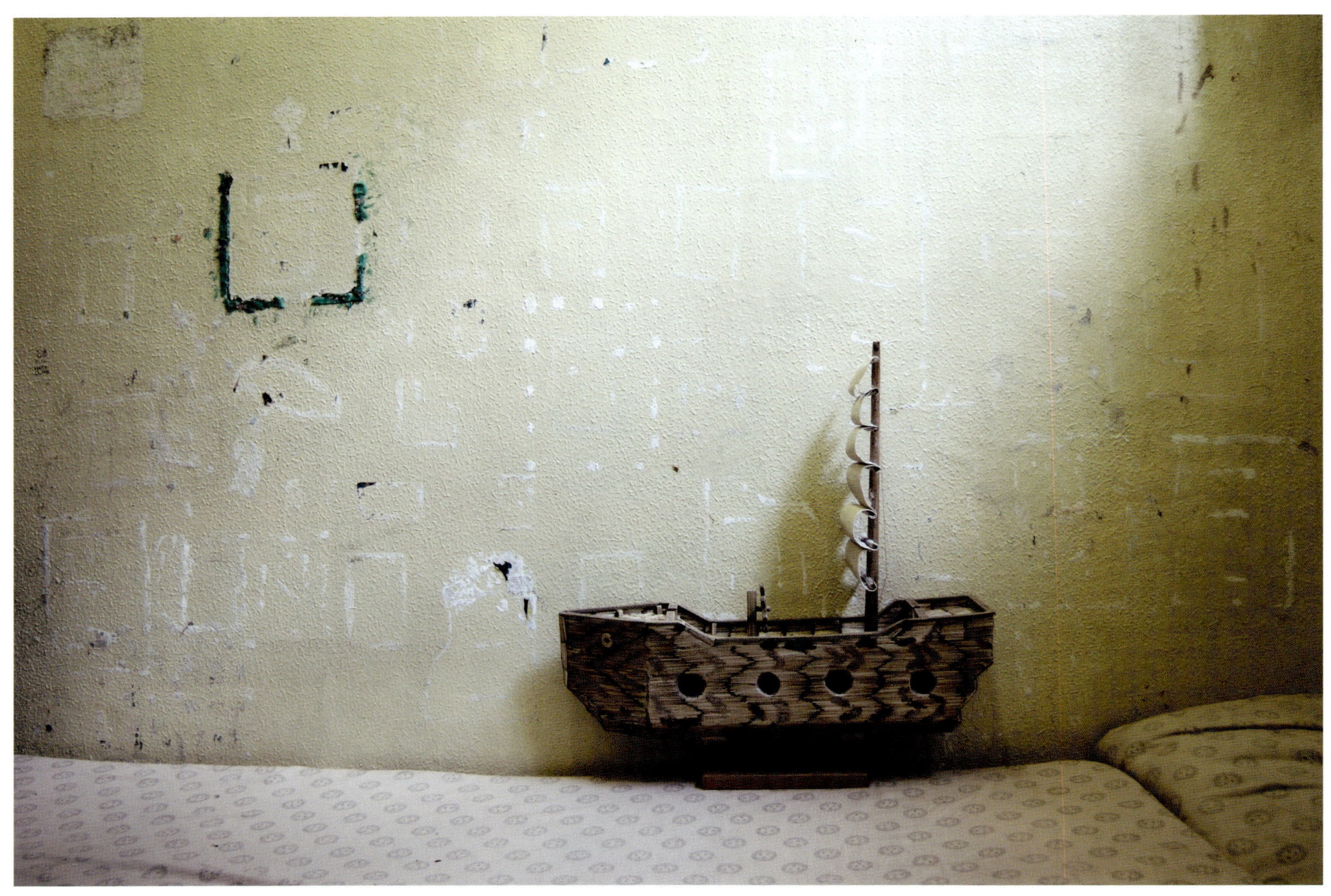

Boat, Pollsmoor Maximum Security Prison,
from the series "Die Vier Hoeke" (The Four Corners), 2004–05
Pigment print on paper, 22 x 30.75 in. (55.9 x 78.1 cm)
Courtesy the artist and Goodman Gallery, Johannesburg

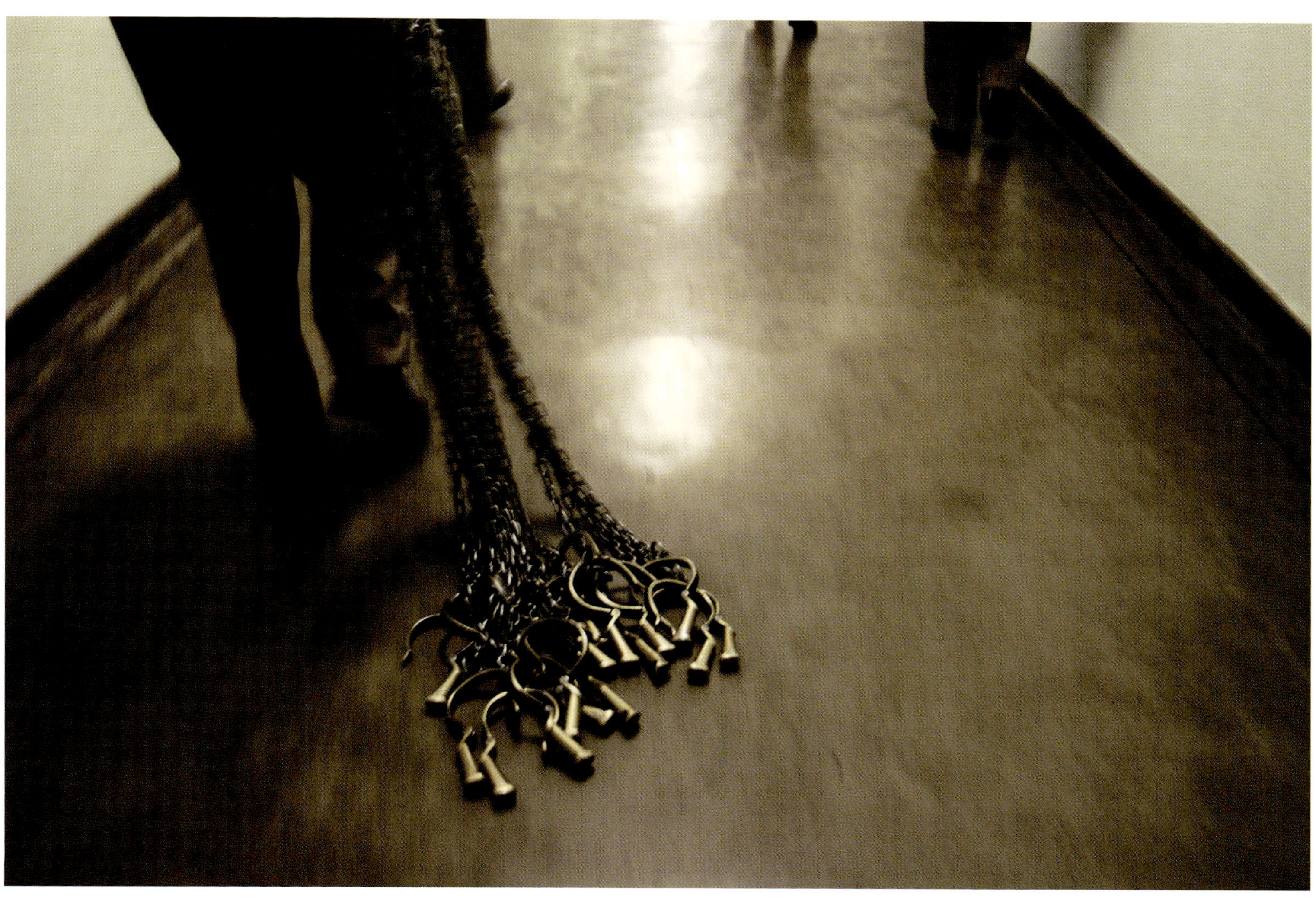

Shackles, Pollsmoor Maximum Security Prison,
from the series "Die Vier Hoeke" (The Four Corners), 2004–05
Pigment print on paper, 22 x 30.75 in. (55.9 x 78.1 cm)
Courtesy the artist and Goodman Gallery, Johannesburg

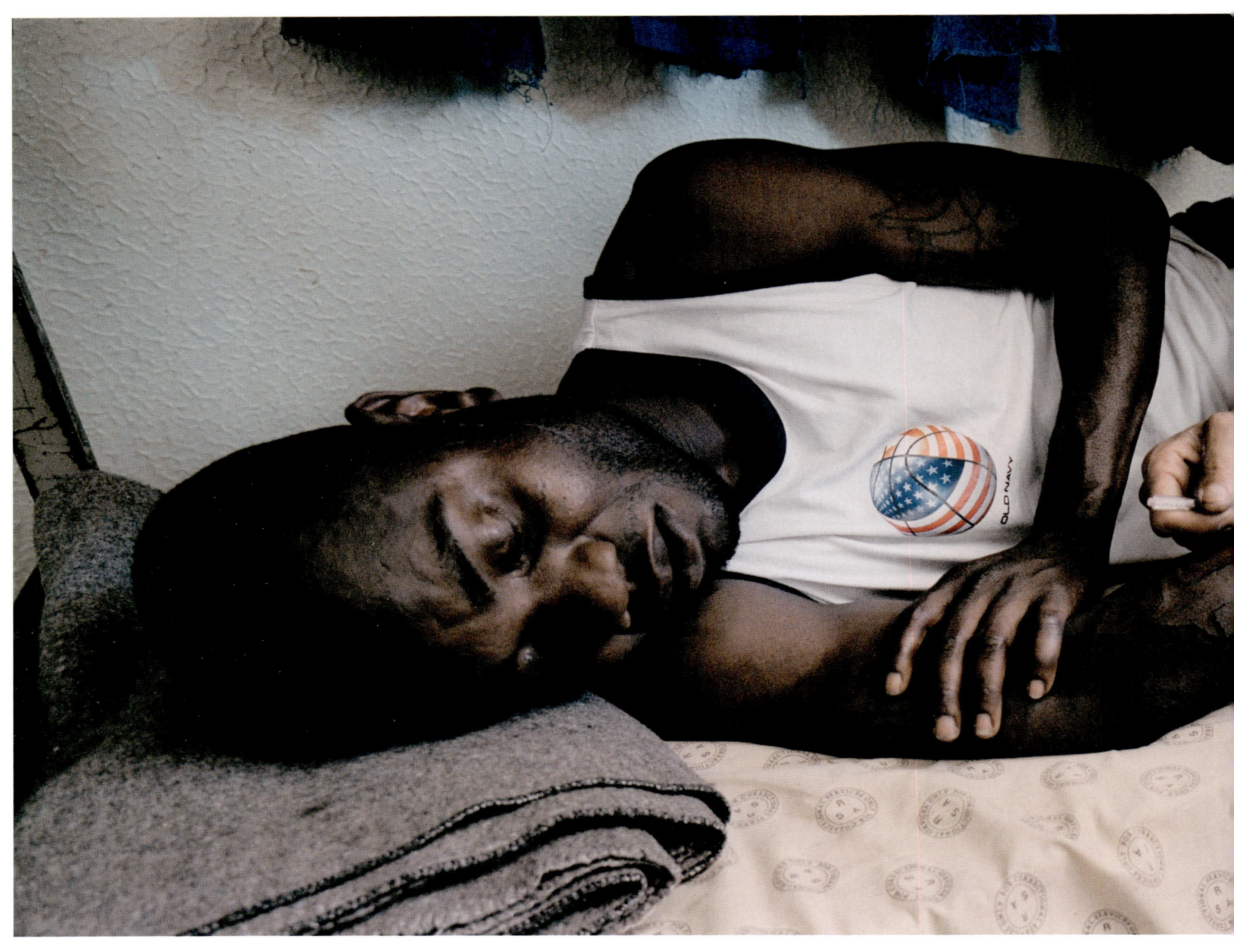
OLD NAVY

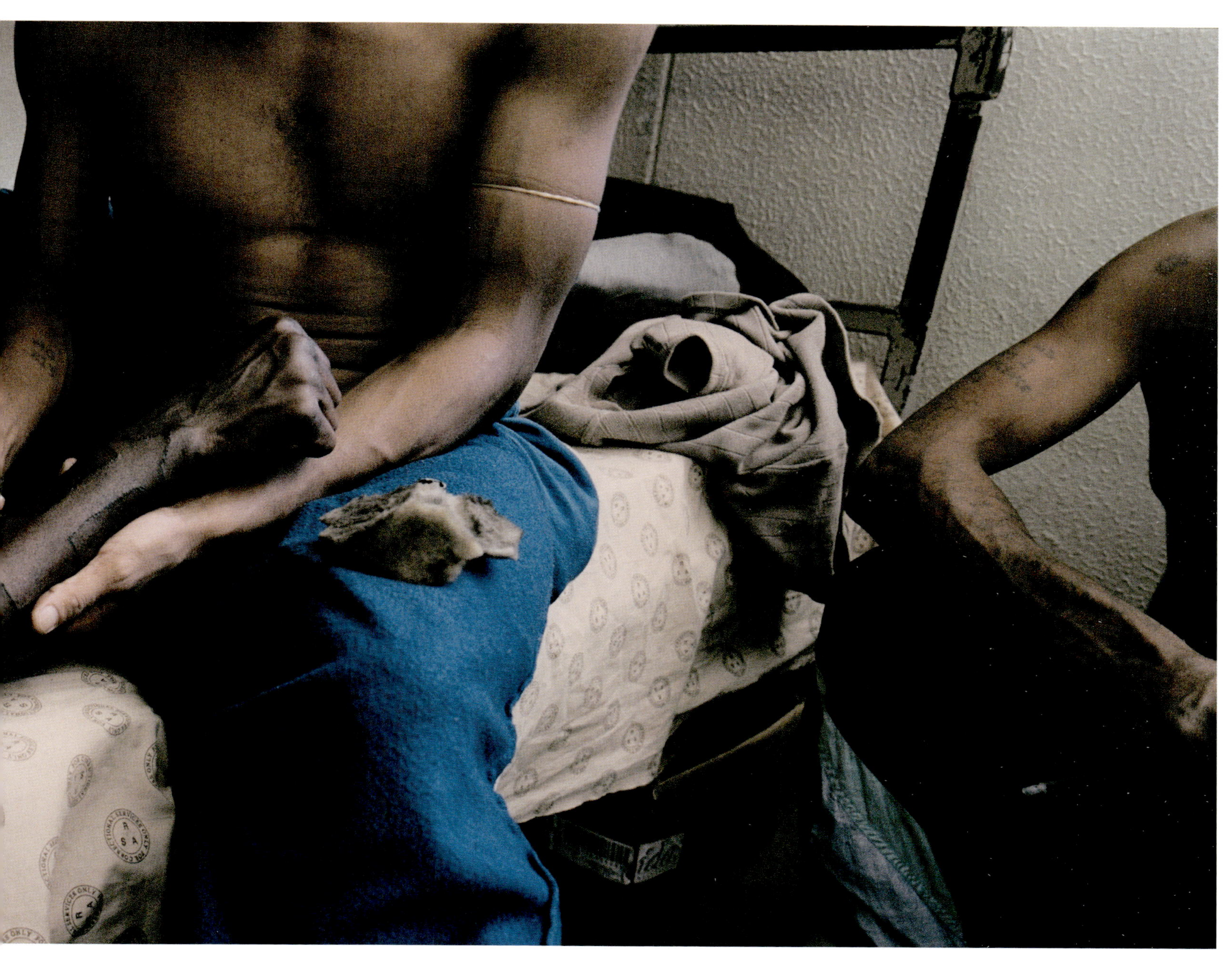

Cell 33, E2 Section, Pollsmoor Maximum Security Prison,
from the series "Die Vier Hoeke" (The Four Corners), 2004–05
Pigment print on paper, 22 x 30.75 in. (55.9 x 78.1 cm)
Courtesy the artist and Goodman Gallery, Johannesburg

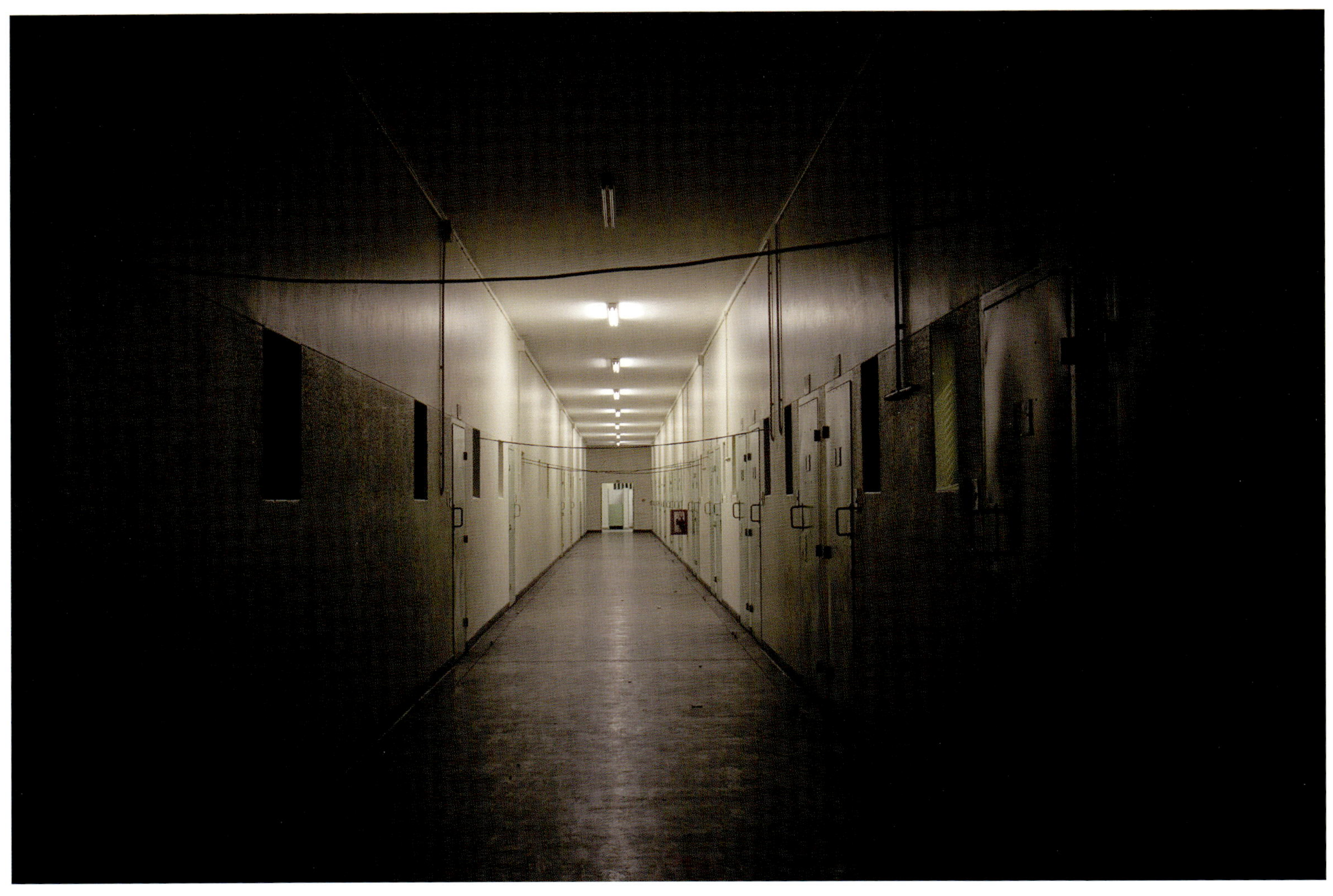

Corridor, E2 Section, Pollsmoor Maximum Security Prison,
from the series "Die Vier Hoeke" (The Four Corners), 2004–05
Pigment print on paper, 22 x 30.75 in. (55.9 x 78.1 cm)
Courtesy the artist and Goodman Gallery, Johannesburg

Sada Tangara

Mamadou Gomis

Romuald Hazoumé

Zohra Bensemra

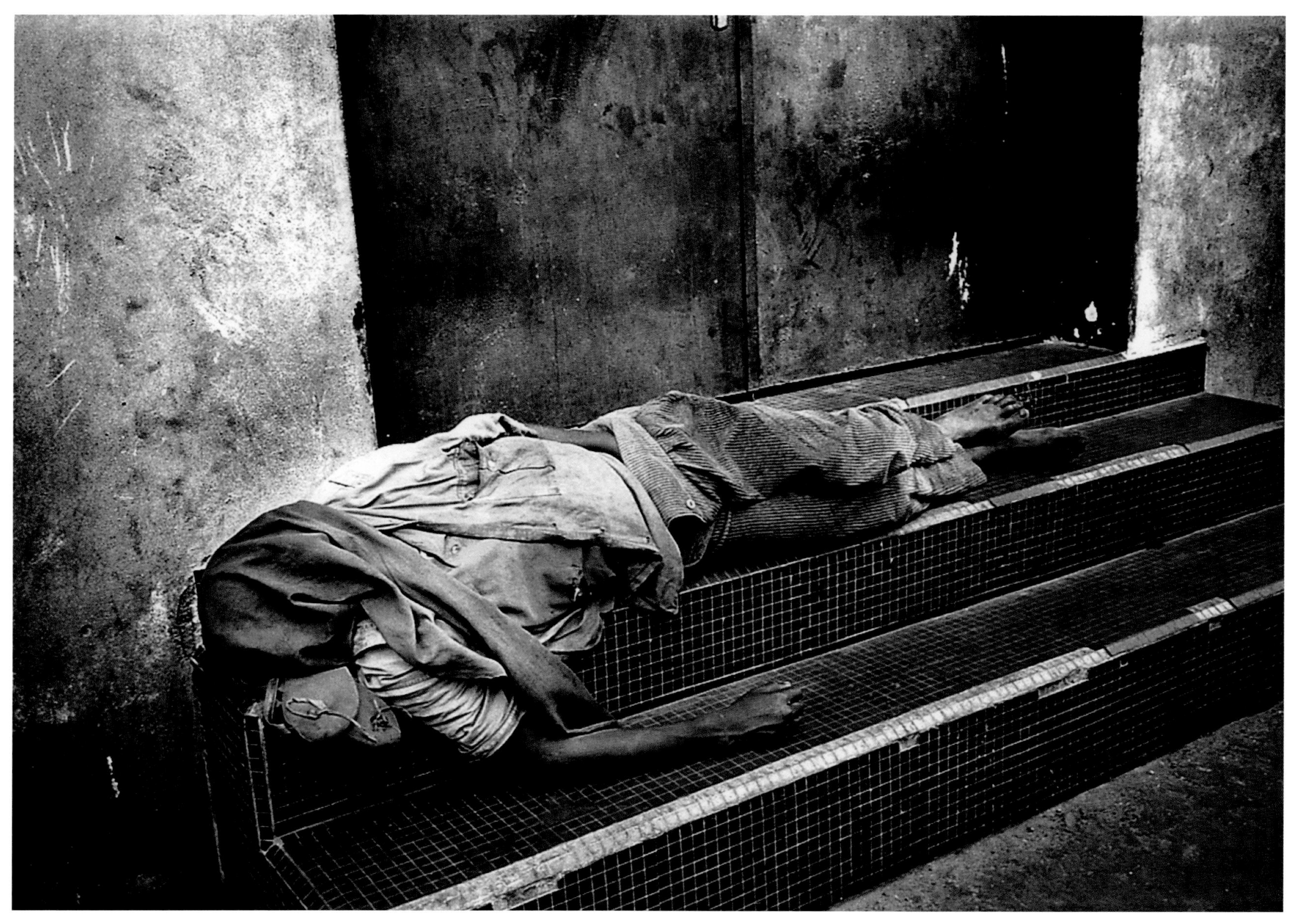

Untitled, from the series "Le grand sommeil" [The Big Sleep], 1998–2003
Gelatin silver print, 11.8 x 15.75 in. (30 x 40 cm)
Courtesy the artist and Serge Aboukrat Éditions, Paris

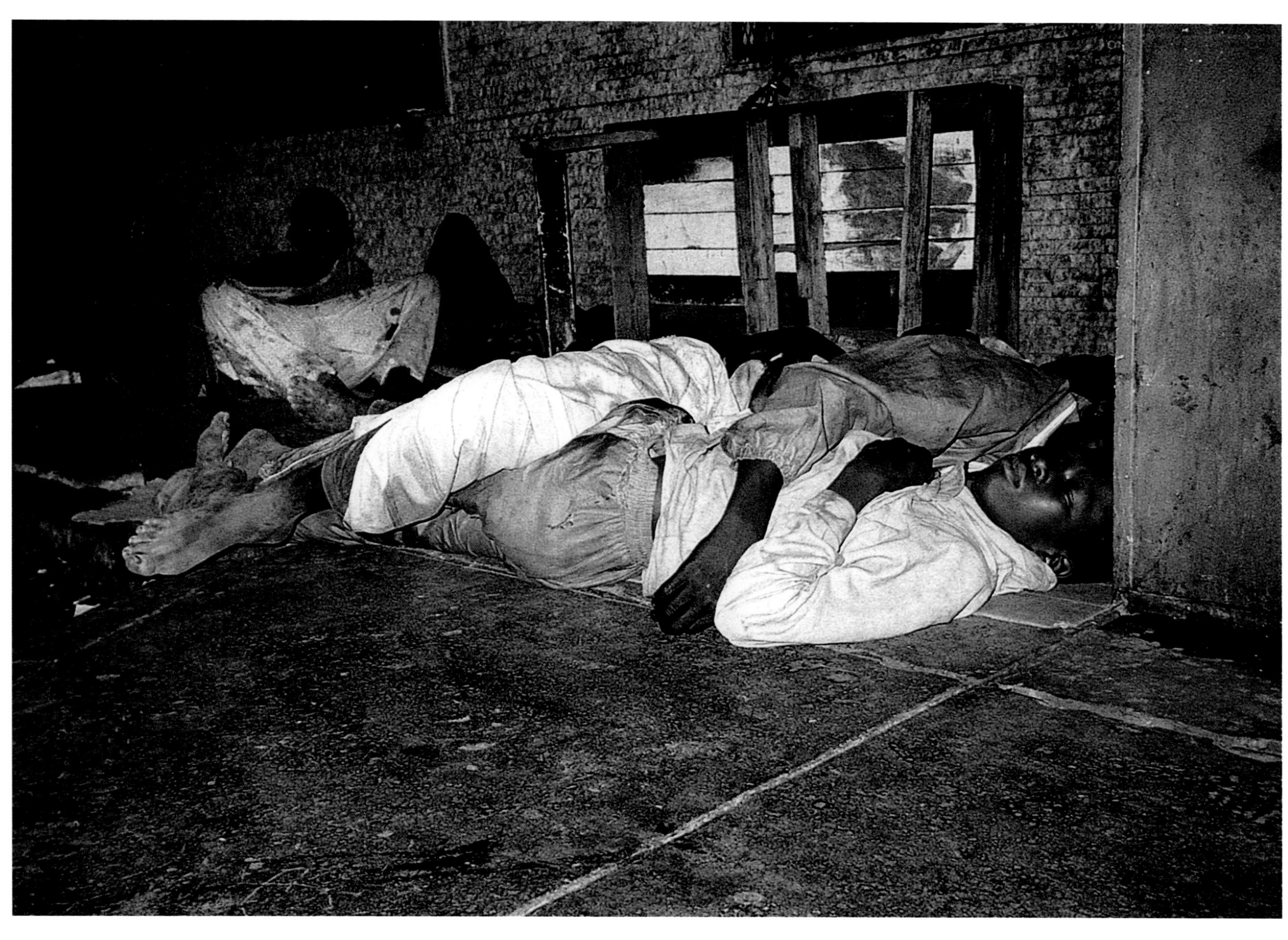

Untitled, from the series "Le grand sommeil" [The Big Sleep], 1998–2003
Gelatin silver print, 11.8 x 15.75 in. (30 x 40 cm)
Courtesy the artist and Serge Aboukrat Éditions, Paris

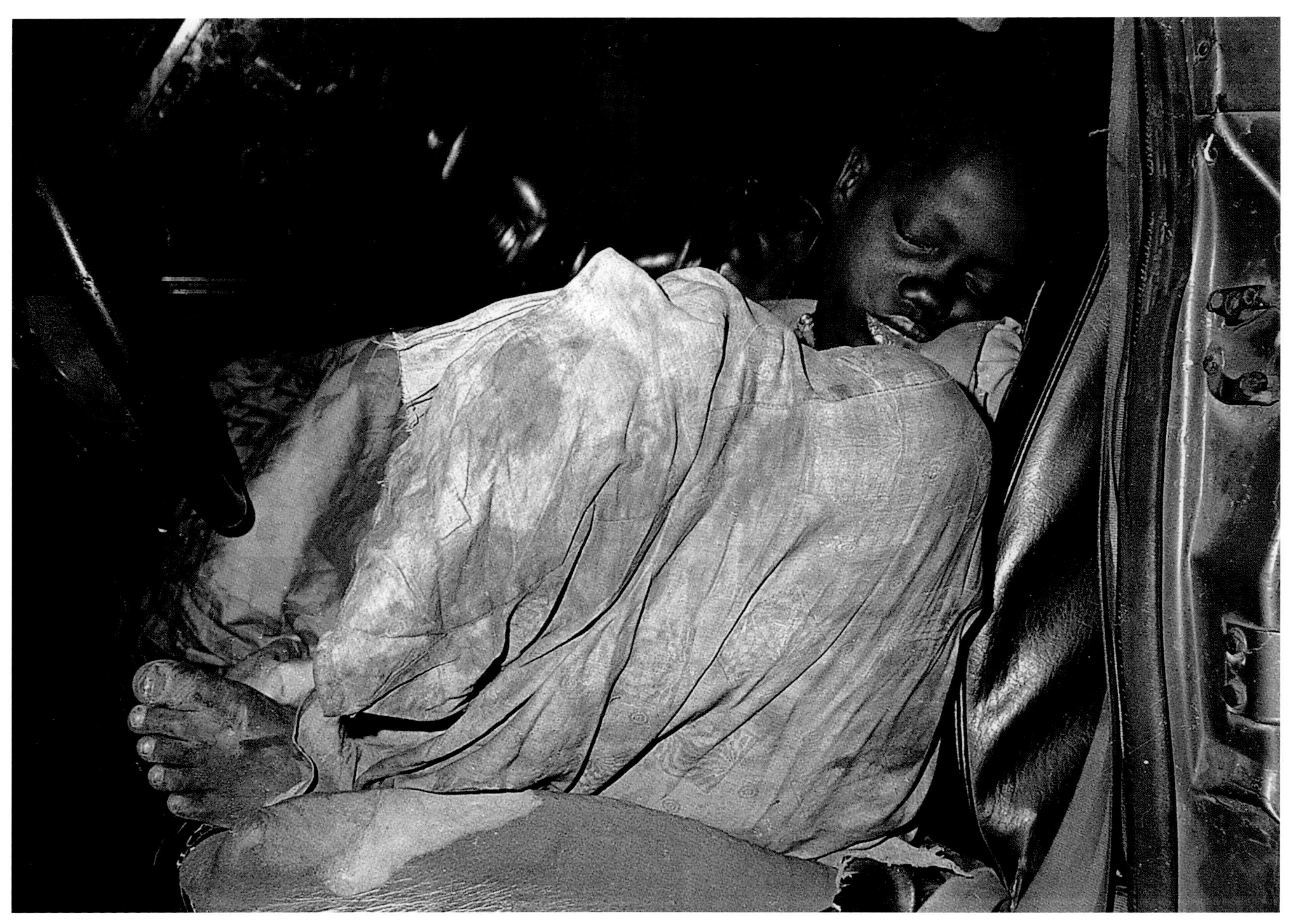

Untitled, from the series "Le grand sommeil" [The Big Sleep], 1998–2003
Gelatin silver print, 11.8 x 15.75 in. (30 x 40 cm)
Courtesy the artist and Serge Aboukrat Éditions, Paris

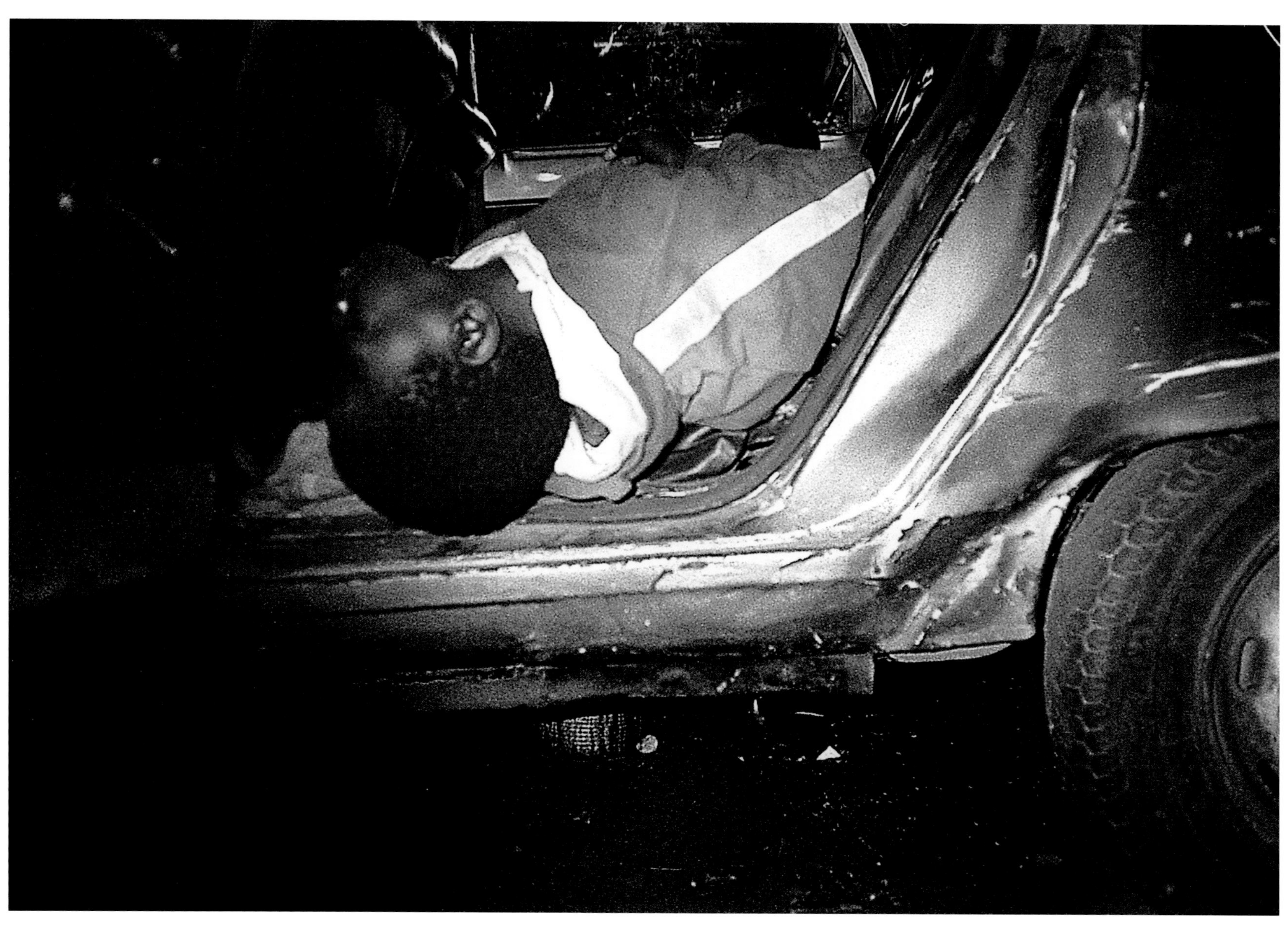

Untitled, from the series "Le grand sommeil" [The Big Sleep], 1998–2003
Gelatin silver print, 11.8 x 15.75 in. (30 x 40 cm)
Courtesy the artist and Serge Aboukrat Éditions, Paris

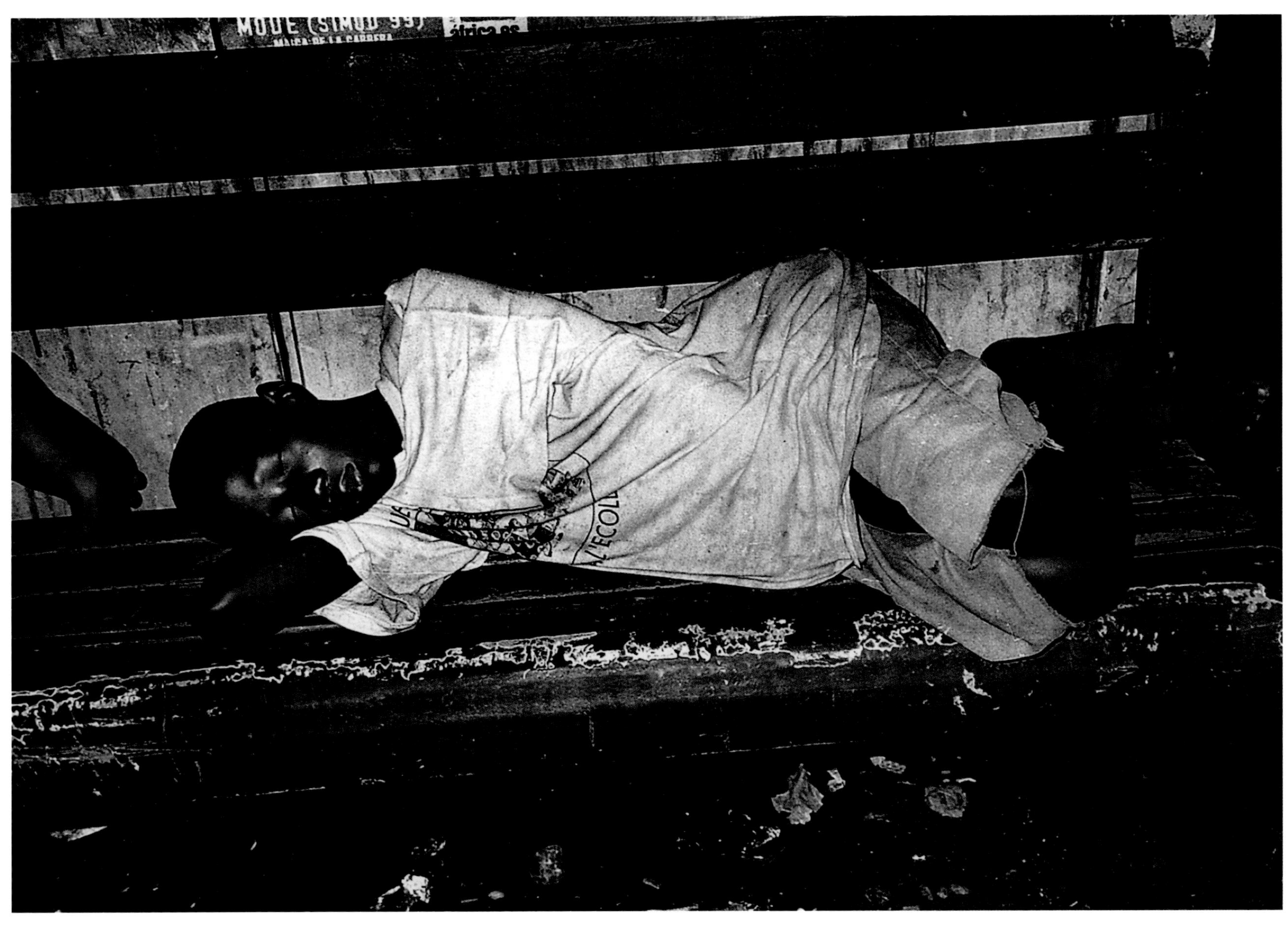

Untitled, from the series "Le grand sommeil" [The Big Sleep], 1998–2003
Gelatin silver print, 11.8 x 15.75 in. (30 x 40 cm)
Courtesy the artist and Serge Aboukrat Éditions, Paris

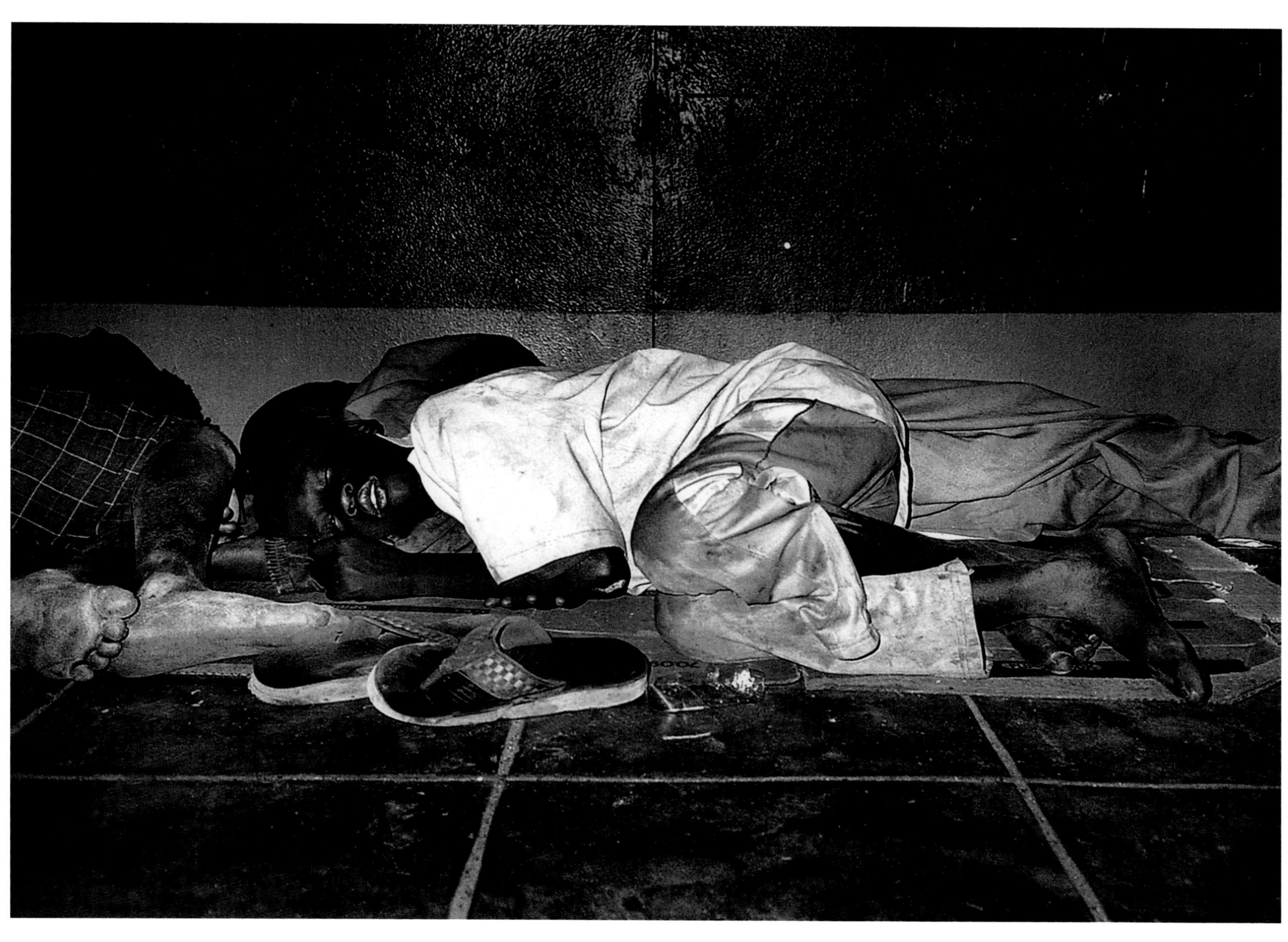

Untitled, from the series "Le grand sommeil" [The Big Sleep], 1998–2003
Gelatin silver print, 11.8 x 15.75 in. (30 x 40 cm)
Courtesy the artist and Serge Aboukrat Éditions, Paris

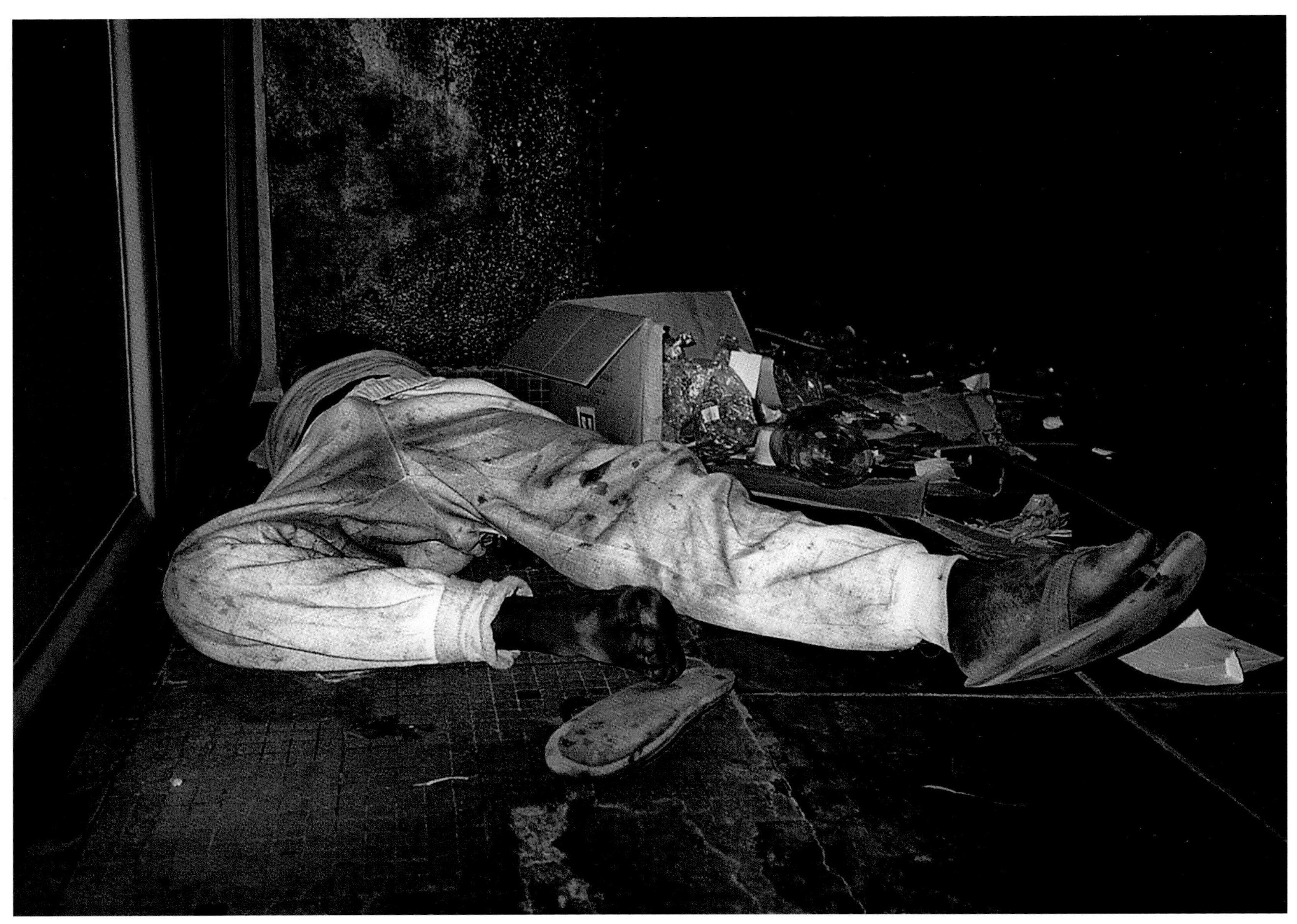

Untitled, from the series "Le grand sommeil" [The Big Sleep], 1998–2003
Gelatin silver print, 11.8 x 15.75 in. (30 x 40 cm)
Courtesy the artist and Serge Aboukrat Éditions, Paris

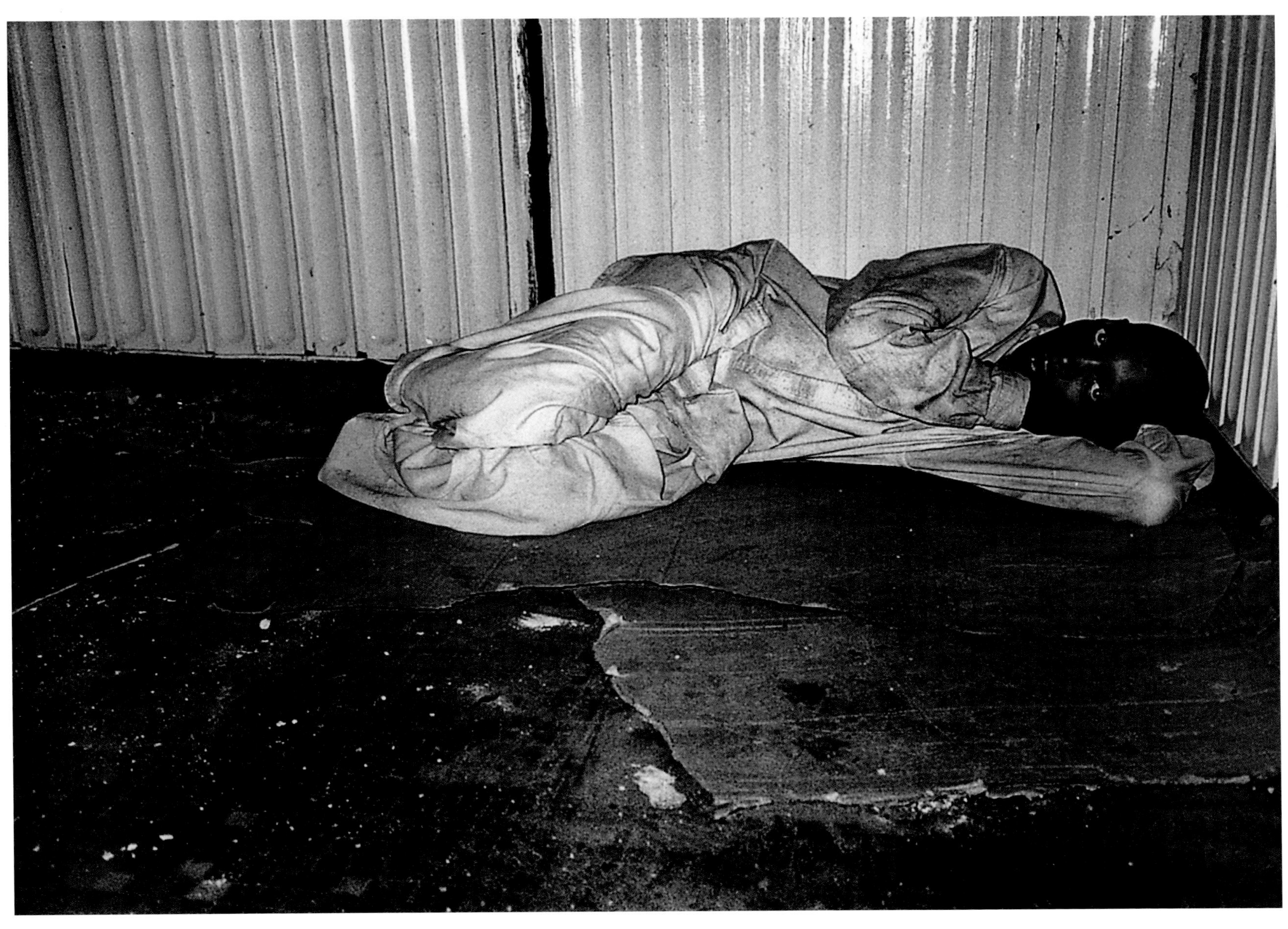

Untitled, from the series "Le grand sommeil" [The Big Sleep], 1998–2003
Gelatin silver print, 11.8 x 15.75 in. (30 x 40 cm)
Courtesy the artist and Serge Aboukrat Éditions, Paris

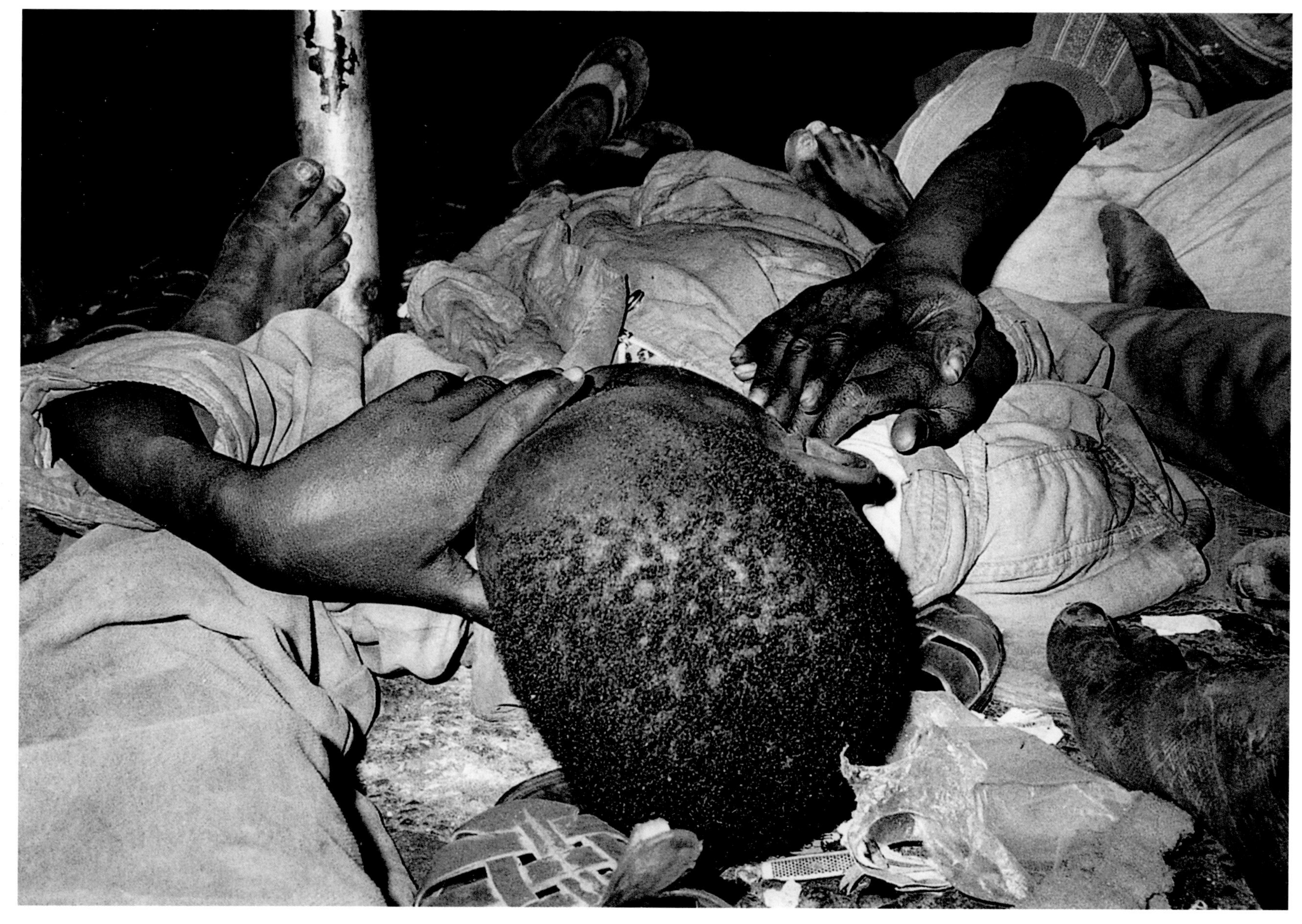

Untitled, from the series "Le grand sommeil" [The Big Sleep], 1998–2003
Gelatin silver print, 11.8 x 15.75 in. (30 x 40 cm)
Courtesy the artist and Serge Aboukrat Éditions, Paris

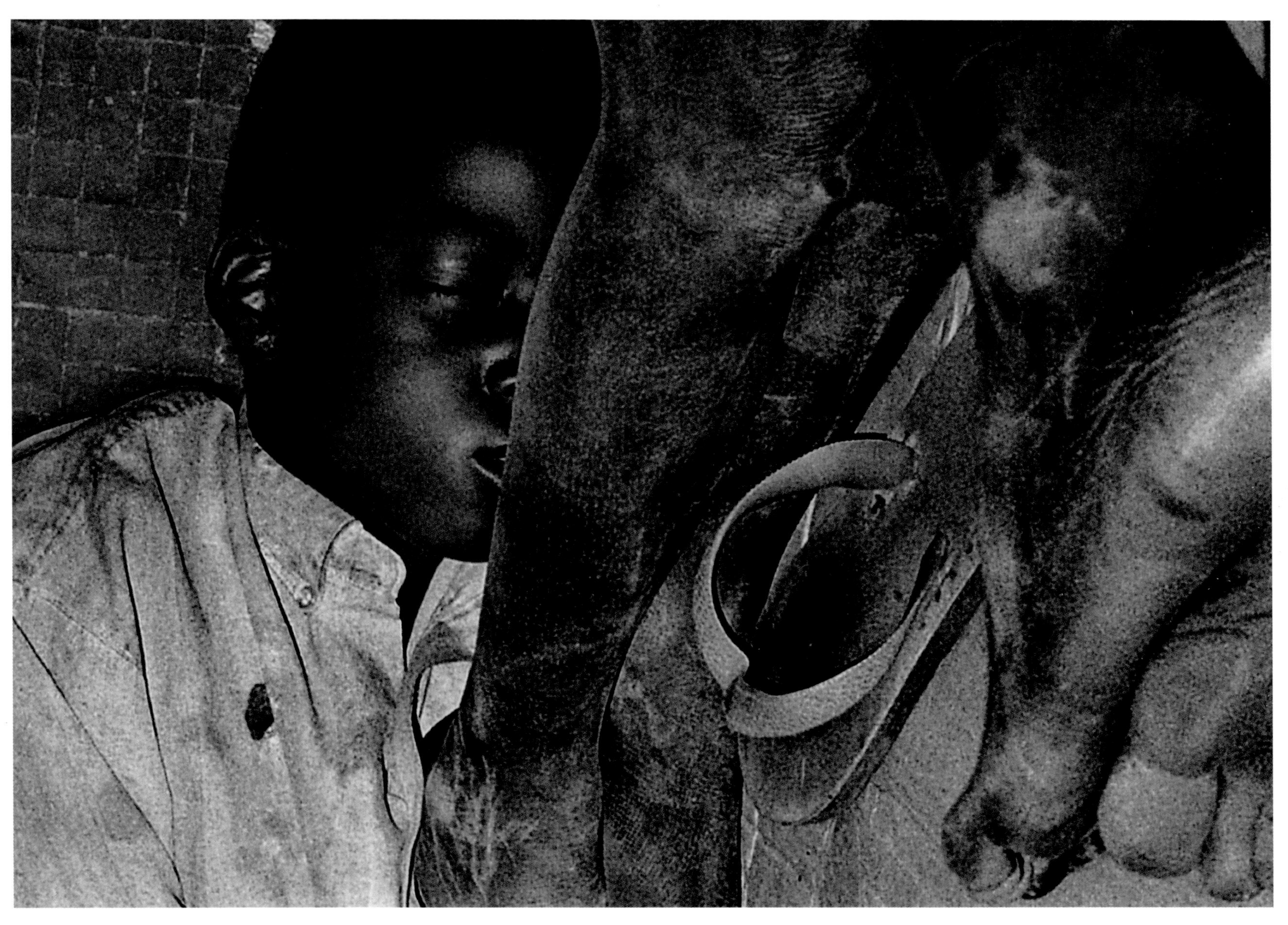

Untitled, from the series "Le grand sommeil" [The Big Sleep], 1998–2003
Gelatin silver print, 11.8 x 15.75 in. (30 x 40 cm)
Courtesy the artist and Serge Aboukrat Éditions, Paris

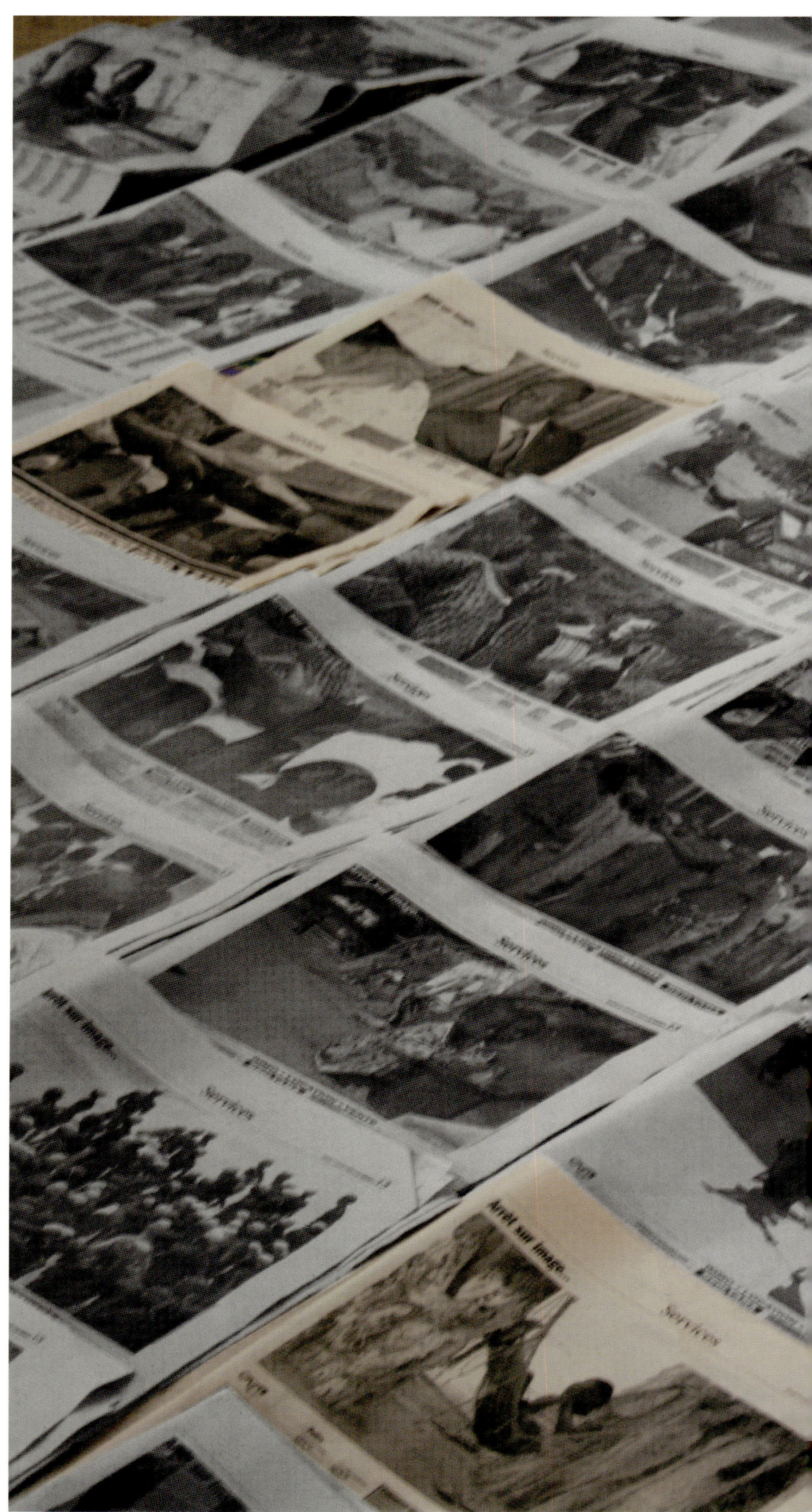

Untitled, 2006
Installation of newspapers
dimensions variable
Courtesy the artist

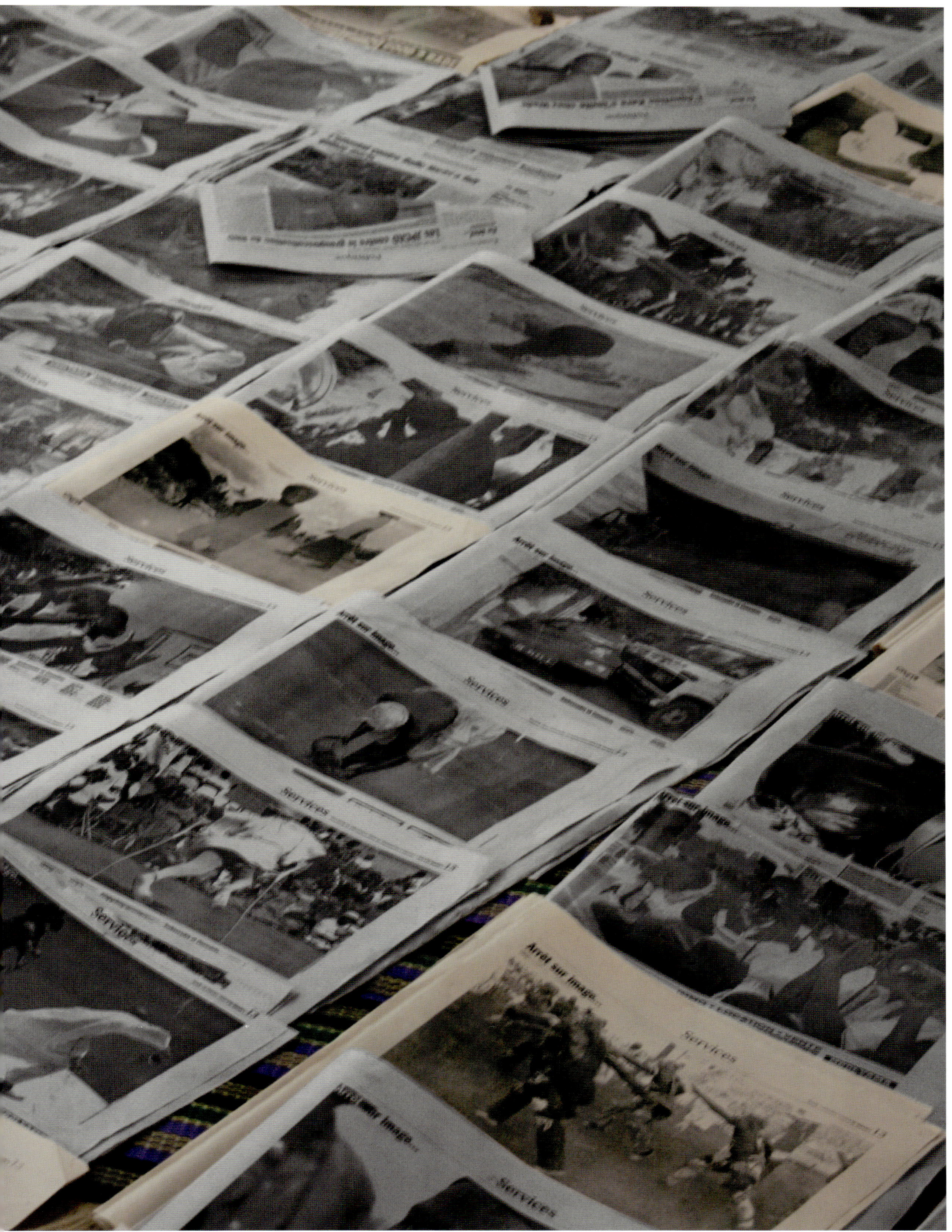
Arrêt sur image...
Services

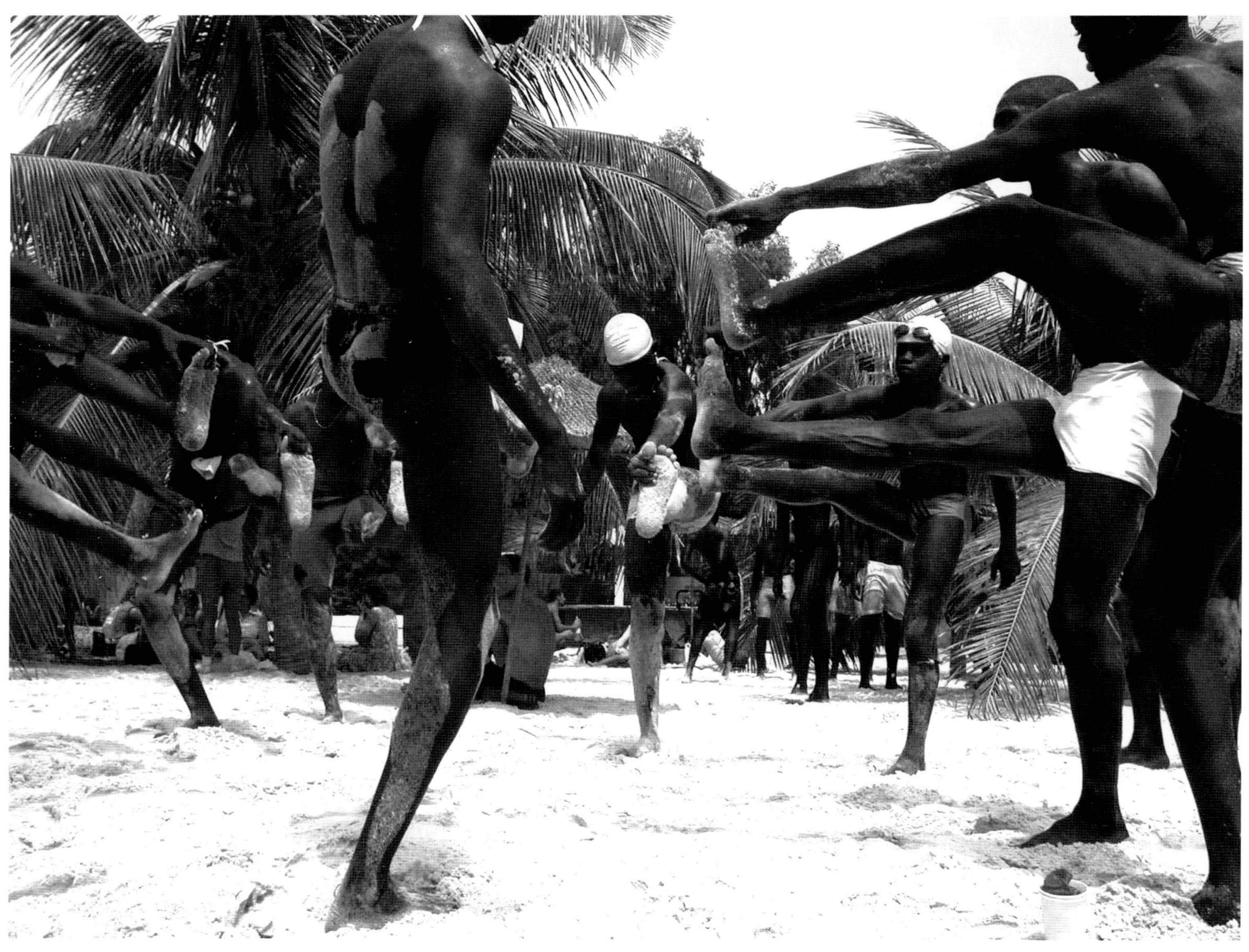

Echauffement de nageurs avant une competition
[Swimmers Warming Up Before a Competition]
Newspaper image, 6.5 x 9.3 in. (16.5 x 23.5 cm)
Courtesy the artist

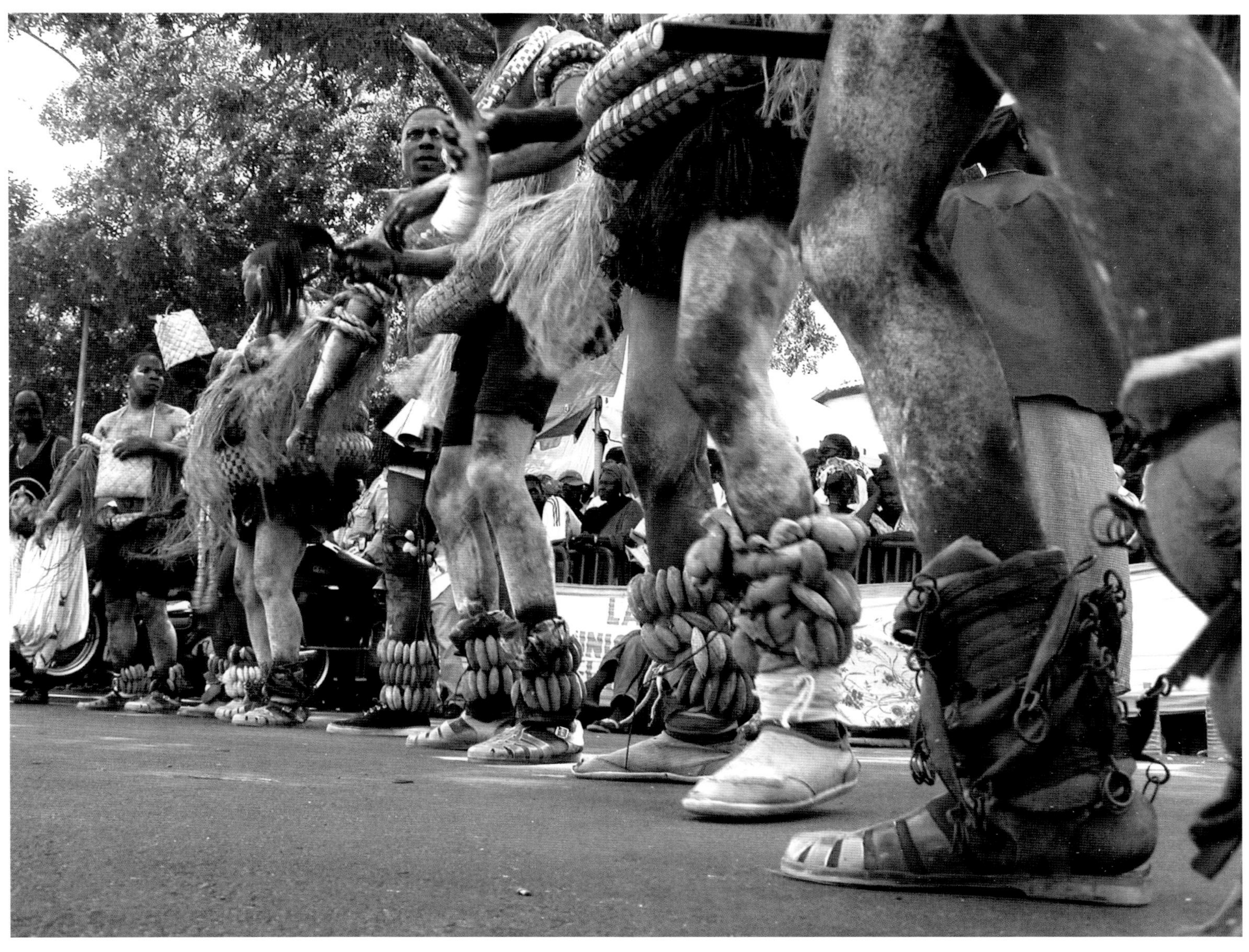

Danse balante
[Balante Dance]
Newspaper image, 6.5 x 9.3 in. (16.5 x 23.5 cm)
Courtesy the artist

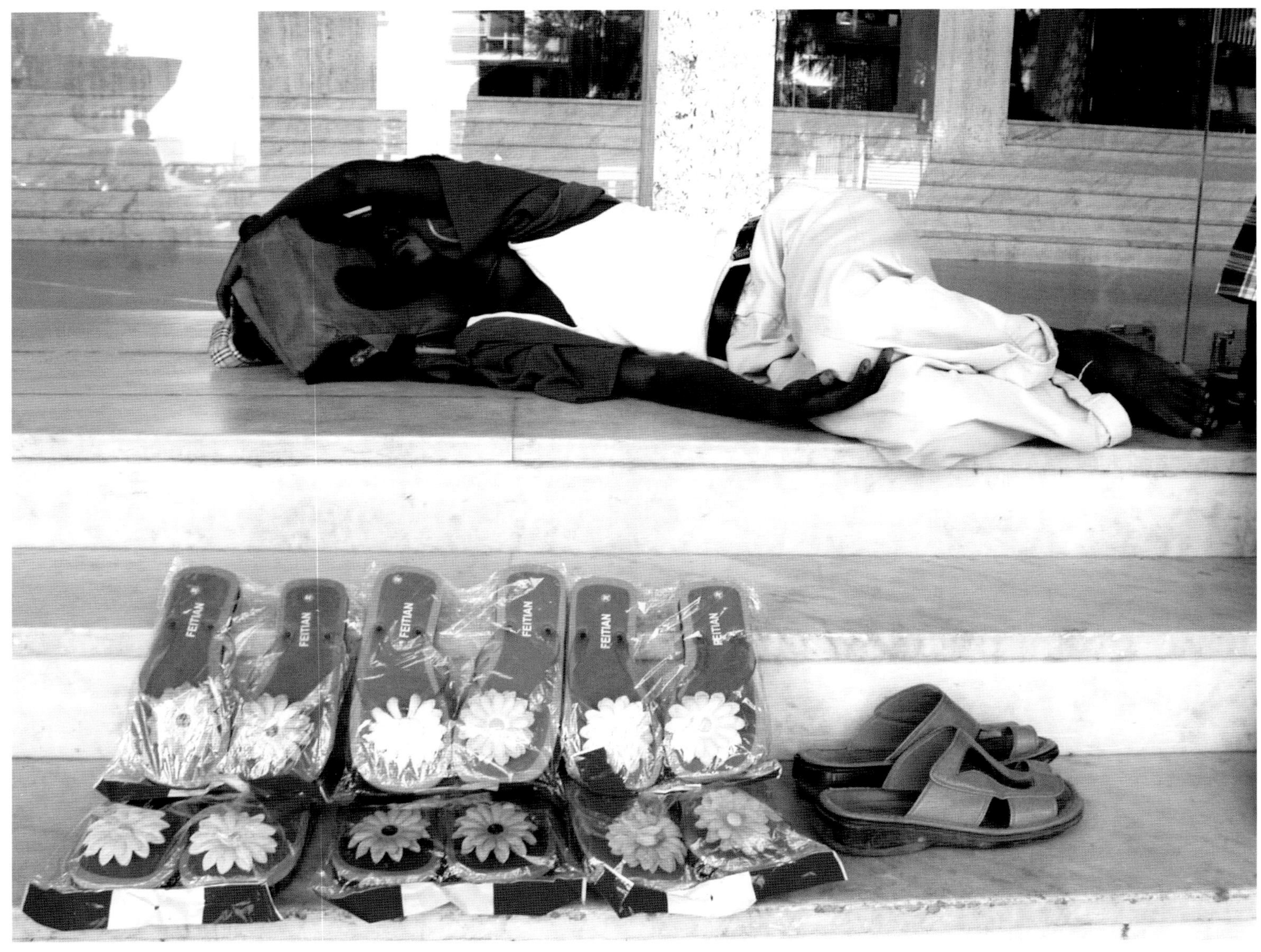

Et qui va parler au client
[And Who Will Talk With the Customer]
Newspaper image, 6.5 x 9.3 in. (16.5 x 23.5 cm)
Courtesy the artist

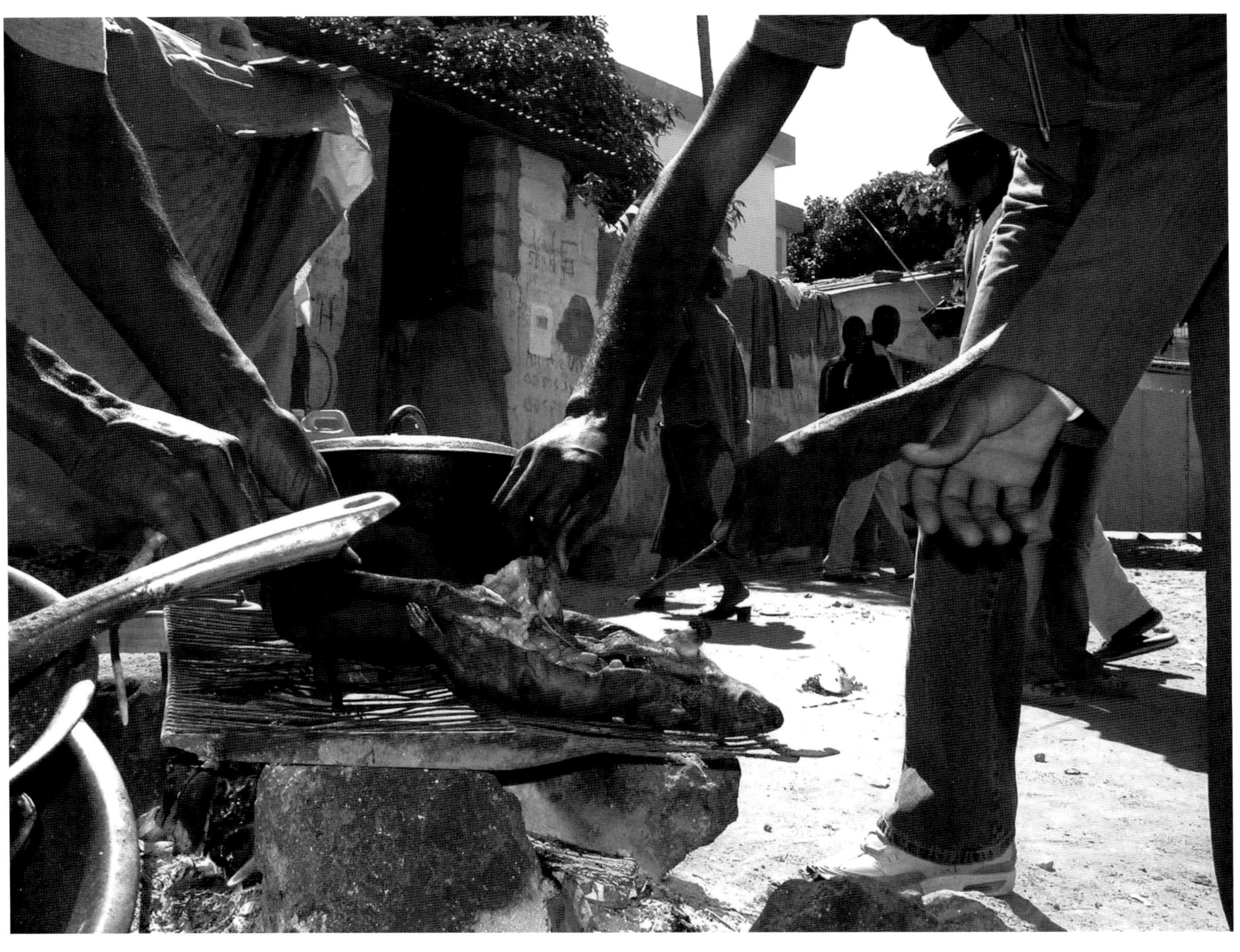

Et si on n'a pas le choix
[And If One Doesn't Have the Choice]
Newspaper image, 6.5 x 9.3 in. (16.5 x 23.5 cm)
Courtesy the artist

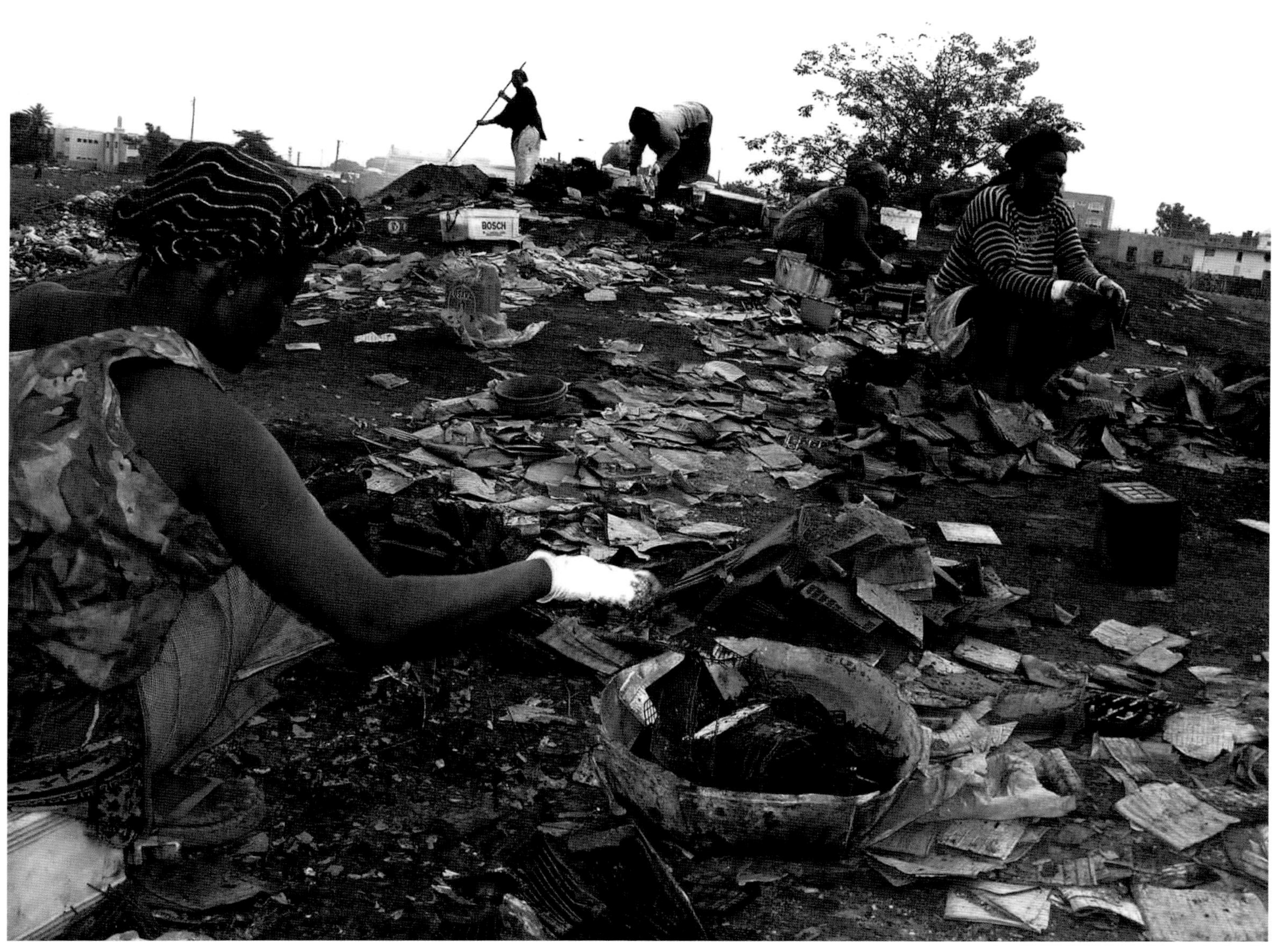

Femmes chercheuses de plomb 1
[Women Looking for Lead 1]
Newspaper image, 6.5 x 9.3 in. (16.5 x 23.5 cm)
Courtesy the artist

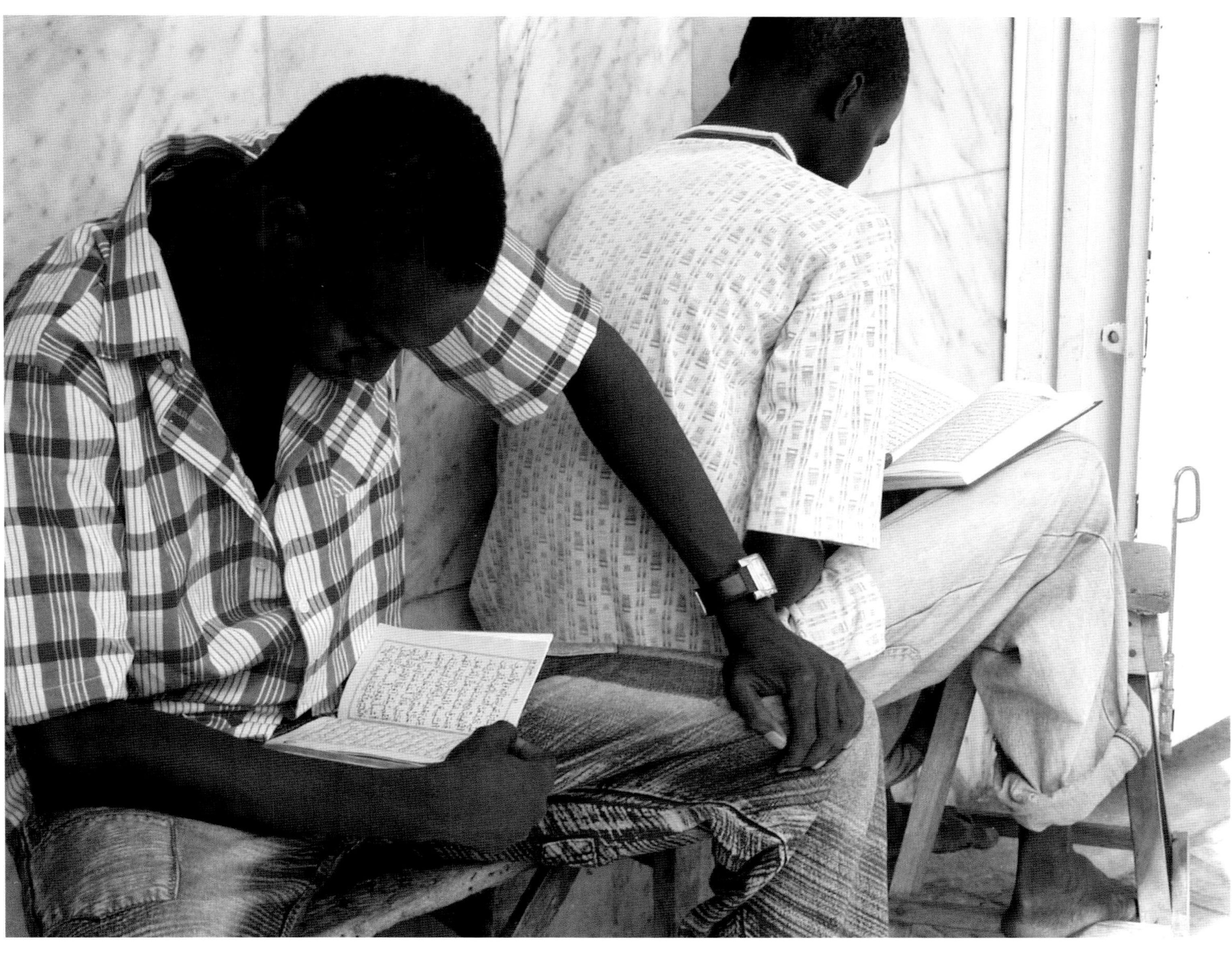

Lectures du coran pendant la ramadan
(Reading the Qur'an During Ramadan)
Newspaper image, 6.5 x 9.3 in. (16.5 x 23.5 cm)
Courtesy the artist

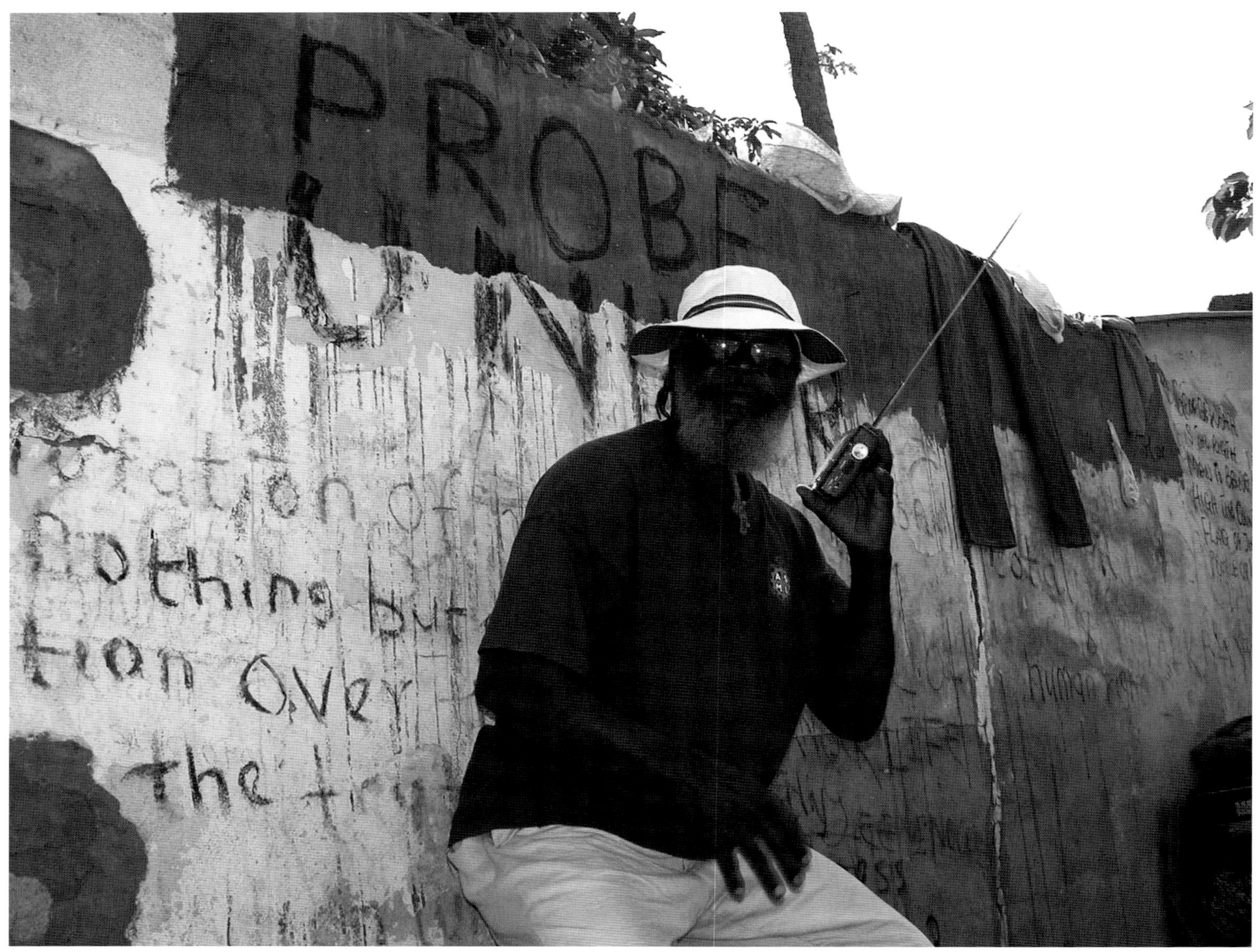

Quand on tient à l'info
(Staying Up On the Info)
Newspaper image, 6.5 x 9.3 in. (16.5 x 23.5 cm)
Courtesy the artist

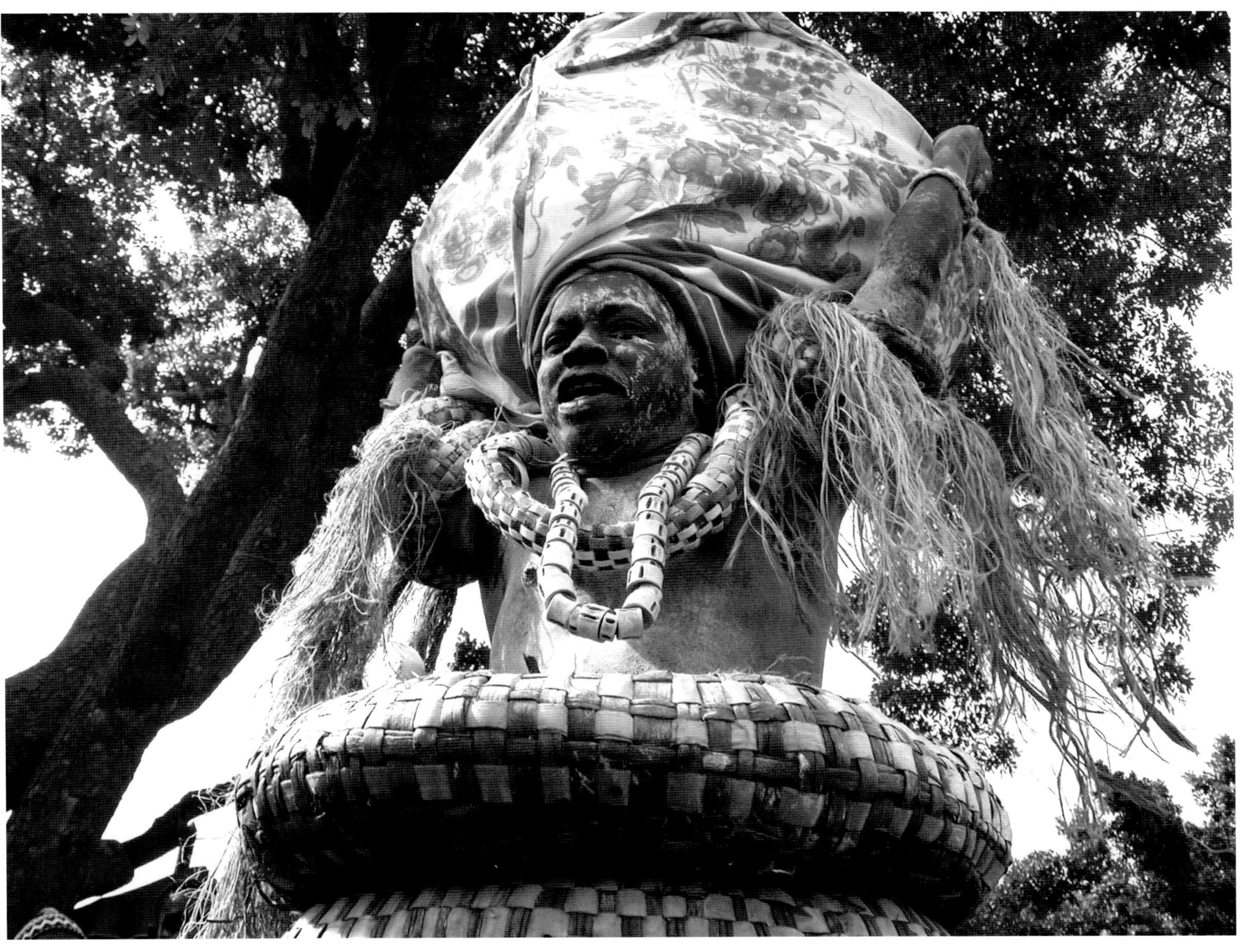

Tradition de la danse balante
(Tradition of the Balante Dance)
Newspaper image, 6.5 x 9.3 in. (16.5 x 23.5 cm)
Courtesy the artist

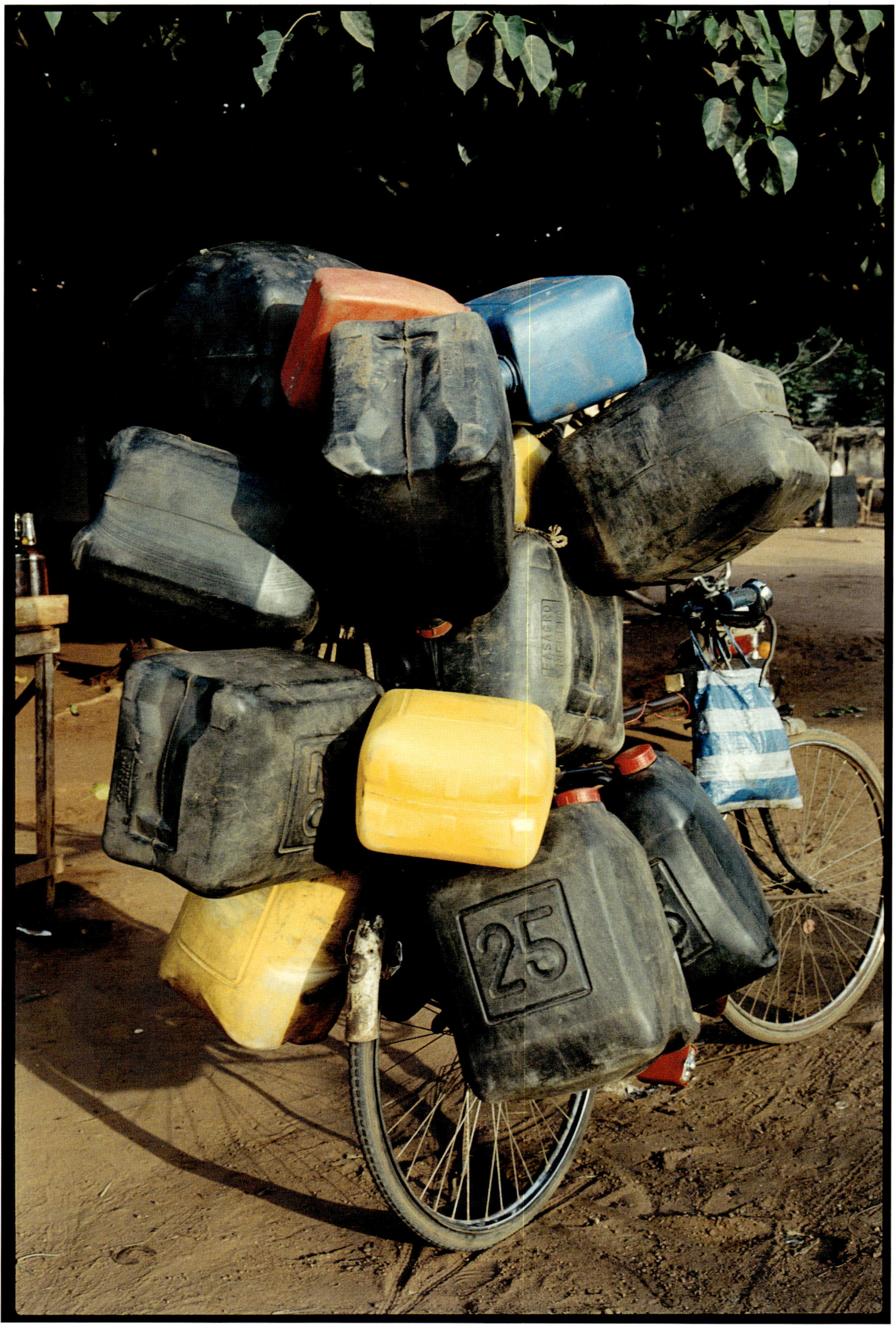

La Roulotte, from the series "Kpayoland," 2004
Chromogenic print, 54.5 x 36.9 in. (138.4 x 93.7 cm)
Courtesy the artist

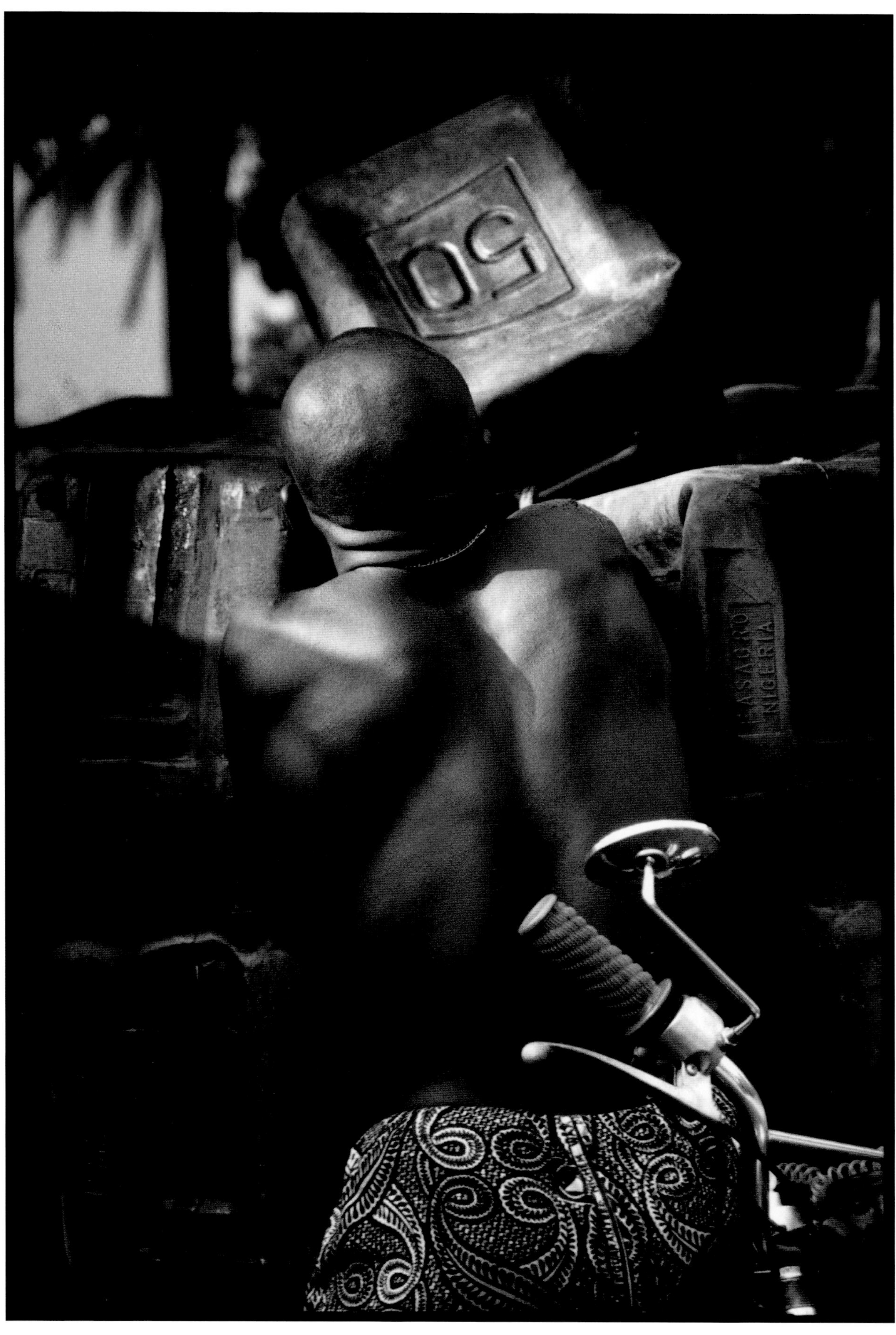

Tyson, from the series "Kpayoland," 2004
Gelatin silver print, 30 x 24 in. (76.2 x 61 cm)
Courtesy the artist

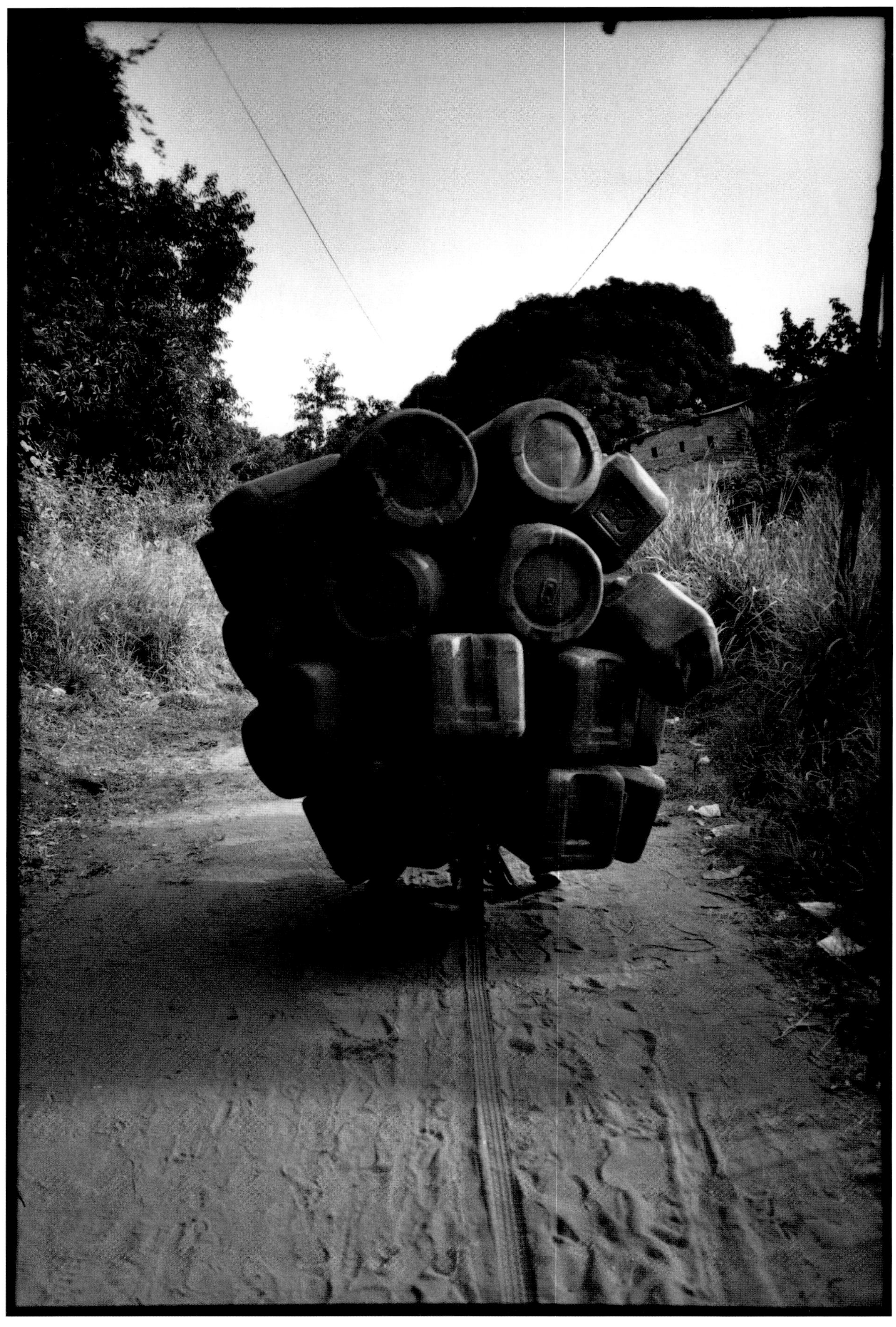

Promenade a Porto-Novo, from the series "Kpayoland," 2004
Gelatin silver print, 30 x 24 in. (76.2 x 61 cm)
Courtesy the artist

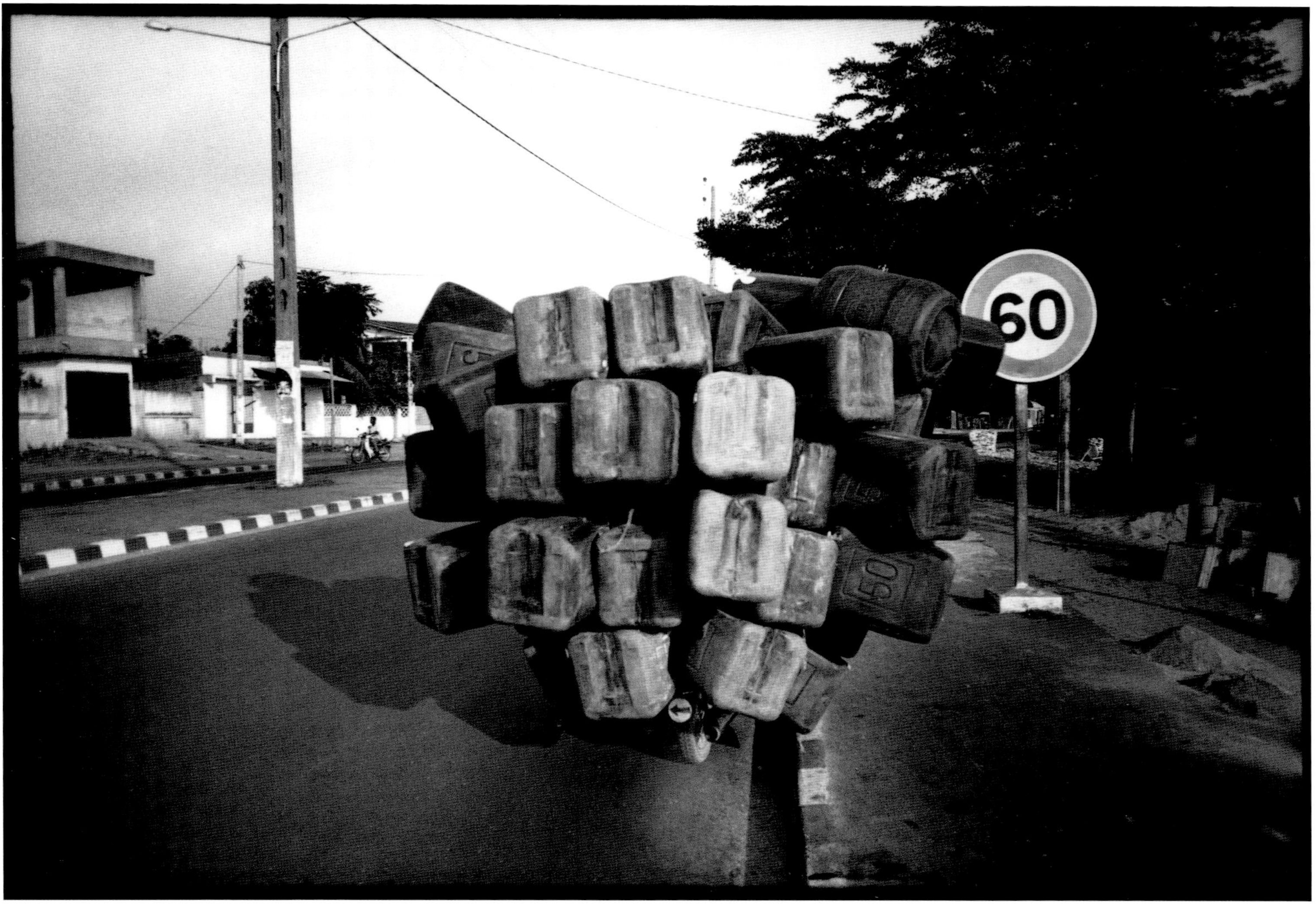

No Limit, from the series "Kpayoland," 2004
Gelatin silver print, 30 x 24 in. (76.2 x 61 cm)
Courtesy the artist

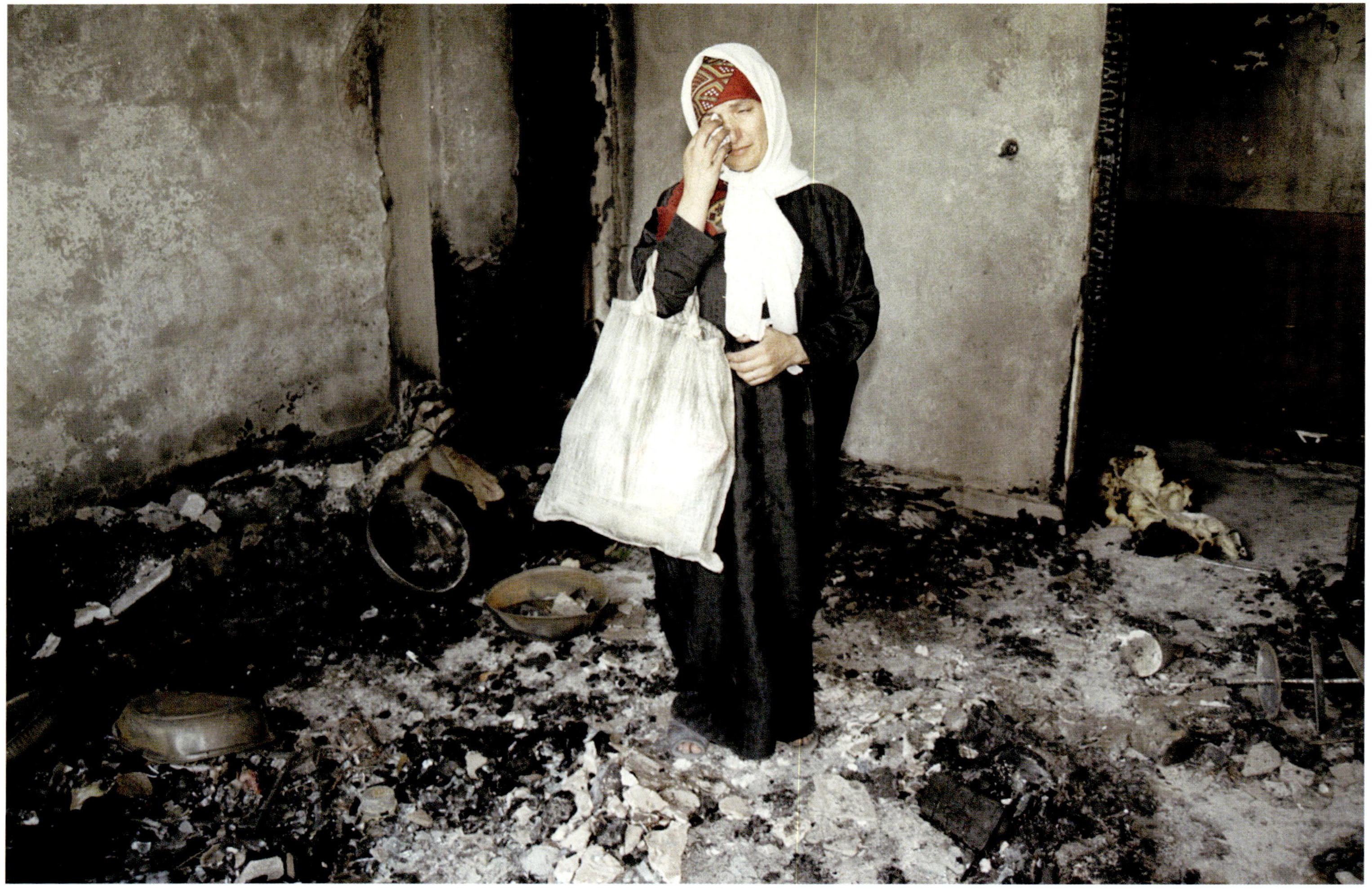

Massacre in Bentalha: over one hundred people were slain in Bentalha, Baraki district, some 15 km from Algiers. Newspapers reported that 252 people, mostly women and children, had been decapitated—September 23, 1997, 1997
Chromogenic print, 11 x 14 in. (27.9 x 35.6 cm)
Courtesy the artist

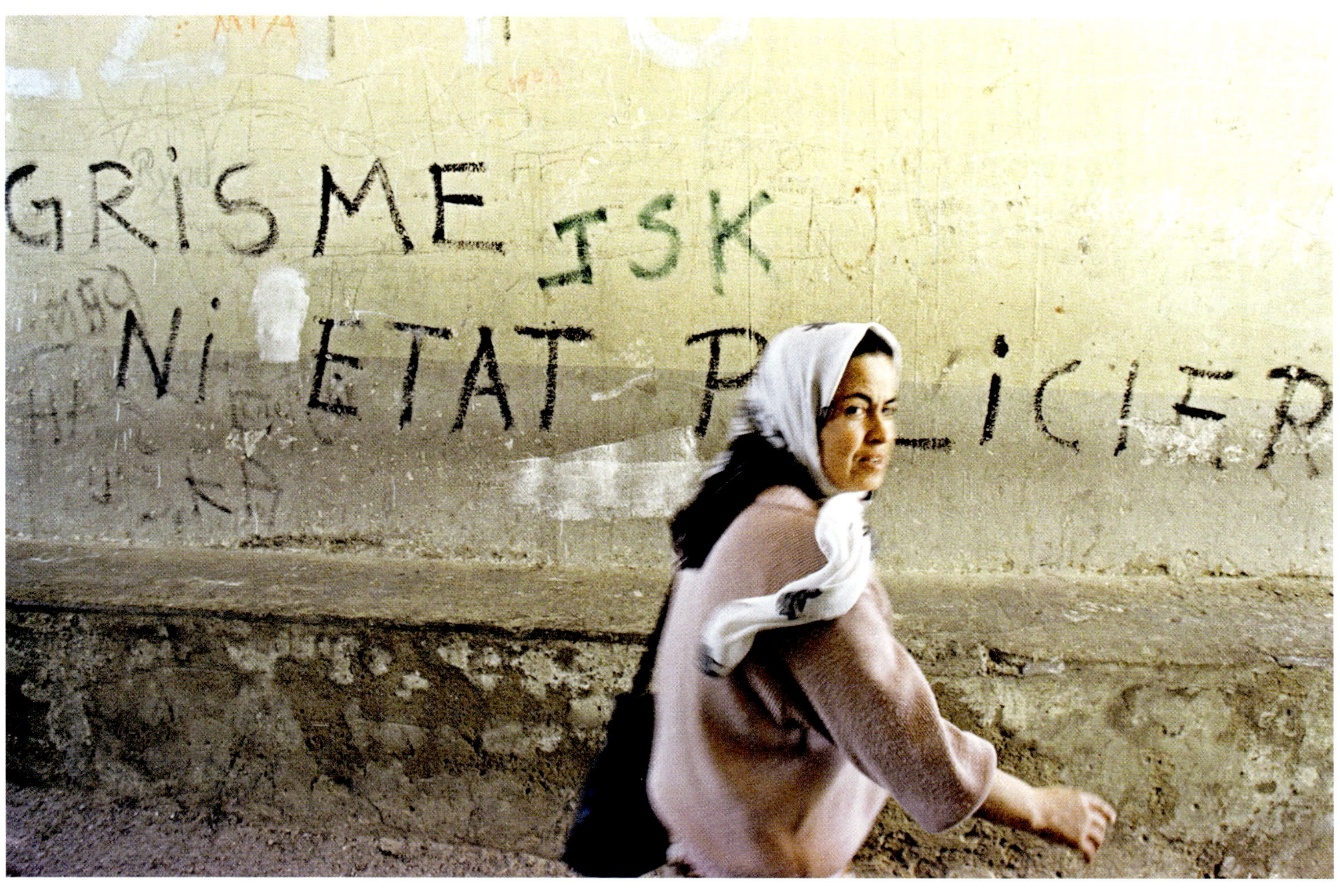

Graffiti on the wall of a low-rent housing project in El Bair, a neighbourhood perched on the hills of Algiers, reads: "No fundamentalism, no police state"—May 27, 1998, 1998
Chromogenic print, 11 x 14 in. (27.9 x 35.6 cm)
Courtesy the artist

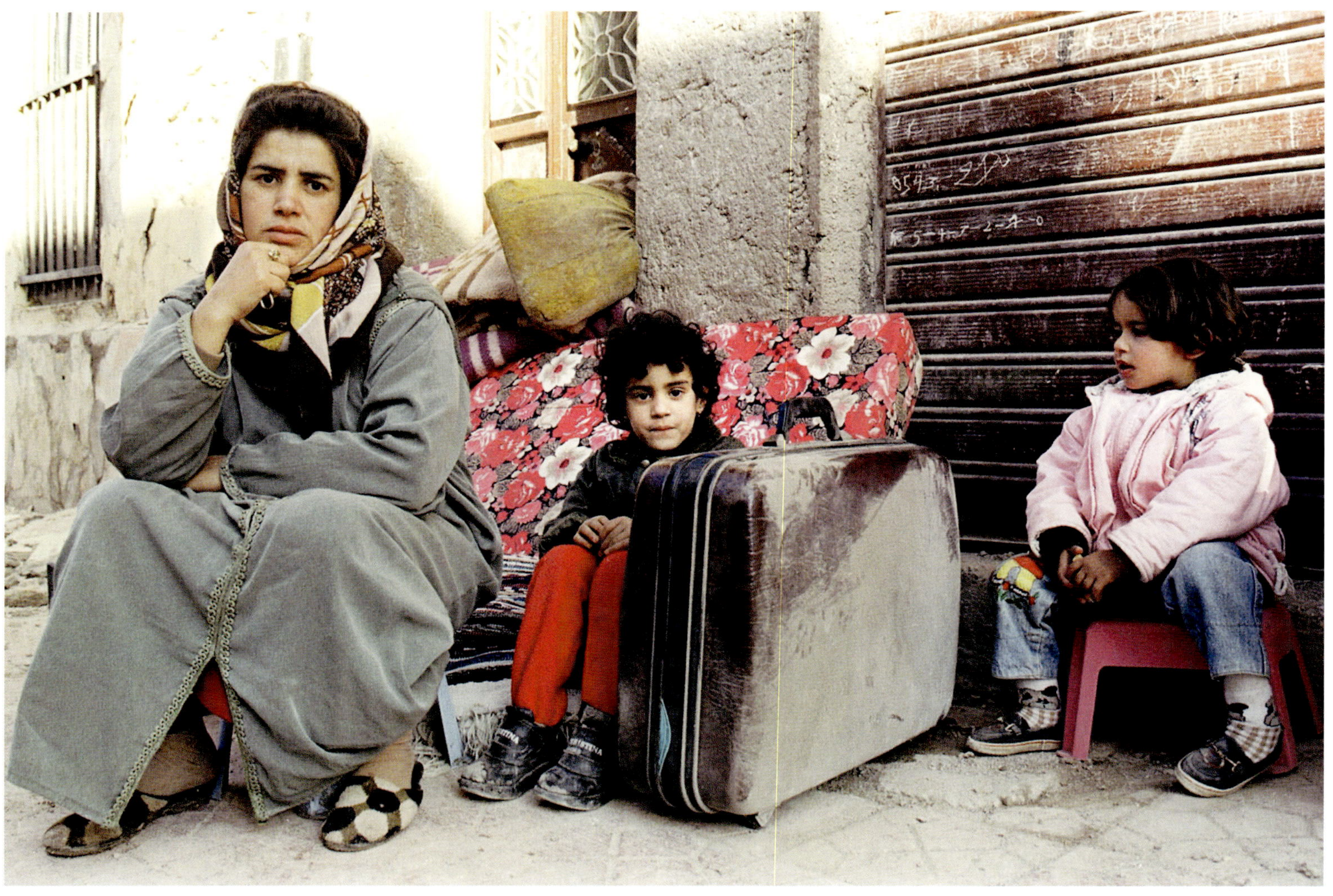

Algerian victims sit with their belongings in a suitcase, one day after an earthquake which caused heavy damage to the town of Ain Timouchant—December 23, 1999. More than twenty people were reported dead in the earthquake which regstered 5.6 on the Richter scale…., 1999
Chromogenic print, 11 x 14 in. (27.9 x 35.6 cm)
Courtesy the artist

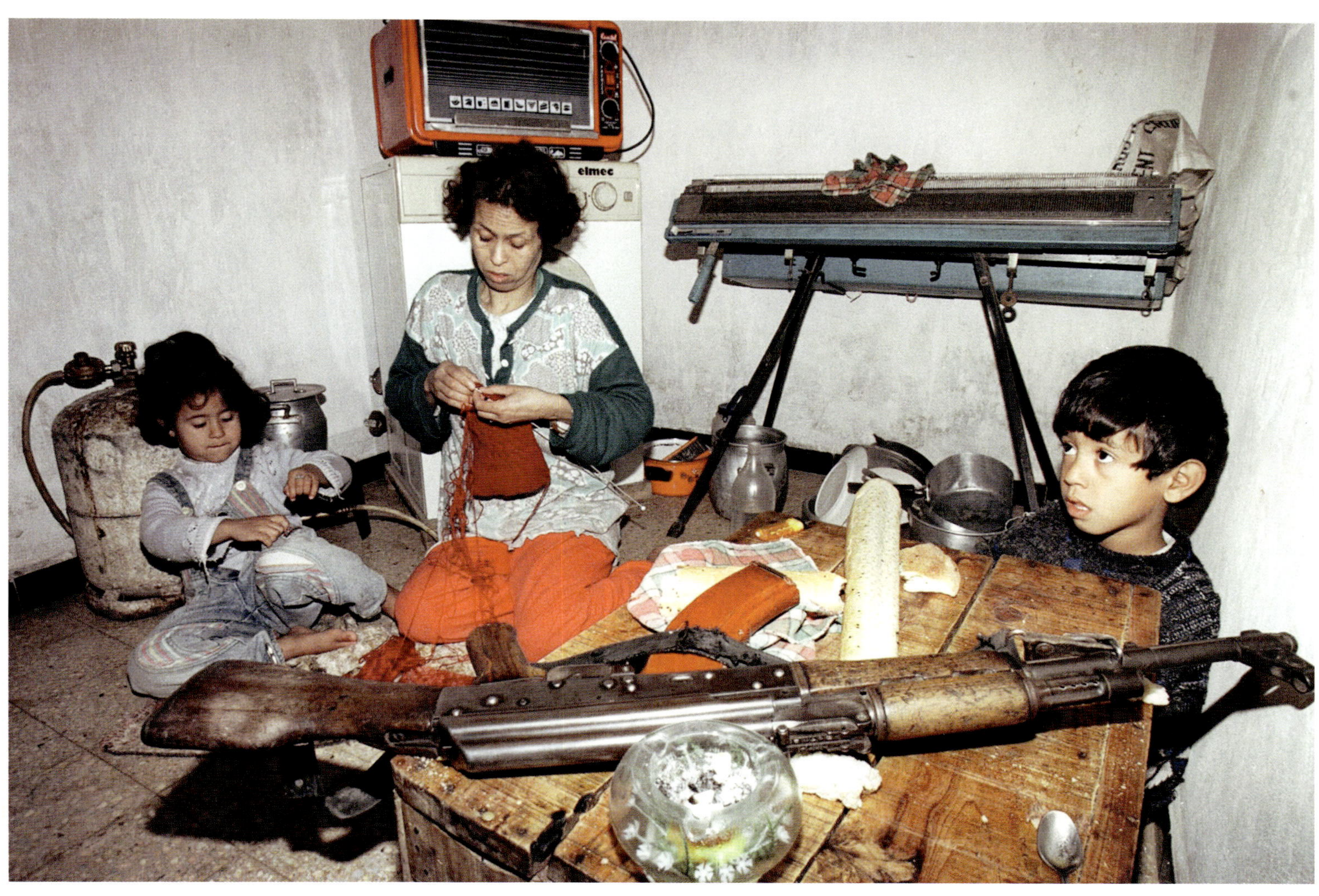

A family in the town of Haouch Omar in the Metidja region of Algeria,
keep an AK-47 automatic weapon at the ready on the living room table—December 8th, 1998, 1998
Chromogenic print, 11 x 14 in. (27.9 x 35.6 cm)
Courtesy the artist

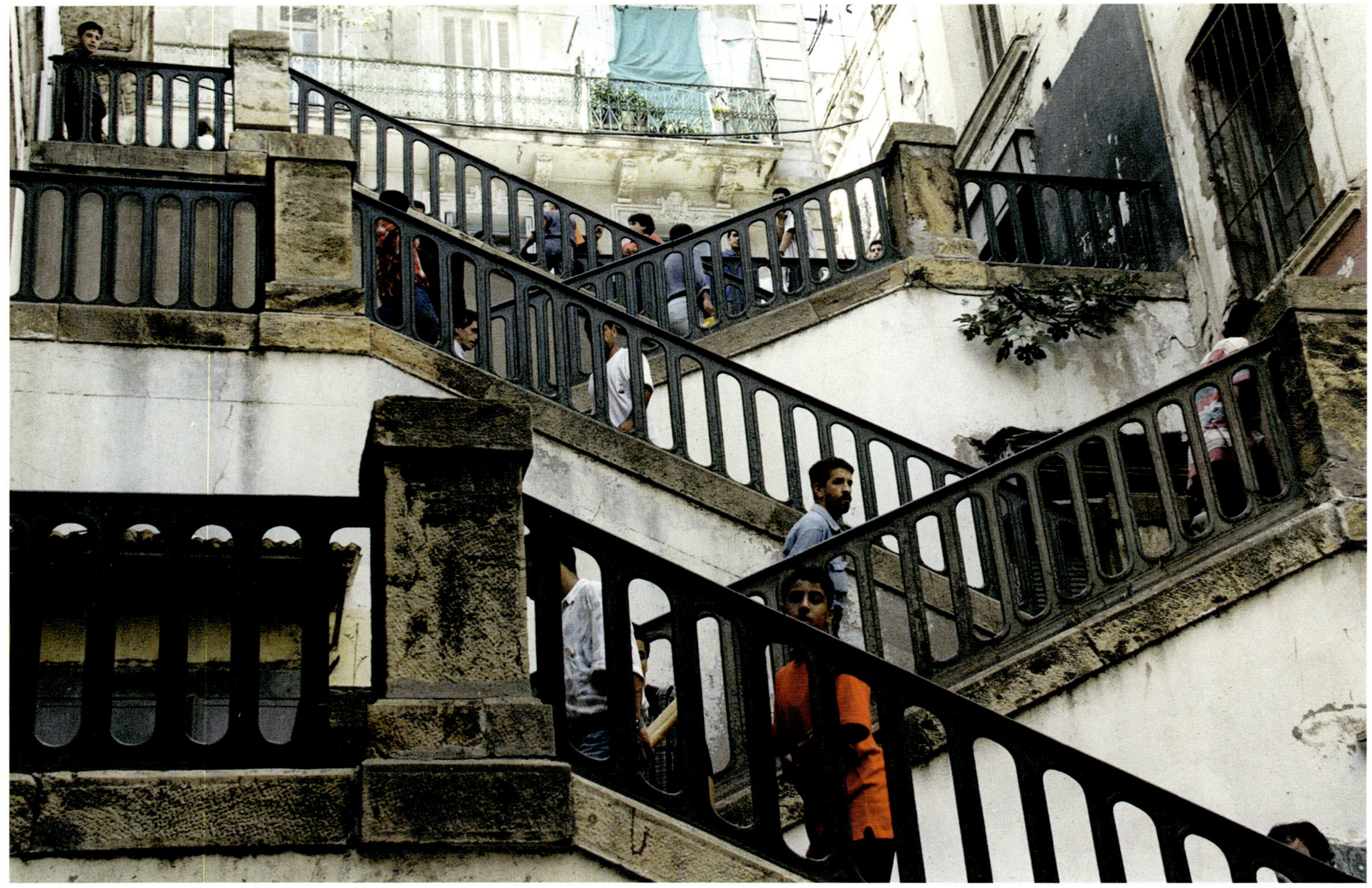

A view of the steps leading from the lower Kasbah, Algiers' oldest quarter, up to the upper Kasbah of Bab Edjdid; the steps are the central feature of this quarter—September 27, 1998, 1998
Chromogenic print, 11 x 14 in. (27.9 x 35.6 cm)
Courtesy the artist

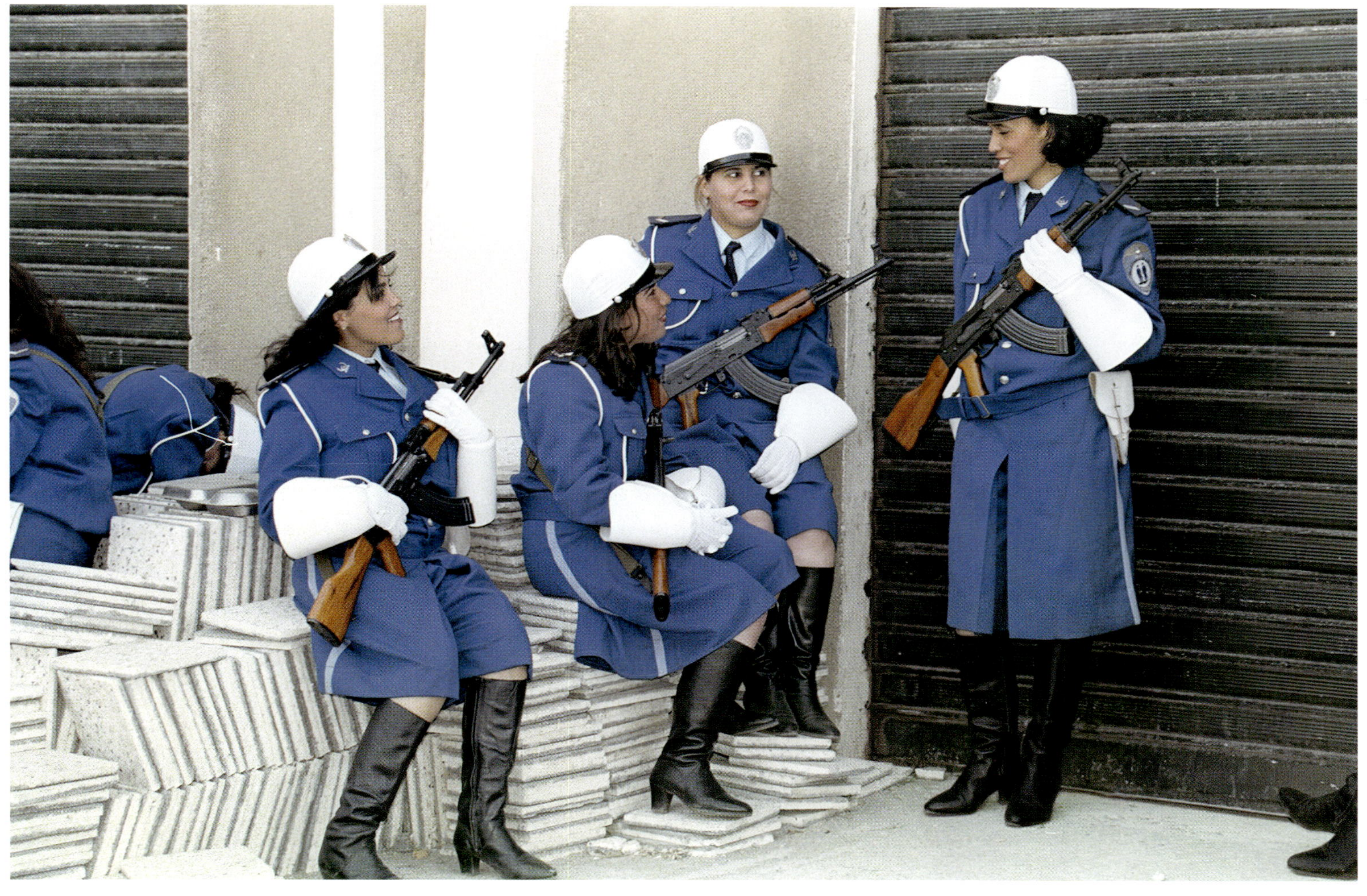

Law-and-order enforcement officers at the Ain Benian police school in Algiers, on the day of graduation of the new self-defence and close combat squad—January 27, 1999, 1999
Chromogenic print, 11 x 14 in. (27.9 x 35.6 cm)
Courtesy the artist

Moshekwa Langa

Michael Tsegaye

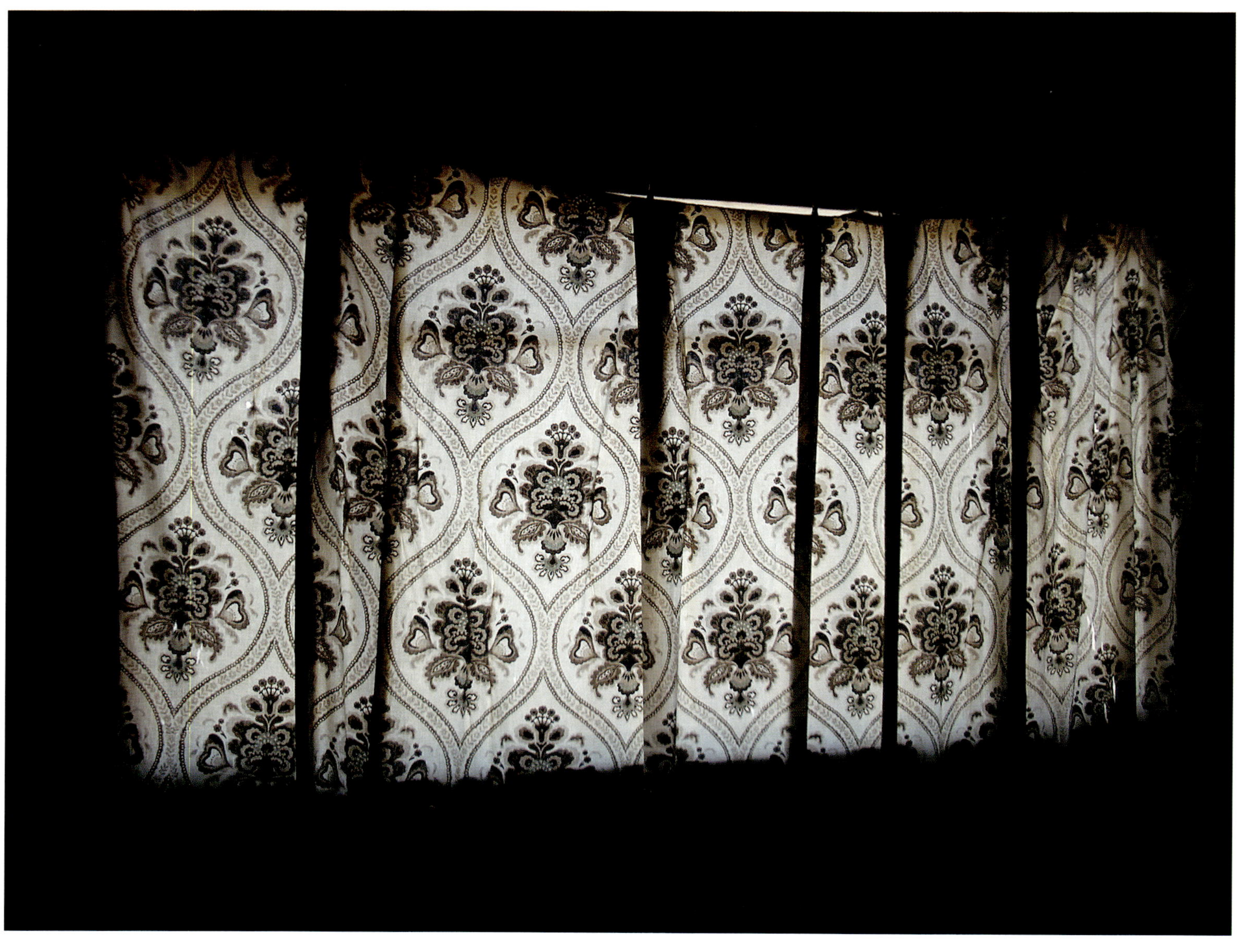

Untitled V, 2005
Chromogenic print, 11 x 14 in. (27.9 x 35.6 cm)
Courtesy the artist and Goodman Gallery, Johannesburg

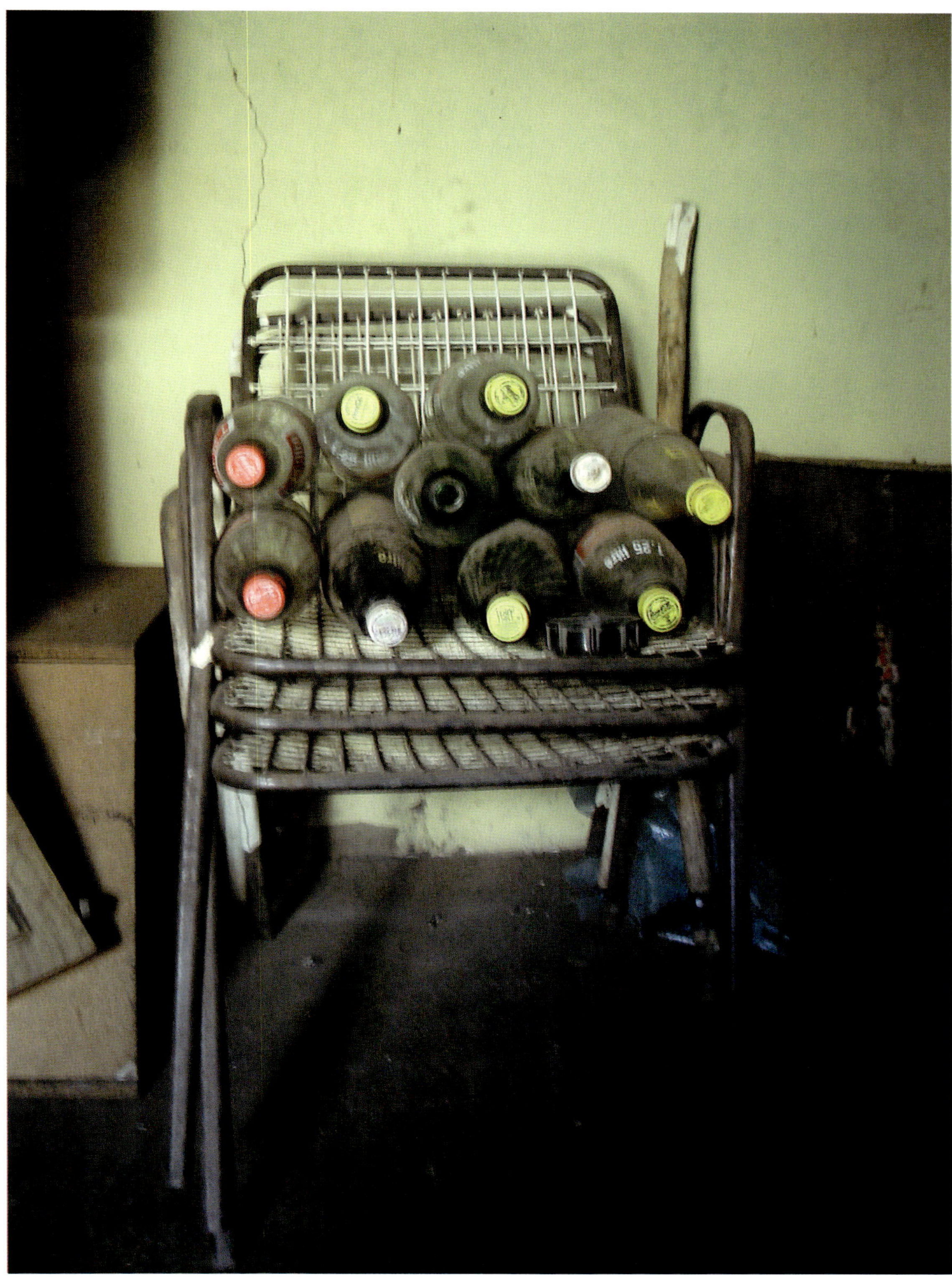

Untitled III, 2005
Chromogenic print, 11 x 14 in. (27.9 x 35.6 cm)
Courtesy the artist and Goodman Gallery, Johannesburg

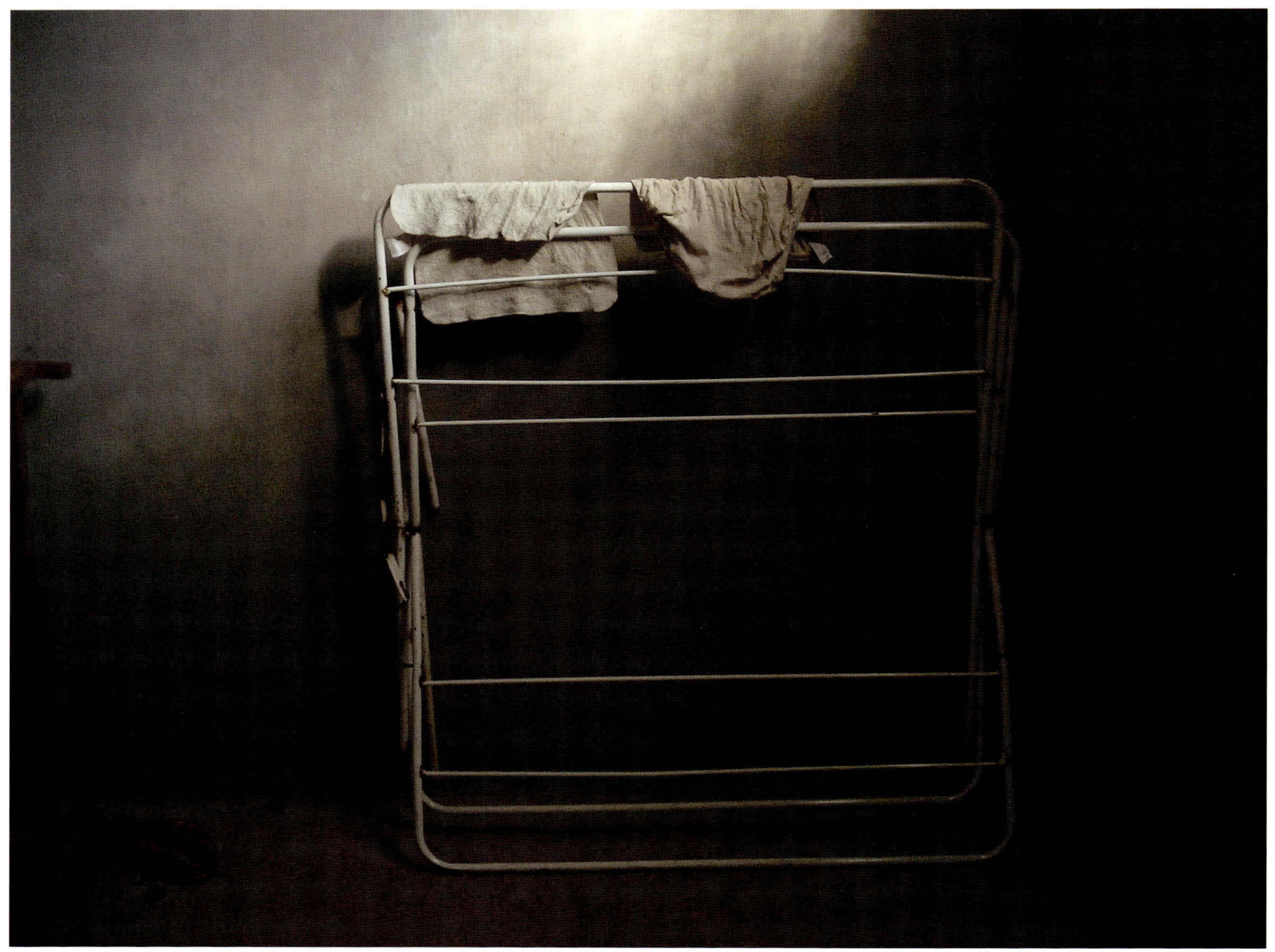

Untitled II, 2005
Chromogenic print, 11 x 14 in. (27.9 x 35.6 cm)
Courtesy the artist and Goodman Gallery, Johannesburg

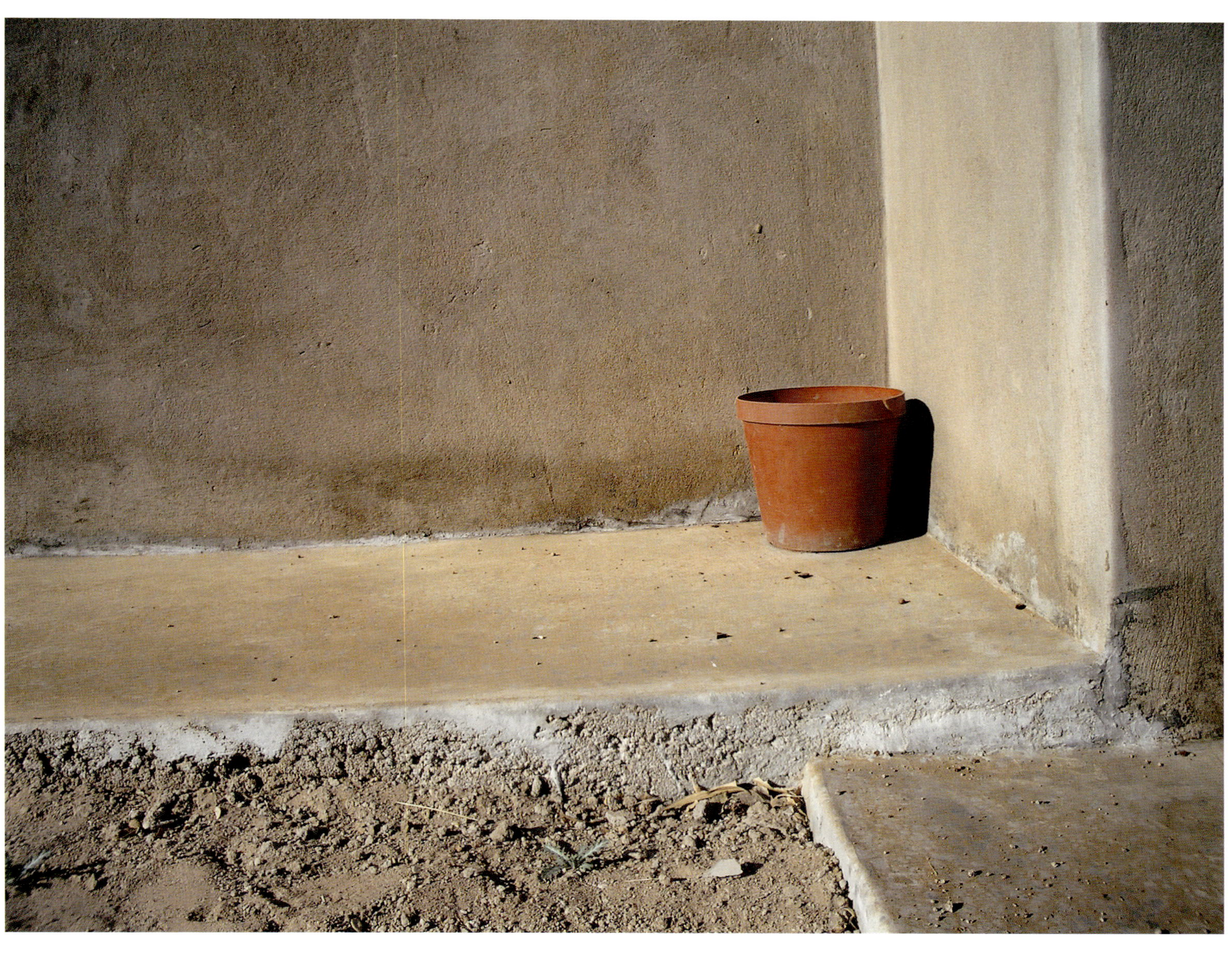

Untitled XIX, 2005
Chromogenic print, 11 x 14 in. (27.9 x 35.6 cm)
Courtesy the artist and Goodman Gallery, Johannesburg

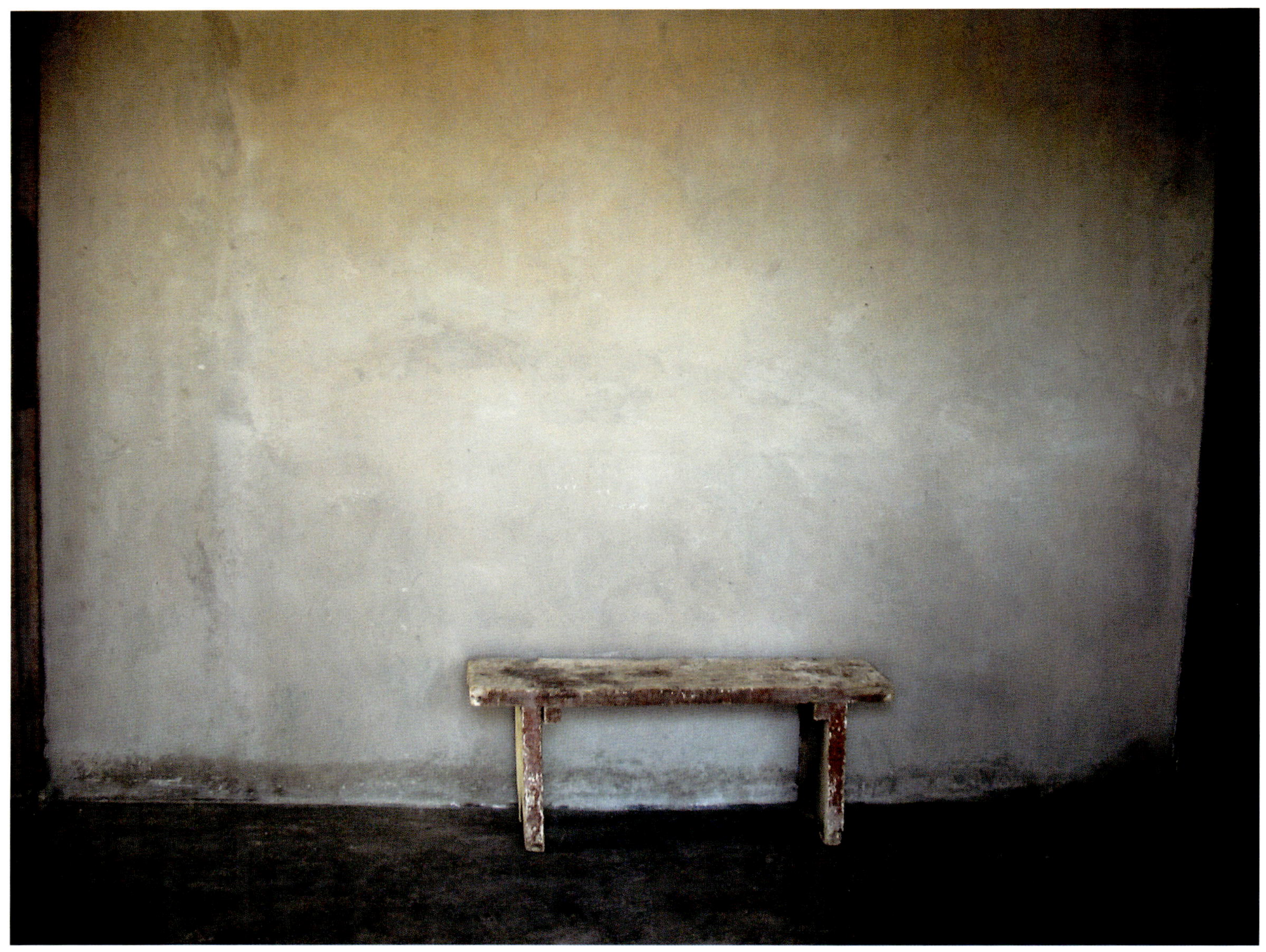

Untitled XVI, 2005
Chromogenic print, 11 x 14 in. (27.9 x 35.6 cm)
Courtesy the artist and Goodman Gallery, Johannesburg

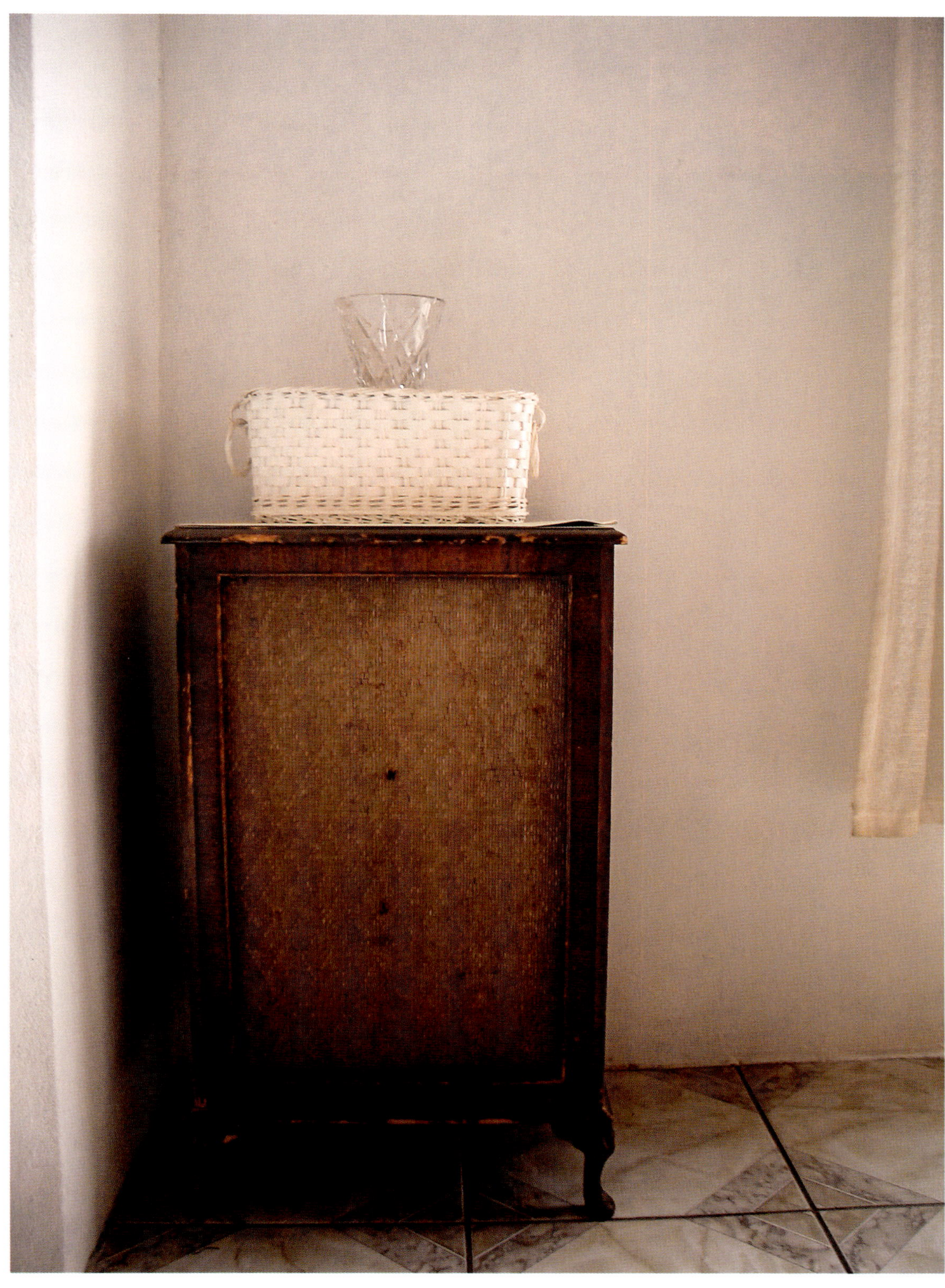

Untitled XX, 2005
Chromogenic print, 11 x 14 in. (27.9 x 35.6 cm)
Courtesy the artist and Goodman Gallery, Johannesburg

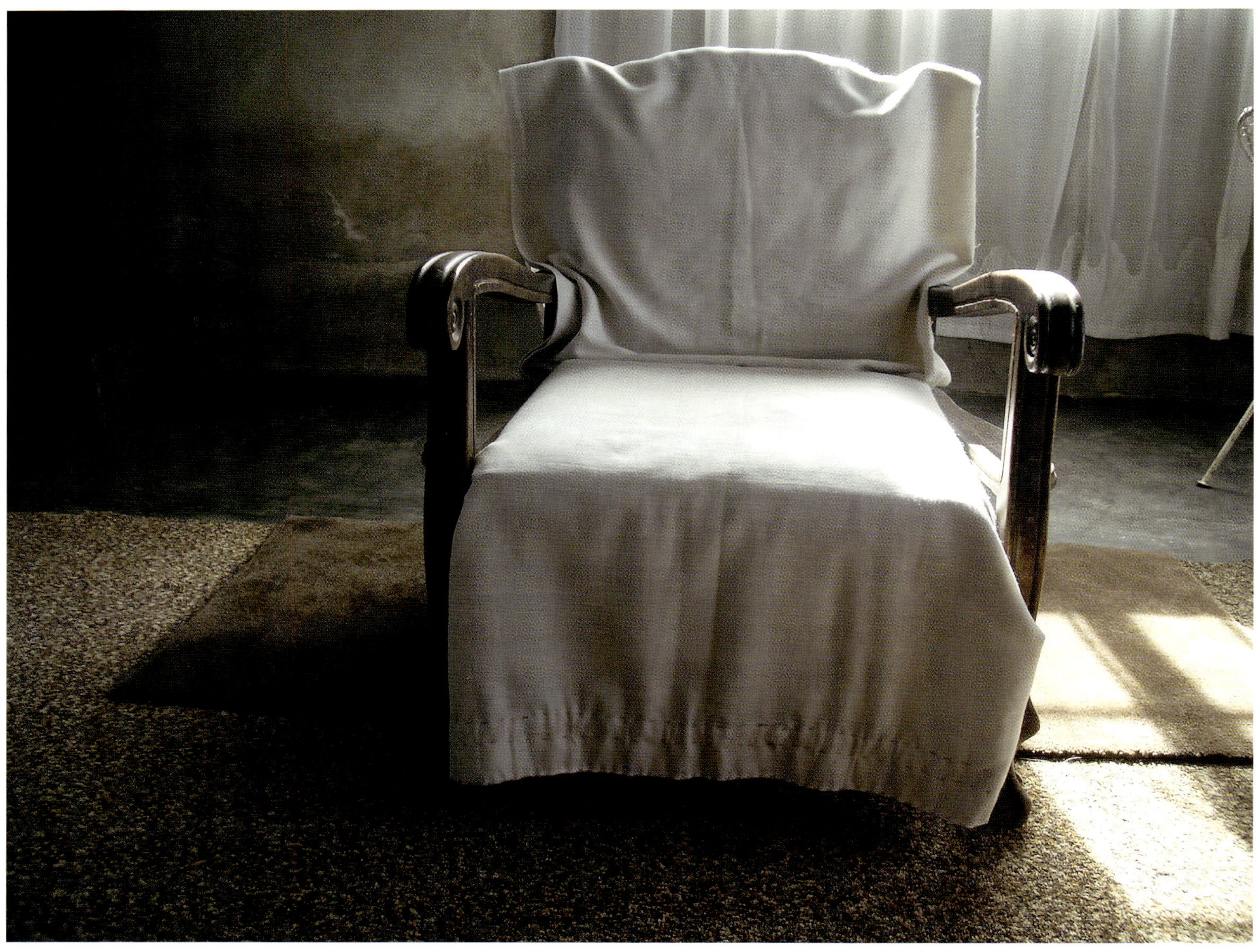

Untitled XXI, 2005
Chromogenic print, 11 x 14 in. (27.9 x 35.6 cm)
Courtesy the artist and Goodman Gallery, Johannesburg

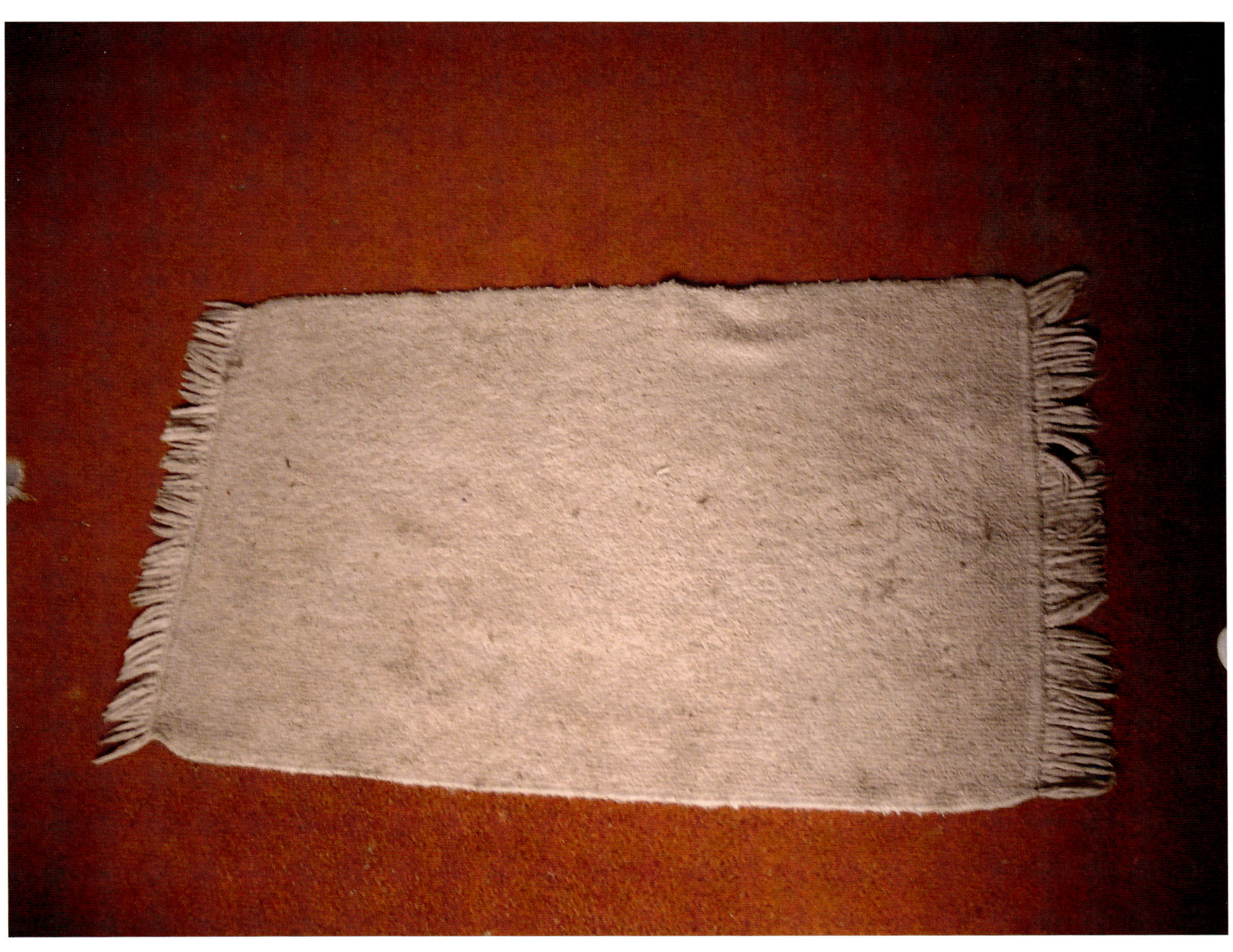

Untitled XIII, 2005
Chromogenic print, 11 x 14 in. (27.9 x 35.6 cm)
Courtesy the artist and Goodman Gallery, Johannesburg

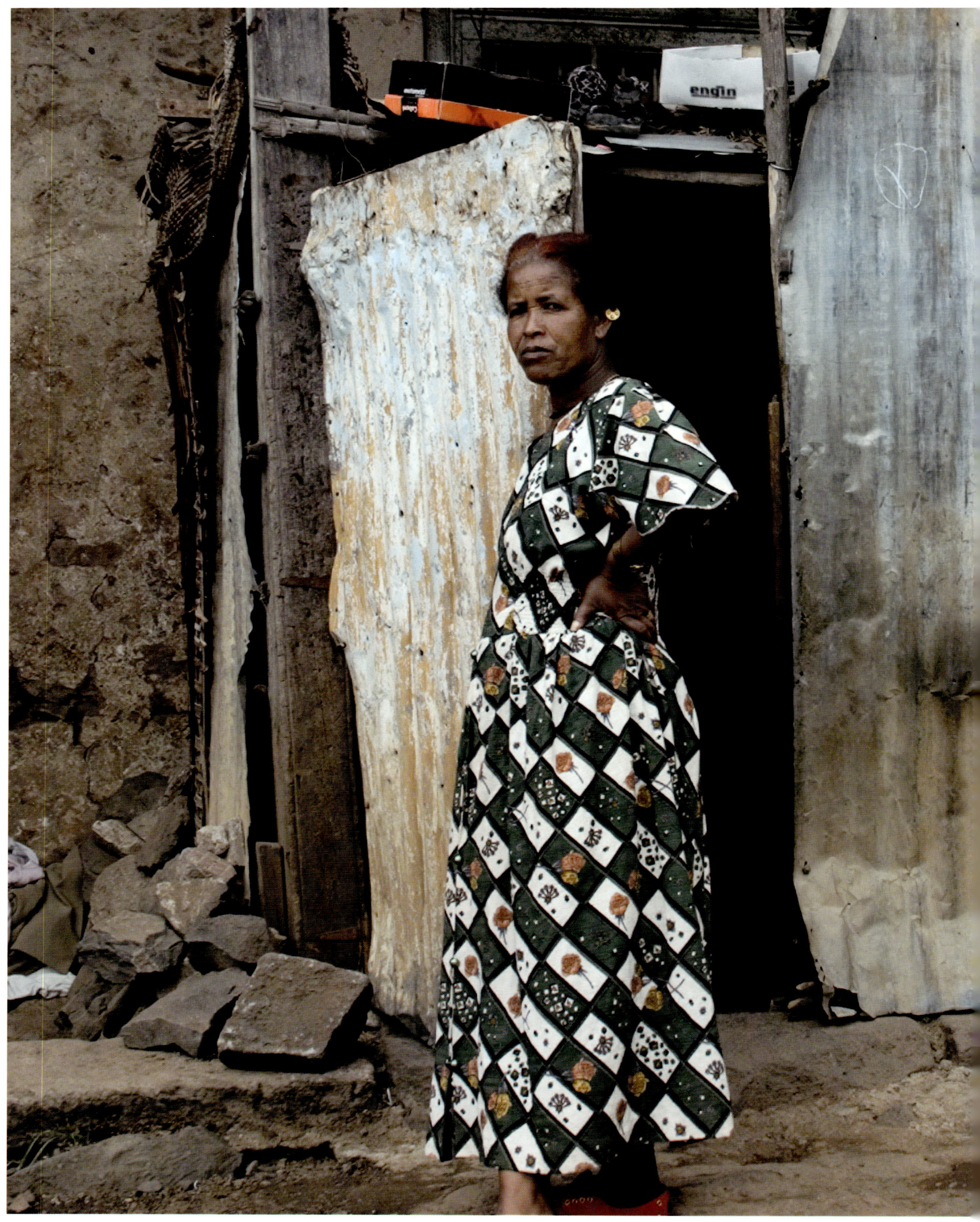
engin

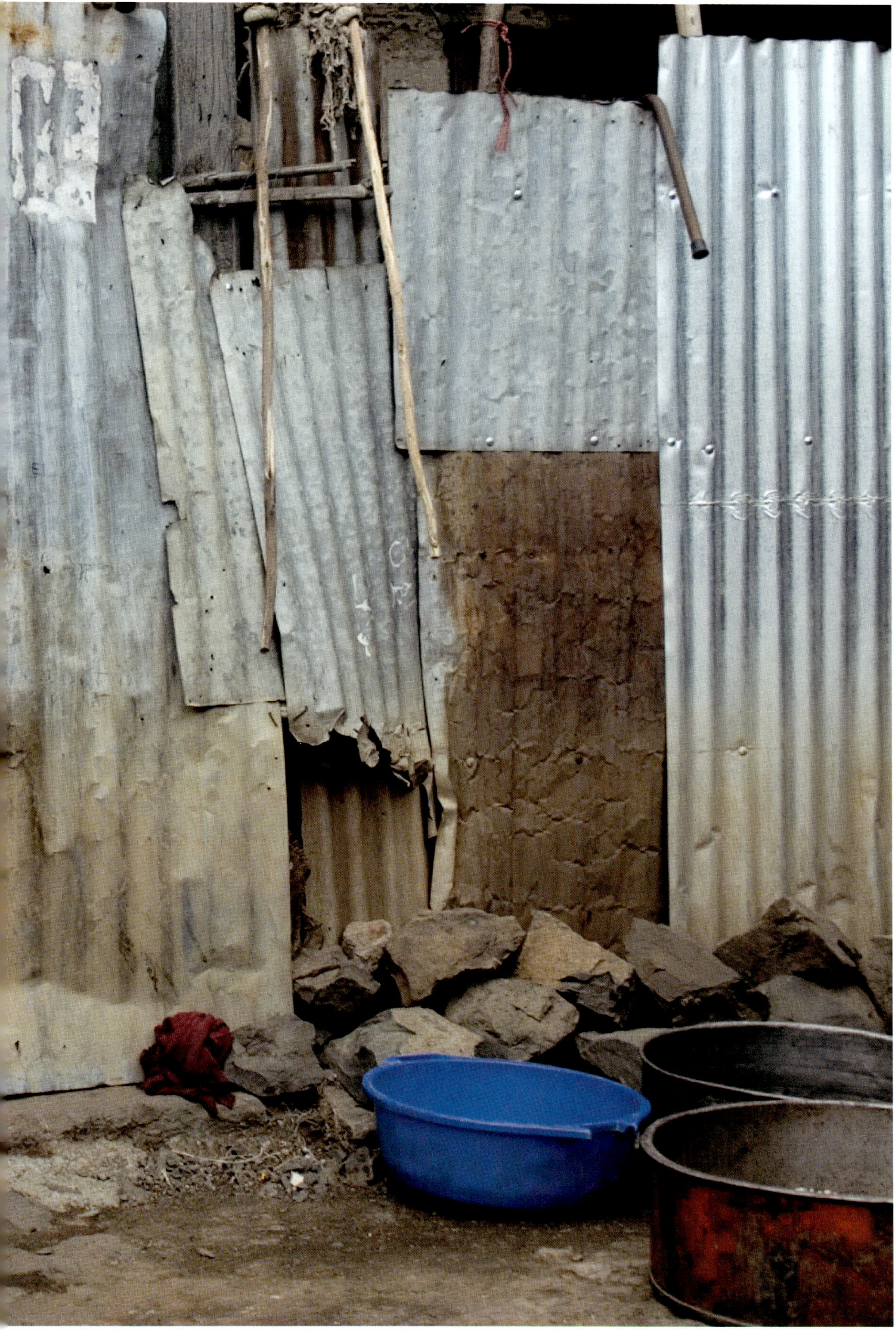

Untitled, from the series
"In and Out," 2005
Chromogenic print
20 x 24 in. (50.8 x 61 cm)
Courtesy the artist

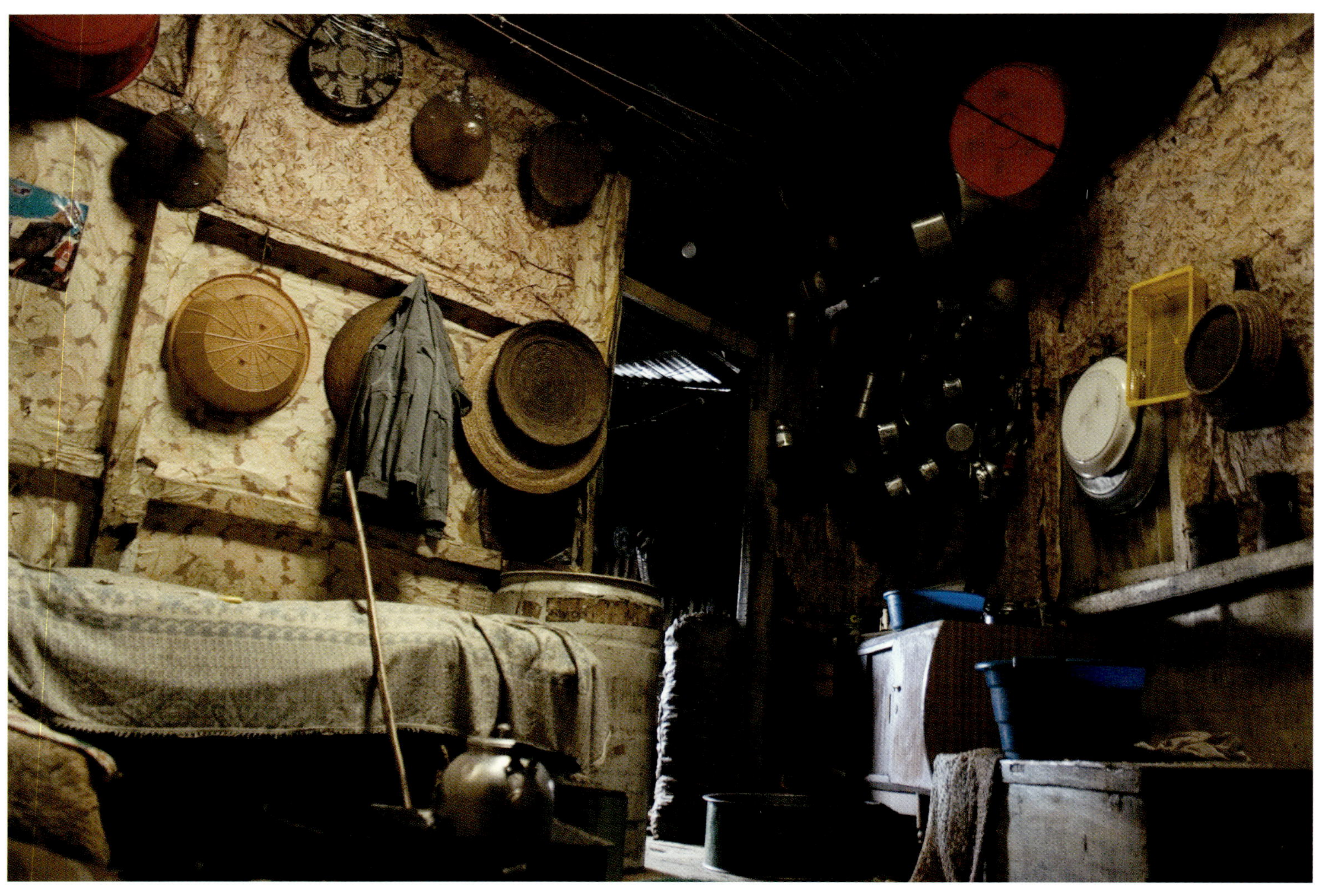

Untitled, from the series "In and Out," 2005
Chromogenic print, 20 x 24 in. (50.8 x 61 cm)
Courtesy the artist

Right:
Untitled, from the series "In and Out," 2005
Chromogenic print, 20 x 24 in. (50.8 x 61 cm)
Courtesy the artist

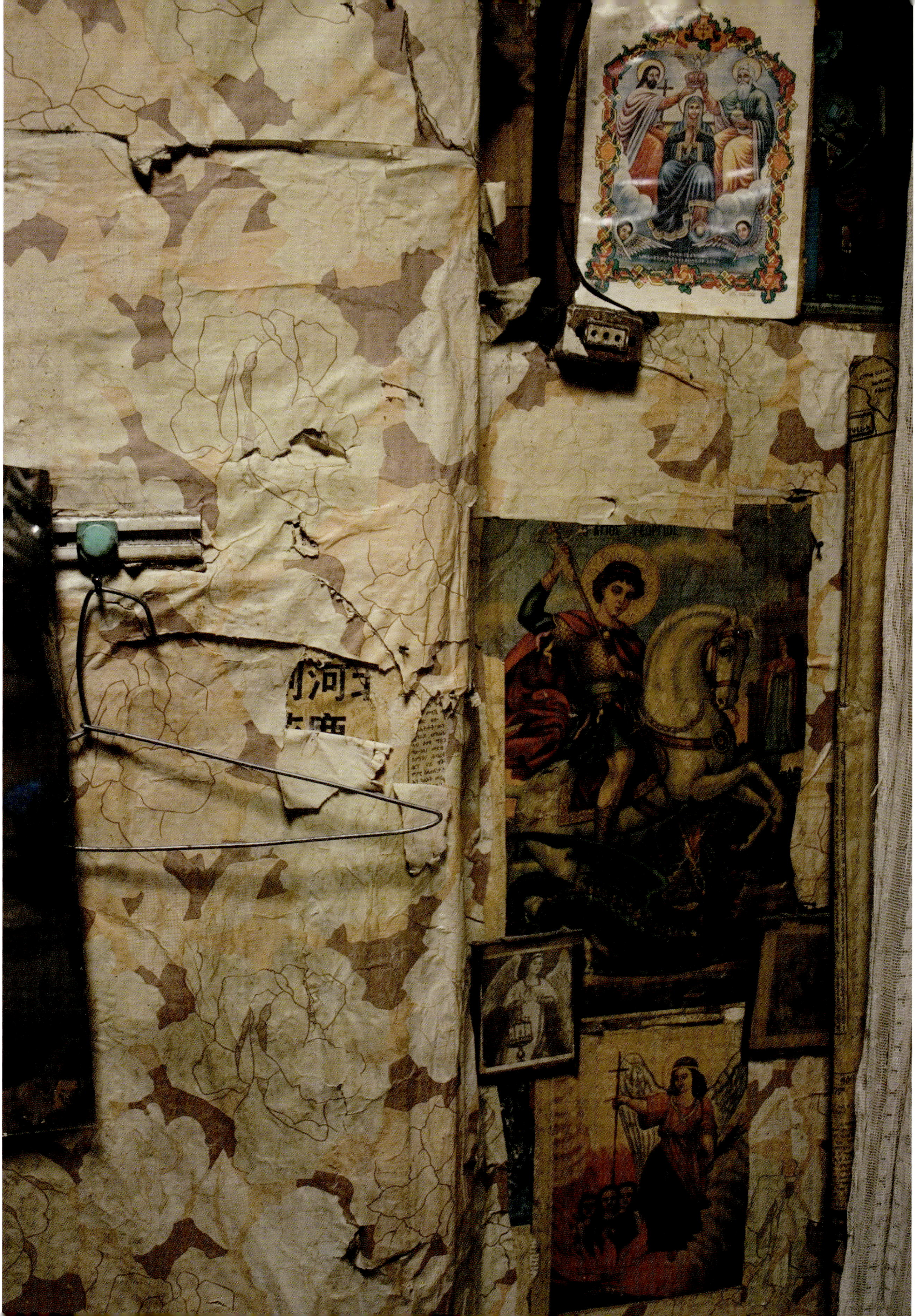
ΑΓΙΟΣ ΓΕΩΡΓΙΟΣ

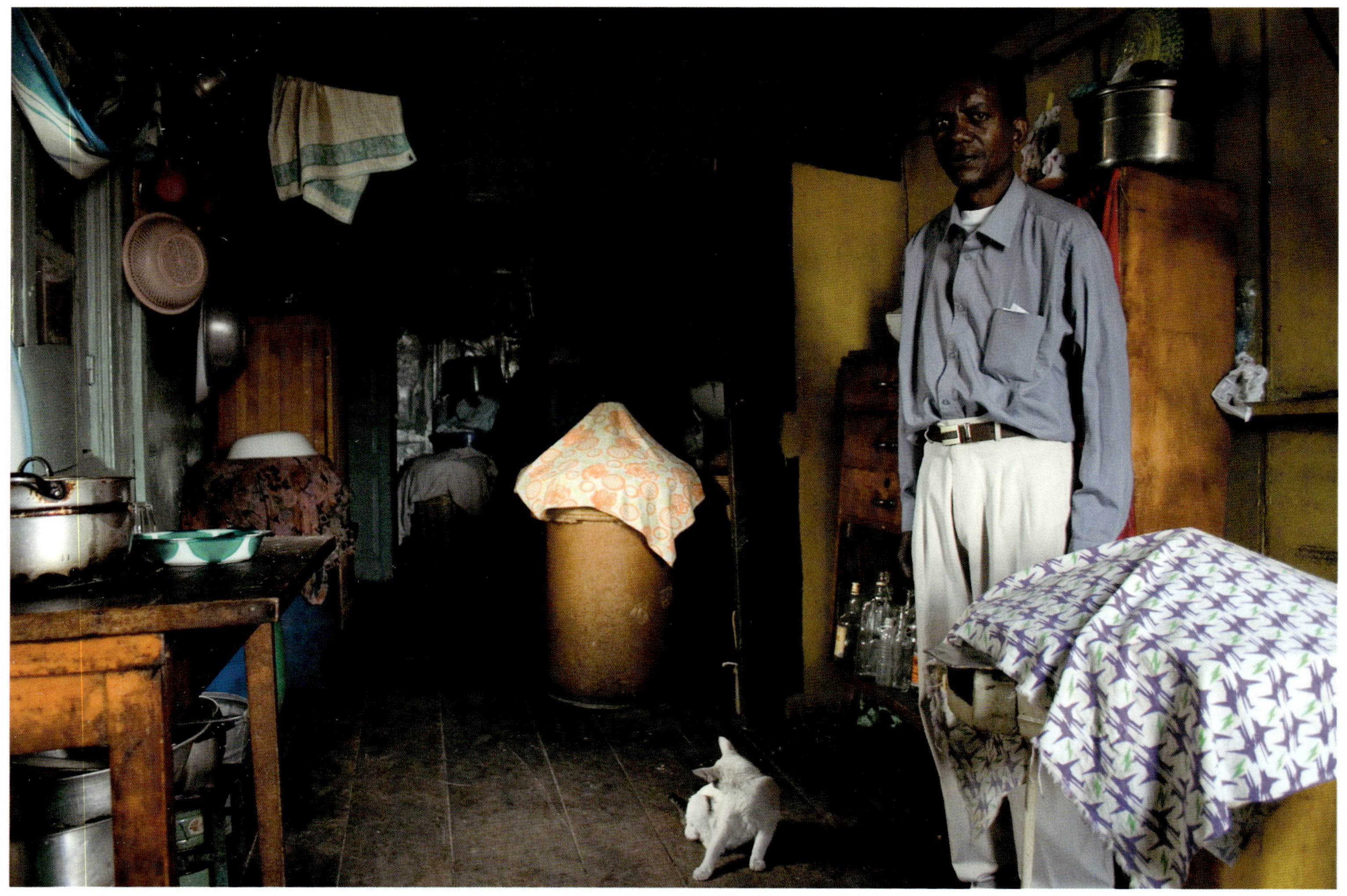

Untitled, from the series "In and Out," 2005
Chromogenic print, 20 x 24 in. (50.8 x 61 cm)
Courtesy the artist

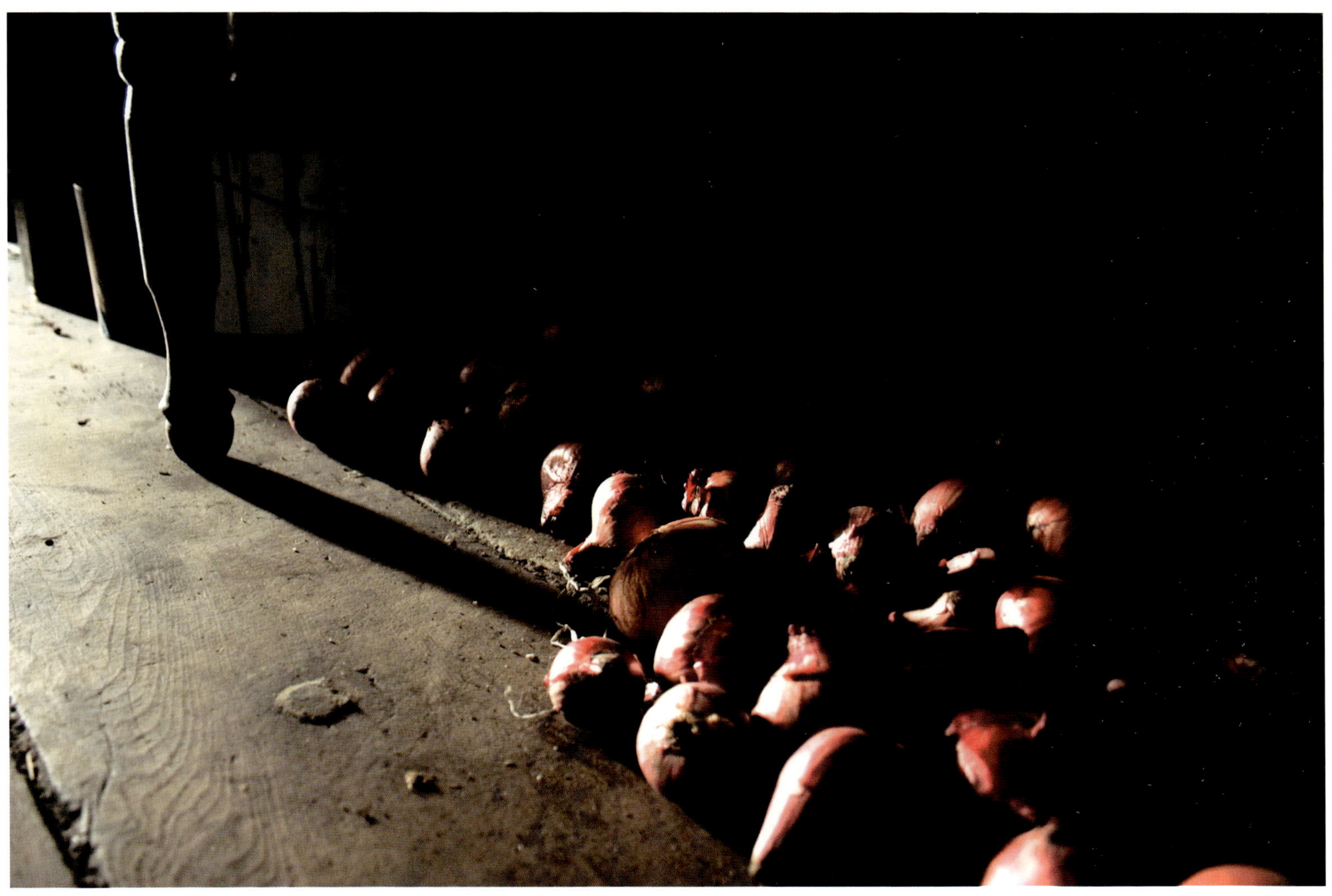

Untitled, from the series "In and Out," 2005
Chromogenic print, 20 x 24 in. (50.8 x 61 cm)
Courtesy the artist

Jo Ractliffe

Randa Shaath

James Muriuki

Boubacar Touré Mandémory

Guy Tillim

Hala Elkoussy

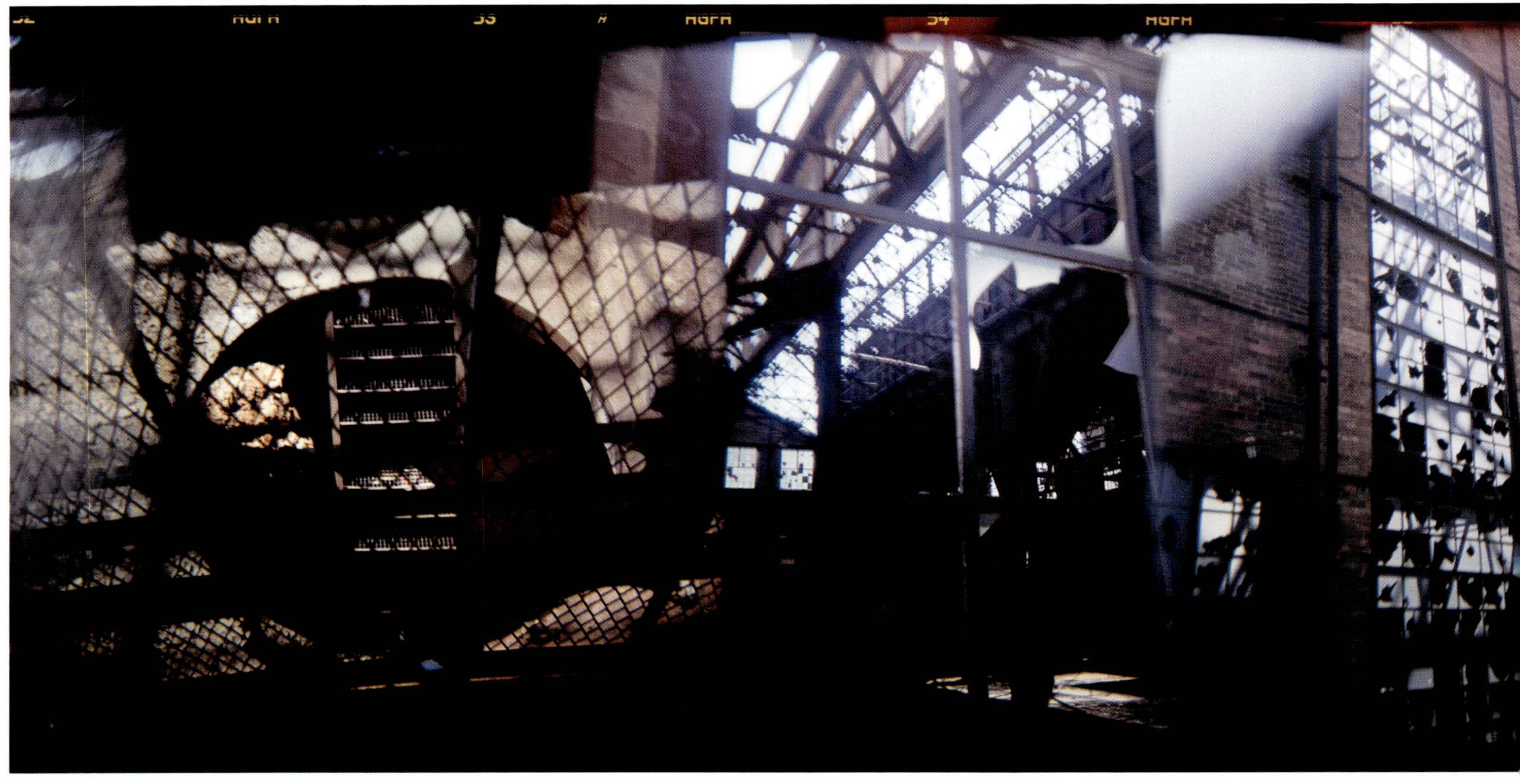

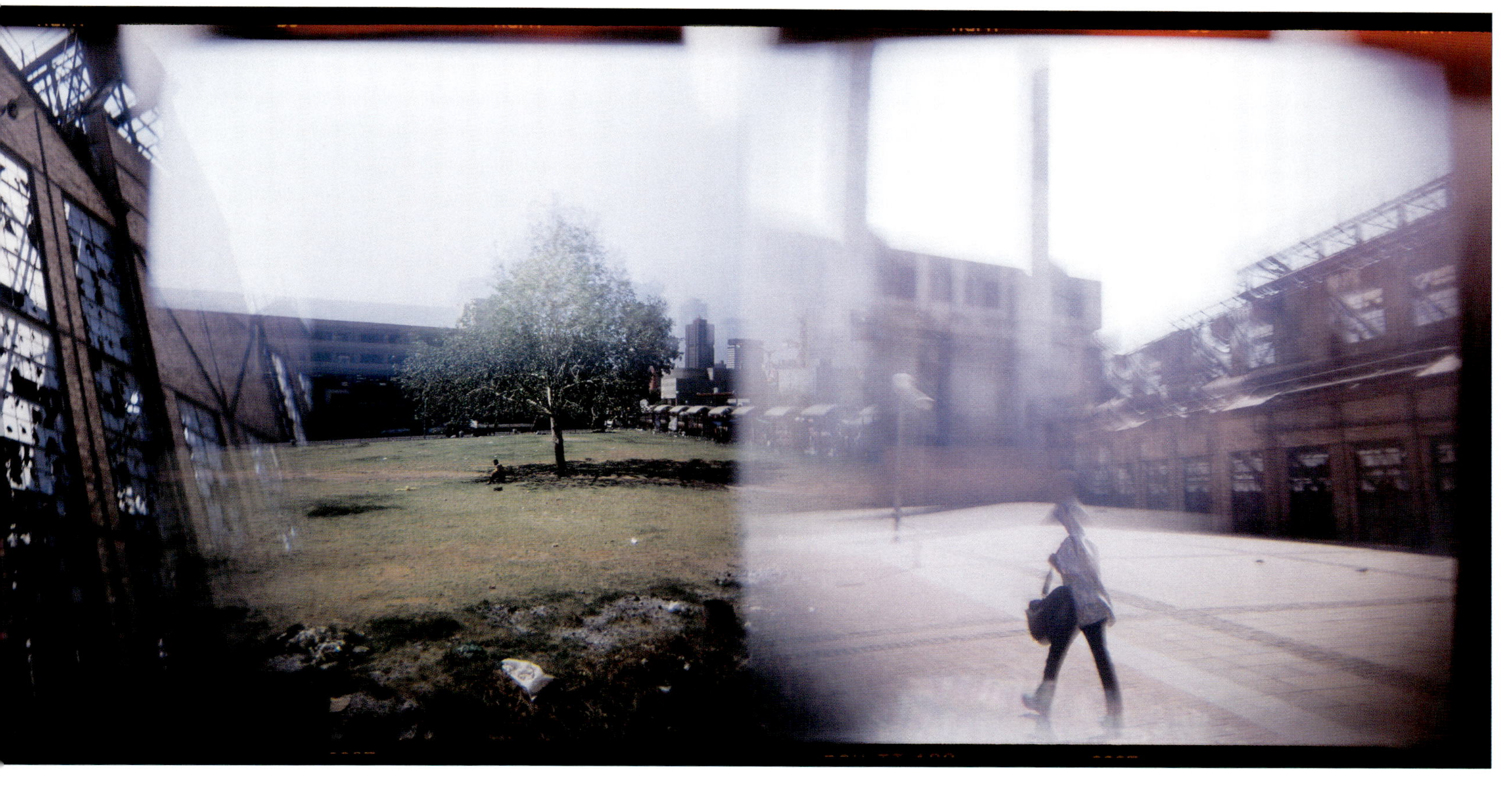

Highlands St, Highlands / Percy St, Yeoville, from the series "Johannesburg Inner City Works," 2000
Pigment print on paper, 20 x 78.9 in. (50.8 x 200.3 cm)
Courtesy the artist and Warren Siebrits Gallery, Johannesburg

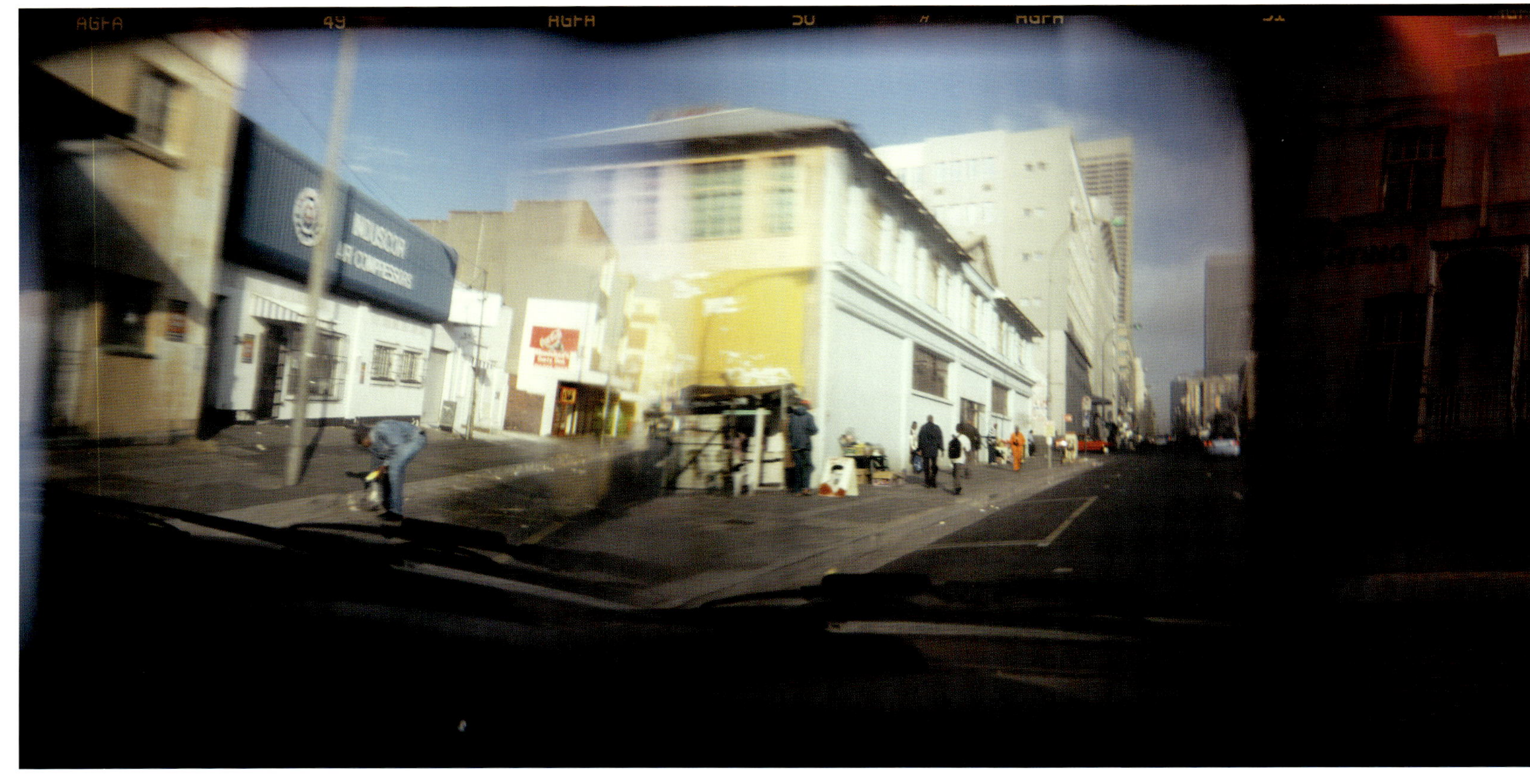
AGFA
49
AGFA
50
AGFA

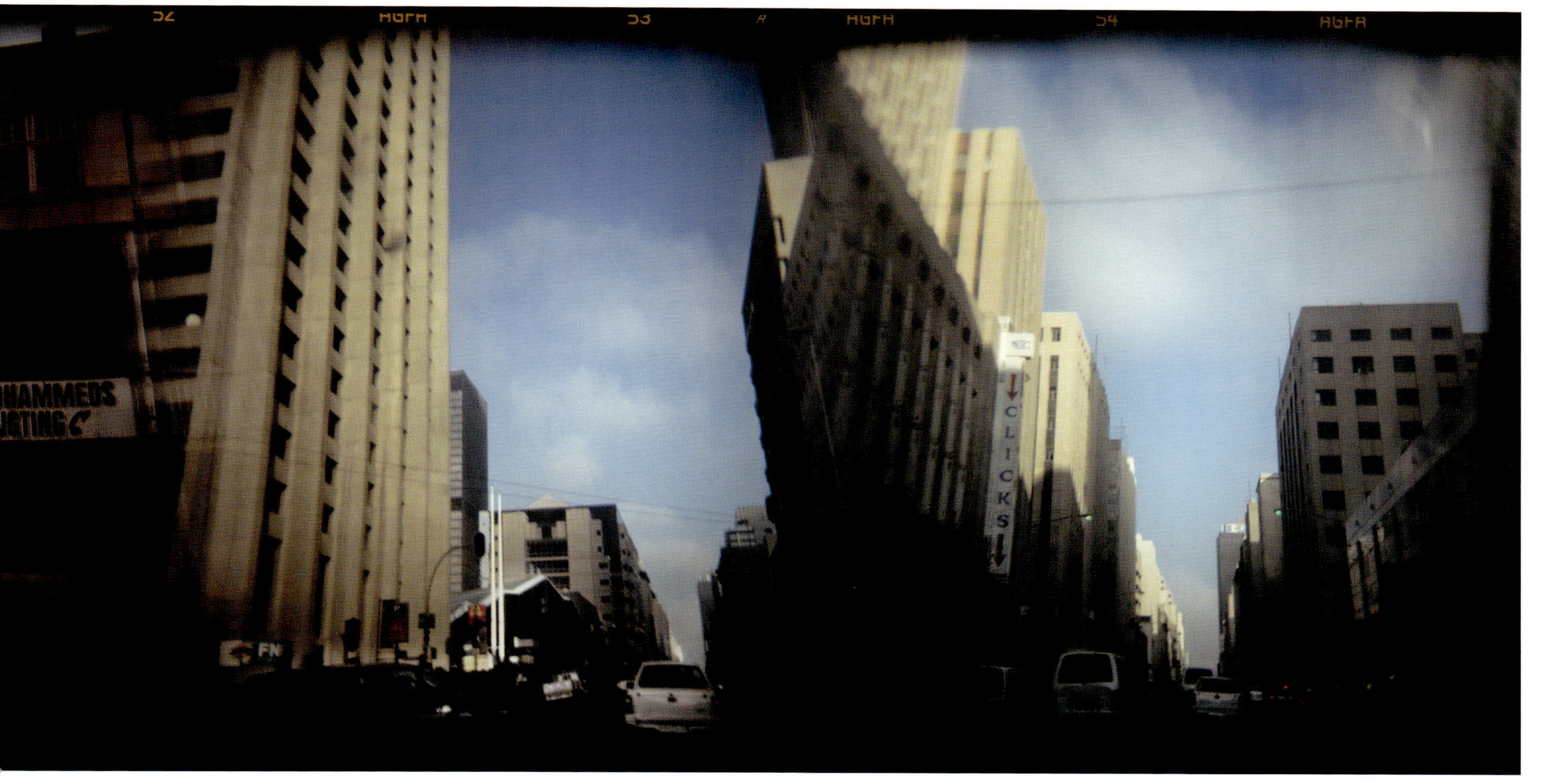

Commissioner St cnr Crown St, Jeppestown / Commissioner St, Marshalltown / Commissioner St cnr Smal St Commissioner St cnr Eloff St, Johannesburg Central
from the series "Johannesburg Inner City Works," 2004
Pigment print on paper, 20 x 78.9 in. (50.8 x 200.3 cm)
Courtesy the artist and Warren Siebrits Gallery, Johannesburg

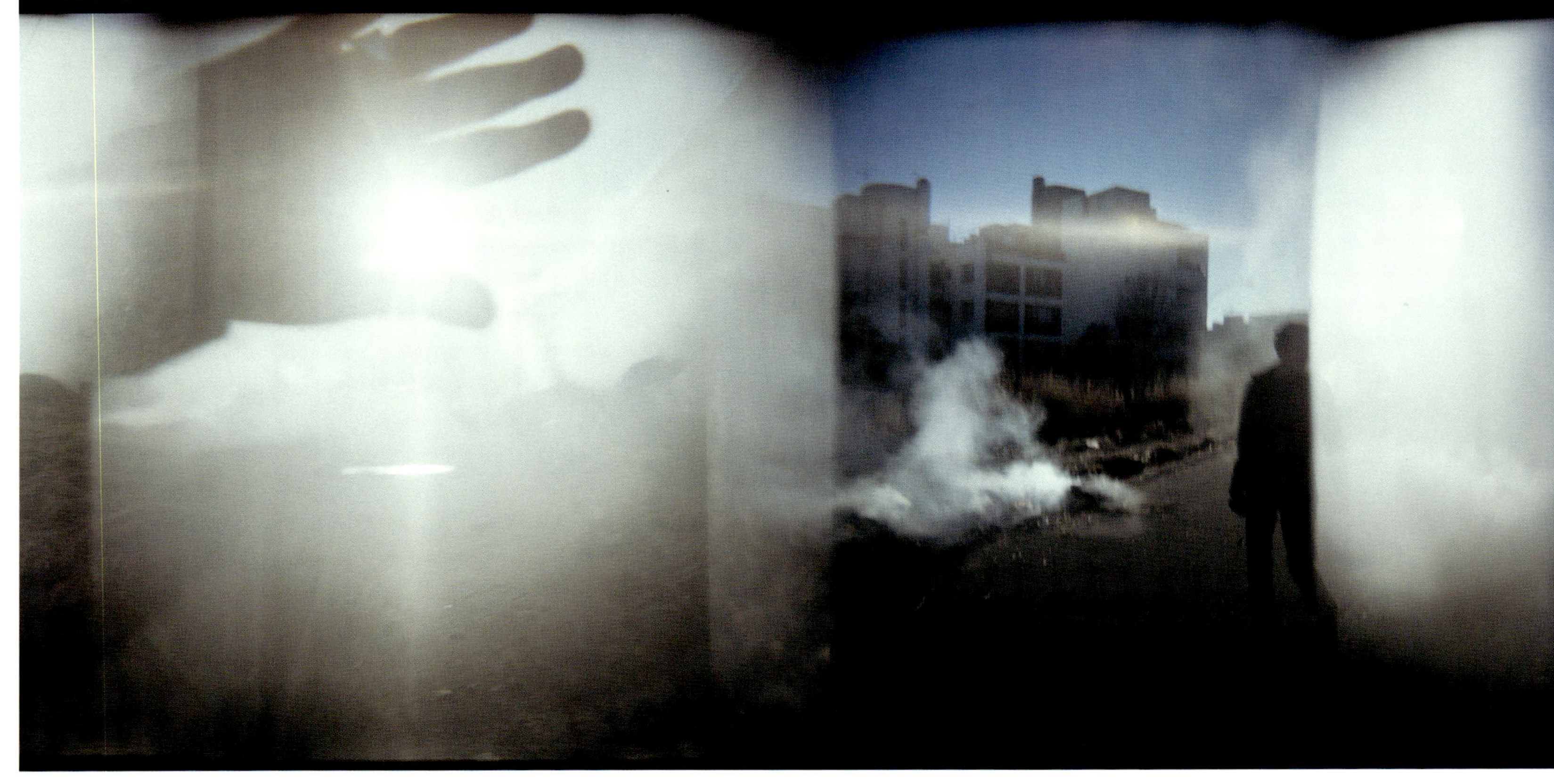

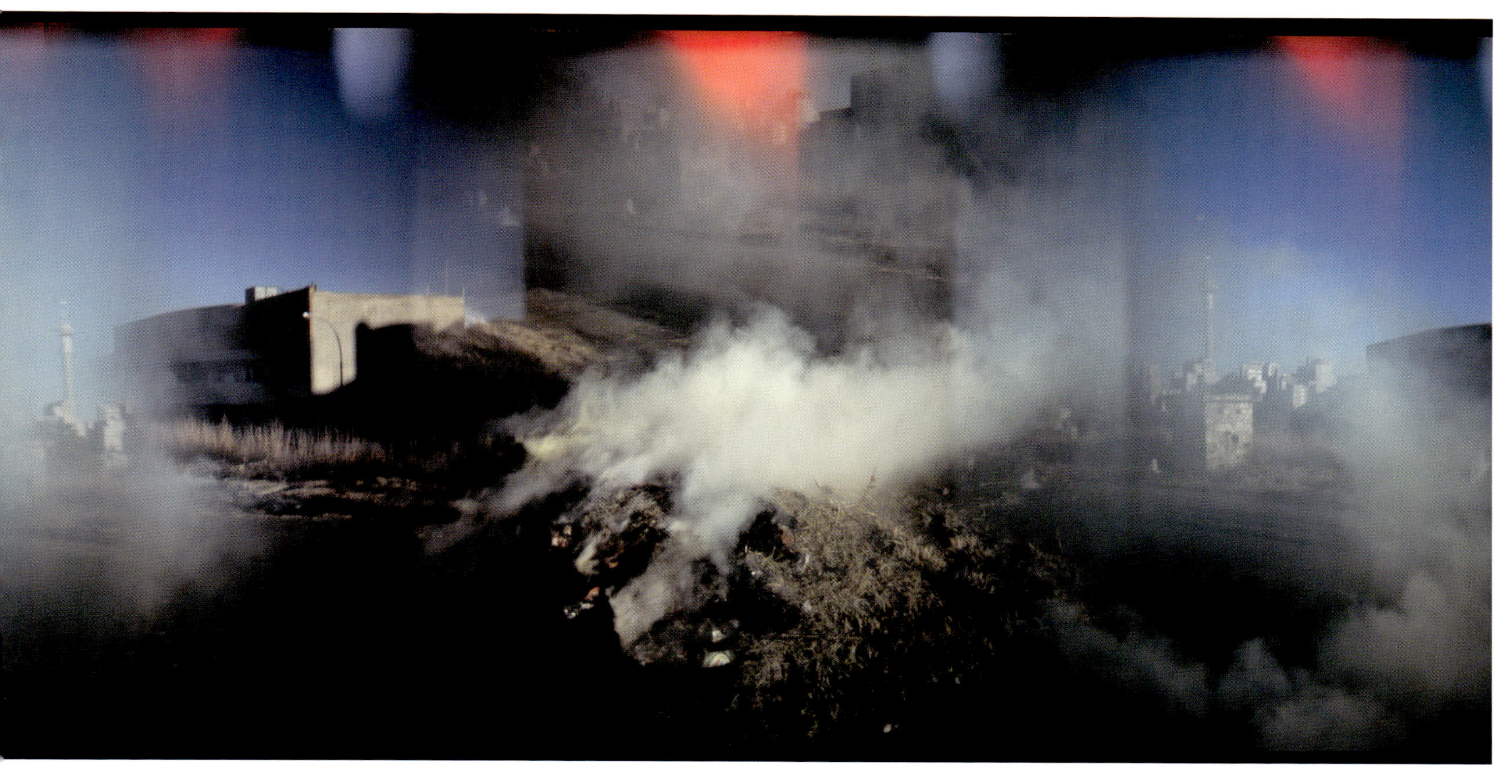

De Beer St, Braamfontein, from the series "Johannesburg Inner City Works," 2003
Pigment print on paper, 20 x 78.9 in. (50.8 x 200.3 cm)
Courtesy the artist and Warren Siebrits Gallery, Johannesburg

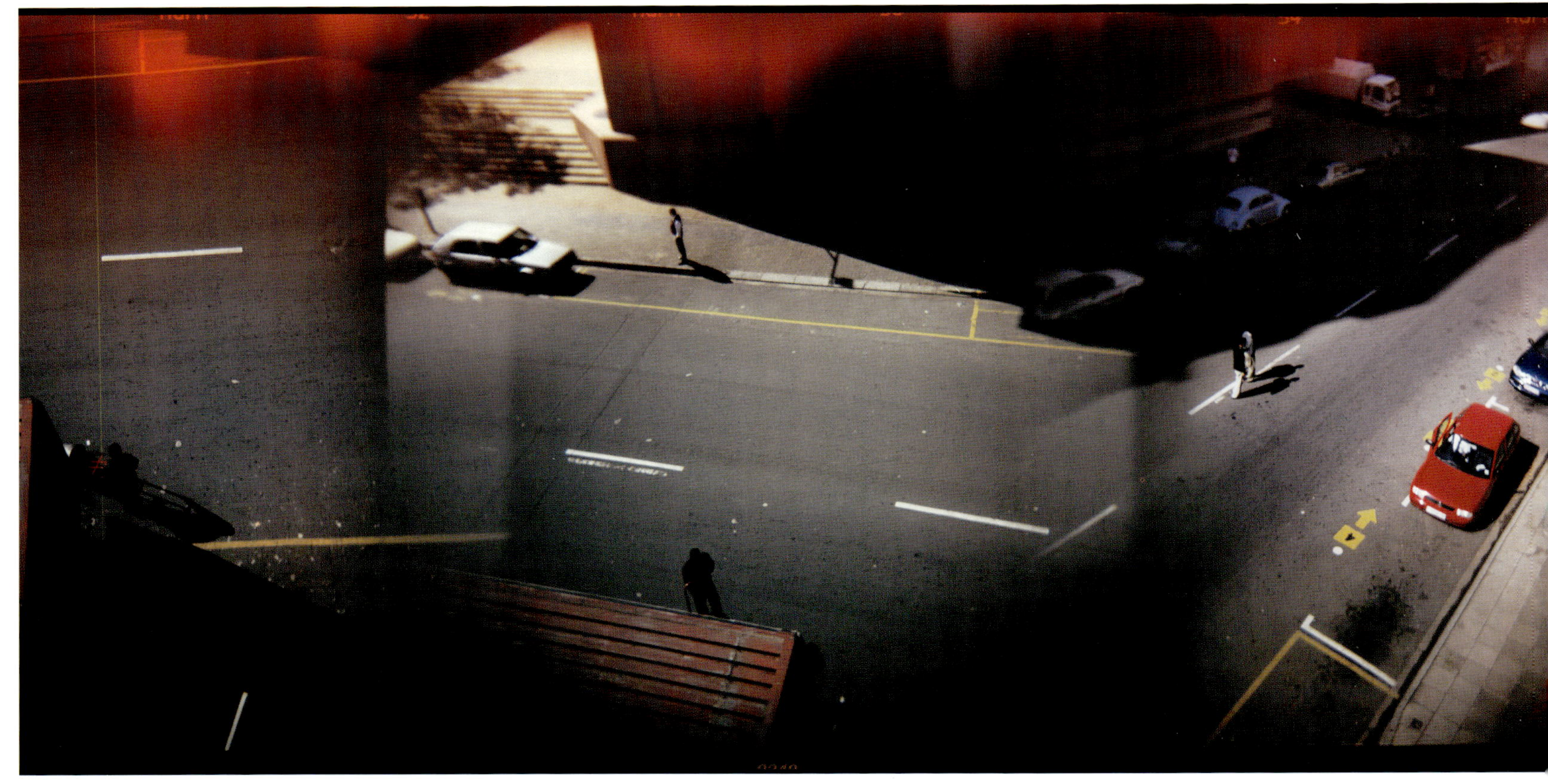

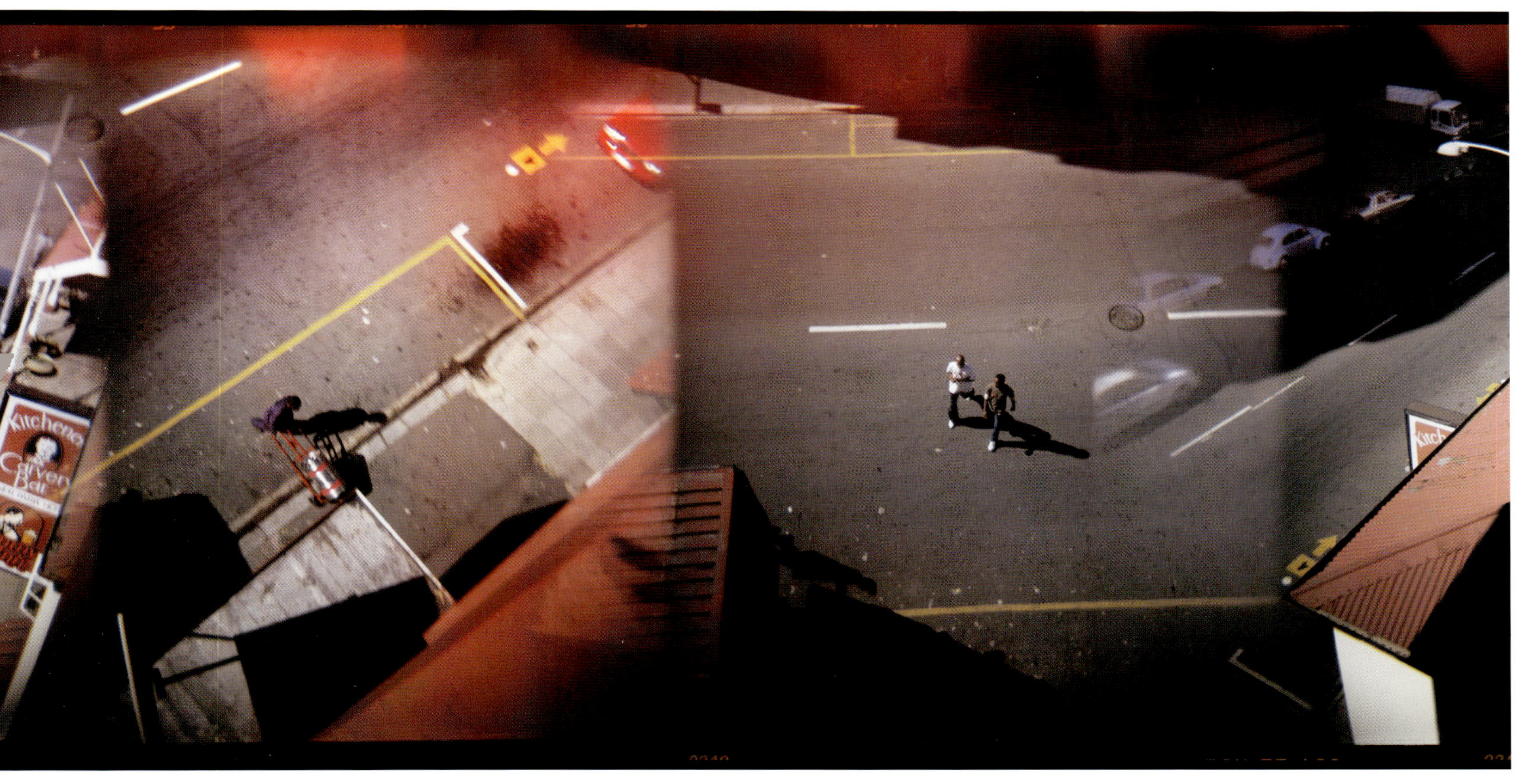

Jeppe St cnr West St, Newtown, from the series "Johannesburg Inner City Works," 2001
Pigment print on paper, 20 x 78.9 in. (50.8 x 200.3 cm)
Courtesy the artist and Warren Siebrits Gallery, Johannesburg

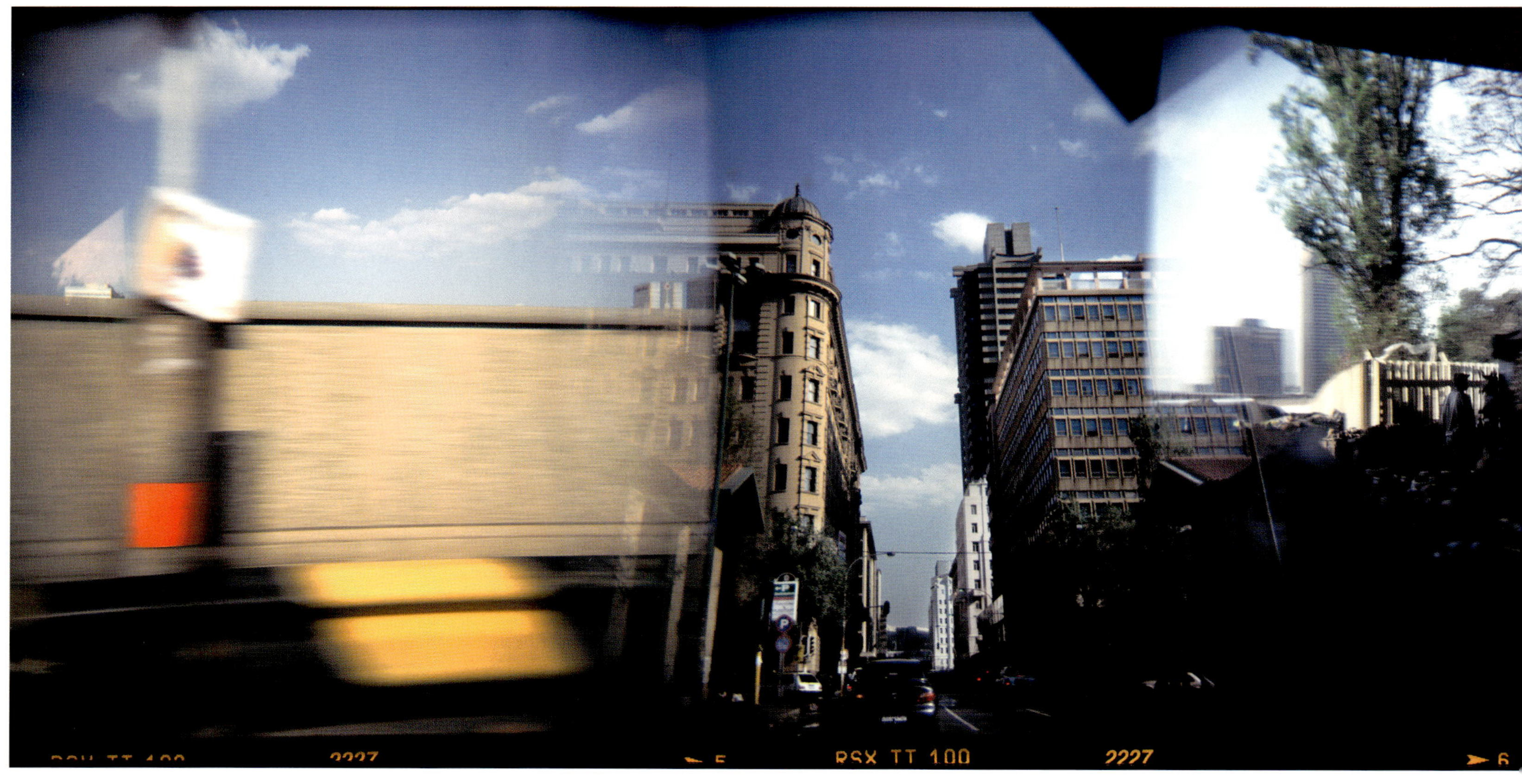
RSX TT 100
2227
6

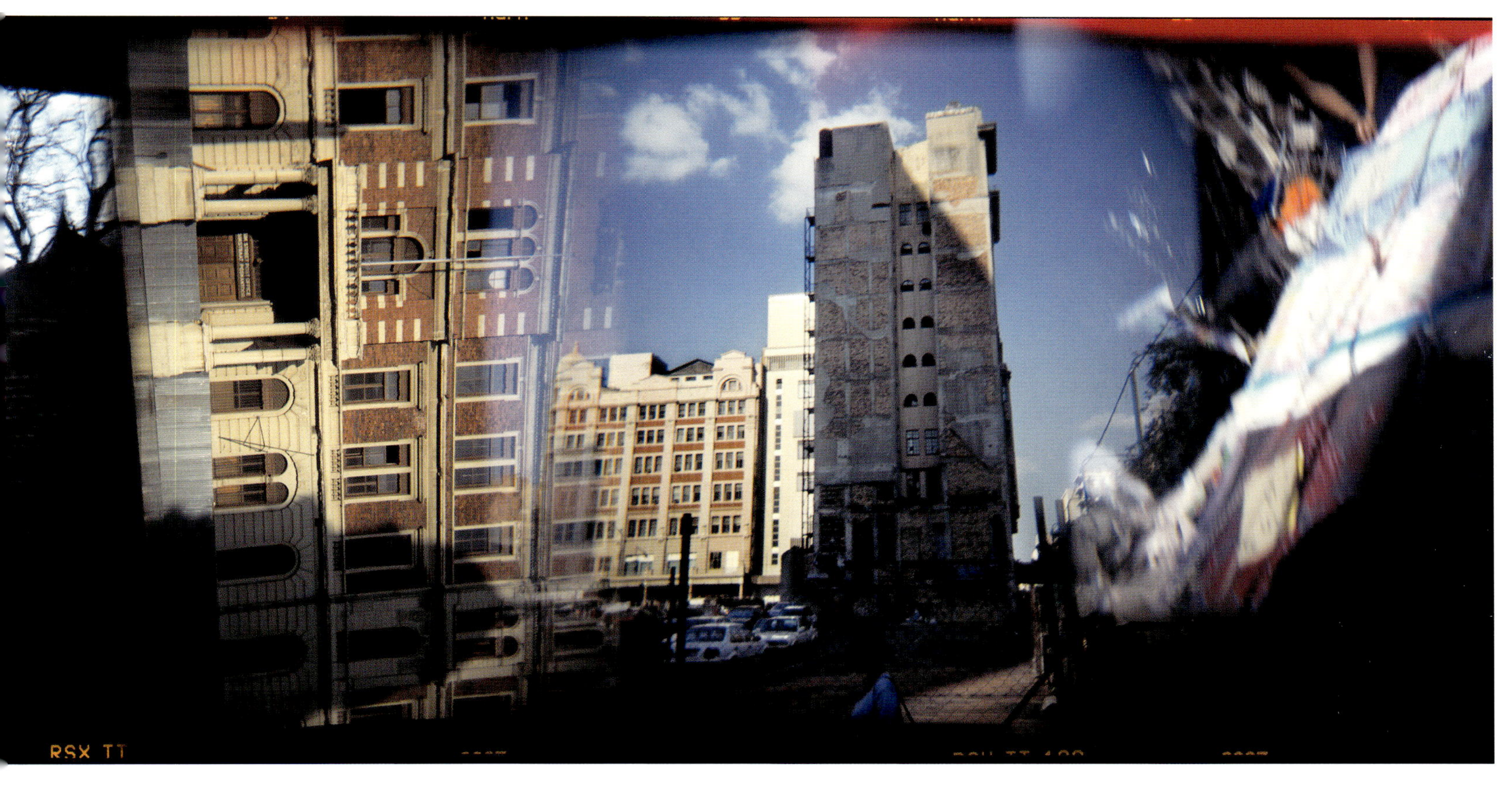

Simmonds St cnr Market St Rissik St Pritchard St, Johannesburg Central, from the series "Johannesburg Inner City Works," 2001
Pigment print on paper, 20 x 78.9 in. (50.8 x 200.3 cm)
Courtesy the artist and Warren Siebrits Gallery, Johannesburg

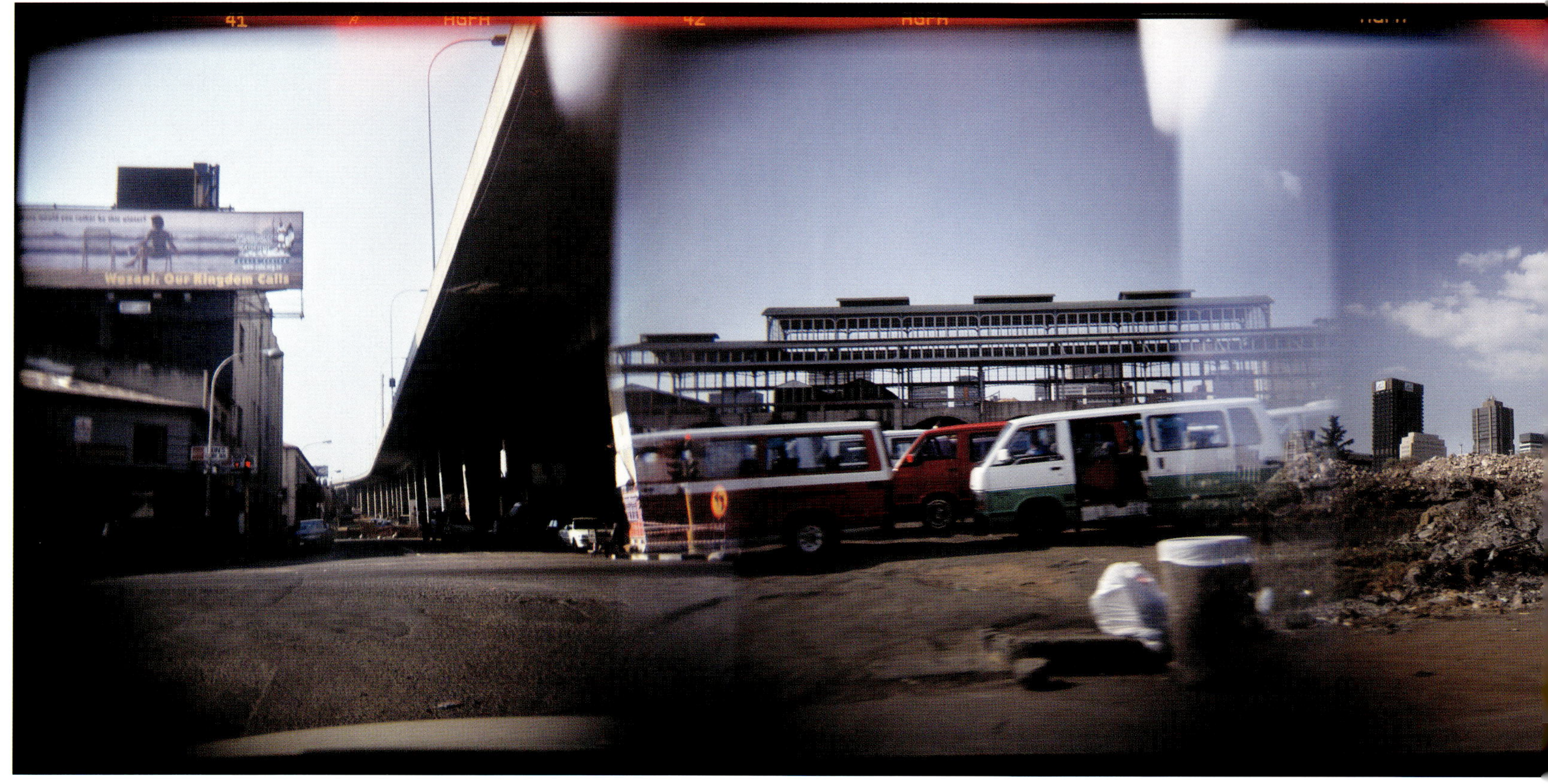
Our Kingdom Calls

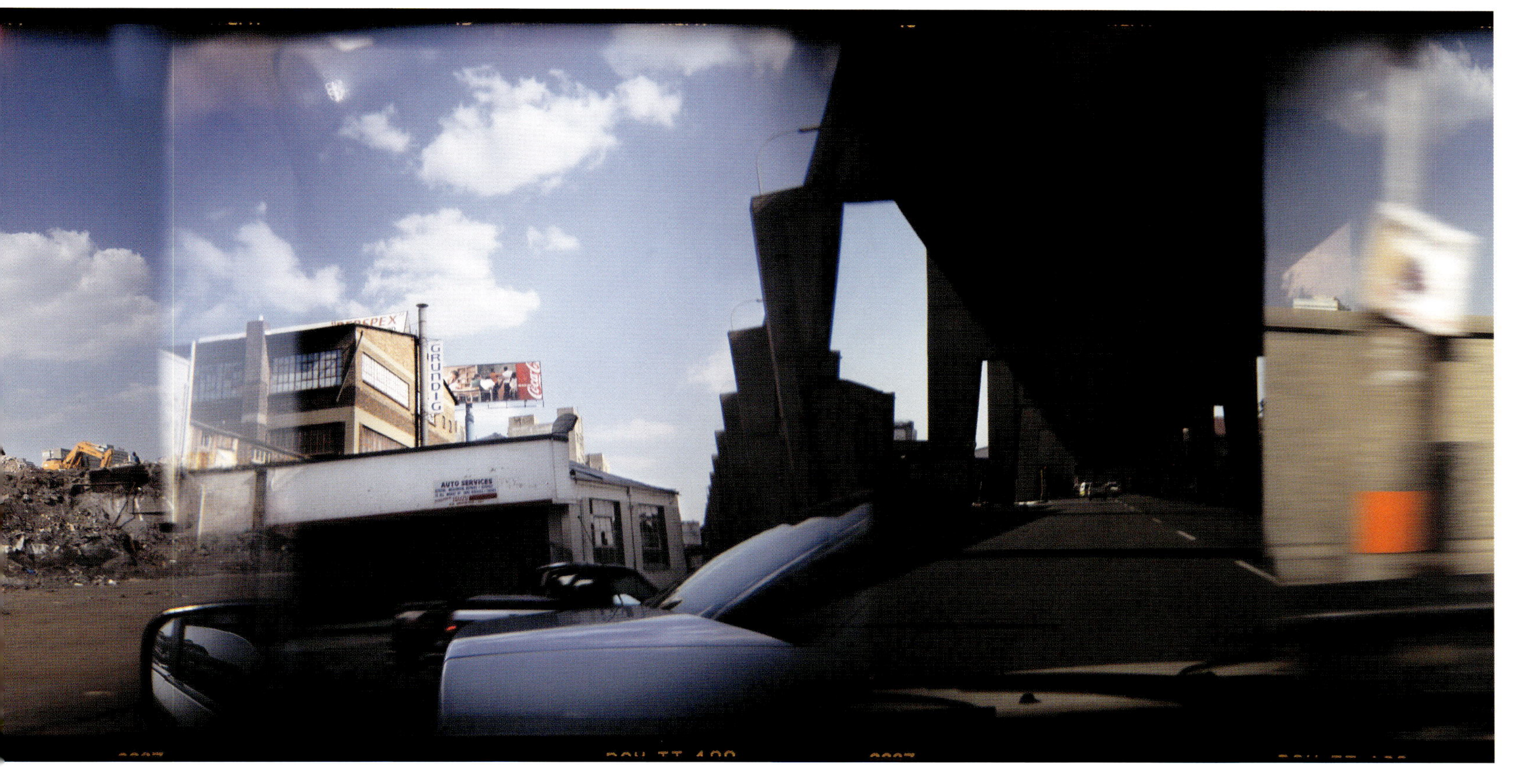

Goch St cnr Bree St Carr St Goch St, Newton, from the series "Johannesburg Inner City Works," 2001
Pigment print on paper, 20 x 78.9 in. (50.8 x 200.3 cm)
Courtesy the artist and Warren Siebrits Gallery, Johannesburg

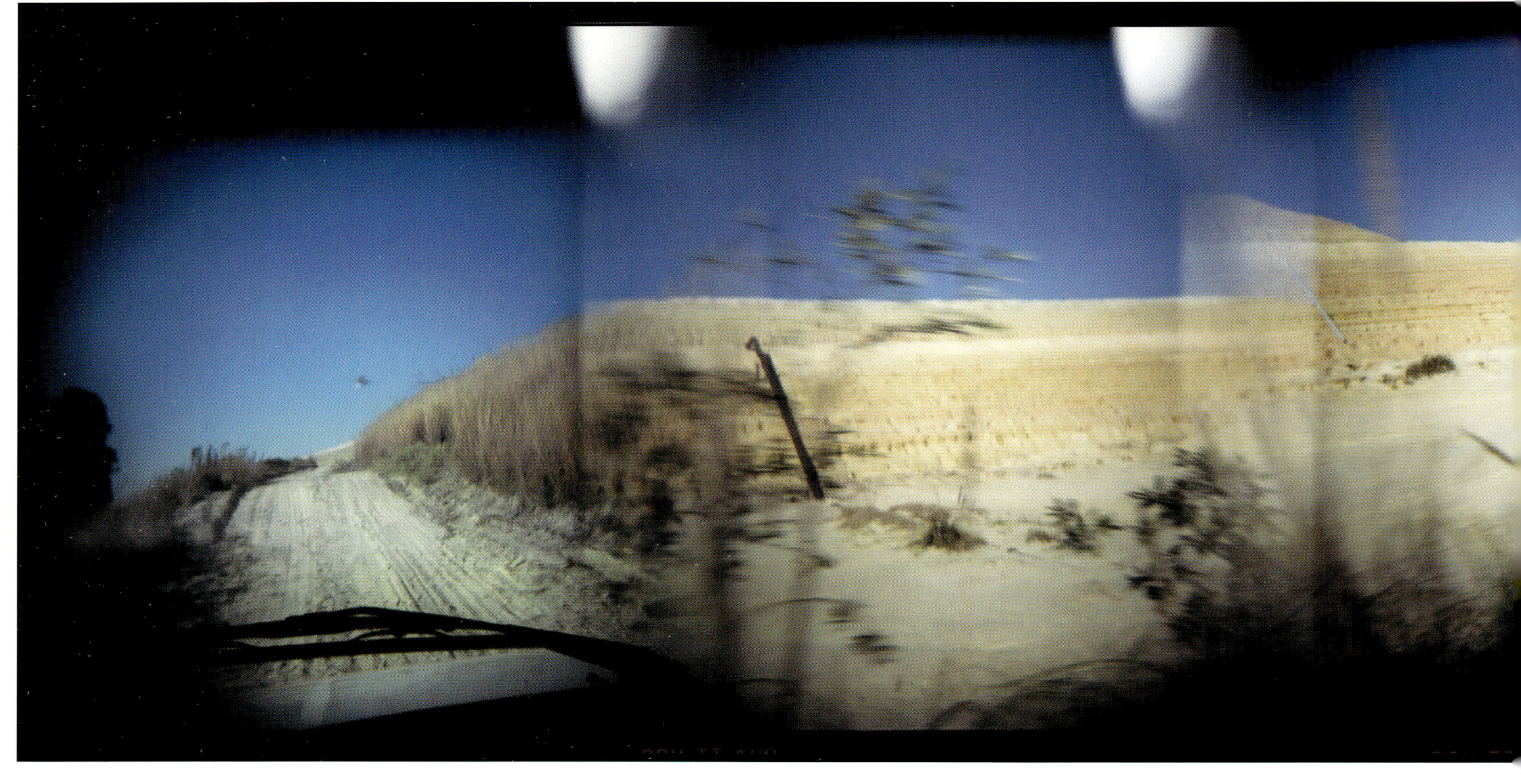

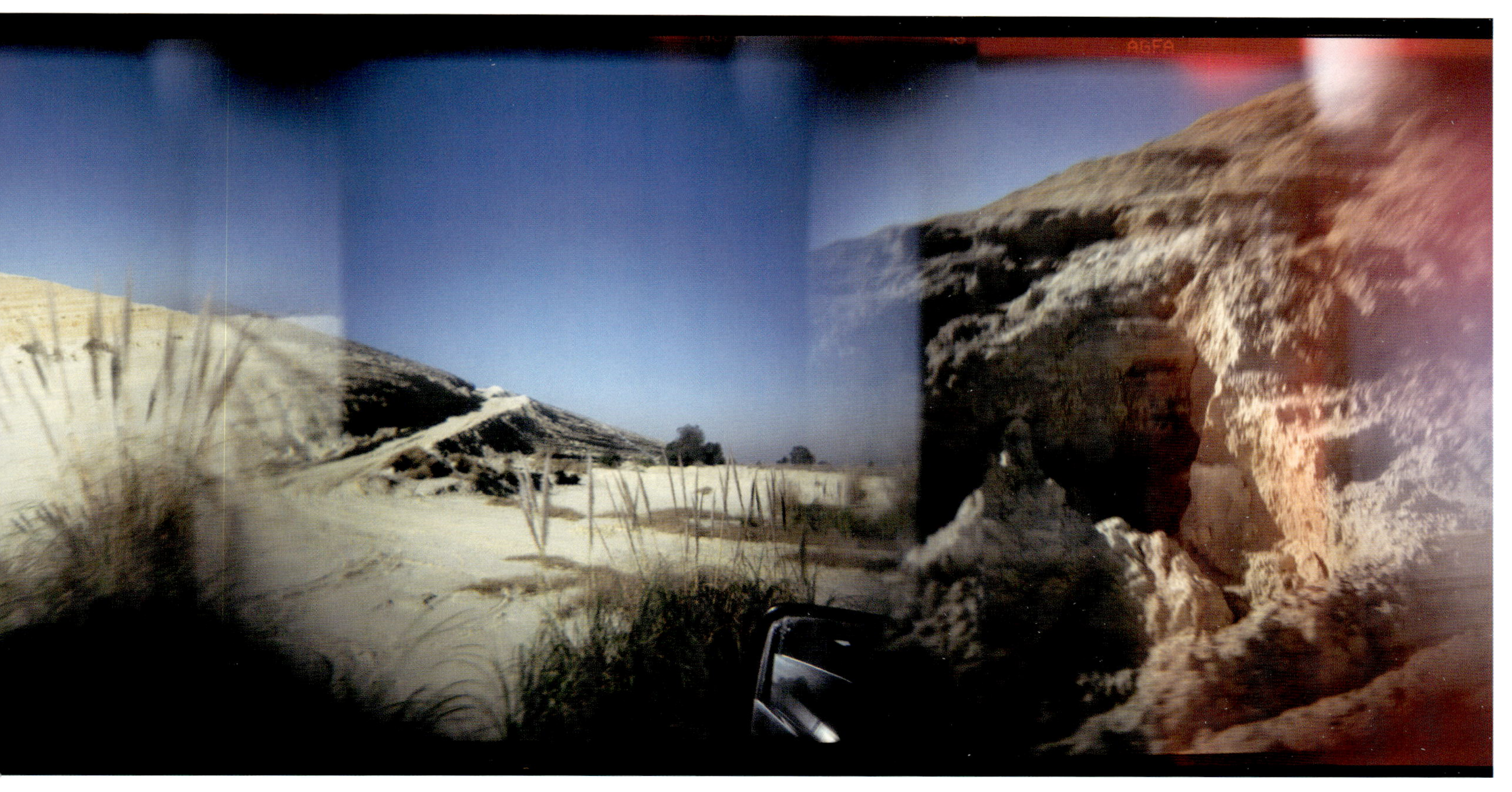

East Rand Proprietary Mines, Germiston, from the series "Johannesburg Inner City Works," 2000
Pigment print on paper, 20 x 78.9 in. (50.8 x 200.3 cm)
Courtesy the artist and Warren Siebrits Gallery, Johannesburg

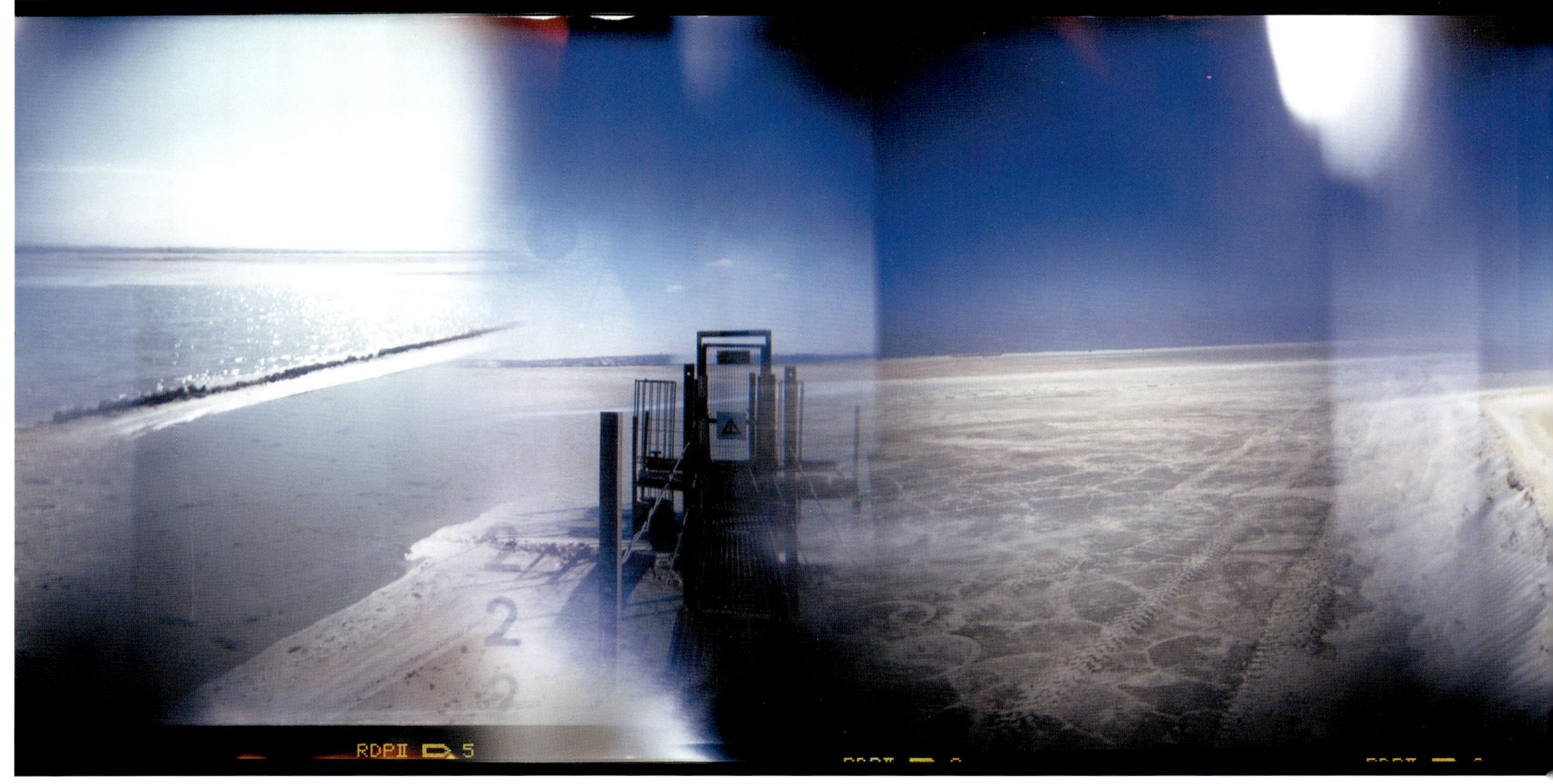
RDPII 5

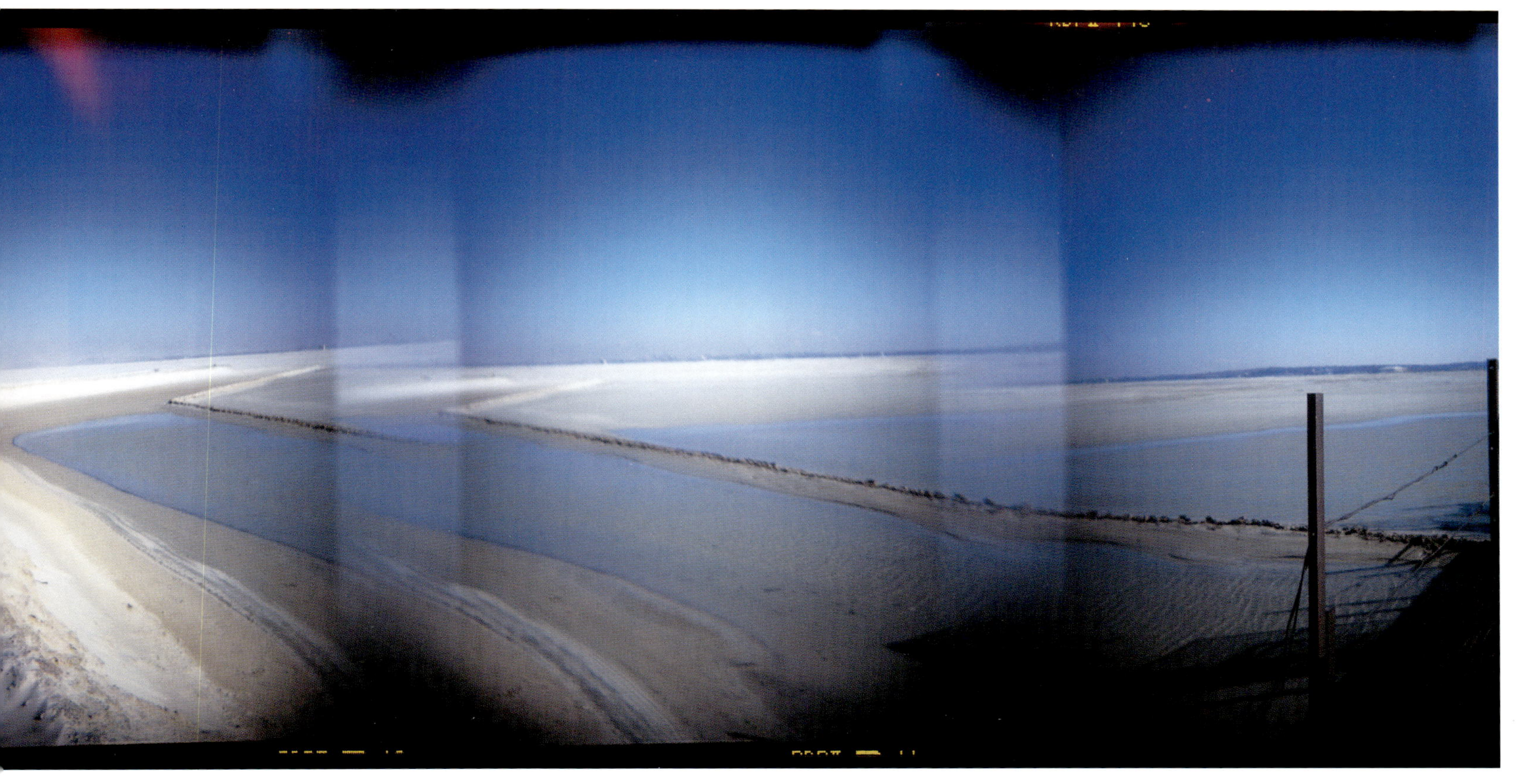

East Rand Proprietary Mines, Germiston, from the series "Johannesburg Inner City Works," 2000
Pigment print on paper, 20 x 78.9 in. (50.8 x 200.3 cm)
Courtesy the artist and Warren Siebrits Gallery, Johannesburg

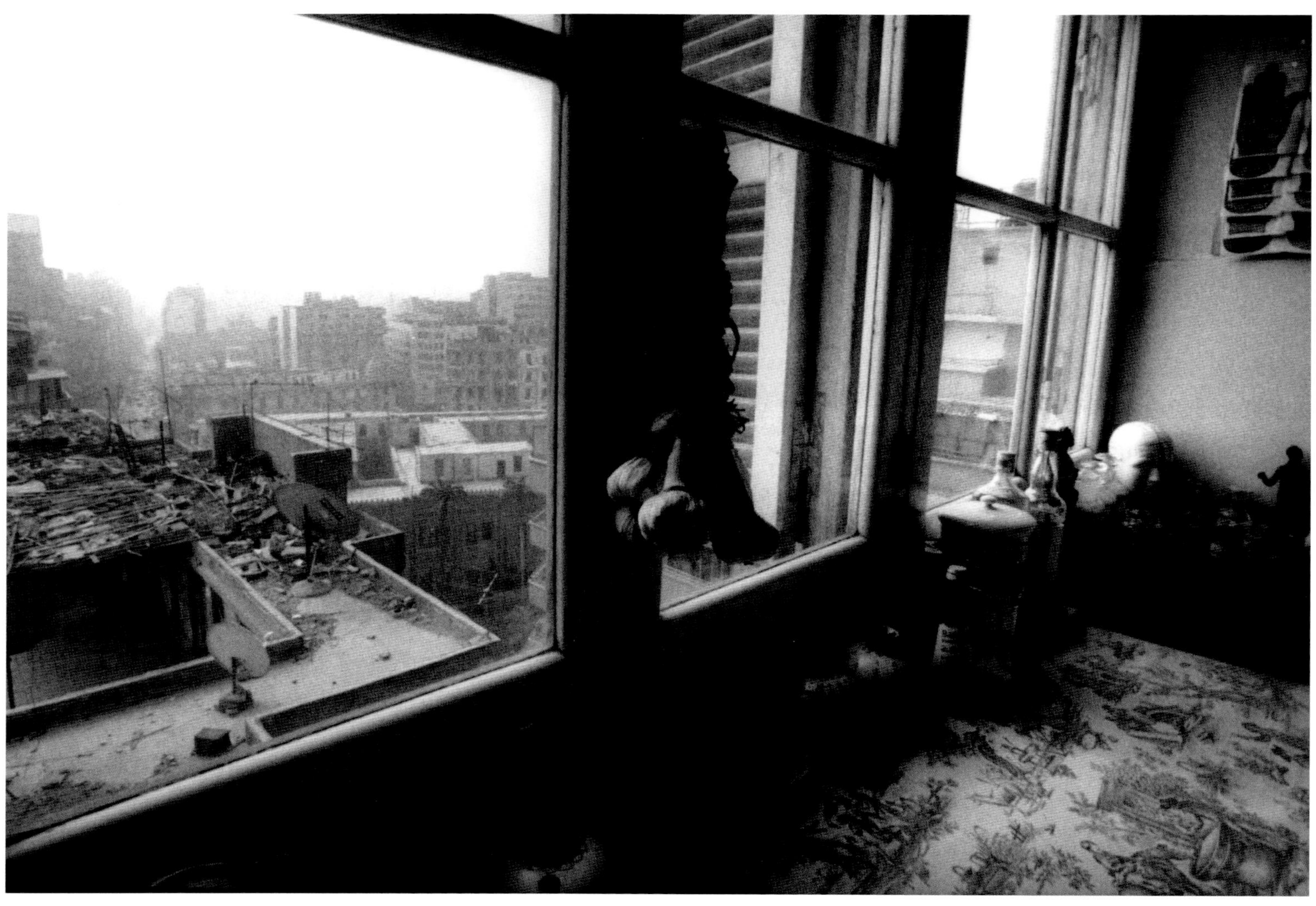

Untitled, from the series "Rooftops of Cairo," 2002–03
Gelatin silver print
Courtesy the artist

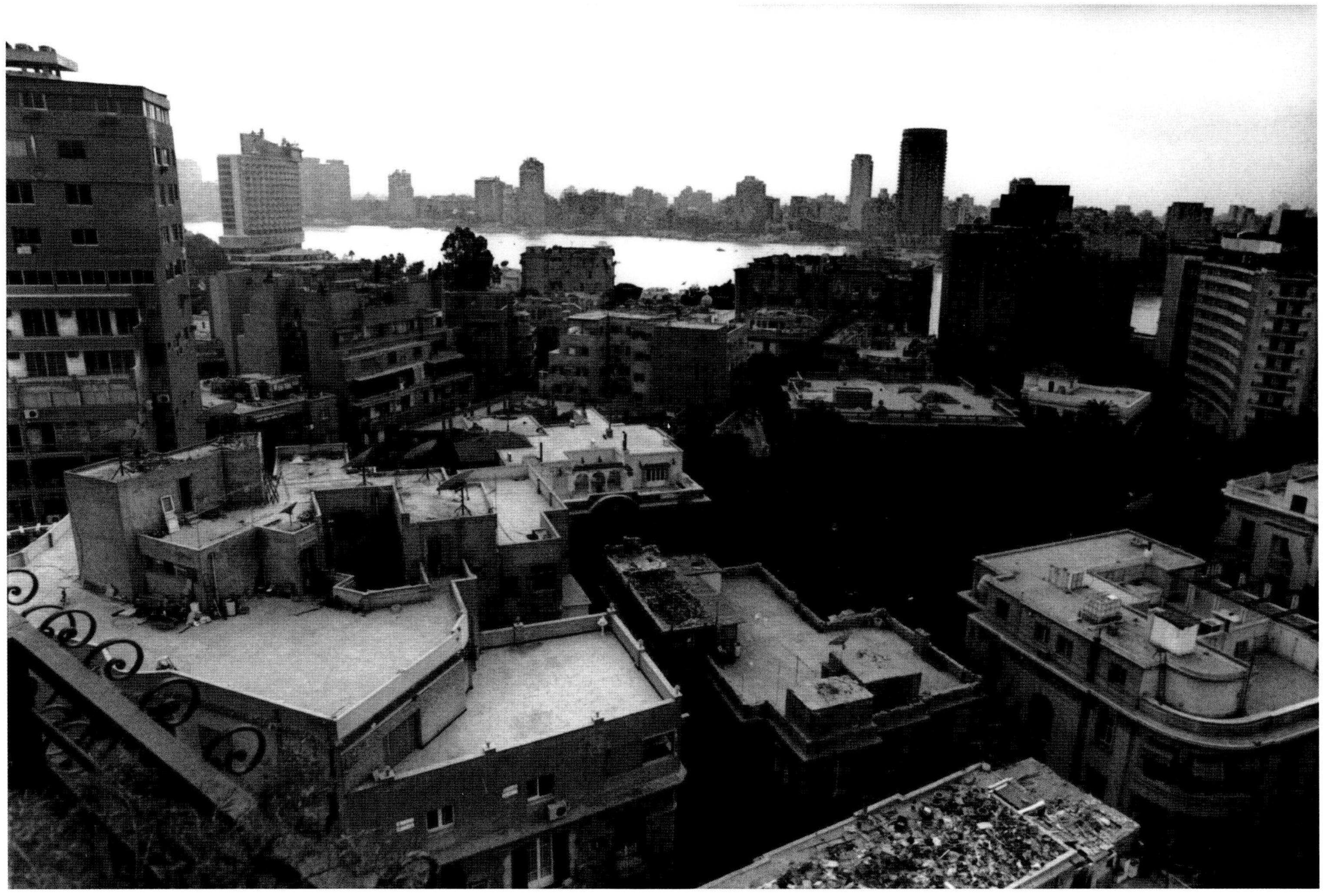

Untitled, from the series "Rooftops of Cairo," 2002–03
Gelatin silver print
Courtesy the artist

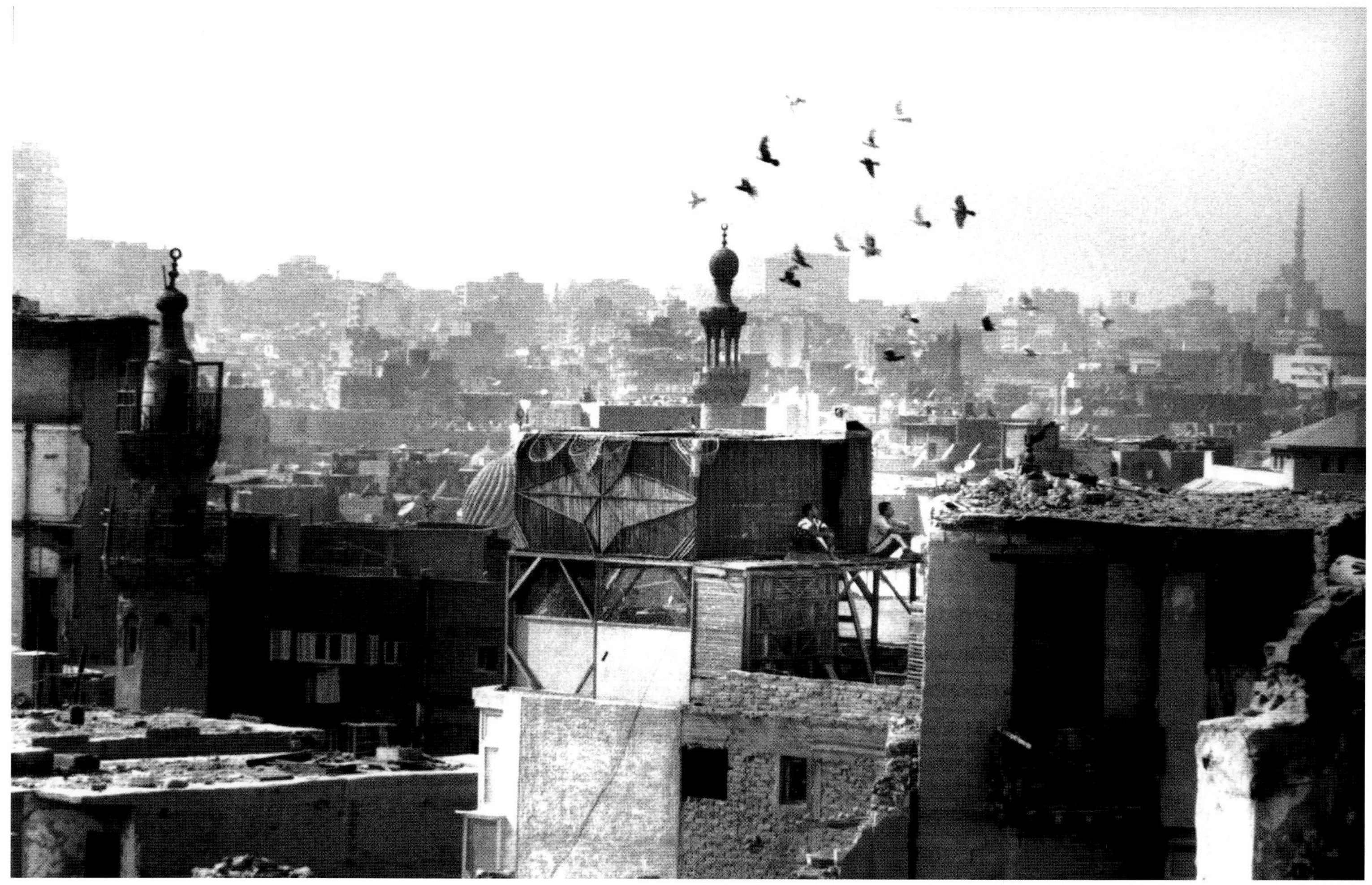

Untitled, from the series "Rooftops of Cairo," 2002–03
Gelatin silver print
Courtesy the artist

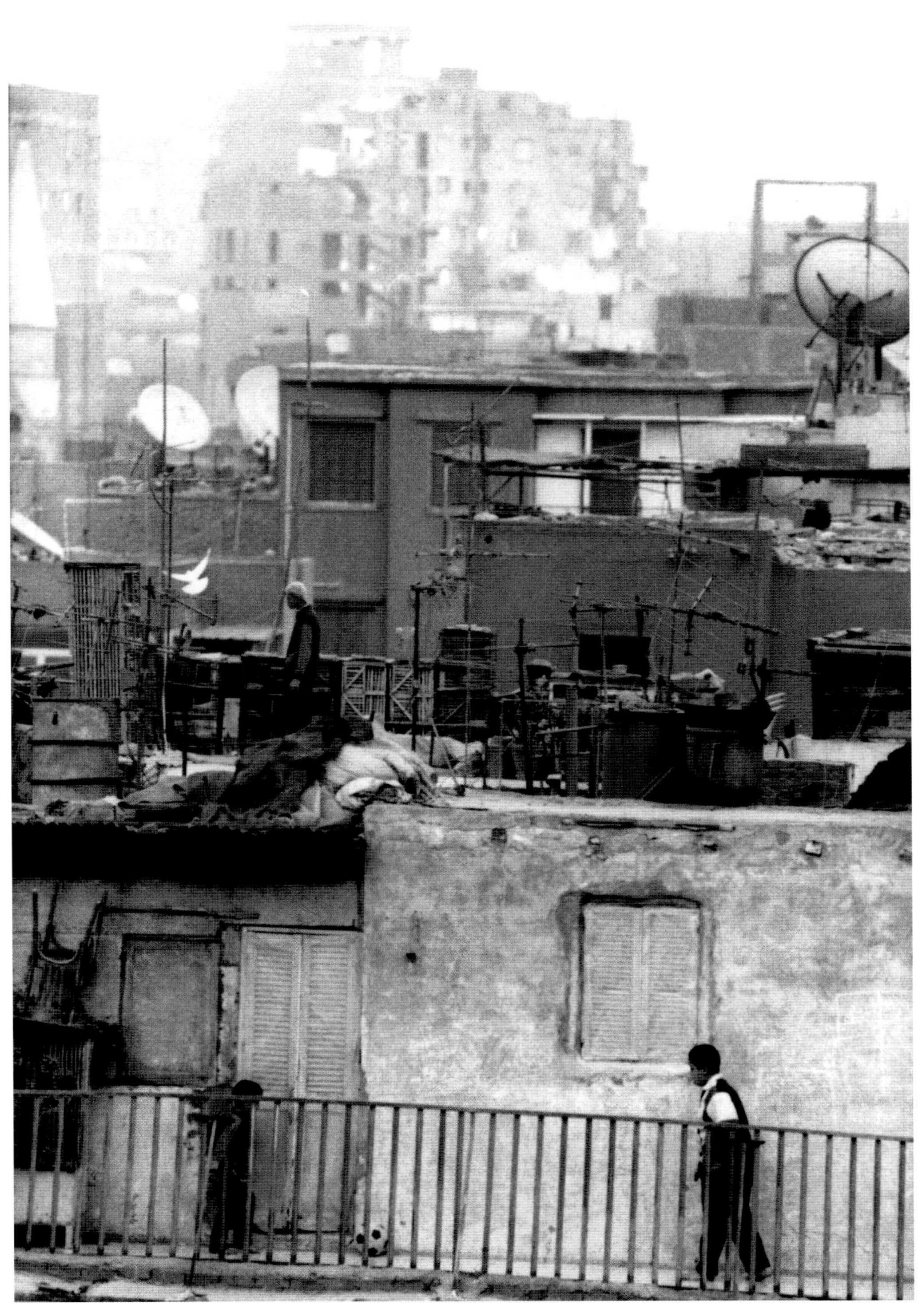

Untitled, from the series "Rooftops of Cairo," 2002–03
Gelatin silver print
Courtesy the artist

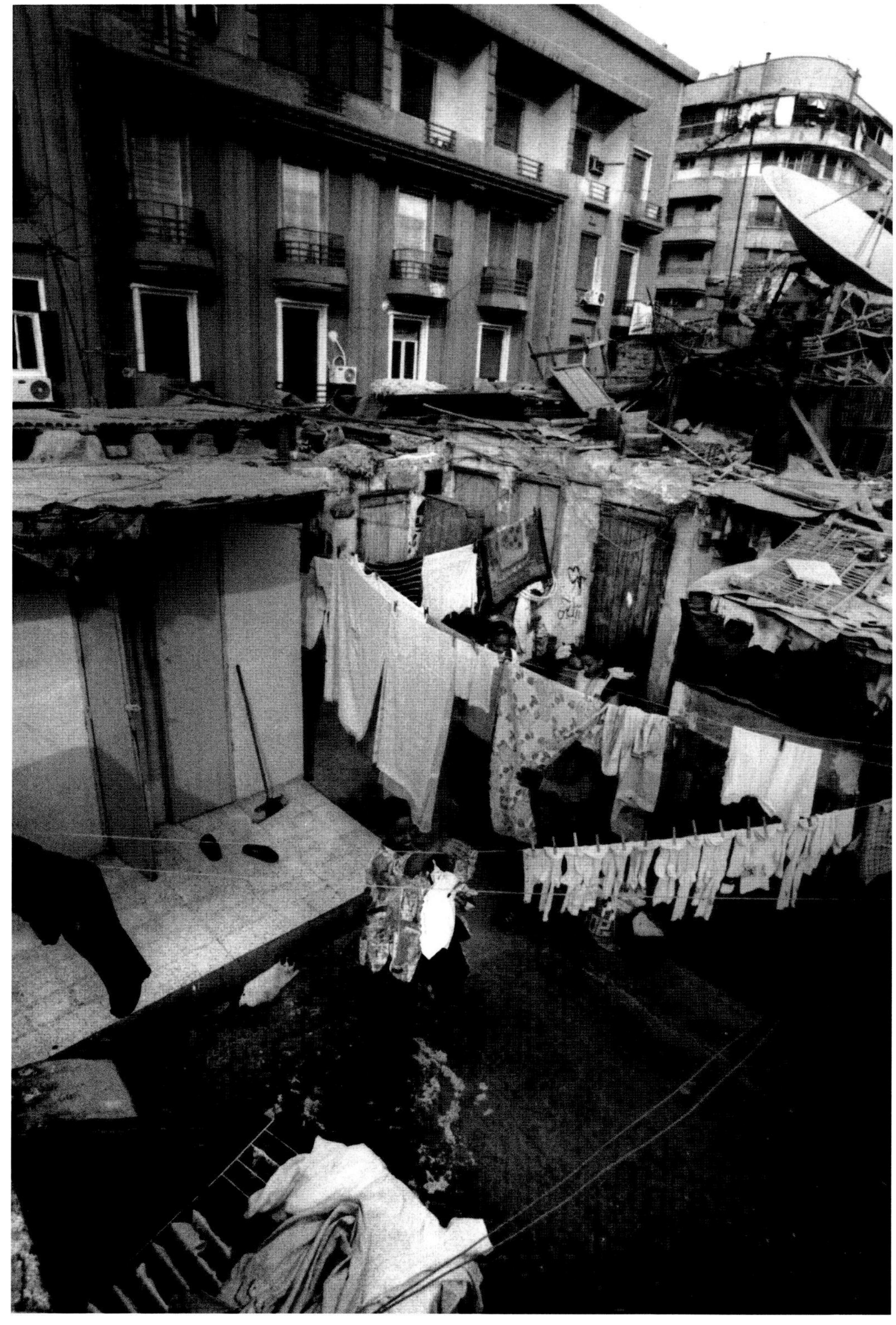

Untitled, from the series "Rooftops of Cairo," 2002–03
Gelatin silver print
Courtesy the artist

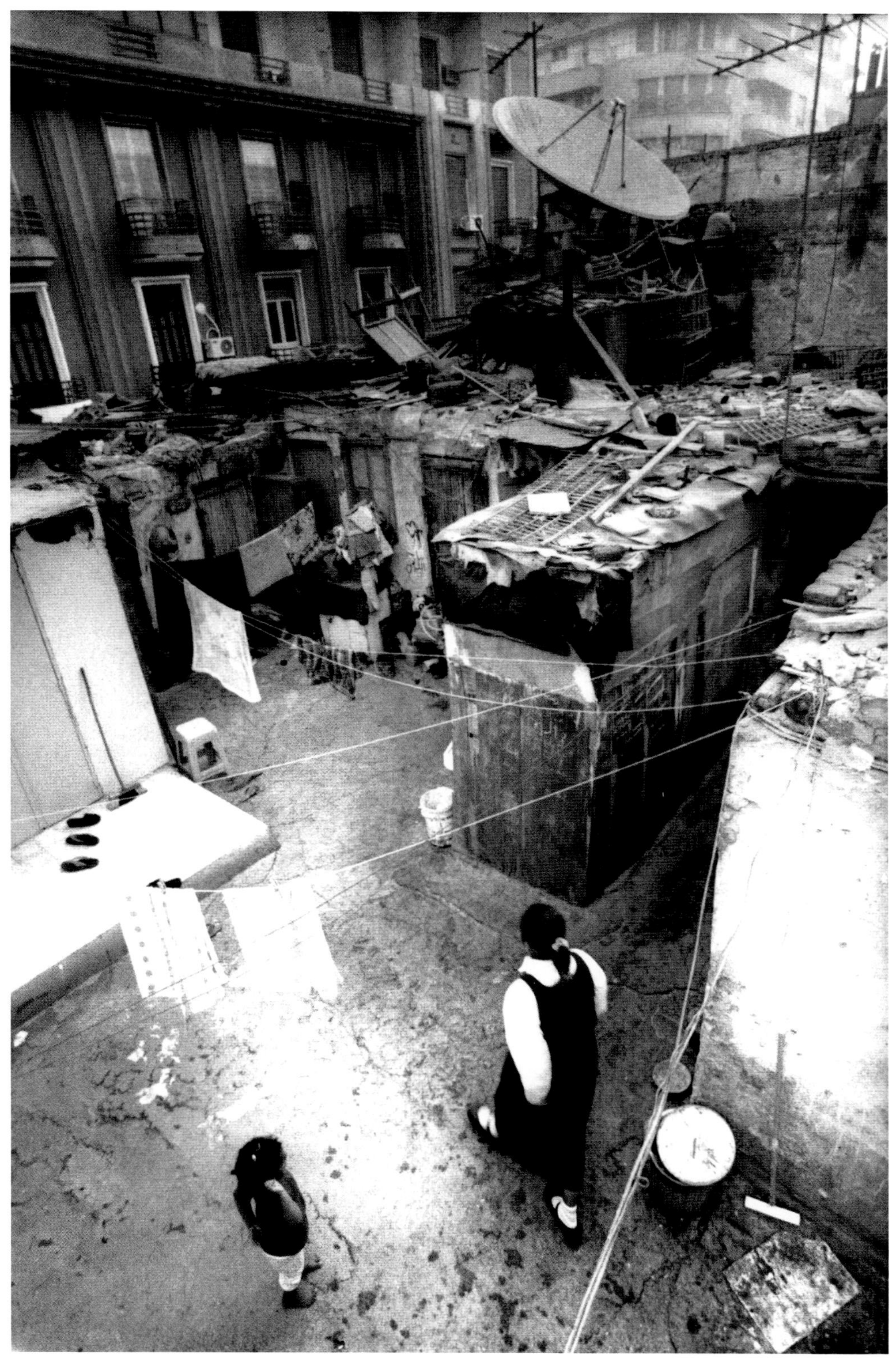

Untitled, from the series "Rooftops of Cairo," 2002–03
Gelatin silver print
Courtesy the artist

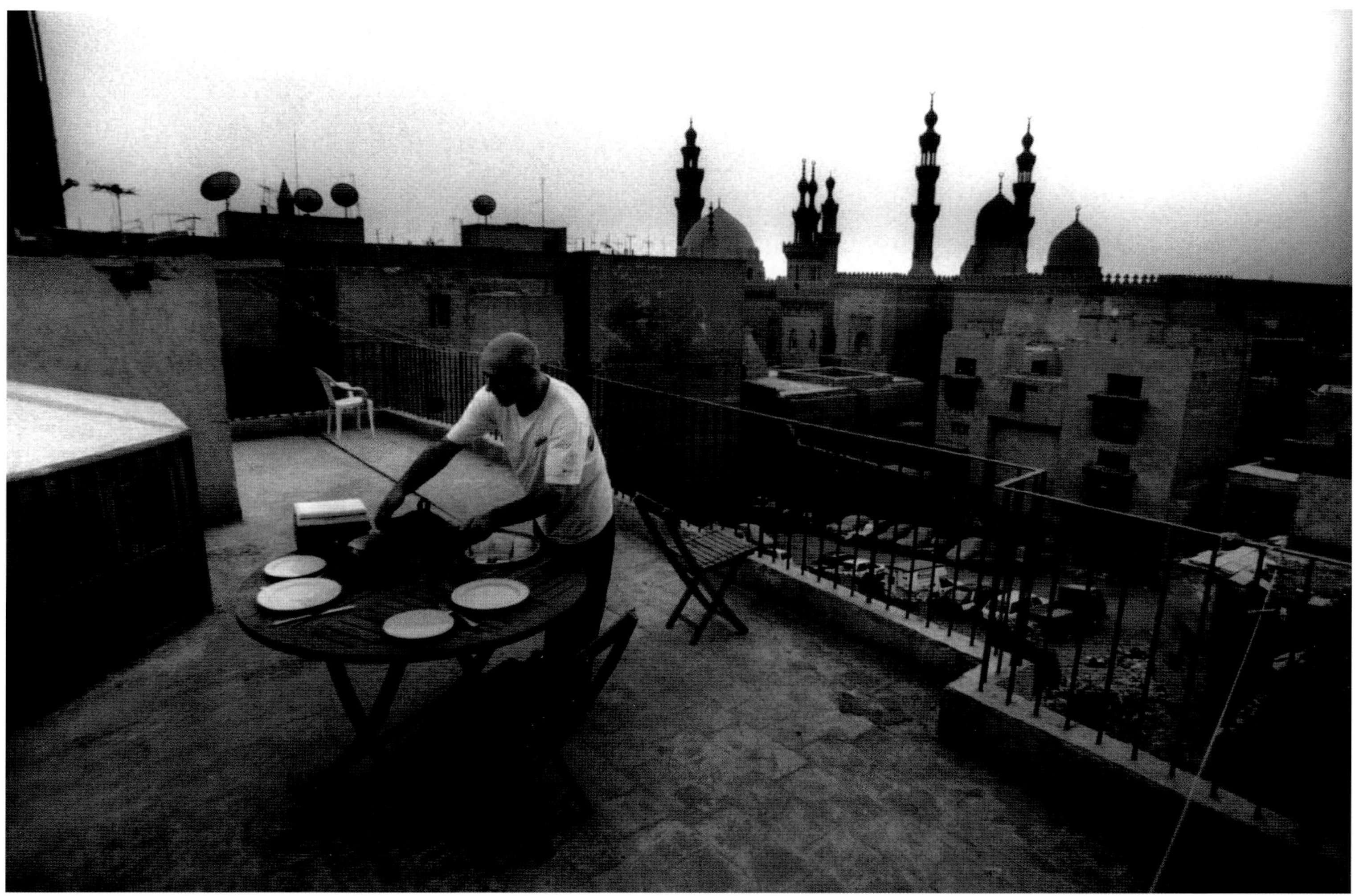

Untitled, from the series "Rooftops of Cairo," 2002–03
Gelatin silver print
Courtesy the artist

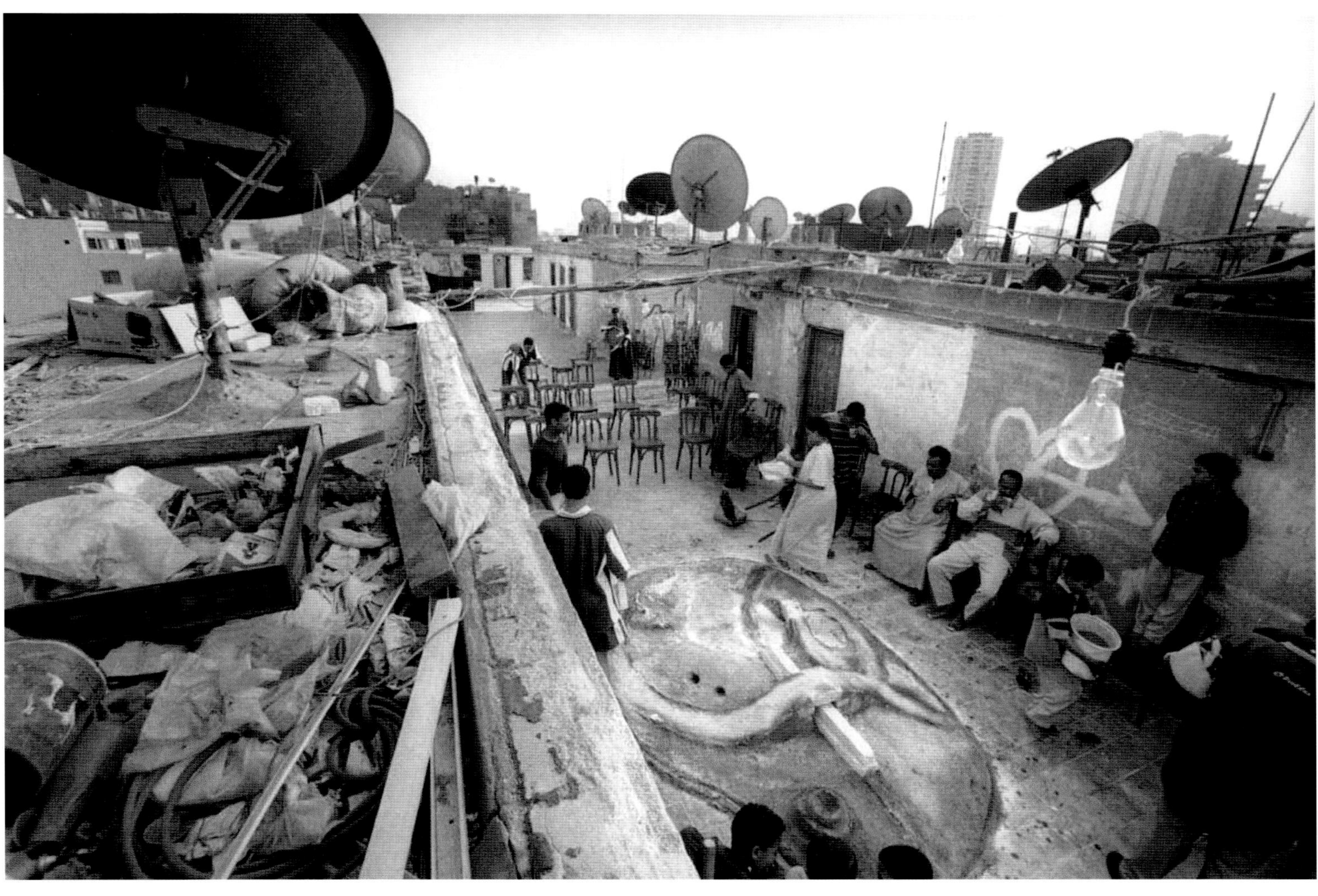

Untitled, from the series "Rooftops of Cairo," 2002–03
Gelatin silver print
Courtesy the artist

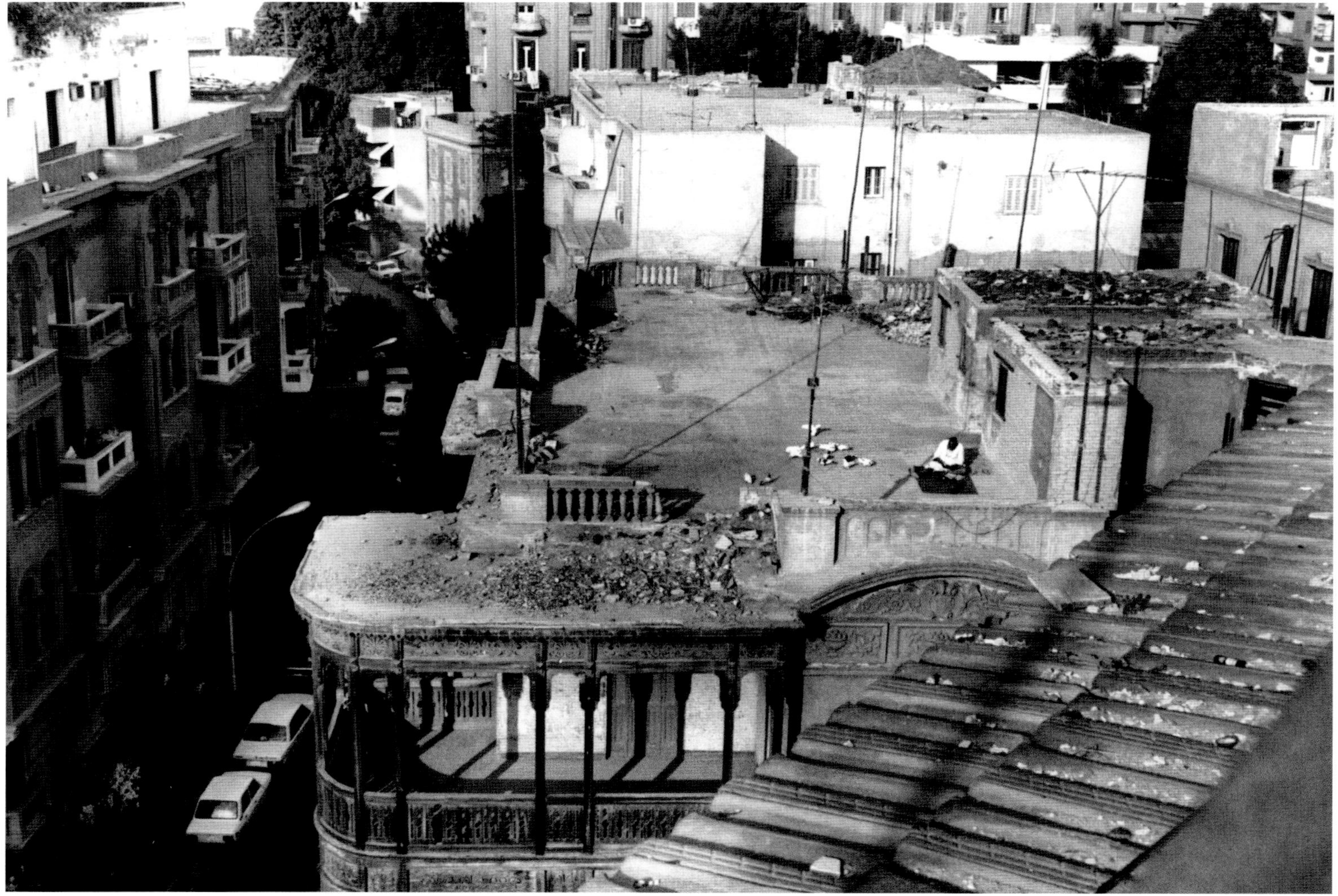

Untitled, from the series "Rooftops of Cairo," 2002–03
Gelatin silver print
Courtesy the artist

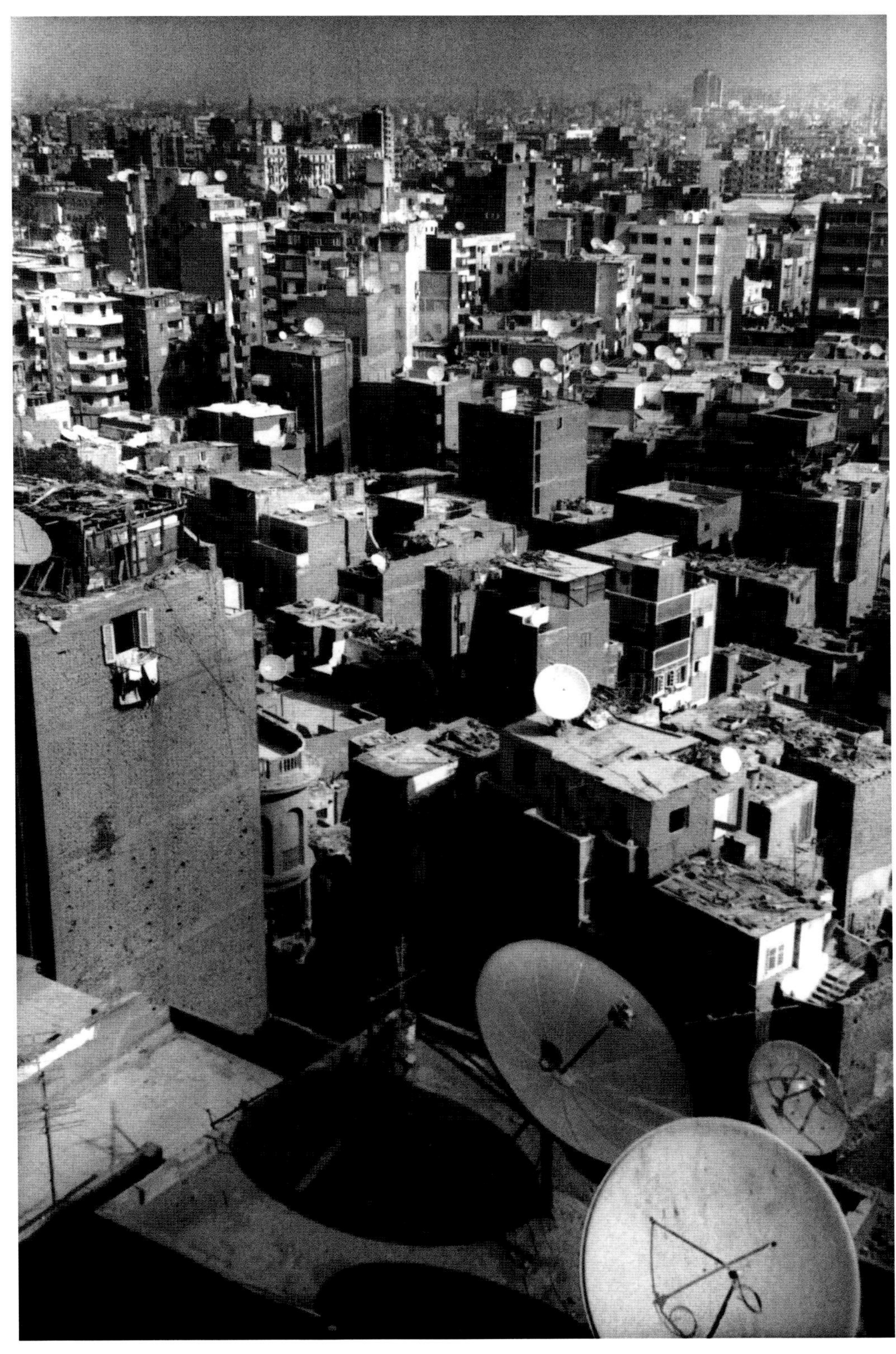

Untitled, from the series "Rooftops of Cairo," 2002–03
Gelatin silver print
Courtesy the artist

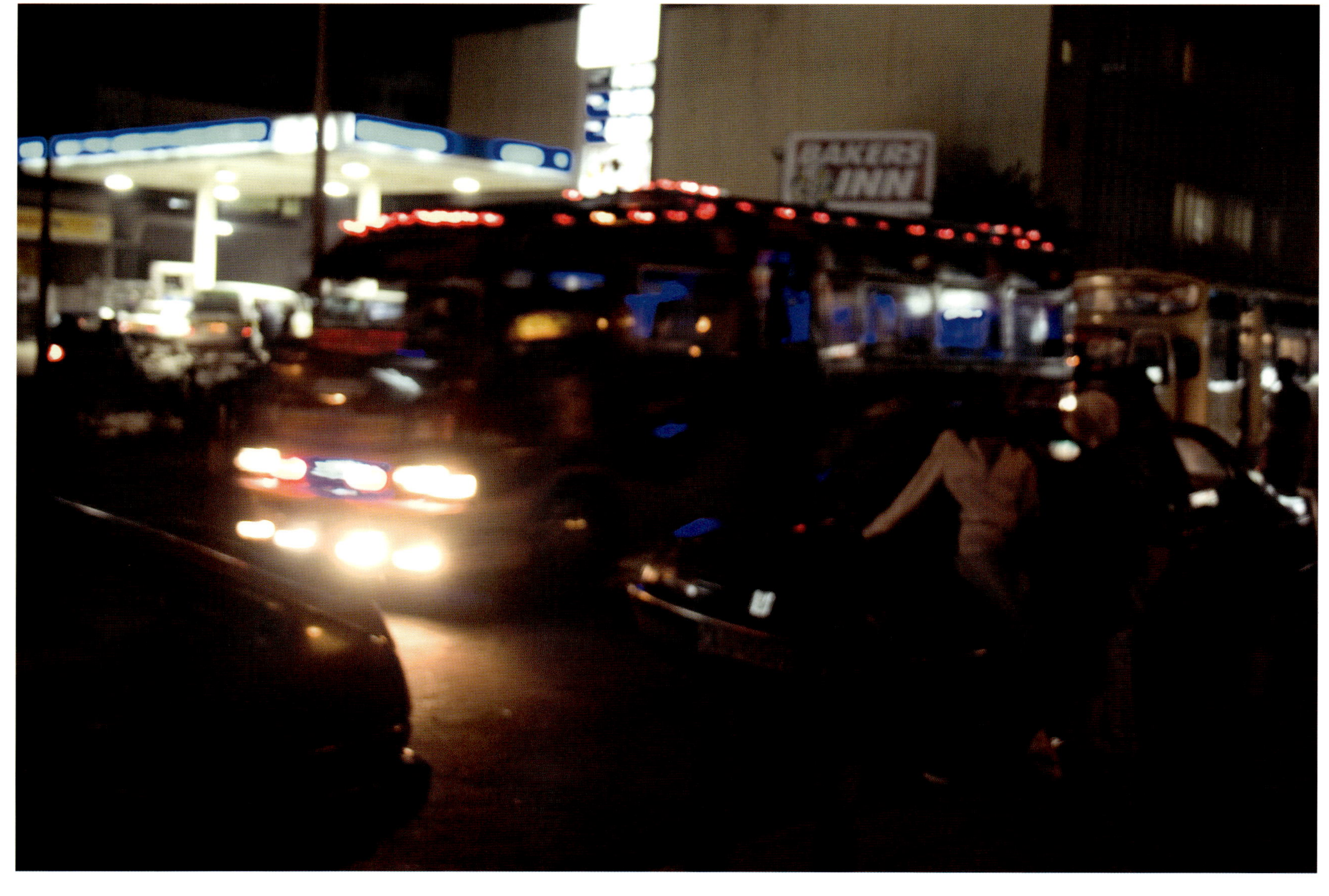

Matatus I, from the series "Town," 2005
Chromogenic print, 20 x 24 in. (50.8 x 61 cm)
Courtesy the artist

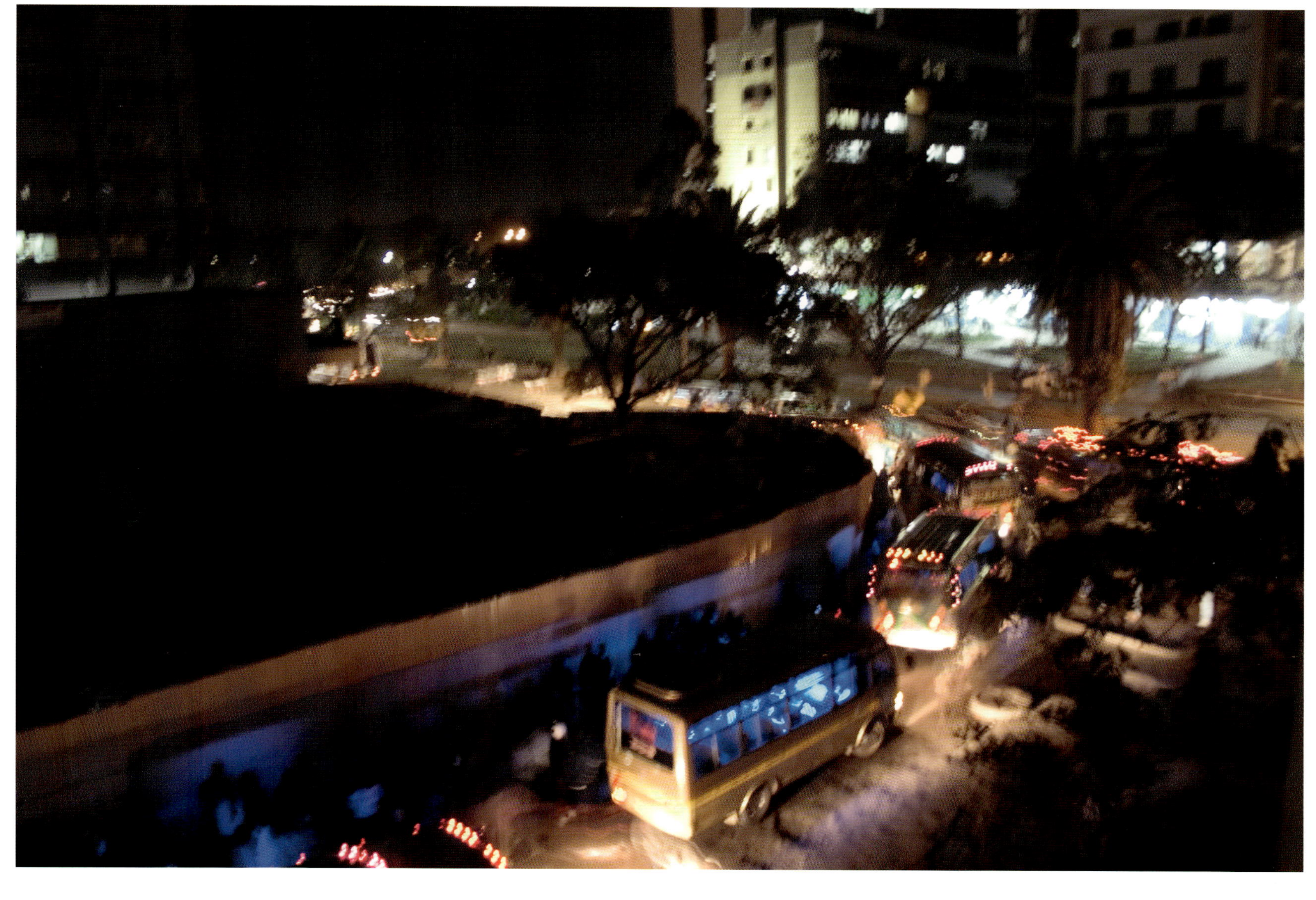

Matatus II, from the series "Town," 2005
Chromogenic print, 20 x 24 in. (50.8 x 61 cm)
Courtesy the artist

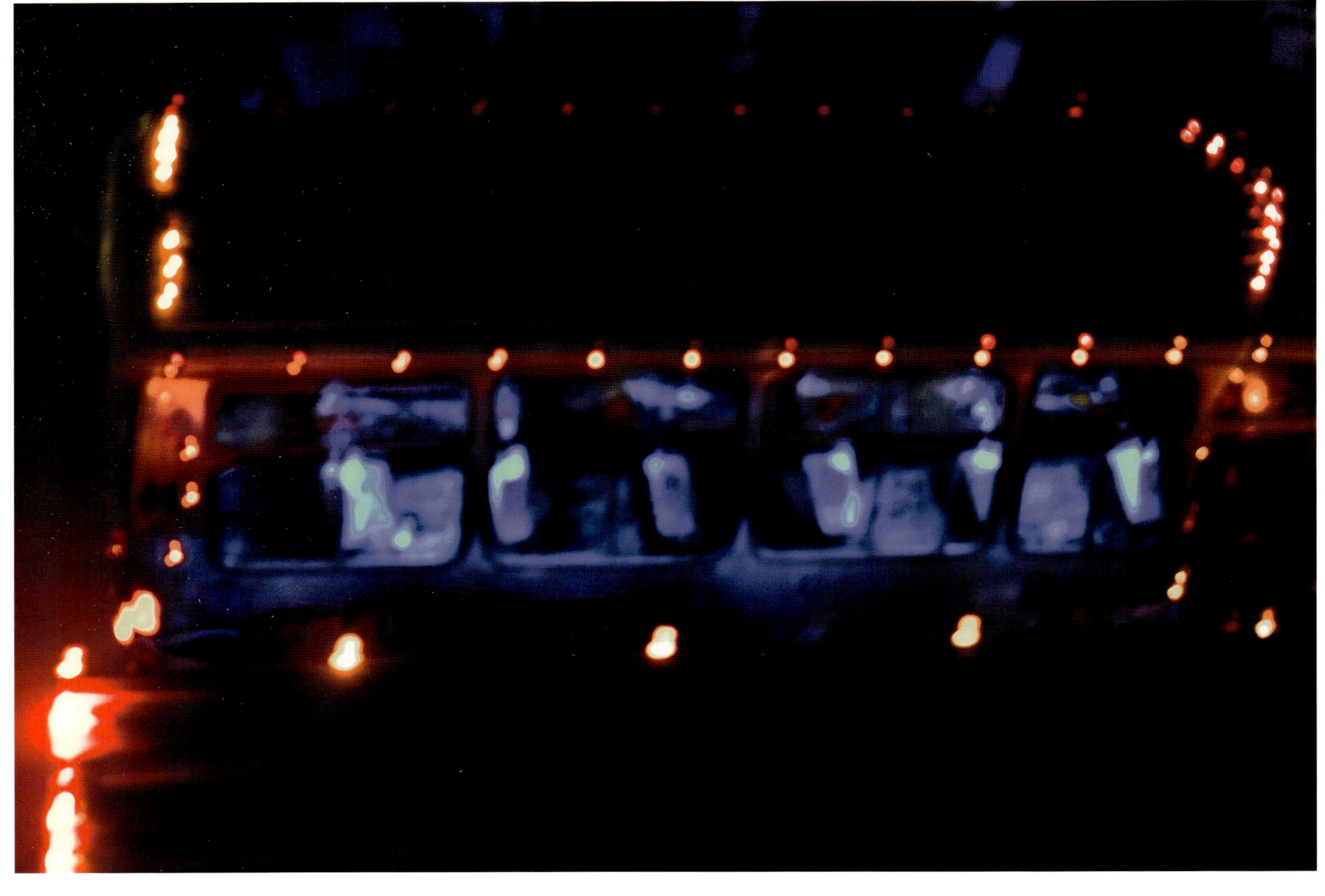

Matatus III, from the series "Town," 2005
Chromogenic print, 20 x 24 in. (50.8 x 61 cm)
Courtesy the artist

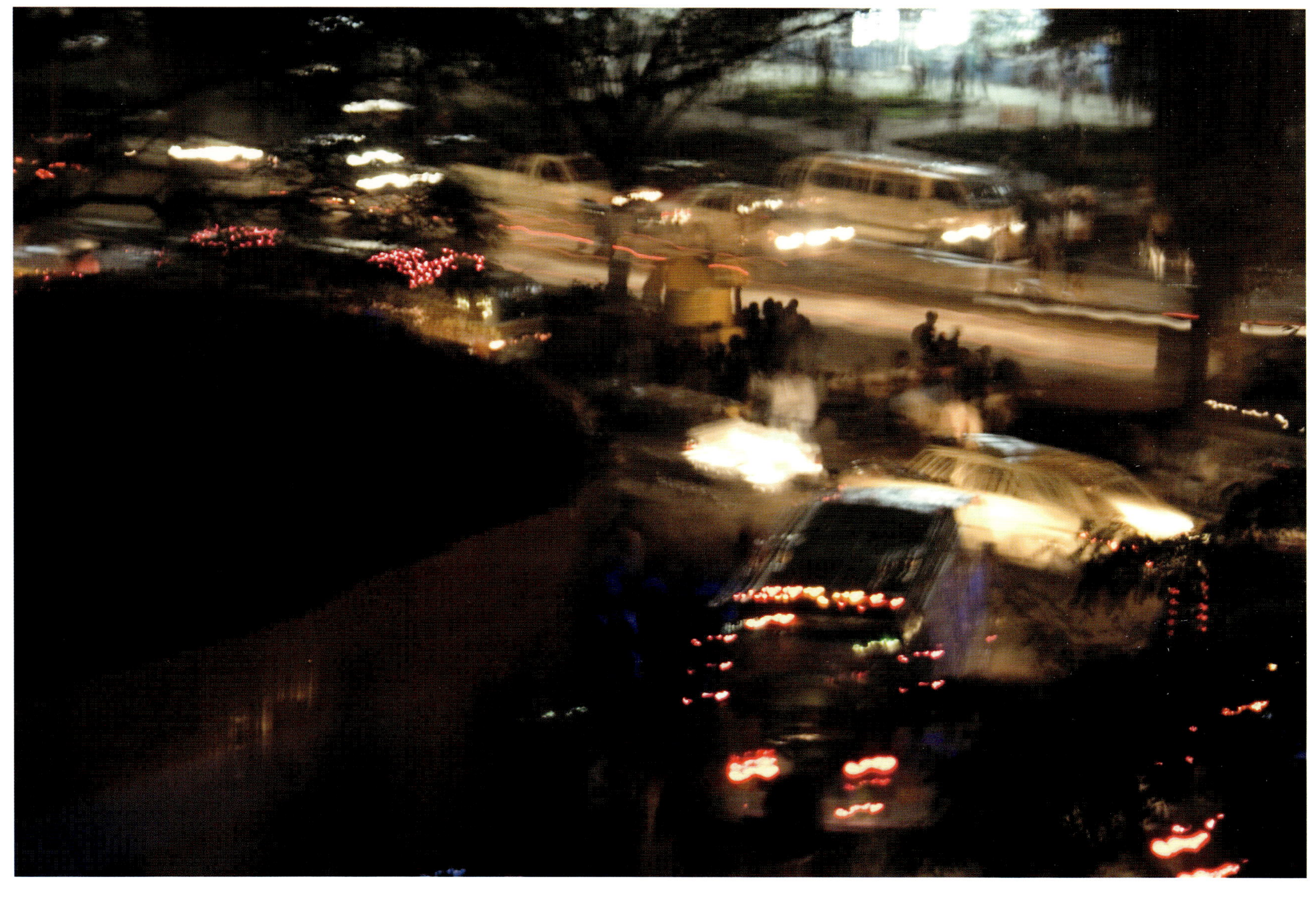

Matatus IV, from the series "Town," 2005
Chromogenic print, 20 x 24 in. (50.8 x 61 cm)
Courtesy the artist

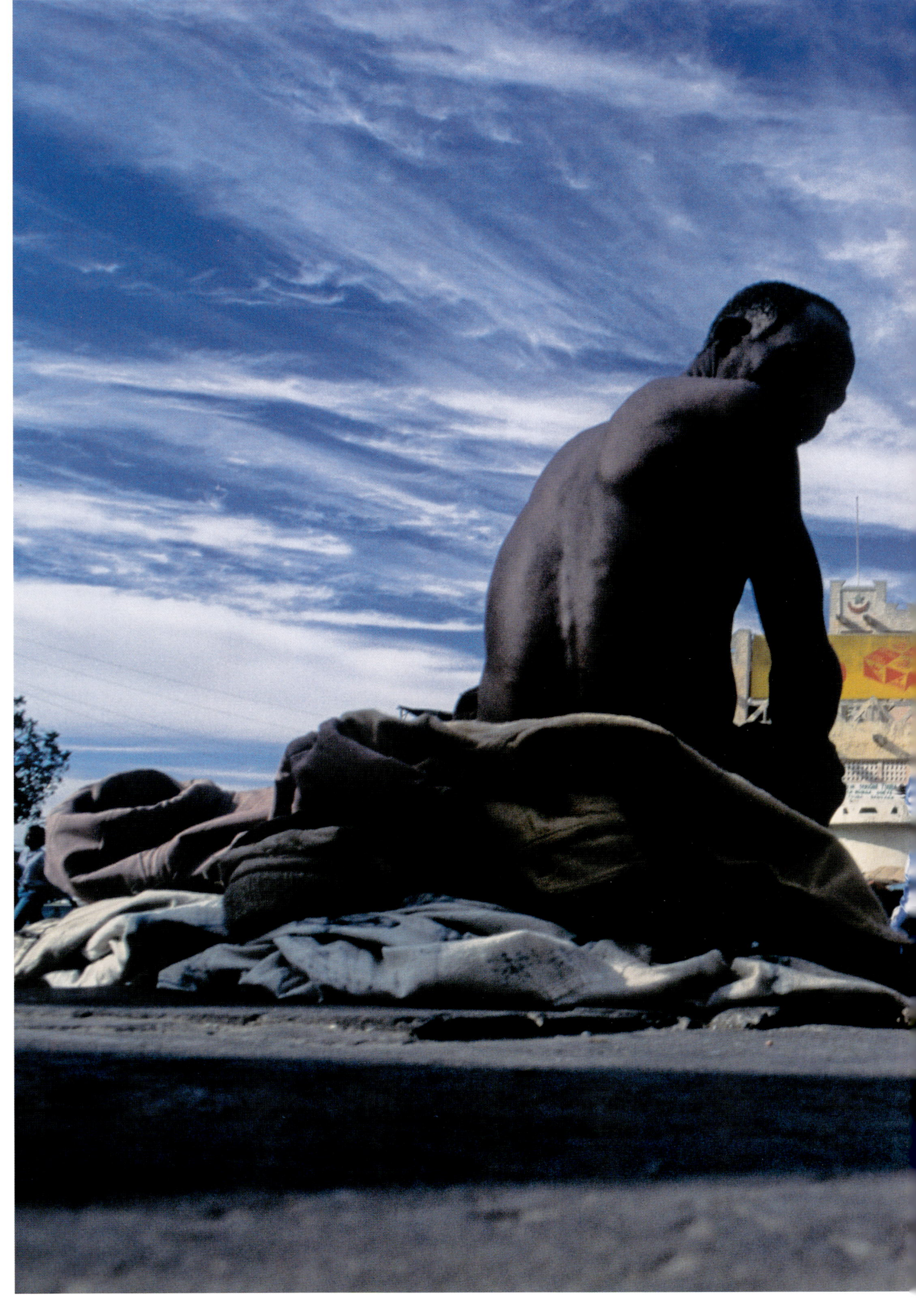

Dakar,
from the series
"Capitales Africaines,"
ca. 2000–05
Chromogenic print
20 x 30 in.
(50.8 x 76.2 cm)
Courtesy the artist

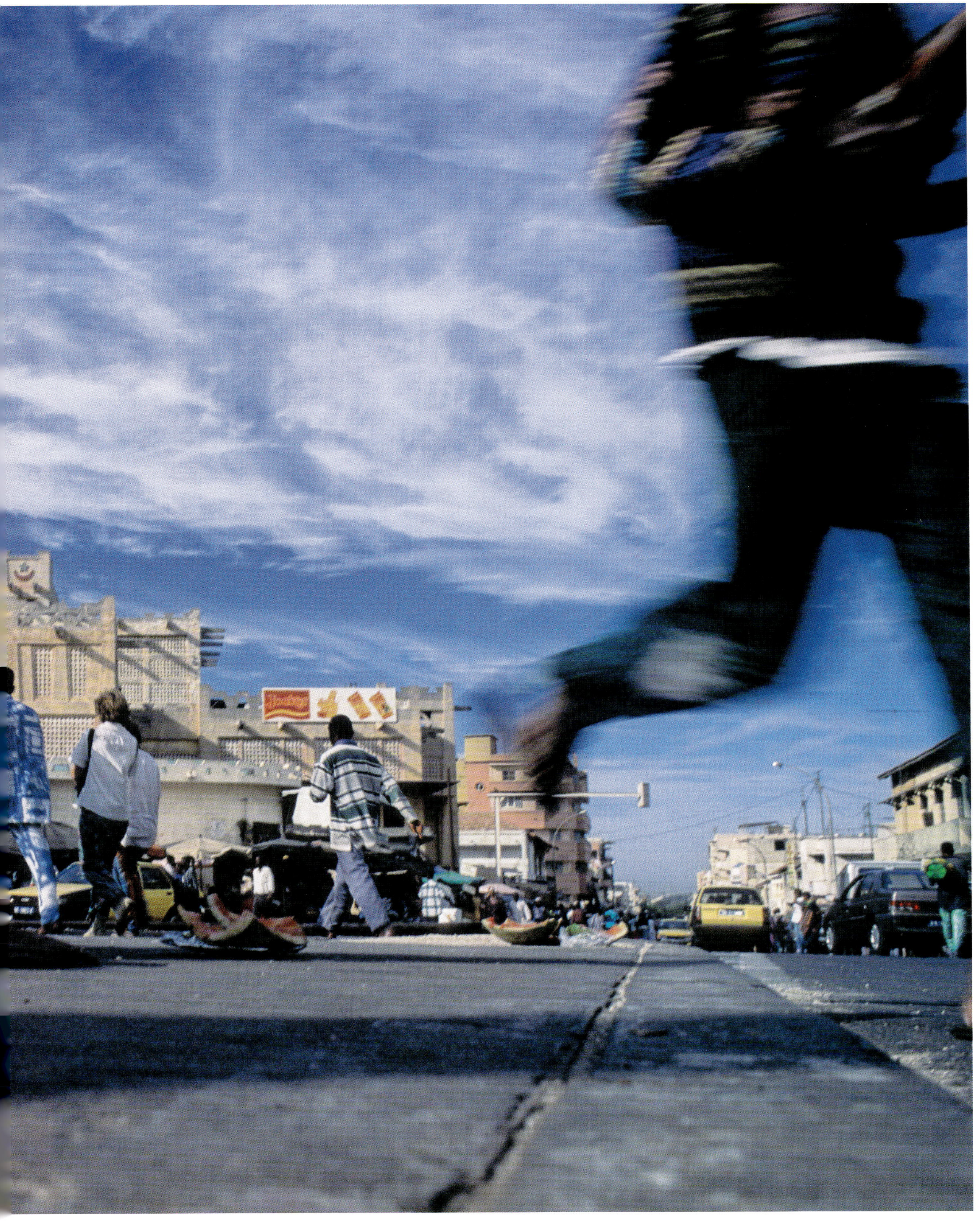

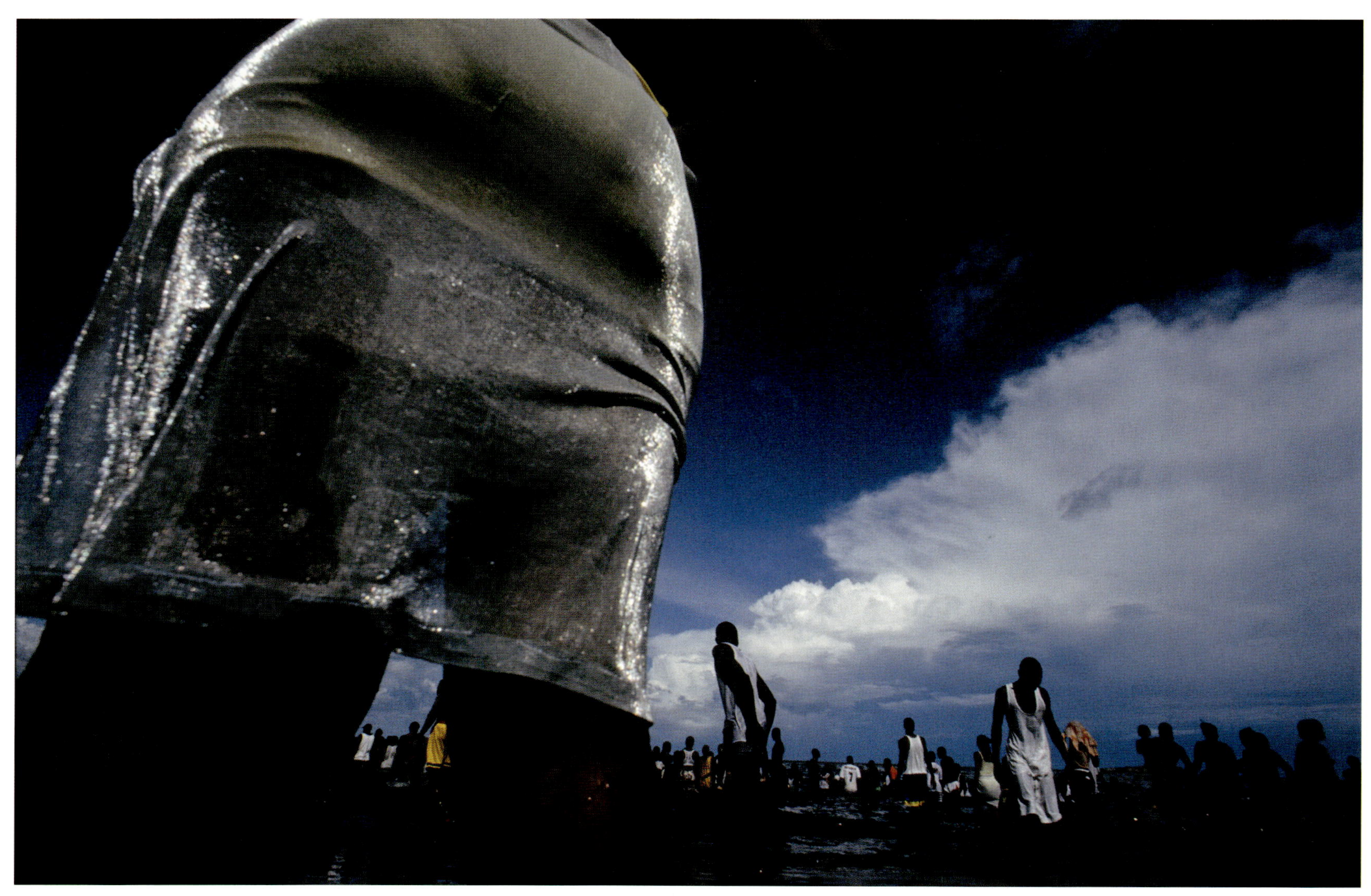

Grandes Vacances [Big Vacation]
from the series "Capitales Africaines," ca. 2000–05
Chromogenic print, 20 x 30 in. (50.8 x 76.2 cm)
Courtesy the artist

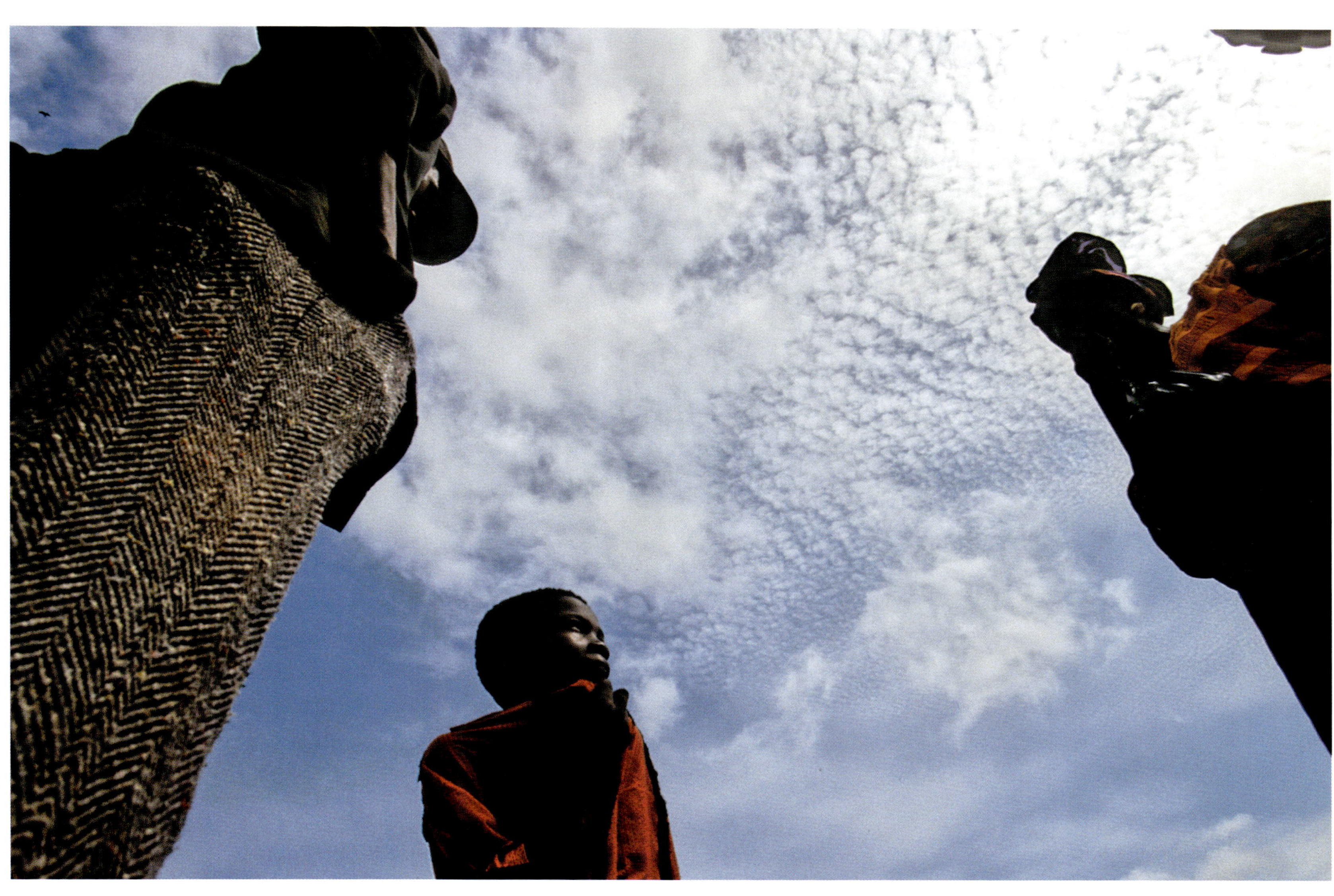

Vendeuse de Petits Pagnes [Seller of Small Cloth Wraps],
from the series "Capitales Africaines," ca. 2000–05
Chromogenic print, 20 x 30 in. (50.8 x 76.2 cm)
Courtesy the artist

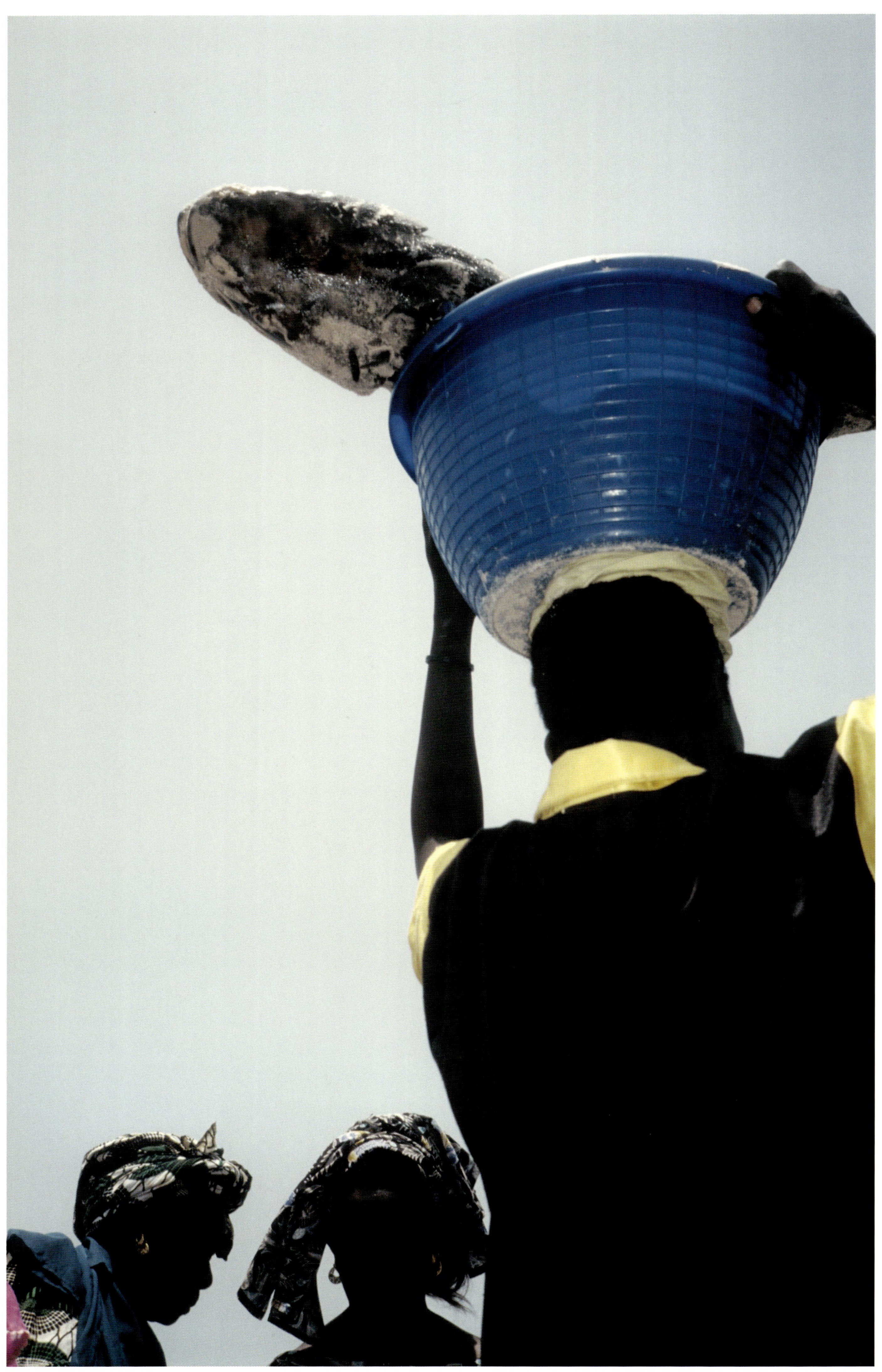

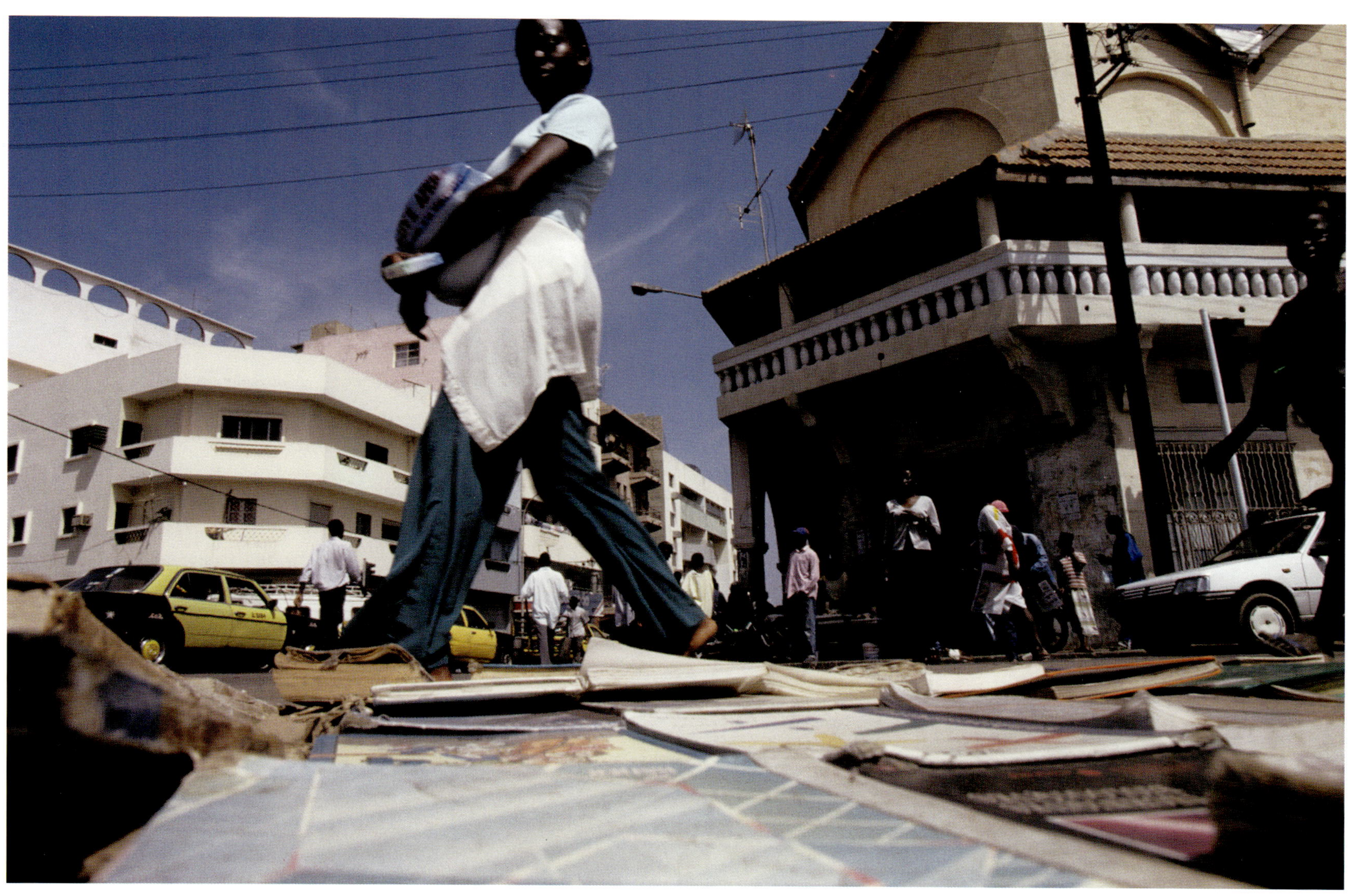

Left:
Littoral, from the series "Capitales Africaines," ca. 2000–05
Chromogenic print, 30 x 20 in. (76.2 x 50.8 cm)
Courtesy the artist

Libraire par Terre 1 [Bookstore on the Ground 1],
from the series "Capitales Africaines," ca. 2000–05
Chromogenic print, 20 x 30 in. (50.8 x 76.2 cm)
Courtesy the artist

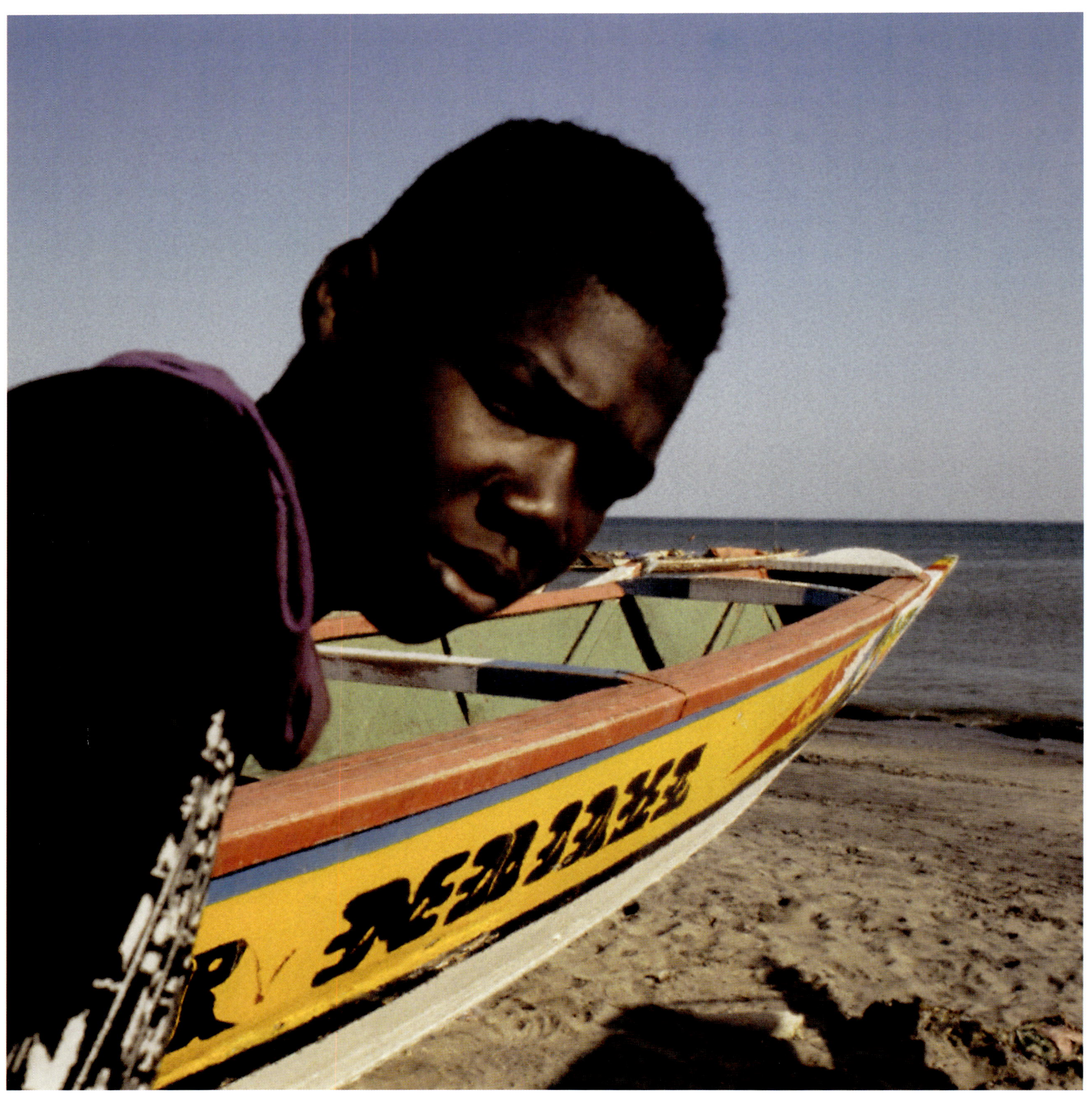

Couleur Littorale 2,
from the series "Capitales Africaines," ca. 2000–05
Chromogenic print, 30 x 20 in. (76.2 x 50.8 cm)
Courtesy the artist

Right:
Couleur Littorale 1,
from the series "Capitales Africaines," ca. 2000–05
Chromogenic print, 30 x 20 in. (76.2 x 50.8 cm)
Courtesy the artist

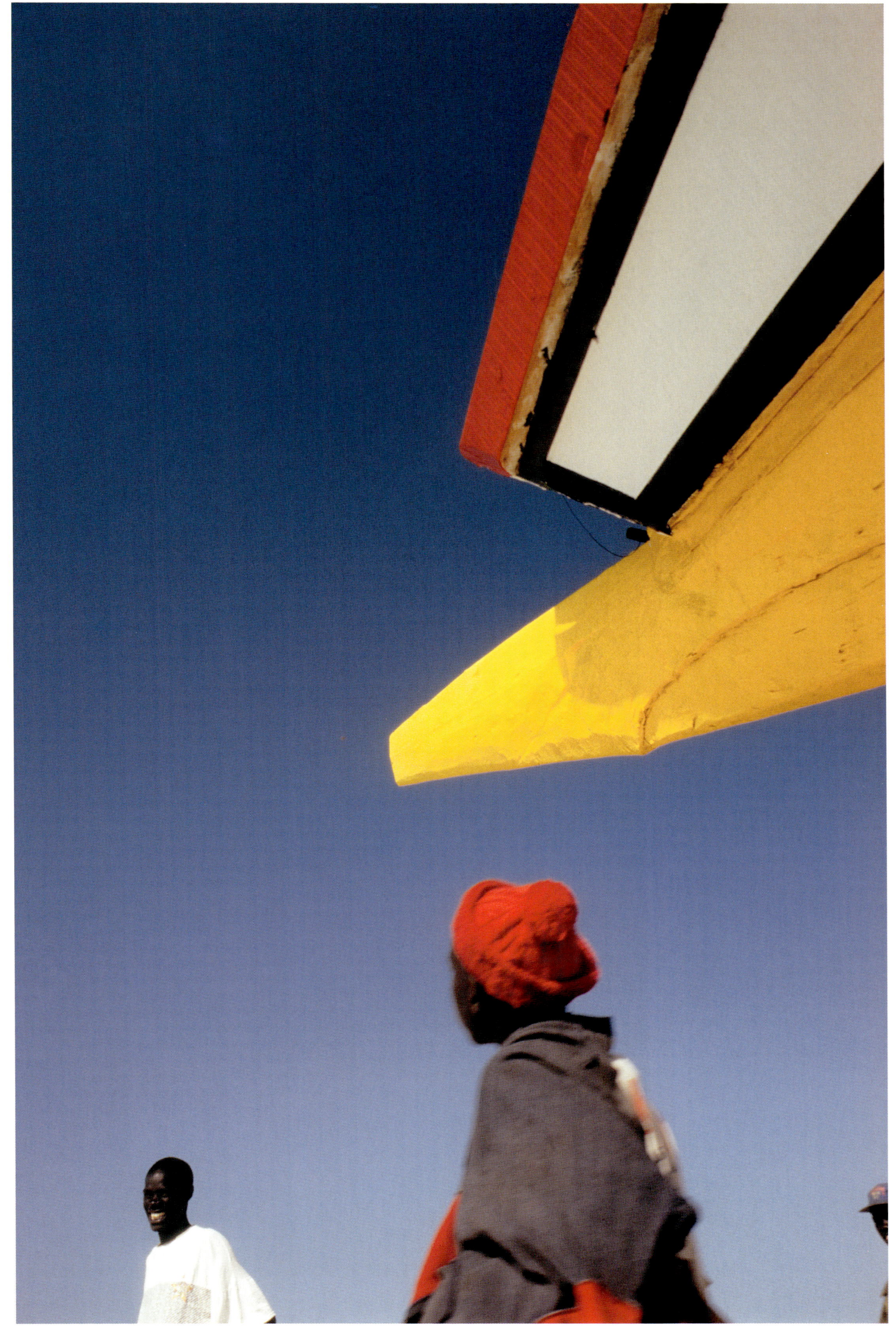

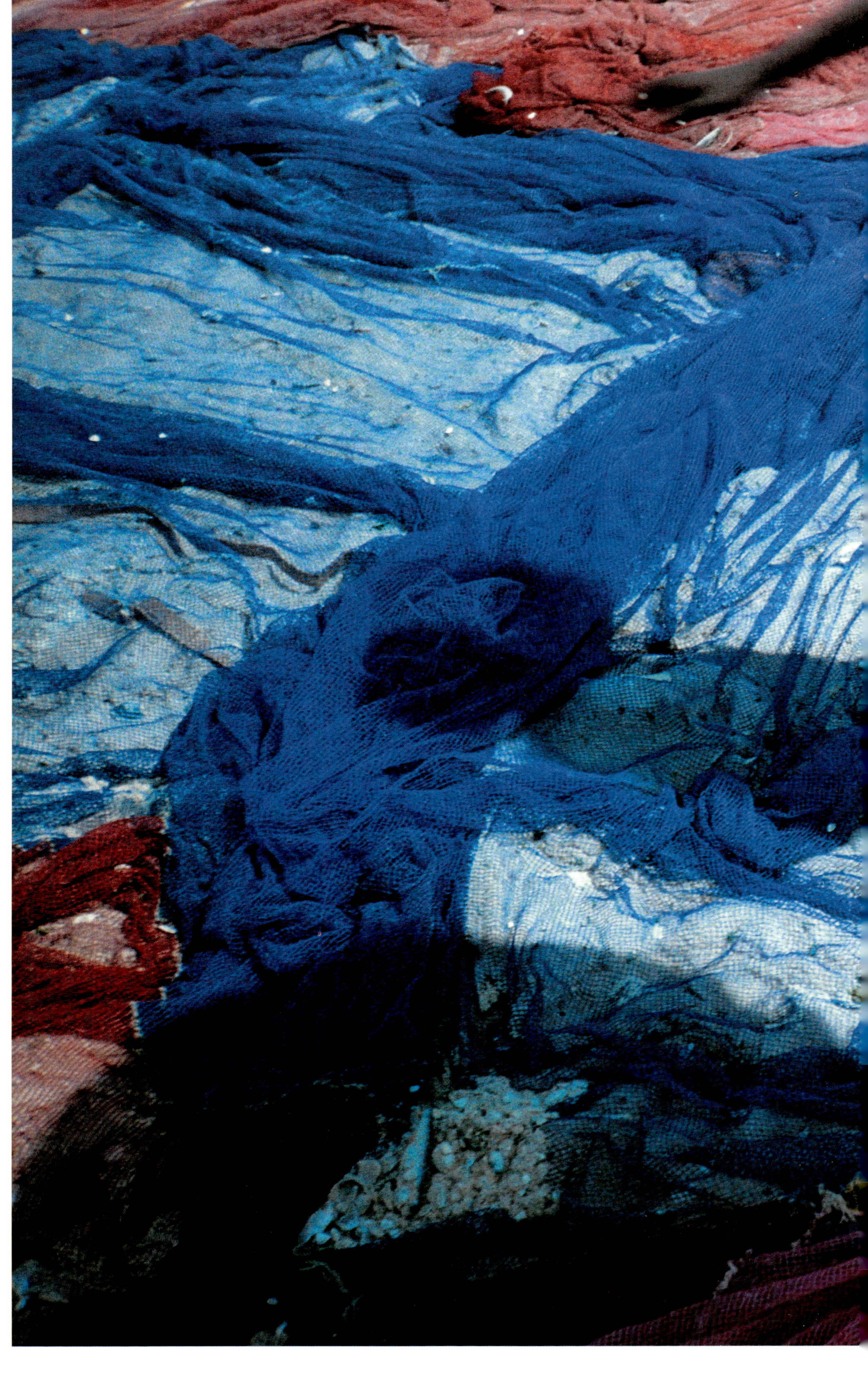

Couleurs de Pêche
[Colors of Fishing],
from the series
"Capitales Africaines,"
ca. 2000–05
Chromogenic print
20 x 30 in. (50.8 x 76.2 cm)
Courtesy the artist

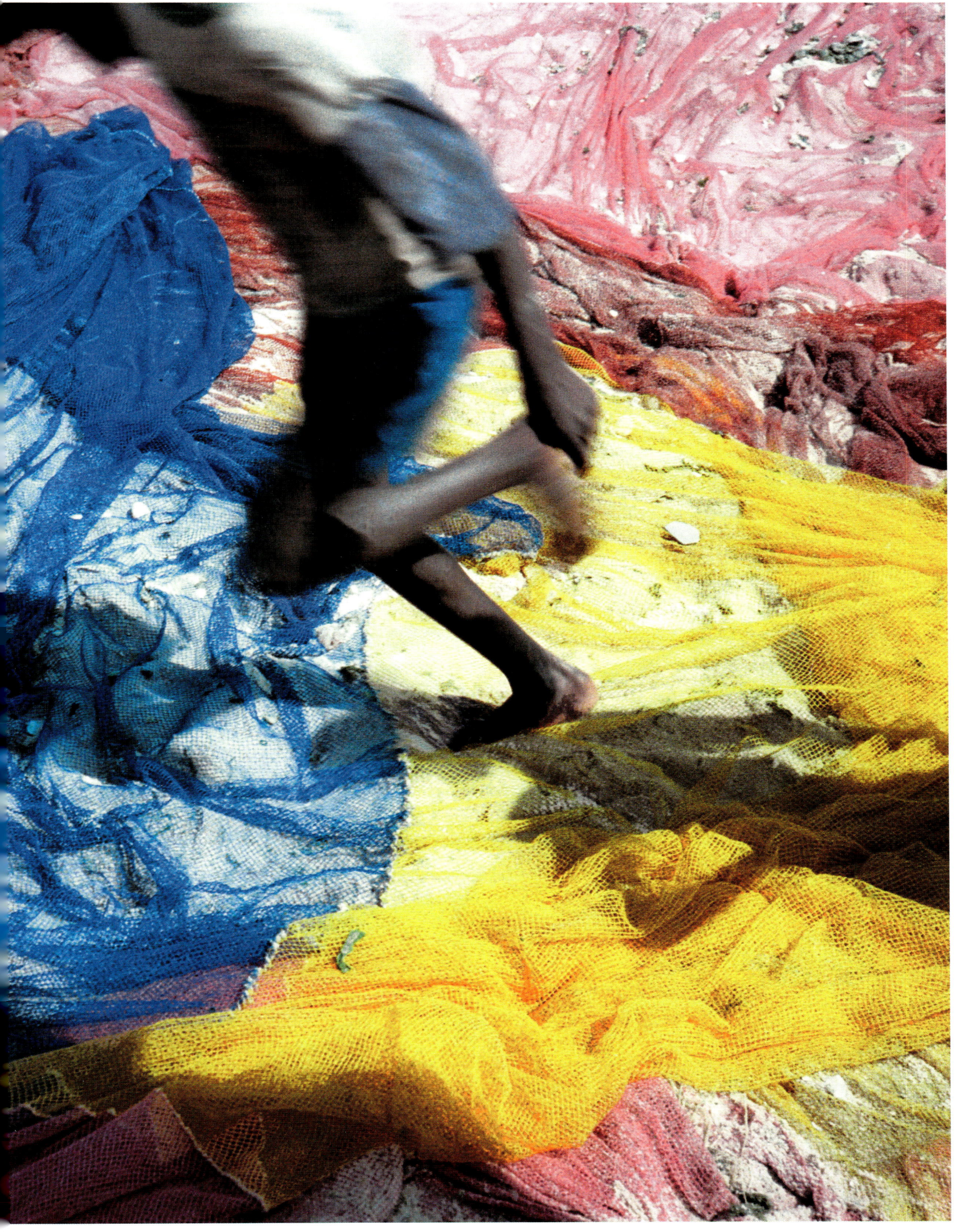

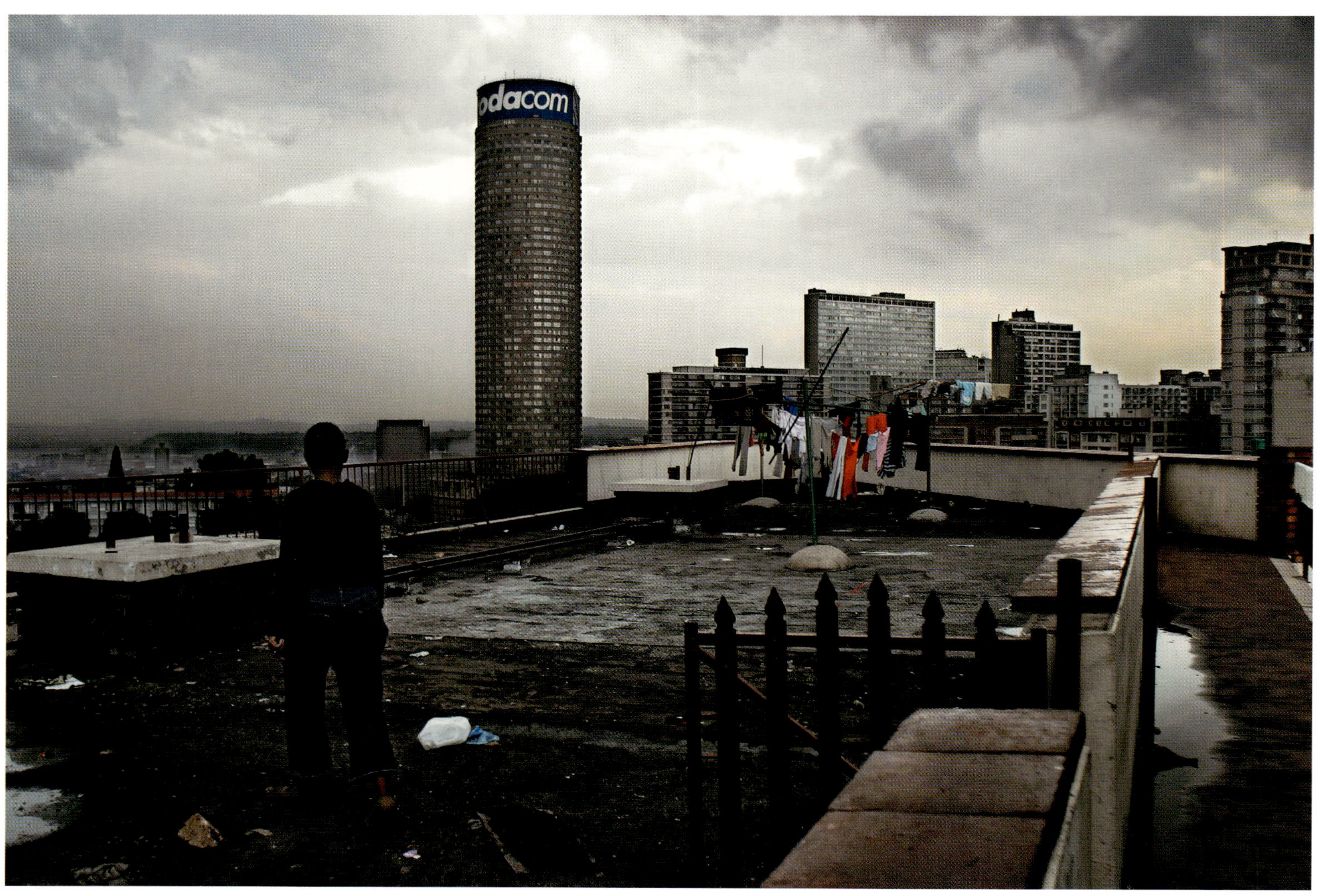

Al's Tower, a Block of Flats on Harrow Road, Berea, overlooking the Ponte Building, from the series "Jo'burg," 2004
Pigment print on paper, 17.2 x 25.8 in. (43.6 x 65.5 cm)
Courtesy the artist and Michael Stevenson Gallery, Cape Town, International Center of Photography, New York

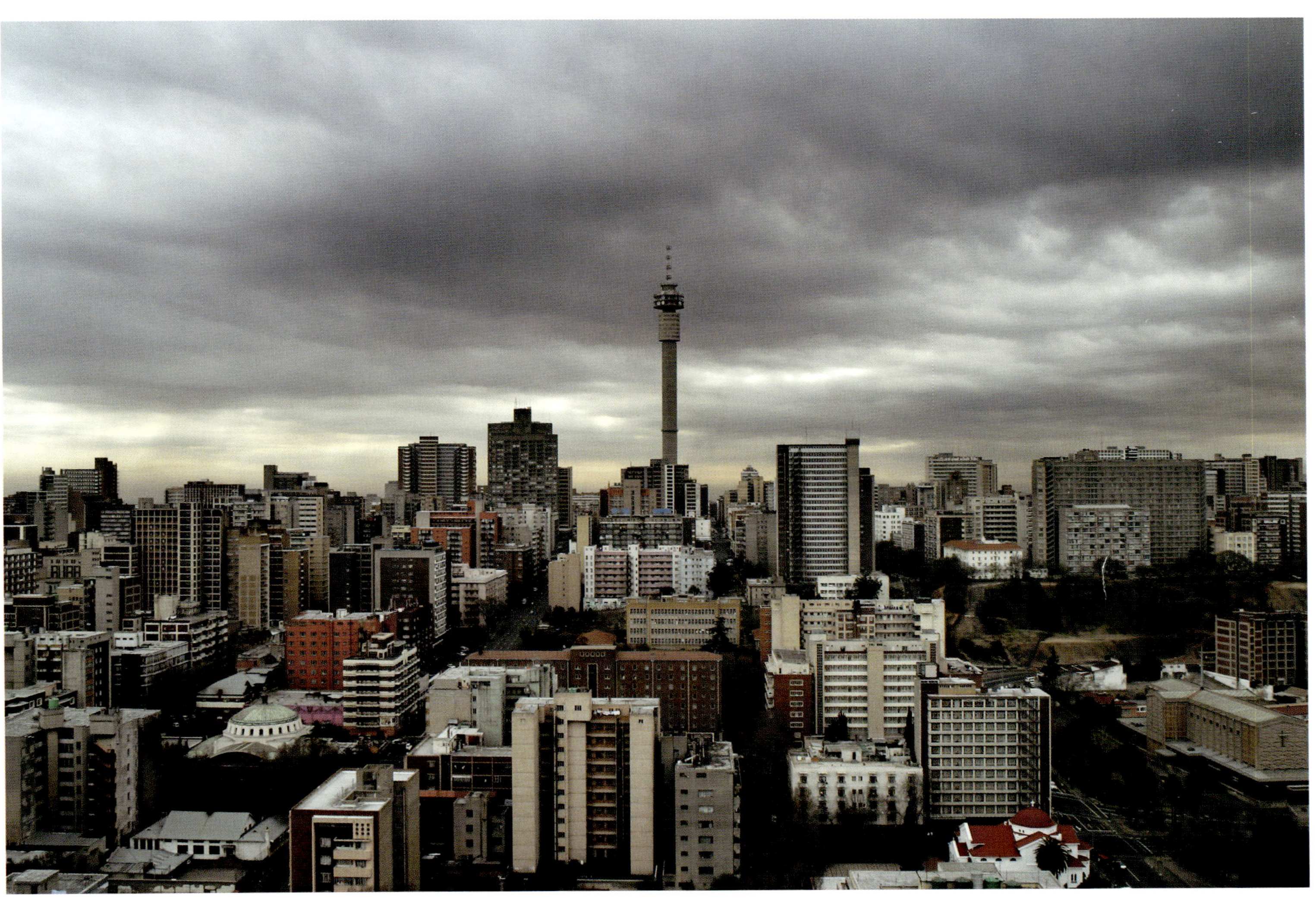

View of Hillbrow Looking North from the Roof of the Mariston Hotel
from the series "Jo'burg," 2004
Pigment print on paper, 13.9 x 20.6 in. (35.3 x 52.4 cm)
Courtesy the artist and Michael Stevenson Gallery, Cape Town, Collection of Artur Walther

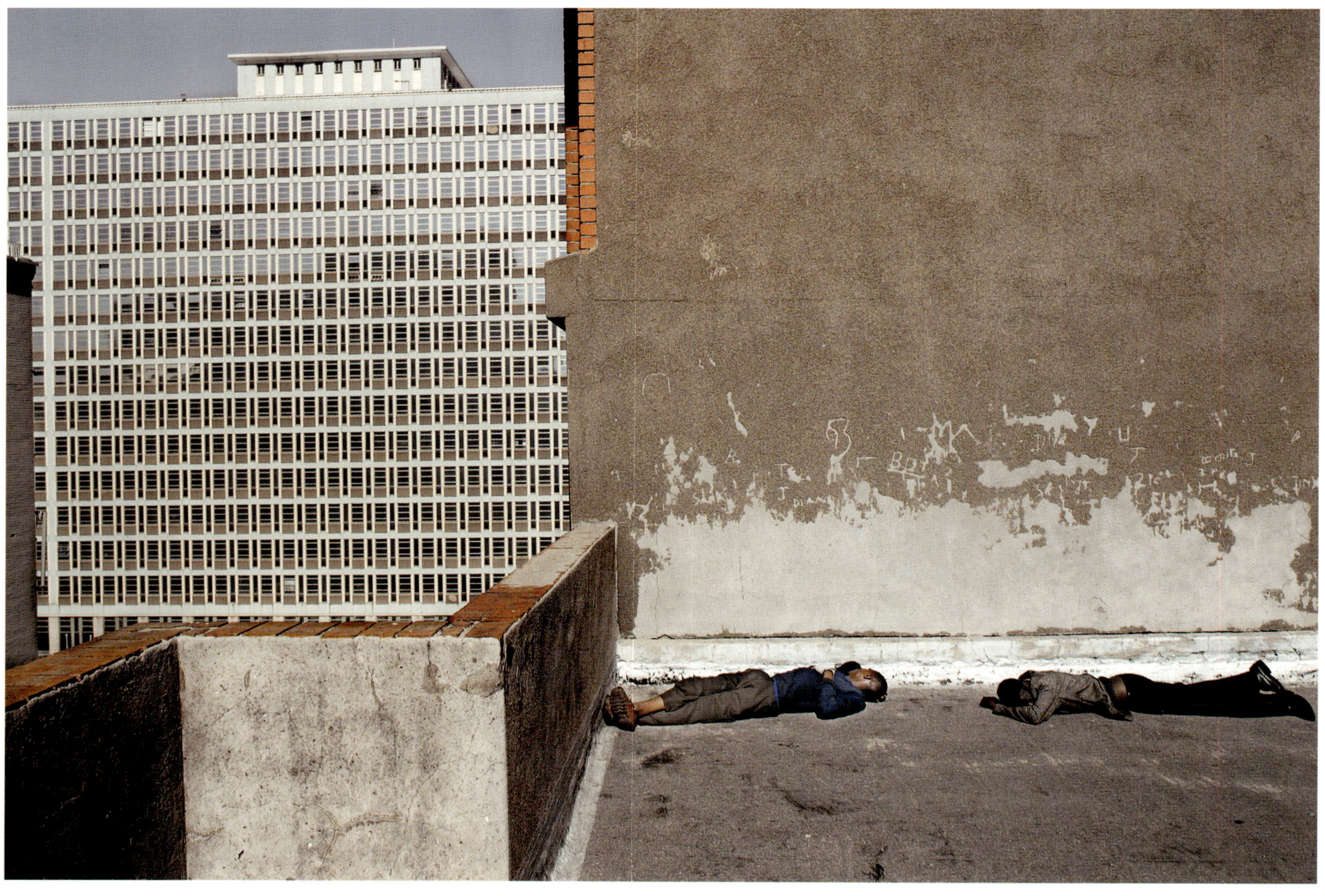

The Roof of Sherwood Heights, Smit Street, from the series "Jo'burg," 2004
Pigment print on paper, 17.2 x 25.8 in. (43.6 x 65.5 cm)
Courtesy the artist and Michael Stevenson Gallery, Cape Town, International Center of Photography, New York

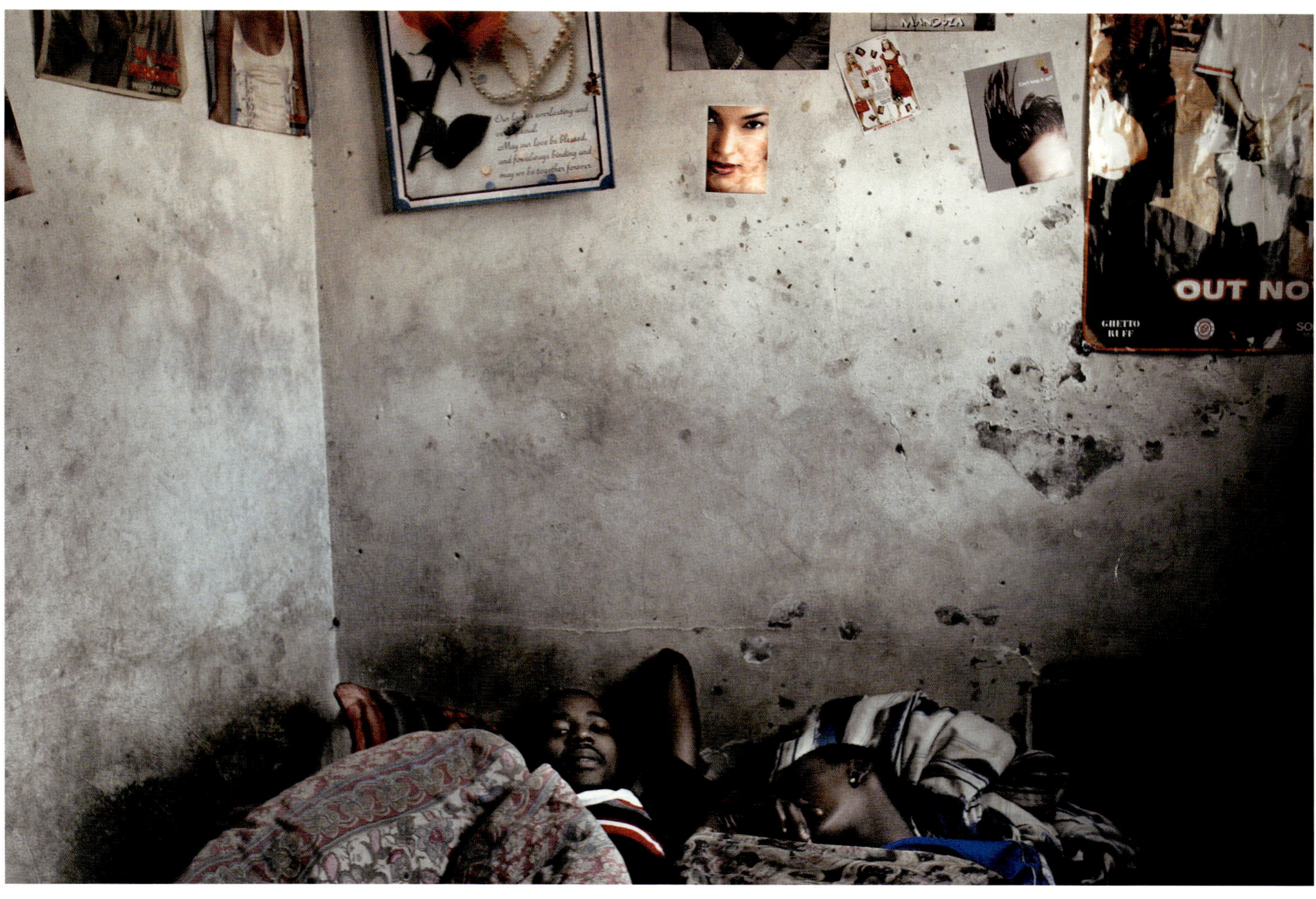

Al's Tower, Joel Road, Berea, from the series "Jo'burg," 2004
Pigment print on paper, 13.9 x 20.6 in. (35.3 x 52.4 cm)
Courtesy the artist and Michael Stevenson Gallery, Cape Town, Collection of Artur Walther

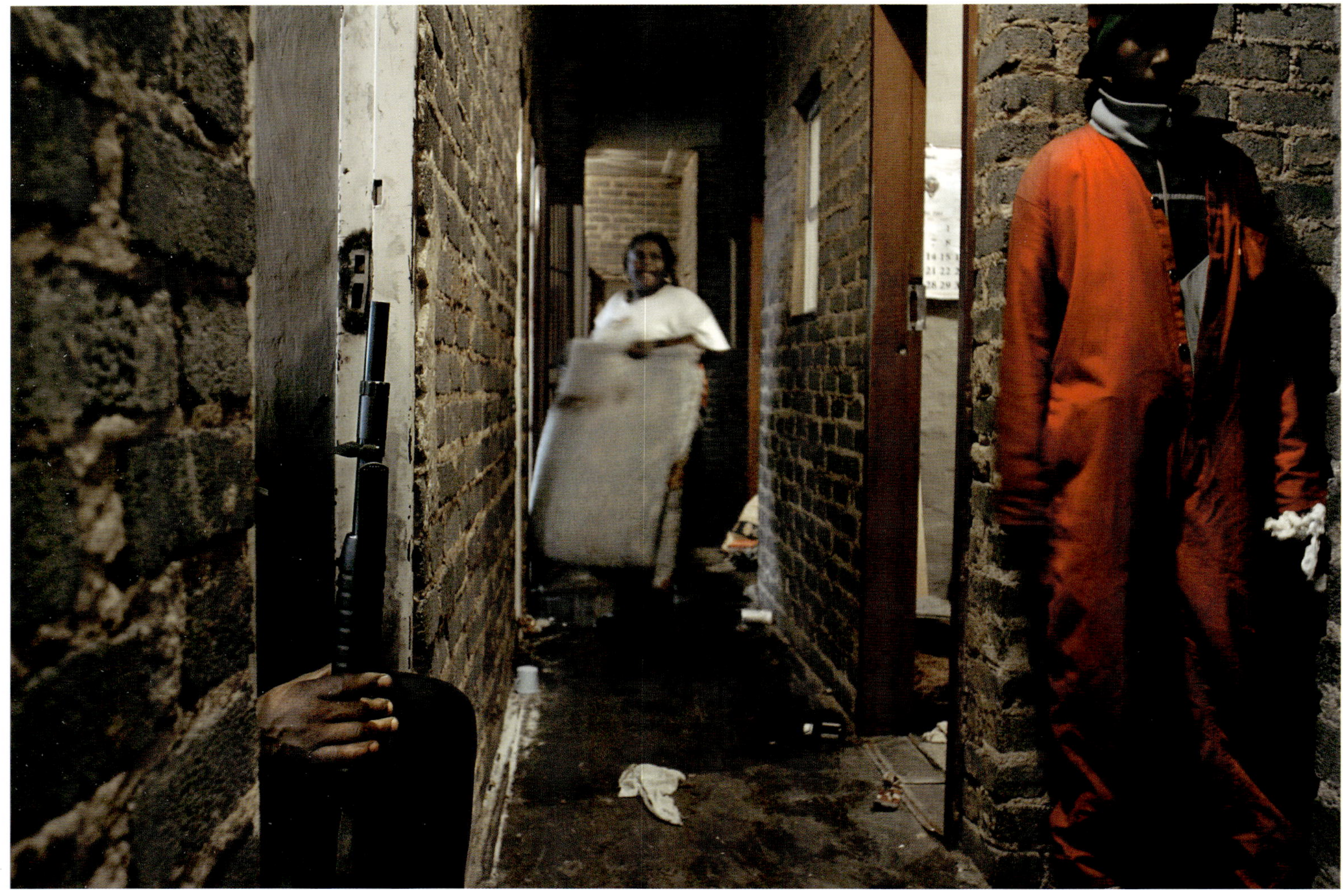

Eviction by the Red Ants, Auret Street Jeppestown, from the series "Jo'burg," 2004
Pigment print on paper, 13.9 x 20.6 in. (35.3 x 52.4 cm)
Courtesy the artist and Michael Stevenson Gallery, Cape Town, Collection of Artur Walther

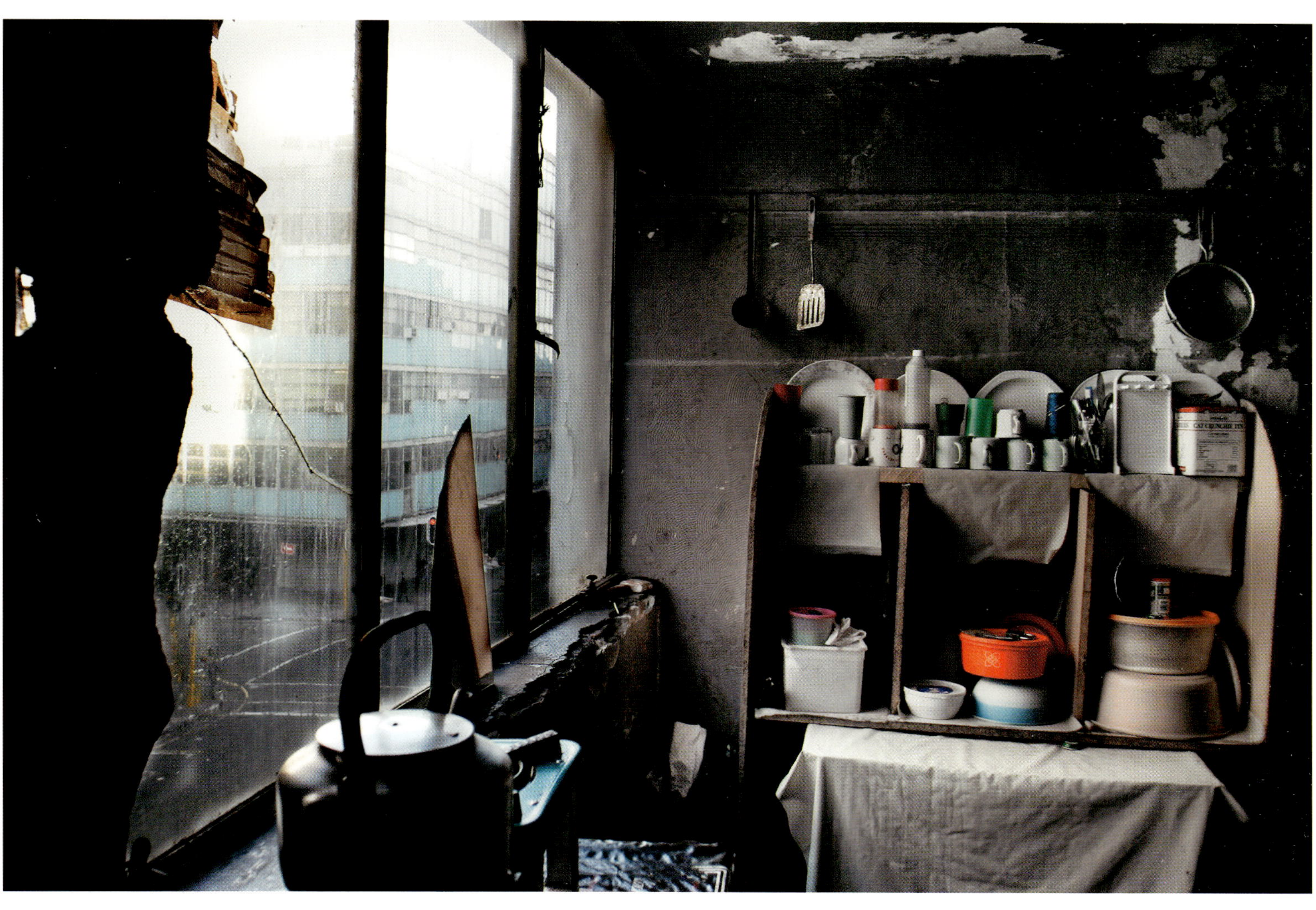

The View from an Apartment in Jeanwell House overlooking the intersection of Nugget and Pritchard Streets, from the series "Jo'burg," 2004
Pigment print on paper, 17.2 x 25.8 in. (43.6 x 65.5 cm)
Courtesy the artist and Michael Stevenson Gallery, Cape Town, International Center of Photography, New York

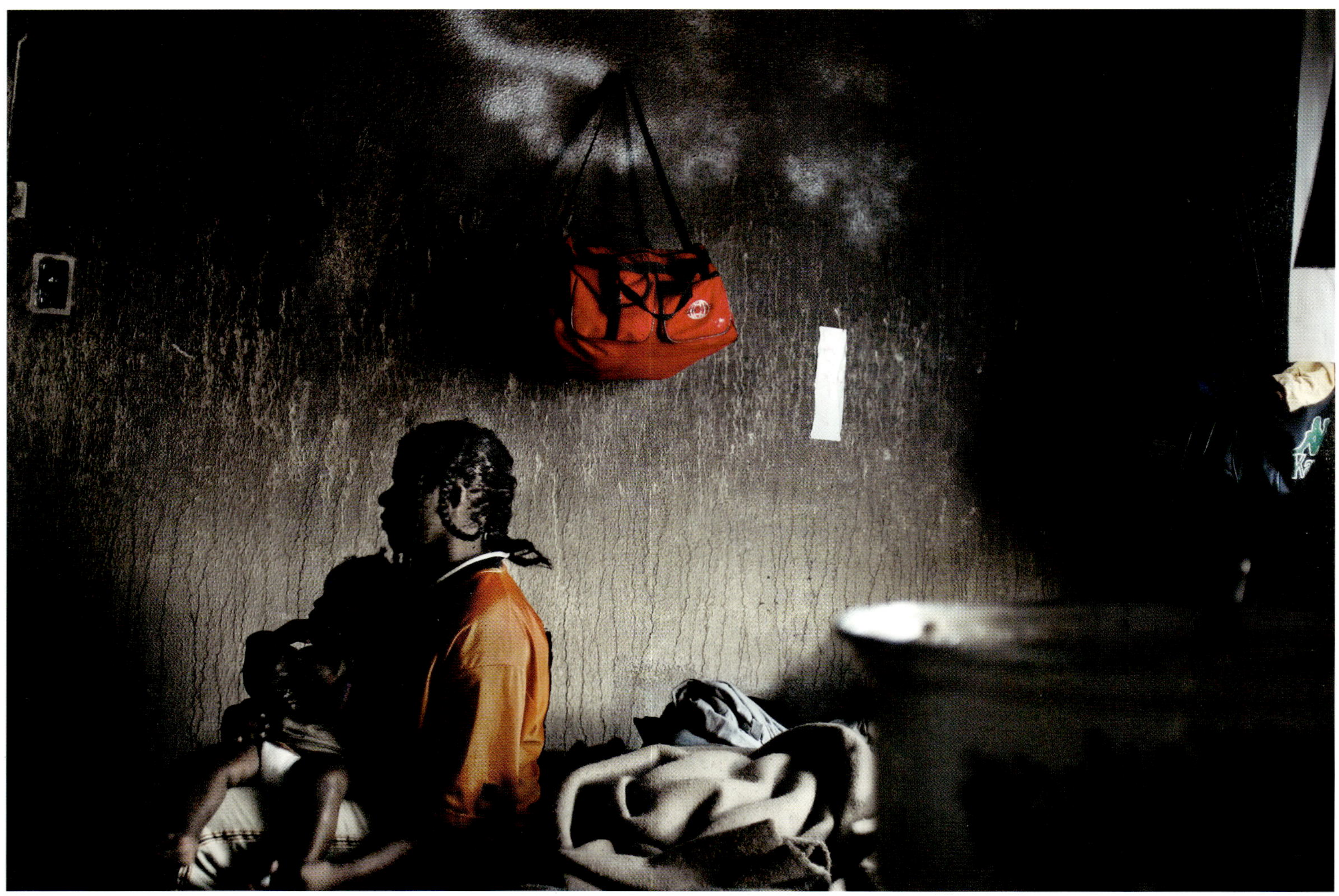

Yonela Kwaza, Grafton Road, Yeoville, from the series "Jo'burg," 2004
Pigment print on paper, 13.9 x 20.6 in. (35.3 x 52.4 cm)
Courtesy the artist and Michael Stevenson Gallery, Cape Town, Collection of Artur Walther

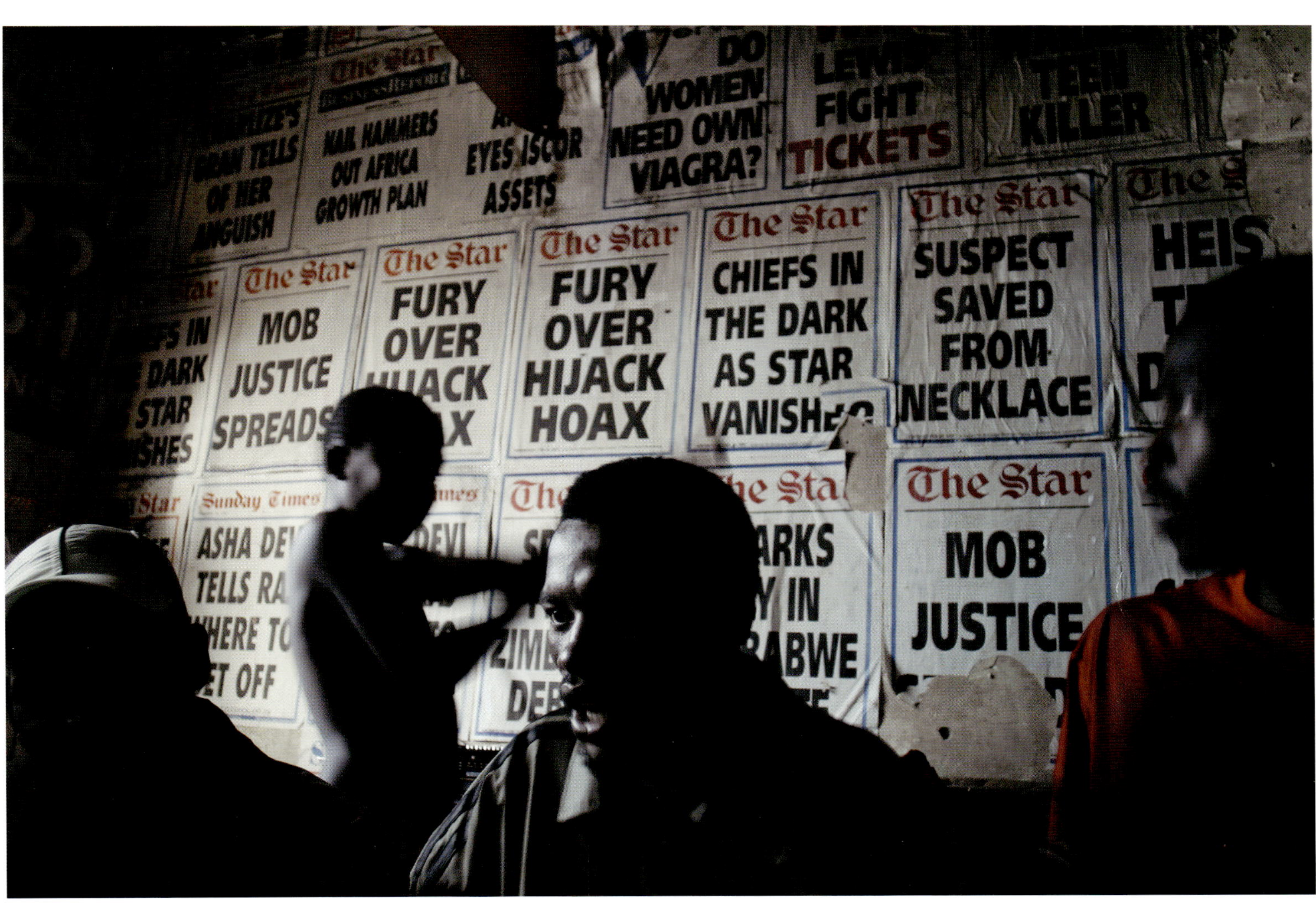

Ntokozo (right) and His Brother Vusi Tshabalala at Ntokozo's Place, Milton Court, Pritchard Street, from the series "Jo'burg," 2004
Pigment print on paper, 17.2 x 25.8 in. (43.6 x 65.5 cm)
Courtesy the artist and Michael Stevenson Gallery, Cape Town, International Center of Photography, New York

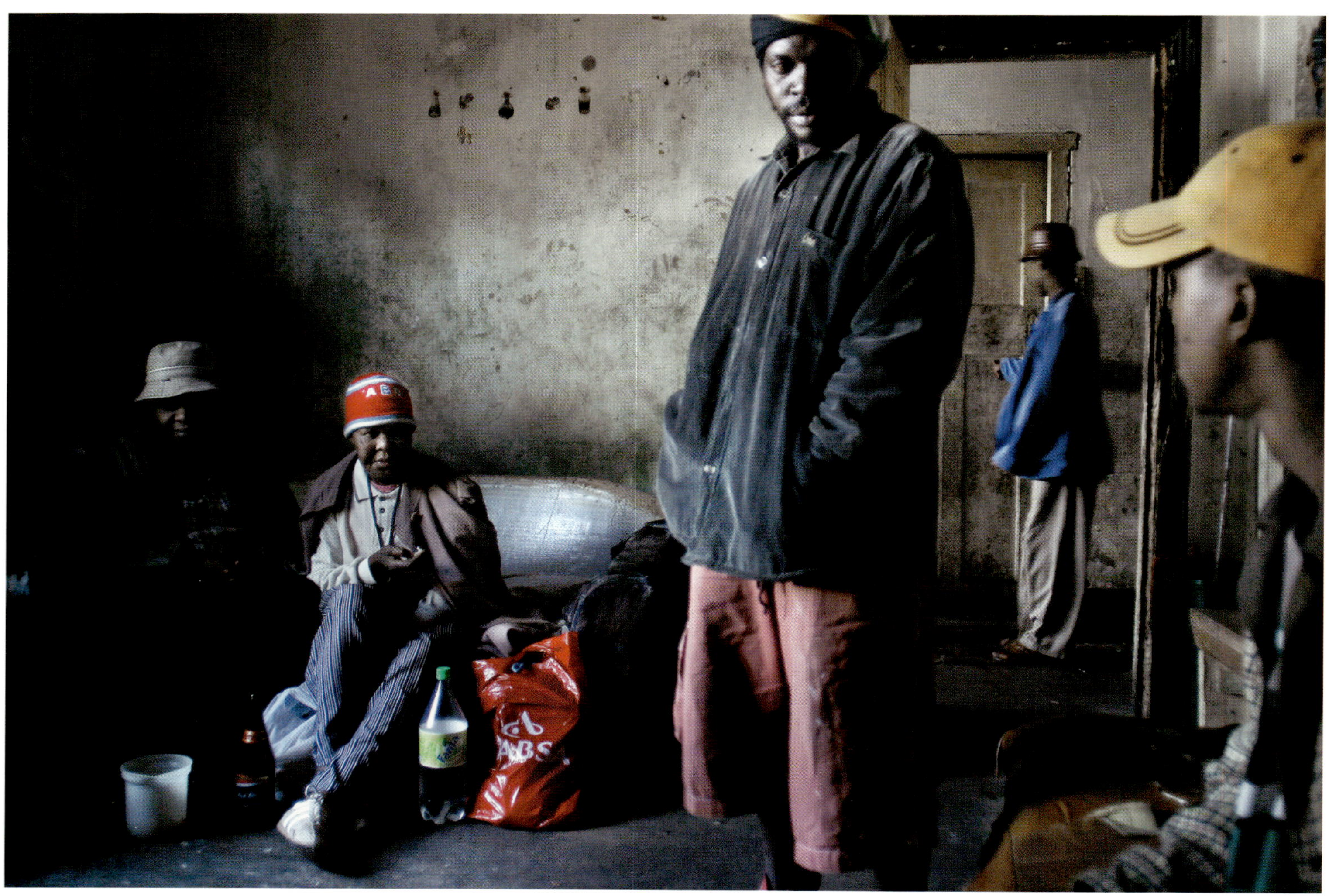

Mbulelo's Bar, Joel Road, Berea. Justice Sibanyone (centre) and His Wife Monica (extreme left), from the series "Jo'burg," 2004
Pigment print on paper, 13.9 x 20.6 in. (35.3 x 52.4 cm)
Courtesy the artist and Michael Stevenson Gallery, Cape Town, Collection of Artur Walther

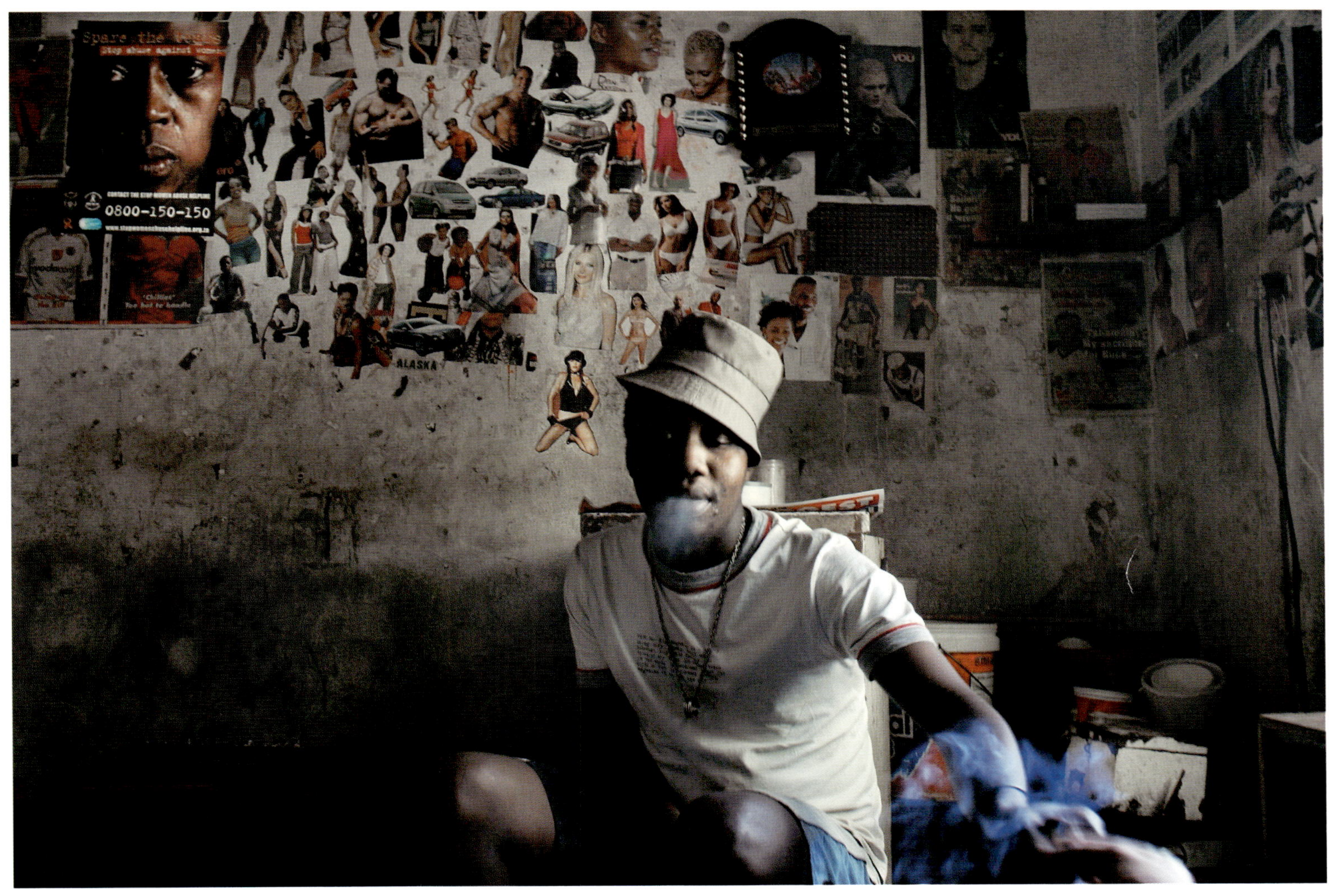

Mbulelo at the Bar He Runs in a House in Joel Road, Berea, from the series "Jo'burg," 2004
Pigment print on paper, 13.9 x 20.6 in. (35.3 x 52.4 cm)
Courtesy the artist and Michael Stevenson Gallery, Cape Town, Collection of Artur Walther

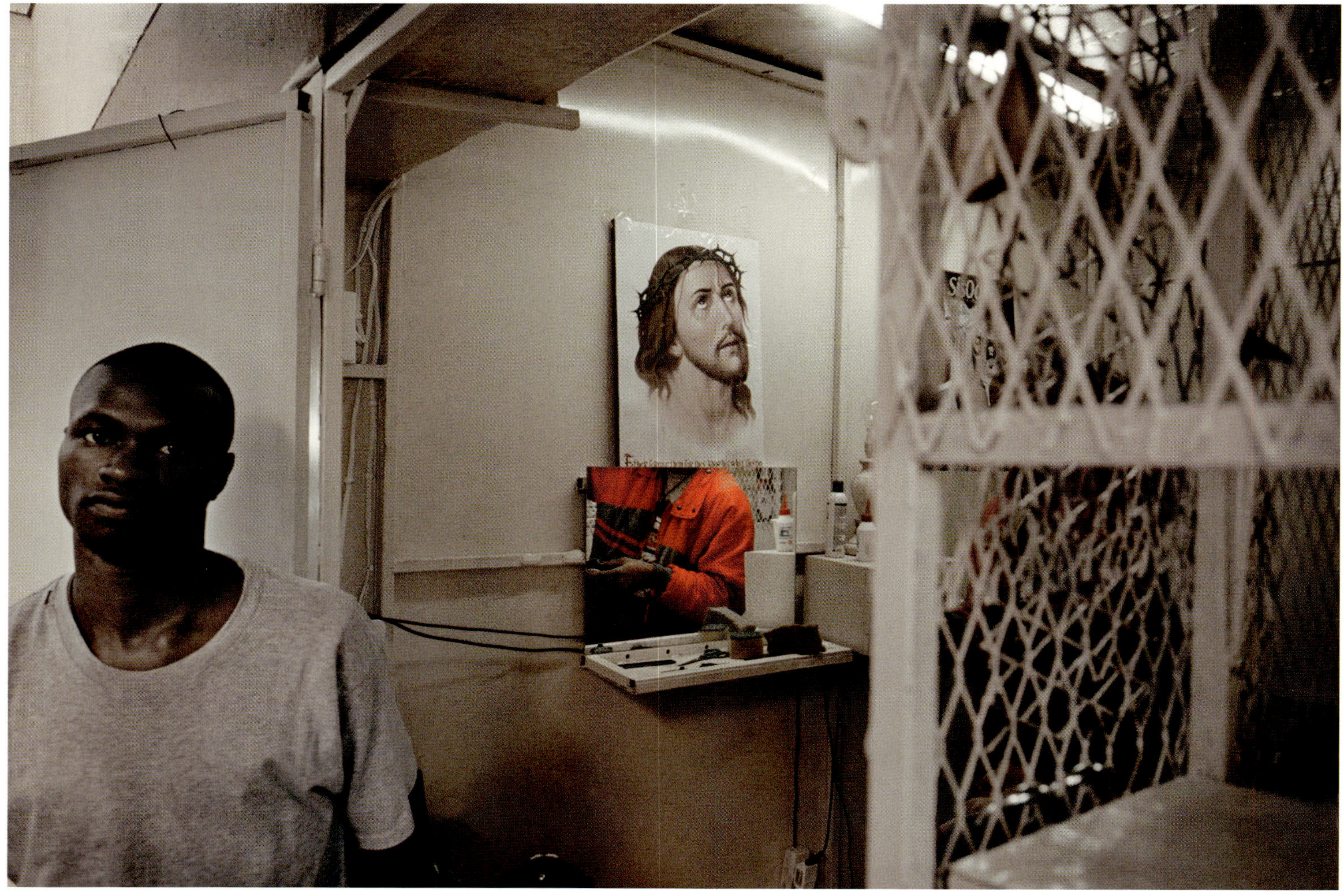

Barber's Shop, Hillbrow, from the series "Jo'burg," 2004
Pigment print on paper, 13.9 x 20.6 in. (35.3 x 52.4 cm)
Courtesy the artist and Michael Stevenson Gallery, Cape Town, Collection of Artur Walther

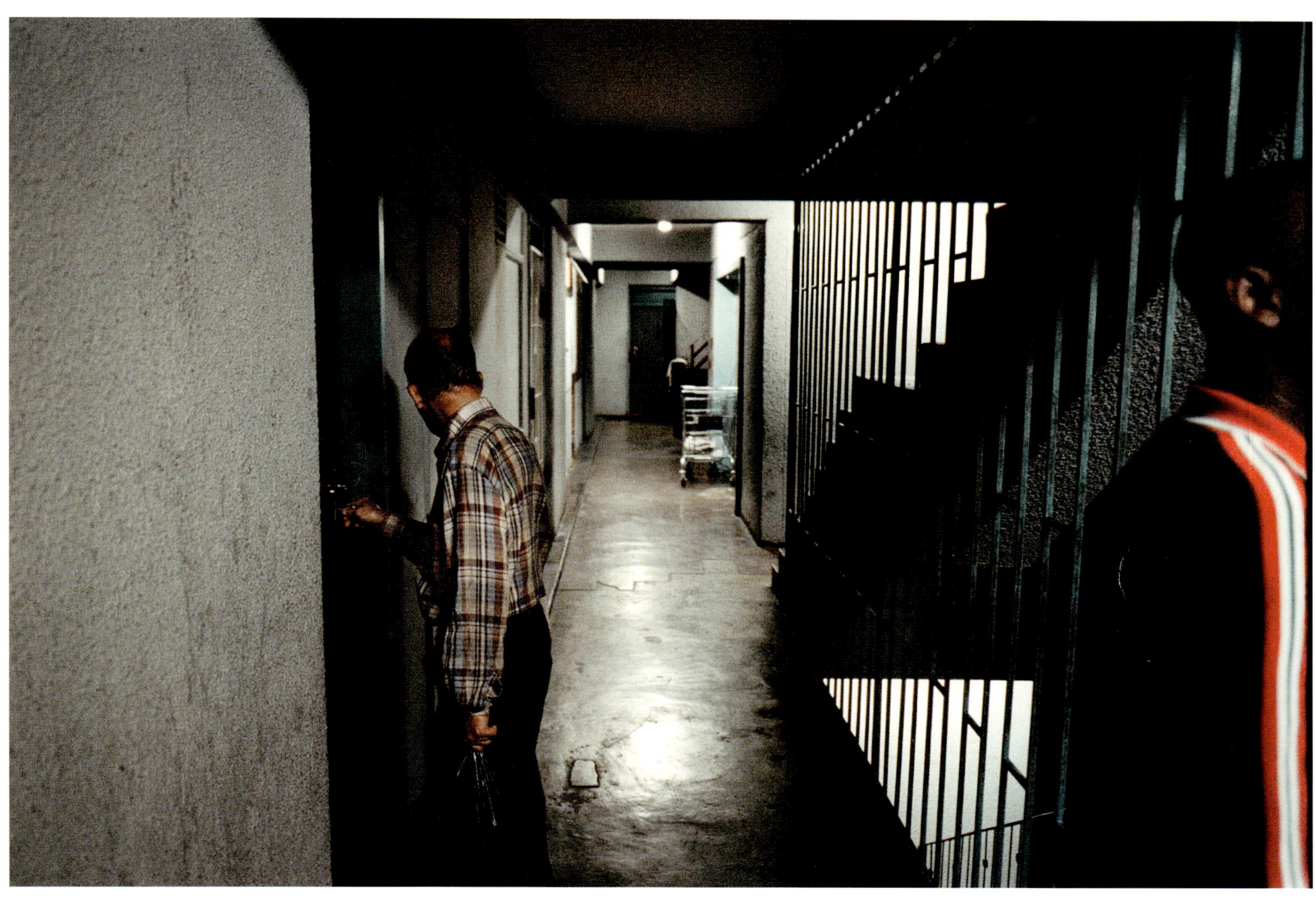

Cape Agulhas, Esselen Street, Hillbrow, from the series "Jo'burg," 2004
Pigment print on paper, 13.9 x 20.6 in. (35.3 x 52.4 cm)
Courtesy the artist and Michael Stevenson Gallery, Cape Town, Collection of Artur Walther

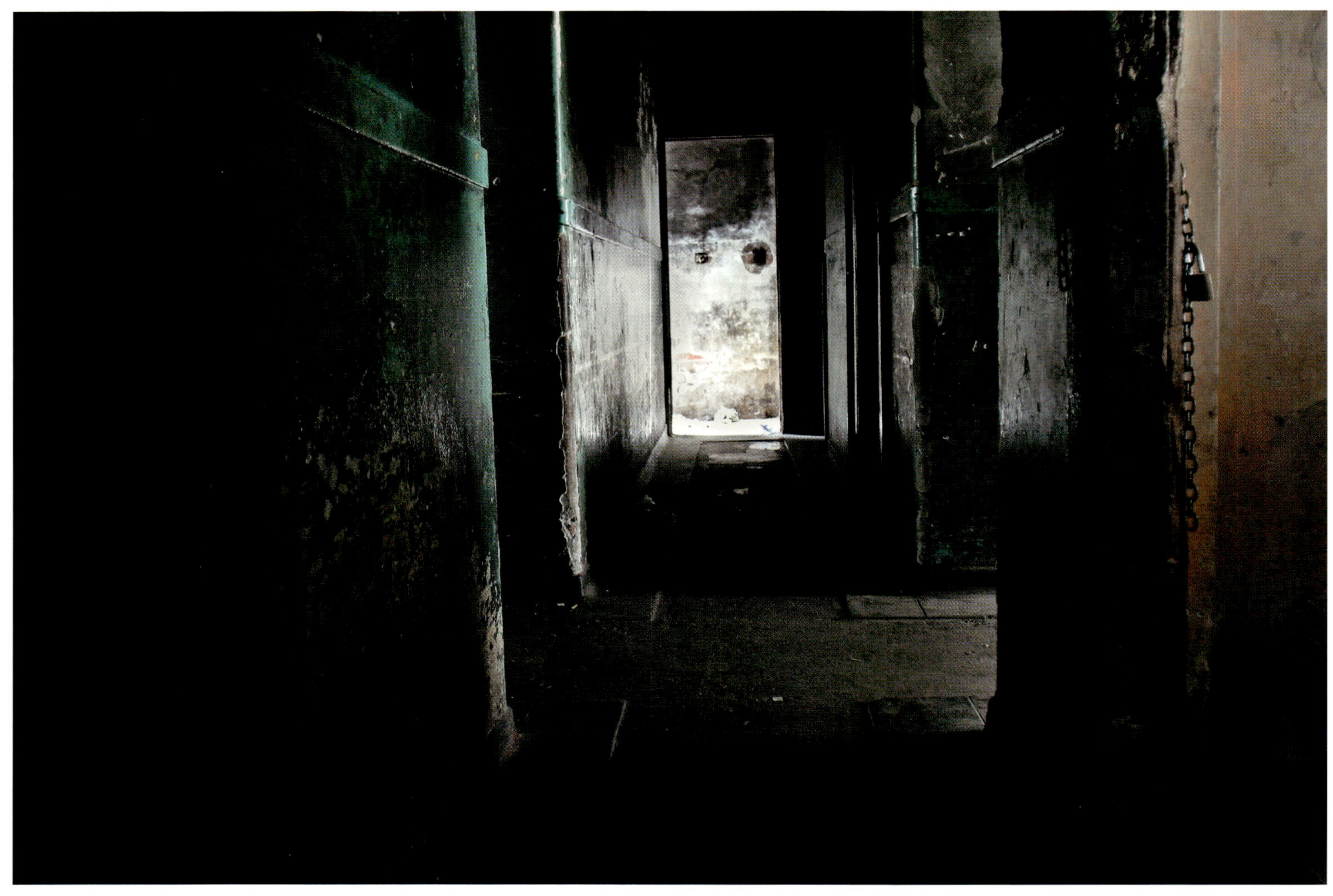

Milton Court, Pritchard Street, from the series "Jo'burg," 2004
Pigment print on paper, 17.2 x 25.8 in. (43.6 x 65.5 cm)
Courtesy the artist and Michael Stevenson Gallery, Cape Town

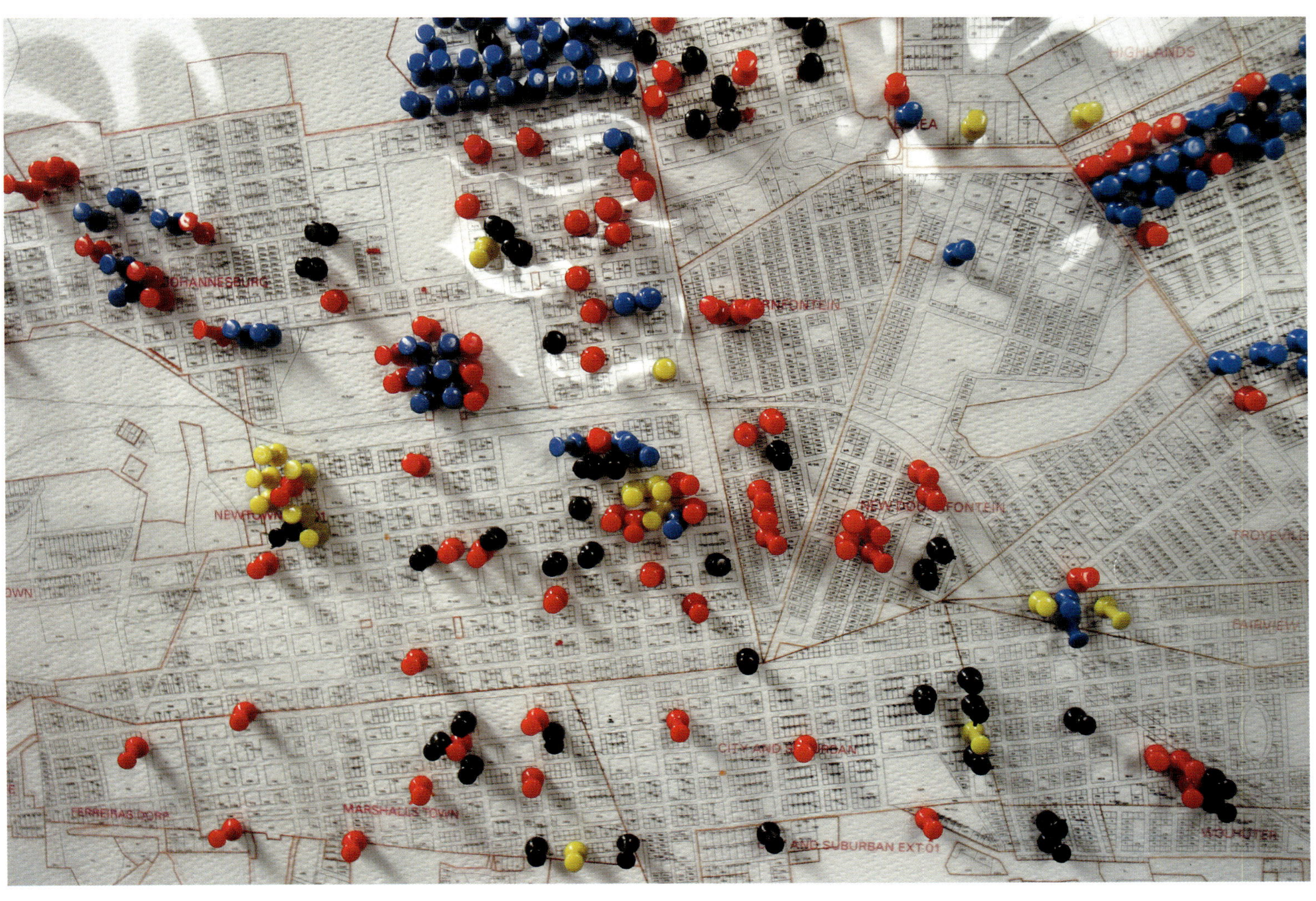

A Map of Central Johannesburg at the Inner City Regeneration Project Office, City Council, Loveday Street, from the series "Jo'burg," 2004
Pigment print on paper, 13.9 x 20.6 in. (35.3 x 52.4 cm)
Courtesy the artist and Michael Stevenson Gallery, Cape Town, Collection of Artur Walther

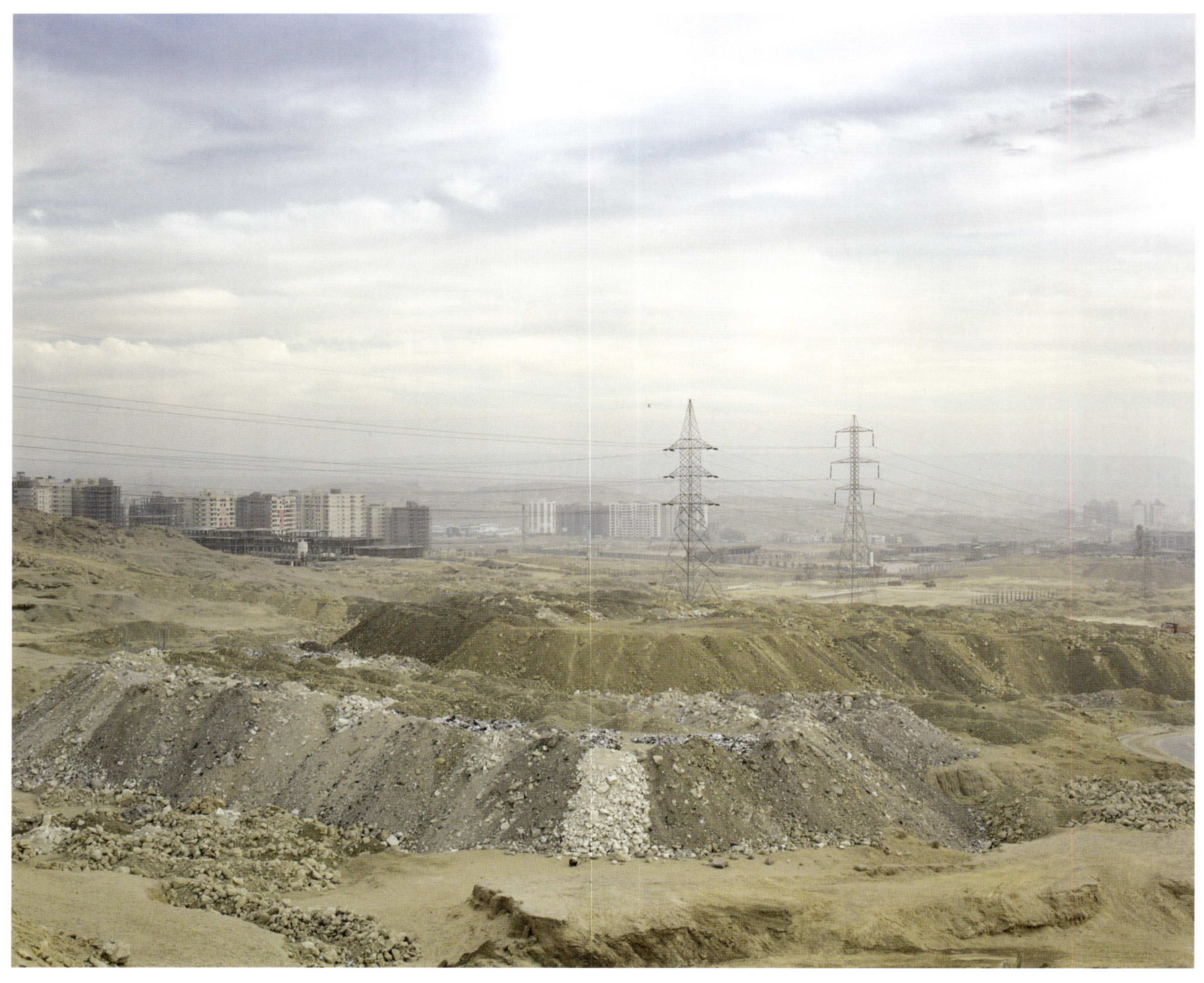

Peripheral landscape #1, Mokattam, 2004
Ink jet print on vinyl, dimensions variable
Courtesy the artist and Townhouse Gallery, Cairo

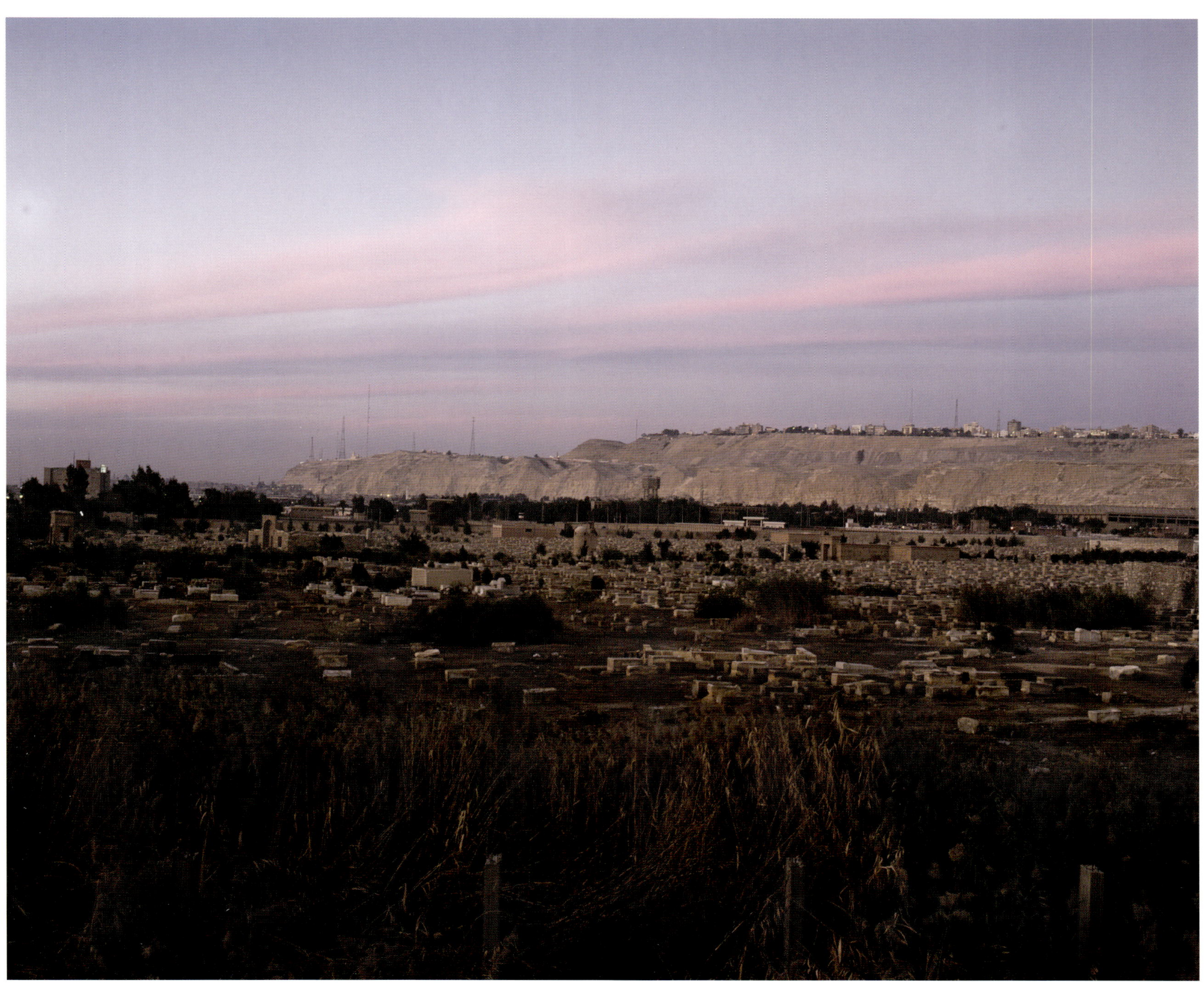

Peripheral landscape #2, Bassateen, 2004
Ink jet print on vinyl, dimensions variable
Courtesy the artist and Townhouse Gallery, Cairo

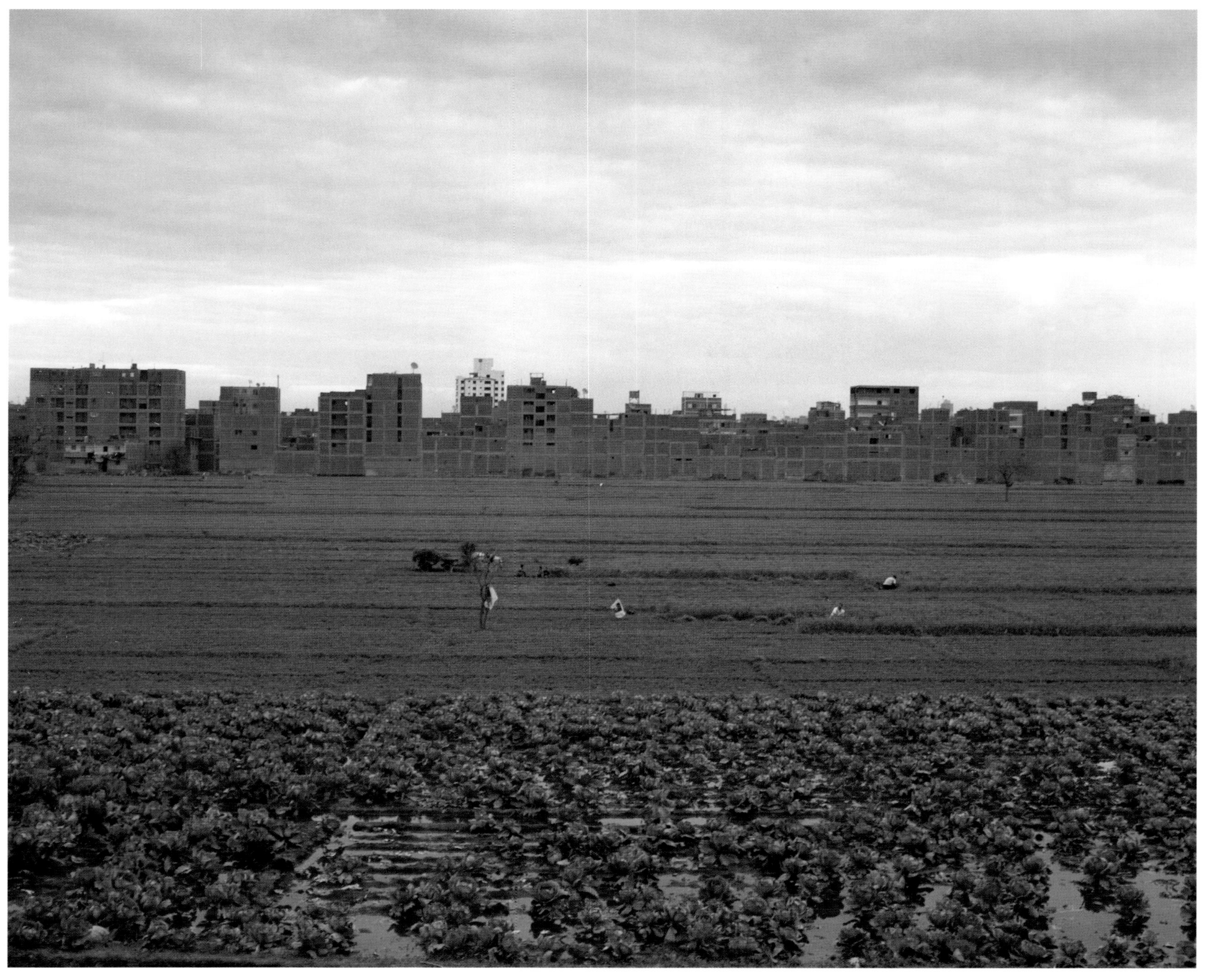

Peripheral landscape #3, Mokattam, 2004
Ink jet print on vinyl, dimensions variable
Courtesy the artist and Townhouse Gallery, Cairo

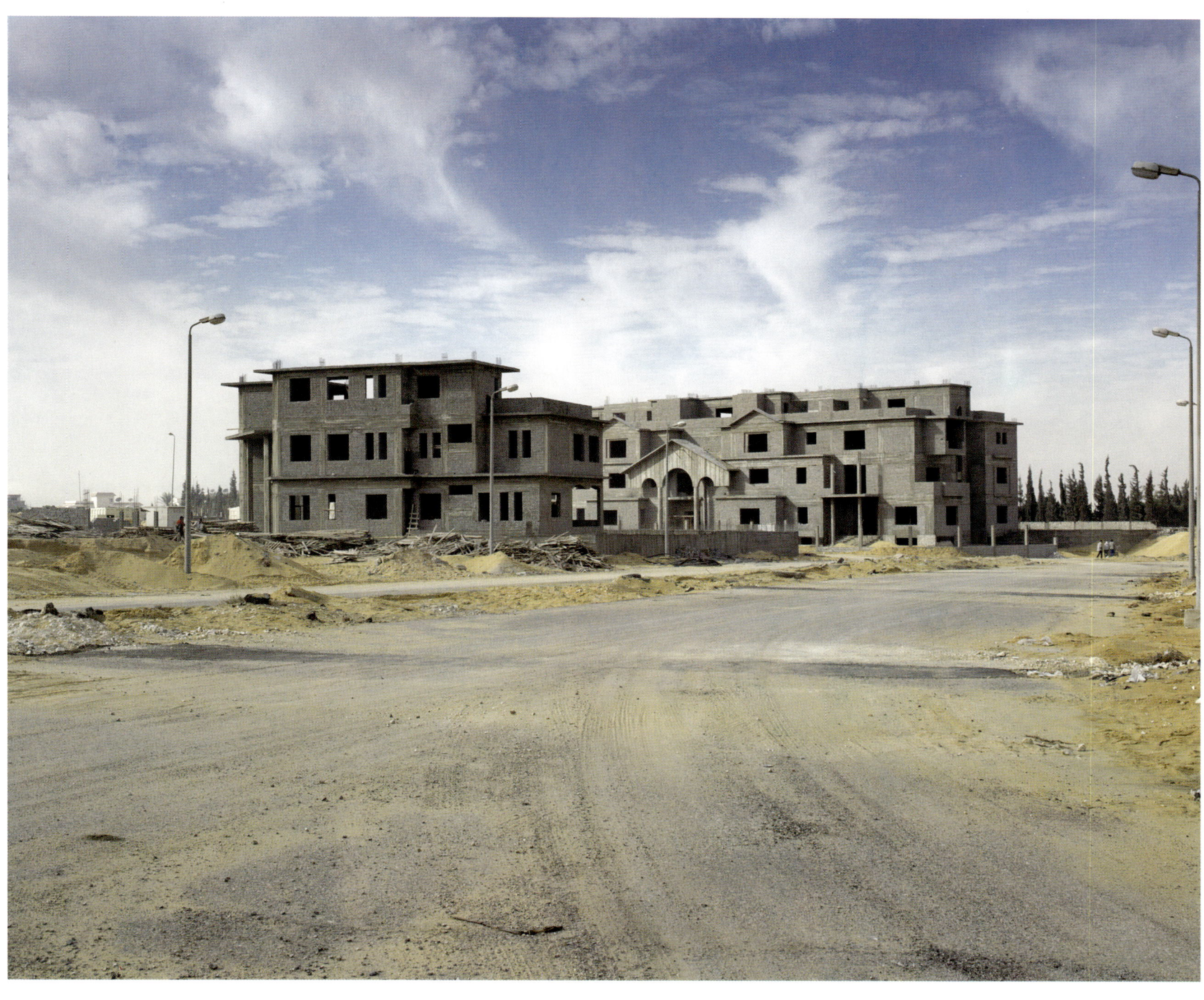

Peripheral landscape #4, El Tagamo' El Khamis, 2004
Ink jet print on vinyl, dimensions variable
Courtesy the artist and Townhouse Gallery, Cairo

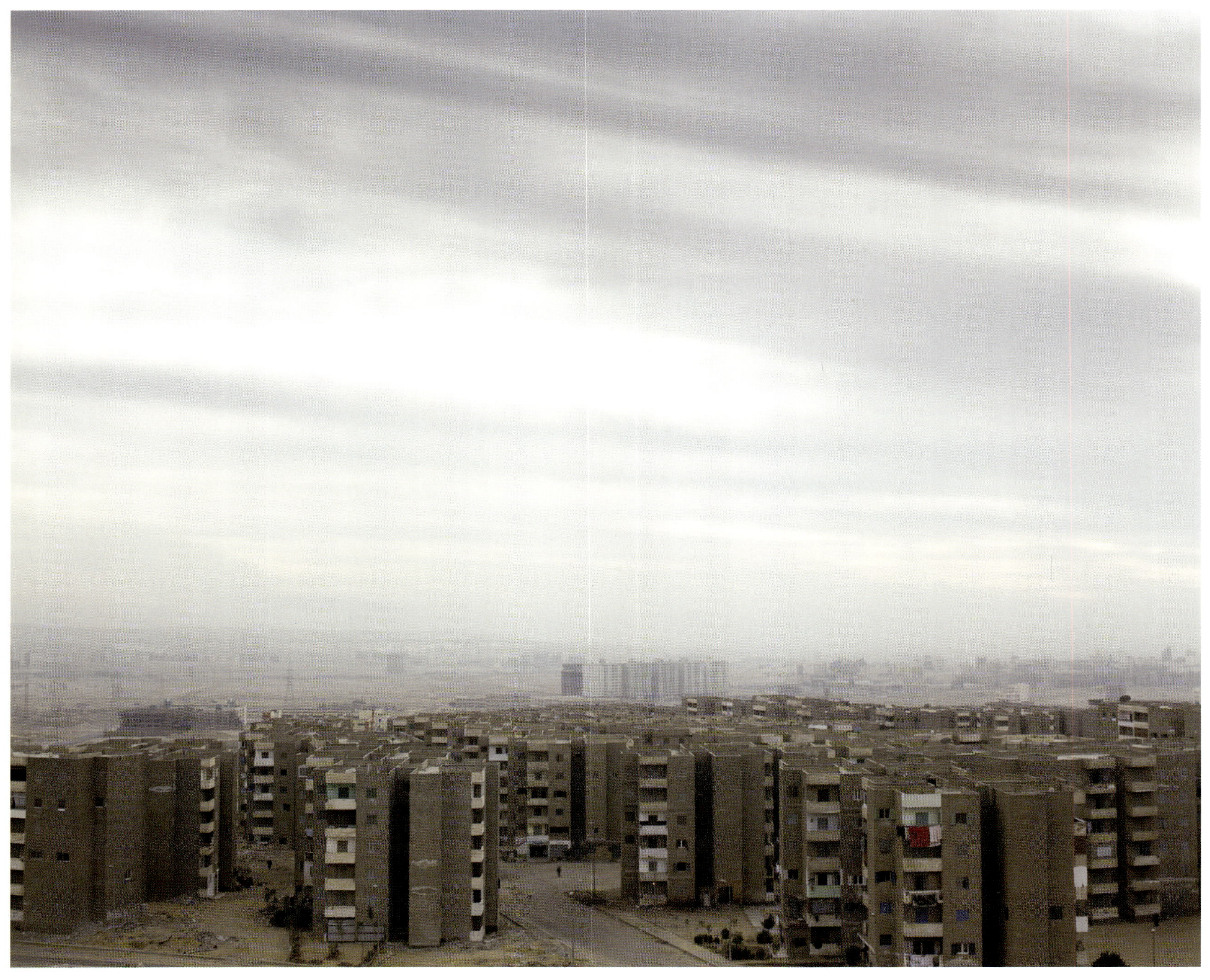

Peripheral landscape #5, Al Warraq, 2004
Ink jet print on vinyl, dimensions variable
Courtesy the artist and Townhouse Gallery, Cairo

Depth of Field

Kelechi Amadi-Obi

Uchechukwu James-Iroha

Toyosi Zaynab Odunsi

Amaize Ojeikhere

Toyin Sokefun-Bello

Emeka Okereke

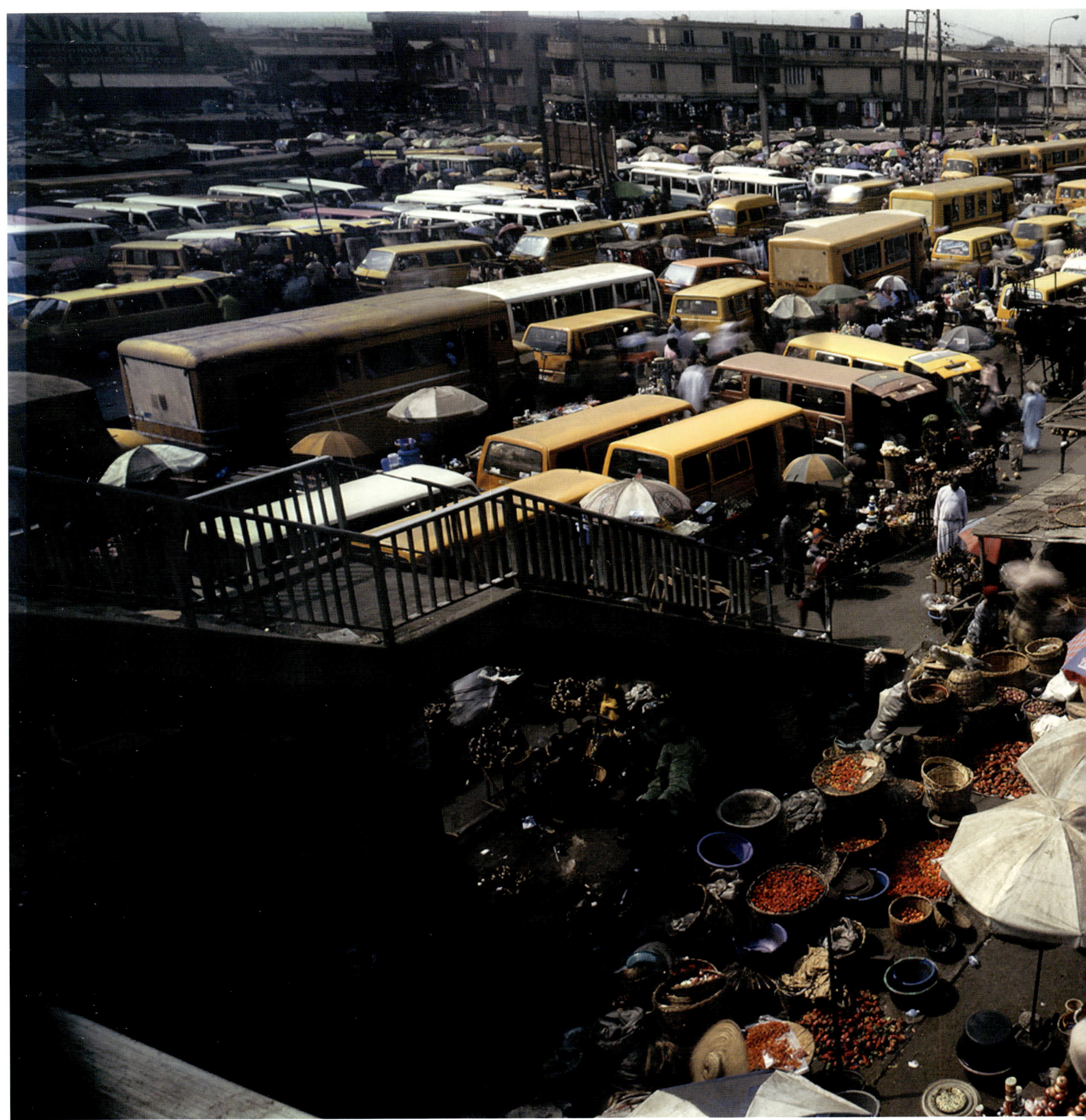

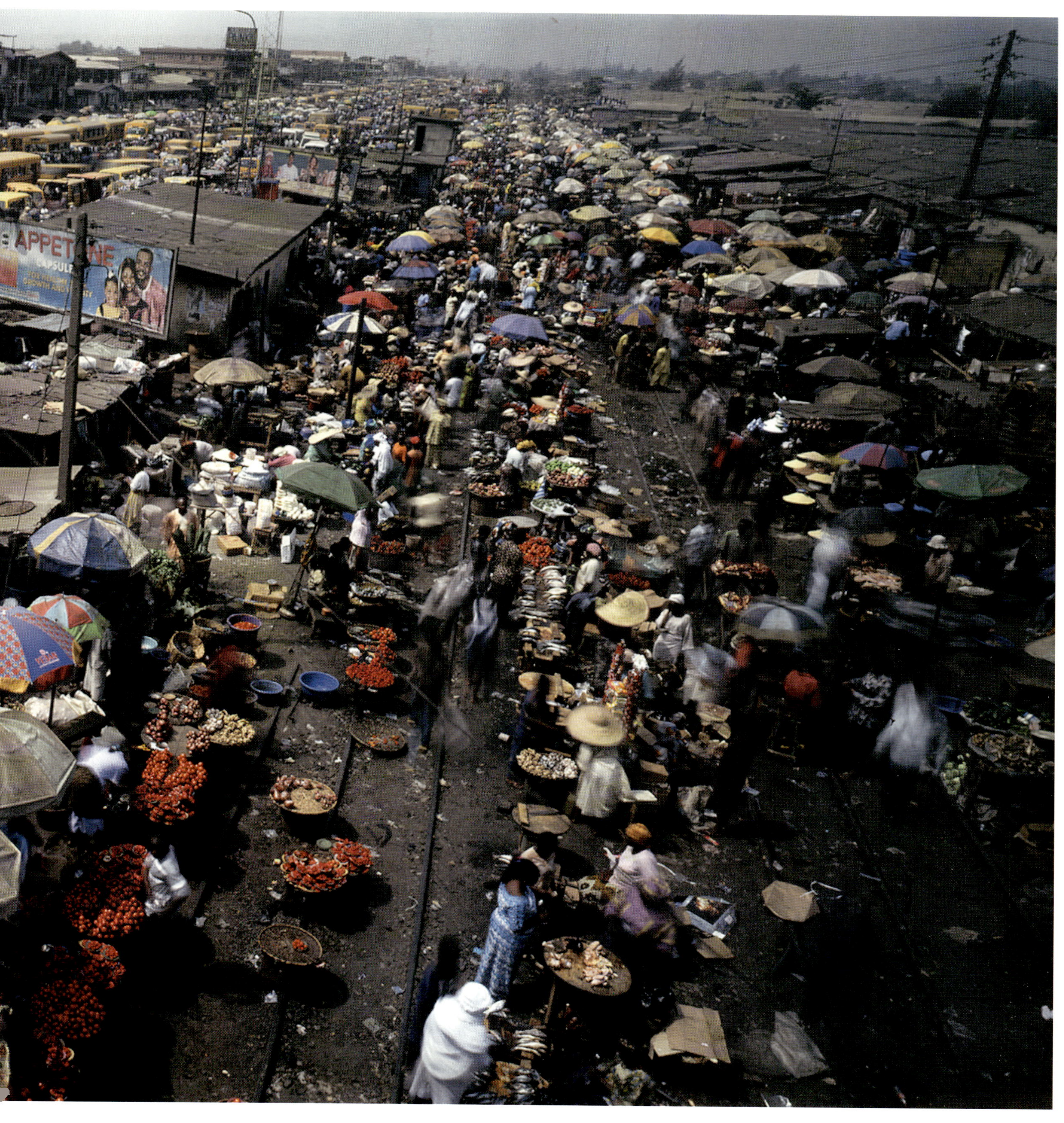

Oshodi, from the series "LAGOS UPTIGHT," 2001–05
Chromogenic print, dimensions variable
Courtesy the artist

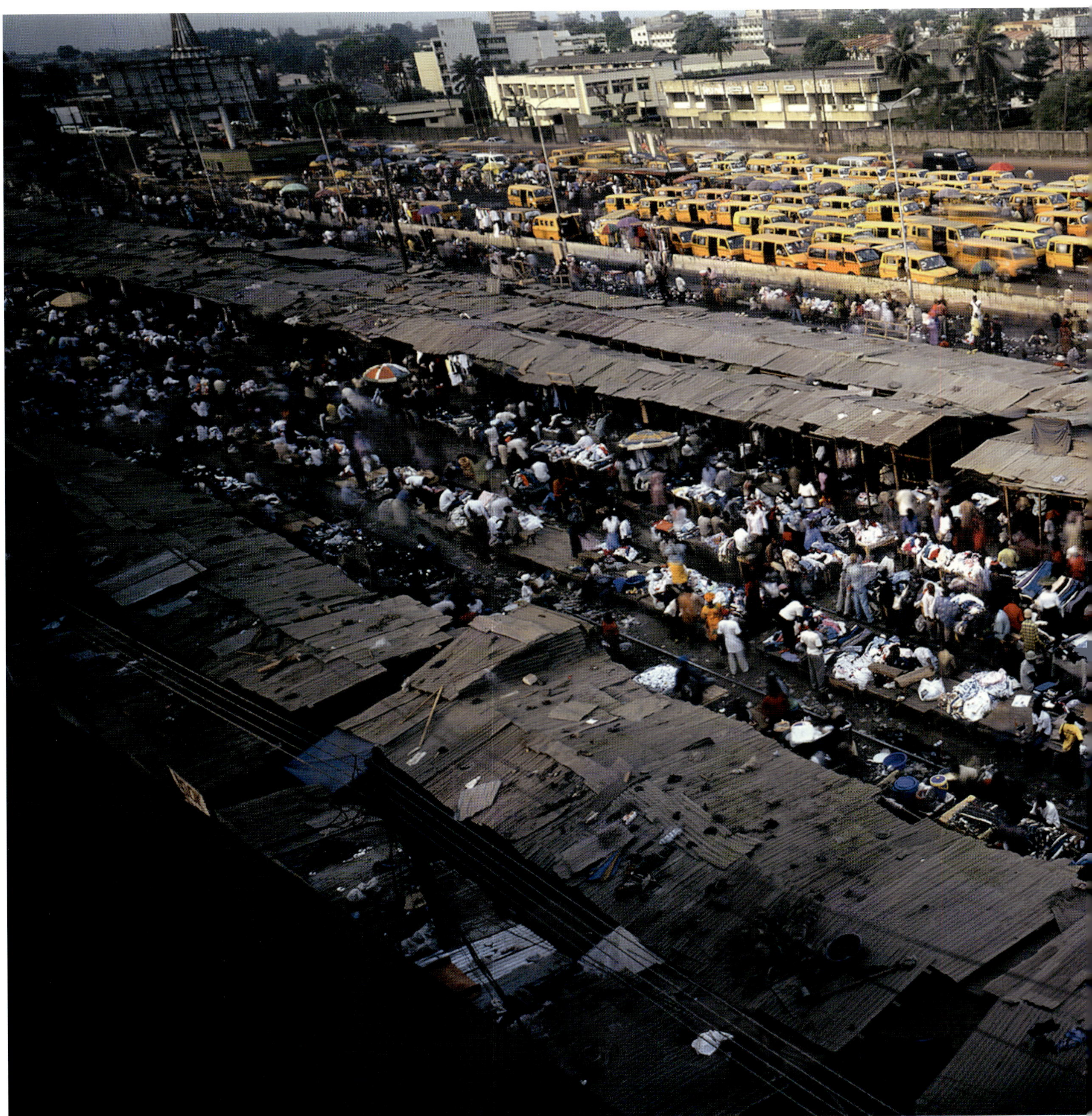

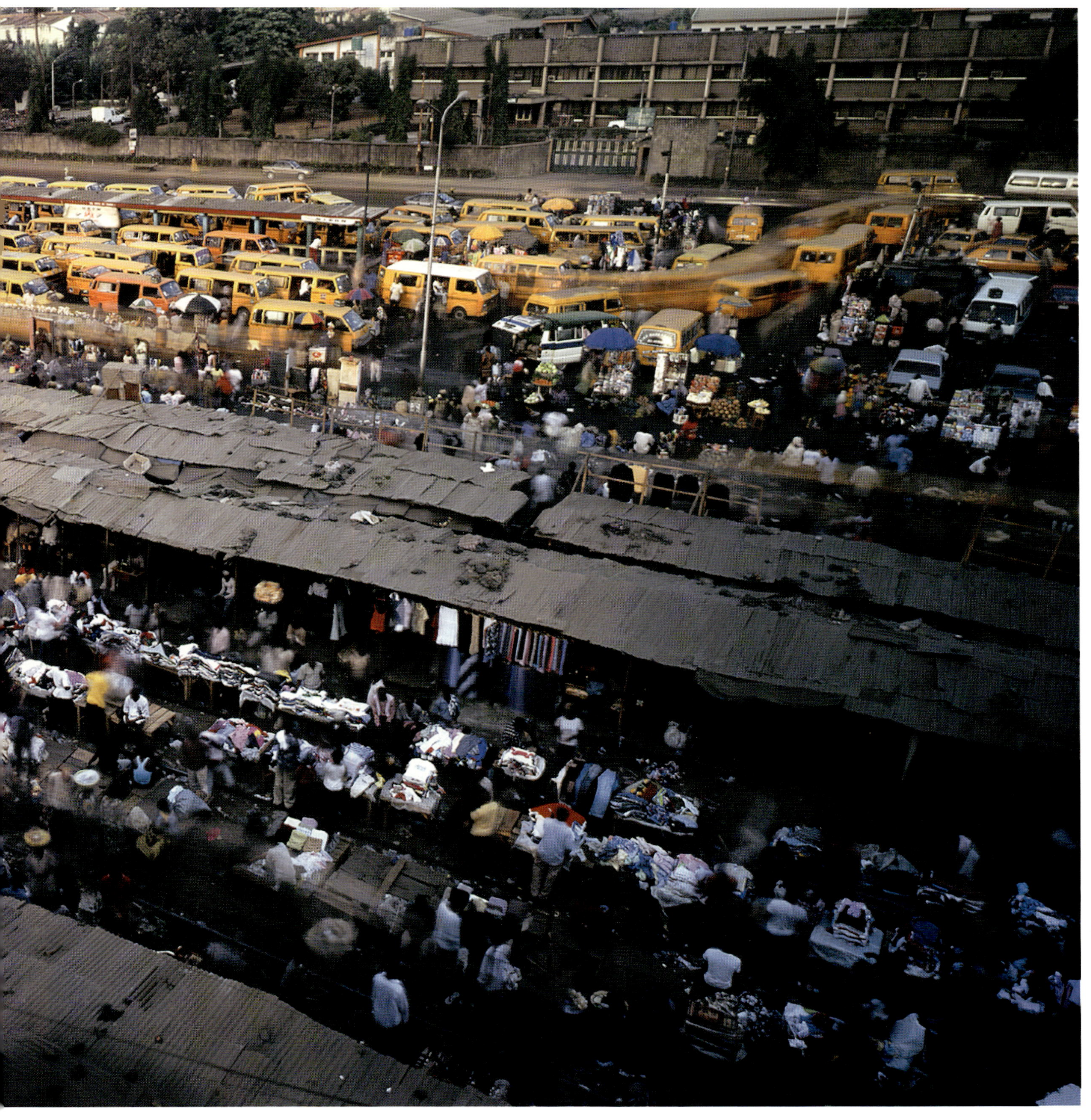

Yaba Market, from the series "LAGOS UPTIGHT," 2001–05
Chromogenic print, dimensions variable
Courtesy the artist

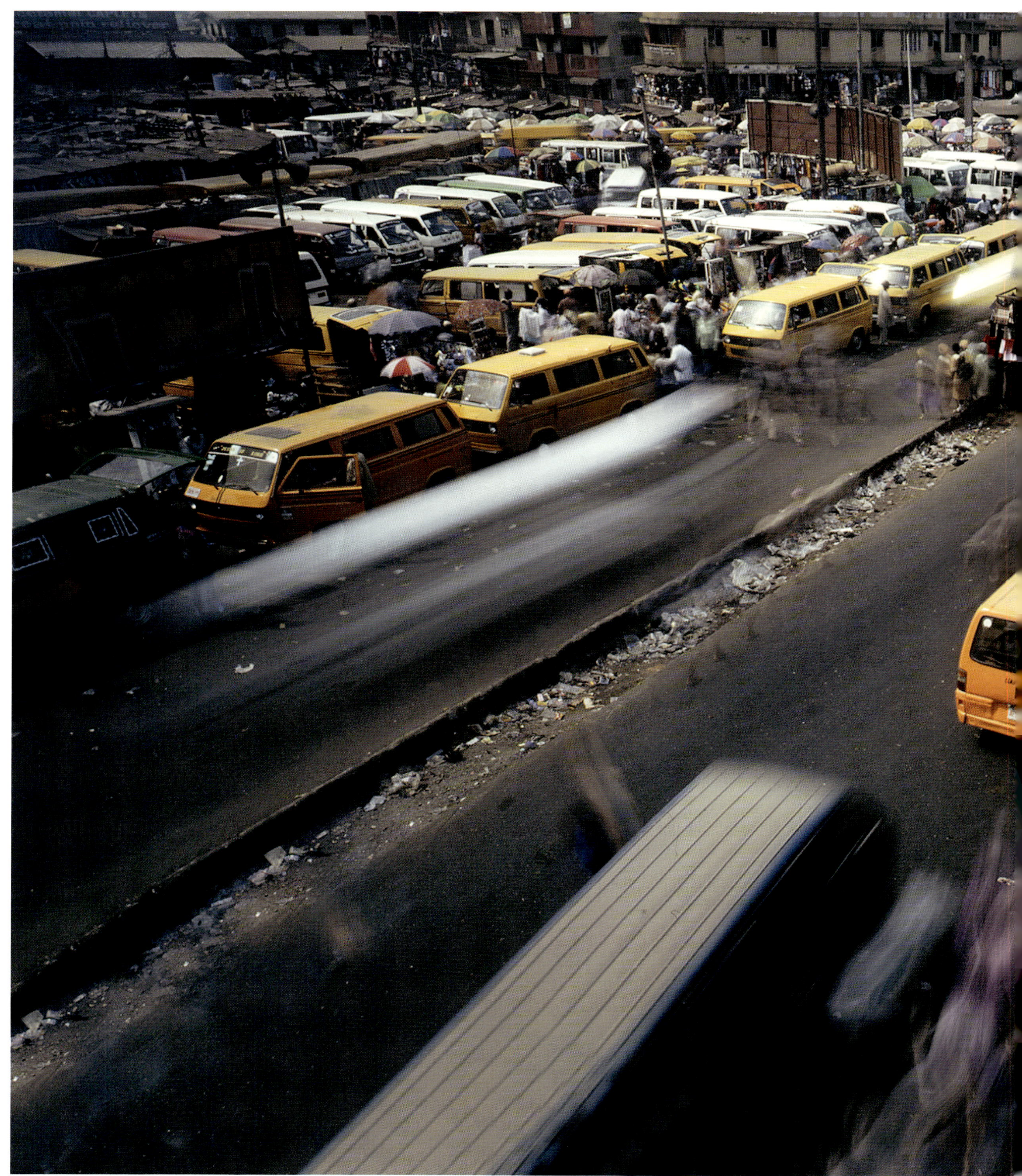

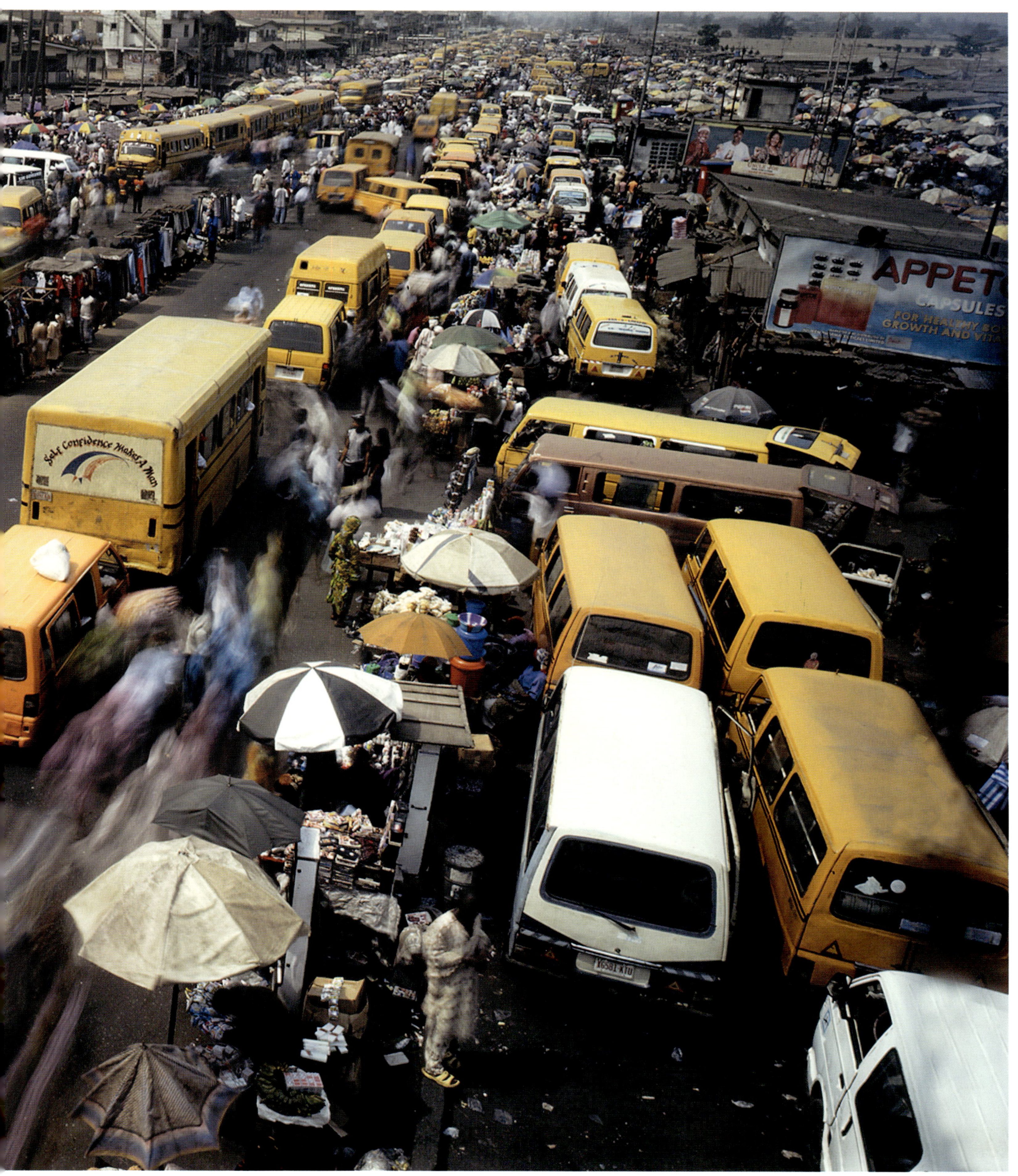

Oshodi 2, from the series "LAGOS UPTIGHT," 2001–05
Chromogenic print, dimensions variable.
Courtesy the artist

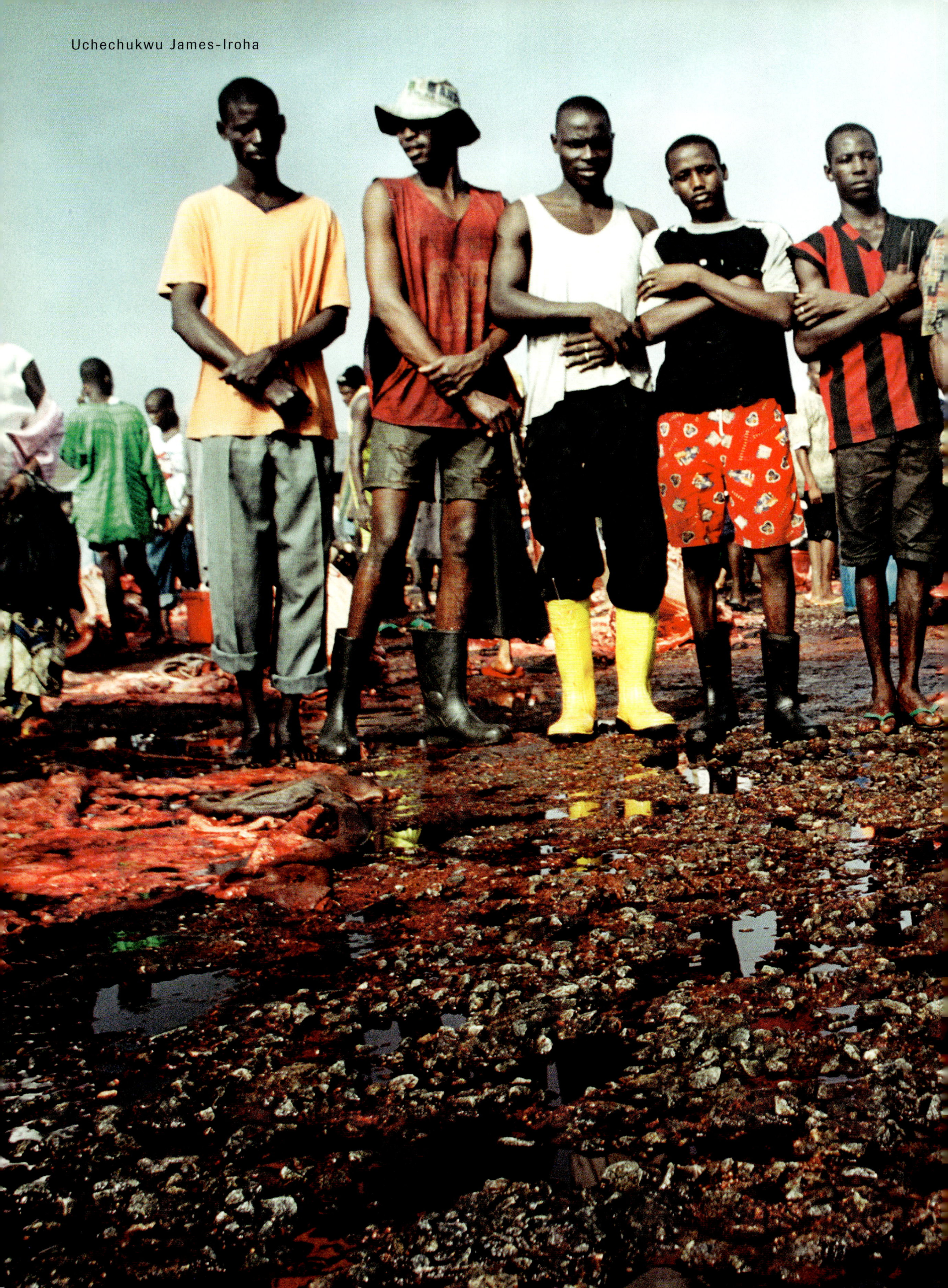

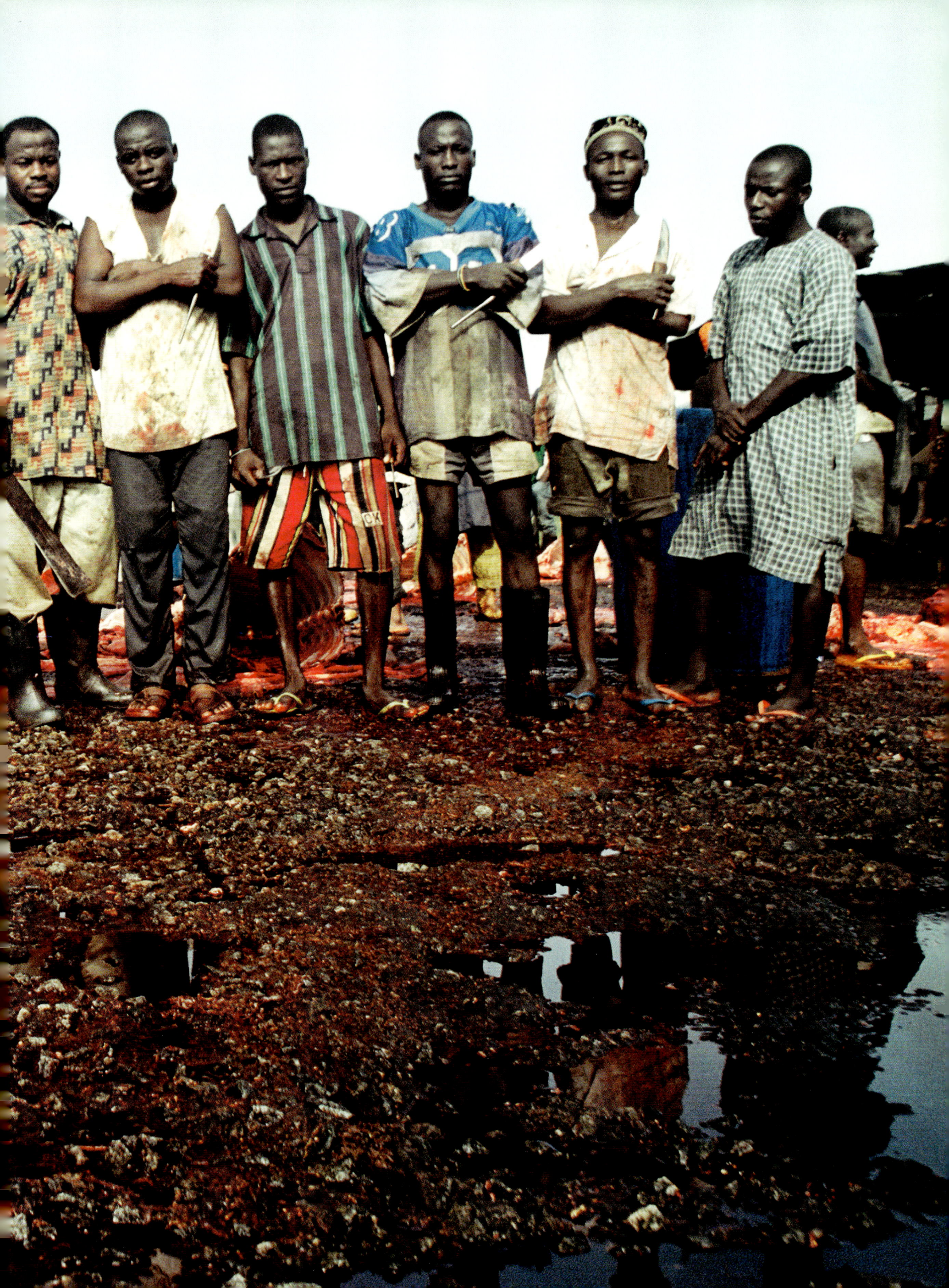

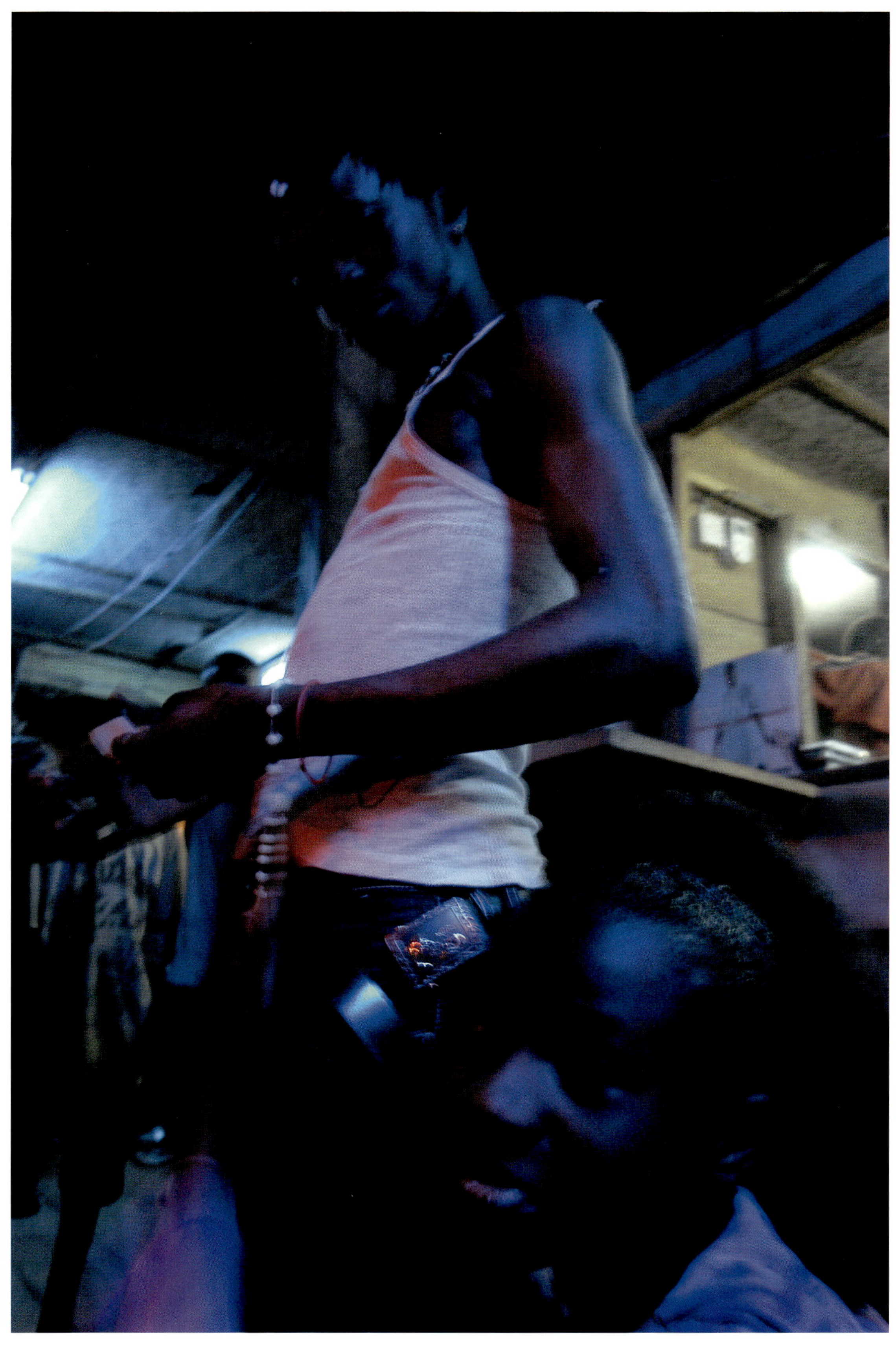

Previous spread:
Uchechukwa James-Iroha, *butchers, Port Harcourt*,
from the series "LAGOS UPTIGHT," 2001–05
Chromogenic print, dimensions variable
Courtesy the artist

oya, from the series "LAGOS UPTIGHT," 2001–05
Chromogenic print, dimensions variable
Courtesy the artist

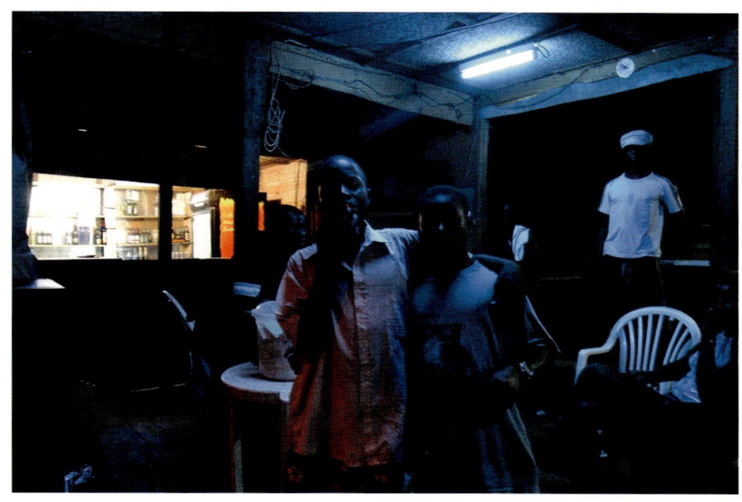

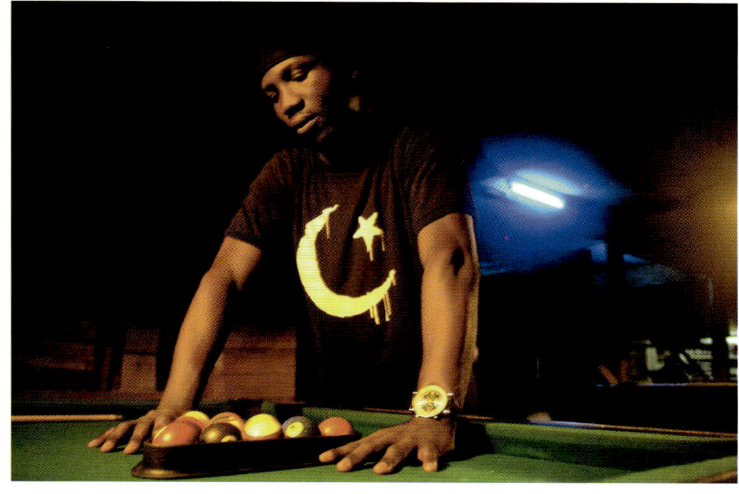

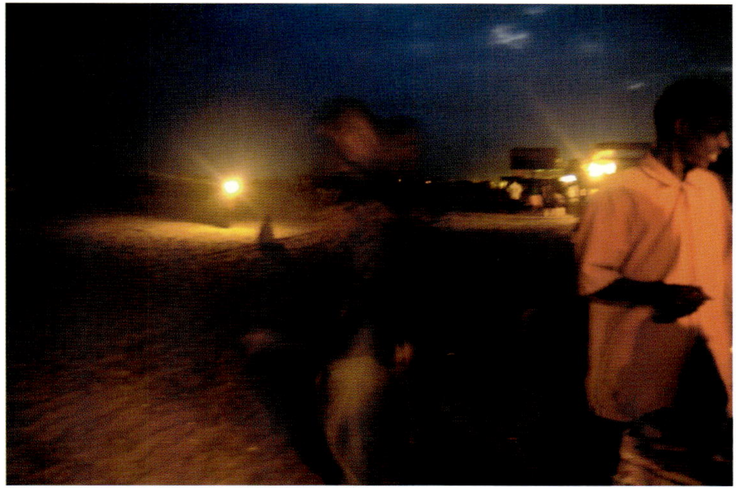

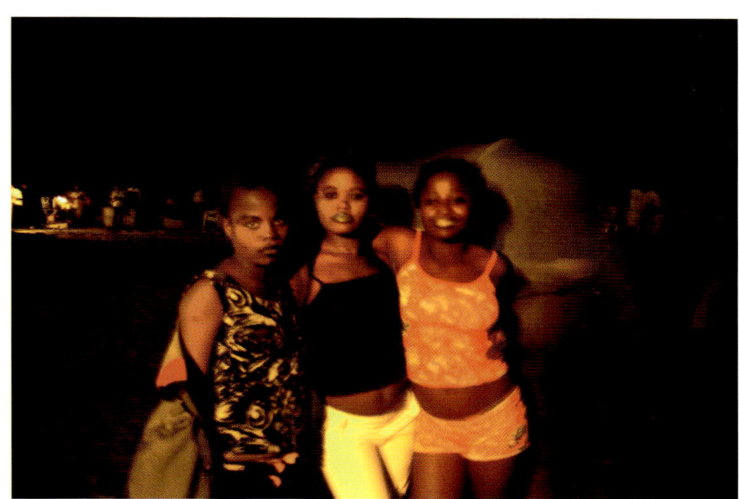

Top left:
varieties' kids 3, from the series "LAGOS UPTIGHT," 2001–05
Chromogenic print, dimensions variable
Courtesy the artist

Top right:
DJ Dizzy P, from the series "LAGOS UPTIGHT," 2001–05
Chromogenic print, dimensions variable
Courtesy the artist

Bottom left:
aboki, from the series "LAGOS UPTIGHT," 2001–05
Chromogenic print, dimensions variable
Courtesy the artist

Bottom right:
runs' girls, from the series "LAGOS UPTIGHT," 2001–05
Chromogenic print, dimensions variable
Courtesy the artist

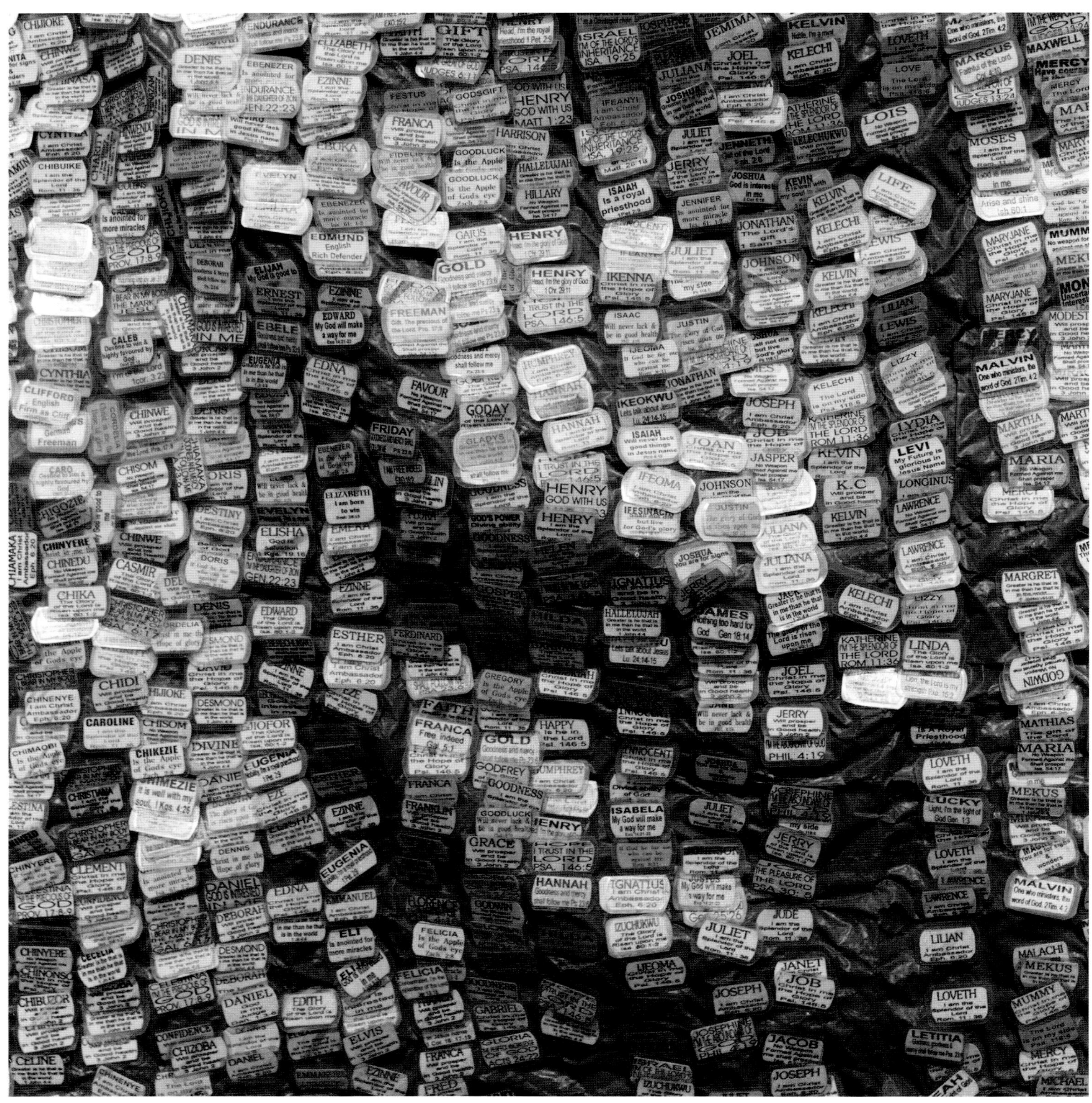

NAME-TAGS, from the series "LAGOS UPTIGHT," 2001–05
Chromogenic print, dimensions variable
Courtesy the artist

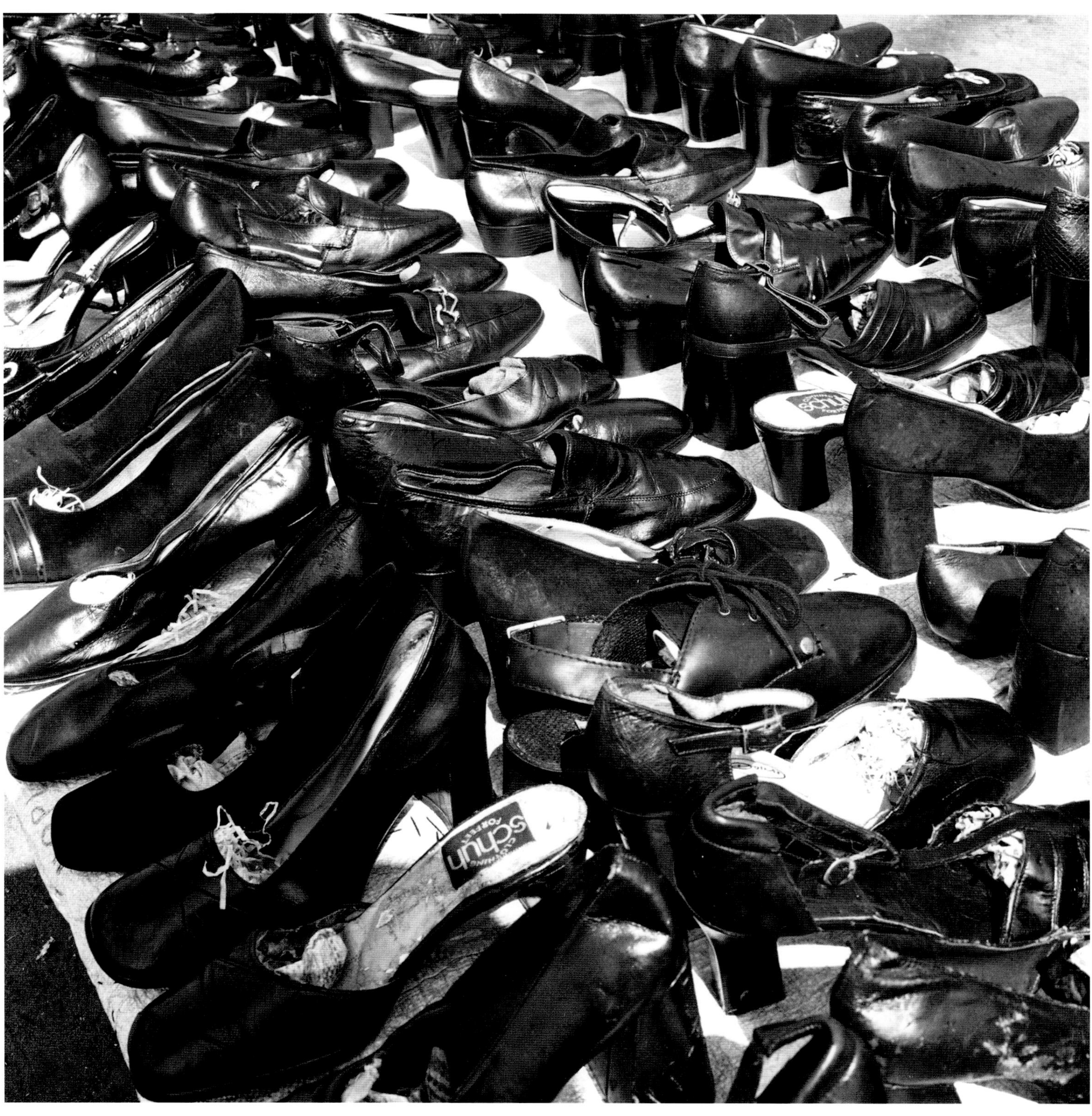

SHOES, from the series "LAGOS UPTIGHT," 2001–05
Chromogenic print, dimensions variable
Courtesy the artist

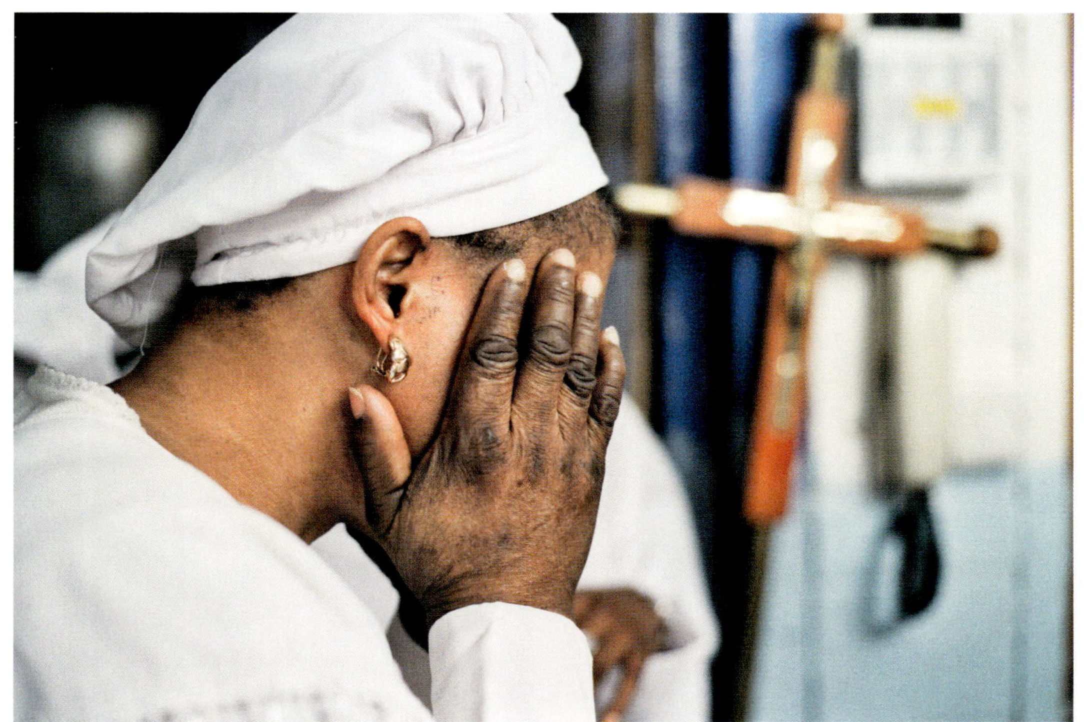

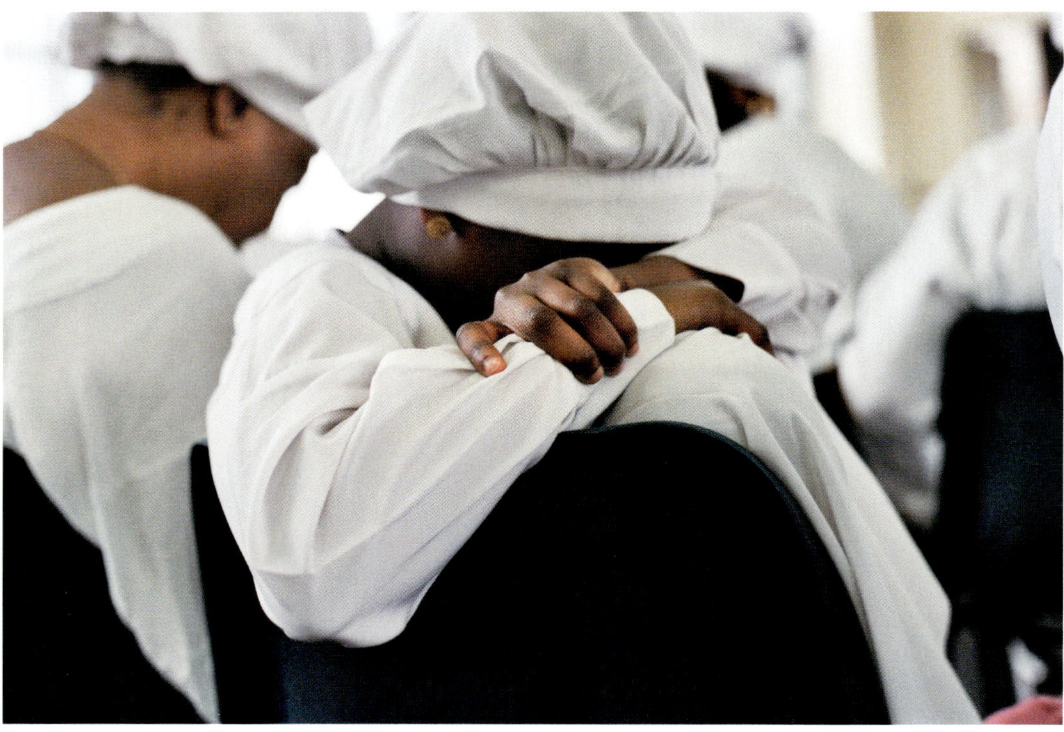

Untitled, from the series "Lagosians in London," 2001–05
Chromogenic print, dimensions variable
Courtesy the artist

Untitled, from the series "Lagosians in London," 2001–05
Chromogenic print, dimensions variable
Courtesy the artist

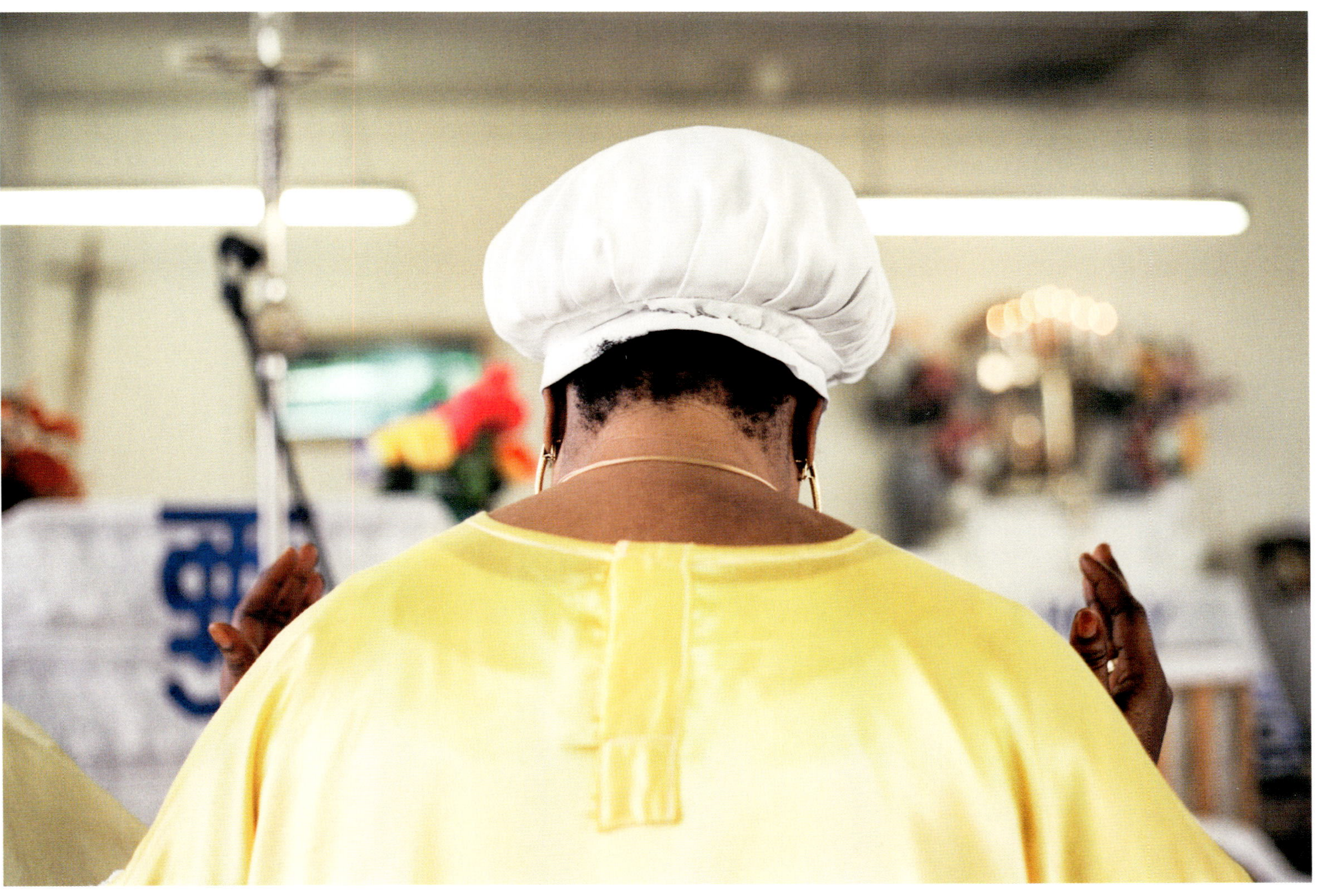

Untitled, from the series "Lagosians in London," 2001–05
Chromogenic print, dimensions variable
Courtesy the artist

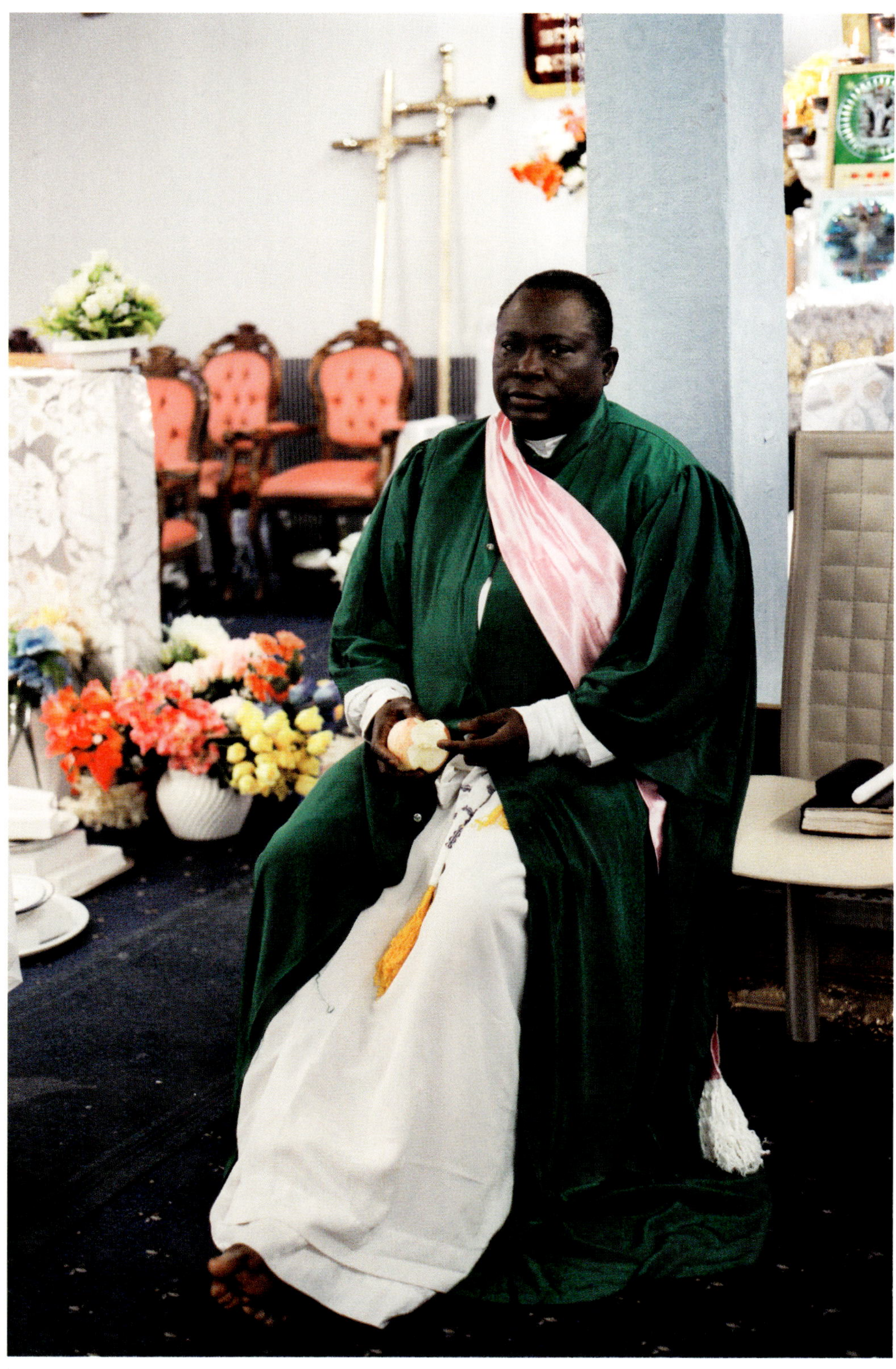

Untitled, from the series "Lagosians in London," 2001–05
Chromogenic print, dimensions variable
Courtesy the artist

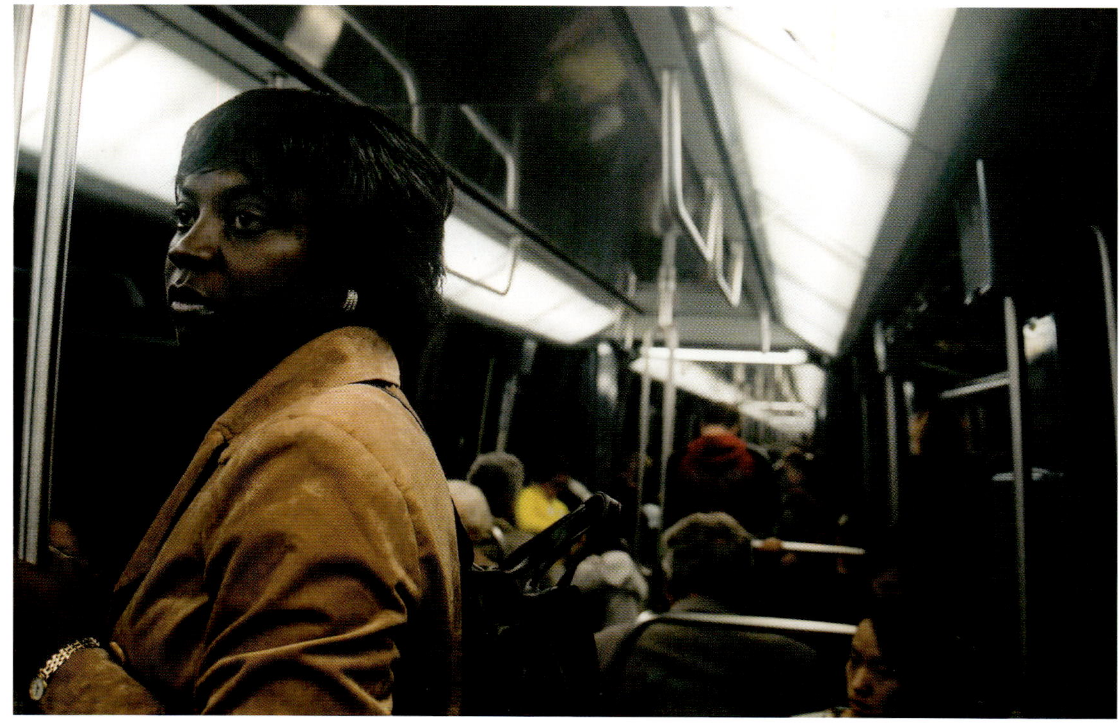

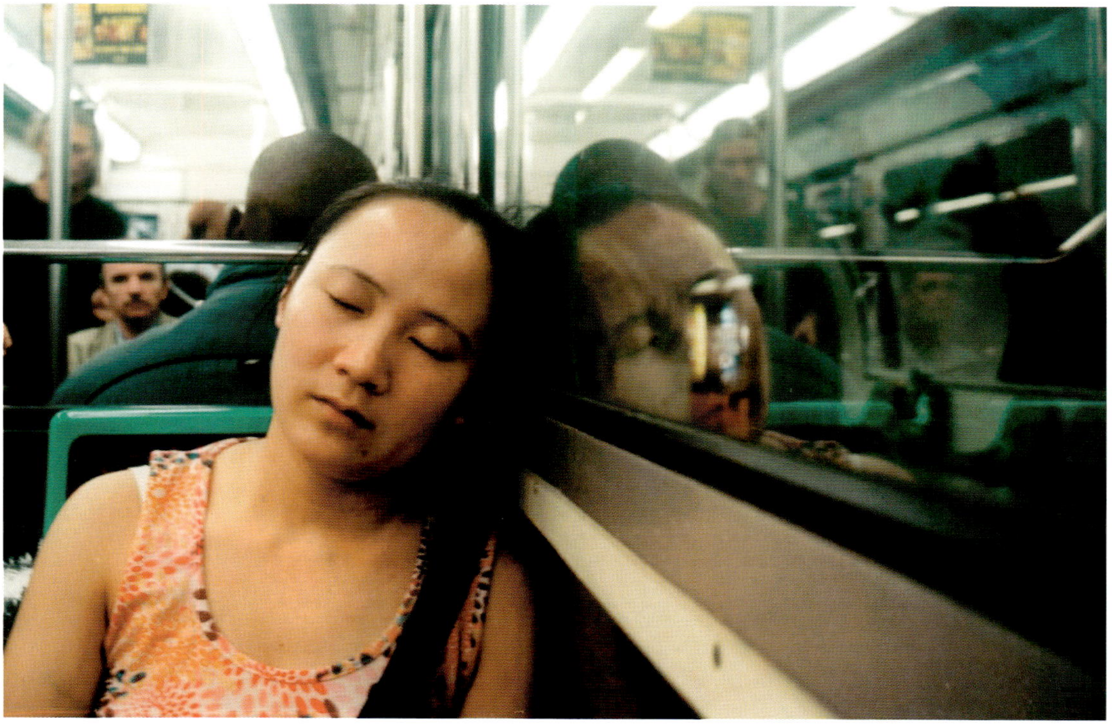

Black Woman, from the series "Paris Metro," 2001–05
Chromogenic print, dimensions variable
Courtesy the artist

Sleeping Woman, from the series "Paris Metro," 2001–05
Chromogenic print, dimensions variable
Courtesy the artist

After *In/sight*: Ten Years of Exhibiting Contemporary African Photography

The Guggenheim exhibition *In/sight: African Photographers 1940 to the Present*, curated by Clare Bell, Okwui Enwezor, Danielle Tilkin, and Octavio Zaya, broke new ground in 1996. Although there had been a marked intensification in the West of major exhibitions of contemporary African art in the wake of *Magiciens de la terre* (1989) at the Centre Pompidou in Paris,[1] none before *In/sight* placed the emphasis squarely on photography, on "the way Africans picture themselves."[2]

The photographs exhibited in *In/sight* demonstrated a burgeoning and self-conscious modernity as anticolonial liberation movements began to flower in the 1940s. This sensibility was exemplified in the portraiture of the great West African studio photographers: Seydou Keïta, who ran a prolific studio from 1948 to 1962, where the citizens of the dynamic city of Bamako would come to be photographed in their finest outfits and with various symbols of prosperity; Malick Sidibé, who photographed all ages of Malians engaged in outdoor leisure activities and in his Bamako studio; and Samuel Fosso, who in the 1970s embarked on his now famous self-portraiture project—casting himself in inventive guises, poses, and costumes after hours in his studio in Bangui, Central African Republic.

Although the emphasis in *In/sight* was perceived in the critical press to be on portraiture,[3] the other tent pole of mid-century African modernism revealed in the exhibition was the documentary impulse represented by a large section devoted to the photo essays of the magazine *Drum*, as well as the photography of David Goldblatt. Goldblatt's piercing series on everyday life in South Africa in the 1950s and '60s, and of Afrikaners in the 1970s, revealed the underlying subtexts of apartheid, following his professed interest in exposing not just the subject at hand but the "conditions of society."[4]

In/sight established a lineage of images and influences within twentieth-century African photography before moving on to how the contemporary artists of the 1980s and '90s had absorbed those influences in their quest to confront their current struggles and issues. Of particular note were the conceptual constructs of Rotimi Fani-Kayode's erotic male nudes, and the interpretive documentary/landscape photography of Santu Mofokeng. That the breadth and newness of the material was revelatory is evinced by the critical response to the show. Holland Cotter wrote in the *New York Times*: "*In/sight* … is an important venture into the terrain. And by sifting themes and raising ideas and remaining determinedly incomplete, it suggests an immense and exciting body of work waiting to be discovered."[5] And John Peffer wrote in *African Arts* that "*In/sight*, the first United States museum exhibit to look critically at the work of African-born photographers, was a valuable and important first step in a new direction."[6]

Enwezor sees crucial shifts taking place from the preponderance of studio and documentary photography shown in *In/sight* to the way photography is used at this moment by the artists in *Snap Judgments*. These shifts are happening both on the level of means—increased use of film, video, and digital media—and motives—photography is now used more as a "probing" tool than an "exposing" tool.[7] In Enwezor's words, an "analytical, postdocumentary photographic work" has emerged, with artists more cosmopolitan and self-aware of being part of the global contemporary art stage, whether they remain working in Africa or work from abroad. Contemporary African photography is also engaged in a broadened range of themes: urban and suburban sites of development, complexities of landscape, the personal and performative, representations of history, and the penetration of photography into everyday life.

The point of this essay is to show the growing momentum of these emphases as they solidified over the last ten years, particularly through the lens of exhibitions of contemporary African photography, both inside and outside the continent, at major museums and international venues. Dissecting such displays is crucial to any analysis of (art) historical shifts. Their central role was summarized by the art historian Salah Hassan, introducing the Third African Photography Festival in Bamako in 1998: "Why show African photography? The response is simple: *if you don't show, you don't exist!* Exhibitions are the very basis for the history of art."[8]

International Exhibitions

In 1998, the exhibition *L'Afrique par elle-même* [Africa: A Self-Portrait] was organized at La Maison Européenne in Paris. The impetus for the project came from the publication of a massive anthology of African photography by Revue Noire, the pioneering press founded in

1991 as a bilingual journal of contemporary African art. In critical notices, the exhibition has been positioned as both a response to and expansion of *In/sight*, extending the years of its overview back to turn-of-the-century portraiture and including more than 300 photographs.[9] It similarly emphasized Keïta, Sidibé,[10] and *Drum* magazine in its mid-century sections, but ended with Zwelethu Mthethwa's contemporary portrait photography. Mthethwa's "Images for Dignity" series (1997–99) from the townships of Cape Town were vividly colorful portraits of black men and women in their homes—shanty homes, but gorgeously decorated—assertively, even aggressively, facing the camera. Unlike *In/sight*, this exhibition traveled extensively in North and South America, as well as Africa, ending in Belgium in 2003.

Many of the recent international exhibitions with substantive sections of contemporary African photography also included historical components or were not devoted exclusively to the medium. *The Short Century: Independence and Liberation Movements in Africa, 1945–1994*, a multimedia show organized by Enwezor in 2001 for the Museum Villa Stuck in Munich,[11] included several *Snap Judgments* artists, as well as the modernist works of Keïta, Sidibé, and Fosso, a mass of documentary material, books, and ephemera.

One of the more striking contemporary pieces—which illustrates the expanded world view of the *Snap Judgments* generation—was produced by Oladélé Bamgboyé, addressing his own diasporic experience in the video *Homeward: Bound* (1995). A double-projection video juxtaposed scenes from Scotland, where Bamgboyé grew up, with a visit to his native Nigeria. As he explained, he aimed to "problematize" his own relationship with Africa vis-à-vis his upbringing in Europe, and challenge the one-sided images of Africa in Western media—"a tragic, phenomenological account of disasters and conflicts, man-made and natural"—which continually victimize the continent and its peoples. In effect, Bamgboyé articulated a position against Afro-pessimism: "It is my intention to destroy the antiquated views of Africa through my works, which offer images challenging those seen in the mass media, a strategy that I believe is necessary for the normalizing of African representation."[12] Moshekwa Langa's contribution to *The Short Century* (*Untitled*, 1996) also took a critical stance against outsiders looking in. His taped montages of maps, newspapers, and magazine layouts included an ad pitch to potential tourists, startling when taken out of context, touting a Kenyan village where humans and wild animals live side by side. Another destination claimed to re-create "original lifestyles" for the visitor.

One confronts the denial of this "touristic eye" in the work of the Senegalese photographer Boubacar Mandémory, who was featured in the 2001 exhibition *Flash Afrique: Photography from West Africa*, organized by the Kunsthalle Wien. The contemporary work—in this case by Mandémory and others—was again displayed alongside the black-and-white studio photography of the previous generation of Keïta and Sidibé. Mandémory's startling colors, oblique angles, and dynamic energy was all the more jarring as a result. This is street photography, but shooting from hip-level and foot-level; blurring the exposures, Mandémory simultaneously aggrandizes his subjects and blocks their individual identities. As explained in his catalogue interview, due to the spontaneity of his output, he does not consider it documentary—contradicting the catalogue's flap text, which describes the show within the previously discussed binary of African studio photography and documentary photography. Koyo Kouoh, writing in the catalogue, places Mandémory in the generation of African photographers tangibly coalescing in the mid-1990s, when "different forms of creative expression became perceptible."[13]

Fault Lines: Contemporary African Art and Shifting Landscapes, a key exhibition that attempted to redefine the terms of modernism and postmodernism in African art and included wide-ranging photographic work, was organized by the Institute of International Visual Arts (inIVA) in London for the 2003 Venice Biennale. In the catalogue preface, Salah Hassan recast the Western modernist strategies of rebellion against the past and artistic experimentation; in Africa, the higher stakes of modernity were the struggles for decolonization and liberation, leading to image-making that "transcended" dependence on the visual language of European modernism. In the work of younger artists, like Ugandan Zarina Bhimji's haunting architectural interiors (pages 157–159)—remnants of Idi Amin's reign of terror which led to her own family's expulsion, along with others of South Asian descent—or Salem Mekuria's video exploration of the layers of religious historicity in Ethiopia—similar to Theo Eshetu's—Hassan outlines a form of "post" modernism, but from the specific viewpoints of African diaspora artists living in Western cities.[14]

The most recent exhibition to feature a number of *Snap Judgments* artists is *Africa Remix*, which opened at the Museum Kunst Palast, Düsseldorf (July 24–November 7, 2004).[15] Like *Snap Judgments*, *Remix* is characterized by an almost complete break with previous generations, with the exception of Fosso's ever-evolving self-portraits. The exhibition was divided into themes: "City and Land," "Identity and History," and "Body and Soul." Simon Njami, the curator and one of the founders of Revue Noire, wrote the short introductory essays to each section, crediting the contemporaneity of themes to the new generation's urban and complex international backgrounds. Beginning in the 1980s, artists began defining their roles "within the more global framework of international contemporary creation": "An opposition thus appeared between a collective memory that sealed their sense of belonging ... and a personal memory where a jumbled combination of sexuality, politics, feminism, race and origins all confronted each other."[16] These qualities could be seen melding in the strong showing of women artists from various regions: Lara Baladi, whose video *Shish Kebab* (2004) combined her created images of Egyptian stereotypes with found media images; Yto Barrada, showing the points where the mythical Moroccan landscape meets the detritus of development in her "A Life Full of Holes: The Strait Project" series (1998– 2004) (pages 96–105); Tracey Rose's poetic and raw full-frontal female nudes in the video *TKO* (2000); and Otobong Nkanga's "Stripped Bare" series (2003), of vacated colonial structures planted in the Nigerian landscape.

South Africa

In the last ten years, there has also been an intensification of photographic exhibition practices within Africa, with particularly robust activity in South Africa and Mali. A generational shift can be further discerned in these exhibitions. In South Africa, this is typified by an acute self-awareness of moving away from the country's straight documentary tradition. Since the official ending of apartheid in 1994, the South African National Gallery (SANG) has undertaken numerous projects examining the liberation's effects on the artistic community, including two key exhibitions devoted exclusively to African photography: *PhotoSynthesis: Contemporary South African Photography* in 1997, and *Lines of Sight: Perspectives on South African Photography* in 1999, as well as the ambitious *Decade of Democracy* in 2004, which included several of the *Snap Judgments* artists along with artists working in all media.

In the introduction to the *PhotoSynthesis* catalogue, Kathleen Grundlingh stressed the need for a reevaluation of photography's place in South African culture. The previously dominant genre of social documentary, a critical element of the struggle against apartheid, had given way to highly individualistic artistic exploration: "freed from their collective political purpose, photographers have had to redefine their individual photographic identities and aims."[17] Grundlingh outlines her view of the subjects that have since come to the fore, which dovetail with Enwezor's concept of "post-documentary analytical": issues of gender, African identity, conceptual works which often conceal their meaning, and the everyday experience of global culture. Jo Ractliffe's mixed-media piece called *Bridges for Baldessari* (1996) typified this shift, a montage of Hollywood-esque film stills of glamorous figures, bisected by industrialized urban sites and close-ups of violent tableaux. Portraits were included by Guy Tillim and Mthethwa, Tillim's of a shopkeeper in Taleni, and Mthethwa's of two women in a kitchen from the "Images for Dignity" series. Both may seem at first strictly documentary, but they are in fact highly stylized juxtapositions of strikingly clad individuals with stacked and arranged commodity goods that show them functioning within their own particular economic systems.

Lines of Sight, which opened at SANG in 1999 and traveled to the Bamako Biennial in 2001, was constructed as an historical overview of South African photography, including essays on colonialism, early twentieth-century Pictorialism, and mid-century Cape Town photo albums. Mthethwa curated the contemporary photography section, "Divergence." His statement emphasized the new fluidity of the photographic medium in post-apartheid South Africa: how photojournalists were now experimenting with art, and how, in turn, trained artists were experimenting with photography. As subjects, race and gender held particular importance for him: "I wanted to compare different concepts and approaches, as well as highlight the play between opposites and the many levels and tones that occur between polarities."[18] He included a series of black-and-white photographs from a family archive, discovered by Hentie van der Merwe, of a special type of karakul sheep coveted for its fur. Van der Merwe's grandfather, who raised the sheep, photographed each with a number before their slaughter, and the artist saw eerie similarities between this and photographic classification systems he had discovered of naked World War II soldiers.[19] This was preceded by Jodi Bieber's saturated color prints of different race groups, each using brightly colored compositions to highlight another type of classification system, that of bourgeois symbols of prosperity: black children at a ballroom dance class in vivid green dresses, white children plainly clothed, driving in bright red trucks.

The 2004 exhibition at SANG, *Decade of Democracy*, was presented by the organizers as a summation of artistic activity in South Africa since the end of apartheid. The editor of the catalogue, Emma Bedford, struck an optimistic tone in the introductory essay; that since the first democratic elections, despite the persistence of poverty, enormous strides had been made and were to be celebrated—and that South African artists had risen to the challenges of these newfound freedoms. This sense of liberation and self-exploration manifested itself in more daring explorations of desire, sexual orientation, and race, as in van der Merwe's photo-lithographs from the "Insatiable" series (1995), showing soft-focus black-and-white photographs of beautiful men in gauzy white shirts with silver pins stuck in them. It is a celebration of the male body but with an underlying subtext of sexual violence. Tracey Rose's loaded photograph *The Kiss* (2001), featuring herself made up as a white woman, naked and embraced by a black man (her American art dealer, Christian Haye), on a marble pedestal, managed to address race, sex, miscegenation, and artmaking in one simple gesture of a couple hugging. This was the cover piece of the catalogue, and the concluding sentence of Ashraf Jamal's essay devoted to *The Kiss* demonstrates how the image encompassed the goals of the exhibition and the newfound self-consciousness of artmaking in South Africa: "That the work possesses a populist appeal, and, at the same time, is able to assist us in rethinking the pathology of our history, makes it all the more significant and durable."[20]

Mali

Since 1994, the Bamako biennials, called *Rencontres* [Encounters], have succeeded in bringing large crowds to a central location to see pan-African photography. The first biennial was brought about by the initiative of French photographers Françoise Huguier and Bernard Descamps after Huguier became familiar with the work of Keïta and Sidibé, both of whom were featured prominently in the exhibition. The second biennial, in 1996, expanded into the realm of photo-reportage. The content of these inaugural exhibitions was described in gallerist Amadou Chab Touré's summation of the first four biennials in very similar terms as the critical reception of *In/sight*, as needing to show the world a previously unknown history: "the first two festivals emphasized the rich visual heritage of early 20th century photographers, but the third one stressed the necessity of opening up to new projects. ... This fourth festival was forced to ... continue the task of opening itself up to contemporary photographic creation and confirm its continental and international dimension."[21]

The third festival (1998), a turning point for the biennial, directly referenced issues raised by *In/sight*. Salah Hassan's introductory catalogue essay ("Toward a Renaissance") opened with a question posed by Enwezor and Zaya two years before: "So how do we address questions of representation, self-imaging, and artistic freedom when those initiatives are counteracted by stronger economic imperativeness, and when the contingencies of social and epistemological control are made to bend to the influence of power and access?"[22] He saw one response to this question in the Bamako biennials themselves, whose purpose is to open up the discourse of defining African photography through the display of work as well as the accompanying seminars and workshops. In addition to the more theoretically searching tone of the organizers' questions, selections were extended for the first time to North Africa, jettisoning the common idea that African photography denoted sub-Saharan production. One of the main exhibitions that year featured Omar D.'s Algerian scenes and landscapes. There was again a large showing of South African documentary, but with a pointed acknowledgment of how photographers' visions had shifted from a specific impulse to enact social change to more personal and introspective approaches.[23]

The fourth *Rencontres* had an elegiac title, *Memories of a Millennium*. It included borrowed exhibitions like the earlier discussed *Lines of Sight*, which traced the full history of photography in Africa back one hundred years. Artistic director Simon Njami's introductory catalogue essay was quite generalist in tone, discussing the fundamental problematic of representation in the history of photography's role in Africa. But he framed the historical material shown in the fourth festival very much within contemporary theoretical language and determined to set it firmly upon the international art world stage: "if an African photography does exist, it is, like the African languages, multiple, ambivalent and contradictory. This is what this fourth edition of the Bamako Meetings will strive to show."[24] In a cover letter to the packet of press material, Njami asserted: "the time has come to project the *Encounters* into the future and strengthen the foundations of both continental and international recognition."[25]

This theme continued into the fifth *Rencontres, Sacred and Profane Rites*, held in 2003 and again directed by Njami. The exhibition included Hala Elkoussy's scenes of urban alienation in cafés and bus stops from her series "(re)construction" (2003); Maha Maamoun's "Cairoscapes" (2001–03), panoramic city shots with parts of women's floral dresses, decontextualized and denying the touristic eye; and Mohamed Camara's conceptual "Chambres Maliennes" (2001–02) series, figures photographed indoors, in impoverished sections of Bamako, but with their faces averted.

Ten years ago, *In/sight* introduced Keïta, Fosso, Sidibé, Goldblatt, and other African modernists to an expanded audience, and they have continued to gain in popularity among museum goers and collectors. For several years after, many exhibitions relied on their work as a crux and a comparative to an emerging generation of artists, a testament to their canonization. More recent shows, however, have examined contemporary African photography without necessarily foregrounding those photographers as a historical support system. Contemporary African artists and photographers have created new dynamics of representation, engaging issues of race, gender, place, but also offering images of urbanity, energy, and variety which counter the bane and monotony of Afro-pessimism. And, to return to Hassan's assertion of the pivotal role of exhibitions in this process, the public audience has seen this progression through them, "the very basis of art history."

Vanessa Rocco
Assistant Curator

Noted Exhibitions

1996 *In/sight: African Photographers, 1940 to the Present*, Guggenheim Museum, New York

1997 *PhotoSynthesis: Contemporary South African Photography*, South African National Gallery, Cape Town

1998 *L'Afrique par elle-même* [Africa: A Self-Portrait], La Maison Européenne de la Photographie, Paris

1999, 2001 *Lines of Sight: Perspectives on South African Photography*, South African National Gallery, Cape Town (July 17–October 31, 1999); Centre de Musée National du Mali, Bamako (October 15–November 30, 2001)

2000 *Translation/Seduction/Displacement: Post-Conceptual and Photographic Work by Artists from South Africa*, White Box Gallery, New York (February 3–April 1); Institute of Contemporary Art at Maine College of Art, Portland (August 17–October 26)

2001 *Flash Afrique: Photography from West Africa*, Kunsthalle, Vienna

2001–02 *The Short Century: Independence and Liberation Movements in Africa, 1945–1994*, Museum Villa Stuck , Munich (February 15–April 22, 2000); Martin-Gropius-Bau, Berlin (May 18–July 22, 2001); Museum of Contemporary Art, Chicago (September 8–December 30, 2001); P.S.1, New York (February 10–May 5, 2002)

2003 *Fault Lines: Contemporary African Art and Shifting Landscapes*, 50th Venice Biennale

2004 *Decade of Democracy: South African Art 1994–2004*, South African National Gallery, Cape Town

2004–06 *Africa Remix: Contemporary Art of a Continent*, Museum Kunst Palast, Düsseldorf (July 24–November 7, 2004); Hayward Gallery, London (February 10–April 17, 2005); Centre Georges Pompidou, Paris (May 24–August 15, 2005); Mori Art Museum, Tokyo (May–August 2006)

Bamako Biennials 1–5

1994 I Rencontres Africaines de la Photographie

1996 IIes Rencontres Africaines de la Photographie

1998 *Ja Taa, Prendre l'image*, IIIes Rencontres Africaines de la Photographie

2001 *Mémoires intimes d'un nouveau millénaire*, IVes Rencontres Africaines de la Photographie

2003 *Rités sacres, rites profanes*, V[es] Rencontres Africaines de la Photographie

2005 *Un autre monde*, VIes Rencontres Africaines de la Photographie

Notes

1 For a summary of how the "floodgates" of contemporary African art exhibitions opened in the 1990s, see Thomas McEvilley, "How Contemporary African Art Comes to the West," in *African Art Now: Masterpieces from the Jean Pigozzi Collection* (London: Merrell Publishers, 2005), p. 35.
2 Carol Squiers, "Seeing Africa Through African Eyes," *New York Times*, May 26, 1996.
3 "Yet over and over, portraiture—the effort to shape and fix an identity in a shifting world—is the theme this show revolves around." Holland Cotter, "Mostly African Scenes, All by Africans," *New York Times*, July 5, 1996.
4 Okwui Enwezor, *Documenta XI: Short Guide* (Osfildern-Ruit: Hatje Cantz, 2002), p. 92.
5 Cotter, "Mostly African Scenes."
6 John Peffer-Engels, review in *African Arts* 30, no. 1 (Winter 1997), p. 73.
7 One of the *In/sight* photographers, Santu Mofokeng, submitted an artist statement to the catalogue which in effect points to the nascent shift that is more fully realized by the artists in *Snap Judgments*: "I had a rationale for documenting the lives of black people in the South Africa of yore, but, now that things have changed, it has become more difficult to legitimize my role as a documentary photographer in the traditional sense. … I see my role becoming one of questioning rather than documenting. The projects I have undertaken recently are about the politics of representation." Quoted in Clare Bell et al., *In/sight: African Photographers, 1940 to the Present* (New York: Guggenheim Museum, 1996), p. 22.
8 "Pourquoi exposer la photographie africaine? La réponse est simple: *Si tu n'exposes pas, tu n'existe pas!* Les expositions sont á la base même de l'histoire de l'art." Salah Hassan, "Vers un renaissance," *Ja Taa, Prendre l'image*, IIIes Rencontres Africaines de la Photographie (Bamako, 1998), p. 9. He goes on to say that exhibitions play an essential role in the diffusion of art objects and in the displacing of private domains into public: "Elles jouent un rôle primordial dans la diffusion de l'objet d'art et dans son déplacement du domaine privé au domaine public."
9 *Africa Remix* (Paris: Centre Pompidou, 2005), p. 244, which describes the Revue Noire team as organizing the project "after" *In/sight*, and that it was "more ambitious."
10 The years immediately after *In/sight* were a fertile time for Keïta/Sidibé scholarship. In 1997 and 1998, art historian André Magnin published substantive monographs on both photographers (see the bibliography). He noted in the text devoted to Keïta that he discovered the photographer when his work was shown, uncredited, in the exhibition *Africa Explores*, organized by Susan Vogel at the Museum for African Art in New York in 1991.
11 It traveled to the Martin-Gropius-Bau, Berlin; Museum of Contemporary Art, Chicago; and P.S.1, New York.
12 "Oladélé Ajiboyé Bamgboyé," in *Documenta X: Short Guide* (Berlin: Cantz, 1997), p. 28.
13 Koyo Kouoh, "Frozen Mobility: A Photographer in Dialogue with His Environment," in *iFlash Afrique! Photography from West Africa*, edited by Thomas Miessgang and Barbara Schröder (Vienna: Kunstalle Wien, 2001), p. 37.
14 Salah Hassan, "Preface," in *Fault Lines: Contemporary African Art and Shifting Landscapes*, edited by Gilane Tawadros and Sarah Campbell (London: Institute of International Visual Arts, 2003).
15 It travels through the summer of 2006 to the Hayward Gallery, London; the Centre Pompidou, Paris; and the Mori Art Museum, Tokyo.
16 Simon Njami, *Africa Remix: Contemporary Art of a Continent* (Ostfildern-Ruit: Hatje Cantz; London: Hayward Gallery, 2005), p. 55.
17 Kathleen Grundlingh, *PhotoSynthesis: Contemporary South African Photography* (Cape Town: South African National Gallery, 1997), p. 6.
18 "… my vision was to reveal different aspects of practice and presentation in contemporary South African photography." Zwelethu Mthethwa, "Divergence," in *Lines of Sight* (Cape Town: South African National Gallery, 2001), p. 98. The catalogue was published on the occasion of the Bamako showing.
19 Correspondence with artist, December 13, 2005. The archive of naked soldiers was shown in the exhibition *Translation/Seduction/Displacement: Post-Conceptual and Photographic Work by Artists from South Africa*, organized by Lauri Firstenburg and John Peffer for the Institute of Contemporary Art at Maine College of Art, Portland, 2000.
20 Ashraf Jamal, "The Bearable Lightness of Tracey Rose's The Kiss," in *Decade of Democracy: South African Art 1994–2004*, edited by Emma Bedford (Cape Town: Double Storey Books; Iziko Museums of Cape Town, 2004), p. 108.
21 Amadou Chab Touré, "Towards Understanding and Being Understood," in *Mémoires intimes d'un nouveau millénaire: IVes Rencontres de la Photographie Africaine, Bamako 2001* (Paris: Éditions Éric Koehler, 2001), pp. 14–15.
22 Hassan, "Vers une renaissance," p. 8.
23 "The developments that the country has undergone in recent years have had a profound effect on the way South African photographers represent reality. Physical, political and psychological changes have led committed and concerned photographers toward a more personal, more introspective approach to photography." *Ja Taa, Prendre l'image*, IIIes Rencontres Africaines de la Photographie (Bamako, 1998), unpag.
24 Simon Njami, "Chronicles of a Millennium," in *Mémoires intimes*, p. 13.
25 Simon Njami, "IVth African Photography Encounters in Bamako," letter, 2001. He also touted the new bilingual (French/English) catalogue. The North African emphasis continued with a national exhibition of Moroccan photographers that included Ali Chraïbi, Yto Barrada, and Lamia Naji.

Artist Biographies

Doa Aly

Born in Cairo, 1976
Lives and works in Cairo

Doa Aly explores the physicality of bodies and the systems that regulate those bodies in public space. In her installation *48 Ballet Classes*, she documents, through photography and video, lessons she took over several months with prima ballerina Sonia Sarkis. Aly had no previous training in the strenuous discipline, so the work depicts the journey of her own untutored, "common" body toward an unobtainable goal: the "skilled" body of the ballerina, which derives from training that begins before the age of nine. Aly's work layers frustration on frustration as she contends with bodily restrictions and the teacher's disappointment at her lack of progress. There is also the viewer's potential irritation with a training document that reaches no climax and finds no resolution. Aly's inclusion of both photographs and video in the installation allows for the scrutiny of isolated moments in time and simultaneously provides a continuous sequence that alludes to the essentially transitory nature of the body. Combined here, these incompatible forms of temporal experience—the frozen versus the continuous—introduce an element of formal irresolution that mirrors the body's slippage between its current and potential existence. It is tempting to relate Aly's analysis of the means of inculcating disciplinary regimes into the body to her status as a female artist in an Islamic society. On the other hand, her work consciously participates in an artistic dialogue that extends beyond parochial boundaries, allowing it to be situated in a context that is both international and multicultural. KM

Education
2001 BFA, Fine Arts Academy, Cairo

Solo Exhibitions
2004 *Grey Matter*, Townhouse Gallery, Cairo
2003 *Puppet Fashion Show*, Townhouse Gallery, Cairo
2002 *Pixels Series*, Mashrabia Gallery, Cairo

Group Exhibitions
2003 *Body*, Falaky Gallery, American University in Cairo
2001 Al Nitaq Festival of Contemporary Art, Cairo
1999 Al Nitaq Festival of Contemporary Art, Cairo

Awards and Residencies
2005 IAAB: International Exchange and Studio Program, Basel
2004 A Single Country Project: Arts Exchange Program, United States
2003 Residency, Open Studio Project, Townhouse Gallery, Cairo

Lara Baladi

Born in Beirut, 1969
Lives and works in Cairo

Lara Baladi applies the aesthetic strategies of collage and montage across the different media of photography, video, and installation. Her work highlights the absurdities, quirks, and contradictions of Egyptian modernity; her aim is to address stereotypes of women and Egyptians that are visible in popular culture, which she does with a humorous criticality. In her billboard-sized collages, a range of images from various media, such as cartoons, magazines, and advertisements, are translated into small photos with similarly colored backgrounds, and pieced together into a regular mosaic design, or sometimes a picture. She uses a wide variety of feminine imagery, from dolls to madonnas, video-game heroines to mermaids, pin-up goddesses, and comic girls. *Oum el Dounia* ("The Mother of the World"—a popular term for Egypt) shows a beach that doubles as desert and a sky/ocean populated with Egyptian caricatures, including a composite of the hookah-smoking caterpillar from *Alice in Wonderland*. *Al Fanous el Sehry* ("The Magic Lantern") takes early photographic motion studies or film strips as a point of departure, cynically showing X-ray babies growing into women, only to toss out more babies in an endless cycle. The reproductive capacity of the medium is conflated with female reproduction in this sardonic take on the inescapable facts of life and on art-making in the age of mechanical reproduction. AM

Education
1990 BA, Business Administration, Richmond University, London

Solo Exhibitions
2004 *Kai'ro*, Bildmuseet, Umeå, Sweden; Porin Taidemuseo, Pori, Finland; Nikolaj Contemporary Art Center, Copenhagen
2002 *Al Fanous al Sehry*, Townhouse Gallery, Cairo
2001 *Sandouk El Dounia*, El Nitaq Festival, Cairo; Ashkal Alwan, Beirut

Group Exhibitions
2005 *On Difference #1: Local Contexts, Hybrid Spaces*, Württembergischer Kunstverein Stuttgart
Water, Water Everywhere…, Scottsdale Museum of Contemporary Art, Arizona
2004 *Africa Remix: Contemporary Art of a Continent*, Museum Kunst Palast, Düsseldorf; Hayward Gallery, London; Centre Georges Pompidou, Paris; Mori Art Museum, Tokyo
2003 *Body Con*, Wanakio Festival, Okinawa; Uplink, Tokyo
DisORIENTation: Contemporary Arab Artists from the Middle East, Haus der Kulturen der Welt, Berlin
Rites sacrés, rites profanes, 5th Rencontres Africaines de la Photographie, Bamako, Mali
1998 *La Saison Photographique Africaine*, Institut du Monde Arabe, Paris; Haus der Kulturen der Welt, Berlin

Residencies and Awards
2002–03 Japan Foundation Fellowship

Bibliography
• *Larabesque Aroussa Baladi*. Madrid: Factum-Arte, 2002.

Oladélé Ajiboyé Bamgboyé

Born in Odo-Eku, Nigeria, 1963
Lives and works in London

Trained as an engineer (his thesis involved the design of a futuristic food-manufacturing plant), Oladélé Bamgboyé has long been concerned with the manner in which new technologies are both redefining and supplanting the sphere of culture. In his various *Unmasking* projects, he uses computers and digital imaging to conduct research into the nature of the digital archive, framing a critical response to its widespread adoption by museums and investigating the literal and virtual movements of artifacts around the globe. In *Unmasking, Part II* (1999), for example, archaeologically unclassifiable objects from the Egyptian collection of the San Antonio Museum of Art in Texas are shown on computer monitors far from their physical location, highlighting the tensions at play between the "original" and its copies. Nearby, videos showing collections of art in the context of museums lay bare the institutional imperatives that maintain the hierarchy of original over copy, and a 3-D object scanner and attached plotter allow Bamgboyé's audience to participate directly in the economy of artifacts by scanning and re-creating their own personal relics. In much of his other work, Bamgboyé pursues the problem of diaspora as both identity and form. In "Arise" (1991/97) and "Celebrate" (1994), he creates works of self-portraiture that might be productively related to long-standing African traditions of studio portraiture. In "Arise," Bamgboyé's body merges confusingly with a visually complex backdrop that calls to mind those used by Seydou Keïta, an exemplar of African photography for European and North American audiences. While Bamgboyé's work considers questions of identity endemic to certain strains of Western art production, it also unsettles the placement of African portrait photography in the canon of Western photographic history. KM

Education

1996–98	MA, Media Fine Art Theory and Practice, Slade College of Fine Art, London
1981–85	BSc, Chemical and Process Engineering, Strathclyde University, Glasgow
1976–81	Woodside Secondary School, Glasgow

Solo Exhibitions

2002	*Oladélé Ajiboyé Bamgboyé*, Thomas Erben Gallery, New York
2000	*Oladélé Ajiboyé Bamgboyé*, Project Gallery, Center for Contemporary Art, Kitakyushu, Japan
	Strangers & Paradise: Oladélé Ajiboyé Bamgboyé: Photo-Videoworks 1991–2000, Witte de With Center for Contemporary Art, Rotterdam
	Oladélé Ajiboyé Bamgboyé: The Unmasking, Part II, Thomas Erben Gallery, New York
	Oladélé Ajiboyé Bamgboyé: Videoworks, Helsinki City Art Museum
1999	*Oladélé Ajiboyé Bamgboyé*, Artpace, San Antonio, Texas

Group Exhibitions

2003	*Looking Both Ways: Art of the Contemporary African Diaspora*, Museum for African Art, New York; Peabody Essex Museum, Salem, Massachusetts; Cranbrook Art Museum, Bloomfield Hills, Michigan; Fundação Calouste Gulbenkian, Lisbon; Edinburgh City Art Centre, Scotland
2001	*The Short Century: Independence and Liberation Movements in Africa, 1945–1994*, Museum Villa Stuck, Munich; Martin-Gropius-Bau, Berlin; Museum of Contemporary Art, Chicago; P.S.1, New York
	Yokohama 2001: International Triennale of Contemporary Art, Pacifico, Yokohama
2000	*New British Art 2000: Intelligence*, Tate Britain, London
	The Vincent van Gogh Bi-Annual Award for Contemporary Art in Europe Exhibition, Bonnefantenmuseum, Maastricht, Netherlands
1997	documenta 10, Kassel, Germany
1996	*In/sight: African Photographers, 1940 to the Present*, Guggenheim Museum, New York

Awards and Residencies

2000–01	Artist-in-Residence, Witte de With Center for Contemporary Art, Rotterdam
2000	Resident Research Professor, Center for Contemporary Art, Kitakyushu, Japan
	Nominated for the Vincent van Gogh Bi-Annual Award for Contemporary Art in Europe
1999	New Works 99:3, Studio Residency Program, Artpace, San Antonio, Texas

Bibliography

• Byvanck, Valentin, and Oladélé Ajiboyé Bamgboyé. "Oladélé A. Bamgboyé." In *Looking Both Ways: Art of the Contemporary African Diaspora*, edited by Laurie Ann Farrell, pp. 62–73. New York: Museum for African Art, 2003.

• Obrist, Hans-Ulrich, and Oladélé Ajiboyé Bamgboyé. "Interview with Oladélé Ajiboyé Bamgboyé." *Nka: Journal of Contemporary African Art*, no. 13–14 (Spring–Summer 2001), pp. 86–91.

• *Oladélé Ajiboyé Bamgboyé: Writings on Technology and Culture*. Rotterdam: Witte de With Center for Contemporary Art, 2000.

Yto Barrada

Born in Paris, 1971
Lives and works in Paris and Tangier

Born in Paris to Moroccan parents, Yto Barrada attended school in Tangier and later studied at the Sorbonne in Paris and the International Center of Photography in New York. She is the founder and director of programming for the newly opened Cinémathèque de Tanger, Morocco's first independent cinema. Barrada's work "A Life Full of Holes: The Strait Project" (1998–2004) addresses the overriding problem of illegal immigration from Morocco to Spain across the narrow Strait of Gibraltar. The attempt to escape a land with few opportunities has become fraught with danger since the 1995 implementation of the European Union's Schengen Agreement closed the strait to Moroccans without visas, which are notoriously difficult to obtain. Like the so-called "corridor of death" in the stretch of the Sonoran desert between Mexico and Arizona—where hundreds of Central American immigrants have died from dehydration and heat en route to the U.S.—the strait is extremely dangerous to cross. Its high winds and strong currents claim thousands of African lives every year. Barrada's photographs obliquely examine the powerful desire to leave despite the danger of crossing and the hardships of illegal existence on the other side. Her pictures convey the barricaded strait's compelling physical and psychic presence that overshadows all aspects of Moroccan life. AM

Solo Exhibitions

2006	*Yto Barrada*, Jeu de Paume–Site Sully, Paris
2004	*A Life Full of Holes: The Strait Project*, Witte de With Center for Contemporary Art, Rotterdam; Open Eye Gallery, Liverpool; Centre de la Photographie, Geneva; Mead Gallery, University of Warwick, Coventry, UK
2003	*Gran royal turismo*, Galerie Polaris, Paris

Group Exhibitions

2006	*Deutsche Börse Photography Prize 2006*, The Photographers' Gallery, London
2005	*Territoires croisés*, 7th Festival Cultures du Maghreb, Caen, France
	Transphotographiques 2005: Hors circuits, Lille, France
2004	*Africa Remix: Contemporary Art of a Continent*, Museum Kunst Palast, Düsseldorf; Hayward Gallery, London; Centre Georges Pompidou, Paris; Mori Art Museum, Tokyo
	Fabbrica dell'immagine, Villa Medici, Rome
	Premieres, Museum of Modern Art, New York
	Tour-ismos: La derrota de la disensión / Tourisms: The Defeat of Dissent, Fundació Antoni Tàpies, Barcelona

2003 *Global Detail*, 10th Noorderlicht Photofestival, Groningen, The Netherlands
Strangers, The First ICP Triennial of Photography and Video, International Center of Photography, New York

Awards
2006 Shortlisted for the Deutsche Börse Photography Prize 2006, The Photographers' Gallery, London

Bibliography
• Barrada, Yto. *A Life Full of Holes: The Strait Project.* London: Autograph ABP, 2005.
• Masson, Anaïs, Yto Barrada, and Maxence Rifflet. *Fais un fils et jette-le à la mer: Marseille/Tanger.* Paris: Éditions Jean-Michel Place, 2004.

Luis Basto
Born in Lourenço Marques, Portuguese East Africa (now Maputo, Mozambique), 1969
Lives and works in Maputo, Mozambique

A self-taught photographer, painter, and sculptor, Luís Basto learned his trade in the difficult years after Mozambique's independence in 1975 and has lived both there and in Zimbabwe. He is representative of and heir to a rich tradition of Mozambican documentary photography. Spurred by the work of Ricardo Rangel (b. 1924), Mozambique's documentarians have recorded that country's complex and conflict-ridden history, from the long fight for independence, which began in earnest in the 1960s, to the catastrophic civil war that followed, from the mid-1970s to 1992. Today, as Mozambique's people fight to maintain their hard-won democracy and to preserve the still-vulnerable peace, Basto documents urbanization and the vibrant cosmopolitanism of the contemporary African metropolis. Basto's portraits of fellow countrymen reveal the complexity of Mozambique's culture, which has been forged from a mix of African, Asian, and European peoples brought together by centuries of war, trade, and migration. KM

Group Exhibitions
2004 *Africa Remix: Contemporary Art of a Continent*, Museum Kunst Palast, Düsseldorf; Hayward Gallery, London; Centre Georges Pompidou, Paris; Mori Art Museum, Tokyo
Les Afriques, Musée des Arts Derniers, Paris
2003 *El arte con la vida*, 8th Bienal de la Habana, Havana
Photographie africaine contemporaine, Mestna Galerija, Ljubljana, Slovenia
Rites sacrés / rites profanes, 5th Rencontres Africaines de la Photographie, Bamako, Mali
2002 *Iluminando Vidas: Fotografia Moçambicana 1950–2001 / Ricardo Rangel & the Next Generation*, Photoforum PasquArt, Seevorstadt, Switzerland; Museo Cantonale d'Arte, Lugano; Schule für Gestaltung, Basel; Galeria da Associação Moçambicana de Fotografia (AMF), Maputo, Mozambique
Photofesta, Associação Moçambicana de Fotografia (AMF), Maputo, Mozambique
2001 *Afriques: L'artista i la ciutat / Africas: The Artist and the City*, Centre de Cultura Contemporània, Barcelona
Kunst aus Zimbabwe / Kunst in Zimbabwe, Iwalewa-Haus, Afrikazentrum der Universität Bayreuth, Germany
Mémoires intimes d'un nouveau millenaire, 4th Rencontres Africaines de la Photographie, Bamako, Mali
2000 *Through Our Own Eyes*, National Gallery of Zimbabwe, Harare
1998 *eyeAfrica: African Photography, 1840–1998*, South African National Gallery, Cape Town

Bibliography
• *Luis Basto: Photographe.* Montreuil: Éditions de l'Oeil, 2004.

Zohra Bensemra
Born in Algiers, 1968
Lives in Algiers and works internationally

As an Algerian journalist who has worked for Reuters since 1998, Zohra Bensemra has documented the aftermath of atrocities committed in her country during the recent years of Islamic terrorist activity. Conflict began in the mid-1980s with the clash between the Armed Islamic Group (GIA) and Algeria's repressive socialist government. Violence increased in the early 1990s after the Islamic Salvation Front (FIS) overwhelmingly won the popular vote, only to be denied power. A decade of de facto civil war ensued, with civilians caught in the crossfire; by 2002, an estimated 80,000 people had died. An uneasy peace was achieved after a controversial pardoning of Islamic prisoners by the government in early 2000 and the disarmament of the FIS military wing; but a violent struggle over Berber civil rights in the Kabylia region erupted a year later. Bensemra's courageous photographs particularize different moments in this troubled history, especially emphasizing female experiences. In a nation criticized by international Islamic activists for its restrictions against women, Bensemra reveals a surprisingly multifaceted view of Algerian women against the backdrop of political bloodshed. They appear as mourners, mothers, glamorous passersby, and police; victims, but also protectors. AM

Solo Exhibitions
2002 *Algérie–Algerien*, Friedrich-Ebert-Stiftung, Berlin/Bonn
1998 Fnac, Brussels

Group Exhibitions
2005 *Un autre monde*, 6th Rencontres Africaines de la Photographie, Bamako, Mali
2004 *Women by Women: 8 Women Photographers from the Arabic World*, Kommunale Galerie im Leinwandhaus and Fotografie Forum International, Frankfurt
2003 *Passeurs d'images: Photographes algériens dans la presse internationale*, Galerie de la Fnac Montparnasse, Paris
Visa pour l'image, Festival International du Photojournalisme, Perpignan, France
1997 *Visa pour l'image*, Perpignan, France

Bibliography
• *Zohra Bensemra: Algérie. La vie quotidienne des années 1992–2002.* Berlin/Bonn: Friedrich-Ebert-Stiftung, 2002.

Zarina Bhimji
Born in Mbarara, Uganda, 1963
Lives and works in London

In Zarina Bhimji's images, the work of the visual artist dovetails with that of the geographer. Frequently, her projects investigate the movements of people spurred by trade and colonization. Of particular interest to her are the long-standing connections between South Asia and East Africa. Born in Uganda, of South Asian descent, Bhimji often uses photography to examine her own history. In the process, autobiographical elements are generalized into a statement on the multiple displacements of the former South Asian population of Uganda. At the end of the nineteenth century, Asians arrived in Uganda in large numbers to support Britain's colonial endeavors (specifically, building railroads). Many Asians in Uganda prospered through trade, but in 1972 the dictator Idi Amin made them into scapegoats for the country's economic problems and all Asians were expelled. Bhimji's most recent body of work, which is still in process, aims to create a "landscape of malaria" in the broadest possible sense, yielding a visual geography that encompasses the scientific, cultural, and emotional aspects of the disease. Malaria and other diseases are embedded in the history of cross-cultural contact in East Africa, and the development of effective antimalarial drugs helped open up the continent to European colonization in the nineteenth century. Bhimji explores this story and also looks at how, today, malaria is bringing together parts of the world that seem quite disparate: rural Africa, where a largely preventable disease kills more than a million people annually, and the high-tech laboratories of the developed world, where new drugs are being concocted and the malaria genome is being sequenced. KM

Education

1987–89	Higher Diploma in Fine Art, Slade School of Fine Art, London
1983–86	BA, Fine Art, Goldsmiths' College, London
1982–83	Leicester Polytechnic, Leicester, England

Solo Exhibitions

2004	*Out of Blue*, Baltic Art Center, Visby, Sweden
	Zarina Bhimji, inIVA–Institute of International Visual Arts, London
2003	*Zarina Bhimji: MATRIX 150*, Wadsworth Atheneum Museum of Art, Hartford, Connecticut
	Zarina Bhimji: Out of Blue, Tate Britain, London
2001	*Cleaning the Garden*, Talwar Gallery, New York

Group Exhibitions

2005	*British Art Show 6*, BALTIC Centre for Contemporary Art, Gateshead, England
2004	*Experiments with Truth*, The Fabric Workshop and Museum, Philadelphia
2003	*Fault Lines: Contemporary African Art and Shifting Landscapes*, 50th Venice Biennale
	Poetic Justice, 8th International Istanbul Biennial
2002	documenta 11, Kassel, Germany
2001	*The Short Century: Independence and Liberation Movements in Africa, 1945–1994*, Museum Villa Stuck, Munich; Martin-Gropius-Bau, Berlin; Museum of Contemporary Art, Chicago; P.S.1, New York
1996	*In/sight: African Photographers, 1940 to the Present*, Guggenheim Museum, New York

Awards and Residencies

2003	Infinity Award for Art, International Center of Photography, New York
2002–03	Artist-in-Residence, DAAD (German Academic Exchange Service), Berlin
2001	Sciart, Research Award for Artist/Scientist Collaboration, UK
2000	Artist-in-Residence, National Institute for Medical Research, London

Bibliography

• Bhimji, Zarina. "Imaging the Body: The Work of Zarina Bhimji." *Lancet* 355 (April 15, 2000), p. 1377.
• Dewan, Deepali. "Tender Metaphor: The Art of Zarina Bhimji." In *Fault Lines: Contemporary African Art and Shifting Landscapes*, edited by Gilane Tawadros and Sarah Campbell, pp. 131–37. London: Institute of International Visual Arts, 2003.
• *Zarina Bhimji*. Cambridge: Kettle's Yard, 1995.

Mohamed Camara

Born in Bamako, Mali, 1985
Lives and works in Paris and Bamako

At age sixteen, Mohamed Camara began taking pictures of family, friends, and interiors with a borrowed digital camera. His early series "Chambres Maliennes" (2001–2) earned him a solo exhibition at the Tate Modern three years later. This work revealed a locally rooted, poetic sense of place that was nevertheless oddly intelligible to an international audience. Camara's new pictures herald the artist's peregrinations through foreign lands, now depicting the dislocation of place. In the images, Camara's subject is strangely juxtaposed with his surroundings, evoking a sense of uprootedness perhaps familiar to the vast population of migrants and expatriates who are a central feature of the globalized economy. In one image, an African "Everyman" experiences snow for the first time, facing a mountainous winter panorama in shorts. In other pictures, kitschy Christmas decorations attain a dreamy beauty as Camara revels in the trappings of Western rituals. The artist's staged photographs blend spirituality, irony, and humor in an amused shuffling of stereotypes and realities, both noting and blurring the supposed boundaries between Africa and the West. AM

Solo Exhibitions

2005	*Mohamed Camara: Photographies*, Château du Grand Jardin, ORCCA, Joinville, France
2004	*Untitled: Mohamed Camara*, Tate Modern, London
2003	*Transfert(s)*, Africalia 2003, Brussels
2002	*Chambres Maliennes*, Mois de la Photo, Galerie Pierre Brullé, Paris; Galerie Chab, Bamako, Mali

Group Exhibitions

2005	*Critic's Choice*, FACT, Liverpool
2004	*Bamako 03: Fotografia africana contemporània*, Centre de Cultura Contemporània, Barcelona
	Beauté.Afriques@Nantes, Le Lieu Unique, Nantes, France
2003	*Mali: Photographs and Contemporary Textiles*, MuDAC–Musée de Design et d'Arts Appliqués Contemporains, Lausanne, Switzerland
	Rites sacrés, rites profanes, 5th Rencontres Africaines de la Photographie, Bamako, Mali; Barcelona; Kornhausforum, Bern; Salon International du Livre, Geneva

Bibliography

• *Mohamed Camara, photographe*. Text by Colette Fellous. Montreuil: Éditions de l'Oeil, 2002.

Ali Chraïbi

Born in Marrakech, Morocco, 1965
Lives and works in Marrakech

Ali Chraïbi began working as a photographer in 1995, after taking a course at the Institut Français in Marrakech. Chraïbi's pictures in *Snap Judgments* were selected from the series "Modern Times" (1998), which consists of eighty-five black-and-white images taken in soap and oil factories in Ain Harrouda and Ain Sebâa, suburbs of Casablanca. This poetic and metaphorical series documents the lives of factory workers in their current political and historical conditions, while at the same time employing an overarching symbolic theme that refers to the natural cycle of birth, life, death, and rebirth. "Modern Times" begins with close-up portraits of the factory workers, whose faces are inscribed with a dignity and inscrutability emphasized by a close attention to detail. Then, as the camera is pulled back to incorporate the workers' surroundings, the darkened, blurred background begins to take shape, resolving itself into factory walls with switches and machinery. The figures often appear as shadows or ghostly reflections in glass, becoming inseparable from and engulfed by the machines that they operate. The final pictures offer a fleeting glimpse of freedom, overshadowed by the inevitability of the next working day. The juxtaposition of the natural human life cycle with the forced structure and mechanical routine of the factory reminds us of the uneasy coexistence of modernity and nature. AM

Solo Exhibitions

2005 *Dries* & *Driss, Katja* & *Kadija*, Centre Culturel de l'Agdal, Rabat, Morocco (with Bernice Siewe)
2003 Institut Français de Rabat, Morocco; Real Sociedad Fotográfica, Zaragoza, Spain

Group Exhibitions

2005 *Afinidades–Affinités*, Fundación Cristóbal Gabarrón, Valladolid, Spain; Institut Europeu de la Mediterrània, Barcelona
Purity and Danger, kbp (Klein Blue Productions), Brooklyn, New York
Traces and Omens, 12th Noorderlicht Photofestival, Groningen, The Netherlands
2004 Fundación Antonio Pérez, Cuenca, Spain
2003 Villa des Arts, Casablanca
2002 Dak'Art 2002: Biennial of Contemporary African Art, Dakar; European Parliament, Brussels
2001 *Mémoires intimes d'un nouveau millenaire*, 4th Rencontres Africaines de la Photographie, Bamako, Mali

Awards

2002 "Au Sud du Sud" prize, Centre Culturel SAREV, Marseille, France
1999 Award from the Salon National d'Art Photographique, Association Marocaine d'Art Photographique (AMAP), Meknès, Morocco

Bibliography

• *Suites marocaines: La jeune création au Maroc* Paris: Revue Noire, 1999.

Allan deSouza

Born in Nairobi, 1958
Lives and works in Los Angeles

Allan deSouza's performances, photography, and sculpture typically address themes of colonialism, memory, and sexuality in a corporeal fashion. Shortly after Kenya's independence from Great Britain in 1963, the deSouza family, like many Indian families in East Africa, emigrated to the United Kingdom. Seven years old at the time, deSouza did not return to his birthplace until shortly before his mother's death in 2003. Drawing on the experience of this return, he conceptualized "The Lost Pictures." For the series, deSouza had prints made from old slides taken by his father of his mother, grandmother, and siblings in Nairobi. The artist taped the family pictures to heavily trafficked surfaces in his Los Angeles home such as the bathroom shower, sink, and kitchen counter. Bits of food, dirt, hair, soap, and blood—the bodily detritus of daily life—coagulated on the pictures, which became worn, damaged, and blurred. DeSouza then scanned the ruined prints and digitally manipulated them, obscuring the beloved subjects almost beyond recognition. The resulting abstracted surfaces of "The Lost Pictures" function as a memorial to the artist's early childhood in Kenya, an acute comment on photography's inability to fully resuscitate memory, and a poignant reminder of the inadequacy of memory itself to resurrect the past. AM

Education

1997 MFA, Photography, University of California, Los Angeles
1993–94 Critical Studies, Whitney Independent Study Program, New York
1983 BA (Hons), Fine Art, Bath Academy of Art, England
1976–77 Foundation Art, Goldsmiths' College, London

Solo Exhibitions

2005 *The Lost Pictures*, Talwar Gallery, New York
2004 *The Lost Pictures*, Pomona College Museum of Art, California
2003 *people in white houses*, Talwar Gallery, New York
2002 *Will **** for Peace*, collaboration with Yung Soon Min, Mezzanine Gallery, University of Minnesota, Minneapolis; Oboro Gallery, Montreal

Group Exhibitions

2005 *Un autre monde*, 6th Rencontres Africaines de la Photographie, Bamako, Mali
Lasting Foundations: The Art of Architecture in Africa, Courtyard Gallery, New York, organized by the Museum for African Art, New York
2004 *Africa Remix: Contemporary Art of a Continent*, Museum Kunst Palast, Düsseldorf; Hayward Gallery, London; Centre Georges Pompidou, Paris; Mori Art Museum, Tokyo
African Art, African Voices: Long Steps Never Broke a Back, Philadelphia Museum of Art
Masala: Diversity and Democracy in South Asian Art, William Benton Museum of Art, Storrs, Connecticut
2003 *Looking Both Ways: Art of the Contemporary African Diaspora*, Museum for African Art, New York; Peabody Essex Museum, Salem, Massachusetts; Cranbrook Art Museum, Bloomfield Hills, Michigan; Fundação Calouste Gulbenkian, Lisbon; Edinburgh City Art Centre, Scotland

Awards, Residencies, and Professional Experience

2005 Artist in Residence, University of Southern Maine, Portland
Visiting Artist, School of the Art Institute of Chicago
2004–05 Faculty, Vermont College, Montpelier
2003 Commission, Museum for African Art, New York
2002 Lecturer, Photography Department, California Institute of the Arts
Visiting Artist, University of Minnesota, Minneapolis
2001 Artist in Residence, Art in General, New York
Photography Residency, Light Work, Syracuse, New York
Individual Artist's Award, Durfee Foundation, Los Angeles
1998–2003 Lecturer, Studio Art Department, University of California, Irvine

Bibliography

• *Allan deSouza: The Lost Pictures*. New York: Talwar Gallery, 2005.

Depth of Field (DOF)

Collective formed in Lagos in 2001
Kelechi Amadi-Obi (born in Lagos, 1969)
Uchechukwa James-Iroha (born in Enugu, Nigeria, 1972)

Toyosi Zaynab Odunsi (born in Lagos, 1975)
Amaize Ojeikere (born in Lagos, 1966)
Emeka Okereke (born in Aba, Nigeria, 1980)
Toyin Sokefun-Bello (born in Lagos, 1978)

The collective known as Depth of Field formed when four friends from Nigeria—Kelechi Amadi-Obi, Uchechukwa James-Iroha, Toyin Sokefun-Bello, and Amaize Ojeikere—attended the fourth photography biennial in Bamako, Mali. They decided to join forces in their home city of Lagos to support their common photographic aims, and to encourage each other's work in a city where conditions for photographing are difficult and, due to Nigeria's politically troubled past, photography is viewed with suspicion. Toyosi Zaynab Odunsi and Emeka Okereke joined DOF in 2003, while photographer and curator Akinbode Akinbiyi and photojournalist Jide Adeniyi-Jones act as mentors to the young but influential collective. DOF takes as its "field" the sprawling Lagos metropolis—with an estimated population of 13 million it is one of the largest cities in the world—where, in DOF's words, "textures, movement, compressed energy and colours find themselves in a fusion of visual chaos that holds a latent order and organization." DOF's body of work includes images of Port Harcourt butchers who resemble champion soccer players; nighttime scenes of adolescent exploration into adult preoccupations; the commercial tension between redistributed Western cast-offs and local products being sold alongside each other in markets that stretch for miles; a Christian ceremony; and subway scenes encountered on travels abroad. AM

Education

	Kelechi Amadi-Obi
1992–93	BL Nigerian Law School, Lagos
1988–92	LLB, Law, University of Nigeria, Enugu Campus
	Uchechukwa James-Iroha
1990–95	BA, Visual Arts, University of Port Harcourt, Nigeria
	Toyosi Zaynab Odunsi
	BA, Visual Communications, Westminster University, UK
	Amaize Ojeikere
	HND, Business Administration and Management
	Emeka Okereke
2003–4	Alliance Française, Lagos
1992–99	Government College Umuahia, Abia State, Nigeria
	Toyin Sokefun-Bello
1996–99	BSc, University of Lagos

Solo Exhibitions

2005	*After the Fact*, Berlin Photography Festival, Martin-Gropius-Bau, Berlin
	Depth of Field: Images of Lagos and London, South London Gallery; Open Eye Gallery, Liverpool
2004	*STADTanSICHTen / URBANreVIEWS*, ifa-Galerie, Berlin and Stuttgart

Bibliography

• *STADTanSICHTen*. Geislingen/Steige: C. Maurer, 2004.

Andrew Dosunmu

Born in London, mid-1960s
Lives and works in New York

Raised and educated in Nigeria, Andrew Dosunmu began his career as a design assistant at the fashion house of Yves St. Laurent, subsequently working as a creative director and fashion photographer whose images have appeared in a variety of international magazines. In addition to his photographic practice, Dosunmu works in cinema and television. His award-winning documentary *Hot Irons* (1999) showcases a rich corner of Detroit's African American visual culture, featuring the artistry of some of the city's finest hairstylists as they prepare for the annual "Hair Wars" competition. In South Africa, Dosunmu directed episodes of the widely acclaimed and wildly successful television series "Yizo Yizo," which dramatizes the policy debates around education in post-apartheid South Africa through a frank presentation of the social crises and conflicts at a Johannesburg high school. Dosunmu has also served as creative director for album covers (for such artists as Erykah Badu and Public Enemy) and directed music videos, including his first for Isaac Hayes in 1996 and others for Angie Stone, Wyclef Jean, Kelis, Aaron Neville, Maxwell, and Tracy Chapman. KM

Group Exhibitions

2004	*Schrumpfende Städte / Shrinking Cities*, Kunst-Werke, Berlin
2003	*D Troit*, GAS Gigantic Artspace, New York
2000	African Film Festival, Lincoln Center, New York, and the Brooklyn Museum
1999	FESPACO Pan-African Film Festival, Ouagadougou, Burkina Faso
	Los Angeles Independent Film Festival
	Toronto International Film Festival

Awards and Residencies

2005	Sundance Screenwriters Lab
	Sundance Filmmakers Lab
1999	Laurent Award for Best Documentary Film, for *Hot Irons*, FESPACO Pan-African Film Festival, Ouagadougou, Burkina Faso
	Reel Film Video Award, Toronto International Film Festival

Hala Elkoussy

Born in Cairo, 1974
Lives and works in Cairo and Amsterdam

In the world's growing cities, particularly in Africa, relations between the center and periphery are of central importance, and peripheries become places in which an exploding urban population must be accommodated. Hala Elkoussy's series "Peripherals" examines the contemporary landscape of Cairo through large-scale images in which urban edifices rise uncannily from rural and desolate surroundings. This stark juxtaposition encapsulates the inexorable spread of the African megalopolis. Elkoussy's photographs offer a specific visual account of the effects of the last century's demographic shift in Cairo—an inflow of peasants from the countryside that increased the city's population from around 1.3 million in 1937 to more than 15 million today. In her compositions, the buildings sit on the edge of a city struggling to house its residents: some are government-built housing for the underprivileged; others are private residences that remain unfinished because their owners have run out of money. Formally, Elkoussy's photographs subvert the conventions of the sublime landscape that was so typical among European photographers' nineteenth-century Orientalist visions of North Africa. Those visions obscured the signs of modernity that are, by contrast, so present in "Peripherals." In her work as a whole, Elkoussy addresses the broader concept of the peripheral or the marginal by foregrounding the placement in the international art world of contemporary work from Africa and the Middle East. Works from the "periphery" are read through art historical narratives that have been authored in Europe and North America, and such works are too often seen through the frame of their geographical place of origin. Elkoussy aims to challenge this mode of integration, insisting instead on a practice that articulates the periphery as a fluid space of complex interaction among personal, social, conceptual, and aesthetic concerns. KM

Education

2002 MA, Image and Communication, Goldsmiths' College, London

1996 BA, Business Administration and Economics, American University in Cairo

Solo Exhibitions

2005 *Peripheral*, Townhouse Gallery, Cairo

2003 *Magda & Nevine: Two Women from Egypt*, Khalil Sakakini Art Centre, Ramallah, Palestine
A place, a house, a square [site-specific work], Aarau, Switzerland

Group Exhibitions

2005 *hotspots*, Sammlung Essl–Kunsthaus, Klosterneuburg, Austria
Incontri Mediterranei, Castello dei Ruffo, Scilla, Italy
9th International Istanbul Biennial

2004 *Bamako 03: Fotografia africana contemporània*, Centre de Cultura Contemporània, Barcelona
Dak'Art 2004: The Biennial of Contemporary African Art, Dakar
In a furnished flat in Cairo [curator and exhibitor], Cairo
Nazar: Photographs from the Arab World, 11th Noorderlicht Photofestival, Fries Museum, Leeuwarden, The Netherlands

2003 PhotoCairo 2, Townhouse Gallery, Cairo
Rites sacrés, rites profanes, 5th Rencontres Africaines de la Photographie, Bamako, Mali; Kornhausforum, Bern

2001 Al Nitaq Festival of Contemporary Art, Cairo

Residencies

2005–06 Rijksakademie van Beeldende Kunsten, Amsterdam

2004 Founding member of the Center for the Contemporary Image, Cairo

2003 Artists in Residence Programme, Aarau, Switzerland
Open Studios, Townhouse Gallery, Cairo

Theo Eshetu

Born in London, 1958
Lives and works in Rome

A videographer who examines conceptions of identity and modes of perception, Theo Eshetu draws on a surprising array of themes and disciplines in the creation of his work, including anthropology, art history, popular culture, and religious iconography. Indeed, those unfamiliar with Christianity's long history in Ethiopia may be surprised by Eshetu's video *Trip to Mount Ziqualla*. In it, he depicts an annual pilgrimage to an ancient monastery perched on the rim of the crater of an extinct volcano. Pilgrims climb the steep mountain road on foot behind richly dressed priests and a *tabot*, a sacred representation of the Ark of the Covenant, the chest in which the shattered tablets of the Ten Commandments are believed to be kept. While Ziqualla is an important pilgrimage site for Ethiopia's Christians, the annual festivities also attract animists and Muslims, who comprise the other strands of the country's rich cultural tapestry. Eshetu, an Ethiopian born in London and now living in Rome, is clearly a product of the dizzying cultural syncretism that is emerging in our globalized, transnational world. In his video, he combines glimpses of the specificity of Ethiopian culture with echoes of his immersion in global popular culture. We see a multipaned effect, structurally reminiscent of Byzantine-influenced Ethiopian panel painting, yoked to video editing techniques that suggest the kaleidoscopic visual style of contemporary music videos. The soundtrack is similarly disorienting: at one moment we hear the ululations of pilgrim women and, at another, raps by the New York–based group Cypress Hill. KM

Education

1981 Degree in Communication Design, North East London Polytechnic

Solo Exhibitions

2004 *Films of Theo Eshetu*, BAMcinématek, Brooklyn

2003 *Blood*, Museo Laboratorio d'Arte Contemporanea, Rome
Digital Africa, African Film Festival and Electronic Arts Intermix, New York

2002 *Africanized*, 58th Venice Film Festival

1999 *Brave New World*, Galleria Comunale d'Arte Moderna e Contemporanea, Rome

Group Exhibitions

2005 *Living for the City*, Brooklyn Institute of Contemporary Art; Jack Shainman Gallery, New York

2004 *On Air*, Galleria Comunale d'Arte Contemporanea, Monfalcone, Italy

2000 African Film Festival, Lincoln Center, New York, and the Brooklyn Museum
INPUT 2000, Halifax, Canada
TransAfricana [video installation], Chiesa di San Giorgio, Bologna

1999 Golem Video Festival, Galleria Civica d'Arte Moderna e Contemporanea, Turin
Sithengi, Cape Town

Awards, Residencies, and Professional Experience

2003–present Faculty, Accademia dell'Immagine, L'Aquila, Italy

2002 Best Biographical Documentary for *Dialogue with Yves Klein*, Asolo Art Film Festival
Fellowship, Civitella Ranieri Center, Umbertide, Italy

2000–03 Faculty, Accademia di Belle Arti di Carrara, Italy

1999 Award of Merit, African Film Festival of Verona
Second Prize, International African Film Festival, Milan
Prix du Conseil de l'Europe, VideoArt Festival, Locarno

Mamadou Gomis

Born in Ndoulo, Senegal, 1976
Lives and works in Dakar

Mamadou Gomis has worked for over fourteen years as a photojournalist in Senegal for international agencies such as Agence France-Presse, Panapress, and Reuters. He is currently the director of photography services for the Dakar-based daily *Le Journal*. In August 2004, that newly launched newspaper commissioned Gomis to follow in Boubacar Touré Mandémory's footsteps by publishing one photograph in the paper on every day except Sunday. Gomis's pictures appear on page 13 under the heading "Arrét sur image..." ("Freeze frame...") and show a snapshot of life from somewhere in Senegal's capital. Whether of swimmers stretching before a race, performers of a ritual dance, women digging through the trash, men reading the Qur'an during the holy month of Ramadan, or people cooking and eating a monkey, the photographs have an unpretentious yet striking aesthetic that makes them accessible to local readers. Limited to one image per day—but potentially limitless in the length of the project—Gomis's quotidian enterprise captures not only the vibrancy and difficulty of life in Dakar, but also reflects the city back to its inhabitants in its moments of ritual, celebration, excitement, desperation, routine, and quietude. AM

Kay Hassan

Born in Johannesburg, 1956
Lives and works in Johannesburg

Kay Hassan is an impressively adaptable artist. He works with photography, video, large-scale multimedia installations, and paper constructions. Though, in his own words, he ventures to "reflect what is happening in South Africa," his work is also "a reflection of what is happening in the world." In the large-scale photocollage *Negatives* (2006), Hassan uses Polaroid backings scavenged from itinerant photographers as the raw material for a composite image that grapples with the central role of photography in mediating between personal identity and state regulation. In many parts of Africa, it is common for itinerant photographers to work outside public buildings, supplying customers with photo IDs for government documents. The identity portrait is one of the most commonly distributed forms of photography in Africa, and they have a particularly resonant history in South Africa, where, under apartheid, they were ubiquitous reminders of the state's power to enforce laws based on race. A collective portrait of South Africa emerges in *Negatives,* which acknowledges both the shared history of apartheid and the transitory, migratory life experienced by so many contemporary South Africans. KM

Education

1988–89	Guest student, Schule für Gestaltung, Basel
1978–80	Evangelical Lutheran Art and Craft Centre, Rorke's Drift, South Africa

Solo Exhibitions

2003	*Everyday People,* Gallery Momo, Johannesburg
	Kay Hassan, Kunsthalle Bern, Switzerland
2000	*Kay Hassan,* Württembergischer Kunstverein, Stuttgart; Haus Huth, Berlin; Pretoria Art Museum; South African National Gallery, Cape Town; Durban Art Gallery, South Africa

Group Exhibitions

2005	*10 Years 100 Artists: Art in a Democratic South Africa,* Bell-Roberts Gallery, Cape Town
	Urban Cocktail, Walker Art Center, Minneapolis
2004	*Negotiated Identities: Black Bodies,* Johannesburg Art Gallery
	New Identities: Contemporary South African Art, Museum Bochum, Germany
2003	*The African Exile Museum,* Migros Museum für Gegenwartskunst, Zürich
2002	*Exposition Collective,* Palais de Tokyo, Paris
	Playtime, Museum Africa, Johannesburg
2001	*The Short Century: Independence and Liberation Movements in Africa, 1945–1994,* Museum Villa Stuck, Munich; Martin-Gropius-Bau, Berlin; Museum of Contemporary Art, Chicago; P.S.1, New York
2000	Dak'Art 2000: Biennial of Contemporary African Art, Dakar

Awards, Residencies, and Professional Experience

2000	Recipient of first DaimlerChrysler Award for South African Contemporary Art
1990–93	Faculty, Academy of the Federated Union of Black Artists (FUBA), Johannesburg
1986–88	Scholarship to study printmaking with S. W. Hayter at Studio 17, Paris (awarded by the French government)

Bibliography

- Bester, Rory. "Kay Hassan: Borders and Borderlands." *Nka: Journal of Contemporary African Art,* no. 10 (Spring–Summer 1999), pp. 18–23.
- *Kay Hassan.* Bonn: DaimlerChrysler AG, 2000.
- *Kay Hassan: Kunsthalle Bern, 21.3–27.4.2003.* Bern: Kunsthalle, 2003.
- Meerali, Shaheen. "Cape of Longing: South Africa and Kay Hassan." *Third Text,* no. 55 (Summer 2001), pp. 85–92.

Romuald Hazoumé

Born in Porto Novo, Benin, 1962
Lives and works in Porto Novo

In his sculptures and installations, Romuald Hazoumé considers the place of Africa in the world economy, often using plastic gas cans that he has altered to resemble traditional African masks. In *La Bouche du Roi* (1994–2004), for example, the gas containers are cut and arranged to evoke the human cargo of a nineteenth-century slave ship. Hazoumé also includes masks representing the current king of Benin and a colonial regent. The work is completed with items like beads, tobacco, and spices, which were traded for slaves. By using jerry cans to describe the commerce of slavery, Hazoumé draws attention to West Africa's historical role as a supplier—at great cost to itself—of raw materials to the global economy: slaves in the past, oil today. Hazoumé's photographic project is an outgrowth of these same concerns. In the images that comprise the ongoing series "Kpayoland," which he began in 2004, Hazoumé depicts the containers used in the lucrative and widespread smuggling of gasoline from Nigeria into the Republic of Benin, where the price of fuel is higher and official supplies are often nonexistent. *Kpayo* means "poor quality" in the Goun language, which is spoken along the border between the two countries, and the cheap gas it refers to fouls the air and is a constant fire hazard. Hazoumé's series documents informal, cross-border trade, part of an unofficial economy that thrives across Africa as a result of weak states and government corruption. He depicts *kpayo* vendors, who are often breadwinners for poor families hard hit by Benin's high unemployment. The government has largely tolerated this black market for decades, even though a clampdown on *kpayo* sellers would yield economic benefits for well-connected official fuel distributors and more tax revenue for the state. In Hazoumé's photographs, plastic jerry cans symbolize the difficult negotiations Africa's citizens and states must make in order to navigate the complex economic networks that link localities to one another and stitch West Africa into a global system. KM

Solo Exhibitions

2006	*Romuald Hazoumé,* Fondation Zinsou, Cotonou, Benin
2005	*Romuald Hazoumé: ARTicle 14—débrouilles-toi, toi-même,* October Gallery, London
	Romuald Hazoumé: La Bouche du Roi, The Menil Collection, Houston
2002	*Romuald Hazoumé,* Centre Culturel Français, Turin
2000	*Romuald Hazoumé,* Art & Public, Geneva
1999	*Romuald Hazoumé, Vor-Sicht,* Dany Keller Galerie, Munich; Museum für Konkrete Kunst, Ingolstadt, Germany; The Project, New York

Group Exhibitions

2005	*African Art Now: Masterpieces from the Jean Pigozzi Collection,* Museum of Fine Art, Houston; The Grimaldi Forum, Monaco
2004	*Africa Remix: Contemporary Art of a Continent,* Museum Kunst Palast, Düsseldorf; Hayward Gallery, London; Centre Georges Pompidou, Paris; Mori Art Museum, Tokyo

2001 *TRADE*, Fotomuseum Winterthur, Switzerland; Nederlands Foto Institut, Rotterdam
2000 *d-sign*, Dany Keller Galerie, Munich
Partage d'exotisme / Sharing Exoticism, 5th Biennale d'Art Contemporain de Lyon
Romuald Hazoumé / Paul Pfeiffer, Duke University Museum of Art, Durham, North Carolina

Bibliography

• *Romuald Hazoumé*. Cotonou: Fondation Zinsou, 2006.
• *Romuald Hazoumé: La Bouche du Roi*. Houston: Menil Collection, 2005.
• Volkwein, Peter. *Romuald Hazoumé "Vor-Sicht."* Ingolstadt: Städtische Galerien, 1999.

Moshekwa Langa

Born in Bakenberg, South Africa, 1975
Lives and works in Amsterdam

While some of Moshekwa Langa's art seems to be grounded in an interrogation of his African identity, some of his other work clearly refuses to be labeled as African art at all, rejecting the "burden" of identity. The arc of his artistic career is marked by so many unpredictable shifts in focus that variability might rightly be considered the hallmark of his practice. Perhaps this mobility stems from his constant navigation of the passage between home and abroad, a navigation that, in his case, calls into question the very stability of such concepts. Though he is from South Africa, Langa has lived in Amsterdam since 1997. In either place, his predilection is for using materials readily at hand and for opening his practice to conceptual imperatives derived from the locale in which he finds himself. Working in all media (collage, installation, painting, photography, and mixed media) and in modes that are sometimes poetic and sometimes jarring, Langa is a prolific creator. He was born in KwaNdebele, one of the segregated, theoretically autonomous "homelands" created by South Africa's apartheid government, and an important early project responded directly to this environment. Wishing to create charcoal drawings on a grand scale, he used discarded cement bags that he rubbed with soap or wax and stained with organic materials. Hanging them on laundry lines to dry, he realized they looked like skins—his drawings had taken on physical presence and become nightmarish, visceral bodies. Similarly, in his new, nostalgia-tinged photographs shown in *Snap Judgments*, simple household items are given powerful iconic significance as spare still-life compositions. Though the processes used to create these two projects differ greatly, in both, Langa strives for a dreamlike quality that is at once spectral and tangible and objects appear simultaneously as manifestations of memory and palpable artifacts. KM

Education
1997–98 Participated in the Rijksakademie van Beeldende Kunsten, Amsterdam

Solo Exhibitions
2005 *Moshekwa Langa*, Goodman Gallery, Johannesburg
2002 *Fresh: Moshekwa Langa*, South African National Gallery, Cape Town
1999 *Moshekwa Langa*, Centre d'Art Contemporain, Geneva
Moshekwa Langa—Live and in Person, The Renaissance Society, Chicago

Group Exhibitions
2004 *Africa Remix: Contemporary Art of a Continent*, Museum Kunst Palast, Düsseldorf; Hayward Gallery, London; Centre Georges Pompidou, Paris; Mori Art Museum, Tokyo
2003 *Black President: The Art and Legacy of Fela Anikulapo-Kuti*, New Museum of Contemporary Art, New York
Fault Lines: Contemporary African Art and Shifting Landscapes, 50th Venice Biennale
A Fiction of Authenticity: Contemporary Africa Abroad, Contemporary Art Museum, St. Louis; Purnell Center for the Arts, Carnegie Mellon University, Pittsburgh; Blaffer Gallery, Art Museum of the University of Houston
How Latitudes Become Form: Art in a Global Age, Walker Art Center, Minneapolis
Looking Both Ways: Art of the Contemporary African Diaspora, Museum for African Art, New York; Peabody Essex Museum, Salem, Massachusetts; Cranbrook Art Museum, Bloomfield Hills, Michigan; Fundação Calouste Gulbenkian, Lisbon; Edinburgh City Art Centre, Scotland

Awards
2001 First Prize, FNB Vita Art Prize

Bibliography

• Langa, Moshekwa, and Kobena Mercer. "Moshekwa Langa: In Conversation." In *Looking Both Ways: Art of the Contemporary African Diaspora*, edited by Laurie Ann Farrell, pp. 93–113. New York: Museum for African Art, 2003.
• *Moshekwa Langa*. Chicago: Renaissance Society; Geneva: Centre d'Art Contemporain, 2002.
• Walker, Hamza. "The Global Village Revisited." In *Fault Lines: Contemporary African Art and Shifting Landscapes*, edited by Gilane Tawadros and Sarah Campbell, pp. 205–17. London: Institute of International Visual Arts, 2003.

Maha Maamoun

Born in Cairo, 1972
Lives and works in Cairo

Egypt has been a site of tourism since the ancient Greeks beheld the pyramids across the Mediterranean. In the nineteenth century, it was a major stop on the Grand Tour, a place where Europeans would travel for a taste of the exotic and a glimpse of the picturesque. Photography encouraged this travel and was in some sense its aim: the medium allowed visitors to return home with tangible proof of their journey or permitted armchair travelers to imagine such an adventure from the privacy of their homes. Photography allowed foreigners to take figurative possession of Egyptian views, and the Orientalist imagery that accompanied tourism in the age of empire presented a highly mediated vision of Egypt, which situated its people as objects to be contemplated, as part of the scenery. Maha Maamoun's series "Domestic Tourism" (2005–6) challenges viewers who are accustomed to the "postcard view" of her country. Responding to images proffered by the tourism industry of monuments, friendly smiling locals, or families enjoying themselves at the beach, Maamoun re-creates and overturns these scenes with manipulation and choreography that is sometimes subtle, sometimes obvious, and always unexpected. This is not the first time that Maamoun has sought to negate the pictorial codes prevailing in depictions of Egypt. In "Cairoscapes" (2001–3), an earlier series of panoramic photographs, she depicted isolated fragments of dresses with floral motifs found in the streets of Cairo. In the images, patches of flora, seemingly unattached to bodies, erupt into the highly urban and largely anonymous city that surrounds them. By isolating these floral patterns and employing the form of the panoramic photograph, so popular for nineteenth-century landscapes and cityscapes, she creates a new vision of Cairo that is surprisingly decontextualized and strikingly contemporary. KM

Education

2001 MA, Middle Eastern History, Arabic Studies Department, American University in Cairo

1993 BA, Economics, American University in Cairo

Solo Exhibitions

2004 *Retake*, Fabrica Gallery, Brighton, England

Group Exhibitions

2006 *Regards des photographes arabes contemporains*, Institut du Monde Arabe, Paris

2004 Dak'Art 2004: Biennial of Contemporary African Art, Dakar
In a furnished flat in Cairo, collaborative project between Egyptian and Swiss artists, Cairo
Made in Africa Fotografia 2004, Musei di Porta Romana/Galleria Arteutopia, Milan
Nazar: Photographs from the Arab World, 11th Noorderlicht Photofestival, Fries Museum, Leeuwarden, The Netherlands

2003 *Going Places*, commission for public transport buses, Cairo
PhotoCairo 2, Townhouse Gallery, Cairo
Rites sacrés, rites profanes, 5th Rencontres Africaines de la Photographie, Bamako, Mali; Kornhausforum, Bern

2002 4th Nile Salon for Photography, Palace of Arts, Cairo Opera House

Awards and Residencies

2004 Dak'Art Biennial jury award, Prix du Centre Culturel SAREV, Marseille
Residency, Visiting Arts/Brighton International Fellowship, Brighton, England

Boubacar Touré Mandémory

Born in Dakar, 1956
Lives and works in Dakar

Boubacar Touré Mandémory's color photographs capture street life in Dakar, Senegal's capital, as part of a series entitled "Capitales Africaines." Self-taught, Mandémory came to photography after a career in advertising. His typical use of low camera angles results in striking views with looming figures and strong contrasts of shadow and light that suggest an estrangement of the familiar. Often a brilliant blue sky, sometimes with an attendant explosion of clouds, plays a strong compositional role in his work. Although he has documented various ethnic groups in Mali and Sierra Leone, Mandémory blurs the line between artistic venture and documentary project, offering a highly aesthetic, composed view of daily life that still provides a wealth of visual details. Mandémory is interested in questions of modernity, tradition, and religion; he pitches his work to a European audience and views it as an ongoing project to challenge the stereotypic representations of ethnographic photography. AM

Solo Exhibitions

2002 *Quotidiens d'ailleurs*, Centre Wallonie-Bruxelles, ParisGroup Exhibitions

2003 *In faccia al mondo / Facing the World*, Museo d'Arte Contemporanea di Villa Croce, Genoa
Photographie africaine contemporaine, Mestna Galerija, Ljubljana, Slovenia

2002 *Made in Africa Fotografia 2002*, Musei di Porta Romana, MilanPhotofesta 2002, Associação
Moçambicana de Fotografia (AMF), Maputo, Mozambique

2001 *Flash Afrique*, Kunsthalle, Vienna
Mémoires intimes d'un nouveau millenaire, 4th Rencontres Africaines de la Photographie, Bamako, Mali
Regards croisés: Regards intérieurs, 11th Aubenades de la Photographie, Aubenas, FranceRencontres Internationales de la Photographie, Palais de l'Archevêché, Arles, France

2000 Mois de la Photo, Dakar

1997 19th Festival des Trois Continents, Nantes, France

1996 Rencontres du Cinéma du Réel, Centre Georges Pompidou, Paris

Bibliography

• "B. T. Mandémory Interviewed by Gerald Matt: 'I Do Not Like the Cinema'" In *iFlash Afrique! Photography from West Africa*, edited by Thomas Miessgang and Barbara Schröder, pp. 78–80. Vienna: Kunsthalle, 2001.

• Kouoh, Koyo. "Frozen Mobility: A Photographer in Dialogue with His Environment." In *iFlash Afrique! Photography from West Africa*, edited by Thomas Miessgang and Barbara Schröder, pp. 37–40. Vienna: Kunsthalle, 2001.

Zwelethu Mthethwa

Born in Durban, South Africa, 1960
Lives and works in Cape Town

One of South Africa's premier photographers, Zwelethu Mthethwa first garnered international attention for his dignified color portraits of migrants living in shantytowns outside of Cape Town. Mthethwa's two recent "Untitled" series of 2003 and 2005, depicting sugar cane workers and gold miners, respectively, continue the respectful collaboration between photographer and subject in the portrayal of ordinary South Africans. Here, however, Mthethwa investigates sites of labor as post-apartheid locales of exploitation that are key to a global economy. South Africa's mines, long a source of the nation's wealth, account for 40 percent of the world's gold exports and were a focal point for bitterness over racial exploitation under apartheid. Some of the deepest mines in the world, they reach almost two miles into the earth and are extremely expensive to operate. Today a certain percentage of the mines are now owned by blacks as part of a post-apartheid government agreement to shift economic benefits into the hands of those who were formerly denied any share of the profits. However, miners still labor under extreme conditions in almost 100 percent humidity for the equivalent of about $400 per month, and job security fluctuates with the price of gold. Given these circumstances, it is not surprising that many strikes occurred during the two years in which Mthethwa photographed the miners. AM

Education

1989 MFA, Imaging Art, Rochester Institute of Technology

1985 Advanced Diploma in Fine Art, Michaelis School of Fine Art, University of Cape Town

1984 Diploma in Fine Art, Michaelis School of Fine Art, University of Cape Town

Solo Exhibitions

2005 *Ticket to the Other Side*, Galerie Hengevoss-Dürkop, Hamburg
Women in Private Spaces, Andréhn-Schiptjenko, Stockholm

2004 *Lines of Negotiation*, Jack Shainman Gallery, New York

2003 *Interior Portraits: Zwelethu Mthethwa Photographs*, Cleveland Museum of Art

2002 *Staging*, Contemporary Art Museum, St. Louis, Missouri

Group Exhibitions

2005	*Click*, Goodman Gallery, Johannesburg
	The Experience of Art, 51st Venice Biennale
	Ipermercati dell'arte: Il consumo contestato / Art Hypermarkets: Contesting Consumerism, Palazzo delle Papesse, Siena
	New Work/New Acquisitions, Museum of Modern Art, New York
	Significant Works Within Reach, Schneider Gallery, Chicago
	The Whole World Is Rotten: Free Radicals and the Gold Coast Slave Castles of Paa Joe, Jack Shainman Gallery, New York
2004	*Africa Remix: Contemporary Art of a Continent*, Museum Kunst Palast, Düsseldorf; Hayward Gallery, London; Centre Georges Pompidou, Paris; Mori Art Museum, Tokyo
	African Photography, 26th Bienal Internacional de São Paulo
	Made in Africa Fotografia 2004, Musei di Porta Romana/ Galleria Arteutopia, Milan
2003	*The African Exile Museum*, Migros Museum für Gegenwartskunst, Zürich
	Rites sacrés, rites profanes, 5th Rencontres Africaines de la Photographie, Bamako, Mali; Kornhausforum, Bern
	Strangers, The First ICP Triennial of Photography and Video, International Center of Photography, New York
2002	*The Gift: Generous Offerings, Threatening Hospitality*, Scottsdale Museum of Contemporary Art, Arizona; Bronx Museum of the Arts, New York; Govett-Brewster Art Gallery, New Plymouth, New Zealand; Art Gallery of Hamilton, Ontario
2001	*Africas: The Artist and the City*, Centre de Cultura Contemporània, Barcelona
	The Short Century: Independence and Liberation Movements in Africa, 1945–1994, Museum Villa Stuck, Munich; Martin-Gropius-Bau, Berlin; Museum of Contemporary Art, Chicago; P.S.1, New York
2000	*Fun Five Fun Story*, Art Gallery of New South Wales, Sydney

Awards, Residencies, and Professional Experience

2000	Research Associate, Michaelis School of Fine Art, University of Cape Town
1999	Nominee, FNB Vita Art Prize, South Africa
1994–99	Lecturer in Photography and Drawing, Michaelis School of Fine Art, University of Cape Town
1993	Bertrams VO Art for Africa Award, South Africa
	City of Abidjan Prize, Abidjan Biennale, Ivory Coast

Bibliography

• Dhlomo, Bongi. "Zwelethu Mthethwa Talks about His Photographs." In *Liberated Voices: Contemporary Art from South Africa*, edited by Frank Herreman, pp. 66–75. New York: Museum for African Art, 1999.

• Godby, Michael. "The Dreams of Color: Zwelethu Mthethwa's Portraits." *Nka: Journal of Contemporary African Art*, no. 10 (Spring–Summer 1999), pp. 46–49.

• *Zwelethu Mthethwa*. Texts by Octavio Zaya, Michael Godby, and Teresa Macri. Turin: Marco Noire Editore, 1999.

James Muriuki

Born in Kenya, 1977

Lives and works in Nairobi

James Muriuki's position as gallery manager and assistant program coordinator at the Rahimtulla Museum of Modern Art (RaMoMA) in Nairobi, Kenya, has informed his interest in how symbols of culture function. *Matatu* is a Kiswahili term referring to the colorful minivans, brightly painted with trendy images and slogans, that dominate Nairobi's traffic. The privately owned *matatus* function as public transportation in the city, as the state-owned bus system cannot cope with Nairobi's increasing population and transportation needs. The minivans pack in as many customers as possible, well beyond safety limits; little is done to enforce legal regulations. Many Nairobians use the *matatus*, which are especially popular among young people, for their daily commute. Proprietors compete for customers by showing off the trendiest paint jobs and blaring the hottest music—hip-hop, rap, African reggae—from powerful and expensive speakers; it is said that teenagers will hop on just to hear the latest hits. With their adoption of loud Western music, their cool aesthetic, and sense of danger, the *matatus* symbolize Nairobi's cultural modernity for Muriuki, who sees the vehicles as the creative outlet of a striving city. He finds the buses especially beautiful at night, when shining lights and thumping bass beats herald their approach. AM

Education

2001	BA, Design, University of Nairobi
1998	Diploma and Higher Diploma, Institute for the Management of Information Systems (IMIS), Kent, UK

Group Exhibitions

2005	1st Indian Ocean Photography Biennial, Alliance Française, Madagascar
2004	*KENYAart*, Brooklyn Public Library

Lamia Naji

Born in Casablanca, 1966

Lives and works in Casablanca

Formally employing strong contrasts, Lamia Naji's black-and-white photography often searches for spiritual meaning in the modern world. *Couleurs Primaires* (2005) documents an all-night Sufi ceremony called *lila* that is comprised of dances performed for saints and spirits. The work's composition breaks down the distinction between video and photography, as still photographs replace each other to the rhythms of electronic trance music. Though trance is a form of contemporary rock usually played at nightclubs, here Naji puns on its connection to traditional forms of music meant to induce an ecstatic state. *Lila* ceremonies are associated with the Gnawa, a black Muslim sect descended from enslaved or conscripted Sudanese who were brought to Morocco in the eleventh century. The Gnawa people's shared sub-Saharan ancestry has united them in exile. The Gnawa belief system is syncretic, derived from a mixture of Islam and West African religions like Bambara and Fulani. In Gnawa ceremonies, dancers and musicians perform with castanets, lutes, clapping, and chanting to enact healing rites; specific colors have important meanings and are accompanied by distinct chants and beats. By updating the Gnawa ecstatic healing tradition with modern trance music, Naji seems to suggest that both cultural forms induce a similar rapture. AM

Solo Exhibitions

2005	*Couleurs Primaires*, Galería Rafael Pérez Hernando, Madrid
2001	*I Love Cats*, Institut Français de Casablanca, Rabat, Fez, and Meknès, Morocco

Group Exhibitions

2005	*Interruptus*, La Boca Espacio de Cultura, Madrid
2003	*IES Luis de Góngora. Exposición retrospectiva 1992–1996*, Festival Sensexperiment, Córdoba, Spain
2002	*Buen Rotllo*, MACBA, Musée d'Art Contemporain de Barcelona

	Made in Africa Fotografia 2002, Spacio Oberdan, Milan
2001	*Mémoires intimes d'un nouveau millenaire*, 4th Rencontres Africaines de la Photographie, Bamako, Mali
2000	*Artistes de la Casa de Velázquez*, Institut Français de Casablanca
	Nuits urbaines, Institut Français de Marrakech, Morocco
1999	Casa Velázquez, Madrid
	Maroc: Médina, Médinas, La Friche la Belle de Mai, Marseille, France
	Paris-Casa: Suites marocaines, Couvent des Cordeliers, Paris
1997	*Casablanca, Fragments d'imaginaire*, Institut Français de Casablanca
1996	*In/sight: African Photographers, 1940 to the Present*, Guggenheim Museum, New York

Bibliography

• *Voyage intentionnel = Overcoming Tourism: Hakim Bey, Lamia Naji, Hassan Massoudy*. Carcassonne, France: Musée Lilim, 1994.

Otobong Nkanga

Born in Kano, Nigeria, 1974
Lives and works in Paris and Amsterdam

Presented individually, Otobong Nkanga's abandoned or lushly overgrown landscapes might connote an ominous premonition of the ruins of civilization. But while each photograph may conjure a timeless and eerily symbolic present, taken as a whole, Nkanga's project reveals a concern not simply with landscape but with the often unspoken politics of human effort in relation to the land. Bland and with few distinguishing features, these photographs taken in Nigeria and Germany at first appear geographically nonspecific; only the odd palm tree or conifer reveals their locale. But the surprising juxtaposition of images from the two nations—obscure landscapes, derelict buildings, sites of construction and maintenance—suggests questions such as: who paid for these landscapes, who creates and cares for them, and who has abandoned them? *Workmen in pool 1* (2005), which shows two men cleaning the pool on a golf course, speaks to the high expense of water in dry African nations like Nigeria, where only resort hotels catering to wealthy internationals can afford to use and waste so much water. Other photographs taken in Nigeria, like *Emptied Remains: Check point* (2004–5) and *Things have fallen III* (2004–5), seem to function symbolically in their reference to nature's ability to obliterate human effort; the contrast between abandoned buildings and functioning landscapes suggests the political and economic differences between Germany and Nigeria. In *Emptied Remains: Check point*, the struggle between nature and culture acquires a political edge; yet that photograph could easily connote Cold War politics as well, as it recalls Checkpoint Charlie in Berlin. Landscape photographs of Africa have predominated as pure, spectacular nature, but Nkanga's pictures deny the magnificent and seemingly untouched nature of many a travel book, hinting instead at the political forces that shape social and literal geography. AM

Education

2005–present	DasArts, Advanced Research in Theatre and Dance Studies, Amsterdam
1995–2001	École Nationale Supérieure des Beaux-Arts, Paris
1992–94	Obafemi Awolowo University, Ile-Ife, Osun State, Nigeria

Solo Exhibitions

2004	*Fokus 2*, Kunstverein Springhornhof, Neuenkirchen, Germany (with Jens Haaning)
	On Fragile Grounds, objectif_exhibitions, Antwerp, Belgium

Group Exhibitions

2005	*Belonging*, Sharjah International Biennial 7, Sharjah, United Arab Emirates
	North/South Lab, Tanzquartier, Vienna
2004	*Africa Remix: Contemporary Art of a Continent*, Museum Kunst Palast, Düsseldorf; Hayward Gallery, London; Centre Georges Pompidou, Paris; Mori Art Museum, Tokyo
	African Photography, 26th Bienal Internacional de São Paulo
	Do You Believe in Reality?, Taipei Biennial, Taiwan
	Epifyten: De Klassieke hortus als voerdingbodem voor hedendaagse kunst, Hortus Botanicus, Amsterdam
	Flash Right, Turn Left Artwalk, Amsterdam
	Flying Circus Project 04, TheatreWorks, Singapore
2003	*El arte con la vida*, 8th Bienal de la Habana, Havana
2002	*The Classical Eye and Beyond*, FotoFest 2002, Project Row Houses, Houston
	Dessins XXL, Le Lieu Unique, Nantes, France
2001	*Mémoires intimes d'un nouveau millenaire*, 4th Rencontres Africaines de la Photographie, Bamako, Mali

Awards and Residencies

2005	DasArts, Trustfund Stichting/Dutch Ministry of Education, Culture, and Science
2003	Dutch Ministry of Foreign Affairs/DCO/IC
	Rijksakademie van Beeldende Kunsten/Dutch Ministry of Education, Culture, and Science
2002	Ministère des Affaires Étrangères (AFAA) and Ministère de la Culture et de la Communication (DAP), France
	Rijksakademie van Beeldende Kunsten/Dutch Ministry of Education, Culture, and Science
2000	Residency Program, Houilles, France

Bibliography

Smokescreen: Otobong Nkanga. Neuenkirchen: Kunstverein Springhornhof, 2004.

Omar D. (Daoud)

Born in Annaba, Algeria, 1951
Lives and works in Algiers and Paris

For over thirty years, Omar D. has acted as a witness, taking pictures of his fellow citizens during a time in which Algeria's political upheavals exploded into a brutal civil war whose brokered peace remains tentative. The photographer was persecuted, as were many journalists, artists, and intellectuals, during the worst years of conflict between Algeria's repressive socialist government and fundamentalist Islamic terrorists. In his own words, the theme of Omar D.'s work is *"dénoncer la dictature et l'humiliation subie par tout un peuple malgré la richesse du pays"* ("to denounce the dictatorship and the humiliation inflicted on the people in spite of the prosperity of the country"). Deeply sympathetic, but enigmatic in their refusal of narrative, his portraits can be seen as a protest for humanity in the face of oppression and injustice. The photographer's early training as an ophthalmologist may have influenced his emphasis on the eyes as a literal and symbolic conduit for understanding the world in his series "The Algeria of Yesterday and Today" (1998–2005). References to the existentialist philosophers Jean-Paul Sartre and Albert Camus (who grew up in Algeria) throughout Omar D.'s work give a philosophical bent to his photographs, acknowledging and at the same time contesting the bleak political situation. AM

Solo Exhibitions

1999	*Algérie de touts les silences*, Fnac, Paris; traveled to Madrid, Lisbon, Ghent, Bamako, and Algiers

Group Exhibitions

2005 *Paris Photo 2005*, Musée du Louvre, Paris
T'saouar: Photographes du Maghreb, Château de Sainte-Suzanne, France

2004 *Africa Remix: Contemporary Art of a Continent*, Museum Kunst Palast, Düsseldorf; Hayward Gallery, London; Centre Georges Pompidou, Paris; Mori Art Museum, Tokyo
Nazar: Photographs from the Arab World, 11th Noorderlicht Photofestival, Fries Museum, Leeuwarden, The Netherlands

2003 *Algérie portraits*, Musée d'Art Moderne, Saint-Étienne, France; Théâtre du Muselet, Chalon en Champagne, France

2002 *En direct de Bamako: Une sélection des 4e Rencontres de la Photographie Africaine*, Fnac, Paris
Gens de Berbérie, Festival International de Biarritz, Terres d'Images Grâce, Biarritz, France

2001 *Enfants de Bagdad, exil & création*, Grasse, France
Mémoires intimes d'un nouveau millenaire, 4th Rencontres Africaines de la Photographie, Bamako, Mali

Bibliography

• *L'Algérie antique: De Massinissa à saint Augustin.* Text by Serge Lancel. Photographs by Omar Daoud, Pierre Salama, and Cornelis Van Voorthuizen. Paris: Mengès, 2003.
• *Algérie portraits.* Paris: Éditions Éric Koehler, 2003.
• *Enfants de Bagdad* Paris: Éditions Miroirs de l'Oeil, 2001.
• *Mémoires de disparus.* London: Autograph Londres, 2005.

Jo Ractliffe

Born in Cape Town, 1961
Lives and works in Johannesburg

For Jo Ractliffe, photography is "a resistant and unforgiving medium." Ractliffe probes the intersection between photography's documentary mode and a more poetic and personal visual language. Opposing any semblance of fixity in her images, she embraces transience, often by emphasizing the medium's technical limitations. To create "Johannesburg Inner City Works" (2000–2004), a series of large-scale cityscapes, Ractliffe used a plastic toy Holga camera. Very unpredictable, the manual-spooling Holga allows Ractliffe to create a cinematic effect, splicing together discontinuous shards of the constantly shifting landscape of Johannesburg, a city whose ever-altering character and visage is remarkable even by African standards. In a previous body of work executed with the toy camera, Ractliffe turned its lens on Vlakplaas, a farm outside Pretoria that was the home of brutal apartheid death squads. There, the strip of unbroken negative printed in black and white captures both the facade of normalcy behind which apartheid's evil was allowed to operate, and the difficulty of ever coming to a satisfactory resolution about the "truth" of that era's atrocities. "Johannesburg Inner City Works," on the other hand, employs color and unexpected shifts in perspective to suggest the collision of cultures and the structural regeneration that is forging today's Johannesburg. KM

Education

1988 MFA, University of Cape Town
1985 BA, Fine Art, University of Cape Town
1982 Diploma in Fine Art, Ruth Prowse School of Art, Cape Town

Solo Exhibitions

2005 *Jo Ractliffe: Selected Colour Works 1999–2005*, Warren Siebrits Modern and Contemporary Art, Johannesburg

2004 *Jo Ractliffe: Selected Works 1982–1999*, Warren Siebrits Modern and Contemporary Art, Johannesburg

2002 *Snow White*, École Cantonale d'Art du Valais, Sierre, Switzerland

1999 *End of Time*, Ibis Art Gallery, Nieu-Bethesda, South Africa; Mark Coetzee Fine Art Cabinet, Cape Town

1997 *Guess Who Loves You*, Goodman Gallery, Johannesburg

Group Exhibitions

2005 *Prepossession*, Ivan Dougherty Gallery, University of New South Wales, Sydney; Golden Thread Gallery, Belfast
10 Years 100 Artists: Art in a Democratic South Africa, Bell-Roberts Gallery, Cape Town
Unsettled: 8 South African Photographers, The Regional Museum, Kristianstad, Sweden; Reykjavik Museum of Photography; Durban Art Gallery, South Africa; Nationale Fotomuseum, Copenhagen

2004 *A Decade of Democracy: South African Art 1994–2004*, South African National Gallery, Cape Town
Mine(d)fields, Stadtgalerie, Bern

2003 *Coexistence: Contemporary Cultural Production in South Africa*, Rose Art Museum, Brandeis University, Waltham, Massachusetts

2002 *Iconografias metropolitanas: Cidades*, 25th Bienal Internacional de São Paulo

Awards and Professional Experience

2003 Finalist, DaimlerChrysler Creative Photography Award
1999 Nominee, FNB Vita Art Prize, South Africa
1991–present Faculty, University of the Witwatersrand, Johannesburg

Bibliography

• Atkinson, Brenda. *Jo Ractliffe: Artist's Book* [taxi series 001]. Johannesburg: David Krut Publishing, 2000.
• Ractliffe, Jo, and Brenda Atkinson. *Jo Ractliffe: End of Time.* Cape Town: Mark Coetzee Fine Art Cabinet, 1999.
• Ractliffe, Jo, and Terry Kurgan, eds. *Johannesburg Circa Now: Photography and the City.* Johannesburg, 2005.
• Ractliffe, Jo, and Warren Siebrits. *Jo Ractliffe: Selected Works 1982–1999.* Johannesburg: Warren Siebrits Modern and Contemporary Art, 2004.

Tracey Rose

Born in Durban, South Africa, 1974
Lives and works in Johannesburg

Tracey Rose uses photography, film, video, and performance to examine racial, gender, ethnic, and national identity. The colorful and fantastic series "Lucie's Fur Version 1:1:1" (2003–4) embeds a critique of the racist and sexist biases of Christianity within a broader critique of Western Christian art. Rose's title refers to Lucy, an ancient hominid discovered in Ethiopia in 1974, whose resemblance to an ape sparked controversy over prevailing concepts of evolution, religion, and race. In "Lucie's Fur," Rose juxtaposes the scientific origins of humanity and Christianity's version of the story. With Adam and Eve portrayed as young homosexual Zulu men, the Messiah as a black woman in leopard-print underwear on a floating carpet, and the archangel Gabriel as a literally multicolored female, Rose's imagery effects a campy reversal of Christianity's most revered themes, and provides mocking critiques of African stereotypes in the same breath. AM

Education

2004 The South African School of Motion Picture Medium and Live Performance, Cape Town

1996 BA, Fine Arts, University of the Witwatersrand, Johannesburg

Solo Exhibitions

2004 *Lucie's Fur, Version 1:1:1*, The Project, New York
The Thieving Fuck and the Intagalactic Lay, Goodman Gallery, Johannesburg

2002 *Ciao Bella*, Goodman Gallery, Johannesburg; Gallery in the Round, Grahamstown, South Africa
TKO, Yvon Lambert Le Studio, Paris; The Project, New York

2001 *Tracey Rose / Uri Tzaig*, La Panaderia, Mexico City

Group Exhibitions

2005 *10 Years 100 Artists: Art in a Democratic South Africa*, Bell-Roberts Gallery, Cape Town

2004 *Africa Remix: Contemporary Art of a Continent*, Museum Kunst Palast, Düsseldorf; Hayward Gallery, London; Centre Georges Pompidou, Paris; Mori Art Museum, Tokyo
Camoufleurs, Kunstverein Springhornhof, Neuenkirchen, Germany
A Decade of Democracy: South African Art 1994–2004, South African National Gallery, Cape Town
How Can You Resist?, L. A. Freewaves, Museum of Contemporary Art, Los Angeles
Negotiated Identities: Black Bodies, Johannesburg Art Gallery
Seeds and Roots: Selections from the Permanent Collection, The Studio Museum in Harlem, New York

2003 *The African Exile Museum*, Migros Museum für Gegenwartskunst, Zürich
The Squared Circle: Boxing in Contemporary Art, Walker Art Center, Minneapolis
Terror Chic, Monika Sprüth Philomene Magers, Munich

2002 *Africaine*, The Studio Museum in Harlem, New York

2001 *in the meantime ...*, De Appel, Amsterdam

Residencies

2005 Africa 05 Residency, October Gallery, London

2004 Hollywood Hills House Residency, Los Angeles

2001 Fresh Residency, South African National Gallery, Cape Town

Bibliography

• Coombes, Annie E. *History after Apartheid: Visual Culture and Public Memory in a Democratic South Africa.* Durham: Duke University Press, 2003.

• Jones, Kellie. "Tracey Rose: Post-Apartheid Playground." In *Fresh: 7 Young South African Artists at the South African National Gallery.* Cape Town: SANG, 2003.

Fatou Kandé Senghor

Born in Dakar, 1971
Lives and works in Dakar

Founder of a platform for dialogue called the Waru Studio in Dakar, Fatou Kandé Senghor takes a feminist and activist stance against injustice in Senegal that incorporates various media, including performance, film, video, radio, and writing. The forty-eight transparencies of Senghor's *Palais de Justice* (2005) offer strikingly formal, highly composed views of the interior and exterior of the Dakar Court of Law, a modernist structure conceived by French architect Robert Boy under colonial rule in the late 1950s. Abandoned in 1994 because of its instability, the building is now falling into ruin. Although Senegal is often espoused as a model state for African postcolonial rule, with four decades of self-elected socialism and a recent change to electoral democracy, Kandé Senghor criticizes the state's justice system, accusing it of corruption and incompetence. She has also created a series documenting the lives of prisoners in Senegal as part of her ongoing critique. Austerely beautiful, *Palais de Justice* metonymically conflates the utopian dimension of the modernist project with its ruin, evoking a bitter nostalgia for the heady dreams of a just society heralded by President Léopold Senghor in the early years after Senegal's liberation in 1960. AM

Group Exhibitions

2005 *Bamako V, Continuação*, FotoRio 2005, Centro Cultural Justiça Federal, Rio de Janeiro
The Sneeze, Gazon Rouge Gallery, Athens

2004 Dak'Art 2004: The Biennial of Contemporary African Art, DakarResidencies

2004 Residency, Visual Arts, Banff Center, Alberta, Canada, on the theme of "Intranation"

Bibliography

• Kandé Senghor, Fatou. "On the Predicament of the Sign: The Modern African Woman's Claim to Locality." *Public Culture* 12, no. 1 (Winter 2000), pp. 205–6.

Randa Shaath

Born in Philadelphia, 1963
Lives and works in Cairo

As chief photographer for an Egyptian weekly, Randa Shaath covers Cairo in its many guises. In the 1920s, the city's newly built modern highrises incorporated extra rooms on the roof for laundry and service facilities. After the Egyptian revolution of 1952 and the monarchy's fall, such buildings were nationalized, and the open roofs and tiny rooms became available as living spaces. During the next decades, migrants from the countryside crowded Egypt's capital, living where rent was cheap or even nonexistent—in the old servant quarters of Cairo's former luxury highrises. From her fourteenth-floor apartment, Shaath became fascinated by the population living mostly in the open air on the roofs below her. "Rooftops of Cairo" (2002–3) documents the everyday experience of these spaces, whose liminal position between indoor and outdoor mirrors their inhabitants' peripheral social status. The rooftops lack privacy, forcing neighbors to share bathrooms and public areas, yet at the same time are hidden from the busy street below, providing the solace of fresh air in the heart of the city. During Shaath's project, some inhabitants refused to reveal their names for fear of eviction, while others evinced shame over their home's historical association with servitude. For some rooftop dwellers, however, the benefits outweigh the stigma; artists and pigeon keepers alike enjoy the light and access to the sky. AM

Education

1987 MA, Visual Mass Communication, University of Minnesota, Minneapolis

1985 BA, American University in Cairo

Solo Exhibitions

2004 *Staying or Leaving / Ostati ili otiá*, Umjetnički Paviljon, Zagreb, Croatia; Camera Austria, Kunsthaus Graz

2002 *Being There*, Forum on Cultural Practices in the Region, Beirut
The Spice Route Islands of Cairo, ifa-Gallery, Stuttgart

1995 *Views (Rooftops)*, Al-Hanager Gallery, Cairo; Museum of Fine Arts, Alexandria, Egypt

Group Exhibitions

2005 *Labyrinth Trap*, DOK für Moderne Kunst, St. Pölten, Austria

2004 *Nazar: Photographs from the Arab World*, 11th Noorderlicht Photofestival, Fries Museum, Leeuwarden, The Netherlands; Aperture Foundation, New York; FotoFest at Vine Street Studios, Houston

2003 *Contemporary Arab Representations: Cairo*, Witte de With Center for Contemporary Art, Rotterdam; Venice Biennale; Fundació Antoni Tàpies, Barcelona; Bildmuseet, Umeå, Sweden

2002 *Fragments*, PhotoCairo, Townhouse Gallery, Cairo

2001 *Borders and Beyond*, Photoforum PasquArt, Biel, Switzerland; toured to nine other countries

1993 *Women Photographers*, French Cultural Center, Jerusalem

Residencies and Professional Experience

1995–96 Pro Helvetia Artist in Residence, Boswil, Switzerland

1994–2005 Chief Photographer, *Al Ahram Weekly* (Egyptian English-language newspaper)

1994 Photo Stringer, Agence France-Presse, in Egypt and Palestine

Bibliography

• Golia, Maria. *Cairo, City of Sand.* London: Reaktion Books, 2004

• Hanna, Nelly, and Randa Shaath. *Misr umm al-dunya* (On the History of Islamic Cairo). Cairo: Dar al-Fata al-Arabi, 1990.

• *Randa Shaath: Under the Same Sky, Cairo.* Rotterdam and Barcelona: Witte de With and Fundació Tàpies, 2003.

• Shaath, Randa. *Watani ala marma haggar* (Life in a Refugee Camp). Cairo: Dar al-Fata al-Arabi, 1988.

Mikhael Subotzky

Born in Cape Town, 1981
Lives and works in South Africa

A young South African who has recently completed an undergraduate degree, Mikhael Subotzky debuts in the United States with photographs from one of his first major series, "Die Vier Hoeke" (The Four Corners; 2004–5). The series is the product of Subotzky's extended analysis of conditions at South Africa's Voorberg and Pollsmoor prisons. Pollsmoor was the site of four of Nelson Mandela's twenty-seven years of political imprisonment, and the Nelson Mandela Cell there provided an apt setting for the first exhibition of Subotzky's prison photographs. When viewed at Pollsmoor, which now houses more than 7,000 inmates, the work could be seen as both social reportage about prison life in the new South Africa and as an institutional critique of the prison system. Visitors to the exhibition were forced to navigate dimly lit corridors and pass through elaborate security checks, experiencing for themselves aspects of the world glimpsed in Subotzky's photographs. Exhibited elsewhere, the photographs offer both specific commentary on South Africa and a general contribution to a global debate on the role of prisons in a democratic, multiracial society. KM

Education

2004 BA, Michaelis School of Fine Art, University of Cape Town

Solo Exhibitions

2005 *Die Vier Hoeke*, Nelson Mandela Cell, Pollsmoor Prison, South Africa

Group Exhibitions

2005 Art 36 Basel

Un autre monde, 6th Rencontres Africaines de la Photographie, Bamako, Mali

Cape Town Month of Photography, South African Centre for Photography, Cape Town

Click, Goodman Gallery, Johannesburg

Vyf Kurators, Vyftien Kunstenaars (Five Curators, Fifteen Artists), Klein Karoo National Arts Festival, Oudtshoorn, South Africa

2004 Exhibited Finalist, Brett Kebble Art Awards, Cape Town International Conference Centre

Awards

2004 Michaelis Prize and Simon Girson Prize for *Die Vier Hoeke*

Sada Tangara

Born in Mali, 1984
Lives and works in Dakar

Sada Tangara was born in Mali but came to neighboring Senegal as a child. At the age of thirteen, he entered Man-Keneen-Ki, an art school and charity for homeless and abandoned children founded in 1997 in Dakar, Senegal's capital. Tangara and other children were given disposable cameras and encouraged to take pictures of their surroundings, providing them with a valuable means of representing themselves and their environment. In Tangara's series "Le grand sommeil" (The Big Sleep; 1998–2003), the young photographer documented children like himself, who have no choice but to sleep in the streets of Dakar. Tangara shot the series over the five-year period that he lived in Man-Keneen-Ki, capturing the psychological as well as physical difficulty of the miserable conditions experienced by Dakar's homeless children. Yet Tangara's poetic formal approach lends dignity to his subjects, signaling empathy rather than pity. Indeed, he knows many of his subjects personally. "Le grand sommeil" has been exhibited in Senegal, France, Switzerland, and Germany, publicizing these children's plight to an international audience. AM

Solo Exhibitions

2003 *Sada Tangara*, MAMCO–Musée d'Art Moderne et Contemporain, GenevaCentre Culturel Français de Saint-Louis, Senegal

2002 *Le grand sommeil*, MEP–Maison Européene de la Photographie, Paris

Group Exhibitions

2005 *Fotonoviembre 2005*, 8th Bienal Internacional de Fotografía, Centro de Fotografía, Santa Cruz de Tenerife, Spain

2004 Dak'Art 2004: Biennial of Contemporary African Art, Dakar

2002 *Enfants de nuit*, Festival Perspectives Nouvelles, Saarbrücken, Germany

Enfants de nuit, Festival d'Avignon, FranceMois de la Photo, MEP–Maison Européenne de la Photographie, Paris

2000 Dak'Art 2000: Biennial of Contemporary African Art, DakarRencontres Internationales de la Photographie, Palais de l'Archevêché, Arles, France

1999 *La Passerelle*, Scène Nationale de Saint-Brieuc, France

1998 Dak'Art 1998: Biennial of Contemporary African Art, DakarAwards

2003 Lauréat du Prix Gilles Dusein for "le grand sommeil," MEP–Maison Européene de la Photographie, Paris

Bibliography

• Bruyère, Jean-Michel, ed. *L'envers du jour: Monde réels et imaginaires des enfants errants de Dakar.* Paris: Édition Léo Scheer, 2001.

Guy Tillim

Born in Johannesburg, 1962
Lives and works in Cape Town

Because of the onrush of events that provide the subjects of photojournalism, the genre is often the ephemeral first draft of history. When not showing his photographs in museums, Guy Tillim disseminates his work through the international news media, and he has worked with press agencies such as South Africa's Afrapix, Reuters, and Agence France-Presse. Nevertheless, his photojournalism is atypical. He captures contemporary moments but labors in his photo-essays to root these moments in those that have come before, using seriality, posed images, and visual juxtapositions to narrate long-standing and closely linked historical configurations, like colonialism, economic underdevelopment, and patterns of violence. As Rory Bester has pointed out, though Tillim is often considered a war photographer, his subject is more likely to be the aftermath of war. This point is apt in relation to the "Jo'Burg" series of 2004. There, we see the still very present after-effects of apartheid in the Johannesburg suburb of Hillbrow. White flight in the 1990s from a previously integrated neighborhood, coupled with neglect by landlords, have created an area in which residents—a few holdovers and many recent arrivals, almost all black—are trapped in appalling conditions that they are trying to alleviate through community cooperation. As Tillim's photographs show, the residents' fight for their homes is an uphill battle, and regentrification may be the final fate of the neighborhood. Tillim maintains a self-effacing and modest authorial presence in his images: he photographs his subjects after several visits and only with their permission, using a tripod to allow them the opportunity to situate themselves in relation to the camera. With minimal interference from the photographer, the residents of Hillbrow relate their collective and individual stories through the best available means: their expressions, postures, gestures, and general demeanors. As a series, "Jo'Burg" represents a practice of post-apartheid documentary photography that links contemporary South Africa to its own history. KM

Education

1985	BCom, University of Cape Town

Solo Exhibitions

2005	*Guy Tillim*, South African National Gallery, Cape Town
2004	*Guy Tillim, Südafrika*, Mercedes-Benz Museum, Stuttgart; DaimlerChrysler Contemporary, Berlin
	Kunhinga Portraits, Sala Uno, FotoGrafia: Festival Internazionale, Rome
	Leopold and Mobutu, Michael Stevenson Contemporary, Cape Town; The Photographers' Gallery, London
2003	*Congo Democratic Republic*, Bell-Roberts Gallery, Cape Town; Fotofiesta, Medellín, Colombia
	Departure, Bell-Roberts Gallery, Cape Town; NSA Gallery, Durban, South Africa; Photo ZA Gallery, Johannesburg
	Kunhinga Portraits and Congo Democratic Series, Photo ZA Gallery, Johannesburg
2001	*Kuito, Angola*, South African Museum, Cape Town; Gallerie Dupon, Paris; Société des Auteurs Multimedia, Paris

Group Exhibitions

2005	*Un autre monde*, 6th Rencontres Africaines de la Photographie, Bamako, Mali
	A Journey Around My House, Círculo de Bellas Artes, Madrid
	Outside Europe, DaimlerChrysler Contemporary, Berlin
	10 Years 100 Artists: Art in a Democratic South Africa, Bell-Roberts Gallery, Cape Town
2004	*Africa Remix: Contemporary Art of a Continent*, Museum Kunst Palast, Düsseldorf; Hayward Gallery, London; Centre Georges Pompidou, Paris; Mori Art Museum, Tokyo
	Staged Realities: Exposing the Soul in African Photography, 1870–2004, Michael Stevenson Contemporary, Cape Town
	Unsettled: 8 South African Photographers, National Museum of Photography, Copenhagen; The Regional Museum, Kristianstad, Sweden; Reykjavik Museum of Photography
2003	*Unveiled / Enthüllt*, OMC Galerie für Gegenwartskunst, Düsseldorf

Awards

2005	Leica Oskar Barnack Award
2004	DaimlerChrysler Award for South African Photography
2003	Higashikawa Overseas Photographer Award
2002	Prix SCAM (Société Civile des Auteurs Multimedia)
2001	Finalist, Prix Care for Humanitarian Reportage, France
1999	Mondi Award South Africa for Photojournalism
1998	Mondi Award South Africa for Photojournalism

Bibliography

• Badsha, Omar, and Guy Tillim. *Amulets* & *Dreams: War, Youth* & *Change in Africa*. Pretoria: South African History Online in cooperation with Unisa Press and the Institute for Security Studies, 2002.
• *Guy Tillim: Daimler Chrysler Award for South African Photography*. Pretoria: DaimlerChrysler South Africa, 2004.
• Tillim, Guy. *Departure*. Cape Town: Michael Stevenson Contemporary, 2003.
• ——. *Jo'Burg*. Johannesburg: STE Publishers, 2005.
• ——, Adam Hochschild. *Leopold and Mobutu*. Trézélan, France: Filigranes Editions, 2004.

Michael Tsegaye

Born in Addis Ababa, Ethiopia, 1975
Lives and works in Addis Ababa

The photographs of Michael Tsegaye, a painter whose allergy to paint led him to the medium of photography, take as their subject one of Africa's great cities, Ethiopia's capital Addis Ababa. A relatively new center in a region with a long tradition of urbanism, Addis Ababa was founded in 1886 by Emperor Menelik II, and bears the marks of a century of dramatic change, both political and demographic. Its architecture and patterns of urban settlement reflect periods of imperial rule, a brief Italian occupation, years of brutal socialist dictatorship under Mengistu Haile Mariam, and finally a nascent democracy in place at the turn of the twenty-first century. Over that period, the city's population grew from around 40,000 in 1900 to more than 1.6 million. Everyday Ethiopians have made a constant effort to customize the interiors of their private spaces, to make these spaces livable in spite of population explosion and political turmoil. In Tsegaye's photographs, which focus particularly on Addis Ababa's interiors, we see richly layered accretions of material artifacts. While the buildings depicted are often quite rudimentary in construction, the possessions they house are always arrayed practically and with great care, taking on simultaneously decorative and iconic qualities. Tsegaye's images stake the fierce claims of owners for the dignity of their private spaces. KM

Education

1998–2002	Diploma in Painting, Addis Ababa University

Solo Exhibitions

2005	*Religious Ceremonies*, Royal Netherlands Embassy, Addis Ababa

2003 *Foreign*, Goethe-Institut, Addis Ababa
Out of the Blue, Goethe-Institut, Addis Ababa
2002 *Visions of Addis*, Goethe-Institut, Addis Ababa
2001 *Faces and Identities*, Goethe-Institut, Addis Ababa

Group Exhibitions
2004 *Expressions 2*, Bulgarian Embassy, Addis Ababa
Guramayle, Alem Art Gallery, Addis Ababa
Expressions, Alem Art Gallery, Addis Ababa
2003 *Self Portrait*, Alliance Ethio-Française, Addis Ababa

Hentie van der Merwe

Born in Windhoek, Namibia, 1972
Lives and works in Antwerp, Belgium

A conceptually rigorous photographer who has previously engaged critically with issues of identity and gender construction, Hentie van der Merwe's new series "Trappings" (2000) grapples with the place of militarism in the construction of masculine identity. Under apartheid in South Africa, compulsory service in the armed forces played a central role in the ideological construction of a militarized, pathologized white masculinity. While those who wished to escape enforced complicity in the violent imposition of white rule might flee abroad, this option was not open to all. Most young men became, willingly or not, a cog in the regime's military machine. In "Trappings," van der Merwe considers the South African National Museum of Military History in Johannesburg as a site for the communication of an apartheid ideology that was as masculinist and heterosexist as it was racist. Historical military uniforms from the museum's displays are transfigured by van der Merwe into floating, blurred apparitions, made ghostly by the photographer's use of slow exposure times and a handheld camera. Van der Merve reinserts these archived military artifacts—the very trappings of the era of white rule—into the contemporary cultural moment, twisting their meaning by historicizing (and denaturalizing) the ideological tethering of masculine identity to the commission of violent acts. KM

Education
2001 Skowhegan School of Painting and Sculpture, Maine
2000–02 Hoger Instituut voor Schone Kunsten (HISK), Antwerp
1996–2000 MA, Fine Arts, University of the Witwatersrand, Johannesburg
1991–94 BA, Fine Arts, University of the Witwatersrand, Johannesburg

Solo Exhibitions
2005 *Hentie van der Merwe*, Van Laere Contemporary Art, Antwerp, Belgium
2004 *graph*, Galerie Gabriele Rivet, Cologne
2003 *Hentie van der Merwe*, Galerie Gabriele Rivet, Cologne; Van Laere Contemporary Art, Antwerp, Belgium
2001 *Trappings*, Goodman Gallery, Johannesburg

Group Exhibitions
2005 *(my private) HEROES*, MARTa Herford, Germany
2004 *10 anni 10 voci*, IsIAO–Istituto Italiano per l'Africa el'Oriente, Rome
2003 *Body and the Archive*, Artists Space, New York
Sexualität und Tod: AIDS in der Zeitgenössischen afrikanischen Kunst, Rautenstrauch-Joest-Museum, Cologne
2001 *Mémoires intimes d'un nouveau millenaire*, 4th Rencontres Africaines de la Photographie, Bamako, Mali
2000 *Emotions and Relations* [curated by Hentie van der Merwe], Sandton Civic Gallery, Johannesburg; Klein Karoo National Arts Festival, Oudtshoorn, South Africa
Translation/Seduction/Displacement, White Box Gallery, New York
1999 *Lines of Sight*, South African National Gallery, Cape Town

Awards and Residencies
2000–01 Ernest Oppenheimer Memorial Trust Overseas Study Grant
2000 Nominee, FNB Vita Art Prize, South Africa
1999 National Arts Council Bursary for Overseas Study

Bibliography
• Coulson, Amanda. "Hentie van der Merwe at Galerie Gabriele Rivet." *Art on Paper* 9, no. 3 (January–February 2005).
• Reindl, Uta M. "One to Seven: Galerie Gabriele Rivet, Köln." *Kunstforum International* 157 (November–December 2001), pp. 342–43.
• van der Merwe, Hentie. "The Difference Between Colonisation and Desire." In *Grey Areas: Representation, Identity, and Politics in Contemporary South African Art*, edited by Brenda Atkinson and Candice Breitz. Johannesburg: Chalkham Hill Press, 1999.

Nontsikelelo "Lolo" Veleko

Born in Cape Town, 1977
Lives and works in Johannesburg

Nontsikelelo "Lolo" Veleko is among the vibrant group of photographers associated with the Market Photography Workshop, a hands-on program founded by David Goldblatt to teach photography and visual literacy to people historically disadvantaged by apartheid. An outgrowth of the Market Theatre, an independent company committed to nonracial culture during the apartheid era, the Photography Workshop has attempted to create a collaborative environment in which all races can come together to forge new photographic practices capable of documenting a changed South Africa. Veleko is well positioned to participate in the group's project. Fluent in three languages in addition to her native Xhosa, she endeavors in her photography to recognize and question the construction of identity in a radically altered society. Her recent work has considered both graffiti and fashion as mechanisms of cultural communication and as signs of identity allegiance, and she employs the format of fashion photography specifically to pose and complicate the question of what is considered "black enough"—both in her country and abroad. Indeed, in her series "Beauty Is in the Eye of the Beholder" (2004), Veleko captures the vibrant fashion culture of young people in Johannesburg whose stylish and sophisticated clothing confronts stereotypes dictating how the young, black, and urban ought to look. KM

Education
1999–2004 Student and Project Manager, Market Photography Workshop, Johannesburg

Solo Exhibitions
2003 *"The Ones on Top Won't Make It Stop!" An Ongoing South African Graffiti Exhibition*, Women's Arts Festival, Market Theatre Galleries, Johannesburg; The Kuppel, Basel; Johannesburg Art Gallery; Cine Africa, Maputo, Mozambique

Group Exhibitions
2005 *Click*, Goodman Gallery, Johannesburg
10 Years 100 Artists: Art in a Democratic South Africa, Bell-Roberts Gallery, Cape Town
2004 *Is Everybody Comfortable? A Market Photography Workshop*

Exhibition, Bensusan Museum of Photography, Johannesburg; Fortaleza, Maputo, Mozambique
Mine(d)fields, Kunsthaus Baselland, Muttenz/Basel
Negotiated Identities—Black Bodies, Johannesburg Art Gallery
Photofesta, Associação Moçambicana de Fotografia (AMF), Maputo, Mozambique
Sondela: A Decade of Democracy: Witnessing South Africa, Museum of the National Center of Afro-American Artists, Boston; African American Museum, Dallas; Florida A&M University, Tallahassee; NSA Gallery, Durban, South Africa
Unsettled: 8 South African Photographers, National Museum of Photography, Copenhagen; The Regional Museum, Kristianstad, Sweden; Reykjavik Museum of Photography
Urban Life: Beauty Is in the Eye of the Beholder: A Market Photography Workshop Exhibition, Johannesburg Art Gallery; Jahnitos, Maputo, Mozambique

2003 *Fragments of the City: 6 Women Photographers Defining the City and Popular Culture in South Africa*, Bensusan Museum of Photography, Johannesburg

2002 *SHARP: A Market Photography Workshop Exhibition*, Market Theatre, Johannesburg

2001 *MOVE: A Market Photography Workshop Exhibition*, Market Theatre, Johannesburg

Awards

2003 Nominee, MTN New Contemporary Artist

Written and compiled by Allison Moore and Kevin Mulhearn

Checklist of the Exhibition

As of February1, 2006

Doa Aly (b. 1976)
48 Ballet Classes, 2005
Installation of 40 chromogenic prints
(each 10 x 8 in. [25.4 x 20.3 cm]) and
4 DVD monitors
Courtesy the artist and Townhouse Gallery, Cairo

Lara Baladi (b. 1969)
Perfumes & *Bazaar*, 2005
Photographic montage, pigment print on self-adhesive vinyl and duratrans print for light box
94 x 212 in. (239 x 539 cm)
Technical production and printing, Factum Arte, Madrid
Courtesy the artist

Oladélé Ajiboyé Bamgboyé (b. 1963)
Arise I and II, 1991/1997
Diptych, two gelatin silver prints
Each 75 x 50 in. (190.5 x 127 cm)
Courtesy the artist and Thomas Erben Gallery, New York

Yto Barrada (b. 1971)
Meriem—A spelling class at the Darna day centre for street children—Tangier 1999, from the series "A Life Full of Holes: The Strait Project," 1998–2004
Chromogenic print
29.1 x 29.1 in. (74 x 74 cm)
Courtesy the artist and Galerie Polaris, Paris

Belvédère 1—Tangier 2003, from the series "A Life Full of Holes: The Strait Project," 1998–2004
Gelatin silver print
22.8 x 19.5 in. (58 x 49.5 cm)
Courtesy the artist and Galerie Polaris, Paris

Le Détroit—Avenue d'Espagne—Tangier 2000, from the series "A Life Full of Holes: The Strait Project," 1998–2004
Chromogenic print
23.6 x 23.6 in. (60 x 60 cm)
Courtesy the artist and Galerie Polaris, Paris

Man Sitting—Boulevard Mohamed V, Casablanca 2001, from the series "A Life Full of Holes: The Strait Project," 1998–2004
Chromogenic print
31.5 x 31.5 in. (80 x 80 cm)
Courtesy the artist and Galerie Polaris, Paris

Marks left by a football—Tangier 2002, from the series "A Life Full of Holes: The Strait Project," 1998–2004
Chromogenic print
31.5 x 31.5 in. (80 x 80 cm)
Courtesy the artist and Galerie Polaris, Paris

Girl with red hair—Ferry from Algeciras to Tangier—2002, from the series "A Life Full of Holes: The Strait Project," 1998–2004
Chromogenic print
31.5 x 31.5 in. (80 x 80 cm)
Courtesy the artist and Galerie Polaris, Paris

Factory 2—Canteen—Tangier 1998, from the series "A Life Full of Holes: The Strait Project," 1998–2004
Chromogenic print
40.6 x 40.6 in. (103 x 103 cm)
Courtesy the artist and Galerie Polaris, Paris

Luis Basto (b. 1969)
Feira Popular de Maputo, 2005
Fiber-based photographic print
13.8 x 19.3 in. (35 x 49 cm)
Courtesy the artist

G.G. Down Town, Maputo, 2005
Fiber-based photographic print
13.8 x 19.3 in. (35 x 49 cm)
Courtesy the artist

Rashid, Maputo, 2004
Fiber-based photographic print
13.8 x 19.3 in. (35 x 49 cm)
Courtesy the artist

Isidine (The Green Man), Maputo, 2004
Fiber-based photographic print
13.8 x 19.3 in. (35 x 49 cm)
Courtesy the artist

Bus Stop, Old Harare, 2001
Fiber-based photographic print
13.8 x 19.3 in. (35 x 49 cm)
Courtesy the artist

Zohra Bensemra (b. 1968)
Massacre in Bentalha: over one hundred people were slain in Bentalha, Baraki district, some 15 km from Algiers. Newspapers reported that 252 people, mostly women and children, had been decapitated—September 23, 1997, 1997
Chromogenic print
11 x 14 in. (27.9 x 35.6 cm)
Courtesy the artist

Graffiti on the wall of a low-rent housing project in El Bair, a neighbourhood perched on the hills of Algiers, reads: "No fundamentalism, no police state"—May 27, 1998, 1998
Chromogenic print
11 x 14 in. (27.9 x 35.6 cm)
Courtesy the artist

Algerian victims sit with their belongings in a suitcase, one day after an earthquake which caused heavy damage to the town of Ain Timouchant—December 23, 1999. More than twenty people were reported dead in the earthquake which regstered 5.6 on the Richter scale...., 1999
Chromogenic print
11 x 14 in. (27.9 x 35.6 cm)
Courtesy the artist

Law-and-order enforcement officers at the Ain Benian police school in Algiers, on the day of graduation of the new self-defence and close combat squad—January 27, 1999, 1999
Chromogenic print
11 x 14 in. (27.9 x 35.6 cm)
Courtesy the artist

A family in the town of Haouch Omar in the Metidja region of Algeria, keep an AK-47 automatic weapon at the ready on the living room table—December 8th, 1998, 1998
Chromogenic print
11 x 14 in. (27.9 x 35.6 cm)
Courtesy the artist

A view of the steps leading from the lower Kasbah, Algiers' oldest quarter, up to the upper Kasbah of Bab Edjdid; the steps are the central feature of this quarter—September 27, 1998, 1998
Chromogenic print
11 x 14 in. (27.9 x 35.6 cm)
Courtesy the artist

Zarina Bhimji (b. 1963)
Untitled (Uganda), 2002
Chromogenic print
51.2 x 66.9 in. (130 x 170 cm)
Courtesy ARS, New York

Untitled (Uganda), 2002
Chromogenic print
51.2 x 66.9 in. (130 x 170 cm)
Courtesy ARS, New York

Untitled (Uganda), 2002
Chromogenic print
51.2 x 66.9 in. (130 x 170 cm)
Courtesy of ARS, New York

Mohamed Camara (b. 1985)
Cactus de Noël 1: Dans mes rêves à Bamako c'était Noël. [In my dreams in Bamako it was Christmas.], 2001–02
Chromogenic print
11 x 14.7 in. (27.9 x 37.3 cm)
Courtesy the artist and Galerie Pierre Brullé, Paris

Cactus de Noël 2: Quand je prendrai la place du Père Noël, tu verras. [When I take the place of Santa Claus, you will see.], 2001–02
Chromogenic print
11 x 14.7 in. (27.9 x 37.3 cm)
Courtesy the artist and Galerie Pierre Brullé, Paris

Cactus de Noël 3: Au secours Blachère, Tarzan s'est pris dans ses lianes! [Help! help! Mr. Blachère. Tarzan got caught in his lianas!], 2001–02
Chromogenic print
11 x 14.7 in. (27.9 x 37.3 cm)
Courtesy the artist and Galerie Pierre Brullé, Paris

Cactus de Noël 4: Il est où mon cerf? [Where is my stag?], 2001–02
Chromogenic print
11 x 14.7 in. (27.9 x 37.3 cm)
Courtesy the artist and Galerie Pierre Brullé, Paris

Cactus de Noël 5: Merci la Chance de me suivre dans mes rêves. [Thank you, Lady Luck, for following me in my dreams.], 2001–02
Chromogenic print
11 x 14.7 in. (27.9 x 37.3 cm)
Courtesy the artist and Galerie Pierre Brullé, Paris

Nora 2: Quand j'ai éternué elle a disparu. [When I sneezed she disappeared.], 2001–02
Chromogenic print
14.7 x 11 in. (37.3 x 27.9 cm)
Courtesy the artist and Galerie Pierre Brullé, Paris

Nora 4: Même la marchande de sable fait sa corvée d'eau avant de m'endormir.
[Even the sandgirl makes her water before lulling me to sleep.], 2001–02
Chromogenic print
11 x 14.7 in. (27.9 x 37.3 cm)
Courtesy the artist and Galerie Pierre Brullé, Paris

Cactus de Sibérie 1: Mohamed à la montagne: le cactus de Sibérie!
[Mohamed in the mountains: the cactus of Siberia!], 2001–02
Chromogenic print
11 x 14.7 in. (27.9 x 37.3 cm)
Courtesy the artist and Galerie Pierre Brullé, Paris

Ali Chraïbi (b. 1965)
Untitled, from the series "Modern Times," 1998
Gelatin silver print
12.6 x 17.7 in. (32 x 45 cm)
Courtesy the artist

Untitled, from the series "Modern Times," 1998
Gelatin silver print
12.6 x 17.7 in. (32 x 45 cm)
Courtesy the artist

Untitled, from the series "Modern Times," 1998
Gelatin silver print
12.6 x 17.7 in. (32 x 45 cm)
Courtesy the artist

Untitled, from the series "Modern Times," 1998
Gelatin silver print
12.6 x 17.7 in. (32 x 45 cm)
Courtesy the artist

Untitled, from the series "Modern Times," 1998
Gelatin silver print
12.6 x 17.7 in. (32 x 45 cm)
Courtesy the artist

Untitled, from the series "Modern Times," 1998
Gelatin silver print
12.6 x 17.7 in. (32 x 45 cm)
Courtesy the artist

Untitled, from the series "Modern Times," 1998
Gelatin silver print
12.6 x 17.7 in. (32 x 45 cm)
Courtesy the artist

Untitled, from the series "Modern Times," 1998
Gelatin silver print
12.6 x 17.7 in. (32 x 45 cm)
Courtesy the artist

Untitled, from the series "Modern Times," 1998
Gelatin silver print
12.6 x 17.7 in. (32 x 45 cm)
Courtesy the artist

Untitled, from the series "Modern Times," 1998
Gelatin silver print
17.7 x 12.6 in. (45 x 32 cm)
Courtesy the artist

Omar D. (b. 1951)
Untitled, 1998–2005
Gelatin silver print
17.6 x 12.5 in. (44.7 x 31.8 cm)
Courtesy the artist

Untitled, 1998–2005
Gelatin silver print
17.6 x 12.5 in. (44.7 x 31.8 cm)
Courtesy the artist

Untitled, 1998–2005
Gelatin silver print
17.6 x 12.5 in. (44.7 x 31.8 cm)
Courtesy the artist

Untitled, 1998–2005
Gelatin silver print
17.6 x 12.5 in. (44.7 x 31.8 cm)
Courtesy the artist

Untitled, 1998–2005
Gelatin silver print
17.6 x 12.5 in. (44.7 x 31.8 cm)
Courtesy the artist

Untitled, 1998–2005
Gelatin silver print
17.6 x 12.5 in. (44.7 x 31.8 cm)
Courtesy the artist

Untitled, 1998–2005
Gelatin silver print
12.5 x 17.6 in. (31.8 x 44.7 cm)
Courtesy the artist

Depth of Field (collective formed in 2001)
"LAGOS UPTIGHT," 2001–05
Four LCD screens
Courtesy the artists

Allan deSouza (b. 1958)
Bike, from the series "The Lost Pictures," 2004
Chromogenic print
40 x 60 in. (101.6 x 152.4 cm)
Courtesy the artist and Talwar Gallery, New York

Car, from series "The Lost Pictures," 2004
Chromogenic print
40 x 60 in. (101.6 x 152.4 cm)
Courtesy the artist and Talwar Gallery, New York

Fountain, from series "The Lost Pictures," 2004
Chromogenic print
60 x 40 in. (152.4 x 101.6 cm)
Courtesy the artist and Talwar Gallery, New York

Lechko, from series "The Lost Pictures," 2004
Chromogenic print
40 x 60 in. (101.6 x 152.4 cm)
Courtesy the artist and Talwar Gallery, New York

Tomorrow, from series "The Lost Pictures," 2004
Chromogenic print
40 x 60 in. (101.6 x 152.4 cm)
Courtesy the artist and Talwar Gallery, New York

House, 2004
Mixed media
32 x 48 x 4 in. (81.3 x 121.9 x 10.2 cm)
Courtesy the artist and Talwar Gallery, New York

Andrew Dosunmu (b. mid-1960s)
Untitled fashion photography, 2005
Gelatin silver prints and chromogenic prints
Dimensions variable
Courtesy the artist

Hala Elkoussy (b. 1974)
Peripheral landscape #3, Mokattam, 2004
Ink jet print on vinyl
Dimensions variable
Courtesy the artist and Townhouse Gallery, Cairo

Peripheral landscape #4, El Tagamo' El Khamis, 2004
Ink jet print on vinyl
Dimensions variable
Courtesy the artist and Townhouse Gallery, Cairo

Peripheral landscape #5, Al Warraq, 2004
Ink jet print on vinyl
Dimensions variable
Courtesy the artist and Townhouse Gallery, Cairo

Theo Eshetu (b. 1958)
Trip to Mount Ziqualla, 2005
DVD projection
Courtesy the artist

Passage (Version 2), from *Trip to Mount Ziqualla*, 2005
Inkjet print
15.75 x 106.3 in. (40 x 270 cm)
Courtesy the artist

Wild Tress, from *Trip to Mount Ziqualla*, 2005
Inkjet print
15.75 x 106.3 in. (40 x 270 cm)
Courtesy the artist

Mamadou Gomis (b. 1976)
Untitled, 2006
Installation of newspapers
Dimensions variable
Courtesy the artist

Kay Hassan (b. 1956)
Negatives 1-6, 2006
Installation
6 pieces, each 22.4 x 29.9 in. (57 x 76 cm)
Courtesy the artist

Romuald Hazoumé (b. 1962)
La Roulotte, from the series "Kpayoland," 2004
Chromogenic print
54.5 x 36.9 in. (138.4 x 93.7 cm)
Courtesy the artist

No Limit, from the series "Kpayoland," 2004
Gelatin silver print
30 x 24 in. (76.2 x 61 cm)
Courtesy the artist

Tyson, from the series "Kpayoland," 2004
Gelatin silver print
30 x 24 in. (76.2 x 61 cm)
Courtesy the artist

Promenade a Porto-Novo, from the series "Kpayoland," 2004
Gelatin silver print
30 x 24 in. (76.2 x 61 cm)
Courtesy the artist

BB, from the series "Kpayoland," 2004
Chromogenic print
30 x 24 in. (76.2 x 61 cm)
Courtesy the artist

Fatou Kandé Senghor (b. 1971)
Palais de Justice, 2005
48 transparencies on light table
Each 4 x 5 in. (10.2 x 12.7 cm)
Courtesy the artist

Moshekwa Langa (b. 1975)
Untitled II, 2005
Chromogenic print
11 x 14 in. (27.9 x 35.6 cm)
Courtesy the artist and Goodman Gallery, Johannesburg

Untitled III, 2005
Chromogenic print
11 x 14 in. (27.9 x 35.6 cm)
Courtesy the artist and Goodman Gallery, Johannesburg

Untitled V, 2005
Chromogenic print
11 x 14 in. (27.9 x 35.6 cm)
Courtesy the artist and Goodman Gallery, Johannesburg

Untitled X, 2005
Chromogenic print
11 x 14 in. (27.9 x 35.6 cm)
Courtesy the artist and Goodman Gallery, Johannesburg

Untitled XIII, 2005
Chromogenic print
11 x 14 in. (27.9 x 35.6 cm)
Courtesy the artist and Goodman Gallery, Johannesburg

Untitled XVI, 2005
Chromogenic print

11 x 14 in. (27.9 x 35.6 cm)
Courtesy the artist and Goodman Gallery, Johannesburg

Untitled XIX, 2005
Chromogenic print
11 x 14 in. (27.9 x 35.6 cm)
Courtesy the artist and Goodman Gallery, Johannesburg

Untitled XX, 2005
Chromogenic print
11 x 14 in. (27.9 x 35.6 cm)
Courtesy the artist and Goodman Gallery, Johannesburg

Untitled XXI, 2005
Chromogenic print
11 x 14 in. (27.9 x 35.6 cm)
Courtesy the artist and Goodman Gallery, Johannesburg

Maha Maamoun (b. 1972)
The Park, from the series "Domestic Tourism," 2005
Chromogenic print
19.7 x 29.5 in. (50 x 75 cm)
Courtesy the artist and Townhouse Gallery, Cairo

The Beach, from the series "Domestic Tourism," 2005
19.7 x 29.5 in. (50 x 75 cm)
Chromogenic print
Courtesy the artist and Townhouse Gallery, Cairo

Boubacar Touré Mandémory (b. 1956)
Libraire par Terre 1 [Bookstore on the Ground 1], from the series "Capitales Africaines," ca. 2000–05
Chromogenic print
20 x 30 in. (50.8 x 76.2 cm)
Courtesy the artist

Dakar, from the series "Capitales Africaines," ca. 2000–05
Chromogenic print
20 x 30 in. (50.8 x 76.2 cm)
Courtesy the artist

Couleurs de Pêche [Colors of Fishing], from the series "Capitales Africaines," ca. 2000–05
Chromogenic print
20 x 30 in. (50.8 x 76.2 cm)
Courtesy the artist

Vendeuse de Petits Pagnes [Seller of Little Cloth Wraps], from the series "Capitales Africaines," ca. 2000–05
Chromogenic print
20 x 30 in. (50.8 x 76.2 cm)
Courtesy the artist

Grandes Vacances [Big Vacation], from the series "Capitales Africaines," ca. 2000–05
Chromogenic print
20 x 30 in. (50.8 x 76.2 cm)
Courtesy the artist

Littoral, from the series "Capitales Africaines," ca. 2000–05
Chromogenic print
30 x 20 in. (76.2 x 50.8 cm)
Courtesy the artist

Zwelethu Mthethwa (b. 1960)
Untitled, 2005
Chromogenic print
49 x 76.75 in. (124.5 x 195 cm)
Courtesy the artist and Jack Shainman Gallery, New York

Untitled, 2005
Chromogenic print
49 x 76.75 in. (124.5 x 195 cm)
Courtesy the artist and Jack Shainman Gallery, New York

Untitled, 2005
Chromogenic print
49 x 76.75 in. (124.5 x 195 cm)
Courtesy the artist and Jack Shainman Gallery, New York

James Muriuki (b. 1977)
Matatus I, from the series "Town," 2005
Chromogenic print
20 x 24 in. (50.8 x 61 cm)
Courtesy the artist

Matatus II, from the series "Town," 2005
Chromogenic print
20 x 24 in. (50.8 x 61 cm)
Courtesy the artist

Matatus III, from the series "Town," 2005
Chromogenic print
20 x 24 in. (50.8 x 61 cm)
Courtesy the artist

Matatus IV, from the series "Town," 2005
Chromogenic print
20 x 24 in. (50.8 x 61 cm)
Courtesy the artist

Lamia Naji (b. 1966)
Couleurs Primaires, 2005
DVD, 4 mins. 22 seconds running time
Courtesy the artist and Galería Rafael Pérez Hernando, Madrid

Otobong Nkanga (b. 1974)
Things have fallen III, 2004–05
Chromogenic print
23.6 x 35.4 in. (60 x 90 cm)
Courtesy the artist

Emptied Remains: Check point, 2004–05
Chromogenic print
23.6 x 35.4 in. (60 x 90 cm)
Courtesy the artist

Emptied Remains: Barn, Hertel–Rutenmühle, 2004
Chromogenic print
34.25 x 45.7 in. (87 x 116 cm)
Courtesy the artist and Leader+, Kunstverein & Stiftung Springhornhof, Neuenkirchen, Germany

Emptied Remains: Gas field vestige, Wisselshorst, 2004–05
Chromogenic print
34.25 x 45.7 in. (87 x 116 cm)
Courtesy the artist and Leader+, Kunstverein & Stiftung Springhornhof, Neuenkirchen, Germany

Workmen in pool 1, 2005
Chromogenic print
23.6 x 35.4 in. (60 x 90 cm)
Courtesy the artist

Working men II, 2005
Chromogenic print
23.6 x 35.4 in. (60 x 90 cm)
Courtesy the artist

Jo Ractliffe (b. 1961)
East Rand Proprietary Mines, Germiston, from the series "Johannesburg Inner City Works," 2000
Pigment print on paper
20 x 78.9 in. (50.8 x 200.3 cm)
Courtesy the artist and Warren Siebrits Gallery, Johannesburg, Collection of Artur Walther

Goch St cnr Bree St Carr St Goch St, Newton, from the series "Johannesburg Inner City Works," 2001
Pigment print on paper
20 x 78.9 in. (50.8 x 200.3 cm)
Courtesy the artist and Warren Siebrits Gallery, Johannesburg, Collection of Artur Walther

Carr St, Newtown, from the series "Johannesburg Inner City Works," 2001
Pigment print on paper
20 x 78.9 in. (50.8 x 200.3 cm)
Courtesy the artist and Warren Siebrits Gallery, Johannesburg, Collection of Artur Walther

Tracey Rose (b. 1974)
Lucie's Fur Version 1:1:1—La Messie, 2003
Lambda photograph
58.3 x 40.2 in. (148 x 102 cm)
Courtesy the artist and The Project, New York

Lucie's Fur Version 1:1:1—The Messenger, 2003
Lambda photograph
31.5 x 23.6 in. (80 x 60 cm)
Courtesy the artist and The Project, New York

Lucie's Fur Version 1:1:1—L'Annunciazione (After Fra Angelico) c. 1434–2003, 2003
Lambda photograph
48.4 x 61 in. (122.9 x 154.9 cm)
Courtesy the artist and The Project, New York,

The Prelude: The Garden Path, 2004
Iris print
58.3 x 40.2 in. (148 x 102 cm)
Courtesy the artist and The Project, New York

Randa Shaath (b. 1963)
Untitled, from the series "Rooftops of Cairo," 2002–03
Gelatin silver print
Courtesy the artist

Untitled, from the series "Rooftops of Cairo," 2002–03
Gelatin silver print
Courtesy the artist

Untitled, from the series "Rooftops of Cairo," 2002–03
Gelatin silver print
Courtesy the artist

Untitled, from the series "Rooftops of Cairo," 2002–03
Gelatin silver print
Courtesy the artist

Untitled, from the series "Rooftops of Cairo," 2002–03
Gelatin silver print
Courtesy the artist

Untitled, from the series "Rooftops of Cairo," 2002–03
Gelatin silver print
Courtesy the artist

Untitled, from the series "Rooftops of Cairo," 2002–03
Gelatin silver print
Courtesy the artist

Untitled, from the series "Rooftops of Cairo," 2002–03
Gelatin silver print
Courtesy the artist

Untitled, from the series "Rooftops of Cairo," 2002–03
Gelatin silver print
Courtesy the artist

Untitled, from the series "Rooftops of Cairo," 2002–03
Gelatin silver print
Courtesy the artist

Mikhael Subotzky (b. 1981)
'Reception,' Pollsmoor Maximum Security Prison, from the series "Die Vier Hoeke" [The Four Corners], 2004–05
Pigment print on paper
22 x 92 in. (55.9 x 233.7 cm)
Courtesy the artist and Goodman Gallery, Johannesburg, Collection of Artur Walther

Abbatoir, Voorberg Prison, from the series "Die Vier Hoeke" [The Four Corners], 2004–05
Pigment print on paper
22 x 92 in. (55.9 x 233.7 cm)
Courtesy the artist and Goodman Gallery, Johannesburg, Collection of Artur Walther

Cell 508b, A Section, Pollsmoor Maximum Security Prison, from the series "Die Vier Hoeke" [The Four Corners], 2004–05
Pigment print on paper
22 x 92 in. (55.9 x 233.7 cm)
Courtesy the artist and Goodman Gallery, Johannesburg, Collection of Artur Walther

Sada Tangara (b. 1984)
Untitled, from the series "Le grand sommeil" [The Big Sleep], 1998–2003
Gelatin silver print
11.8 x 15.75 in. (30 x 40 cm)
Courtesy the artist and Serge Aboukrat Éditions, Paris

Untitled, from the series "Le grand sommeil" [The Big Sleep], 1998–2003
Gelatin silver print
11.8 x 15.75 in. (30 x 40 cm)
Courtesy the artist and Serge Aboukrat Éditions, Paris

Untitled, from the series "Le grand sommeil" [The Big Sleep], 1998–2003
Gelatin silver print
11.8 x 15.75 in. (30 x 40 cm)
Courtesy the artist and Serge Aboukrat Éditions, Paris

Untitled, from the series "Le grand sommeil" [The Big Sleep], 1998–2003
Gelatin silver print
11.8 x 15.75 in. (30 x 40 cm)
Courtesy the artist and Serge Aboukrat Éditions, Paris

Untitled, from the series "Le grand sommeil" [The Big Sleep], 1998–2003
Gelatin silver print
11.8 x 15.75 in. (30 x 40 cm)
Courtesy the artist and Serge Aboukrat Éditions, Paris

Untitled, from the series "Le grand sommeil" [The Big Sleep], 1998–2003
Gelatin silver print
11.8 x 15.75 in. (30 x 40 cm)
Courtesy the artist and Serge Aboukrat Éditions, Paris

Untitled, from the series "Le grand sommeil" [The Big Sleep], 1998–2003
Gelatin silver print
11.8 x 15.75 in. (30 x 40 cm)
Courtesy the artist and Serge Aboukrat Éditions, Paris

Untitled, from the series "Le grand sommeil" [The Big Sleep], 1998–2003
Gelatin silver print
11.8 x 15.75 in. (30 x 40 cm)
Courtesy the artist and Serge Aboukrat Éditions, Paris

Untitled, from the series "Le grand sommeil" [The Big Sleep], 1998–2003
Gelatin silver print
11.8 x 15.75 in. (30 x 40 cm)
Courtesy the artist and Serge Aboukrat Éditions, Paris

Guy Tillim (b. 1962)
A Map of Central Johannesburg at the Inner City Regeneration Project Office, City Council Loveday Street, from the series "Jo'burg," 2004
Pigment print on paper
13.9 x 20.6 in. (35.3 x 52.4 cm)
Courtesy the artist and Michael Stevenson Gallery, Cape Town, Collection of Artur Walther

The View from an Apartment in Jeanwell House overlooking the intersection of Nugget and Pritchard Streets, from the series "Jo'burg," 2004
Pigment print on paper
17.2 x 25.8 in. (43.6 x 65.5 cm)
Courtesy the artist and Michael Stevenson Gallery, Cape Town, International Center of Photography, New York

View of Hillbrow Looking North from the Roof of the Mariston Hotel, from the series "Jo'burg," 2004
Pigment print on paper
13.9 x 20.6 in. (35.3 x 52.4 cm)
Courtesy the artist and Michael Stevenson Gallery, Cape Town, Collection of Artur Walther

Al's Tower, a Block of Flats on Harrow Road, Berea, overlooking the Ponte Building, from the series "Jo'burg," 2004
Pigment print on paper
17.2 x 25.8 in. (43.6 x 65.5 cm)
Courtesy the artist and Michael Stevenson Gallery, Cape Town, International Center of Photography, New York

Cape Agulhas, Esselen Street, Hillbrow, from the series "Jo'burg," 2004
Pigment print on paper
13.9 x 20.6 in. (35.3 x 52.4 cm)
Courtesy the artist and Michael Stevenson Gallery, Cape Town, Collection of Artur Walther

Barber's Shop, Hillbrow, from the series "Jo'burg," 2004
Pigment print on paper
13.9 x 20.6 in. (35.3 x 52.4 cm)
Courtesy the artist and Michael Stevenson Gallery, Cape Town, Collection of Artur Walther

Yonela Kwaza, Grafton Road, Yeoville, from the series "Jo'burg," 2004
Pigment print on paper
13.9 x 20.6 in. (35.3 x 52.4 cm)
Courtesy the artist and Michael Stevenson Gallery, Cape Town, Collection of Artur Walther

Mbulelo at the Bar He Runs in a House in Joel Road, Berea, from the series "Jo'burg," 2004
Pigment print on paper
13.9 x 20.6 in. (35.3 x 52.4 cm)
Courtesy the artist and Michael Stevenson Gallery, Cape Town, Collection of Artur Walther

Mbulelo's Bar, Joel Road, Berea. Justice Sibanyone (centre) and His Wife Monica (extreme left), from the series "Jo'burg," 2004
Pigment print on paper
13.9 x 20.6 in. (35.3 x 52.4 cm)
Courtesy the artist and Michael Stevenson Gallery, Cape Town, Collection of Artur Walther

Al's Tower, Joel Road, Berea, from the series "Jo'burg," 2004
Pigment print on cotton paper
13.9 x 20.6 in. (35.3 x 52.4 cm)
Courtesy the artist and Michael Stevenson Gallery, Cape Town, Collection of Artur Walther

Eviction by the Red Ants, Auret Street Jeppestown, from the series "Jo'burg," 2004
Pigment print on paper
13.9 x 20.6 in. (35.3 x 52.4 cm)
Courtesy the artist and Michael Stevenson Gallery, Cape Town, Collection of Artur Walther

The Roof of Sherwood Heights, Smit Street, from the series "Jo'burg," 2004
Pigment print on paper
17.2 x 25.8 in. (43.6 x 65.5 cm)
Courtesy the artist and Michael Stevenson Gallery, Cape Town, International Center of Photography, New York

Ntokozo (right) and His Brother Vusi Tshabalala at Ntokozo's Place, Milton Court, Pritchard Street, from the series "Jo'burg," 2004
Pigment print on paper
17.2 x 25.8 in. (43.6 x 65.5 cm)
Courtesy the artist and Michael Stevenson Gallery, Cape Town, International Center of Photography, New York

Stanhope Mansions, Plein Street, from the series "Jo'burg," 2004
Pigment print on paper
13.9 x 20.6 in. (35.3 x 52.4 cm)
Courtesy the artist and Michael Stevenson Gallery, Cape Town, Collection of Artur Walther

Tayob Towers, Pritchard Street, from the series "Jo'burg," 2004
Pigment print on paper
17.2 x 25.8 in. (43.6 x 65.5 cm)
Courtesy the artist and Michael Stevenson Gallery, Cape Town, International Center of Photography, New York

Grafton Road, Yeoville, from the series "Jo'burg," 2004
Pigment print on paper
17.2 x 25.8 in. (43.6 x 65.5 cm)
Courtesy the artist and Michael Stevenson Gallery, Cape Town, International Center of Photography, New York

Michael Tsegaye (b. 1975)
Untitled, from the series "In and Out," 2005
Chromogenic print
20 x 24 in. (50.8 x 61 cm)
Courtesy the artist

Untitled, from the series "In and Out," 2005
Chromogenic print

20 x 24 in. (50.8 x 61 cm)
Courtesy the artist

Untitled, from the series "In and Out," 2005
Chromogenic print
20 x 24 in. (50.8 x 61 cm)
Courtesy the artist

Untitled, from the series "In and Out," 2005
Chromogenic print
20 x 24 in. (50.8 x 61 cm)
Courtesy the artist

Untitled, from the series "In and Out," 2005
Chromogenic print
20 x 24 in. (50.8 x 61 cm)
Courtesy the artist

Hentie van der Merwe (b. 1972)
WW I Service Jacket, Lieutenant, from the series "Trappings," 2002–03
Photo-installation
70.9 x 47.2 in. (180 x 120 cm)
Courtesy the artist

Cape Town Highlanders, Officer (1921–1958), from the series "Trappings," 2002–03
Photo-installation
70.9 x 47.2 in. (180 x 120 cm)
Courtesy the artist

State President's Guard (Formed 1967–Deactivated 1990), Riflemen, from the series "Trappings," 2002–03
Photo-installation
70.9 x 47.2 in. (180 x 120 cm)
Courtesy the artist

TA member of 32 Battalion Reconnaissance Wing, from the series "Trappings," 2002–03
Photo-installation
70.9 x 47.2 in. (180 x 120 cm)
Courtesy the artist

Transvaal Scottish (8th Infantry) Sergeant (1945–1951), from the series "Trappings," 2002–03
Photo-installation
70.9 x 47.2 in. (180 x 120 cm)
Courtesy the artist

Cape Mounted Rifles (Dukes), Bandsman (1913–1926), from the series "Trappings," 2002–03
Photo-installation
70.9 x 47.2 in. (180 x 120 cm)
Courtesy the artist

Transvaal Horse Artillery (Colonial), Officer (1903–1913), from the series "Trappings," 2002–03
Photo-installation
70.9 x 47.2 in. (180 x 120 cm)
Courtesy the artist

Parade Uniform (1967–1990), from the series "Trappings," 2002–03
Photo-installation
70.9 x 47.2 in. (180 x 120 cm)
Courtesy the artist

Nontsikelelo "Lolo" Veleko (b. 1977)
Cindy & Nonkululeko, 2004
Pigment print on paper
8 x 12 in. (20.3 x 30.5 cm)
Courtesy the artist, International Center of Photography, New York

Hloni, 2004
Pigment print on paper
8 x 12 in. (20.3 x 30.5 cm)
Courtesy the artist, International Center of Photography, New York

Nonkululeko, 2004
Pigment print on paper
8 x 12 in. (20.3 x 30.5 cm)
Courtesy the artist, International Center of Photography, New York

Thato J, 2004
Pigment print on paper
8 x 12 in. (20.3 x 30.5 cm)
Courtesy the artist, International Center of Photography, New York

Thulani, 2004
Pigment print on paper
8 x 12 in. (20.3 x 30.5 cm)
Courtesy the artist, International Center of Photography, New York

Bibliography

Adenaike, Carolyn Keyes. "Contextualizing and Decontextualizing African Historical Photographs." *History in Africa*, no. 23 (1996), pp. 429–37.

Adeniyi, Dapo. "Art Photography by Okhai Ojeikere." *Position: International Arts Review* (Lagos) 1, no. 1 (2000), pp. 13–27.

Adeniyi, Dapo, and Guy Hersant. "Telephone Conversation." *Position: International Arts Review* (Lagos) 1, no. 1 (2000), pp. 29–40.

Adès, Marie-Claire and Pierre Zaragozi, eds. *Photographes en Algérie au XIXe siècle.* Exh. cat. Paris: Musée-Galerie de la Seita, 1999.

Alloula, Malek. *The Colonial Harem.* Minneapolis: University of Minnesota Press, 1986.

Apter, Andrew. "Tarrying with Our Negatives (and Positives)." *African Arts* 36, no. 2 (Summer 2003), pp. 1–3.

Archibong, Maurice, and Dapo Adeniyi. "Making Photographs, a Roundtable of Four Nigerian Photographers: Jide Adeniyi-Jones, Don Barber, Chris Nwokedi and Sunday Tumo-Ojelabi." *Glendora Review* (Lagos) 1, no. 4 (1996), pp. 102–17.

Atkinson, Brenda, and Candice Breitz, eds. *Grey Areas: Representation, Identity, and Politics in Contemporary South African Art.* Johannesburg: Chalkham Hill Press, 1999.

Attal, Robert. *Juifs du Maghreb: Catalogue de la collection de cartes postales du fonds Gérard Lévy déposé à l'Institut Ben Zvi à Jérusalem.* Jérusalem: L'Institut, 1990.

Aubral, François. *Touhami Ennadre: Black Light.* Munich: Prestel, 1996.

Augustt Azaglo, Cornelius Yao. *Cornélius Yao Augustt Azaglo: Photographies, Côte d'Ivoire, 1950–1975.* Paris: Revue Noire, 1996.

Badsha, Omar, ed. *South Africa: The Cordoned Heart.* New York: W.W. Norton, 1986.

——, and Charles Hagen. "Making a New Culture: An Interview with Omar Badsha." *Aperture* (New York), no. 119 (Summer 1990), pp. 62–65.

——, and Guy Tillim. *Amulets & Dreams: War, Youth & Change in Africa.* Pretoria: South African History Online in cooperation with Unisa Press and the Institute for Security Studies, 2002.

——, and Heather Hughes. *Imijondolo: A Photographic Essay on Forced Removals in the Inandra District of South Africa.* Johannesburg: Afrapix, 1985.

Bailey, David A. "Photographic Animateur: The Photographs of Rotimi Fani-Kayode in Relation to Black Photographic Practices." *Third Text* (London), no. 13 (Winter 1990–91), pp. 57–62.

Ballen, Roger. *Platteland: Images from Rural South Africa.* London: Quartet, 1995.

Bannister, Andrew, and Kelly Morris. "Choose Your Weapons." *Lancet* 355 (March 4, 2000), pp. 851–52.

Banta, Melissa, and Curtis M. Hinsley. *From Site to Sight: Anthropology, Photography, and the Power of Imagery.* Exh. cat. Cambridge, MA: Peabody Museum Press, 1986.

Barnwell, Andrea D., and Isolde Brielmaier. *Engaging the Camera: African Women, Portraits and the Photographs of Hector Acebes.* Exh. cat. Atlanta: Spelman College Museum of Fine Art, 2004.

Baxter, Ian A. *Blitzkrieg: The Unpublished Photographs, 1939–1942.* London: Brassey's, 2002.

Beaugé, Gilbert, and J.-F. Clément. *L'image dans le monde arabe.* Paris: CNRS Éditions, 1995.

Bedford, Emma, ed. *A Decade of Democracy: South African Art 1994–2004.* Exh. cat. Cape Town: Double Storey Books; Iziko Museums of Cape Town, 2004.

Behrend, Heike. "'Feeling Global': The Likoni Ferry Photographers of Mombasa, Kenya." *African Arts* 33, no. 3 (Autumn 2000), pp. 70–77.

Behrend, Heike. "Fragmented Visions: Photo Collages by Two Ugandan Photographers." *Visual Anthropology* 14, no. 3 (2001), pp. 301–20.

——. "Imagined Journeys: The Likoni Ferry Photographers of Mombasa, Kenya." In *Photography's Other Histories*, edited by Christopher Pinney and Nicolas Peterson, pp. 221–39. Durham, NC: Duke University Press, 2003.

——. "Photo Magic: Photographs in Practices of Healing and Harming in East Africa." *Journal of Religion in Africa* 33, no. 2 (2003), pp. 129–45.

——, and Jean-François Werner. "Photographies and Modernities in Africa." *Visual Anthropology* 14, no. 3 (2001), p. 241.

Bell, Clare, et al. *In/sight: African Photographers, 1940 to the Present.* Exh. cat. New York: Guggenheim Museum, 1996.

Berry, Ian. *Living Apart: South Africa Under Apartheid.* London: Phaidon, 1996.

Bessire, Mark H. C., and Lauri Firstenberg, eds. *Beyond Decorum: The Photography of Iké Udé.* Cambridge, MA: MIT Press, 2000.

Bester, Rory, and Barbara Buntman. "Bushman(ia) and Photographic Intervention." *African Arts* 32, no. 4 (Winter 1999), pp. 50–59.

Biass-Fabiani, Sophie, ed. *Venise, Alger, Le Caire, Constantinople: Photographies de la collection Félix Ziem.* Martigues: Musée Ziem, 1998.

Bigham, Elizabeth. "Issues of Authorship in the Portrait Photographs of Seydou Keïta." *African Arts* 32, no. 1 (Spring 1999), pp. 56–67.

Bleach, Gordon. "Between the Fine Print and a Hard Place: David Goldblatt's South African Artifacts." *Nka: Journal of Contemporary African Art* (Ithaca, NY), no. 9 (Fall–Winter 1998), pp. 52–57.

Blocker, Jane. "A Cemetery of Images: Meditations on the Burial of Photographs." *Visual Resources* 21, no. 2 (June 2005), pp. 181–91.

Bollig, Michael, and Heike Heinemann. "Nomadic Savages, Ochre People and Heroic Herders: Visual Presentations of the Himba of Namibia's Kaokoland." *Visual Anthropology* 15, no. 3–4 (July 2002), pp. 267–312.

Bonetti, Maria Francesca, and Guido Schlinkert. *Samuel Fosso.* Exh. cat. Milan: 5 Continents, 2004.

Bourdieu, Pierre, et al. *Images d'Algérie: Une affinité élective.* Exh. cat. Arles: Actes Sud, 2003.

Bowles, Paul. *Paul Bowles Photographs: How Could I Send a Picture into the Desert?* New York: Scalo, 1994.

Buckley, Liam. "Objects of Love and Decay: Colonial Photographs in a Postcolonial Archive." *Cultural Anthropology* 20, no. 2 (May 2005), pp. 249–70.

——. "Self and Accessory in Gambian Studio Photography." *Visual Anthropology Review* 16, no. 2 (Fall–Winter 2000–2001), pp. 71–91.

Campbell, David. "Horrific Blindness: Images of Death in Contemporary Media." *Journal for Cultural Research* 8, no. 1 (January 2004), pp. 55–74.

Cape Town Month of Photography Festival (1999). *100XC: Photography in South Africa.* Exh. cat. Cape Town: University of Cape Town Press, 1999.

Çelik, Zeynep. "Framing the Colony: Houses of Algeria Photographed." *Art History* 27, no. 4 (September 2004), pp. 616–27.

Clarke, Theo. "Contrasts and Contradictions in South Africa." *Leadership* (Cape Town) (September 2000), pp. 66–76.

Cohen, John Brett, and David Goldblatt. "Forgotten Fields: The Photographs of John Brett Cohen." *Leadership* (Cape Town) (February 2000), pp. 66–77.

Convert, Pascal. "Medea the Algerian." *Art Press* 286 (January 2003), pp. 19–23.

Cook, John. "One-Man Truth Squad." *Mother Jones* 22, no. 3 (May–June 1997), pp. 15–16.

Coombes, Annie E. *Reinventing Africa: Museums, Material Culture, and Popular Imagination in Late Victorian and Edwardian England.* New Haven: Yale University Press, 1994.

Corbey, Raymond. "Alterity: The Colonial Nude." *Critique of Anthropology* 8, no. 3 (1988), pp. 75–92.

Cornwall-Jones, Hermione. "The Photographic Heritage of West Africa." *Anthropology Today* 15, no. 3 (June 1999), pp. 23–26.

Courtellemont, Guy. "Jules Gervais-Courtellemont (1863–1931): Autochromist." *History of Photography* 20 (Fall 1996), pp. 255–57.

Daly, M. W., and L. E. Forbes. *The Sudan: Photographs from the Sudan Archive, Durham University Library.* Reading, UK: Garnet, 1994.

David, Philippe. *Hommage à Alex A. Acolatse, photographe togolais: 1880–1975.* Lomé, Togo: Editions HAHO, 1992.

Diawara, Manthia. *The 1960s in Bamako: Malick Sidibé and James Brown.* New York: Andy Warhol Foundation for Visual Arts, 2001.

Diawara, Manthia. "Talk of the Month." *Artforum* 36, no. 6 (February 1998), pp. 64–72.

Downer, Christine. "King Radama II of Madagascar." *History of Photography* 24, no. 2 (Summer 2000), p. 185.

Dumont, Fabienne, and Linda Givon. *Sue Williamson: Selected Work.* Exh. cat. Johannesburg: Goodman Gallery, 2003.

Dunaway, Finis. "Hunting with the Camera: Nature Photography, Manliness, and Modern Memory, 1890–1930." *Journal of American Studies* 34, no. 2 (August 2000), pp. 207–30.

Durand-Evrard, Françoise, and Lucienne Martini. *Archives d'Algérie: 1830–1960.* Paris: Hazan, 2003.

Edwards, Elizabeth, ed. *Anthropology and Photography, 1860–1920.* New Haven: Yale University Press, 1992.

——. "The Working of Miracles: William Ellis, Photography in Madagascar 1853–1865." *Journal of Museum Ethnography* (Oxford), no. 8 (May 1996), pp. 125–28.

——. *Raw Histories: Photographs, Anthropology and Museums.* Oxford and New York: Berg, 2001.

——, et al. "Anthropology and Colonial Endeavour." *History of Photography* 21, no. 1 (Spring 1997), pp. 1–80.

Egypt: Dream and Realities. Cairo: Aujourd'hui l'Égypte, 1993.

Eiblmayr, Silvia, ed. *Georges Adéagbo: Archäologie der Motivationen, Geschichte neu schreiben.* Exh. cat. Ostfildern-Ruit: Hatje Cantz, 2001.

Elder, Tanya. *Capturing Change: The Practice of Malian Photography, 1930s–1990s.* Linköping: Linköping University, 1997.

Encounters with Photography: Photographing People in Southern Africa, 1860–1999. Rondebosch: University of Cape Town, 2000.

Enwezor, Okwui. "The Postcolonial Constellation: Contemporary Art in a State of Permanent Transition." *Research in African Literatures* 34, no. 4 (Winter 2003), pp. 57–82.

——, ed. *The Short Century: Independence and Liberation Movements in Africa, 1945–1994.* Exh. cat. Munich: Prestel, 2001.

——, and Colin Richards, eds. *Trade Routes: History and Geography: 2nd Johannesburg Biennale.* Johannesburg: Thorold's Africana Books, 1997.

Essaydi, Lalla, and Amanda Carlson. *Converging Territories.* Exh. cat. New York: powerHouse Books, 2005.

Fair, Jo Ellen, and Lisa Parks. "Africa on Camera: Television News Coverage and Aerial Imaging of Rwandan Refugees." *Africa Today* 48, no. 2 (Summer 2001), pp. 35–57.

Fairbrother, Trevor. "Gary Schnieder: Facing Time." *Art in America* (New York) 93, no. 2 (February 2005), pp. 112–16.

Fall, N'Goné, and Pascal Martin Saint Léon, eds. *Anthology of African and Indian Ocean Photography.* Paris: Revue Noire, 1999.

Fani-Kayode, Rotimi. *Black Male/White Male.* London: Gay Men's Press, 1988.

Farrell, Laurie Ann, ed. *Looking Both Ways: Art of the Contemporary African Diaspora.* Exh. cat. New York: Museum for African Art; Ghent: Snoeck, 2003.

Fayemi, A. Olusegun. *Windows to the Soul: Photographs Celebrating African Women.* White Plains, NY: Albofa Press, 2003.

Fechner, Elisabeth. *Alger et l'Algérois.* Paris: Calmann-Lévy, 2002.

Figueira, Tony, Marx Hipandwa, and John Liebenberg. "Namibia." *Revue Noire* (Paris), no. 4 (March–May 1992), pp. 28–32.

Firstenberg, Lauri. "Postcoloniality, Performance, and Photographic Portraiture." In *The Short Century: Independence and Liberation Movements in Africa, 1945–1994,* edited by Okwui Enwezor, pp. 175–79. Munich: Prestel, 2001.

——. "Representing the Body Archivally in South African Photography." *Art Journal* 61, no. 1 (Spring 2002), pp. 59–67.

——. "A Stylist of Subjectivities: Interface in the Photography of Iké Udé." *Third Text* (London), no. 46 (Spring 1999), pp. 53–60.

——, and John Peffer, eds. *Translation/Seduction/Displacement: Post-Conceptual and Photographic Work by Artists from South Africa.* Exh. cat. Portland: Institute of Contemporary Art, Maine College of Art, 2000.

Fitzgerald, Shannon, et al. *A Fiction of Authenticity: Contemporary Africa Abroad.* Exh. cat. St. Louis: Contemporary Art Museum St. Louis, 2003.

Fletcher, David. *Tanks in Camera: Archive Photographs from the Tank Museum: The Western Desert, 1940–1943.* Gloucestershire: Sutton, 1998.

Fondation Arabe pour l'Image. *Histoires intimes: Liban, 1900–1960.* Arles: Actes Sud, 1998.

Fosso, Samuel, Seydou Keïta, and Malick Sidibé. *Portraits of Pride: West African Photography.* Exh. cat. Stockholm: Raster Förlag, 2002.

Foster, Jeremy. "Capturing and Losing the 'Lie of the Land': Railway Photography and Colonial Nationalism in Early-20th-Century South Africa." In *Picturing Place: Photography and the Geographical Imagination,* edited by Joan M. Schwartz and James R. Ryan, pp. 141–61. New York: I.B. Tauris, 2003.

Fosu, Kojo. *Lens Eye: Exhibition of Photographs by Browning, Diko, Garba, Oluyitan, Gbedema, Owuna, January 27–February 14, 1983.* Exh. cat. Zaria, Nigeria: Department of Fine Arts, Ahmadu Bello University, 1983.

Gabous, Abdelkrim. *La Tunisie des photographes: 1875–1910.* Tunis: Éditions CERES, 1994.

Garanger, Marc. *Femmes algériennes 1960.* Biarritz: Atlantica, 2002.

Gasteli, Jellel. *En Tunisie.* Paris: Éric Koehler, 1997.

Gaule, Sally. "Poor, White, South African: Artistic Photography in South Africa." *Afterimage* 24, no. 4 (January–February 1997), p. 21.

Geary, Christraud M. "Different Visions? Postcards from Africa by European and African Photographers and Sponsors." In *Delivering Views: Distant Cultures in Early Postcards,* edited by Christraud M. Geary and Virginia-Lee Webb, pp. 147–77. Washington, DC: Smithsonian Institution Press, 1998.

——. "Early Images from Benin at the National Museum of African Art, Smithsonian Institution." *African Arts* 30, no. 3 (Summer 1997), pp. 44–53.

——. *Images from Bamum: German Colonial Photography at the Court of King Njoya, Cameroon, West Africa, 1902–1915.* Washington, DC: Smithsonian Institution Press, 1988.

——. *In and Out of Focus: Images from Central Africa, 1885–1960.* Exh. cat. Washington, DC: National Museum of African Art, Smithsonian Institution, 2003.

——. "The Incidental Photographer." *African Arts* 36, no. 2 (Summer 2003), pp. 66–81.

——. "Missionary Photography: Private and Public Readings." *African Arts* 24, no. 4 (October 1991), pp. 48–59, 98–100.

——. "Photographing in the Cameroon Grassfields, 1970 to 1984." *African Arts* 33, no. 4 (Winter 2000), pp. 70–77.

——. "Views from Outside and Inside: Representations of Madagascar and the Malagasy, 1648–1935." In *Objects as Envoys: Cloth, Imagery, and Diplomacy in Madagascar,* edited by Christine Mullen Kreamer and Sarah Fee, pp. 148–79. Washington, DC: National Museum of African Art, Smithsonian Institution, 2002.

Geraci, Joseph. "Lehnert and Landrock of North Africa." *History of Photography* 27, no. 3 (Autumn 2003), pp. 294–95.

Gervereau, Laurent, et al. *Photographier la guerre d'Algérie.* Paris: Marval, 2004.

Godby, Michael. "After Apartheid: 10 South African Documentary Photographers." *African Arts* 37, no. 4 (Winter 2004), pp. 36–41.

——. "Framing the Colonial Subject: The Photographs of W. F. P. Burton (1886–1971) in the Former Belgian Congo." *Social Dynamics* (Cape Town) 19, no. 1 (June 1993), pp. 11–25.

Goldblatt, David. *Fifty-One Years.* Exh. cat. Barcelona: Museu d'Art Contemporani, 2001.

——. *South African Intersections.* Munich: Prestel, 2005.

——. *The Transported of Kwandebele: A South African Odyssey.* New York: Aperture, 1989.

Gordimer, Nadine, and David Goldblatt. *Lifetimes: Under Apartheid.* New York: Viking, 1986.

Graffenried, Michael von. *Journal d'Algérie, 1991–2001: Images interdites d'une guerre invisible.* Paris: Autrement, 2003.

Graham-Brown, Sarah. *Images of Women: The Portrayal of Women in Photography of the Middle East, 1860–1950.* New York: Columbia University Press, 1988.

Grundlingh, Geoffrey, ed. *The Cape Town Month of Photography, 2002.* Gardens, Cape Town: South African Centre for Photography, University of Cape Town, 2002.

——, ed. *The Cape Town Month of Photography, 2005.* Gardens, Cape Town: South African Centre for Photography, 2005.

Grundlingh, Kathleen, ed. *Lines of Sight: Perspectives on South African Photography.* Cape Town: South African National Gallery, 2001.

——, ed. *PhotoSynthesis: Contemporary South African Photography.* Cape Town: South African National Gallery, 1997.

Guy, Jeff. "A Paralysis of Perspective: Image and Text in the Creation of an African Chief." *South African Historical Journal* 47 (October 2002), pp. 51–74.

Hales, Kevin Joseph. "A Matter of Record: Black Photography in Ghana." *American Visions* 13, no. 6 (December 1998-January 1999), pp. 22–26.

——. "The Origin and Development of Black Commerical Photography in Ghana." *West African Research Association Newsletter* (Madison, WI) (Fall 1997), pp. 13–14.

Hall, Stuart, and Mark Sealy. *Different: A Historical Context: Contemporary Photographers and Black Identity.* London: Phaidon, 2001.

Hammer, Deborah Stokes. "The William B. Fagg Archive." *African Arts* 27, no. 3 (July 1994), p. 84.

Hardin, Kris L. "Representing Africa: Whose Story Counts?" *Expedition* 35, no. 3 (Winter 1993), pp. 19–33.

Hartmann, Wolfram, ed. *Hues between Black and White: Historical Photography from Colonial Namibia, 1860s to 1915.* Windhoek, Namibia: Out of Africa Publishers, 2004.

Hartmann, Wolfram, et al., eds. *The Colonising Camera: Photographs in the Making of Namibian History.* Cape Town: University of Cape Town Press, 1999.

Hassan, Salah M., and Olu Oguibe, eds. *Authentic/Ex-centric: Conceptualism in Contemporary African Art.* Exh. cat. Ithaca, NY: Forum for African Arts, Prince Claus Fund Library, 2001.

Hébrard, Jean-Louis, and Marie-Claude Hébrard. *L'Algérie autrefois.* Le Coteau: Horvath, 1990.

Hilton-Barber, Steve. "In Good Photographic Faith." *Staffrider* (Fordsburg) 9, no. 3 (1991), pp. 34–39.

Hirsch, Faye. "Subjective State." *Art in America* (New York) 93, no. 2 (February 2005), pp. 66–71.

Houlberg, Marilyn Hammersley. "Feed Your Eyes: Nigerian and Haitian Studio Photographs." *Photographic INsight* (Winter–Spring 1988), pp. 3–8.

——. "Ibeji Images of the Yoruba." *African Arts* 7, no. 1 (Autumn 1973), pp. 20–27, 91–92.

İhsanoğlu, Ekmeleddin. *Egypt: As Viewed in the 19th Century.* Istanbul: Research Centre for Islamic Art, History, and Culture, 2001.

Jenkins, Paul. "The Earliest Generation of Missionary Photographers in West Africa: The Portrayal of Indigenous People and Culture." *Visual Anthropology* 7 (1994), pp. 115–45.

——. "In the Eye of the Beholder: An Exercise in the Interpretation of Two Photographs Taken in Cameroon Early in This Century." In *West African Economic and Social History: Studies in Memory of Marion Johnson,* edited by David Henige and T. C. McCaskie, pp. 93–103. Madison: African Studies Program, University of Wisconsin, 1990.

——. "On Using Historical Missionary Photographs in Modern Discussion." *Le Fait Missionaire* 10 (2001), pp. 71–89.

——, and Christraud M. Geary. "Photographs from Africa in the Basel Mission Archive." *African Arts* 18, no. 4 (August 1985), pp. 56–63.

Jonge, Ingrid Fischer, et al. *Unsettled: 8 South African Photographers.* Exh. cat. Copenhagen: Nationale Fotomuseum, 2004.

Kaplan, Flora S. "Some Uses of Photographs in Recovering Cultural History at the Royal Court of Benin, Nigeria." *Visual Anthropology* 3, no. 2–3 (1990), pp. 317–41.

Karmazyn, Jean-Claude. *Le Maroc en cartes postales, 1900–1920.* Cahors: Publi-fusion, 1994.

Kasfir, Sidney Littlefield. *Contemporary African Art.* New York: Thames & Hudson, 1999.

Kasfir, Sidney Littlefield, and Olabiyi B. J. Yai. "Authenticity and Diaspora." *Museum International* 56, no. 1–2 (May 2004), pp. 190–97.

Köpke, Wulf, and Bernd Schmelz, eds. *Ethnographie Afrikas, Ethnographische Photographie: Festschrift für Jürgen Zwernemann zum 65. Geburtstag.* Bonn: Holos, 1999.

Krauss, Rosalind. "'The Rock': William Kentridge's Drawings for Projection." *October* 92 (Spring 2000), pp. 3–35.

Lamore, Jean. "Samuel Fosso." *Nka: Journal of Contemporary African Art* (Ithaca, NY), no. 13–14 (Spring–Summer 2001), pp. 34–39.

Lamunière, Michelle. "Ready to Wear: A Conversation with Malick Sidibé." *Transition: An International Review* 10, no. 4 (2001), pp. 132–59.

——. *You Look Beautiful Like That: The Portrait Photographs of Seydou Keïta and Malick Sidibé.* Exh. cat. Cambridge, MA: Harvard University Art Museums; New Haven: Yale University Press, 2001.

Laronde, André. *La Libye à travers les cartes postales, 1900–1940.* Paris: Paris-Méditerranée, 1997.

Leakey, Richard. "Africa: The Dark Continent." *Royal Geographical Society Illustrated* (London) (1997), pp. 94–159.

Ledochowski, Chris. *Cape Flats Details: Life and Culture in the Townships of Cape Town.* Pretoria: South African History Online and UNISA Press, 2003.

Lehnert, Rudolf, and Ernst Landrock. *L'Orient d'un photographe.* Lausanne: Favre, 1987.

Lenz, Iris, and Monika Winkler, eds. *Malick Sidibé: Fotografie, 1962–76.* Exh. cat. Stuttgart: ifa-Galerie, 1997.

Light, Ken. "Peter Magubane: A Black Photographer in Apartheid South Africa." In *Witness in Our Time: Working Lives of Documentary Photographers,* edited by Ken Light, pp. 54–61. Washington, DC: Smithsonian Institution Press, 2000.

Loos, Jacky. "E. H. Allis: Early Cape Photographer." *Quarterly Bulletin of the South African Library* 51, no. 2 (December 1996), pp. 53–57.

Lundström, Jan-Erik, and Katarina Pierre. *Demokratins Bilder: Fotografi och Bildkonst efter Apartheid / Democracy's Images: Photography and Visual Art after Apartheid.* Umeå: Bildmuseet, 1998.

Lyons, Robert, and Chinua Achebe. *Another Africa.* New York: Anchor Books, 1998.

Mack, John. "Documenting the Cultures of Southern Zaire: The Photographs of the Torday Expeditions, 1900–1909." *African Arts* 24, no. 4 (October 1991), pp. 60–69.

Magnin, André. *J. D. 'Okhai Ojeikee: Photographies.* Paris: Actes Sud, 2000.

——. *Malick Sidibé.* Zürich: Scalo, 1998.
Magnin, André. *Seydou Keïta.* Zürich: Scalo, 1997.

——, et al. *African Art Now: Masterpieces from the Jean Pigozzi Collection.* Exh. cat. London: Merrell, 2005.

Magubane, Peter. *South Africa—South Bronx.* Old Westbury, NY: Amelie A. Wallace Gallery, 1981.

——. *Soweto: The Fruit of Fear.* Grand Rapids, MI: Eerdmans, 1986.

——. *Vanishing Cultures of South Africa.* New York: Rizzoli, 1998.

——, and Sandra Klopper. *African Renaissance.* London: Struik, 2000.

Marinovich, Greg, and João Silva. *The Bang-Bang Club: Snapshots from a Hidden War.* London: Heinemann, 2000.

Martin, Douglas. "From Apartheid to Another Kind of Apartness." *New York Times,* March 3, 1990, sec. 1, p. 25.

Masiza, Jacqui, and Mothobi Mutloatse, eds. *Tauza: Bob Gosani's People.* Bedfordview: Mutloatse Arts Heritage Trust, 2005.

McClusky, Pamela, and Robert Farris Thompson. *Art from Africa: Long Steps Never*

Broke a Back. Princeton: Princeton University Press, 2002.

Melis, Wim, ed. *Africa Inside.* Groningen: Aurora Borealis, 2000.

——, ed. *Nazar: Photographs from the Arab World.* New York: Aperture, 2005.

Mendel, Gideon. *A Broken Landscape: HIV & AIDS in Africa.* Barcelona: Blume in association with ActionAid, 2002.

——. "Lines of Sight: Gideon Mendel's Photographs." *Leadership* (Cape Town) 5, no. 5 (1986), pp. 66–67.

Mesplié, Louis. "Bamako: The Capital of African Photography." *Cimaise* 42, no. 244 (November–December 1996), pp. 5–28.

Messikh, Mohamed-Sadek. *L'Algérie des premiers photographes.* Paris: Éditions du Layeur, 2003.

Middleton, John. "Aspects of Tourism in Kenya." *Anthropology Southern Africa* 27, no. 3-4 (2004), pp. 65–74.

Miessgang, Thomas, and Barbara Schröder, eds. *¡Flash Afrique! Photography from West Africa.* Exh. cat. Vienna: Kunsthalle, 2001.

Mngadi, Sikhumbuzo. "Rereading and Resistance." *Afterimage* 26, no. 3 (November–December 1998), pp. 7–8.

Moeller, Susan D. *Compassion Fatigue: How the Media Sell Disease, Famine, War, and Death.* New York: Routledge, 1999.

Mofokeng, Santu. "Like Shifting Sands." In *On Shifting Sands: New Art and Literature from South Africa,* edited by Kirsten Holst Petersen and Anna Rutherford, pp. 73–81. Portsmouth, NH: Heinemann, 1992.

——. *Santu Mokokeng.* Johannesburg: D. Krut, 2001.

——. "Trajectory of a Street Photographer." *Nka: Journal of Contemporary African Art* (Ithaca, NY), no. 11–12 (Fall–Winter 2000), pp. 40–46.

Monnier, Nicolas, and Didier Péclard. *Mission et photographie: Retour en images sur un siècle d'histoire missionnaire.* Exh. cat. Dorigny: Le Fait Missionnaire, 2001.

Monti, Nicolas, ed. *Africa Then: Photographs, 1840–1918.* New York: Alfred A. Knopf, 1987.

Moraes, José Augusto da Cunha, and Nicolas Monti, António Pedro Vicente, et al. *Cunha Moraes: Viagens em Angola, 1877–1897.* Coimbra: Casa Museu Bissaya Barreto, 1991.

Naoum, Nabil. *Impressions d'Afrique du Nord.* Photographs by Laziz Hamani, Lara Baladi, Nabil Boutros, Yto Barrada, and Jellel Gasteli. Paris: Revue Noire, 1998.

Nelson, Steven. "Transgressive Transcendence in the Photographs of Rotimi Fani-Kayode." *Art Journal* 64, no. 1 (Spring 2005), pp. 4–19.

Nicol, Mike. *The Invisible Line: The Life and Photography of Ken Oosterbroek, 1962–1994.* London: Global, 1999.

Nimis, Érika. *Félix Diallo, photographe de Kita.* Toulouse: Toguna, 2003.

——. *Photographes de Bamako de 1935 à nos jours.* Paris: Revue Noire, 1998.

Njami, Simon. *Africa Remix: Contemporary Art of a Continent.* Exh. cat. Ostfildern-Ruit: Hatje Cantz, 2005.

——, ed. *Un autre monde: VIes Rencontres de la Photographie Africaine, Bamako 2005.* Exh. cat. Paris: Éditions Éric Koehler, 2005.

——, ed. *Mémoires intimes d'un nouveau millénaire: IVes Rencontres de la Photographie Africaine, Bamako 2001.* Exh. cat. Paris: Éditions Éric Koehler, 2001.

——, ed. *Rites sacrés, rites profanes: Ves Rencontres de la Photographie Africaine, Bamako 2003.* Exh. cat. Paris: Éditions Éric Koehler, 2003.

Oguibe, Olu. "Finding a Place: Nigerian Artists in the Contemporary Art World." *Art Journal* 58, no. 2 (Summer 1999), pp. 31–41.

Oguibe, Olu. "Gordon P. Bleach: From Zimbabwe to Xanadu." *Nka: Journal of Contemporary African Art* (Ithaca, NY), no. 11–12 (Fall–Winter 2000), pp. 28–33.

——, and Okwui Enwezor, eds. *Reading the Contemporary: African Art from Theory to the Marketplace.* Cambridge, MA: MIT Press, 1999.

Ostrow, Saul. "Olu Oguibe [Interview]." *Bomb,* no. 87 (Spring 2004), pp. 30–37.

Özendes, Engin. *Abdullah Frères: Osmanlı Sarayının Foto_rafçıları.* Beyo_lu, Istanbul: Yapı Kredi Yayınları, 1998.

Pankhurst, Richard, and Denis Gerard. *Ethiopia Photographed: Historic Photographs of the Country and Its People Taken Between 1867 and 1935.* London: Kegan Paul, 1996.

Parry, James. "Egypt's New Glamour: Photographer Youssef Nabil." *Arts & the Islamic World (London),* no. 35 (2001), pp. 36–38.

Peers, Simon. "William Ellis: Photography in Madagascar, 1853–65." *History of Photography* 21, no. 1 (Spring 1997), pp. 23–31.

——. *The Working of Miracles / Ny fiasan'ny fahagagana: William Ellis, Photography in Madagascar, 1853–1865.* London: British Council, 1995.

Perrella, Cristiana, and Valentina Bruschi, eds. *I ka nyì tan: Seydou Keïta e Malick Sidibé fotografi a Bamako.* Exh. cat. Rome: Castelvecchi, 2001.

Perryer, Sophie, ed. *10 Years, 100 Artists: Art in a Democratic South Africa.* Cape Town: Bell-Roberts Publishers in association with Struik Publishers, 2004.

Photofesta, Maputo 2002: Primeiros Encontros Internacionals de Fotografia Maputo 2002. Exh. cat. Maputo: Associação Moçambicana de Fotografia, 2002.

Pinney, Christopher. "Notes from the Surface of the Image: Photography, Postcolonialism, and Vernacular Modernism." In *Photography's Other Histories,* edited by Christopher Pinney and Nicolas Peterson, pp. 202–20. Durham, NC: Duke University Press, 2003.

Pivin, Jean Loup. "La redemption du Mal: Le photographe artiste." *Revue Noire* (Paris), no. 3 (December 1991), pp. 16–23.

——. "Touhami Ennadre: Photographie, Maroc." *Revue Noire* (Paris), no. 12 (March–May 1994), pp. 32–37.

Powell, Ivor. "Stories from Beyond." *ArtSouthAfrica* (Cape Town) 2, no. 3 (Autumn 2004), pp. 32–38.

Prochaska, David. "Every Picture Tells a Story: Picture Postcards from Colonial Algeria." In *Photographs as Sources for African History,* edited by Andrew Roberts, pp. 66–79. London: S.O.A.S., 1988.

——. "Fantasia of the Photothèque: French Postcard Views of Colonial Senegal." *African Arts* 24, no. 4 (October 1991), pp. 40–47.

Putter, Andrew, and Sue Williamson. *Sue Williamson at the Goodman Gallery, March 1994.* Sandton (Johannesburg): Goodman Gallery, 1994.

Rammant-Peeters, Agnès, ed. *Palmen en tempels: La photographie en Égypte au XIXe siècle.* Exh. cat. Leuven: Peeters, 1994.

Rangasamy, Jacques. "White Mischief." *Creative Camera,* no. 335 (August–September 1995), pp. 8–9.

Richards, Dan. "Platteland." *Popular Photography* 62, no. 7 (July 1998), pp. 98–100.

Roberts, Allen F. Review of *In and Out of Focus, Photography's Other Histories,* and *Hector Acebes: Portraits in Africa, 1948–1953. African Arts* 37, no. 3 (Autumn 2004), pp. 87–89.

Roberts, Allen F., and Mary Nooter Roberts. "A Saint in the City." *African Arts* 35, no. 4 (Winter 2002), pp. 52–73.

Rosen, Rhoda. "The Documentary Photographer and Social Responsibility." *De Arte* (Pretoria) 45 (April 1992), pp. 4–14.

Rovine, Victoria L. "Exporting Identities Through Art." *African Arts* 37, no. 4 (Winter 2004), pp. 48–55.

Ryan, James R. *Picturing Empire: Photography and the Visualization of the British Empire.* Chicago: University of Chicago Press, 1997.

Samb, Issa. "Photographes: Dakar, Sénegal." *Revue Noire* (Paris), no. 7 (December 1992), pp. 38–43.

Sampson, Anthony. *Drum: The Making of a Magazine.* Johannesburg: Jonathan Ball, 2005.

Schadeberg, Jürgen. *The Black and White Fifties: Jurgen Schadeberg's South Africa.* Menlopark, South Africa: Protea, 2001.

Schildkrout, Enid. "The Spectacle of Africa Through the Lens of Herbert Lang: Belgian Congo Photographs, 1909–1915." *African Arts* 24, no. 4 (October 1991), pp. 70–85.

Schoeman, Karel. *The Face of the Country: A South African Family Album, 1860–1910.* Cape Town: Human & Rousseau, 1996.

Sealy, Mark, and Jean Loup Pivin, eds. *Rotimi Fani-Kayodé & Alex Hirst.* Paris: Revue Noire, 1996.

Searle, Berni, and Rory Bester. *Berni Searle.* Cape Town: Bell-Roberts Publishing, 2003.

Sebbar, Leïla, and Jean-Michel Belorgey. *Femmes d'Afrique du Nord: Cartes postales, 1885–1930.* Saint-Pourçain-sur-Sioule: Bleu Autour, 2002.

Serhane, Abdelhak. *Maroc médina, médinas.* Marseille: Métamorphoses, 1999.

Seye, Bouna Medoune. *Mama Casset et les précurseurs de la photographie au Sénégal, 1950: Meïssa Gaye, Mix Gueye, Adama Sylla, Alioune Diouf, Doro Sy, Doudou Diop, Salla Casset.* Paris: Revue Noire, 1994.

Shumard, Ann M. *A Durable Memento: Portraits by Augustus Washington, African American Daguerreotypist.* Washington, DC: National Portrait Gallery, 1999.

Sidibé, Malick. *Clubs of Bamako.* Exh. cat. Houston: Rice University Art Gallery, 2000.

Smith, Bob, and Salim Amin. *The Man Who Moved the World: The Life & Work of Mohamed Amin.* Nairobi: Camerapix, 1998.

South African National Gallery. *Through a Lens Darkly: 6 Portfolios by South African Photographers.* Exh. cat. Cape Town: The Gallery, 1993.

Sprague, Stephen F. "How I See the Yoruba See Themselves." *Studies in the Anthropology of Visual Communication* 5, no. 1 (Fall 1978), pp. 9–28.

——. "Yoruba Photography: How the Yoruba See Themselves." In *Photography's Other Histories,* edited by Christopher Pinney and Nicolas Peterson, pp. 240–60. Durham, NC: Duke University Press, 2003.

Squiers, Carol. "Fatal Wrath." *American Photo* 5, no. 5 (September–October 1994), pp. 34–40.

——. "The Lost Children of Rwanda." *American Photo* 8, no. 1 (January–February 1997), pp. 50–54.

——. "Seeing Africa Through African Eyes." *New York Times,* May 26, 1996.

Stein, Sylvester. *Who Killed Mr. Drum?* London: Corvo Books, 2003.

Steiner, Christopher B. "Authenticity, Repetition, and the Aesthetics of Seriality: The Work of Tourist Art in the Age of Mechanical Reproduction." In *Unpacking Culture: Art and Commodity in Colonial and Postcolonial Worlds,* edited by Ruth B. Phillips and Christopher B. Steiner, pp. 87–103. Berkeley: University of California Press, 1999.

Stétié, Salah, and Jean-Michel Belorgey. *Égyptiennes: Cartes postales (1885–1930).* Saint-Pourçain-sur-Sioule: Bleu Autour, 2003.

Stevenson, Michael, and Michael Graham-Stewart. *Surviving the Lens: Photographic Studies of South and East African People, 1870–1920.* Vlaeberg, South Africa: Fernwood Press, 2001.

Storr, Robert. "Bamako: Full Dress Parade." *Parkett,* no. 49 (1997), pp. 24–34.

Suolinna, Kirsti, et al. *Portraying Morocco: Edward Westermarck's Fieldwork and Photographs, 1898–1913.* Åbo: Åbo Akademis Förlag, 2000.

Tanger et Tétouan: Les débuts de la photographie, 1870–1900. Exh. cat. Paris: Somogy, 2003.

Taraud, Christelle. *Mauresques: Femmes orientales dans la photographie coloniale, 1860–1910.* Paris: Albin Michel, 2003.

Tawadros, Gilane, and Sarah Campbell, eds. *Fault Lines: Contemporary African Art and Shifting Landscapes.* Exh. cat. London: Institute of International Visual Arts, 2003.

Theye, Thomas, ed. *Der Geraubte Schatten: Die Photographie als ethnographisches Dokument.* Munich: C.J. Bucher, 1989.

Thompson, T. Jack. "Light on the Dark Continent: The Photography of Alice Seely Harris and the Congo Atrocities of the Early Twentieth Century." *International Bulletin of Missionary Research* 26, no. 4 (October 2002), pp. 146–49.

Triulzi, Alessandro, ed. *Fotografia e storia dell'Africa.* Naples: I.U.O., 1995.

Ugiomoh, Frank. "Photo-Logos and/or Narrative Semiotics." *Third Text* (London) 18, no. 1 (January 2004), pp. 1–11.

Van Gelder, Alex, ed. *Life & Afterlife in Benin.* London: Phaidon, 2005.

Viljoen, Shaun, and Andrew Barker. "Untitled." *Leadership* (Cape Town) (December 2000–January 2001), pp. 68–75.

Vine, Richard. "Report from Mali: The Luminous Continent." *Art in America* (New York) 92, no. 9 (October 2004), pp. 68–73.

Vogel, Susan. *Africa Explores: 20th Century African Art.* Exh. cat. New York: Center for African Art, 1991.

Vogl, Mary B. "It Was and It Was Not So: Edmond Amran El Maleh Remembers Morocco." *International Journal of Francophone Studies* 6, no. 2 (2003), pp. 71–86.

——. *Picturing the Maghreb: Literature, Photography, (Re)Presentation.* Lanham, MD: Rowman & Littlefield, 2003.

Waselchuk, Lori. *Is Everybody Comfortable? A Market Photo Workshop Exhibition.* Johannesburg: Market Photo Workshop, 2004.

Webster, Christopher. "The Portrait Cabinet of Dr. Bleek: Anthropometric Photographs by Early Cape Photographers." *Critical Arts Journal* 14, no. 1 (2000), pp. 1–15.

Weinberg, Paul. "Apartheid–A Vigilant Witness: A Reflection on Photography." In *Culture in Another South Africa,* edited by Willem Campschreur and Joost Divendal, pp. 60–70. London: Zed, 1989.

Wendl, Tobias. "Entangled Traditions: Photography and the History of Media in Southern Ghana." *RES: Anthropology and Aesthetics* 39 (Spring 2001), pp. 78–100.

——, and Heike Behrend, eds. *Snap Me One! Studiofotografen in Afrika.* Exh. cat. Munich: Prestel, 1998.

Werner, Jean-François. "Photography and Individualization in Contemporary Africa: An Ivoirian Case-Study." *Visual Anthropology* 14 (2001), pp. 251–68.

Wilkerson-Barker, Donna. "Photographic Memories in Leila Sebbar's 'Le Chinois vert d'Afrique.'" *Research in African Literatures* 34, no. 2 (Summer 2003), p. 28.

Williams, Graeme. *The Inner City.* Johannesburg: Ravan Press, 2000.

——. "The Inner City of Graeme Williams." *Leadership* (Cape Town) (March 2000), pp. 54–61.

Williamson, Sue. *Sue Williamson: Selected Work.* Cape Town: Double Storey, 2003.

Zaatari, Akram, ed. *Portraits du Caire: Van Leo, Armand, Alban.* Arles: Actes Sud, 1999.

Zaya, Octavio. "Meaning in Transit: Framing the Works of Boutros, Dridi, Ennadre, Gasteli and Naji." *Nka: Journal of Contemporary African Art* (Ithaca, NY), no. 5 (Fall 1996), pp. 50–53.

Zervigon, Andres Mario. "The Weave of Memory: Siemon Allen's Screen in Postapartheid South Africa." *Art Journal* 61, no. 1 (Spring 2002), pp. 68–81.

Z'Graggen, Bruno, and Grant Lee Neuenberg. *Iluminando Vidas: Ricardo Rangel e a fotografia Moçambicana, 1950–2001.* Zürich: Christoph Merian Verlag, 2002.

Compiled by Allison Moore and Kevin Mulhearn

INTERNATIONAL CENTER OF PHOTOGRAPHY